HENRY GEORGE

by CHARLES ALBRO BARKER

New York · ROBERT SCHALKENBACH FOUNDATION · *1991*

ROBERT SCHALKENBACH FOUNDATION
41 East 72nd Street, New York, NY 10021

Reprinted with permission of Oxford University Press, Inc.
Original edition published in 1955 by Oxford University Press, Inc.,
New York. Paperback edition published in 1974 by Greenwood Press,
Westport, Connecticut.

Library of Congress Cataloging-in-Publication Data

Barker, Charles A. (Charles Albro), 1904-
    Henry George / by Charles Albro Barker.
    716 p.
    Reprint. Originally published: New York : Oxford University
Press 1955.
    Includes bibliographical references and index.
    ISBN 0-911312-85-4 : $15.00
    1. George, Henry, 1839-1897.   2. Economists--United States-
-Biography.   I. Title.
HB119.G4B3   1991
330'.092--dc20   91-661
[B]   CIP

Portrait of Henry George, on dustjacket, by Peter Van Valkenburgh
Courtesy, The Bancroft Library, University of California

1006328047

Printed in the United States of America

HENRY GEORGE   1884

HENRY GEORGE

for
J.G.B. *and* L.A.B.
children of California
and democrats with passion

PREFACE

———————

THREE GENERATIONS AGO Henry George electrified great numbers of our ancestors on both sides of the Atlantic and in Australia and New Zealand. In the history of the English-speaking world there is no other figure who quite compares with him. Driven by a demon of the spirit, an inner force which combined love of God with love of man and desire for fame, George managed to find the language with which to say what many men were ready, and some were longing, to hear.

This was especially true, and early true, in England. *Progress and Poverty* has fallen 'on old and deep lines of thought in my mind,' Philip Wicksteed wrote the author in 1882, from an inner circle of liberal thought and conscience in London. It lit the light he 'vainly sought for' himself. Through minds as keen as Wicksteed's, and through leadership as gifted as Joseph Chamberlain's, the ideas of Henry George influenced English thought, and, more than a little, England's policy. George's ideas deepened the Fabian movement; they helped to give force to trade unions; and they inspired the Radicals who were rising in the Liberal party.

The influence of George on the United States was hardly slower in becoming effective. By the middle '80s surges of acceptance and rejection delighted or dismayed Americans, according to their sentiments. Then gradually his ideas worked their way into the deeper strata of public thought and conscience. When Georgism seized minds of legalistic bent, like Thomas Shearman's, it impelled the single-tax movement, which began during 1887 and 1888 in New York. When it seized practical and political minds, Tom Loftin Johnson's most notably, Georgism entered near its source the stream that later broadened to become the progressive movement of the twentieth century. When, at their farthest reach, the ideas of Henry George engaged literary and philosophical minds, such as George Bernard Shaw's and Leo Tolstoy's abroad, and Hamlin Garland's and Brand Whitlock's in the United States, the moral appeal of *Progress and Poverty* extended with added charm beyond the circle of those who had read George's books or listened to his lectures or joined organizations, and had pondered his argument for themselves. No other book of the industrial age, dedicated to social reconstruction and conceived within the Western traditions of Christianity and democracy, commanded so much attention as did *Progress and Poverty*. Only *Das Kapital,* conceived outside that tradition, is fairly comparable in purpose of reconstruction, but this book was much slower to catch on than *Progress and Poverty*.

In one respect like *Progress and Poverty* itself, the present biography was begun in California; and more than half the time required for investigation and writing has been devoted to the regional origination of Henry George's thought. Perhaps I should explain that I determined to do this book in the wake of the depression of the '30s, but that I began without the slightest hostage in the Henry George camp. My family had been Republican since 1856; I had cast my first vote for Norman Thomas; and I believed, as I still do, that at the time the New Deal was essentially what the United States needed. I know now that if I had designed my own background to avoid contact with Georgism, I could have chosen no points of political attachment more indifferent to the ideas of the subject of this biography than these three — traditional Republicanism, Thomas socialism, and the New Deal. Only international communism, or some fascism like Huey Long's, would have been wider of the present subject. The nearest American national politics has ever come to George — and that not very close — was the democracy of Woodrow Wilson. Wilson and George, each in his own way, the later figure not uninfluenced by the earlier, did have a magnificent purpose in common. They each devoted a career to establishing a Jeffersonian ideology and policy for the America, and for the world, of the industrial age.

Although the effort that follows is a historical biography, my first incentive was a moral, rather than a historical, appreciation of Henry George. At an early stage of the investigation a professor of literature addressed me in a lowered voice one day, in the Huntington Library cafeteria, to inquire what is wrong with the argument of Henry George. He always gave a little time to *Progress and Poverty,* in the annual cycle of teaching, he said, and every year he was embarrassed because he knew no satisfying reply to the reform idea he thought must be mistaken. The question reassured me, because I had begun at about the same place. By that time, which was during the war summer of 1944, I was committed to examine the circumstances of Henry George: to try to discover the sources of his somehow persuasive and disturbing book, and to report the reactions of acceptance, rejection, and criticism with which his contemporaries did him honor. For a decade, Henry George has wearied me many days, but those days have always been interesting ones, and I retain the conviction with which I started, that moral problems are the most important problems to which an historian can address himself.

It would be wrong to try to reduce to some formula the California story of the growth of Henry George's ideas, during his years in the state as journalist, observer, and servant of the Democratic party. Most of Part One is an embryology of the philosophy of *Progress and Poverty,* and such a study requires stage-by-stage reports of his western life. Yet the reader will have an easier time with those reports if he is told beforehand that from the very first until the very last, from the political ideas acquired in his parents' home to the campaign that made him a martyr, seventeen years after he had left California, the axioms of his thought were always the same. They were the Jeffersonian and Jacksonian principles of destroying private economic monopolies and of advancing freedom and equal opportunity for everyone.

We shall of course discover a few exceptions along the way. The most glaring one will be Henry George's Californian attitude toward Chinese immigration. But his liberal first principles inform every one of the major items of the economic program he conceived on the West coast: absolute free trade, the abolition of private-property values in land, the repeal of discriminatory taxes, and the public ownership of telegraph lines and other public utilities. The same principles underlay also the eight books he wrote, two in California and six in New York; and they are at the moral center of all the main causes for which he labored and fought, after *Progress and Poverty* was published: land reform in the British Isles, the labor party of 1886–8 in the United States, the exposing of the Roman Catholic hierarchy in New York politics, the single-tax movement, the establishing of a free-trade policy for the Democratic party, the Bryan candidacy of 1896, and the party he called the Democracy of Thomas Jefferson.

The reformer's many undertakings were linked on a chain of consistent purpose, but much of the fascination of his life derives from the incredible largeness and flexibility with which at different times and in different situations he appeared the same actor in contrasting roles. During the Civil War he was a Republican but at other times a Democrat; between 1886 and 1896 he was, successively, a party bolter, a Cleveland man, and a Bryan man. He was an admirer of Roman Catholicism, and yet an extreme and effective critic of bishops and pope; indirectly he assisted socialism, but he fought socialists and their doctrines; the single-tax reform for which he is remembered was supported by lawyers and businessmen, principally, but the interest of working men was Henry George's prime loyalty. In one lifetime he drew the threads together, and when he died he received a salute of the people's affection as did no other American between Lincoln and Franklin Roosevelt.

Time, money, access to books and manuscripts, and the sympathy of family and colleagues are needed to write a book. For enough of the first and second, and for a wealth of the third and fourth, I am more grateful than I can say.

Serious expenditures on behalf of this research and writing began while I was a member of the faculty of Stanford University. The Council for Research in Social Science of that university made possible the microfilming for me of the best of the Henry George Collection of manuscripts in New York. During the second half of 1944, a research fellowship at the Henry E. Huntington Library allowed me time free from my regular duties, and a wonderful opportunity to study the California background of my subject. This award, which like the Stanford one was derived from Rockefeller funds, was allotted from the Huntington's grant for the study of the civilization of its own region of the United States.

In addition to the summer and autumn of 1944, I had time largely free from duty during the university year 1949–50. This was made possible, after only four years of service at the Johns Hopkins, by that university's uncommonly generous policy toward members of the faculty. For a travel grant and other assistance during that year, I am indebted to the American Philosophical Society.

The libraries I have called on have been many. Though for years I have been accustomed to handsome treatment by library people, the quick responses I received to letters of inquiry concerning George materials, the aid efficiently given during stop-over visits, have been for me a revelation of efficiency and help. For this kind of accommodation, I owe thanks, on the West coast, to the California State Library, both the main institution in Sacramento and the branch in San Francisco, and to the library of the Sacramento *Bee*. For similar help in the Middle West and in the East, I thank the Wisconsin State Historical Society, the John Crerar Library in Chicago, the Historical Society Library of Illinois, the State Library of Indiana, the University of Michigan Library, and the libraries of Smith College, and Yale, Columbia, and Princeton universities. In nearly every case the goal of inquiry has been unique manuscripts, and these collections are mentioned in detail in the 'Notes on the Sources' at the back of the book.

For library hospitality sustained over long periods of investigation, my first West coast debt is to Stanford. At the Huntington, I had the use of rich and rare Californiana, both manuscript and printed, principally of the 1850s and 1860s. On many occasions, but specially during the summers of 1945 and 1948, the Bancroft Library of the University of California has helped me use its unique California newspaper and manuscript materials. On home ground, since 1945 the Johns Hopkins Library has provided, from its rich Hutzler Collection of American economic writings, a set of Henry George's *Standard* and a number of rare editions of his works. The officials of Dartmouth College, in a region I have come to love, have made me feel that the Baker Library is a home institution also. I have used its generous resources freely for six summers of the present task.

Without any one of the libraries just mentioned, this biography would be less complete. Without the Library of Congress, especially the manuscript and newspaper materials, the book would be shorter than it is but would have taken a longer time to write. Without the unique Henry George Collection, given by Anna George de Mille to the New York Public Library, the book would not and could not have been written at all.

During the course of a decade — in the libraries, among colleagues in the universities, and among those I have consulted as participators in the Henry George movement — I have accumulated obligations which are quite as personal as professional. I should have liked to turn a phrase for each person in the list below; I hope that anyone who sees his name there will remember what he did, over and beyond the call of ordinary obligation, for I shall not forget. I am recalling ideas suggested, manuscripts, articles, and books turned up I had not the knowledge to seek for, uncommon courtesies and encouragements, criticisms that made a difference — and other forms of generosity. I thank: Thomas A. Bailey, Peter J. Coleman, Thomas I. Cook, Henry E. Cottle, Albert J. Croft, Father John Tracy Ellis, Ralph H. Gabriel, John D. Hicks, Robert C. Hill, Richard Hofstadter, Louis C. Hunter, Jeter A. Iseley, Sherman Kent, Edward Kirkland, Frederic C. Lane, Arthur S. Link, Will Lissner, Clarence D. Long, Margaret Lough, J. Rupert Mason, Broadus Mitchell, Fulmer Mood, Sidney Painter, Claude W. Petty, Belle Dale Poole, M.D., Robert E. Riegel, J. E. Wallace Sterling, Carl B. Swisher, Paul S. Taylor, Francis J. Thompson, and Louis B. Wright. For the memory of Anna George de Mille, Henry George's youngest child, who answered every question I asked, and who enthused over the idea of my book, though she was writing another, I am deeply grateful.

Six associates, who otherwise would appear in the list above, have rendered freely those time-consuming professional services by which scholars help one another. Professors Merle Curti of the University of Wisconsin and C. Vann Woodward of the Johns Hopkins have read the manuscript entire. Professor Robert Cleland of the Huntington Library counseled an inexpert student of California, at the beginning, and read Part One in manuscript; and Professor G. Heberton Evans, Jr., of Hopkins read the same part from an economist's point of view. Professor David Spring of Hopkins read chapters xi, xii, and xiii; and Professor Howard Quint of the University of South Carolina, chapters xiv, xv, and xvi. Miss Lilly Lavarello, department secretary, editor, and associate, has put up with the delays and met the deadlines, and in every case improved the manuscript. During a year while I was a visitor at the American University of Beirut, Miss Siham Haddad ably carried on that work. My wife has borne with the strains of authorship from first to last; and, at the stages of pencil draft and typescript, she took on the duties of critic and editor in addition to all else.

The responsibility for what follows is mine alone. But whatever achievement may be discovered there is to be attributed, in a proportion for which the words above are far from sufficient, to those who are named, and to others, whose help may have been less in amount, but whom I no less sincerely thank.

C.A.B.

The Johns Hopkins University
24 December 1954

Now, thirty-seven years later, I equally thank the Schalkenbach Foundation, publishers of the works of Henry George, for this second reprint edition. I hope it will draw many new readers, including those whose governments are in flux, to George's ideas on economic justice.

C. A. B.

Santa Barbara, California
April 1991

CONTENTS

———

Preface, vii

PART **I** 1839–1879

A CALIFORNIA PROTEST

I

A Boy from a Christian Home

1839–1855

A MAN's world contains the world he knew as a boy, and when things are right the legacy is strength-giving, a resource for life. Surely it was good fortune that Henry George was born and brought up in Philadelphia, during the age we name for Andrew Jackson. 'Drawing my first breath almost within the shadow of Independence Hall,' he said to the San Francisco audience which heard his first notable oration, 'the cherished traditions of the Republic entwine themselves with my earliest recollections, and her flag symbolizes to me all that I hold dear on earth.'

It is hard to think that he could have had a more appropriate heritage. Had he been blessed to be born to the inspired circle of the village of Concord, and had he learned the ideas of freedom walking beside Ralph Waldo Emerson and listening to town-meeting debate and Unitarian sermon, he would, we may think, have reached the heights younger than he did, and commenced earlier his career of writing and speaking. A latter-day Transcendentalist he might well have become, for he had that kind of sympathy and impulse; and in the Concord group he would have wanted Henry Thoreau for mentor and friend. Rephrasing American principles under these auspices, though, if environment suggests anything, he would have said more about religion than he did, and less about the social condition of man, less about land and population and trade, according to his best gifts.

Better for George's first growth, it is reasonable to think, than

3

even the community of the Transcendentalists could have been, was the bustling city where the great Declaration and the federal Constitution were written. In Philadelphia an idealist's mind turns naturally to events of state and society; remembrance of things past attaches uniquely to the birth of the Republic and connects with the rise of common people. Philadelphia recalls Benjamin Franklin; it suggests Quaker inspiration and civic growth; it brings to mind congresses and conventions, Jefferson's ideas and Washington's strength, occasions of battle and victory, and the historic statement of great principles. Philadelphia's buildings, especially the very greatest, have a meaning for Americans that monuments elsewhere can in no way rival. 'I've seen the shackled slave under the shadow of Independence Hall carried by federal arms back to his master,' Henry George told a Philadelphia audience thirty-six years after he had left the city.

Above all the place of his origin gave George as birthright the right to speak for the people of the world's great cities. Philosopher of the land though he became, he was always a city man. The burden of the present history is to tell how he executed that spokesmanship, first in San Francisco and much in New York and London and Glasgow, but also around the world — in Sacramento, Dublin, Edinburgh, Birmingham, Liverpool, Paris, Melbourne, Cleveland, Chicago, and Minneapolis, and in perhaps a hundred other cities.

Life began for Henry George on 2 September 1839, in a brick row house on Tenth Street near Pine. This was close to mid-city then, as it is today. But what is now a blighted area was a century ago a good and convenient place to live. The distances of everyday life had to be walking distances; and the Tenth Street house was six blocks from Market Street, and about a mile from St. Paul's Church. Somewhat nearer, nine blocks from home to be exact, the old statehouse known and loved as Independence Hall stood in matchless dignity. During Henry's boyhood it was still as tall or taller than the near-by buildings, and of course gave Philadelphia its architectural climax. The Customs House, where Henry's father worked many years, itself a classic in marble of Greek revival architecture, occupied an adjoining square. The fascinating waterfront of the nation's second largest city — also second commercial and financial center — lay ten blocks from home, straight down Pine, or Spruce, or Lombard.

Though born the oldest son, Henry never knew an uncrowded household. At the time of his birth the family numbered six. Besides the parents and year-old sister Caroline, there was an older sister perhaps in her teens, Harriet, whom his father had adopted during his earlier marriage. Then there was Mrs. George's sister Mary Vallance, an arthritic, who was to be the beloved Aunt Mary of thirty years of raising the George children, and who seemed to Henry the very embodiment of sacrificial love. During the 1840s and '50s there came eight children more. A year after Henry, Jane, a lively girl and in time a great student, always his favorite sister; then four other girls, two of whom died in infancy, and three boys. The boys were too much younger than Henry for companionship, though family legend has it that they worshipped him, and that five-year-old Morris cried the most bitterly of anyone when he sailed away to California. During childhood and youth it was the three girls nearest his age with whom he shared most fully. But he never lost track of any of the family, and in due course the middle brother, John Vallance, became an associate, and in later life Caroline came to live in his household.

Back of the growing family known genealogical lines were short, but even so we may guess that they were more than average length for that time and place. Henry's two grandfathers had come as immigrants of the later eighteenth century, and both had married and succeeded in the city. His father's father had been born a Yorkshireman and trained a seaman under British colors. In America he became a shipmaster and in a small way a shipowner. Married here to Mary Reid, and the father of three children, of whom Richard Samuel Henry George, our Henry's father, was youngest, Captain George had lived well, according to his prosperity. In the long reminiscence of Richard George, his home had been a bustling happy place, supplied to overflowing with good things to eat and enjoy, and amply tended by servants. Regrettably this backlog of family fortune had disappeared before Henry George's day. His father's brother, Duncan George, a businessman — whose son James preceded Henry to California — is the only relative on the paternal side who at all entered Henry's young life in Philadelphia.

On the maternal side, Henry's grandfather John Vallance had been brought as an infant from Glasgow to America. Trained as an engraver, Mr. Vallance achieved some prominence in his craft; and, to the advantage of the family which concerns us, he married Margaret Pratt. This grandmother of Henry George supplied the one quarter-section of his family which connected him deeply with Philadelphia history. She was a great-granddaughter of a member of Benjamin Franklin's Junto, which had been made up of men of mind and enterprise; and she was related to many businessmen and artist-craftsmen of the city.

Unfortunately Margaret Pratt Vallance was widowed at forty and died a decade before her daughter, Henry's mother, had married and settled. But her children and their families, two or three of them in Philadelphia, surrounded the Richard Georges. We shall hear especially of the Latimers — Aunt Rebecca Vallance Latimer, Uncle Thomas, and Cousin George. So, though Henry and his sisters and brothers never had grandparents to know and visit, they had plenty of relatives close at hand, who made life lively and sufficient in the city. None of the kin seems to have been at all wealthy. The one legacy of money mentioned in the family came to the sisters Catharine George and Mary Vallance in 1858, and probably amounted to little. Yet as Henry's luck in his teens will indicate, the Vallance connections had not infrequently a favor to bestow, to ease the strains of a family's struggle.

Before marriage, 19 April 1837, both Richard George and Catharine Vallance — he thirty-eight, she twenty-six — had been earning a living in small businesses of education. Indeed it was by reason of the school which she and her sister ran that Miss Catharine became acquainted with her husband. After the death of the first Mrs. George, the widower placed Harriet under the care of the Misses Vallance. This connection overlapped another. During the 1830s and most of the '40s Richard George earned a living by publishing Sunday school and other books for the Episcopal Church; and for a while he had as partner Thomas Latimer, a brother-in-law of the teachers. These relationships indicate that things economic were essentially equal between the life partners; and they explain how fortune provided beforehand a school-teacher mother and a school-teacher maiden aunt for the conscientious training of the children. And, in a broader view, Richard and Catharine George, humble people by temperament both of them, derived from that creative, working and small-owning element in Philadelphia society, which Professor Bridenbaugh now tells us was one of the earliest growing beds of social democracy in American city life.

The kind of living that the devoted father of the family could make for wife, sister-in-law, and nine children has been variously estimated by students of Henry George, but always with emphasis on poverty and insecurity, and with some implication that hard times during childhood embittered the mind of the future social critic and reformer. And indeed the solemn picture can be darkly drawn: the man who denied Ricardo suffered as a child from pressure of population in the family; the economist who offered to cure depressions was brought up in a household pressed by the crisis of the late '30s and early '40s; and as a teen-ager he was thrust from his parents' home by the hard times of 1857.

But these unshaded lines sketch too impressionistically from the surface, and the picture requires lightening. Before 1831 Mr. George had been a clerk in the Customs House. Then he turned to publishing. Although there is no record of the business's income, there is of its activities: Mr. George's firm operated a bookstore, and for some time it had the depository of the General Episcopal Sunday School Union, the Bible and Prayer Book Society, and the Tract Society. Church publishing was a going business in America's most enthusiastic age for missions and Sunday schools. Episcopalianism was growing, notably so in the middle states, and Mr. George was as active as a layman could be. His business weathered the depression of 1837 and after — the period of his marriage and the birth of several children. Only in 1848, when general economic conditions had improved, did he give up the firm and return to work in the Customs House. At that time large publishers were invading church publishing. Whether or not Mr. George was driven completely to the wall, all the arguments of common sense must have been on the side of a salaried job.

But abandoning one's own enterprise is hard, and the point of change fixed the memory of poverty in the family mind. The father now became an ascertaining clerk; and, with seven or eight dependents, his government salary was $800 a year. Yet this austere statistic requires both understanding and revision. Besides his office duties, Mr. George took on extra work at Parkinson's, the finest restaurant in the city, probably doing some bookkeeping.

From this source he made about $250, more than enough for a year's house rent. Also by the '50s his salary had risen to about $1100. Though it is true that the depression of 1857 caused him many anxieties, this was not until after Henry had left home; and then apparently Mr. George's only immediate deprivation was his side earnings, a loss he felt he could bear. In 1859 a government economy measure withheld one month's salary at the Customs House. The real risks of his job were political, and they did not materialize for him, as a Democrat, until 1861. Altogether his ordinary income of $1300 or $1400 during the '50s, when Henry was of an age to worry about such matters, compares very favorably with the incomes of clergymen and teachers at the time. The whole period of Henry George's childhood and youth was happily one of prevailingly low prices and rising standards of living; and Mr. George seems to have made a fair living. At darkest estimate it was genteel deprivation, not want or catastrophe, that pressed upon the George family during Henry's childhood years.

This impression is confirmed by the way in which the family lived. Their first home, the house on Tenth Street, they equipped attractively and well. The Georges had their share of good furniture, mahogany upholstered with mohair; and on the walls, beside needlework and engravings, they hung family portraits in oil appropriate to Vallance family history. Apparently they suffered some loss of situation when the size of the family compelled them to move, during the '40s, to a larger house of the same type on South Third Street, three doors north of Queen. This placed the family farther from Market Street than before, but about the same distance from the Customs House and Independence Hall, and only half a mile from church; and it brought the boy within three blocks of the water. The house was in the Southwark District, and likely most of the residents were working people; at any rate there were riots in the neighborhood on the tail of the 1837 depression. But rioting has no part in the George record; and this home was the one to which the cousins flocked, and to which, a quarter-century later when he was beginning to see the ugliness of slums, Henry George was happy to visit from California, and to send his young wife and babies for a long stay. Mr. George rented the Third Street house, gaslit and stove-heated, for $200 a year.

Letters to Henry written after he had left home in his teens tell us most of what we know about how life was lived in the place where he grew up. Of course the house was congested. With eight to a dozen people under the one roof, Henry and later his brothers chose to sleep in the attic and have a private headquarters where boys could read and talk. The other possibility, preferred but not commanded by the mother, was to sleep on a sofa downstairs, where temperatures were less extreme. Although Mrs. George had hired help at least part of the time, everyone had to share in the housework. A letter to Henry described mother, aunt, and one sister doing the family ironing. An evening caller discovered a full circle of Georges: the father reading the newspaper in a big rocking chair, the mother with a magazine, Aunt Mary and Caroline sewing, Jane writing, Tom painting pictures, and the smallest brother happy with a birthday present of candy and a quarter-peck of apples. These must have been familiar scenes, full of nostalgia for Henry.

The family's pleasures were pretty seasonal. Puritanical though they were, their Christmases combined festivity with worship: excitement, surprises, toys, guests, and turkey made the order of the day. They celebrated the Fourth of July with the enthusiasm and noise and fireworks which were habitual and appropriate in Philadelphia. Back of the house they kept a garden heavily planted; at fifteen Henry had certain rosebushes all his own. Some summers members of the family went to the country for a vacation, either to visit relatives in the Wyoming valley of northern Pennsylvania or to rest at a hotel. The family's standards Mrs. George once summed up with authority: 'neither poverty nor riches that is the happy medium. If only we can live comfortable and make both ends meet that is all I ask for. I hope that we will all possess the true riches, have an inheritance beyond the skies. This alone will bring true happiness.' By other standards the family lacked many things: travel to distant places, higher education, large expenditures or possessions of any kind. But within the family's natural orbit, Mr. George's dollars somehow afforded a medium way of life and supported a loyal and happy family.

Looking backward we may reasonably associate much of the goodness of their life together with the domestic capacities of the mother and aunt, and with the steady habits of the father. Yet if asked the older Georges would have attributed the family's soli-

darity not to themselves but to their Heavenly Father's guiding
hand. The family Bible on a pedestal table made a shrine at home,
and there they all repaired for morning and evening prayers. Even
a skeptical friend of Henry's later teens said that Richard George's
family worship affected him deeply; and probably three out of
four of the letters written to Henry in California contained
passages which tell us that questions of salvation, worship, and
Christian behavior were the ideas of greatest concern to the family.
Caroline and Jane were as anxious for Henry's spiritual well-being
as were his parents.

The historic well where they refreshed their faith was St. Paul's
Protestant Episcopal Church, one of the most influential churches
in Philadelphia. Only a few blocks from Independence Hall —
roughly halfway between it and the Third Street house — St. Paul's
occupied a handsome brick and plaster building, which had been
built before the Revolution in the great period of Philadelphia
brick architecture. Splendid iron gates at the street and a gold
and white interior stated the principles of eighteenth-century taste
and simplification within the Church of England. Henry's church
attendance made an impression on Ignatius Horstmann, a contemporary who became a Roman Catholic bishop. He remembers
the boy as, 'every Sunday, walking between his two older sisters,
followed by his father and mother, all of them so neat, and trim
and reserved.'

A family could hardly have found more ways to become closely
attached to a city church than the ways that connected the Georges
with this one. Mrs. George's mother was buried in the crowded
church lot; her father and two brothers-in-law served as vestrymen;
and her nephew George Latimer was called to the ministry there.
But no member of the Vallance family served St. Paul's longer
than did Mr. George himself. While he was still in publishing, he
taught the infant school. Thus Henry's familiarity with the Bible
ran back to church and home in his earliest days, but to the same
teacher in the two places. Beginning in 1852, Mr. George served
a seventeen-year term as vestryman, a term which included those
of his brothers-in-law and also that of Jay Cooke, the famous banker
(and Sunday school worker) who is said to have improved his contacts by moving from the Methodist to the Episcopal Church.

The Georges' absorption in St. Paul's meant more than Bible

and church and conscience in Henry's upbringing. Then as now these three could be lightly taken in a mild blend, in an Episcopal or other church. At St. Paul's the blend was heady. The age of Jackson and Emerson was the age also of the fullest flow in American history of the spirit of evangelism. Some of the flamboyant achievements of religion, more often on the frontier than not — the Mormons, the Finney revivals in New York and Ohio, the camp meetings — have unduly obscured evangelism in the cities, and in the more conservative churches. St. Paul's, appropriate to the name, illustrates the story of this little known side of the movement.

To sense the power of it, a word about Episcopal Church history is required. During the first half of the nineteenth century, the American Episcopalians, like the Church of England people, divided into High Church and Low Church inclinations. In this country High Church meant a maximum persistence of Anglican traditions and ceremonies, near to the Catholic order; and Low Church meant considerable assimilation of the less formal habits of Methodists and other evangelicals. The whole history of St. Paul's placed it in a position of Low Church leadership. The first minister of the parish had led a sort of come-outer movement from Christ Church, the oldest and in the end the most famous and aristocratic High Church parish in the city. On the eve of the Revolution St. Paul's got into 'continuous difficulty' with the Bishop of London, who had general discipline over all the Church of England parishes in America. Symbolically as well as physically, St. Paul's stood near Independence Hall.

This momentum carried forward into Henry George's day and life. During the first quarter of the nineteenth century St. Paul's became the largest parish in the state; new parishes of the Low Church kind proliferated from it in the Philadelphia area; and, under the rectorship of a man inspired by John Wesley, the early Sunday school developed. Yet the climax of evangelicalism and Americanization in the parish waited for the rector of the Georges' own time. This was Dr. Richard Newton, English-born American-trained member of a family of clergymen, his sons better remembered than himself. Dr. Newton conducted the services with 'almost rural simplicity'; there was no bowing during the recitation of the creed, and there was much attention to Sunday school work

and strong support for foreign missions, especially one in Liberia
about which Henry heard a great deal. Year after year he preached
a popular series of sermons on personalities of the Bible — and
just possibly Henry George's address on Moses, given on three con-
tinents during the last two decades of the century, was in some
degree an echo of his pastor's voice. Any radicalism that Dr. Newton
may have entertained seems to have concentrated on church
polity, where he took and debated very advanced grounds
for an Episcopalian. Like his church generally, he took no prominent role in the slavery controversy; apparently he acquiesced in
the institution and did no more for the Negro than sending
assistance to Liberia. How well the elder Georges loved his emphasis on the saving of individual souls, and loved the preacher
they made perfectly clear in letters to Henry during his first year
in California. During the extensive revivals of 1858, St. Paul's
was holding daily services, they reported joyfully, and unbelievers
in numbers were falling to their knees.

It is impossible to look forward to any period of Henry's adult
life, least of all to the twenty years after *Progress and Poverty,* and
not believe that a main line of evangelical feeling runs continuously from the spirit of St. Paul's to the spirit of his effort of
the '80s and '90s for a transforming social change. We shall discover no more persuasive evidence of this continuity than his
natural and easy renewal with Heber Newton, Dr. Newton's son, in
New York City, after they had both become prominent men. As
children they had played together at the rectory, and had gone to
school together; then in the '50s they had separated into different
courses of life which kept them apart for three decades. Yet, when
they met, they converged in common effort. Heber Newton as
minister had moved in the logic which by that time was carrying a
segment of Episcopalianism, and Protestantism generally, from his
father's evangelical emphasis on the saving of souls to the new
emphasis on bringing into being the Kingdom of God on earth. In
the long run the two men, Henry George and Heber Newton, drew
on a common source of energy and moved in a common direction.

In the shorter view, though, scraps of evidence tell us that Henry
as a youngster bucked the current of piety at home. He was never
confirmed at St. Paul's, and after he left home his parents had a
couple of years of worry about his spiritual condition. Perhaps

there is a flash of antagonism in a story from catechism class, when he was seven or eight. Dr. Newton asked the boys why the grocery-man keeps netting over dried peaches. 'To keep the flies out,' sallied young Henry. Yes, to prevent stealing, the minister replied, his own face reddening. And shortly after arriving in California, still in his teens, Henry begrudged his admiration for Dr. Newton: 'I like him better than any other minister I have ever heard,' he told his sister, with some ambivalence. By that time Henry George was capable of thinking ill of a man who acquiesced in slavery. Perhaps only by reason of a streak of aversion for an intense man, or of a youngster's feeling that he had been overdosed with religion, Henry at home had some reservation about St. Paul's, and never reached full commitment of faith under its auspices.

Yet he was not to delay long in making a Christian commitment. And as for his loyalty to the church in which he was reared, he made an almost unconscious declaration in California. Editorializing during his thirties — at a stage when he was altogether concerned with public affairs and the least concerned with religion of any period of his life — his eye was caught and irritated by a comment on Episcopalian worship in the San Francisco *Chronicle*. Contrary to that paper, he declared in his own columns, American Episcopalianism had not always been highly ritualistic; the services of the church were often even plainer than those of Methodists, Baptists, and Congregationalists. Let us hope, he said, that the Episcopal Church may ever go its way, 'meeting the child with words of promise, and soothing the mourner at the grave, and daily expressing in its liturgy the needs and aspirations of the human heart.'

The story of Henry George in school, though it is very short, gives the first line of individual record along which to follow his boyhood growth. After learning the R's at home under the school teachers of the family, he was sent at about six to a private school in the Third Street vicinity, run by a Mrs. Graham. He remained three years. Then he transferred for a short term in the Mount Vernon School, a public grammar school in the rapidly growing and recently reformed Philadelphia system.

At the age of nine he changed to the Episcopal Academy of Philadelphia, which next to the older Friends' schools was as historic as any in the city. It was housed in a handsome eighteenth-century building, and it represented the social and intellectual character of Episcopalianism generally. In the years just preceding Henry's attendance, the curriculum had been reformed under the leadership of Bishop Alonzo Potter as chairman of the board. Modern languages, penmanship, drawing, and 'graphics' were offered the younger boys; a Divinity Department taught Latin, Greek, and Hebrew to the older students; and there was instruction in science as well. Unfortunately we have no way of following Henry's course in this curriculum, three years and a half from February 1849 to June 1852, and no knowledge of the grades he made. Most likely his studies were all elementary, possibly with some beginning work (if so, all he ever had) in foreign languages.

For no plain reason the boy did not do well at the Academy and became so unhappy that he asked to be withdrawn. The family remembers that he was uneasy because his father paid only a reduced tuition fee, the same as for sons of Episcopal ministers. But the full fee was only $60 a year, and there were many free scholars. Possibly Henry used the fee question to cover some resistance to school piety, or to the Divinity Department looming ahead; or not unlikely at age thirteen he felt self-conscious at the Academy, coming from the Southwark District and being associated with sons of the city's mansions. Whatever the reason, his withdrawing asserts for the first time a disinclination, which became lifelong, for education that was not vocational, or practical in some immediate way. Knowledge as tradition and cultivation, though in time he was to become a reader of poetry and the literature of ideas, never at any stage of his development appealed to Henry George.

After Henry left the academy, Mr. George placed him under a coach, a Mr. Henry Lauderbach, to prepare him for the public high school. This led to a half-year of good study. The pupil enjoyed the teacher; and the teacher found the boy apt and well equipped in basic knowledge. Much later Henry George looked back on this interval as the most effective part of his education, and in due course he tried to arrange to have his own son study under the same man.

The last stage of his formal education proved very brief. On 5 February 1853, at thirteen and a half, he entered Philadelphia's new and excellent high school. His average score in the entrance examinations was 67, which placed him in the middle of the group of 115 boys admitted at the same time. Unfortunately the school records, which are so precise at the point of entering, become as silent as those of the Episcopal Academy about the quality of work he did. From the curriculum of the period, a present official of the school thinks that Henry must have studied the history of England, English composition, Latin grammar, bookkeeping, natural philosophy, phonography (stenography, correspondence style), and penmanship and drawing. But whatever he took, Henry did not sustain the diet. On 20 June, after only four and a half months, still less than fourteen years old, he quit school for good. His next full-time studies would not come until a quarter-century had passed, and he settled down to *Progress and Poverty*.

Amply, perhaps more amply than any other American city at the time, Philadelphia offered a boy chances for self-education, outside school doors. A century after Benjamin Franklin, the city's good libraries, the American Philosophical Society, and the Franklin Institute sustained the effort to achieve a people's culture which the great civic benefactor had been proud to start. Henry was a reading boy. The very last thing he did before going to sea in 1855 was to get a friend to return a book, and to arrange his withdrawing from the Apprentices Library. Like his mother he loved the romantic novels and poetry of the time, and both he and Jane read them avidly. Yet in this category of literature we have an instance of his boy's taste straying beyond the orbit of the family: he had to smuggle the *Scottish Chiefs* to his bedroom for secret reading.

By the time he reached his middle teens he was reading at least a little history and contemporary thought. A diary which is dated 1855 but which includes entries from the next few years contains notes on Emerson's new essays, the now famous *Representative Men*. Under a heading for English history, Henry listed dynasties and sovereigns; and, under American history, events from 1487 to 1777, and the presidents and vice-presidents from Washington to Pierce. Also in the diary, it would seem with a mind that was noticing affairs in Europe, he jotted down the areas and populations of Great Britain, France, Austria, and the principal Italian states. At the time when he was keeping these notes Henry belonged to a literary club, so styled, by the name of the Lawrence Society. Even in the midst of none too literary proceedings, Henry and his contemporaries wagged their tongues about Aristophanes and Byron,

and had their say about public affairs. The sum of scattered indications is that by sixteen Henry George had read a fair amount
and perhaps a great deal, and that much of what he read came from
outside the domain of his family's dominant, evangelical and
Biblical, thought.

Much the same applies to the other varieties of his young experience in Philadelphia. Dancing and cards were forbidden in the
family, and the theater also; but with the aid of Barnum, who
disguised plays for the Philadelphia pious by announcing lecture-
performances, Henry had a share of fun. He went also to the
Franklin Institute, where his uncle Thomas Latimer was a member
and able to get him in. The diary of 1855 shows that in the early
months of that year he attended lectures on science three times a
week, and enjoyed most the lectures on climatology and organic
chemistry. Thus the legacy Benjamin Franklin left to the people
of Philadelphia became in some way the boy's own.

A good heritage and culture were Henry George's during his
childhood, not glittering and not overrich, yet more historic, more
deeply informed by principle and tradition, and more varied and
ample than first statements about family income, and austerity,
and his own schooling would naturally suggest.

II

Independence by Sea

1855–1857

OUT of school Henry found a job with Asbury and Company, importers of china and glass. They paid him $2 a week for long hours of copying papers, wrapping parcels, and running errands, and he stuck it out for a year or so, performing to satisfaction. Then he moved to a clerkship in a marine adjuster's office. 'Don't you remember our conversations about the pitiful sums of your weekly earnings?' his mother asked years later, when it was his brother Val's turn to be dissatisfied, making $1.50 a week.

The way out was the water route. Though breaking from the family circle at age fifteen sounds pretty extreme for a proper George, going to sea was really not at all unnatural. It was only one step from his father's office to the offices where Henry had his first jobs, and one step more from clerking in a maritime business to a ship's deck. As a little fellow Henry had loved the sea stories his father told from the lore of Captain George — particularly the patriotic ones of his grandfather's valor during the War of 1812 — and father and son had roamed the Philadelphia waterfront together. 'One of our chief playgrounds,' remembers William Newton, brother of Heber, 'was about the wharves of the city. [Henry] had a friend who was a sea captain and I a cousin, and both of us had our minds set on a sea voyage.' And in his own much later retrospections, Henry George cherished the education he had had, knowing and loving the port. He had seen the first iron steamship ever to put into Philadelphia, he once told an audience, and the fact of

iron afloat had astounded him: in time the boy had thought of
the hollowness within, and conceived for himself a notion of the
displacement of water by a floating body. He made model brigs
for the mantlepiece at home; and for the rest of his days he loved
to sail, and to make sketches of sailing vessels.

Opportunity came in 1855, and he must have been watching
for it. About the middle of January Henry noticed in the *Herald*
that the Indiaman *Hindoo* had put into New York after a voyage
from the Orient. This was the vessel on which a twenty-four-year-
old fellow parishioner of St. Paul's, Samuel Miller, sailed as mate.
With the assistance of George Latimer the two met, at St. Paul's
Church it seems likely, and talked out Henry's hopes. The boy
learned that Miller expected by spring to be put in command of
the *Hindoo* and sent to Australia and India; and Henry was
promised that if the promotion came off he too could ship. Within
a month or so, the friend, now Captain Miller, wrote that they
could go ahead. He would gladly help with gathering a sea-going
outfit; his one anxiety was that should anything go wrong the
George family would never forgive him. 'Any trouble would be my
misfortune not my fault.'

At the point of decision making, Henry's diary takes on a flavor
of secrecy and conspiracy. Yet it is more likely that the elder Georges
fooled the boy, by being undeceived, than that he brought off anything very secret. The fact that his cousin, who within a few weeks
was to be ordained a minister, sat in on the conference, makes it
pretty clear that family affairs never slipped out of adult supervision. At any rate, when Henry broached the matter, his parents,
who had had a recent experience of his being willful around the
house, did not object too much; and the arrangements of detail
were made rather between Mr. George and Captain Miller than
by Henry himself. He was to sail as foremast boy. In the hope that
he would not have too good a time and want to go to sea again, the
father asked that things not be made too soft. As his mother later
reviewed the matter: 'We had perfect knowledge of the Captain and
he promised to watch and protect you as a brother which he did.'

On Sunday, 1 April, the day before leaving, St. Paul's Sunday
school gave Henry a new Bible, and George Latimer presented a
copy of James's *Anxious Inquirer*. (Some Sundays later the young
minister pleased the family by praying for Henry during church

service.) On Monday the moment of going was hard, and the boy almost faltered. But his father, two uncles, and half a dozen cousins and friends went with him to the Delaware river ferry; and from there he traveled with Sam Miller, 'four hours brooding' to New York. Some of the farewell letters from Philadelphia were pretty doleful, such as the one from a chum who told his 'Dear Mackerel' that he hoped this parting would not be the last one. Doubtless the railroad journey gave Henry his first and most emotional opportunity to read a poem signed 'F. C.,' and written out in the prettiest and primmest hand a girl could manage.

> *Thou Henry still art young,*
> *And does not see the wonder Thou wilt tread*
> *The buoyant deck, and look upon the flood,*
> *Unconscious of the high sublimity . . .*
> *Blest be thy passage o'er the changing sea*
> *Of life; the clouds be few that intercept*
> *The light of joy. The waves roll gently*
> *Beneath thy bark of hope, and bear thee safe*
> *To meet in peace, thine other father, — God.*

The blurs and creases and turned down corners of the good paper on which this message is inscribed are the first signs of record that Henry was interested in Florence Curry, who was the daughter of a family friend, or in any girl.

The youngster bucked up in New York City. He signed the shipping articles at $6 a month, three-quarters as much net as he had earned gross at home. He had a few days for sight-seeing. The great city struck him much more happily in 1855 than it was to in 1869, when we shall find him making his next and crucial visit. He liked everything, perhaps excepting the Customs House, which he compared unfavorably with the one where his father worked. His eye was pleased by the regularity of the streets, and the brownstone houses and the city gardens; and from the Battery the views of land and water entranced him. First experiences of living and working as a seaman were 'a great deal easier than expected': he mentioned sleeping in the after-house with carpenter and cook, and eating meals prepared by hands as clean as kitchen hands at Parkinson's. With a 'God bless you all' he ended his good-bys on 10 April as the *Hindoo* was pulled downstream for the long voyage.

The vessel, though twenty-five years old, was good size for then —
586 tons register, 1200 tons burden — and the outward cargo comprised half a million feet of lumber for Australia. The normal
crew, Henry had understood beforehand, was nineteen men: fourteen able seamen, the cook, the steward, two mates, and the captain.
On this trip the foremast boy, and possibly also the carpenter, was
extra. The crew, the members of which Mr. Miller had some
trouble picking up, was a properly mixed lot, men from the West
Indies, a Spaniard, and an Englishman among them, and they all
looked interesting to the youngest member.

Henry George's fifteen months on the *Hindoo* became the
natural occasion of his doing his first sustained writing. There was
opportunity to mail letters at only three points: before sailing from
New York, at Melbourne, the port of call, and from Calcutta, the
destination. But for everyday a sailor may keep a journal, and
Henry did a remarkable job. In interesting detail he put down his
routine duties, keeping watch and doing odd jobs; and he recorded
his introspections also — homesickness at first, Sunday thoughts
of St. Paul's, and remembrance of the pies his mother baked. It
was all very normal: no emotions to excess, hard work but not too
much to do.

Best of all the youngster's mind reached out, noticing things
and putting them down with clarity and force and economy of
word. For instance, the story in his Sea Journal of the Fourth of
July in the South Atlantic: 'Weds. July 4. At 12 o'clock last night the
day was ushered in by three discharges from a small swivel, which
made a great deal of noise, rousing up all who were asleep. As soon
as the smoke cleared away and the dead and wounded were mustered, it was found that it had not been without execution, all
the glass on one side of the house being shattered (a loss not easily
repaired), a port blown out; and the waddings (made of rope yarn,
and very hard) had passed, one through the head of the new water
cask, and another through the new foretopsail, which had not
been bent a week . . . At 12 m. all hands were called to reef.
While reefing the foretopsail the parrel of the yard gave way, causing a great deal of trouble and keeping all hands from dinner. It
was 2:30 p.m. before our watch got below to their plum duff, which
had been allowed in honour of the day. The rest of the day was
rainy, with wind constantly varying, keeping us hawling on the

braces. Thus closed the most miserable 4th of July that I have ever yet spent.'

Not often in the journal did he turn from the facts to the feeling of what he saw. But we may look ahead, near to journey's end, to see that at sixteen he could express an emotion and an impression too. On 28 May 1856, he noted: 'I witnessed this afternoon one of the most beautiful storms that I have ever seen. It was about 4 p.m., the sun shining brightly. The squall or rather shower came up astern: the space over which it extended seemed not above ¼ mile in width and its bounds were as clearly marked on the water as those of a sandy beach. Where it was raining the sea seemed as though it were molten silver which contrasted strongly with the deep blues adjoining. The wind curling the tops of the waves made a most beautiful appearance. On the whole was suspended a small but most beautiful rainbow. The shower quickly came on us, but it was light, and as quickly departed.' Evidently writing was fun; certainly there was no other reason than doing a task because he liked to do it, for Henry to keep this journal.

Outward bound the *Hindoo* swung far southeast. Far out of sight of land all the way, the vessel rounded the Cape of Good Hope about the middle of July, and from there ran into cold and gales in the southern Indian Ocean. At last on 24 August, the 137th day at sea, the ship put into Hobson's Bay, the port of Melbourne. Here occurred the most difficult event of the voyage, apparently Henry's very first experience of the conflict of working men with property and authority.

According to his Sea Journal, the sailors planned to leave the *Hindoo* in Australia, and they were in a hurry. He heard them talk about the region around Melbourne as a 'Land of Promise, where gold was to be had by all.' He sympathized with their haste, on the day of putting in, as he heard the men discussing 'What they would do, where they would go, and how they would spend their money when they got it.' But under their articles they were not free until the cargo had been unloaded, and here the crew balked. Fearing that, if they put the lumber ashore, Captain Miller would not pay them, they demanded immediate discharge. Of course this played right into the captain's hands: he regarded the whole crew as a miserable lot, and naturally refused the demand.

Three days of tension passed aboard the *Hindoo,* riding anchor well out in Hobson's Bay. Then as the crew had wanted, the American consul was brought aboard. Seated on the booby-hatch, he heard grievances and commitments. 'Some complained of bad food,' Henry recorded without stating his own judgment, 'others of bad language and threats used to them by the officers, and some of blows and one of sickness caused by falling from aloft.' The consul found in favor of the ship's master; and Captain Miller followed the judgment by saying that once the cargo was unloaded, 'he would pay them their wages and let them go in peace.' Yet authority somehow lost power. The sailors demanded the captain's promise in writing; he refused, and the men refused to work. The struggle ended with the striking sailors' being convicted and taken to prison ship for a month's hard labor. The lumber was discharged and ballast taken aboard, doubtless at lower cost to the business venture than paying sailors' wages from New York.

We gather that, though legal right seems to have been all on the side of the young captain, Henry George tacitly sympathized with the strikers. Perhaps it was simple shock and resentment at first seeing maritime law, or any kind of labor law, in action. Or it may have been more: Henry may have felt some truth in the sailors' incidental complaints and have judged Sam Miller too truculent in young authority. We may take the word of Henry George, Jr., and Anna George de Mille that his championing sailors' rights, as an editor nearly twenty years later, connected in his mind with unforgettable scenes in Hobson's Bay. In 1840, American enlightenment, in the person of Richard Henry Dana, had begun stating the facts and making the fight for seamen, demanding that they be treated essentially like other laborers and citizens. Henry George, in this as much as anyone Dana's successor, made his background observations in Australia.

Though the *Hindoo* lay over nearly a month, Henry went to Melbourne only once, just long enough to remember at his visit of 1890 the city's earlier San Francisco-like appearance: 'its busy streets, its seemingly continuous auctions, its crowds of men with flannel shirts and long high boots, its bay crowded with ships.' When the time came for economic writing, he always had an eye for what was going on in Australia and New Zealand.

In the Sea Journal, a couple of periods of being becalmed, one of them at the crossing of the equator, were the only matters of note for the remainder of the outward voyage. Then, in one of his most effective passages, he described the approach up the Hooghly River to Calcutta: 'Mon. Dec. 3 . . . About 5 a.m. we were taken in tow by the steamer and proceeded up the river. The night air was misty and chilly and a monkey jacket proved very comfortable. The day soon began to break, revealing a beautiful scene. The river at times very broad and again contracting its stream into a channel hardly large enough for a ship of average size to turn in, was bordered by small native villages, surrounded by large fruit trees, through which the little bamboo huts peeped . . . On the banks the natives began to go to their daily toil, some driving cattle along, others loading boats with grain, while the women seemed busy with their domestic affairs. As we approached the city, the banks on both sides were lined with handsome country residences of the wealthy English . . . The river which [at Garden Reach] takes a sudden bend was crowded with ships of all nations, and above nothing could be seen but a forest of masts. On the right hand or Calcutta side, are the East India Company's works, for repairing their steamers, numbers of which, principally iron, were undergoing repairs . . . One feature which is peculiar to Calcutta was the number of dead bodies floating down in all stages of decomposition, covered by crows who were actively engaged in picking them to pieces. The first one I saw filled me with horror and disgust, but like the natives, you soon cease to pay any attention to them.'

The *Hindoo* lay nearly all of December and the first half of January in Calcutta harbor, and Henry had freedom to explore a great deal in city and countryside. But the first matter for a boy away from home was a batch of letters, the only ones to reach him on the voyage. His mother had asked friends and relatives to write, and his father had made a packet of the letters: the effort seems to have been planned as group persuasion that Henry should stay at home next time. The letters brought an ocean of affection. From home, humor and teasing as well as words on the sadness of separation, and news of all the relatives; and, from a friend, the not too distressing item that Henry's 'dear Florie' had cried the entire day of his departure, and now was looking 'awful' as she had grown 'several feet.' Thus reminded, the boy wrote the long letters which still tell the story of his visit to India. He shopped for presents to take home, and accumulated in Calcutta a parrot and many handkerchiefs, boxes, fans, and other 'nic nacks.' For himself he selected a pet monkey, a lively and comforting little beast which turned out to be the only member of a considerable menagerie brought aboard the *Hindoo* to survive the passage to New York.

In port the captain and the foremast boy were free to be friends and have their fun together. They suffered a little from change of diet at first, but the weather was beautiful, and during the ten days before Christmas they visited both Calcutta and Barrackpore, sixteen miles away. They saw a juggler perform, and a dwarf dance; and in a park Henry climbed a giant banyan tree. The captain thought it curious to see white and colored people mix promiscuously on the streets and was tempted to thump a colored gentleman walking with three white girls. Henry recorded no reaction to his commander's attitude. The two found the stores open late on Christmas eve, and the churches crowded on Christmas day. They attended an early service in the cathedral of the Church of England, and then a late service in another Anglican church. They presented themselves with a holiday dinner and really must have had a glorious time. But most of their thoughts that day, the captain insisted, went back to Philadelphia. India was never mystic India to Henry George after this visit; it was an actual, grim, and suffering India. And in course of time, when as social critic he was ready to compare peoples and their problems, having seen the land was to make the literature of India the more fascinating to him, and his argument the more effective.

For the return voyage once again new sailors had to be signed, and Henry noticed that, though they came from more diverse origins than the outgoing crew, almost to a man they had been in the United States and now considered themselves to be Americans. There was room for thought in this: the fourteen 'Americans' included men from England, Ireland, Scotland, Wales, Holland, and Russia. As they were about to sail the boy noticed that the cargo was very 'tight' and the ship 'deep.' He predicted a long voyage, about 120 days, which would bring them into New York about the middle of May. He predicted his own situation also: on arrival home he would have about $50, 'not much for 13 or 14 months.' But not a bad net gain, either, one may think, considering that his total wages would have come to about $85 or $90, and that he had already seen the sights of New York, Melbourne, and Calcutta, on funds advanced.

The worst of the return voyage came at the very start, when adverse winds kept the *Hindoo* three weeks beating down the eighty-six mile stretch of the Hooghly River, a terrible annoyance. The Philadelphians were made happy though on 4 February, the day when at last the pilot could be dropped, because, as they were about to leave the river's mouth, Captain Miller's father brought in his splendid new ship, an American clipper. There was much visiting back and forth, in a small way a St. Paul's reunion, before the *Hindoo* put out to sea.

During the first month the cook sickened and died, and for a few days the captain gave Henry duty in the galley, a job he hated. Otherwise the voyage home lacked much event. The monkey kept him company, and, says Henry, prevented the cockroaches from crawling on his face while he slept. On 13 April the *Hindoo* rounded the Cape of Good Hope again, two weeks later sighted St. Helena, and on 14 June put safely into New York harbor. An April entry in the Sea Journal, the last that requires quoting, tells us that the writer was relishing his adventure: 'One year has passed since the Sunday when I took farewell of my friends — to me an eventful year; one that will have a great influence in determining my position in life; perhaps more so than I can at present see. O that I had it to go over again! Homeward bound! In a few months I hope to be in Philadelphia once more.'

It was a browned and much grown-up young fellow who returned to the Third Street home as summer came on, less than three months short of seventeen. Though he was proud of having gone to sea, in some degree his parents won their point. He showed no sign of wanting to go again; and in the future he thought of seaman-ship for himself only as the means to earn a passage, or in hard times as a very temporary make-do. Final advice against seamanship as a possible career for Henry George was written by Sam Miller, as he was about to sail again: 'I hope you will find some agreeable and profitable employment before long, take my advice and never go to sea. You know the troubles of a sailor's life before the mast, it never gets any better. [The] 2d mate leads proverbially a dog's life, the mate and Captain's very little better.' Henry had now to set a new course for himself, and he knew it; but his bearings were far from clear.

Of course the first question was a job, but finding one was slow. Some unnamed errand took him on an overnight trip to Baltimore in August. He seems to have been doing some work for the uncle who paid his way, rather than looking for a position; and Henry put down in his diary only that he talked politics and wandered about the waterfront of the city. At last in September, and this time again through his father's arranging, he got a job sufficient for the time being. This was an apprenticeship in the printing shop of King and Baird, and once more the pay was only $2 a week. But Mr. George thought of the printing trade as educational, and one to open doors, and Henry fell into step. They never did a wiser thing together.

As printer's apprentice the boy learned fast. After eight months he could set 4000 ems a day 'on common news work,' an amount which would earn a journeyman printer about $10 a week, he boasted. He made friends and picked up ideas. 'Henry George was a remarkably bright boy always in discussion with other boys in the office,' Ned Wallazz tells us. 'He got into the habit of appealing to me (I am seven or eight years older) for support as to his dates and facts, historical and political.' This was 1857, the year when Pennsylvania's James Buchanan became President, the year also of Dred Scott, and of the beginning of a depression. Henry George's own recollection of print-shop talk fixes on an economic idea taught him by an old printer of the firm, the proposition — which might have been concocted out of the pages of Adam Smith himself, and which certainly conformed with the ideas of the *laisser faire* school, which prevailed in the United States almost as uniformly as in England — that in old and settled countries workmen are paid low wages, and that in new countries they are paid high. It was an idea to disturb a boy who remembered Australia, and who was beginning to hear and think about the American West coast. Philadelphia was an old city; and Henry had three years ahead at $2 a week, before at twenty-one he could become a journeyman and earn an independent living of his own.

The dimness and distance of his prospects in the printing office were matched by a certain incompatibility at home. Not that there was a sharp break, nor that the Georges failed to allow leeway for a lad in his later teens. Jo Jeffreys, one of Henry's more spirited contemporaries, gives us an attractive description of how Henry entertained his friends in the attic bedroom, the gaslight dim and books spread around, with hours on hours of talk. When the host drowsed off, the friends filed out and let him rest. But Henry had not been home long when his father quarreled with him about the hours he kept; and he and his mother argued, not far from election time, about slavery. In this Democratic family the parents condoned slavery as sanctioned by Scripture, and they rejected abolitionism in the way President Buchanan did, as an altogether exaggerated and impractical movement. Henry retorted that his mother's attitude rested 'on policy not principle,' and that the ownership of human beings gave slave masters too much power. Henry George was thinking of home and church in 1857, we may be sure, when he recalled much later, 'how over and over again I have heard all questions of slavery silenced by the declaration that the negroes were the *property* of their masters, and that to take away a man's slave without payment was as much a crime as to take away his horse without payment.' Very likely Henry's going one Sunday to the Swedenborgian Church of the New Jerusalem was a bit of a declaration of moral and spiritual independence.

During his months at home Henry's most particular friends were Ned Wallazz, of King and Baird's, Joseph Jeffreys, who was about to take up the study of law, and two old chums, the brothers Charles and Collins Walton. All shared in the Lawrence Society. Now, as apparently not before the voyage to India, that organization indulged in gay activities, some of them surprising for members and friends of the George family. What with boxing and fencing and general horseplay, 'the exercises tended to promote the muscular rather than the literary character,' says Charlie Walton; and there came times 'when the test of merit, and the standard of membership, was the drinking of the most Red Eye, the singing of the best song, and the smoking of the most segars.' Henry did not refuse. Writing to an absent member he explained that his letter would 'savor the filthy weed,' for he was smoking 'one of the longest kind of pipes filled with Stead's,' and he told about 'a drunk last Saturday night, when Jeffreys laid down in the street to be carried home and put to bed.' The Georges knew that Henry smoked, and probably knew that he drank too. Certainly they knew about Jo Jeffreys, whom Jane George liked. 'Confound it,' Jo told Henry after a call, 'when we are drunk we go just where we ought not to.'

Yet the Lawrence Society's original interest in books and ideas persisted, and the boys did compositions on serious subjects. From 1857 we have two contributions by Henry, the very earliest known essays of his writing. The first deals with Mormonism. With a gay 'Ho Brothers' for salutation, Henry launched into denunciation: polygamy, he said, exposed the Mormons to incredible temptations; and their organizing and colonizing activities created for the leaders of the movement extra temptations, to exploit the common membership. (Was this already recurrent theme, that power corrupts, so soon even a half-serious idea with Henry George?) To his moralizing without benefit of facts Henry added unflattering estimates of Joseph Smith and Brigham Young; and he ended by arguing that the Latter-day Saints should somehow be brought to submit to government authority. Except for his anti-slavery feeling, this bit of social judgment is the first instance in the record of Henry George's proposing to change the ways of men.

His other Lawrence Society composition concerns 'The Poetry of Life,' and it takes us closer to the inner man. Poetry, said Henry, belongs to him who sees life round and who nurtures the divine flame. It is denied to those whose views are narrowed 'to the sole end of wealth.' He alone knows the poetry of life who can withdraw from the noise and hustle, and 'who strips the idols of common adoration to their nakedness, [and] views man as he was created, a being a little lower than the angels, but crowned in glory and honour, as a being awful in his powers and sublime in the rightly directed use of them.' Poetry occurs in the universal experiences: in the hopes of youth, 'in the first dawning of love,' in 'the fierce struggles of man with his fellows,' at last in death itself. 'If we would view men and things in their true effects and relations, we must withdraw from the turmoil and let the soul take her stand.'

We could easily say that as first essays the Lawrence Society papers, certainly the 'Mormonism' one, are better forgiven and forgotten. But the Sea Journal of 1855 and 1856 places them from the outset in the sequence of Henry George's writing; and they demand notice as they fix the point of turning from the clear flow of descriptive expression, which first came bountifully to him, into more turgid channels of thought and writing. Aboard the *Hindoo* at fifteen and sixteen he had written with little self-consciousness, for himself alone, about external things; but now, and for a while in the future, self-consciousness and self-assertiveness were the order of the day. It may or may not be significant that Henry's reading pieces of Emerson — exhortations toward self-expression, every line of them — occurred almost certainly between writing the Sea Journal and the Lawrence Society essays. As of 1857, the important thing is that, nearly a decade before he began to earn his living by his pen, Henry George had spontaneously phrased his boy's thoughts in both the precise and objective and the hortatory and subjective modes of expression common in his day. It is only normal that at eighteen he was yet making no effort toward that difficult goal: welding the two together into a powerful tool of expression and persuasion. It would take a quarter-century and the writing of a great book to do just that.

Besides family, job, friends, and ideas, Henry had time for one other interest, Florence Curry and her family. The family as a whole was important to him: the widowed mother, Mrs. Rebecca Curry, who heard his troubles; the older daughters, Martha and Emma, especially Emma who wrote him when Florence did not, and who was an intimate of his sister Caroline; and Florence, apparently a few years his junior, who fascinated him. The Currys were friends of the family and fellow parishioners at St. Paul's, and they had connections. Born a Kelley, Mrs. Curry had as brother no less a person than the Philadelphia judge who, as Republican Congressman, would presently be known as 'Pig Iron' Kelley, the most famous spokesman for the iron interests of the state. More to the concern of Henry, the widow's nephew, George Curry, was now territorial governor of Oregon, and he invited his aunt and cousins to join him. Accordingly, in March 1857, Mrs. Curry packed up her family and left Philadelphia, to take charge of a new home on the Pacific coast.

On seeing the family depart, Henry was quite as desolated as Florence had been in 1855. He let his feelings be hurt because, though he stood by until their boat sailed, he received no farewell wave or glance, a deprivation he may have misunderstood; and he trudged back to the printing office in the doldrums, pondering 'the mutability of human affairs.' But within a month Emma was writing about an expectation which they had discussed at home; and during the summer Florence herself, 'stony-hearted' about letter writing though Henry called her, was mentioning it

too: 'We will have a home to offer you and warm hearts to welcome
you.' The girls wrote most of the letters, but Mrs. Curry approved.
Indeed the family could hardly have reached Portland before
Henry wrote the mother that he was 'still of the same opinion about
going West; you know my reasons . . . I only wait for your promised account of Oregon, and advice to determine where and
when I shall go.' So it appears that during the winter of 1856–7,
perhaps no more than six months after returning from India, again
in conference with St. Paul's people, Henry George decided to leave
home for more than just a voyage.

His determination to go West, at a time to depend on circumstances and the advice of his friends, became the more important
on 10 June. On that day he quarreled with the job-room foreman
at King and Baird's and had to quit. Possibly he was given extra
courage by the latest word from the Currys: one of their friends,
the editor of the Oregon *Statesman,* had said that if Henry would
come he would pay him journeyman's wages, $4 or $5 a day in the
new territory. But no letter from Oregon put travel money in his
pocket, and only after stalling a couple of days did he nerve himself to confess to his family that he had got himself out of a job. He
returned home low spirited, he confessed to his diary, 'and told
Pop that I had left K & B. * * * * * * .' To the distant friends
he wrote that he had been 'learning little and making little . . .
and would not quietly submit to the impositions and domineering
insolence of the foreman.' It was still too early for him to sense
that he was unemployed in a year of economic contraction,
and that opportunities western or eastern might close up on him
at an abnormal rate, as presently they did.

For a short while he made do in Philadelphia. For six days he was
hired to do the work of a journeyman compositor who was out on
strike; the work ended when the strike ended, and he was paid
$7.50, his largest wages to date, and the only scab wages of his
life. Next, in July, he worked on a weekly sheet, *The Merchant,*
and was paid only 'better than nothing.' Meanwhile his father discovered a possibility for him in the printing firm of Stavely and
McCalla, at $2.25 a week, with more promised in the second year.
But this was on condition that he stay with the firm until he became twenty-one, and Henry would have none of it. He was tired
of being an apprentice. The stop-gap job he took in late summer,

shipping to Boston and return on a coal barge, at least spared him more of that humiliation. He proved to a doubting skipper that he had strength and skill to man the wheel, and so earned the wages of an able seaman.

By fall the hard times had hit and he knew it. In a letter written but not sent to a brother in the Lawrence Society, Henry grieved: 'The times are damned hard, and are practically getting worse every day . . . There are thousands of hard-working mechanics now out of employment in this city. And it is to the fact that among them is your humble servant, that you owe this letter. If you will send on without delay the V. you owe me, you will be doing the State a service by lessening the pressure of the hard times upon one of the hard-fisted mechanics who form her bone and muscle.' And Henry demanded also to be told of any rich men or corporations his friend happened to know ('I should much prefer the latter, especially if their rules and regulations are a little lax') who might want 'a nice young man of my well known talents and capacities.' He was ready for a canal boat, he said, if only it would pay.

Yet even at this moment of anxious temporizing, Henry saw better things ahead. If we may trust a much later recollection, he had learned by the time of the Boston trip that a steamer was being fitted out in the Philadelphia Navy Yard for lighthouse service on the Pacific coast — a marvelous chance for a free passage. With his parents fully in counsel, he wrote to Congressman Thomas B. Florence, a Philadelphian who was interested in navy business. He wanted to become an 'ordinary seaman or first-class boy' on the *Shubrick,* he petitioned. His father backed him up with a personal appeal; and Mr. Florence promised to help. In addition Henry besought his uncle Thomas Latimer to influence people in the Lighthouse Bureau in Washington, so that he might be permitted to earn his way on the *Shubrick* without the normal commitment to remain on the crew after arrival. In due course he submitted testimonials; and he even stretched the truth to represent himself as 'a graduate of the Philadelphia High School.'

The pressure moved the wheels. About six weeks after the approach to Representative Florence, Henry George was appointed steward of the bright new craft. The only hitch was that he was obliged to sign for a full year's service; but even this was sweetened by a promise of $40 a month, much the best he had ever earned. He could now make his way to the Currys if he chose; or he would probably have a chance to settle into federal-government service, as his father had. Certainly he would see his married cousin James George, an older contemporary who was fairly well situated now as bookkeeper in a San Francisco clothing firm. In that distant western land, infinite possibilities lay open.

Things moved fast. Henry had to leave suddenly three days before Christmas; his orders came so late that there was no time for proper farewells. A picture was taken, disappointing compared to the daguerreotype of 1855. Though Ned Wallazz learned what was happening in time to write Henry a letter, Jo Jeffreys missed him, calling on the evening of departure. The lovable scamp, now his best friend, comforted the family by lending a picture he had, better than the new one, for duplication.

The parting was hard for the affectionate pious family. Aunt Mary and sister Caroline put solemn thoughts into their good-by letters, like those of 1855: their hopes that nephew and brother would do nothing dishonorable, and their faith that the day would come soon 'when our dear Henry will be one of the lambs of Christ.' Yet we may cheerfully doubt that in the rush such thoughts were said aloud. More likely spoken were the things the parents chose to write: they were completely satisfied with the job on the *Shubrick,* and they were confident that it would lead to good results. Though in a New Year's letter the mother said how dreadfully she had missed Henry on Christmas day, she admitted that if she could she would not now wish him back: 'I want you to be something and somebody in the world.'

As for the young man's own view of how he would succeed in the future, he set himself in entire seriousness a thirty-seven point introspective examination of capacities. He used the scheme of phrenology, the fad and pseudo-science of the day. He judged himself to be 'large' or 'full' on the points of amativeness, combativeness, destructiveness, self-esteem, firmness, secretiveness, conscientiousness, hope, and individuality. Correct so far, we may judge, according to the record of his early years. He found himself lacking or 'small' in concentrativeness, acquisitiveness, mirthfulness, and calculation. Accurate again, he seems, though of all men he would be 'concentrative' in future years. He contradicted himself with

his 'large' for caution; there is room to question his 'moderate' for
language; and one would wish that he had not left blank the spaces
on veneration, benevolence, and ideality, among others.

His one-word answers he enlarged by free self-characterization.
He included the following comments: 'An ardent, devoted, and
constant lover; he will defend the object of his love with boldness,
protect his or her rights with spirit. Will feel much stronger attachment than he will express . . . Is not very fond of children . . .
Chooses as his friends the talented, intellectual and literary, and
avoids the ignorant . . . Is extremely fond of travelling. Has an
insatiable desire to roam about and see the world and afterwards to
settle down . . . Is patriotic and ready to sacrifice all in defence of
his country . . . May get angry quickly, but, unless the injury is
deep or intended, cannot retain his anger . . . Will be more likely
to make a general than a critical scholar. May have bold and
original ideas upon a variety of subjects yet will not without effort
or excitement have a train of connected thoughts upon any . . .
Is qualified to meet difficulties, overcome obstacles, endure hardships, contend for privileges, resent insults and defend his rights to
the last . . . Desires money more as a means than an end . . . Is
inclined to enter largely into business and push his projects with
so much energy and zeal as to appear rash and nearly destitute of
caution; yet will come out about right in the end, and will seldom
fail entirely in his projects, though he may be obliged to retrace
his steps.'

In like vein of assurance Henry wrote his parents, aboard the
Shubrick on 6 January, the eighteenth day from home, and asked
them not to share the letter outside the family. After requesting
them to write Mrs. Curry that he would see her soon, he declared:
'I know my dear parents that you felt deeply the parting with me —
far more so than I did. But let the fact that I am satisfied and that
my chances are more than fair comfort you. As for me, for the
first time in my life, [I] left home with scarcely a regret and without a tear. I believed that it was my duty both to myself and to you
to go, and this belief assuaged the pain of parting.

'I am now about setting out for myself in the world, and though
young in years I have every confidence in my ability to go through
whatever may be before me. But of that I will say nothing, let
the future alone prove . . . I remain your Loving child.'

III

New Californian: Immigrant and Wage Earner

1858–1861

JUST to be taken on the crew of the *Shubrick* was a promise of adventure for Henry, and it gave an assurance of safety for the comfort of the people at home. Named for the admiral who was chairman of the Lighthouse Bureau, the vessel was a 'first' in two or three particulars. She was the first tender in the lighthouse service to be sent to the Pacific coast, and the first to be powered with steam. She was a hybrid, with a square-rigged foremast, yet was accounted good-looking, with black hull and funnels, and great red side wheels. She was armed with half a dozen cannon, and with a hot-water gun specially designed to discourage prowling Indians. Henry's father went over the vessel with him and met certain members of the crew, a few days before sailing.

The start was auspicious, and so were the first three days at sea. But on Christmas day, at a point off Hatteras, the *Shubrick* ran into such a storm as Henry had never experienced on the India voyage. The little tender, 'cockleshell' he called her — she was 140 feet long, and carried a 371-ton burden — got caught in the trough of the waves and took a dreadful battering. Deck engine, deck lumber, and extra spars went overboard, and the seas stove in the starboard bulwarks and part of the wheelhouse. When the call came, between ten and eleven at night, for all hands to put overboard whatever would lighten the load, Henry worked with a Negro deckhand heaving sacks of coal. It was a perilous Christmas. But by daylight seas were calming, and five or six days later the

34

Shubrick put into Charlotte Amalie, the port of St. Thomas, one of the Virgin Islands, for refueling and refitting.

To spare his parents anxiety Henry made no mention of the hurricane. To them he admitted no more than 'head winds and a rough sea' so far — a not very successful ruse, for, when news of the storm came out in the *Evening Journal,* or 'Evening Disturber' as Collins Walton called the paper, it excited the Georges greatly. Writing home Henry slipped into the peaceful pictorial vein of the Sea Journal, and his description is not to be improved upon: 'Here I am this winter's afternoon (while you are gathered around the parlour stove, perhaps thinking and talking of me) sitting in the open air in my white sleeves almost roasted by the sun. I wish that you could view the scene which surrounds us. The noble mountains rising from the water, covered with perpetual vegetation of the tropics and varied in colour by the shadows of the clouds which seem to climb their sides; and the little town with its square red-roofed, Dutch houses and white forts, surrounded by the palm and cocoanut trees which line the head of the bay; the ships and steamers which deck the harbour; and the boundless sea stretching away to the edge of the horizon, glittering in the sunlight — form a picture which I know you would enjoy.'

While the *Shubrick* lay in the harbor, Henry had an interview with the commanding officer. Apparently before leaving Philadelphia he had been in some way disappointed about the $40 wages. At any rate Captain de Camp now promised 'that if he could hit on any plan which would enable him to raise my wages to their original standard ($35.00) [sic] for the time occupied going out, he would do so, and I am certain of getting more as soon as we reach our destination.' Putting to sea again, 9 January, Henry wrote the letter to his parents quoted at the end of the last chapter: the boy had his face to the wind, confident for the future as never before.

Rounding Barbados, the *Shubrick* touched Pernambuco and put into Rio de Janeiro. This should have been a high point of the voyage for an enthusiastic traveler. Yet all that Henry managed to write, and this in a letter not sent, was that he had paddled the harbor, 'from one island to another in a canoe, the exact model of the famous one constructed by Crusoe,' and that he had gone ashore in Rio only once, and then seen very 'little of the town, for it was too infernally hot to walk the narrow streets.'

Again a failure to report to his parents was a covering up of unfortunate events. There was reason, for this time the crew of the *Shubrick* faced a more appalling danger than a storm at sea. Yellow fever was raging in Rio — a dread disease for a Philadelphian. No case developed before the *Shubrick* sailed, but after twelve hours at sea three men were stricken, and during the five-day run to Montevideo five or six more went down. All survived except one, a lovable fellow named Martin, the second engineer, whose agonies made the last few hours out of Montevideo a race for help. But, before the tender slipped into the mouth of the La Plata, Martin died piteously, in the presence of his young cousin, a fireman on the crew.

This was Henry's first knowledge of tragic death. It turned him to his pen immediately, and in time he made it an event in his literary life. In two letters to Philadelphia — Engineer Martin was one of the crew whom Mr. George had met and liked — he told the story simply and with feeling. The stricken man had wished to be buried ashore, and his mates had sympathized; after he died Captain de Camp had consulted with the cousin, and burial at some lonely spot along the coast, from which the body could be removed home whenever opportunity availed, had been the decision. But when Uruguayan officials refused under quarantine regulations, that plan had to be set aside, and after a short run to sea the crew of the *Shubrick* gave Engineer Martin a sailor's burial. Their effort failed. Though bored with holes and weighted with coal, the coffin floated, and a kedge anchor had had to be attached. Then, after 'the desired effect' had occurred and the vessel had returned to moorings, the tide brought the box back, right up to the side of the *Shubrick*. This decided the crew and captain. Now evading the watch of the port officials, they quietly took the body to a little valley not far from Montevideo and buried it as they had wanted to do. Henry's account of all this shows him to have been deeply moved but not at all superstitious: his letters explain the failure of sea burial by the simple errors of insufficiently weighting the box and insecurely attaching the anchor.

Yet the event grew on him, and in time, with the encouragement of the interest in the occult which prevailed in California, it took on mystery and terror. Eight years after the voyage Henry George retold the little tragedy in one of his earliest pieces of published writings. Under the title, 'Dust to Dust,' he described a wild sky and scudding clouds as the background of Martin's dying; he said that at the moment of death a prayer rose spontaneously from the crew, and instantly the sun came through and the heavens were crossed by a rainbow 'of everlasting promise.' The author had it that the crew had been quite superstitious. The coffin had 'seemed almost instinct with life and striving to elude' the anchor; and then, 'as we steamed up the river, it was more than hinted among many of us that the strong desire of the dying man had something to do with the difficulty of sinking his body.' The return of the corpse to the *Shubrick* gave the magazine story its climax: 'Onward it came, through all the vessels that lay beyond us — now lost to our view, now coming into sight again — turning and tacking as though piloted by life, and steadily holding the course for our steamer. It passed the last ship and came straight for us. It came closer, and every doubt was dispelled. It was, indeed, the coffin. A thrill of awe passed through every heart as the fact became assured.' For Henry George as writer, the magazine story signifies a beginner's effort to join the company of writers, Melville the greatest, who, in that day better than in any other period of American letters, were putting into fiction the power and the mystery of the sea. In the words of the story, 'There is something in the vastness with which nature presents herself upon the great waters which influences in this direction even minds otherwise sceptical.'

After Montevideo the passage through the Strait of Magellan, and a brief anchorage there, left a magnificent memory of dark water, great rocks, evergreens, and snow on distant mountains. It left also a poignant one of missionaries working with the 'not at all attractive' Tierra del Fuegians — missionaries whom, he later learned, were killed for their efforts and eaten by cannibals of the vicinity. On the passage north the *Shubrick* touched at Panama, apparently nowhere else, before it came to its destination. Though a bold salute from Henry George's pen on entering the Golden Gate would have been appropriate to the mood of his leaving home, he seems rather to have been a little appalled by San Francisco. All we have is a couple of lines sent off to Mrs. Curry. Plans and moves would have to be worked out, he told this friend. He added that San Francisco struck him as 'a dashing place, rather faster than Philadelphia.'

Within an hour of the *Shubrick*'s putting in, 27 May, James George met him and took him home. At once his letters began to indicate that he was ready for anything, and not too strongly determined for Oregon after all. His mother had guessed this before he left home. To be sure, Mrs. Curry wrote immediately; and she was warm and cordial as ever, and full of regret that he had not reached the West coast in time for Martha's wedding. But she conspicuously had nothing to offer in the way of a job, on the Oregon *Statesman* or any other paper. On Henry's side, 'the old Oregon fever has not entirely died,' he said; and certainly he had not forgotten Florence. A month after arrival he charmingly told Martha that Florence had kissed him in a dream, and added that 'I will be almost afraid to meet her for I know she will awe me into bashfulness and silence at once.' Yet at the same writing he showed that he was becoming excited, as San Francisco was, by Frazer River gold, and said that come spring he might go to the diggings far away.

All this projecting took for granted both that he would disregard his father's advice to stay more or less permanently in government employment, and that he could somehow make himself free of his commitment to a full year of service — seven months to go — aboard the *Shubrick*. According to family record, the eighteen-year-old steward enlisted the sympathy of Ellen George, his cousin's wife. At their home he went to bed, and she herself went to interview Captain de Camp. One may imagine a woman's story of an ailing youngster who needed care, and one may think that the three concerned — Henry, cousin, and ship's commander — all acted in full knowledge that desertion was a habit that had been more or less condoned in San Francisco Bay since Gold Rush days, when sailors, even sailors in the United States Navy, had hit for the mountains in droves. Whatever the pretense, the captain accepted Henry's 'retirement' without effort to bring him back. Though the record of the *Shubrick* showed other desertions, it made no mention of Henry's leaving; and the only damaging document in the dossier is an envelope addressed to him from Philadelphia and sent back with the marking, 'Run away.' His mother worried, and his father moralized a little; but it was his friend Jo Jeffreys who summed up the episode. 'I think you did make a decided "jump" when you left the *Shubrick* so suddenly, though I hope you did not do so before you received what was due you. You must have been in a state of great anxiety when waiting for the expected visit of Captain de Camp, though I think the fact does credit to your ingenuity.' Presumably Henry never received any of his accumulated wages.

Certainly the young man was in a risk-taking state of mind, and San Francisco was the place for it. We have the word of a future governor that the financial crisis of the late '50s had hit earlier and harder there than in New York; and an editorial in the San Francisco *Hesperian* immediately after Henry's arrival, trying hard to be optimistic, contained such not completely cheerful observations as these: that the new gold rush to the Frazer River in British Columbia had given work to many unemployed, that it was beginning to stimulate business, and that recently there had been fewer suicides in California. If it was true of nineteenth-century America generally, it was triply true of California during Gold Rush days that people gambled recklessly with their jobs. Positions were bandied as freely as stock certificates, and even those most vulnerable wage earners, the white-collar men, exchanged them readily as new chances offered.

Henry acted that way, quitting the *Shubrick,* and now his cousin did the same. The responsibility of wife and young children notwithstanding, James George abandoned his bookkeeping and entered a Frazer River venture with a San Francisco merchant. A century earlier, in days of Atlantic colonization, James would have been called 'factor' rather than partner, and the San Francisco man the 'principal.' The George side of the bargain called for setting up a store in Victoria, to do business with the miners. 'Trade acknowledges no political boundaries,' the *Hesperian* was now boasting, as California capital sought investment in British Columbia; and the magazine added that the boundaries of San Francisco's commercial 'empire will be as wide as those of western civilization.' As enterpriser in this forward movement, James offered Henry a job as store clerk. And by August, possibly late July, Henry was on the job selling goods across the counter, under the British flag another thousand miles from home. Perhaps he had been in California long enough to know that some of the biggest money of the earlier '50s, and some of the more stable accumulations, Leland Stanford's among others, had been made by

the storekeepers of Sacramento just behind the lines of the great
gold diggings.

Yet Henry sailed from San Francisco none too anxious for store
work; and at first he was probably more than half inclined to try
on his own for river gold and a big find. Certainly his letters about
getting rich quick, and the fact that he had to work his way north
as a sailor, distressed the good people in Philadelphia. But by the
time he arrived on Vancouver Island, floods on 'the terrible Frazer'
had brought gold mining to a standstill, from which it never really
recovered. He was lucky to have the store job to resort to, and to
have the store for home. By putting up a sign for late and early
customers, 'Please give this door a kick,' he offered something
like twenty-four-hour service to his customers.

He had a very good time, at least for a while, and he seems to
have thought there might be a prosperous future in the store.
Thrusting his chest out a bit, he had printed a business card which
brought a desirable reaction from Jo Jeffreys: 'It looks quite important for you, old fellow. I wish I could lend you $500.' Even
members of the family who disliked the venture got some exaggerated ideas; Uncle Joseph van Dusen's firm considered sending the George cousins a shipment of Philadelphia goods for sale.
'Bless you, my dear little sister,' wrote Henry after Jane had said
something naïve about his residence, 'I had [no bed] to make.
Part of the time I slept rolled up on my blanket on the counter, or
on a pile of flour, and afterwards I had a straw mattress on some
boards. The only difference between my sleeping and waking
costumes was that during the day I wore boots and cap, and at
night dispensed with them.' The fun of the venture came many
ways: he attended an Indian wedding and a powwow; a returning
miner gave him a 'big boat with sails'; and he looked forward to
the ice-skating season.

But a British Columbia winter never came for Henry George.
In the late fall some quarrel or difference, not permanent but
painful, occurred between the cousins. We are told only that later
he was contrite and admitted he had 'behaved badly towards Jim
George.' He abandoned the store, borrowed money, and sailed
steerage from Victoria back to San Francisco. He had never before
been so completely alone in the world as at the end of 1858.

The one visible increment of the northern venture was a good start on his later famous set of chin whiskers. Years afterward he told audiences that on the voyage to Victoria he had for the first time had his eyes opened to the meaning of Chinese immigration on the West coast. An old miner, whom he quizzed, admitted that for the present the Chinese were merely working the diggings abandoned by white prospectors. But the workingman foresaw that in time Chinese competition would bring wages down for everyone. Though this kind of anxiety had not yet become the daily operation of Henry's mind, he remembered later how deeply the prognosis had impressed him: 'The idea that as a country grew in all that we were hoping it might grow the condition of those who had to work for a living must become not better but worse.' In the wilderness this was the Adam Smith lesson of the Philadelphia printer again, but made ominous by the threat of the Orient, not too far away for its huge labor force to affect matters crucially. The lesson of old countries and low wages was relearned at an impressionable time for the learner. During the British Columbia interval, Henry George turned nineteen and went out of a job, almost simultaneously.

One phase of his affairs, his relations with the Currys, the northern trip had clarified completely. During the summer Martha, the oldest sister, had come with her new husband to Victoria, and the old friends had had a good visit and an exchange of confidences. Martha reported that Florence was not in love. Not in love with anyone else, appears to have been the idea Henry was to get; and the hint that the young lady was keeping an open mind about him, this year and a half since coming to Oregon, seems to have been strengthened by a bright letter which Florence herself wrote a little later. 'Remember, Hen,' invited the girl who had been on his mind for years, 'if you ever come to Portland, that our hearts and homes are ever open to welcome you. I shall expect a letter in return to this, and expect to have the correspondence continued.'

Yet Henry delayed writing, and perhaps never wrote again to Florence Curry. When he took passage to San Francisco he passed up an opportunity to stop in Portland. And if a low state of pocketbook and wardrobe possibly explains his not visiting at the governor's residence, this would not have prevented him from writing later from San Francisco. One recalls a self-judgment in the phrenological examination: Henry believed himself 'strong in his

attachments . . . yet may occasionally fall out of them.' By all
the signs, he had fallen out of attachment to Florence; and the
possibilities of Oregon, for love or for work, never seriously entered
his calculations again.

During the winter of 1858 and 1859, moreover, a series of hard
events underscored the fact of personal isolation. On his return to
San Francisco the boy had the comfort and security of visiting Ellen
George, who was teaching school until decision could be made
that she should take her children and move to Victoria. Apparently
Henry's trouble with James did not change his relationship with
Ellen. But in February, James's business having improved, she
went to join him; and presently Henry learned that she had taken
sick and died in British Columbia. Meanwhile word came from
Philadelphia that, under depression stringency, his father's salary
was being withheld for a month — the aging clerk went to the
Customs House every day nonetheless — and the family was
strained and worried. And finally, later in the year, came the news
of the sudden death of Joseph Jeffreys. Jane's attachment to Henry's
old friend made the event doubly sad, and Mrs. George grieved
also. 'Oh his bright mind,' she wrote her son, 'his lonelyness, his
sensitiveness, his love for you, made me feel an interest in him of
no common kind.'

Henry owed Jo a great debt for understanding and counsel.
Wishing him luck when he left Philadelphia, this friend had said
things no one else could very well say. On the matter of liquor:
'You and I have different natures, Harry, and what I may leave
without regret you are too apt to cling to with all the ardency of
your too-ardent soul . . . You have enjoyed yourself — that is
right — you have endeavored to repay yourself for restraint and
confinement . . . and in the wild excitement you have perhaps
forgotten your aims, your hopes, your ambitions, and here you
have been wrong.' About the Frazer River move, and Henry's
shuttling around generally, Jo judged harshly, but admonished in
affection: 'If you enter a house as a clerk, stay at it, in God's name.
If you should unfortunately resolve to follow printing, follow it
with all your abilities and energy until there shall no longer be any
necessity for it. You will allow me to say that your great fault (and
I think it is your worst one) is that of half-doing things, *in this
sense,* that you vacillate about the execution of that which alone

secures permanent success and lasting fame . . . Now you are competent for any labour to which your inclinations may direct you. You are not competent to succeed at a dozen employments, nor can you expect to amass a fortune by labouring at them alternately.' Not even his worried parents spoke to Henry half so sternly, nor understood the hazards of his zigzag course quite so well. His friend's death must have seemed to Henry the greatest loss he had suffered so far.

On the side of his West coast career, moreover, the year following his leaving Victoria brought him twice within a hairbreadth of disaster. He was a forlorn fellow who came back to San Francisco laden with debts instead of with nuggets, and possessed of very little beside the hand-me-down coat he wore and a blanket. Up to now, whether in Philadelphia or Calcutta, in San Francisco or Victoria, Henry George had operated always as a member of the George family. Every job and every adventure, possibly excepting the voyage to Boston, had hinged on the influence of his father or his uncles or his cousin. But now on his own, he was reduced to a human unit on the job market in San Francisco, which was during that year an especially crowded and lonesome place to be. As one among thousands returning from the Frazer River, he might well have had no choice except to go to sea again.

A stroke of luck saved him for the winter. By pure accident Henry met in San Francisco David Bond, an old friend from King and Baird's. The printing-house connection led to a printing-house job. Henry was soon at work in Frank Eastman's office, at $16 a week, the best wages he had ever made. There was no reason not to luxuriate a little. He settled comfortably in the What Cheer House, a temperance hotel for men which he described as 'the largest if not the finest hotel in the place.' Nine dollars a week paid for 'a beautiful little room and first-class living.' It was a grand relief. At this stage of great satisfaction with San Francisco he sounded out Jane, who was completing a teacher-training course at home, about possibly coming on. 'Women are sadly wanted here,' he urged, and school-teachers are well paid — fifty dollars a month for 'A, B, C teachers,' and one hundred dollars, Ellen's salary, not unusual and not the highest pay. Only the desolation of the Christmas and New Year's holidays dampened Henry's spirit at this stage. One year away from home, he reacted to recent freedom with a season of austerity: he cut out smoking, paid no attention to girls, and even lacked the inclination for the theater or other amusements, he wrote his people.

For two or three months — about long enough for Mr. George to congratulate his son on returning to his trade and to confess his own reverses — this pleasant situation held. Then, coincidentally with Ellen's departure, business slackened in the Eastman shop and Henry lost his job. He got by for the rest of the winter as a weigher in a rice mill. But in the hard spring of 1859 the mill closed, and on top of this Mrs. Curry wrote that, even if she heard of newspaper jobs in Oregon, she was 'afraid that your free spirit would be disgusted' with the work.

Evidently Henry was too discouraged to write home. We have only the unnecessarily shamefaced confession, decades later, that for a couple of months he was 'in fact what would now be called a tramp.' Like thousands before and since, he set out for the gold country, for Placerville — often called Hangtown — in the region of the Mother Lode east of Sacramento. He did not get that far. At some point in the interior he picked up farm work and he slept in barns, regular California hobo style. An exact contemporary, a self-confessed tramp who worked four months on a ranch near Sonoma, earned $26 per month and keep. In the early summer Henry made his way back to San Francisco. As ill chance had it, he arrived too late to follow up the one real job opportunity the Currys ever arranged for him — could it have been their reply to a distress signal? — a place like the one they had half offered him before he left Philadelphia, setting type on a Portland paper. He considered going to sea once more; and then again David Bond came to the rescue.

The new job this time was with a weekly newspaper of a kind that flourished with peculiar exuberance in San Francisco. Though the *California Home Journal*, subtitled *California Literature, Romance, and the Arts,* is an unknown in the larger history of journalism, the one available remaining issue — one on which we may be quite sure Henry George labored — suffices, with other evidence, to place it in the general class of literary papers of which the *Golden Era* is the most renowned. These papers existed on quite a different footing from that of such regular newspapers as the *Alta California* and the *Bulletin,* with their daily, weekly, and other editions, and their main attention given to commercial and political news. As business undertakings the literary papers were generally a risky, short-lived lot. Yet somehow Henry's particular paper, which sold for 12½ cents — 'a bit' — an issue, kept going for several years; and in his eyes the proprietor, Joseph C. Duncan, was a friendly employer and an admirable one.

Months earlier, while he was working at Eastman's and living at What Cheer House, young George had had an urge to do a lot of reading, some of it the new literature of California; and now working on the *Home Journal* he had special reason to expand that interest. In the first instance the need to read had come from within himself, after a year at sea and at storekeeping; and the hotel he lived in gave him easy access to a collection of books famous in California history. As a kind of moral substitute for a bar, the proprietor of the What Cheer House, a New England Yankee, maintained a library and a museum of California wild life, for the edification of his guests. Among two or three thousand books and a generous supply of European, East coast, and California newspapers, Henry had a splendid opportunity. Biographies, Greek and Roman classics in translation, histories, and such British and American fiction of the century as the works of Scott, Dickens, and Thackeray, and Irving, Cooper, and Hawthorne were all available to him. Perhaps we should discount his own later impression that he actually read most of the books on What Cheer shelves. But we know that sometime he did a lot of reading, and the What Cheer House library may account for at least a part of it. One book he did not read demands mention: though Henry spotted Adam Smith's *Wealth of Nations* in the hotel library, he passed by a future favorite book, and it is safe to say that he had not read one line of book economics at this stage of his life.

To the satisfaction of discovering books in California for his pleasure, the job on the *California Home Journal* added the interest of first contact with literature in the making, and with literary criticism. Though the weekly invited 'tales, romances, historical sketches, and articles on science' without restriction to region, in San Francisco style Mr. Duncan made a policy of stressing California interests, and his columns contained such items as articles on Chinese gambling and reports of notable persons who came to the state. Regionalism with rainbows of local color was

the essence of early California literature, and Henry George's
first durable and interesting job connected him with that kind of
thought at a point of grass-roots origin.

Not only his work but the incidentals of his life indicate that by
now George was becoming fond of the state where he had chosen
to try his fortune. By temperament Henry was the kind of young
man to delight in the spectacle San Francisco has always offered,
and to let it grow on him. On Sundays, free from the composing
room, he rambled in the hills outside the city. Telegraph Hill,
before it became popular, charmed him most: the clouds and fog,
sun and shadow, the green hills of springtime — he loved the
whole color and feeling. Now finding a group of friends whom
he enjoyed, he went to the theater occasionally; and with Isaac
Trump, known to him since *Shubrick* days, he took a room on
Dupont Street for a while, in the most polyglot section of town.
The boys equipped themselves more or less Bohemian style with a
couple of cots and chairs, a trunk for a table, a bottle for a candle-
stick, and a Dutch scene print for a window curtain. There they
entertained their friends — when the rent was not overdue —
with talk and fooling reminiscent of the Lawrence Society. Years
afterward Henry George recollected with nostalgia their table-
tipping and their talk about the mysteries of life, up and down
the scale from ghost stories to the ideas of the Swedenborgians.

In this kind of life the young immigrant's 1859 gave way to 1860;
and 1860 meant in his anticipation September and the age of
twenty-one, when he would cease to be an apprentice and as a
journeyman could command twice as much as his present $12
wages. In this case the realization proved no less than the hope.
When he did come of age he promptly joined the typographical
union, and during a short interlude off the *Home Journal* he
earned his first full California wages as a substitute printer on the
San Francisco dailies. Then before the year's end Mr. Duncan took
him back and made him foreman printer. His wages jumped to $30
a week, and for a few months Henry George had one of the more
prosperous intervals of his life. All in all he owed a great deal to the
Home Journal: it had tided him over in San Francisco from
the crisis period of his relocation into the crisis period of the
nation; it had restored him to his proper work, and justifying his

coming West the paper had carried him over into a phase of attachment and feeling for California as a place to live.

But an immigrant is an individual with two loyalties of place, and in Henry George's case the home loyalty, though it was a declining one, had vigorous spokesmen in the persons of his mother and his sisters. Naturally the womenfolk could not be easily reconciled to Henry's absence. During his first year away the Victoria business had been distasteful to all the Philadelphia Georges; and then when hard luck hit in early 1859 the women especially begged Henry to come home. They could not bear to think of his settling down and sometime marrying, so far away. The boy's answer was partly money and partly long-run opportunity in the West. Not the cost of passage home, 'the rub isn't there. It's what shall I do when I get home. Wages are low and work is hard to get, and I might be unable to obtain anything for some time, while here I shall always be able to scratch along, at any rate, and have some chance of doing something more.' The wanderer now found a phrase for the destiny that separates families and delays hopes: 'It's all for the best, you know.' He entered it in many letters to Philadelphia.

Two events worked some reconciliation among his people to his being away. One was the secession of South Carolina from the Union, in the fateful November of 1860. From the first fortnight of that crisis Mr. and Mrs. George, more accurately than many others, especially more so than people in California, anticipated bloodshed between South and North. They foresaw that in San Francisco the hazards would be less for a son of military age than in Philadelphia, and they admitted that he had better stay. The mother was not to stick to this judgment, and Henry was to want to go to war. But speaking for her husband and herself she wrote, on the last day of 1860, that they had concluded it was better for him to be on the West coast 'for a little while' at least.

The other event of reconciliation was entirely personal, and had occurred about six months earlier: Henry confessed faith and joined the church. During his early months in San Francisco he had attended the Unitarian congregation, and liked it. Had Thomas Starr King, the Boston preacher who was to make himself the spiritual leader of Civil War patriotism in San Francisco, already taken that pulpit, it is hardly likely that Henry would have pulled himself away. But Unitarianism caused head shaking at home, and probably he had his own reservations. He tried the Episcopal churches, but found them too High Church. In the end he discovered a resting place when a friend took him to a Methodist church. Though he was not moved to much letter writing about his conversion, he assured his parents and sisters that they were not to be concerned about the sectarian location of it. Little difference to what part of the fold one belonged, he said, so long as one felt a true belonging. This confession drew from home heart-felt letters of gratitude and relief and appreciation.

Neither the humble little church in San Francisco nor Methodism as a religious movement was ever to prove a place of great loyalty or activity for Henry George. But his parents were not wrong to rejoice at what he wrote them. For their wandering son, now pretty well transplanted in California, had of his own inclination turned back to their values. This involved a commitment he was to keep in his own special ways of devotion, in crucial times, in historic places, as life advanced.

IV

Suffering and Exaltation

1861–1865

DURING the Civil War the choices that young men of military age had to make were of course less prefigured than in our day. The draft was less certain; and no area of federal activity, from taxes to artillery, was as tightly organized then as now. But we should err if we slipped into saying that for Henry George's generation the anxieties of 1861, the ultimates we phrase as the downfall or survival of civilization, seemed less tragic than the anxieties of 1917, 1941, and 1950 have seemed to people of our own day. Though there had been a generation of crying 'wolf' between North and South, perhaps no nation that has experienced war was ever so unready as the United States then was for compulsion, for the military, for the realities of battle and revolution. When the showdown did come, it was shocking in the extreme, and all that was most dear seemed to hang in the balance.

In George's case awareness of abolitionism in the East gave meaning to the national tragedy, as he viewed its slow unfolding from a distance. As the son of an office-holding Democrat he might in easier times have found the party battles of the new state of his residence to be interesting, and the dominant position of his father's party to be entirely to taste. Recent California politics had been not unlike Pennsylvania's: a successful intrusion of Know Nothing native Americanism in 1855, and a clear victory for the Democrats in 1856. But, very unlike what he would do in the future, Henry at this stage took no notice of state or local politics. Perhaps he was too young and too new in the state to know or care. Certainly he pitched his political concerns at the national and moral level appropriate to his personal history in Philadelphia. In 1859 he wrote to his old opponent in slavery discussion, his mother, that California displayed a contemptible provincial lack of interest in the John Brown affair. And early in the election year he troubled to read a constitutional history of the United States. His letters show him to have been intensely aware of the growing crisis.

Of course he voted for Abraham Lincoln, and we can imagine his home thoughts when letters told him that the older and younger members of the family were at sixes and sevens, variously for Douglas, Bell, and Lincoln. Voting for the first time, he must have experienced a special excitement. It was not only that he was differing from his parents, but the margin in California was so slight as to magnify the responsibility of the individual voter.

Nor did Lincoln's victory end the anxieties of decision making in the state. While proposals were voiced first, that California lead a new secession movement and set up a Pacific republic, and second, that sympathy and aid be extended to the Confederacy, he endured the crisis within his heart. His family kept him informed about sentiment at home: 'You cannot feel it as we do,' his father said, 'All around us is warlike . . . Nothing now but the sound of the drum and the marching of troops South.' But Henry did feel it, as for him personally policy thinking yielded to pondering about the meaning of the war and about what his own duty might be.

He estimated that joining the army in California would lead to nothing more important than frontier duty keeping Indians quiet. In perhaps the longest, surely the most emotional letter of his life, the one written to Jane George on 15 September 1861, which we shall need to consider later as his 'Millennial Letter,' he said that if he were home, and situated as his friends were, he too would go to war. 'Not that I like the idea of fighting my countrymen — not that I think it is the best or pleasantest avocation, or that the fun of soldiering is anything to speak of; but in this life or death struggle I should like to have a hand . . . I have felt a good deal like enlisting, even here, and probably would have done so had I not felt that my duty to you all required me to remain, though I did not, and do not, think our volunteers are really needed or will do any fighting that will amount to anything; but I should like to place my willingness on record, and show that one of our family was willing to serve his country. We cannot tell. It may be my duty yet, though I sincerely hope not.'

All the rest of his life the Civil War was to be for Henry George not a bitterness personally experienced but a tragedy viewed in perspective and deeply felt. Another passage in the same letter should be quoted here, partly because the time of writing was yet so near his religious training and his conversion, and partly because it shows how very early, and also how self-propelling, he was in searching for a Christian point of view on the fratricidal war. 'Truly it seems that we have fallen on evil days. A little while ago all was fair and bright, and now the storm howls around us with a strength and fury that almost unnerves one. Our country is being torn to pieces and ourselves, our homes, filled with distress. As to the ultimate end I have no doubt. If civil war should pass over the whole country, leaving nothing but devastation behind it, I think my faith in the ultimate good would remain unchanged; but it is hard to feel so of our individual cases. On great events and movements we can philosophize, but when it comes down to ourselves, to our homes, to those *we love,* then we can only feel; our philosophy goes to the dogs, and we but look prayerfully, tearfully, to Him who hath more care for us than for all the sparrows.'

Meanwhile during the spring and summer of 1861, the sale of the *California Home Journal* had put Henry George out of his job, and he had risked a business adventure. The opportunity he seized represented neatly the state of affairs in California journalism. Before November 1860 most of the newspapers, like the preponderance of the votes, had been Democratic, but now the change of politics encouraged new ventures and new ideas. Though in later days important papers begun or reorganized during the Civil War period were to concern Henry George, in the season when Lincoln took office he was of course not ready to take up anything very weighty. But he did go into a shoestring proposition, in partnership with four or five other young men. They took over the San Francisco *Daily Evening Journal,* which under the name *Constitution* had supported the Unionist candidates, Bell and Everett, during the election. On terms of investing $100, money which he had saved from recent earnings, George became an equal partner, and an enthusiastic young entrepreneur into the bargain.

He pushed for a policy of literary-interest and human-interest journalism, like that to which he was accustomed on the *Home Journal*. To the bright young sister who was now teaching school he addressed a request, the day before Sumter, that she send a 'nice gossipy letter, once in a while, for the paper. You could do it exquisitely, I know. Try it, and if the paper is going on by that time (which there is little doubt of) I'll pay you well. No political news, but town-talk, sensations among woman-kind, new books, scraps of sentiment, poetry, new fashions.' About his own future he added: 'I think we have a good prospect, and in a little while will have a good property, which will be an independence for a life-time.'

He had his way on *Evening Journal* policy, and Jane actually contributed a few letters, very feminine and bluestocking, during the summer and fall. In June the paper announced a circulation of 3000, a good number to grow on, and for an early-summer season, Henry George's hopes ran high.

At just this point letters from Philadelphia indicated, at first fears, then the certainty, that Mr. George would lose his job at the Customs House. A Republican was now slated as collector and had let it be known that the axe would fall, on 'the ground that with the Victor is the spoil, and rotation in office is just and proper.' To this Henry responded with loyal bravado, assuring his people that he would sell his partnership if need be. In return came an outpouring of gratitude and refusal from home. 'It shows me,' his father said, 'that my Dear Son far away was willing to make any sacrifice to help and assist his parents in distress and so with all my dear children.'

One hazard was passed, yet month by month life was becoming infinitely complicated. In August the *Journal* paid the partners only $6 a week apiece. As a small journal, which could not afford the new telegraphic news service, it confronted mounting wartime disadvantages. Unpaid bills forced Henry to set up a cot in the office and return to austerities reminiscent of British Columbia. Even so he professed to the people at home that the paper was growing and promised 'a certainty (comparatively, of course).' He predicted $30 a week for each partner, within a year. The San Francisco *Call* had been built up that way, why not the *Evening Journal?*

But it was not hope of business success which was really directing Henry's course in the hard fall of 1861. He had no adequate answer for his parents, who, when they learned how the *Evening Journal* was actually going, changed their minds about the wisdom of remaining in California. The printing business was booming in wartime Philadelphia. Now he should come home, they urged. Yet up to this time not even Henry himself, still less the Philadelphians to whom he had given no intimation, quite suspected how fixed in California he was: that a girl was about to become the deciding influence on what he would do, where he would live, in the crucial next few months.

Annie Corsina Fox had entered his life on the evening of 12 October, a year earlier. Reluctantly Henry had let a friend persuade him to go to a party that night at the home of a Mr. and Mrs. Joseph Flintoff and Mrs. Flintoff's mother, Mrs. Henry McCloskey. He had almost balked at the door. A huge crowd, a singing tenor, and altogether more show and side than he had ever been accustomed to quite chilled him off. Then his eye lit on the dainty person to honor whom on her seventeenth birthday the party was being given. 'Let's go in,' proposed Henry George.

The girl who attracted him completely came from a British and Irish overseas background. As one of two children of the marriage in Australia of Elizabeth McCloskey to a major in the British army, Annie Fox had already behind her a story of domestic tragedy and much moving about. Her parents' marriage had broken early. The known facts are: the McCloskeys were pure Irish and Catholic, and Major Fox a redcoat Anglican; Mrs. Fox had married at sixteen, and her husband was twenty years older; after a short while they separated and he disappeared completely; and a few years later, when Annie was ten, the young mother died of what the family called a broken heart. For the little girl this meant a bringing-up by her grandparents, coming and going with grandfather Henry McCloskey, who was a contractor, railroad builder, and speculator. After Australia the family had a year in Hawaii, and then came on to San Francisco. Annie and her sister were sent to school at the convent of the Sisters of Charity in Los Angeles, and Teresa had taken the veil. Annie had reached the point of doing a little teaching there — English for Spanish-speaking girls — when she was called to San Francisco to attend her grandmother, who was now widowed and in declining health. When she met

Henry George, Annie was engaged to be married to some man
about whom the family records tell us nothing — an unhappy
commitment according to the little that is said. In her own much
later retrospect her whole situation in the Flintoff household was
miserable, and she a very lonely girl.

She and Henry reached an understanding almost at once.
Though the grandmother died, apparently in December 1860, two
or three months had been long enough for the old lady to approve
the match in family councils, as Annie must have known. And at
that time — these were still $30-a-week *Home Journal* days for
Henry — Annie's uncle, Matthew McCloskey, who also lived in
San Francisco and acted as a kind of guardian, agreed.

During the winter and afterward the young people kept constant company. We are told that they took walks and memorized
poetry; and the man instructed the girl in the meaning of the
national calamity. Their engagement was no secret to people who
knew them in San Francisco, but Henry said nothing in letters
to his family. Even after a visiting friend aroused suspicions in
Philadelphia, Henry camouflaged the situation by telling a jealous
sister that, 'One thing is certain, if I do marry it will be no one but
an orphan without relatives, so that I can pack her up, and come
home at a moment's notice, and stay as long as I please.'

By all the signs, love would have marched straight to the altar,
and with the blessings of the McCloskeys, perhaps as early as the
summer of 1861, had it not been for Henry's hard times and his
father's. But the shortage of funds was a fact; and to a bad time
of frustration, and to a head whirling with affairs and anxieties,
we owe the Millennial Letter, from which Henry's ideas on the
Civil War and his sense of his own patriotic obligation have been
quoted. To be sure he still refused to share with anyone at home
the fact of the existence of Annie Corsina Fox; but everything else
he poured out, and the concerns of young love penetrated every
line he wrote.

Of course it is not at all unique to discover a young man suffering
a season of sorrows. The war years, and the whole romantic century,
abounded in them. It is scarcely less unusual that Henry took the
comfort he needed, when the facts of life failed to square with hope,
from mankind's ancient comforting beliefs: the promise of immortality and the promise of Utopia. Yet the letter is engaging,

because the boy wrote into it a connected estimate of his roles in life, as citizen, son, and Christian, and as a man of personal ambition. And the ideas and attitudes the writer displayed are important because they exhibit the faith and hope from which moral and intellectual growth — and in time the writing of a great book — sprang.

The passages quoted below will not be injured, nor their meaning twisted, by some rearranging and omitting of phrases and sentences, as the punctuation indicates. Henry began by saying how impatient he felt, as his affairs stood still and he could not make them move, and he drew from a great sea poem:

> *Storm or hurricane,*
> *Anything to put a close*
> *To this most dread monotonous repose.*

What he thought the good society ought to be he called the millennium: 'How I long for the Golden Age — for the promised Millennium, when each one will be free to follow his best and noblest impulses, unfettered by the restrictions and necessities which our present state of society imposes upon him — when the poorest and meanest will have a chance to use all his God-given faculties, and not be forced to drudge away the best part of his time in order to support wants but little above those of the animal.'

George applied local color to his vision of the Golden Age. First, he pictured unselfish family life as showing what human energy rightly disposed might mean. James George's new marriage furnished a lovely illustration: 'His wife is one of those women who makes the happiness and well-being of their husbands and children an art and a study. Whenever I go there in the evening I always find them together — a pretty, happy family.' Then, the California hills he made romantic and millennial, too. 'I had a dream last night . . . I thought I was scooping treasure out of the earth by handfuls, almost delirious with the thoughts of what I would now be able to do, and how happy it would all be . . . Is it any wonder that men lust for gold, and are willing to give up almost anything for it, when it covers everything — the purest and noblest desires of their hearts, the exercise of their noblest powers! What a pity we can't be contented! Is it? Who knows? Sometimes I feel sick of the fierce struggle of our high civilized life, and think I would like to get away from cities and business, with their jostlings and strainings and cares altogether, and find some place on one of the hillsides, which look so dim and blue in the distance, where I could gather those I love, and live content with what nature and our own resources would furnish . . .'

The brother admitted to Jane homesickness in his emotions, a need for the old assurances and security. 'At night when I lie down and think of the old times — when I wake sometimes at midnight, and I can almost feel the kisses that seemed to press my brow a minute or two before, and the voices that I heard in my dreams seem to linger in my ears yet, and I almost cry with mingled pleasure and pain . . . But it will be soon, not so very far off either I hope, though at present I cannot count the time.'

In a climactic passage, which he perhaps felt none too safe in writing, and yet pushed a little hard, Henry inserted a paragraph, his first recorded discussion of the idea of immortality. 'What a glorious thought it is, that at last all will be over — all trial, all care, all suffering forever finished; all desire filled, all longing satisfied — what now is but hope become a reality — perfect love swallowing up all in one boundless sea of bliss. How the old hymn that we used to sing in Sunday School swells and peals through the mind, when one thinks of and realizes its meaning as a living truth, like a glorious burst of heavenly music, telling of the joys of the redeemed and freed.

> *"Oh that will be joyful . . .*
> *To meet and part no more."*

What a thought. What a picture! With all we love or have loved here "to meet and part no more" — one unbroken family around His Throne. Can we be unhappy long, if we believe this?' Although all George's future passion and his sophistication about the idea of immortality had still to be born, his lifelong fascination with it had arrived this early.

With this passage the writer had explored almost every individual escape available to a young man who feels overwhelmed: to join the army, to strike it rich, to live by the soil, to go back home, to die. The fact that he did not even hint at the alternative which made his life famous — that a Christian or a democrat may strive to transform society, not wait but work to see the Golden

Age arrive — shows how far short he was, at twenty-two, from being generally reform-minded as in the future. His only conclusion was for personal action: 'We must struggle, so here's for the strife.' It contained no economics except individualism, and no dedication except to self and the few he loved.

Within a month of the writing Henry tried some new moves. With two partners he dropped out of the *Evening Journal*, while the three who remained bought the shares of the sellers, on credit. He and Annie must have made their decisions together. At the moment of his selling out, she refused to leave San Francisco when Sister Corsina McKay of the Los Angeles convent — whom she loved so much as to have taken her name — invited her back for some duty, presumably teaching again in the school. And also simultaneously, Henry confessed his love to Jane, at first to her alone, to sound out the situation at home.

The sister's reply makes perfectly plain why he had kept up the deception toward Philadelphia. First, Annie's Roman Catholic faith. 'I know that our family will object to that, Ma especially,' Jane wrote, 'but still I do not think she will withhold her consent on that account.' The sister herself regretted the religious difference, and admitted pangs of jealousy; and she argued that the new home be set up in Philadelphia. But the answer Henry craved came unqualified: 'If you *really love Annie, you marry her as soon as you are able to support her* . . . Love is too precious a thing to be thrown away . . . In the meantime do not forget me; do not cease to love me as much as ever, will you? There can be two places in your heart — one for Annie and one for me.'

The intense courtship displeased Annie's guardian, who happened to be a real-estate developer. He troubled to make inquiries in Philadelphia. But reassurances concerning the family did nothing to improve the look of Henry as a provider, and on 2 December Mr. McCloskey forced a showdown. Discovering Henry calling, he ordered the young man to come less often. Tempers flared, and except for Annie's intervening there would have been a fight.

After a night of much praying, Annie Fox decided that she could not bear to remain where she was, and told Henry that she had better go to Los Angeles to teach. This brought the tender decision. Henry George drew a fifty-cent piece from his pocket, and said, 'Annie, this is all the money I have in the world. Will you marry me?' Then she made reply, 'If you are ready to undertake the responsibilities of marriage, I will marry you.'

Before evening the groom made what preparations he could. He borrowed money and clothes and arranged with the James Georges for a couple of weeks board in the home he admired so much. Isaac Trump agreed to go to the Flintoff door and ask for 'Mrs. Brown.' That was the secret signal. Carrying not much more than the books of poetry they loved, Annie rode off with Henry; and they went with Ike and Ike's fiancée for a wedding supper at a restaurant. At about nine they proceeded to the Bethel Methodist Church of Henry's membership. A handful of friends, including Mrs. George, although James could not come, attended the ceremony. Out of consideration for both bride and groom, the minister read the Episcopal service; and on Annie's finger her husband slipped a ring that had belonged to Mrs. McCloskey. The couple announced their marriage in the newspapers, and a month or so later in Sacramento they secured a Catholic sanction.

For three weeks Henry got by on substitute printing. Then from a friend came word of a job in Sacramento, and on Christmas day Henry left bride and cousins for the 100-mile trip up bay and river. Fortune smiled. Though at first he found only substitute printing again, the work was on the Sacramento *Union,* the biggest paper in the state capital. Before long his job became regular and adequate, and even before that Annie, who was desolate at being left behind, joined him in what was then California's second city.

Altogether typical of the coming decades, the couple had an easier time in Sacramento than in San Francisco. They located first in pleasant rooms near the capitol square; they saw the spring high floods without injury to themselves; they enjoyed the summer's aridity and heat. The worst event of the season came early when Annie was obliged to go back to San Francisco to get the personal property she had left at her Uncle Flintoff's. She was already mentioning the possibility of a baby. So soon pregnant, she had to face a family lawsuit; and the bride's worst anguish was to discover how vindictive her uncles could be. Matthew McCloskey would do anything to badger Henry, she reported. That Annie George was not in touch with her sister Teresa for a period of years measures the completeness of her break from the McCloskey family.

Back in Sacramento events went very well. On 3 November

1862 was born a red-headed boy, the future congressman, Henry George, Jr. Meanwhile Henry, Sr., had collected his credit, perhaps a couple of hundred dollars, from the sale of the San Francisco *Daily Evening Journal*. Now earning about $40 a week the young father was ready to take things a little easy for a change, he said.

On the Philadelphia side the parents and sisters in the family which meant so much to Henry George did everything in their power to welcome Annie as beloved daughter. Unfortunately unusual delays in the wartime winter mails had kept them in the dark more than two months about what the oldest son was doing. But then an outpouring of response to Annie's appealing letters began the sealing of her lifelong affection for her husband's family, and Mr. George wrote that he could get Henry a job at home, on the *Inquirer*. To Jane Henry wrote in June that, 'Marriage has certainly benefited me by giving a more contented and earnest frame of mind and will help me to do my best in "whatever station it pleases God to call me." This is the only difference I can perceive. Annie and I are so well matched in years and temperament that there is no violent change in either.' In due course Mrs. George wrote the kind of letters appropriate for a grandmother.

Not unrelated to the values in life ultimately expressed in *Progress and Poverty,* all this devotion was raised to acute consciousness at midsummer, about the time of the Second Bull Run. Word of the sudden death of Jane George struck the newlyweds as though they lived next door. Typhoid fever had taken her. Henry kept his grief to himself one night while he worked at the press; then he told Annie, and wept. 'Henry,' wrote the mother, 'how her mind developed! It was too much for her frail body. She read too much — nearly every day at the library besides bringing home books.' In the Millennial Letter, addressed to Jane less than a year earlier, Henry had discussed immortality as though it were a promise, a rosy vague extension of lives already filled. But now he had to believe, he told his wife as he paced the floor, that the soul of the individual conquers death, and outlasts it, and proves it of no avail.

Altogether the fourteen months from the Millennial Letter to the birth of the baby had contained about all the crises to which young people are subject, and some of the strains had been extreme. Yet all had been the kinds that time does conquer, and in a backward glance the first and second years of marriage — especially the second, the year of Vicksburg and Gettysburg to the east — show a very idyllic side also. The young couple moved from hotel and boarding-house to a comfortable place of their own: a house with four rooms and a garden, for which they paid $8 a month. They came to relish the climate of Sacramento and the wonderful profusion of flowers. Among other gains for security, word came from Philadelphia that Mr. George had found a new position, apparently with a sufficient salary. In every way their two years together were justifying the gamble they had taken, eloping on nothing but love.

As of 1863 the career and money sides of life demanded most of the attention of the man of the family. Little episodes demonstrate that the recent part-proprietor of the San Francisco *Evening Journal* had no mind to be contented for long with the income and status of a workman's wages, and they offer agreeable testimony also that the future critic of speculation began with no immunity to the California disease. With a couple of friends, one of them John Barry of San Francisco, George explored the possibilities of establishing a printing business in Nevada; and with Ike Trump he looked into the chances of opening a Sacramento *Union* agency in Marysville, and also those of trying a newspaper of their own in the Russian River country. Though none of these projects came to risk and trial, George did put some money, with Trump, into mining stocks. He had seen his old boss, Joseph Duncan, make a killing, and many friends invested whatever savings they could spare. Unfortunately or fortunately, a few months of speculating decided him that paying assessments was worse than abandoning hopes for a quick clean-up, so he valued down his stocks from $462.50 to about half, and proposed to sell all but a few which still looked good. Chastened, he told Trump: 'It is now nearly eight months since we determined to make our fortunes, and I am afraid, in spite of our sanguine hopes we have failed . . . I have come to think if I get my money back I will be in luck.'

On the political side of life, one senses from these Civil War years in Sacramento a general influence on Henry George's future, more readily than one discovers any practical and immediate steps in the education of a restless printer. His residence in the state capital coincided with the governorship of Leland Stanford, the successful storekeeper and coming railroad man in politics. As first Republican statesman in California, Stanford stood for the opposite of Pacific secession and fondness for the Confederacy, and under his administration the state made considerable economic, though inconsiderable military, contributions to the Union cause. For all the immediate, patriotic objects of the governor, George the young printer of course had perfect sympathy. At the same time, as is well known, the future president of the Central Pacific took West coast command in the planning and arranging — the famous contact-establishing, contract-making, and statute-passing business in state and nation — that prepared for the transcontinental railroad. Though we have no contemporary comment from George, it is impossible to think that he did not hear a great deal of gossip about Stanford at this time. It is reasonable to assume that the respect which his future philosophy allowed for the role of the imaginative and aggressive capitalist in an industrial system, and the grudging admiration George never denied the man, stemmed in part from personal knowledge of the governor whose humble fellow townsman he had been.

For a future journalist as well as social thinker, Sacramento was a good place to be and work in for a while. San Francisco had all the lead in commercial and literary journalism; but, partly because Sacramento was the state capital and partly because (before the railroads were built) it had much more immediate contact with the mining and agricultural regions, the interior city had a big advantage for political and general newspapers. There were two especially strong ones, the *Union,* on which Henry George set type, and the *Bee,* of which James McClatchy was the famous editor. In later years George was to be intensely interested in the *Bee,* to regard it as an ally of his own paper, to contribute to it, and to become a personal friend of Mr. McClatchy. So far as we know there were few if any beginnings of that connection as early as 1862 and 1863. Yet it is safe to judge that George at this stage became acquainted with the *Bee's* ardency for land reform, which was a parcel of the newspaper's radical Republicanism. McClatchy had worked under Horace Greeley, and in some degree he made the *Bee* a California model of the great nationalistic and reformist *Tribune* of New York City. With Governor Stanford on one hand and the *Bee* on the other, Henry George had close views of the contrasting elements that were going into the forging of the new Republican Party.

Though perhaps George would have become reform-minded

earlier if he had worked for the *Bee* and not the *Union,* it was probably better for him as a journalist that he had his first experience on the larger newspaper. And also the *Union* fitted better with his family's political tradition. Recently developed from Stephen A. Douglas Democracy into strong patriotic unionism, we may be sure that the young typesetter liked the paper's slogan: *'The UNION for the Union.'* Though often critical of the paper in later years, George looked back on the wartime editor, Henry Watson, as having been as great and influential a national patriot in California as Thomas Starr King. George must have been pleased in 1862 when the *Union* defended the Emancipation Proclamation, even though the editorial tone was milder than his own antislavery feeling. It is worth adding that during the Civil War the *Union* supported Governor Stanford and the other railroad builders, and that afterward it suffered regrets. In the postwar wisdom of one of the owners of the paper: 'the railroad men had professed and pretended that everything should be conducted as fairly and squarely towards the people as could be; they were going to benefit the State of California . . . All of which we encouraged.' The trouble was that the paper, like the people, had taken a bear by the tail: 'We found by G-d after warming the [railroad] into life, that it was going to bite.' This was the resentment of hindsight, which George in time would share.

All things considered, the years 1862 and 1863 in Sacramento seem to have been the period of Henry George's California life when his ideas conformed the closest with the policy of the state and with the opinion of the newspapers of the city of his residence. He went with the Republican current during the mid-war period.

A personal conflict, however, suddenly caused him to leave the city and deprived his small family of their pleasant situation. Here once more, as at King and Baird's printshop and in James George's store, Henry George fell out with his boss. Whose fault it was is not known. Henry George, Jr., tells us that like the quarrel in Victoria this one also was later made up. But at the moment the loss of a job returned him to San Francisco and opened a perilous period of his life.

As if to play for a repetition of the good luck of 1858 when he had gotten a new job so easily, George again took a room at the What Cheer House. But no David Bond appeared. The contemporaries who speak of very good times in San Francisco in 1864 speak mainly of speculation and building, and certain war-stimulated enterprises. The other side of the coin was that forces of economic deflation and upset were also at work; and one exact contemporary of Henry George, though he was an engineer, had a very hard time getting and keeping jobs. Do not come to San Francisco, Frank Hinckley advised his brother: 'a surplus of young men in the city [makes conditions] so that it is next to impossible for a man to get into business even with strong influential friends. There are many who would be glad enough to pay their board until better times come.'

Precisely so with Henry George. When Annie and the baby came on he moved from a good hotel to a shabby one; later they took rooms in a private house and finally wound up in a second-story housekeeping flat. George could locate no proper job. His old newspaper, the *Evening Journal,* had nothing better for him than soliciting subscriptions. And his good friend Trump, who had come down from the mining country out of work, had no better scheme than peddling clothes wringers. For a few days George put the two selling projects together, miserably tramping from house to house in Alameda County across the bay. Things must have seemed to be looking up when he found some substitute printing again; but the *Evening Journal* was slow to pay, and the work he got on the big *Evening Bulletin* — the paper he would later assault the most ferociously — did not amount to much.

Only in the spring of 1864 did he turn up anything which at all suited him, a six-month job on the *Daily American Flag.* This was another forgotten paper of the same class as the *Home Journal* and the *Evening Journal.* It was owned and edited by one D. O. McCarthy, an Irishman of vigorous anti-slave and unionist ideas like James McClatchy's. But at best the job was stopgap, and George thought again of going into business in the mining country, perhaps Sonora or Silver Mountain. Finally he decided to try job-printing in San Francisco, in a partnership with Trump. Once more working on a shoestring, the two purchased part of the equipment of the same *Evening Journal* on which Henry had worked, and which had just expired.

The venture could hardly have been more awkwardly timed, or less successful. In December, the month of starting operations,

Annie George was pregnant, seven months or so along. The following is Henry's diary entry for Christmas day, 1864. 'December 25. Determined to keep a regular journal, and to cultivate habits of determination, energy, and industry. Feel that I am in a bad situation, and must use my utmost effort to keep afloat and go ahead. Will try to follow the following general rules for one week:

'1st. In every case determine rationally what is best to be done.

'2nd. To do everything determined upon immediately, or as soon as an opportunity presents.

'3rd. To write down what I shall determine upon doing for the succeeding day.

'Saw landlady and told her I was not able to pay rent.'

In January the question became literally that of having enough to eat. Some days there were twenty-five cents apiece for the partners to take from the printing-office till. Dinners for the Georges and for Ike Trump who ate with them dropped into a routine of cheap fish, corn meal, milk, potatoes, and bread. They continued to get milk by persuading the milkman to trade it for printed cards. Annie George took in sewing as long as she was able, and she carried all her trinkets, except the McCloskey wedding ring, to the pawnshop. Then on the morning of the twenty-seventh she was delivered of her second child, Richard. Possibly she really heard what she thought she heard, the doctor's orders: 'Don't stop to wash the child; he is starving, Feed him.'

On this day of anguish, in a dismal rain, occurred the event often told of Henry George. In his own words: 'I walked along the street and made up my mind to get money from the first man whose appearance might indicate that he had it to give. I stopped a man — a stranger — and told him I wanted $5. He asked what I wanted it for. I told him that my wife was confined and that I had nothing to give her to eat. He gave me the money. If he had not, I think that I was desperate enough to have killed him.'

The ordeal lasted for weeks. In February George surrendered to Trump his interest in the printing establishment with the understanding that, if a sale brought in any money, he would have a share. Next, about the first of March, Henry had several days of typesetting; and Annie paid $9 rent by the earnings of her needle. At this point $20 a week, if they could only have it regularly, looked about ideal to the wife and mother.

The need to redirect his life, which these hard times compelled him to acknowledge, is better expressed in Henry George's words than in any possible rephrasing. 'I am afloat again, with the world before me. I have commenced this little book as an experiment — to aid me in acquiring habits of regularity, punctuality, and purpose . . . I am starting out afresh, very much crippled and embarrassed, owing over $200. I have been unsuccessful in everything. I wish to profit by my experience and to cultivate those qualities necessary to success in which I have been lacking. I have not saved as much ás I ought and I am resolved to practice a rigid economy until I have something ahead.

'1st. To make every cent I can.

'2nd. To spend nothing unnecessarily.

'3rd. To put something by each week, if it is only a five-cent piece borrowed for the purpose.

'4th. Not to run into debt if it can be avoided.'

In the matter of getting on with people, George planned:

'1st. To endeavour to make an acquaintance and friend of everyone with whom I am brought in contact.

'2nd. To stay at home less, and be more social.

'3rd. To strive to think consecutively and decide quickly.'

In this time of greatest trouble Henry George made the trial upon which hinged the decision of his lifetime. His diary dates the event to the hour, on the afternoon of 25 March 1865: 'After getting breakfast, took the wringing machine which I had been using as a sample back to Faulkner's; then went to Eastmans and saw to bill; loafed around until about 2 p.m. Concluded that the best thing I could do would be to go home and write a little. Came home and wrote for the sake of practice an essay on the "Use of Time," which occupied me until Annie prepared dinner.'

The 'Use of Time,' which marks George's decision for a writing career, was the first essay he had tried since the trifling days of the Lawrence Society almost a decade earlier, and the first sustained writing since the very private Millennial Letter. He was writing clearly again but there is little in the essay to indicate either that the young man's natural skill as a writer had held up or that it had declined, in recent years. We do learn something about his values in life. As in 1861, money for himself occupied front position in his mind. Not just $20 or $30 a week but wealth was what he

wanted, in an amount to open the doors to good things: 'more congenial employment and associates,' opportunities 'to cultivate my
mind and exert to a fuller extent my powers,' and real capacity 'to
minister to the comfort and enjoyment of those whom I love most.'

Sizing up his present predicament, he felt remorse for the hours
he had idled. 'If, for instance, I had applied myself to the practice
of bookkeeping and arithmetic I might now have been an expert
in those things; or I might have had the dictionary at my fingers
ends; been a practised, and perhaps an able writer; a much better
printer; or been able to read and write French, Spanish, or any
other modern or ancient language to which I might have directed
my attention, and the mastery of any of these things would give me
an additional, appreciable power, and means by which to work my
end, not to speak of that which would have been gained by exercise
and good mental habits.'

The young man, now twenty-five, recognized of himself that,
entirely apart from the hazards of unemployment, he would never
be satisfied to earn his living by his trade. He did not deceive himself into thinking that writing would build a sure bridge from
poverty to riches, and he was not especially idealistic about that
calling. Yet feeling his own way forward he did begin to generalize
a notion of human capacity — a pretty democratic notion — which
he would enlarge in his greatest writing. As he put it now: 'To
secure any given result it is only necessary to rightly supply sufficient force. Some men possess a greater amount of natural power
than others and produce quicker and more striking results; yet it
is apparent that the majority, if properly and continuously applied,
are sufficient to accomplish much more than they generally do.'
So for himself George determined that, 'I will endeavour to acquire
facility and elegance in the expression of my thoughts by writing
essays or other matters which I will preserve for future comparison.
And in this practice it will be well to aim at mechanical neatness
and grace, as well as at proper and polished language.'

A little surprisingly, because nothing previous, unless it be membership in the printers union, indicates conviction or idea on behalf
of labor, George made his next piece of writing a plea for working
men. He did this in a communication to the editor of the new
Journal of the Trades and Workmen, the short-lived first labor
paper to be published on the Pacific coast. 'We, the workers of

mankind,' he began, live in the brightest day that has ever dawned
for the 'like of us.' Without bothering to justify his optimism, but
complimenting the editor, George estimated the service a labor
journal could render: 'At a time when most of our public prints
pander to wealth and power and would crush the poor man beneath
the wheel of the capitalist's carriage; when one begins to talk of
the "work people" and "farm servants" of this coast, and another
to deplore the high rate of wages [this was true of the *Alta California*] . . . I, for one, feel that your enterprise is one which we
should all feel the necessity of, and to which we should lend our
cordial support.' Hortatory but innocent of program, the piece
contains little foretaste of future ideas, and no suggestion of an
economist's analytical powers in the making. Only the simple identification of himself with a cause appears: in his very first published
writing Henry George spoke for laboring men's improving their
economic situation.

While some time was to pass before the opportunity came to
develop this vein, another effort of 1865 assures us that the paper
in the *Journal of Trades and Workmen* was no sport, no misrepre-
sentation of present interests. This text is lacking, but George's own
word tells us that he did an 'article about laws relating to sailors.'
It appears that in hard times his memory had brought back the
struggle of the crew and captain of the *Hindoo* in Hobson's Bay,
and that he now made his first plea for maritime labor.

George's second publication, which came out only a week after
the first, shifted the scene of thought and elevated the level of publication. This time he did a 'Plea for the Supernatural,' quite in the
California mode of being fond of the esoteric, and it was printed
in the distinguished literary journal, the *Californian,* where Mark
Twain and Bret Harte and 'a lot of other bright young writers'
were appearing. Using the first person singular, George wrote of a
psychological event during a voyage on the Indian Ocean. The sight
of the Southern Cross, he said, had flooded his mind with memories
of what his mother had taught him: the names of the stars, and
ideas of the Creator's love. A meteor had flashed. 'To me it was
an emblem of myself: having no part in the sweet glory around, it
was quenched in darkness . . . A voice called me . . . Before me
stood my mother as she was years ago . . . That I could not hear
and see this, on the trackless Indian Ocean, miles and miles from

land, proves nothing. *I did.* Whether with the sense of the body I
care not; but my soul saw and heard, and it knows.'

There is no way to tell whether, in the writer's mind, the story
was completely fictional or was developed from an experience of
his own aboard the *Hindoo,* but we can be fairly sure that the 'Plea
for the Supernatural' is not to be read as a very literal confession of
belief. In a short interval George cashed in two or three times on
San Francisco's vogue for spiritualism. In the second chapter we
anticipated from 1856 the best of the series, the 'Dust to Dust'
story which, as he wrote it about this time, he embellished with a
supernaturalism not his own at the time of the event. That story,
too, appeared in the *Californian.* The important thing is that in
this beginning of serious writing George picked up emotional
themes, just as he had done as a youngster for the fun of the Lawrence Society. His native skill as reporter of external events, displayed in 1855, he had not yet begun to develop.

Within a fortnight of George's debut in the San Francisco magazines came by wire from Washington the shock of the assassination
of President Lincoln. The word arrived at ten o'clock in the morning, Saturday, 15 April, and the city's chords of feeling vibrated almost out of control. Business stopped, the courts closed, speeches
were improvised, and mourning was quickly displayed. Vengeance
too broke out. Law and order yielded as inflamed persons broke into
pro-Southern newspaper offices and scattered type and destroyed
property. Ike Trump took some degree of leadership in the turmoil, and Henry George seems to have participated. Then in his
little flat, with great emotion, George wrote a letter to the editor of
the *Alta California,* the city's oldest and most conservative paper,
on which he was at the moment 'subbing.'

It is a comment on the excitement of the day that the letter was
printed, not in the regular edition but apparently in an extra,
though perhaps it went no farther than proof. An editor's line explained that the 'stirring article' had been contributed by a printer.
Under the heading, 'Sic Semper Tyrannis!' George pictured the
wounded president against the 'glitter and glare' of the theater.
'They have struck down the just because of his justice, and the
fate they have fixed upon him shall be theirs.' Retributive justice
and Christian atonement, George mixed his moral ideas. 'What a
fitting time! Good Friday! At this very moment . . . sounds the

solemn wail of the Tenebrae. Now . . . again has Evil triumphed,
and the blood of its victim sealed its fate . . . As a martyr of Freedom — as a representative of the justice of a great Nation, the
name of the Victim will live forever . . . *Abraham Lincoln* will
remain a landmark of the progress of the race.'

It was an impulsive way to break into newsprint. Yet despite all
crudities, 'Sic Semper Tyrannis!' won for the writer his first job as
a newspaper reporter. The *Alta* commissioned him to describe the
Lincoln mourning in the city, and the reports in that paper tell us
that he thrilled to the occasion. On Wednesday, 14,000 citizens followed a catafalque through the city; the great Second Inaugural
was read; Horatio Stebbins, Starr King's successor, gave the principal address; the crowd sang thrillingly the *Battle Cry of Freedom*.
The reporter put visual detail and feeling both into the *Alta's*
stories that week.

Then unsolicited, Henry George wrote another letter, a very
thoughtful one, and it was printed as a front-page editorial of the
Alta in the regular Sunday edition, 23 April. The title was simply
'Abraham Lincoln.' 'No common man, yet the qualities which
made him great were eminently common . . . He was one of the
leaders who march alone before the advancing ranks of the people,
who direct their steps and speak with their voice . . . Hot blood
called him slow, and cold blood called him hot; but the universal
current, tempered by the moods and springing from the hearts of
the times, pulsed through his veins . . . No other system could
have produced him; through no crowd of courtiers could such a
man have forced his way . . . And, as in our time of need, the man
that was needed came forth, let us know that it will always be so,
and that under our institutions, when the rights of the people are
endangered, from their ranks will spring the men for the times
. . . Let us thank God for him; let us trust God for him; let us
place him in that Pantheon which no statue of a tyrant ever sullied
— the hearts of a free people.'

Passion had evoked, and a week had brought from incoherency
into coherency, the political affirmations of the young printer who
had just one month earlier determined to write. In the common
anguish he had turned from faddish supernaturalism, in which he
could never have reached maturity, to the folk mysticism which
democracy does produce. Unknowing of course, but in common

with many of the great men of contemporary letters and as early as any, he had made a small but eloquent contribution to the legend of the fallen Lincoln.

The end of the war and his being so little employed very soon provided the occasion of George's nearest approach to service in a military force. California, as the one unionist state adjoining Mexico, was particularly sensitive to the insult to the United States of the presence of the Emperor Maximilian on a throne created by Napoleon III, contrary to the Monroe Doctrine. Henry George felt the humiliation bitterly; and when a San Francisco group formed, in the old filibuster style, he joined it. He became a lieutenant under an Indian fighter named Burn; and a friend, probably John Barry, became a major. The project contemplated an invasion from the west coast of Mexico to help Juarez topple the foreigner from the throne.

Not that this was pure impulse with George, for in this undertaking money was offered at last, after two lean years. The *Alta* agreed to take any newsletters he would write from Mexico, and to pay Mrs. George. On D day Henry and Annie took the new baby to St. Patrick's Church and had him baptized Richard Fox, after his grandfathers. Finally after more prayers at home, Lieutenant George joined his fellow officers in Platt's Hall, where they swore in 'a good many men' at the last moment.

But that evening the Brontes expedition, so called from the name of the vessel to carry the force, collapsed by reason of the *Brontes*. Provisions were inadequate; and word got around that the scheme involved seizing a French transport, and possibly even an American mail vessel off Panama, to make up deficiencies. So the story rumored against Henry George in New York in 1886, that he had been mixed up in a piratical adventure, had a certain grounding in truth; and late in life George himself felt apologetic about it. In San Francisco that spring evening, talk of piracy proved to be more than official leniency could bear, and a revenue cutter dropped anchor in front of the *Brontes*.

For Henry George the episode meant that a zealous, foolish impulse had been frustrated, and that now he must find some new direction for taking his second step into journalism. His mind was not at all changed about Mexico. Very soon he and Annie joined the Monroe League, a fresh and short-lived organization to support a new filibuster; and this time they went through rituals and oath taking on a bare sword and a republican flag of Mexico. Mrs. George, twenty-two years old and the mother of two children, was the only woman member. Later, in the responsible position of editor, he vindicated the execution of Maximilian much as we justify the execution of war criminals. 'It is a protest against the right of Kings to cause suffering and shed blood for their own selfish ends . . . It will teach princes and princelings to be more cautious how they endeavour to subvert the liberties of a free people.'

A literary historian, Professor Franklin Walker, has noted accurately the incorrigible romanticism of Henry George in this period of utopianism and adventure seeking before he became an editor. His mind shared much of the American common lot. With just as much correctness an economic historian might observe that George's periods of unemployment in 1859 and 1861 and 1864 and during his crisis of 1865 were more the normal than abnormal thing for young men in California. Many beaten men went home; others by the hundreds went out of work; probably few of the great fortunes of the state were accumulated without periods of reverse and anxiety in the experience of the accumulators. Yet over the twenty years, and despite his own sense of failure in 1864 and 1865, Henry George's California story is a success story. The periods of defeat were quite temporary. It could be contended that his hard times in the state did not especially make him a man of suffering, no more than his father's low income had made him a child of poverty in Philadelphia.

He had not suffered uniquely, but he had been hurt, and the crisis at the time of Richard's birth was unforgettable. The unique thing in George's case of course is that during Civil War years he reached a high intensity of self-awareness, and an awareness of ideas. His writing shows that he was beginning to see his own reverses as part of a social process, as part of the situation of all laboring men. He was beginning to see poverty in the light and shadow cast by Civil War aims, by Christian ideals, and by the ideals of the national heritage.

V

San Francisco Editor

versus California Ideas

1865–1868

IN DECEMBER 1865 Henry and Annie George returned to Sacramento. Again the state capital had a job for him when San Francisco did not, and again an interval there provided a stabilizing period in the battle for a living.

It was a printing, not a writing, job. Probably some friendship or connection accounts for a bit of preferment: at any rate the work was state printing, getting out the documents of the biennial session of the legislature, which opened on 4 December. George was pleased, and he now wrote his sister Caroline in much the same tone as he had written Jane when happy about an earlier new job: 'I am, for the present, only ambitious of working, and will look neither to the right nor to the left until I have "put money in my purse" — something it has never yet contained. I have abandoned, I hope, the hand to mouth style of living, and will endeavour, if not absolutely forced to do so, to draw no drafts on the future.' In accord with his recent resolutions about being social and making contacts, George in Sacramento belonged to the Odd Fellows and the National Guard, and attended the Lyceum, where matters of public interest were debated.

An early incident of that program tells the story of Henry George's first positive response to a specific economic idea. One

William H. Mills, later a high official of the Central Pacific Railroad, addressed the Lyceum in favor of the protective tariff. He spoke with knowledge of the *laisser faire* economists in the back of his mind — Smith, Ricardo, and Malthus. But the American nationalist, Henry C. Carey, was his mentor, and Mr. Mills stressed ideas familiar in California: that a protective tariff was 'best calculated to produce the broadest industrial skill of our people, develop the natural resources of the country . . . confer the highest intelligence . . . and generally confer industrial and commercial independence upon the country.'

These had been Henry George's own Republican ideas. We have his acknowledgment that, when the Confederate raiders were destroying trade, he considered 'their depredations, after all, a good thing for the state in which I lived . . . since the increased risk and cost of ocean carriage in American ships [then the only way of bringing goods from the eastern states to California] would give to her infant industries something of that needed protection against the lower wages and better established industries of the Eastern states . . .' He had even regretted that the federal constitution prevented a state tariff.

But the protective argument backfired that night in the Sacramento Lyceum. Mr. Mills gave the audience a favorable comparison of the nationalism of the tariff with the cosmopolitanism of free trade. Then, according to the speaker's recollection and friendly judgment of his opponent, George thought fast on his feet. The young printer asked the audience to reject Mr. Mills's preference. He pleaded that protective tariffs were causing 'antagonism between the nations,' and had 'augmented their selfishness' and 'made standing armies and vast navies necessary to the peace of the world.' He contrasted 'free trade, as an evolutionary force,' one which 'made nations dependent, promoted peace among them, and urged humanity on towards a higher plane of universal fraternity.'

It is sometimes forgotten that free trade was the economic dogma second in prominence to the dogma about land in George's ultimate economic teaching and preaching. The episode in the Sacramento Lyceum gives chronological first place to free trade. Though we have no evidence from which to explain the inner reasons for a crucial change in Henry George's mind, the voicing of that change does fix the date of his first taking initiative in economic thought;

he did this a year earlier than his first writing about land policy, and two or three years ahead of his first questioning the rightness of private property in land. Nothing could have been more characteristic of George as an economic thinker than this beginning. Now as later his economic perceptions were inseparable from moral perceptions, in the working of his mind, and economic ideas once accepted assumed with him the force of moral law.

During this nine-month period in Sacramento, George carried on his writing according to program. Before he left that city, both the 'Dust to Dust' story and one other, his third and last in the vein of the mysterious and supernatural, had been finished and printed. 'The Prayer of Kakonah' he constructed from a legend he must have picked up in British Columbia; it is the only piece of his early writing that pretends to moral wisdom. In the allegory as George told it, Kakonah was an Indian chieftain who had learned 'all that can be learned.' When he died his people prayed the Lord of Life to let him come back awhile, for there was no successor to govern wisely. But only seven days of return to earth showed the folly of the arrangement. In Kakonah's heart, now that his natural task was finished, all 'his wisdom seemed foolishness, and his power was weariness . . . Where the Master of Life has set bounds, let none try to pass.' So reflected Henry George, fifteen months after the death of President Lincoln, on the limitations of wisdom and the necessity of a people's producing new leaders for new times.

By midsummer, a year after the fiasco of the Brontes expedition, he had his second try at journalism. This time the Sacramento *Union* took his articles; and, though the pen name he adopted for the series, 'Proletarian,' suggests a reversion to pro-labor preaching like that of 1865, much of what he wrote was quite different from anything up to now. In a sharp criticism of President Johnson, George took the side of the Radical Republicans and presumed for the first time to pass judgment on issues of constitutional procedure. Another article, closer home, criticized the administration of the state library in Sacramento. A splendid kind of public institution and worthy of tax support, he agreed, but the poorest proletarians would be glad of a slight extra public expense if it would make the books available when they could use them, after working hours. Between pieces for the *Union,* George reported the state fair in

Sacramento, including remarks on the productivity of the economy of California, for one of the San Francisco papers.

He was reaching out in every direction and, had he continued free-lancing and supporting his family this way and that, he would probably have tried a novel soon. He considered going east, after all. Yet he felt that he could manage the transition into the kind of life he wanted better where he had made a beginning than where he would have to start at scratch. As he put the matter to his father: 'I want if possible, to secure some little practice and reputation as a writer here before going, which will not only give me introduction and employment there, but help me in going, and enable me to make something by corresponding with papers here. If I do not overrate my abilities, I may yet make position and money.' He was not being too optimistic. The editor of the *Union* commended him strongly for the 'Proletarian' articles, calling them 'clearly, forcibly, and elegantly written, evincing just views, thinking power, good taste, and excellent command of effective expression.' Henry George promised to make 'a valuable aid in the editorial staff of a daily journal,' this editor believed.

The wanted opportunity came in November. On the fifth of that month an independent Republican paper, the San Francisco *Daily Times,* a newspaper completely of the new dispensation of California politics and journalism, brought out its first issue. Likely the paper was owned in part in Sacramento, or at least was planned among Republicans in the capital city. George knew about it long beforehand certainly, and applied for a position as 'reporter or assistant editor.' And, though warned that he was taking considerable chance in moving and though hired at first for the composing room, still a printer not a journalist, George went hopefully back to San Francisco. For once his optimism was justified. His best hope of late summer, 1866, that by early the next calendar year he would be earning $50 or $60 a week writing for the *Times,* proved to be only four or five months ahead of the actual fact.

A public disagreement between prominent people thirty years later, about who deserved the honor of having introduced Henry George to editorial writing, tells us something about that debut. Undoubtedly James McClatchy, the first editor of the *Times,* for a short term absent from the Sacramento *Bee,* was the man. Accord-

ing to information in the *Bee* years later, apparently written by his
son, McClatchy and George were already friends when the *Times*
was started; and, when the printer asked for a chance to show what
he could do, McClatchy gave him some reporting and moved him
into the local room, and very soon assigned him editorial writing.
One guesses that George had talked things out with McClatchy before coming to San Francisco and had been given reasonable assurances that he would have a chance to write.

Noah Brooks, the second editor-in-chief of the *Times,* claiming
to have been Henry George's Columbus, seems rather to have been
his second discoverer but to have been actually the first to advance
him to place and responsibility. At any rate, after McClatchy quit
the *Times,* George returned to the composing room without other
assignment, and he was there when a foreman called him to Mr.
Brooks's attention. At first meeting the editor held off. He thought
that the young man's writing on affairs might have been plagiarized;
and, as he noticed the unimpressive physique, the thinning hair,
he was skeptical. But very soon he had George regularly on editorial work; and shortly, after a death on the staff, George became
the third-ranking editor. This rise accounts for a major event of
George's life, occurring in June 1867, when a disagreement with
the directors caused Noah Brooks and his first assistant to quit, as
McClatchy had done. At that point, at the age of twenty-eight,
Henry George became managing editor of the most interesting
paper in San Francisco.

Unlike Sacramento, the great port city during the Civil War had
not had a strong newspaper to speak the advanced Republican
mind, zealous against slavery and ardent to make the South conform with the economy and civilization of the North. The first
issue of the *Times* announced that it would assume that kind of
spokesmanship. In the vein of policy which history names 'Radical
Republican,' the paper's own words of 5 November 1866: 'The
Times will be pronounced [sic] to aid in securing to the Republic
and to mankind the legitimate fruits of our victorious arms, and
to maintain the control of the State and the Nation in the hands
of unquestioned loyalty.' And three days later, an editorial said,
more specifically, that though the Confederates had surrendered
they had not yet accepted the spirit, and whole intention, of the
North. 'They yielded to our stronger arm, but not to our higher

civilization . . . New ideas, new feelings, new leaders and new laws, must supplant the old. The conflict of ideas rages and will rage; but reason, general information, political integrity and the persuasive ballot, are the weapons of our new warfare.' Later, under Brooks, the *Times* spoke for Negro suffrage and civil rights, though somewhat vaguely: 'Political as well as physical bondage must be annihilated.'

Radical Republican politics and journalism has been much discussed of recent years, often in terms of Thaddeus Stevens, as having lacked the sweetest disposition, as having been needlessly unforgiving toward the recent enemy, and as having incorporated so many self-seeking and corrupt special interests of North and West as to have invalidated its claim to speak a true national idealism. Even after the most adverse judgment of the movement as politics, however, individual Radicals do still command respect as idealists and reformers. Senator Charles Sumner belongs among the sincere tramplers of the vintage; and so does Representative George W. Julian of Indiana, the abolitionist who continued to fight for human equality, as spokesman for land reform and women's rights. Especially when considering the Pacific coast, where the Radical Republican frame of mind naturally lacked much interest in the persecution of defeated Confederates, the idealism of the movement demands high rating. In the West as in the East, Radicalism had power to ignite consciences even against Republican party leadership, and sometimes did.

In this area of opinion the *Times* began. Its editorials demanded reforms reminiscent of the labor propaganda of the Jackson period, and they called for policies quite opposite to recent Republican statute making. It developed the logic of free soil to speak for free land, and even free trade — in this not at all like Thaddeus Stevens. An editorial of 13 December, for instance, under the cautious title, 'The Amelioration of Customs Duties,' explained that 'the abstract principle of free trade is manifestly a correct one.' Working from a phrase Henry George might have written (and there is an indeterminable chance that he *did* write it) — 'Restrictions upon trade and commerce are as antagonistic to the principles which underlie and facilitate the onward progress of the higher forms of civilization, as restrictions on the normal rights of man are destructive to the advancement of human liberty' — the *Times* came out for

downward revision of the customs duties. So arguing, it reported
on, and followed the logic of, Commissioner David Ames Wells, a
supporter of President Johnson, in tariff matters. That is to say it
went with the most informed and liberal American thinking of
the day.

The *Times'* turning to Wells, we may note, was like Henry
George's later habit of studying that economist's federal and New
York state papers; and probably it set the habit for him. The same
may be said of the newspaper's coming out in favor of a slow and
socially conscious policy of paying the federal debt from the Civil
War years. Very rapid payment, however gratifying to creditor interests, would, the editorial page said, penalize the present generation which has already borne an incredible burden of war suffering.
Too fast payment would raise taxes, restrict immigration and land
settlement, and generally constrict the economy — a forceful argument which appealed to George, and which twentieth-century
readers will understand.

Enough has been selected from the comment of the *Times* on
national issues, before George took over editorial responsibility,
to represent its line of thought and to suggest the heterodoxy of its
Republicanism. The paper is so remembered in the larger history
of journalism in city and state. Though it never made money, it
achieved a reputation for good writing. And, under its too rapid
succession of notable chief editors — McClatchy, Brooks, George,
and Dr. Lewis Gunn, three of whom reached fame in the field of
writing — the paper stirred the community. The power-conscious
proprietors of the *Bulletin,* the city's most entrenched newspaper
and a dull one, admitted some admiration of the *Times,* while
George was editor. When the paper failed, in 1869, an Oakland
paper summed up justly. 'The *Times,*' it said, 'certainly did much
to improve journalism in this state by exciting competition; had it
been more vigorous, and marked out a field for itself, instead of
following in the tracks of the *Bulletin* and the *Alta,* it might have
made an early success.'

Being on the *Times,* then, meant for Henry George that his first
editorial responsibility occurred in a vortex of idealism and eco-
nomic-mindedness, as was very appropriate to his own ideas. We
shall need to return to his leading editorials of 1867 and 1868 to
see how he developed those attitudes. But, wheels within wheels,

this phase of his thought cannot be studied with proper understanding of his intellectual growth unless it be connected with his
opinions at the time concerning important state matters. California
affairs were now so special, and so intense, that an analogy from
George's childhood suggests itself. In much the same way as Low
Church evangelicalism had once penetrated his mind, and almost
against his will created values for life, so now the problems of
California's society and economy took over, to be mulled and
generalized for many years to come.

Specifically, these were the questions of labor supply and wages,
and of land settlement, land policy, and landed property, and they
comprised the very essence of current history in the state. Though
earlier in life, beginning in Australia, he had noticed some of the
unstable social phenomena of new-settled lands, and though for a
long time now he had heard predicted disturbing possibilities for
California's future, he had never thought about such matters in
any sustained way. Now he had little choice. All manner of writers
judged the state to be tossed and bobbed in a tremendous economic
storm. This was the period in California affairs when, as in the case
of no other state in the union, state boundaries defined a region of
economic as well as political development. At that time, during
the lifetime of the *Times*, editorials in all the main newspapers,
and thoughtful books as well as pamphlets, assessed economic
problems: so it was really a huge debate of policy which George
entered, ambition aflame, in 1867. An historical parenthesis is required, to explain that debate, before we can understand his role
as editor, and still more to explain the ideas his mind presently
grasped to hold for life.

—2—

It will do no harm to say again what Californians have been saying happily for nearly a century, that during the ten years (and
more) after the Gold Rush the state accomplished some of the most
incredible feats of social and economic building of nineteenth-
century history. How could one think differently from the Methodist missionary, the Reverend Mr. William Taylor who, in the
year of Henry George's arrival, reviewed California's progress during the '50s? The miners in the Sierras, this parson observed, 'are
a hardy, muscular, powerful class of men, possessing literally an

extraordinary development of hope, faith, and patience, and a corresponding power of endurance. They have in my opinion done more hard work in California, within the last eight years, than has ever been done in any country by the same number of men, in the same length of time, and I think I may safely say in double that length of time, since the world was made.'

What is easily forgotten about early days in optimistic California is that, even in that first American decade, the ugliness of the economic process set off criticism in force. A full ten years before Henry George turned somewhat gloomy prophet, a famous minister, Horace Bushnell, who came from Connecticut's land of steady habits and formal villages, protested what the miners were doing to the mountains of the state. The erosion and defacement wrought by diggings, sluices, and flumes were running wounds in nature's breast, to Bushnell. Not the first, he was one of the early eloquent contributors to the cause of conserving the natural resources of California. Even the literature of criticism assumed often that the state could be made into a kind of utopia.

Henry George's life and thought would have been vastly different and his writing would have been less substantial if the regional discussions had not come rapidly down to earth and sometimes been done in a very expert way. In general, the economics of colonization was the appropriate language. Not differently from Iowa and Minnesota at the time, California was reliving, as all American communities have, the old story which had begun on the East coast two centuries earlier: settlement first, with labor and capital risked in hope and expectation; then stages of economic growth toward community productivity, solvency, and a degree of independence. But uniquely California had become a state almost as soon as she became a part of the United States; and her incomparable resources of gold and silver were expected to make her economically independent. These two factors made for an early sense of independence and vigor. And at the same time, the origins of the people who rushed to California — North and South American, English and continental European, and Asiatic — were so disparate as to prevent the occurrence of any future intimacy between the state and any older state or region of the United States such as connected, say, Wisconsin with New England during its early development. Credit came as settlers did, from London and

Paris notably, as well as from across the continent. California was a part of the United States, but as an economic enterprise it depended on the whole capitalistic colonizing world.

This set the frame of economic thought and made natural a rapid development of ideas. Broadly speaking, the 1850s produced promotional economic literature; and the 1860s produced the first sustained flow of economic self-criticism and particularism. Of course these two types of ideas overlapped: a certain amount of criticism, like Bushnell's, cropped up early; and promotion kept up in the '60s, as it has ever since. Nevertheless a distinction of attitude between the '50s and '60s is valid. American history bears a long-run analogy: during the period commonly called colonial, from Queen Elizabeth to George III, first, a century of promoters from Hakluyt to Penn advertised America to Europe; and, second, a group of protesters, among whom Franklin and Jefferson take first rank, argued the side of America's free development and separation from the mother country. Roughly the same alternation occurred in California, but in a cycle of two decades rather than two centuries: a change of impulse, from simple expansion to sentiment in favor of economic solvency and autonomy.

Two illustrations from 1851 will show how early and how naturally, once gold and climate were discovered, California seized men's minds as a place where might be tried daring solutions of economic problems. The first is a letter, now one of the fascinating originals in the Huntington Library, from a statesman and spokesman of the Old South, James Gadsden, to Thomas Jefferson Green, a leader in the California state legislature when it was very new. Gadsden asked for help in getting a big land grant. As he specified: it must be large enough for a self-sufficing community; the conditions must be right for cotton and a variety of other farm products; there must be a town site with available water transportation to the coast; there should be access to the mining country, as an outlet for seasonal operations by Negro slave labor. To come to California from South Carolina, Gadsden proposed to march with a company of immigrants in military order, all the way to whatever location, presumably on the San Joaquin, might be selected for settlement.

At first twentieth-century glance, the Southerner's scheme seems preposterous. By provision of its constitution California was a free-soil state; and, even if that provision could have been nullified,

the free-labor customs of the mining society would have made
western soil poisonous for transplanting a growth of the Old South's
slave economy. Even so, James Gadsden's letter today represents
more than simply that California evoked imaginative varieties of
economic planning among ambitious citizens, a century ago.
Though Gadsden failed, many a Southerner did transmit plantation mores to the state, and adapting those mores — raising other
crops than cotton, using Chinese coolies instead of Negro slaves —
set a permanent pattern of large landholding for California's agricultural society. In time nothing would annoy Henry George
more than this silent, little-challenged victory by the plantation
system, so opposite to his own convictions.

A contrasting northern instance of blueprinting an ideal future
in California appears in a pamphlet published at Benicia, on the
straits of Carquinez, before that little town had had its brief day as
state capital, or had lost its hope of enormous development. The
author was one J. J. Werth, otherwise remembered only as a writer
for the *Alta California*. His title, *A Dissertation on the Resources
and Policy of California, Mineral, Agricultural, and Promotional,*
forecasts many a later and weightier volume. 'Progression, Progression,' he prophesied as 'the Destiny of California.' In three
years since 1848 the state had accomplished what elsewhere would
require a generation, he believed; and in the early future it would
achieve a diversified economy, ample railroads, and cottage residences for a happy population. Thus, opposite the slaveholder's,
a freeman's dream. A couple of years later a New York lawyer, E. S.
Capron, noticed that San Francisco was already manufacturing
jewelry at an amazing rate, and said that the suburbs of that city
promised to develop like Birmingham or Pittsburgh — a prophecy
of present-day industrialization on the fringes of the city.

At least as early as Henry George's arrival in San Francisco, the
promotional stage of regional economic thinking had achieved both
quality in performance and popularity of interest; and, in the case
of one famous writer, the critical spirit too had struck hard. The
signs of popular interest occur everywhere: in the little newspapers
which employed Henry George, for instance, and in books, and
in the major literary magazines, such as the *Pioneer, Hutchings
Illustrated California Magazine,* and the *Hesperian,* which published many an article on questions of economic development and

condition. On the side of book publishing, the French economist, Ernst Seyd, brought out in London in 1858 a detailed economic description, *California and Its Resources, a Work for the Merchant, the Capitalist, and the Lawyer.* To capitalists of roving eye, M. Seyd presented California as 'the fairest and most fertile' land on earth. Interest was made to beckon at 2 or 3 per cent per month; living was represented as cheaper than in Australia, and labor as better paid. To this writer, and to other French writers, the growing cities of the state, with grand opportunities for profit and promises for culture, were peculiarly appealing. This emphasis of course designated one of the special phenomena of California's frontier growth — cities ahead of countryside. This too we shall find important in the mind of Henry George.

Earlier than the social criticism of the '6os, the mordant writing of Hinton Rowan Helper tells us all we need to know about the arrival in California of the economic objector's point of view. The famous North Carolinian's California book, *The Land of Gold, Reality versus Fiction,* published in Baltimore in 1855, won him less reputation than *The Impending Crisis in the South,* partly because in California he made his one-man attacks for the losing not the winning side. If others were promoters, he was the demoter of California. He hated San Francisco for the cold and fog, and he detested the speculators and exploiters in the state's economy. Somewhat foolishly, Helper went to enormous lengths of statistical demonstration to show that California was an economic failure: the costs of acquiring the land, plus the expenditures of emigration from the eastern states, plus labor spent in California were a miracle of waste, to this writer. As outgo they added up to a total greater than the value of the mineral wealth which California had returned to the world to pay those costs: the deficit as of 1855 he found to be 60 millions. Helper's use of figures was absurd. But as in his anti-slavery writing, the cantankerous Southerner had a point not to be dismissed because unpopular. He saw in the speculation and monopolism of California the oppression of free labor, much as he saw in slavery the oppression of white labor in the South. He conceded that California's 'spacious harbors and geographical position are her true wealth.'

Though there is no evidence that George ever read Helper or Seyd, or even knew of Werth or Gadsden, his protest and his utopianism about California came in time to overlap their ideas, and to continue some of them. Professor Paul S. Taylor has wisely noticed that, though California as a sovereign state was confronted by complex social problems which rose in chronological series — slavery or free labor in 1849, Chinese admission or Chinese exclusion, during the '60s, '70s, and early '80s, and land monopoly or free land, a perennial issue — the series embraced just one basic issue: 'What kind of a rural society do Californians want?' Professor Taylor might permit reducing the question to simply: 'What kind of a *society* do Californians want?' At any rate, the 1850s were confronted with major choices. Then in the '60s, Henry George's decade of finding himself, new writers whom he did know, and journals which he did read, and to which he occasionally made contributions, brought the problems into the focus of the changing times. We have seen already, in terms of George's being employed and unemployed, what perilous and depression-filled years the middle '60s were.

Three books of the decade sum up the advance of regional economic analysis. Beginning in 1863, their chronological order is also the order of their importance in policy discussion, as follows: John S. Hittell, *The Resources of California comprising Agriculture, Mining, Geography, Climate, Commerce, etc., etc., and the Past and Future Development of the State* (Roman, 1863, and many later editions); Titus Fey Cronise, *The Natural Wealth of California* (Bancroft, 1868); and Bentham Fabian, *The Agricultural Lands of California; A Guide to the Immigrant as to the Productions, Climate, and Soil of Every County in the State* (Bancroft, 1869). All these were published in San Francisco, not in Europe or in the eastern states as such books often had been in the previous decade; and the authors were all men of much experience and observation in the state. Hittell was by far the best-known and most influential man of the group. As an editor, and a contributor, for years, of economic writing to the *Alta California,* his doing a book on *The Resources of California* was, in that time and place, like, say, Walter Lippmann's doing a book on foreign policy today: it was the gathering of tested data and the publishing of a widely accepted set of ideas. Looked at in the perspective of later time, his book ranks with Professor Ezra S. Carr's *Patrons of Husbandry on the Pacific Coast,* 1875, which included broad discussions of agriculture and landholding in California; and it ranks with the seventh and final volume of Hubert Howe Bancroft's *History of California,* published in 1890, which contains remarkable chapters on contemporary agriculture, manufacturing, business, railroads, mining, and city-growth in the state.

Were this a general history of economic thought in California, a dozen reasons could be discovered for a close examination of all these regional descriptions, histories, and programs. As we are concerned, however, with the frame and setting of one young editor's discovering his role, we may be guided by the time factor. In 1867, when George took over the *Times,* Hittell's was the only one of the three major economic descriptions of the decade already in print. That writer's own words indicate that he regarded himself as a promoter, and he was much like Seyd and other writers of the '50s, although he was also much more critical than they. 'I write of a land of wonders,' he said. 'With many drawbacks, which have been set forth clearly and unreservedly, California is still the richest part of the civilized world. It possesses most of the luxuries of Europe, and many of the advantages which the valley of the Ohio had forty years ago. In the few years of its history it has astonished the world, and its chief glories are still to come.' Hittell and Cronise and Fabian alike put out a very literate propaganda and information that was encyclopedic. Lengthy chapters on the geology, zoology, botany, agriculture, and mining of California were not too much for the writers and readers of the '60s. The improvement over the effusions of J. J. Werth was enormous.

On the critical side, no other regional analyst was quite so severe as was Hittell, and he spoke more strongly in the first than in the later editions of his book. In that edition he demanded no less than a transformation of the state's economy. What was wanted may be understood by analogy with the Radical Republican program for reconstructing the South. To replace the instability of the economy created by the Gold Rush, the *Alta California* writer — and, more mildly, the others also — proposed to encourage social growth based mainly on homestead agriculture, and also on diversified, settled, and productive industries. With variations of their own, Hittell and the others offered the northern conception for the state, not different in principle from Werth's, but now rendered in detailed blueprints. A grand increase in farming, to put to use the state's promising soil and climate, was their principal idea. From that would flow food for the cities; there would be rural markets for industry; and prosperity and loyalty would flourish among the people. Hittell proposed this without especially idealizing farm life, and he certainly did not slip over into radical ideas about property in land. He hoped for prosperity in the mines as on the farms; and he saw the future arriving with deep digging already displacing placer mining, and with more capital equipment being taken into the Sierras. His goal for California was Hamiltonian, or Whiggish rather: a balanced economy, with city and country, extractive industry and refining industry, transport and commerce, labor and employment, all in sound relationships with one another.

Thus, for the long term, the grand strategy of California's economists was based on achieving balance and prosperity by expanding the underdeveloped sectors of economic life. Ideally, according to prevailing economic ideas, the reaching of such a goal would not prove too difficult, but be a more or less automatic evolution. New doses of immigration and investment, the usual tonic for faltering colonies, could be expected to provide the stimulus. But present realities were hard, and the depression of the 1860s forebade leaving the matter on a completely *laisser faire* basis. For the time being the automatic flows were running in reverse: more emigrants were leaving the state than there were immigrants arriving. According to Hittell, a quarter-million workers, representing a million population, had recently departed. So a crisis operation was called for by the doctors — such economic surgery as would stop the bleeding. Once stability was accomplished, the international flow of credit and of population movement could be counted on to nourish California back to health.

This was the general position of economic expectation at which the three principal regional writers converged in agreement, all of them bringing out books within short years of George's beginnings as writer and editor. Strikingly they agreed also about the point indicated for surgery. The situation of land distribution and land policy, they all said, was the festering sore — the specific removable cause of California's depressions and unemployment. In his *Resources of California*, Hittell told the world that 'the unsteadiness of business and the lack of employment of recent years' could be traced mainly to the 'want of unquestioned ownership of the soil.'

Settlers, he charged, had been driven unjustly from the land they occupied, with such disastrous results for themselves, and with such a huge destruction of values, that fifty years of peace would be required to place California where otherwise it would at present be, in point of economic stability and security. Hittell placed the responsibility on Congress. The famous act of 1851, intended to settle land titles, had really upset them, he and many others asserted. That national politics had most particularly damaged the regional economy was common conservative belief in San Francisco.

Since so much of the story in the next few chapters develops the idea of the magnitude of land problems and the seriousness of land policy in California, we need to notice, at this point of Henry George's entering the debate, only that there were present in the state several varieties of political opinion on the matter, and that opinion reflected several facets of actual abuse. McClatchy's *Bee* was already as aware of the problems of land monopolization as any of George's papers would ever be — McClatchy himself had taken personal part in squatter riots near Sacramento, during the previous decade. And in the early '60s a vigorous lobbyist, George Fox Kelly, took up the fight for dispossessed squatters in northern California, and appealed their case in the federal courts and to President Lincoln. The 'most gigantic fraud organization ever known upon earth' had deprived the people of that part of the state of rights in land which properly understood were inalienable, said Fox in his *Land Frauds in California*.

Viewing the state-wide problem (outside the cities) in the most general way, and with the guidance of recent historical research, we may picture a mountain phase and a valley phase of the land question. In the Sierras, the gold miners had set the pattern of landholding in their own way, without benefit of official surveys, registrations, or the taking of titles. Squatting on domain lands, they had simply established mining districts and district regulations, on an entirely voluntary basis. These procedures were well adapted to placer mining, a stage in which men were many and capital goods few. In due course we shall find Henry George praising the mining-district regulations as democratic, and as a successful system of landholding in use, rather than in ownership. But to Hittell and his conservative kind such arrangements were insecure and adverse to capital investment, and unfavorable to permanent settlement and family life in the mountains. Presently Congress did pass a law of the kind Hittell believed in, and freehold tenures, a protection to mining-company investments, became the normal thing in the mountains.

As for the agricultural valleys of the state, Hittell reviewed hard conditions and unintelligent policies. As present-day scholars agree, many of the richest and most convenient farm lands had been granted before 1846, in large and unsurveyed holdings which were intended for Mexican cattle ranchers; these holdings had been recognized by the treaty of Guadalupe Hidalgo; and the federal legislation of 1851 had provided that the Spanish and Mexican grants be examined and confirmed. Thus some of the causes of land aggregation were inherited from Mexico. But as modern scholars also agree, the processes of confirmation had been long and drawn out; they had been so managed as to destroy or place a shadow on titles which should in justice have been valid; and, instead of a normal process of breaking up the Mexican holdings by rapid sale, insecure titles had prevented sales to farmer-owners and had led to all sorts of irregularities — monopolistic speculating, squatting and the evicting of squatters, and tax dodging. Under unhealthy conditions land engrossment had reached proportions under American law never approached under Mexican law, and had entrenched itself in a way particularly repulsive to the settler, and peculiarly difficult to amend.

Hittell's answer to the problem of the aggregation of agricultural lands was the same as his answer to the unusual situation in the mountains. Apply the traditional American system of fee-simple ownership, he advised, and he suggested no further steps in land reform. He did recommend minor reforms of other kinds for stimulating California's economy: to cut out the 'forestalling' or cornering practices of the merchants of San Francisco, which placed unnatural restraints on trade; and to change the West coast habit of depending too much on long-term big-credit operations in business. He also proposed policies, not his alone, which George would later resist strenuously: reducing the interest rate and reducing the rate of wages. Hittell was a deflationist, all round, and one who put much reliance on *laisser faire*. His argument for fee-simple ownership, without further steps to break up the big holdings, rested on that basis. Security of ownership, and a reputation for security, would bring to the state an adequate flow of new settlers and new investment, he believed, and in that way California would soon have the 'permanent improvement, and all these blessings of inestimable value which come only with fixed and happy homes, and the best regulated social order.' In a free, secure market he expected the oversized landed estates to break up by reason of transfers of title, which would occur through sales and inheritances.

To sum up: in 1866 and 1867, when the San Francisco *Times* was taking hold, the problem of land monopolization in the state had been thoroughly discussed. Since by this time the federal courts had at long last given a series of rulings on the Mexican titles, and since, as we have seen, Congress had decided on fee-simple landholding in the mineral-bearing region, the conservative, *laisser faire* answer to the land problem was due to have an extensive trial. The problem of insecure titles had been reduced; the problem of engrossment remained. In San Francisco there was no strong voice, yet, for extensive land reform; the strongest in the state was that of Henry George's friend, James McClatchy.

But at this point, when discussion of land issues might conceivably have quieted for a period, a political situation blew up in San Francisco which, had it been so intended, could hardly have been more accurately designed to heighten the implications of land-title problems before the public eye. A legacy from the Spanish past, this particular land problem was a little different and a little more spectacular than any such problem ever faced by any other city in United States history — unless possibly Los Angeles is a rival in this respect as in others. The public question arose: Did San Francisco as a community own in perpetuity the land onto which urban growth was inevitably pressing it? If possibly Yes, would the rising values of the land actually accrue to the city's credit? Or, if the answer was No, must land speculators and withholders, in a particularly unsavory spot, make a killing according to an American custom which was especially active in California?

To understand how a question of publicly owned land could arise in practical affairs, we must take a last glance at how the United States acquired California, and sense the strain on ancient institutions when Americans burst upon the thinly settled Mexican domain. From Spanish origins descended the tradition that community settlements, called *pueblos,* were provided by the king with grants of four square leagues of land — the equivalent of 17,636 acres. The principal question which this legacy placed before the United States courts was whether or not San Francisco had actually been such a *pueblo* and now retained such an endowment or the residue of such an endowment. There is no need to enter the historical and legal complexities of the issue here; it will suffice to record simply that in the end the federal-court ruling was affirmative: San Francisco had been a *pueblo* and did still possess certain lands in public ownership on that account.

This decision bore a moral suggestion of San Francisco's wealth and responsibility. And quite naturally it involved political consequences. Once the principle was acknowledged, that San Francisco did possess a public domain of its own, the question arose whether the city's property right devolved upon the individuals who had occupied parcels of the old *pueblo* land? The case was not entirely analogous to settlers squatting on, or making purchases from, or establishing homesteads upon, the national domain. United States policy favored quick settlement and individuals taking ownership on domain lands. But the debate about San Francisco's *pueblo* rights, in the courts and on the press, acknowledged that Spanish usage had assigned the *pueblos* a function somewhat like that of steward for the king, and that individual settlers became the occupants and users of land, rather than owners in fee simple. The guaranty in the treaty of peace with Mexico, which promised that the United States would honor prewar property rights, could, moreover, be read to mean that the city of San Francisco owned its domain in perpetuity and could not rightfully permit any of that land to fall into private hands.

But Americans arriving in San Francisco of course never acted in that manner. Even before the Gold Rush, large 'alcalde grants' — so named from the Spanish title of the American officer who issued them — gave permanent titles to United States settlers. Speculation boomed; scandals occurred; litigation went on; and legislation to give firm titles seemed necessary, in both Sacramento and Washington. Certainly there is no other situation in the American record, to which a leading lawyer could refer in a court brief, as William J. Shaw did to this one, in 1860, as follows: 'Thousands of our people in the oldest settled counties have been educated into the belief, and today confidently believe, that the towns and villages existing in California actually owned the lands within their boundaries.'

Long before 1866 the courts made durable law of the early *ad hoc* actions concerning *pueblo* domains: private holdings were ruled to be valid as they had devolved through the city's officers from a royal grant of Spain. But in that year the possibility of San Francisco's retaining and operating at least a residue of city-owned land arose once more. This occurred when municipal authorities demanded that the 'outside lands,' so called, 7000 or 8000 outlying acres near the ocean front, which were claimed by private persons, be retained for the public. In this litigation a famous California judge, Stephen J. Field, who is remembered for his later career on the Supreme Court as a strong spokesman for *laisser faire* economics and law, had the final word. Presiding over the United States Circuit Court in San Francisco he issued decrees, not visibly in the *laisser faire* spirit, upholding the city's right. And later, in Washington, when it seemed likely that the Supreme Court would reverse the decision, he drew the bill which California members introduced in Congress, and which as passed gave the city quiet title to the outside lands.

Today the fraction of the *pueblo* lands that remains in actual public ownership is Golden Gate Park, designed by Frederick Law Olmsted, and for many years one of the most beautiful places of public enjoyment in the country. More important than the park, for Henry George or for any reflective mind, from this legacy of California's Spanish past, was the residue of thought — the city that might have been. Suppose that four square leagues of land, radiating from the center of San Francisco, had in actual history been converted into a public reserve, its rents all going to the city treasury, its benefits all accruing to the people's immediate use, and that use determined by the processes of government rather than those of private ownership! This was an idea for the social imagination to seize and not forget.

–3–

Henry George's navigating the many-forked stream of California economic discussion waited, of course, on his assuming responsible control of the *Times,* in the summer of 1867. The first editorial he did, while working under McClatchy's supervision, has a present-day interest because it concerned American relations with Russia. Three years earlier, when, in a well-remembered international incident, squadrons of the tsar's navy had shown up in New York and San Francisco, their coming had been widely interpreted as expressing a sense of alliance between the United States and Russia. Both of those nations were in serious trouble with Great Britain at the time; and the *Alta California* and other California papers went with the prevailing opinion, as they printed editorials of sentimental friendship between the two.

So likewise Henry George in 1866. He saw the analogy between Russia's expanding east and south, and America's westward movement. He sensed a connection between that country's natural economic growth and its internal reform, as the near coincidence of American Negro emancipation and the tsar's freeing the serfs in 1867 suggested. Better Constantinople in Russian Christian than in Turkish hands, George thought; and wiser for the Western powers to watch with equanimity while Russia built her railroads and improved her social system and government, than to try to circumvent her. This first editorial gives an accurate clue to Henry George's belief, a representative American one, that the Old World was accelerating its march toward liberalism and democracy. Almost a prophecy of his own role in 1882 and after, George editorialized in the *Times* on coming liberations in Europe, especially as the English working classes were now reading the lessons of the Union victory in the United States.

Before George assumed control, the *Times* took an editorial line on the economic problems of the state that in some respects paralleled and in others departed from the Hittell line maintained in the *Alta California*. Land problems, though the paper could rehearse the *pueblo's* history from first to last, McClatchy did not make particularly prominent in the *Times*. In common with the writers of regional economics, the paper bespoke anxiety about the return east of California's immigrants. As a prime remedy it proposed a policy, which Henry George was later to attack, that 'State or National authorities, or both combined' should subsidize the bringing of impoverished Europeans to the state.

As for steps that would help to keep the present labor force in California, the *Times* favored moderately the eight-hour work day, which was just taking hold in the California unions and in politics.

To the *Times'* way of thinking, labor's best hope of improvement lay in the long-run benevolent operation of impersonal economic forces — in the growth of technology and in the supply-and-demand processes of the employment markets. It lay very little in trade unionism or in labor legislation; and the working man's best chance for advancement was to be found in education for the masses and in some participation in the co-operative movement. On the point of improving the condition of seamen — and we can only guess that George was the writer on the subject — the *Times* did take a fighting pro-labor stand. Yet it acquiesced in the Chinese coolie immigration, and in general pattern of policy, the *Times* stood quite close to the *Alta* in 1866 and early 1867.

When George took charge, the editorial concern of the *Daily Times* enlarged with respect to matters of land more than it changed in any other way. We cannot say that this meant that the managing editor had discovered his ultimate focus of interest. It is more likely that the award of the outside lands to the city and city and state politics forced the matter on George, or rather on the *Times*, than that he took great initiative. For now that the lands were legally in San Francisco's domain, the question was whether the city and the state legislature, between which authority was shared, would conserve them for the public good, or whether they would permit another round of distribution to engrossers and graft.

In July 1867 was formed a Pueblo Land Association, the one object of which, according to its advertisements, was to defeat land grabbers by securing the 'free distribution of the unappropriated lands of the *Pueblo* in small tracts to those of its inhabitants who need and will occupy them as homesteads.' Again the Spanish custom was appealed to; the gift of the king was read as *in trust* to the *pueblo*, the lands not to be squatted upon or speculated in, but to be administered for the benefit of the people. The association arranged 'large' meetings in August. At one of them Governor Low presided; and a judge made a principal speech. At another meeting, with bonfires, fireworks, and a brass band, Senator John Conness took credit for having prevented very large speculators from getting control of land belonging to the public.

Henry George's *Times* went no further than the *Alta* when, on 31 August, it applauded Senator Conness and approved the work of the Pueblo Land Association to keep out the speculator. Thus far it was on the common line. The paper's liberalism came to the fore when it supported the bill drawn up by the association for the state legislature. More than just providing for homestead lots, the Pueblo Land Association would have established several sizable permanent city-owned areas: two 500-acre parks, a 200-foot drive and six plazas along the beach, and space for public schools, a college, firehouses, charitable institutions, and churches. The association wanted land classified for commercial use to be auctioned, and the remainder to be distributed gratis as home lots, to those who would build houses worth $200 or more. These proposals sound very much like the future Henry George, and the *Times* praised them, in an editorial of 14 December and at other times, as promising San Francisco a future as 'the greatest, most beautiful and most independent city in the world.'

But the idea was too advanced, required too much state restriction on business operations, for San Francisco and California in those days. The city supervisors issued a famous order, no. 733, which, except for one park, made little reservation for the public and approved private grants without regard for size. The *Times* complained for the ordinary citizens, to whom this perfidy seemed to mean the difference between a 'home or no home, ownership or rent, independence or poverty.' In the issues of 14 and 24 January 1868, it said that a few speculators, men who might have placed a 'ribbon fence' around huge blocks of land, would now become 'millionaires in a short time.' Perhaps this was Henry George's very first comment on the 'unearned increment' of land values in modern city-growth.

Though, in the final step, the state legislature did approve Order no. 733, the result was not as bad as the *Times* had anticipated. 'A powerful organized interest has moved both bodies, and stripped the people of their land,' said the paper, on 25 March, in first hot grief. 'The consequence is that the city of San Francisco, with the richest patrimony of any city on the continent, will be compelled to buy back, for public uses, a few of her eight thousand acres.' On this point the editorials in the *Alta* expressed great satisfaction; titles had been rendered firm, that paper noted, and some reservations for public use, including a 1000-acre park, would serve the city well. When the politics of the matter had cooled, the *Times* acknowledged some satisfaction in the park. From editorials of this time we may note that in the beginning George's ideas about urban land came close to land-use planning; and we may anticipate that, though in the modern sense he never became an economic planner, this affinity of ideas would always persist.

In the education of Henry George the cardinal suggestion of the San Francisco *pueblo*-land problem was of course that the public ownership of land had and could become an actual issue in politics: he learned this almost certainly before he had even heard of the Ricardian theory of rent, or of any proposal, after Ricardo, to capture economic rent for the public. The *pueblo*-land question had an incidental effect of making contact for him in San Francisco's Democratic politics. Against a different story in the *Bulletin,* the Republican *Times* had given Mayor McCoppin credit for having gotten a ruling through the supervisors which secured to San Francisco a certain reservation of land. Henry George's editorial, 'Honor to Whom Honor Is Due,' even though due a Democrat, brought an appreciative letter from the city hall. Actually this was the second round of an exchange between editor and mayor; and their correspondence is the first sign of Henry George's turning aside from the Republican party to the party of his father and Andrew Jackson, as a possible instrument of California reform.

On other phases of the land problem, the *Daily Times* under George had its say, piecemeal as the controversies arose. A series of editorials in March explained and approved proposals before the legislature, which were more or less identified with ex-Governor Milton Latham, and with W. C. Ralston, the glittering president of the Bank of California. The scheme was: to have enacted provision for railroad rights of way and space for terminals in San Francisco, on terms that would encourage the railroad company to skirt the bay and lay track up the peninsula and into the city, and yet would keep within the city, and out of the coffers of the railroad, the benefit of increasing land values near the railroad installations. As in the case of the outside lands, the *Times* took the side of the city's interest. And, on the broader front of the use of agricultural land, the *Times* complained that the very slow dispersal by sale of the Mexican ranchos to immigrant farmers, notably in the Los Angeles and San Bernardino areas, was retarding the settlement of the state.

The young editor threw his weight, too, on the level of national policy. On 2 June 1868, not long before he left the *Times,* he wrote strongly against the gift of federal lands in support of state colleges, the historic policy of the Morrill Act then half a dozen years old. Not that this was a new idea; many objectors, earlier than he, had seen that the Morrill Act favored eastern states more than western, and land speculators more than anyone else. Now the *Times* found it working that way, as operators were engrossing huge chunks of college land in the San Joaquin Valley. Of the prices at which they were selling to settlers, five dollars or more an acre, only a fraction, which the paper estimated at twenty-five to sixty-five cents an acre, was reaching the colleges. This meant that the government's donation was operating as a tax on settlers in California's central valley: the labor of California farmers was supporting schools that were for the most part in the older states and was making rich an absentee class of landlords.

This complaint against the Morrill Act makes a good resting point for the first phase of the development of the editor's ideas about land and land policy. Entering objection, he had shown accuracy and insight. Today high authority supports George's judgment. Professor Paul Gates's researches have recently shown that the Morrill Act has been honored above its deserts; that while doing something for education that law also strengthened a most undemocratic landlordism in American society.

George also showed reach of mind. In the editorial last quoted, discussing the wasteful hurried distribution of San Joaquin Valley land, he inserted a warning: 'And when we cease to have cheap land we shall realize in full force the social evils which affect Europe.' This sentence expresses the anxious thought George was going to make central in *Progress and Poverty,* Book VII, Chapter V, eleven years later; it pinpoints a perception that helped make Frederick Jackson Turner, twenty-five years later, an illuminating interpreter of the nation's history. It is probably impossible to say which anxious observer of American nineteenth-century life happened first to think it necessary to change from Jefferson's hope — that free land would make the republic strong — to Turner's fear — that the end of free land would begin the withering of our liberties and equalities. But so far as California is concerned, Henry George was the early eloquent speaker. Written in a context of economic troubles, his editorials had by 1868 set him on reconaissance for the lifetime mission not yet disclosed: his personal war to bend to compliance with democracy the land institutions and policies of the United States, and of other countries.

Watching this fast development in the young editor, we have seen no reason yet to call him a radical, or to say that he differed from, more than he resembled, his contemporaries of the conservative San Francisco press. Yet the process of Henry George's becoming different, of being a dissenter rather than a conformist, did begin at this time. An interesting early indication dates from June 1867, the month in which George assumed his editorship, when the *Alta* ran a few editorials, probably written by Hittell. These pushed the idea that local wage rates were much too high for California to succeed industrially, in competition with low-wage areas in the eastern states. The *Alta* ridiculed the labor unions' eight-hour program, which the *Times* half-liked; and one of the editorials drew heavily on the wages-fund theory of contemporary economics to assert the priority of capital over labor. Though admitting a mutual dependence — 'Capital cannot reproduce itself without labor, and labor cannot be put into action without capital' — the commercial newspaper argued that capital maintains labor (from the wages fund) until the product becomes exchangeable; thus capital is the essential and controlling factor in economic production. On 8 August another editorial predicted that before long the California labor market would be invaded from outside, and the state would gain by reason of the fall in wages.

Though the time would come, Henry George was not yet ready to buck with opposite theories either the wages-fund theory or the iron law of wages. But he was willing to debate with the *Alta*. How ignorant that paper was, answered the *Times* of 9 August, to think that a result 'detrimental to the interests of the workmen . . . *would be* a great boon to the *State at large.*' The 'fundamental principles of political economy' protested such an absurdity. Then followed, I think for the first time, Henry George's economy-of-abundance ideas which he later developed in his books. 'The interests of the State are the interests of its citizens — the greater the rewards which labor receives, the higher the estimation in which it is held, the greater the equality of the distribution of earnings and property, the more virtuous, intelligent and independent are the masses of the people, the stronger, richer, and nobler is the

state. Free trade, labor-saving machinery, co-operative organizations, will enable us to produce more cheaply, and with a positive
increase of wages; but it would be better for California that she
should retain only her present sparse but independent and comfortable population, than that she should have all of England's
wealth and millions with all of her destitution and pauperism.'
It would be interesting to know what writers or books George had
in mind as the sources of his 'fundamental principles of political
economy.' Perhaps he had drawn on some ideas of Wells or had
been influenced by Henry Carey. His editorial reads more like the
1930s than the 1860s, and more like Henry George's future books
than like the British treatises on economics which might have come
most readily to hand for reference.

The *Times* of course celebrated early in 1868, when the state
legislature passed an eight-hour law, and almost simultaneously
Congress prescribed eight hours as the working day for federal employees. The state law had too little force to deserve much praise;
but even so the *Times* was happy that it had become policy to
promise working people leisure, 'in which to learn, to think, to
plan, and to invent.' Since labor's human rights had been an article
of George's social faith from the time he began to have one, there
was nothing new in his holding this opinion; but it was important
for his development that at the time when he was achieving stature
as an editor and was entering into prominent controversy, he asserted simultaneously land-reform ideas and pro-labor ideas, just
as his Jacksonian predecessors had done.

Outside the orbit of questions of the California economy, yet not
far afield, and nearly as important for George as he entered his
career, a number of questions tangential to land and labor came up
in 1867 and 1868. Railroad policy was one. Before he took control
of the *Times,* the paper had criticized the federal government's
donation of lands to the projected, now building, transcontinental
line. The *Times* professed satisfaction that there should be some
public subsidy, as the roads were sure to benefit western growth;
but it gave reasons why bond credit would have been a sounder
procedure than huge gifts of land. Federal assistance should be
extended 'with a view mainly to reclamation,' it said on 2 March
1867, 'and not to enable corporations or individuals to take advantage of its munificence to promote selfish speculative designs' —

a proposition which, in the light of railroad history and economics, seems not to have been as obvious then as it is today. Rates were another problem involving government policy. That tariffs on California's new and still unconnected lines were five times as high as in the East, though operating expenses were only a little more, was the *Times'* opinion. After George took control, the paper spoke for a rate-fixing commission in the state, on the order of a Wisconsin proposal. Thus a future spokesman for government ownership of all utilities that are natural monopolies began on a pragmatic level — he was a spokesman for immediate, practical, public controls over railroads, in 1868.

But he did not halt with the immediate. In a way that was prophetic, both of national events about to occur and of his own development as thinker, he discussed the conflict of interests natural within the railroad business — and in more recent times, in all big business — between the managers and the owners of corporations. The *Times* considered the proposals of state ownership of railroads which were being advanced in England; and reviewed also the idea, presently put forward by the Sacramento *Union,* the now disillusioned pro-railroad paper, that the United States ought to run the railroads. The *Times* own suggestion was a little special, an idea Henry George most likely drew from the public-works canal and railroad system which the state of Pennsylvania had operated between Philadelphia and Harrisburg during his childhood. Let the railroads be a kind of highway, he proposed in an editorial of 28 April 1868. Let the army make the surveys and lay out the lines, and let the roadbed be built and maintained by private capital on a contract basis. Then let the rolling stock be operated by those who wish to ship privately, and by others who would contract to offer public transportation on appropriate terms.

This was George's first pronouncement on the public ownership of railroads: an archaic half-way proposal brought forward from the Jacksonian day of America's earliest steam transportation. It suggests his future, for he was never really to like either full private ownership and control, or full state ownership. Railroad policy would be a wobbly point with him for life. But he would not wobble on all ideas of public ownership, least of all on the telegraph system. An editorial of the *Times,* brought out five days earlier than the one on railroad ownership — and notably a full year before his

famous New York fight with Western Union officials — called for
a publicly owned and operated telegraph system, a system to be
run by the United States Post Office as an adjunct of the regular
postal service.

Of the many signs, in the *Times*, that Henry George, still under
thirty, was growing fast and gaining confidence as a commentator
on economic affairs, none is more convincing than a series of editorials on a question somewhat removed from the main concerns
of the California economists. These were printed under the heading, 'The Currency Question,' during the last days of April and
early in May 1868. Here George set forth a very full elaboration
of the paper's established idea that paying the Civil War debt
should be a gradual process and should not be hastened and made
upsetting to those who, by living and working through the war
period, had already paid dearly. Questions of public debt and debt
policy are always complex, and notwithstanding that at the time
of writing George had still ahead of him most of his lifetime's reading in economic treatises, he wrote his editorials in language that
was about as technical as any he ever used. It seems wise to discount
his own assertion, late in life, that he had been the original author
of the ideas of federal finance which he developed in the *Times*.
Not unlikely he owed, and later forgot, a debt of ideas to John A.
Ferris, a San Francisco contemporary who wrote on public finance
in a vein very similar to his own. But the greater possibility would
seem to be that he adopted ideas currently being debated in the
eastern states, especially Ohio. This was the time when the so-called
'Ohio idea' sponsored by George H. Pendleton, earlier a Democratic member of Congress and later a senator, was very prominent;
and the *Times* in fact acknowledged a debt to the Ohioans, though
it mentioned the Republican senator, John Sherman, rather than
the Democratic leader.

The nub of the *Times'* proposal — and a point which has a
familiar ring in 1955 after a dozen years of Defense Bonds — was
that United States bonds and United States money be made readily
convertible, the one into the other medium of credit, the bonds to
be purchasable in the ordinary routines of business by any who
wished to buy. Like the Ohioans, the *Times* plotted a mid-course
between such currency contraction as was national policy at the
moment, and such impulse for paper-money inflation as certain

Mid-westerners were beginning to demand. As a Californian and as a pro-labor editor, George had two governing reasons to believe in gold and silver as being the only sound money desirable for the long-run policy of the country. The silver-and-gold-producing state never used any other kinds. And, from the days of Andrew Jackson's struggle with the Bank of the United States, and especially since the appearance of the democratic money theories of Edward Kellogg, which the Ohioans were reviving, American labor had distrusted anything resembling an upper-class manipulation of credit conditions — that is how labor saw the existing system of national bank notes and depreciated greenbacks.

Very skillfully, within these lines of commitment, George argued in the *Times* for discontinuing the national banknotes (this meant reducing the powers and profits of bankers), for making the greenbacks issued by the government the one paper currency, for bringing the greenbacks gradually into equal value with gold, and for having federal money always convertible into bonds at a minimum interest rate, and bonds convertible into money. Interconvertibility would mean that all the people would have resort, in foul economic weather or fair, to a place of safe investment and a just return on savings; and that, in expanding times or as they wished, people could shift from federal credit into private investment and business operation. This was rough-hewn equilibrium economics indeed, by today's understanding of that subject; but equilibrium economics it was, a vein which George explored no further until the very end of his career as writer. His intention of 1867, to promote the people's independence from bankers as credit monopolizers and manipulators, is apparent in the terms of the articles.

In August 1868, with a good first crop of economic opinions raised, Henry George quit the *Times*. He did so without a summary or valedictory such as he came later to like to write, whenever occasion offered. But he could have made a considerable claim. He had taken a Radical Republican paper and maintained to the end its essential politics. A May editorial had regretted that President Johnson would probably not be convicted in the impeachment trial. Yet in the same month the *Times* denied being the 'organ' of any group and claimed to be 'an independent paper,' committed to ideas generally like those of Horace Greeley. This self-judgment rings true to the paper's record of wanting co-operation with reform-minded Democrats, and true to the economic policies of the paper. The notions of Liberal Republicanism, already forming in the East in the minds of such men as Greeley and David Ames Wells, better express the direction of George's *Times* than does any other political line.

Though there is no ground yet for talking about any system of Henry George's ideas, he himself was perfectly aware that he was finding a role in a tradition of protest. On his first Fourth of July as editor — under the title, 'To What Are We Drifting' — he placed the *Times* in the current from Andrew Jackson. Only the iron will of that fighter in the White House, he had the paper say, had dethroned the second Bank of the United States. Jackson's war against those who would have let American wealth and power be aggregated in the hands of a few was the *Times'* answer to the question asked by the editorial. 'Capital is piled on capital, to the exclusion of men of lesser means, and the utter prostration of personal independence and enterprise on the part of the less successful masses . . . In what manner should an individual employ the resources which Providence has entrusted to his keeping? Is he justified in using them to his mere personal advancement to the injury of his less favored fellow beings, by interfering with their political rights?' Nearly every economic editorial in George's *Times,* whether the matter was land or banking, wages or railroads, said one thing: Defeat the monopolizers, let all the citizens have access to the bounty of nature.

Within the not narrow area of his regional perceptions, Henry George did do a summary of his thinking of 1867 and 1868. This was his justly famous article, 'What the Railroad Will Bring Us,' written in anticipation of the great coming event. It was the leader in the fourth issue, October 1868, of the *Overland Monthly,* the new journal which — with the masthead phrase, 'Devoted to the Development of the Country' — quickly achieved stature as the best of the California magazines, in form and style much like the solid eastern reviews. Appearing there, Henry George was keeping company with his recent boss, Noah Brooks, one of the editors, and with John S. Hittell, Mark Twain, and Bret Harte, whose 'Luck of Roaring Camp' had appeared in an earlier issue.

A complacent Californian, George took for granted all the material bounties and developments commonly claimed for the state.

The Great West he conceived as the richest part of the country, and its resources such as to command a flow of capital and labor from abroad 'like pent-up waters seeking their level.' The Central Pacific and Union Pacific system, when completed, would just about fulfill the speculator's hopes. San Francisco must become the second, and possibly the first, city in the country. Look at 'the geographical position of the city, and all doubt of the future rank will be dispelled . . . the irresistible tendency of modern times is to concentration.'

From regional patriotism to regional utopianism, George moved with the current around him. 'What constitutes the special charm of California, which all who have lived here long enough feel?' he asked himself. Not climate, 'heresy though it be to say so'; not the absence of social restraint; not the chance to make money. Not local attachment, for California is deficient in context and culture. 'No: the potent charm of California, which all feel but few analyze, has been more in the character, habits, and modes of thought of her people,' and in that 'certain cosmopolitanism' which 'the peculiar conditions of the young state' were bringing out. George wished to find a precise name for the sense of independence and equality prevailing in California, 'born of the comparative evenness with which wealth was distributed,' or at least of the even caprice by which men were one day well-to-do and the next day deprived of wealth.

But he did not relax his anxieties and criticisms. Working from the economics of the *Times,* he quarreled in the *Overland,* as earlier, with the 'certain school of political economists' which deplored high wages and high interest rates. High rates he asserted to be good: they were signs of natural wealth and effective production. The true evils, he said again, were speculation and monopolization. The fact had to be faced that great and potentially good forces in the economy made for concentration: 'The locomotive is a great centralizer. One millionaire involves the existence of just so many proletarians.' Beware of the 'law that wealth tends to concentration,' George told his readers, for it works in California as everywhere else in the modern world.

The sum of his judgment he rendered as a warning: nostalgia for what was passing, and fear and hope mixed, for what would come. San Francisco had already missed a chance which could never be recaptured. By failing to take up the *pueblo* lands 'in time and in a proper spirit,' the city had let go an opportunity for having 'a population better, freer, more virtuous, independent, and public spirited than any great city the world has ever seen.' Would the state as a whole do better? George predicted, 'No.' The coming railroad, though its benefits be acknowledged, would level California with the outside industrial world. Wages would fall. Especially because of the Chinese immigration, the labor problem would demand public attention. As 'we cannot escape the great law of compensation which exacts some loss for every gain,' Californians should anticipate that personal independence would diminish. Though universities and libraries would rise, and arts and letters flourish, class distinctions would also mount. And, for the city especially, 'the political future is full of danger.' More than ever, an 'enthusiasm of humanity' would be needed to keep the promise of California life.

These were accurate prophecies of 1868. Depression and Kearney's type of labor politics, which we would now call fascist, would ride within a decade. The Nob Hill mansions would go up. And, in the same ten years, the University of California would rise, the Lick bequest for science be made, and the San Francisco public library be founded. Concerning all these events Henry George would have his say, and through them all increase his anxieties. With a mind bigger than Hittell's, and a paper livelier than the *Alta California,* he would sharpen his challenge.

VI

Fighting Monopoly and Pledging Utopia

1869–1871

−1−

THE fewness of the Henry George letters extant for the years 1867 and 1868 accords with the impression of his life given by the job on the *Daily Times*. He was at the grindstone, writing, reading, thinking, and deciding. Doubtless he was too busy, and in off hours too wrapped up in his own family, to send to the people in Philadelphia the old amount of detail about Annie, the children, and himself. And there were complications also.

The San Francisco family had grown by now to be five, for the fall of 1867 had brought them Jennie Teresa, their first daughter, whom they named for Henry's sister who had died and Annie's veiled one. The delight of a new daughter brought a nice coincidence into Henry George's life, along with his increased responsibilities and income. This much is on the surface. But as unfortunate family events usually cast a shadow before, it seems that less cheerful changes which occurred when George left the *Times* must have been somewhat expected, and that the moves the family made must have been planned beforehand to take care of a case of distressing illness at home.

As for George's quitting the *Times*, on 12 August, we are told no more than that he was refused an increase in salary, and that the separation occurred with good will on both sides. The next two events, which seem almost to contradict each other, require factors of long-range planning to explain. Within a week George took a managing editorship with the San Francisco *Chronicle,* then a new paper; and within two weeks he had broken up his household and sent Annie and the three children on to Philadelphia. Of course there were the old pulls toward home. It was high time for his wife and children to get to know his parents; and also, for himself, there was always the chance of a bigger career in the East. These matters entered his letters. Possibly George's moving to the *Chronicle* was mainly a jockeying for position, an effort to broaden journalistic contacts beyond the purely Republican ones the *Times* represented, before he himself departed. He wanted contracts, sometime, to write letters in the East for California papers. Considerations of economy and a willingness to gamble whether he should go a few months sooner or later may tell the whole story of his staying in San Francisco when Annie left. It is more likely, however, that his joining the *Chronicle* indicates simply that he took the best job when it was offered, and that Annie's going east was in large degree a move separate from his career decisions.

Certainly the letter she sent him from Panama exhibited a serious condition. She had been desperately ill on the voyage south, a poor brave penciled scrawl informed him. What she said sounded like epilepsy: five seizures between San Francisco and the isthmus, and eight more on the gulf and Atlantic voyage. Her brother-in-law Tom met her in New York, and her father-in-law embraced her first in Philadelphia. Relief it was to be taken into the grandparents' home, where domestic routines fell mainly on others' shoulders. She and Mr. George established a wonderful relationship from the start; and with Mrs. George there was only a bit of mother-in-law trouble — she had to warn Henry to write more frequently to his mother.

'Harry darling, all is happiness around me, but I am not happy, for "my heart is over the sea." ' Paying $15 a week, Annie contributed something to the family's maintenance while she rested. Mr. George, just seventy, was in the coal business now with a little office opposite St. Paul's, and he was not doing very well. Yet there was another side of the picture: 'The folks home here have no idea of our situation. I spoke of getting a new cloak when I first came and Mother wanted to know which I would get, "cloth or velvet?" I said cloth by all means. It amused me more than a little. They were astonished when they saw my wardrobe. They all dress nicely, have all got silk dresses too, and none of them have any idea of the troubles we have been through.' As of the present she grieved that Henry had sold their furniture, yet thought the decision prudent; and she was pleased with the first news about the *Chronicle,* feeling that financial worries were now behind them. She wanted him not to deny himself too much: chewing tobacco was a poor economy in place of the things he preferred, she said; the amount of smoking he did would not hurt, and 'I think a little liquor is good for you.' About herself, the doctor had said that most of her trouble was in her head, she reported cheerfully, and added that she was really improving.

Before long, with an eye to the possible future, Annie began to size up the situation in Philadelphia. She could not like the climate or the city situation and noted that most people who had been in California wanted to return. She realized that Henry might probably be happier in the East, but warned him that they would have to live in better style than in San Francisco to have such congenial acquaintances as they were accustomed to. The oldest sister, Harriet, was living about as they had lived, yet her circle was a little 'low'; and as for the older Georges and the children at home, though their furniture was no better than what she and Henry had had, they made a better show, and they had the friends and connections of many years. 'They have never had poverty to contend with.' Altogether she succeeded well in becoming a beloved daughter: 'If I was an Episcopalian I think I would be all [Mother] would wish. That I cannot be. I would not exchange my liberal opinion for any creed much as I respect it. I go to church with Mother or Aunt Mary every Sunday, but being a Catholic in name is as bad as being practically a Catholic.' To the pleasure of her new sisters and brothers, Annie succeeded in introducing a melodeon into the home, and even in encouraging a certain amount of dancing and card playing.

Whatever the tug and pull on Henry of those for the most part cheerful letters from an unwell wife, there was always the chance of such bad news as reached him in the late fall, and not from Annie alone. Ned Wallazz, the old friend of King and Baird days, wrote that he was alarmed. The George family doctor had 'clapped the cups' on Annie George's temples. (The old practice of bleeding ill persons continued, in certain places, late in the nineteenth century.) Wallazz and his wife thought Annie to be right in doubting the doctor's diagnosis of epilepsy, and in being dissatisfied with the treatment she was getting. It seemed to them that she was afflicted with some disorder of heart or brain, or possibly of the stomach, and that Henry should stop the cupping. This report fitted all too well with what Annie herself was writing: she once overheard the doctor say ominous things, when he thought her to be unconscious. Her last letters to San Francisco, before Henry George himself came on, were emotional and upset. One told him that three-year-old Dick was very ill. The other was written on their wedding anniversary: 'Seven years of care, trouble, and sorrow,' said Annie, 'but also hope and love. We can look back and say we have indeed been one, sharing each other's troubles and joys. But few husbands and wives are as nearly one as we.'

Meanwhile, on the coast, Henry George's working for the *Chronicle* must not be pictured as though he were managing editor of that big paper today. Only three years of life were behind it, and those not as a regular newspaper but, under the title of the *Daily Dramatic Chronicle,* as a 'theater house bill' supported by advertising and circulated without charge. It had never lacked cleverness, however, and now under Charles de Young it had a large spark of ambition added. When, according to the editorial page of 20 August 1868, 'mysterious controlling influences' on the *Times* led to 'an editorial exodus,' it acted quickly, as up-and-comers do. 'Old brains, relatively speaking, have gone out; new ones come in. The two unfortunate men recently escaped from [the *Times'*] office show great emaciation.' So the *Dramatic Chronicle* hired Henry George.

Immediately the paper changed its name to the *Daily Morning Chronicle* and branched out into general journalism; and in its editorials we see Henry George loosening his tightest Republican attachments. Not that the *Chronicle* was Democratic. But an editorial of 3 September, for instance, announced that it would avoid partisanship as a curse. Look at the *Times* and the *Examiner,* it invited; though the two report identical events and affairs in the South under Reconstruction, they are equally destined to come up with absurdly opposed judgments. Working for this paper, George, the former abolitionist now seeking the middle truth, said the same moderate things about the Negro as President Lincoln had said. Editorials explained that while the Negro deserved economic freedom as much as any man because his labor belonged to himself by right, he should probably not be assimilated into the American social and political community — he was not ready for that.

There was preparation in this for one of the main events of George's next year, 1869: the change of mind that made him an early opponent of the policy of admitting Chinese labor on the West coast. The *Times* had been fairly friendly toward coolie immigration; and, generally, in the East and in the West, a correspondence existed between those who favored Chinese admission, often Republican businessmen who wanted cheap labor, and those who persisted in elevating the southern Negro, the Radical Republicans. In this frame of reference, George's inching out of extreme Republicanism, and out of the Radical line about Reconstruction, fitted him for the future. It would have been an almost impossible thing for a journalist on labor's side not to come to hate the coolie immigration; and in the future it would be hard for him to avoid the web of racism, and easy for him to prefer the Democratic to the Republican line. The *Chronicle* represents a softening-up stage in certain of its editor's first ideas.

Yet George did not shift opinions quickly, or change parties in time for the election of 1868. He worked for the *Chronicle* until late fall, and, with the recommendations of the paper, he voted Republican for one last time. Though the *Chronicle* asserted its character as a 'bold, bright, fearless, and *truly independent* paper,' it announced that it could only prefer 'Grant and peace' to 'Seymour and the prospect of civil disturbance.'

In one respect George's brief editorship molded the *Chronicle* into permanent form. In September and early October the paper hit harder at land speculation and made more of it as a public issue than the *Times* had ever done. In a three-day series of editorials beginning on 8 September, it attacked the San Francisco *Bulletin,* which a year earlier had stood about where the *Times* had stood in regard to the *pueblo*-land problem. Now the *Chronicle* charged the *Bulletin* with having followed the *Alta* into the camp of the speculators. The *Bulletin*'s point that taxation would force land aggregations to fall apart sooner or later, and that 'the purchase of land by capitalists, if pursued in a liberal spirit, may [through sales] prove beneficial to the people,' Henry George scored as 'a Jesuitical defense of land grabbers.' He claimed the Sacramento *Union* as an ally in this protest. And when the Oakland *News* said that Henry George's line sounded very much like robbing the rich to divide the plunder among the poor, the editor was not cowed. Suppose it does, he replied under editorial title of the ominous word, 'Agrarianism': to do that would be better than robbing the poor and dividing among the rich. And when someone said that 'old Californians' had a right to gain by the rise of land values, George responded that old Californians were not profiting. The profits were going to scrip purchasers and eastern capitalists and absentee owners generally. Half a century after these sharp editorials, the San Francisco *Chronicle*'s historian credited Henry George with having originated the paper's opposition to monopoly in landholding, and with probably having contributed editorials on the subject during the '70s, when he was running his own paper.

Henry's leaving the *Chronicle* dismayed Annie — she was ready to blame somebody's spite on the newspaper staff — and her whole attitude enlarges the doubt that husband and wife had any deep-laid plan to move them permanently away from San Francisco. Though nothing much is clear about the break, it is altogether unlikely that George would under any conditions have gotten along well politically with de Young. And surely the husband must have felt impelled to take the chance when a new opportunity of journalism availed to send him across the continent. At any rate, almost before Annie knew what was happening, Henry was at her side in the old Third Street home. He came a couple of days too late to be a Christmas present, and before New Year's he was off to New York on business. But for half a year, nearly, he was in and out of the city; and at the end of that period she was a stronger and more stable woman, and he a better known and more experienced man.

−2−

George crossed the continent in the employ of the San Francisco *Herald,* with a business rather than a writing assignment. He came the new way, by the not quite completed transcontinental railroad, and had an interesting time of it. The first leg of the journey, on the Central Pacific from Sacramento to the summit of the Sierras, he liked best; the engineering surpassed anything else he saw. But across the Nevada upland, the Central Pacific was guilty of hurry-up construction, and travel was incredibly slow. The wood for the locomotive was so green it would hardly burn; and, waiting for the steam pressure to rise, the passengers amused and warmed themselves by burning sagebrush along the right of way. Unnecessary curves had been put in the track, George believed, just to qualify for the higher government subsidy for difficult construction. On the Union Pacific leg of the journey east into Omaha, a berth was a relief though the traveler had to share it; and he said that the Union Pacific did better as to roadbed and speed than the Central Pacific in Nevada.

Sitting beside a talkative driver, during the cold ride on the 'mud wagon' stagecoach which connected the two railroads, George took the opportunity to ponder what American business and engineering were accomplishing, and the costs. As he summed up, the citizen and the ticket purchaser had plenty of reason to complain. With Central tariffs at ten cents a mile in coin, and Union at seven and a half, greenbacks accepted, the railroads had not lowered the expense of travel from coast to coast. Of all operations, he judged the Wells Fargo's handling of the United States mails to be the most scandalous. And over and above all manner of visible inefficiencies and high charges for transport, George did not forget the costs to the public of the subsidies and land grants to the railroads, and the demoralization of the legislatures that had enacted them. Monopoly, monopoly now struck Henry George as being a national phenomenon rather than one especially concentrated in California.

His assignment for the San Francisco *Herald* doubled his reasons for being alert to monopoly questions. He was working now for John Nugent, 'a very determined man and a very determined Democrat,' in the judgment of a writer for the *Alta California*. An Irishman born who had worked for the New York *Herald* under James Gordon Bennett, this newspaperman had entered San Francisco journalism in the middle '50s, bringing out his own paper under the famous name. Speaking of the staff he then assembled, one contemporary made him seem like the employer of a circle of latter-day Benjamin Franklins: a group of practical printers, but men wonderfully informed in languages and literatures, some of the sciences, and 'indeed nearly all the garnerings of human information.' But Nugent's quick success with the San Francisco *Herald* had been practically wiped out in 1856, during the rule of San Francisco's most famous vigilance committee. As is well known, the murder of the editor of the San Francisco *Bulletin*, rival of the *Herald*, was the sensational incident that called this committee into life. So corrupt and so impotent to control crime had San Francisco government been that historians have often judged that particular vigilantism favorably, as did most of the solid citizens at the time, the New Englanders of the Congregational Church, for example. But one aspect of the affair had been the suppression of free opinion in the city's journalism. When Nugent dared speak for the minority party which opposed vigilantism, advertising was withdrawn and the San Francisco *Herald* was humbled. Nugent was able to fight back, to be sure, and he kept the paper alive, on a reduced basis, until 1860, the summer before the election of Lincoln. Motives and intentions are not clear, but the facts are that the *Herald* was killed by the combined opposition of businessmen and rival papers, and that Nugent was forced from the field somewhat in the role of a martyr.

He decided to try to come back in 1868. He doubtless forecasted improving political weather for Democrats in California. He said that he was assured plenty of venture capital for a new *Herald*, and that he counted on the increasing supply of national and international news, which since the Civil War was being distributed by news agencies, as a factor in favor of making a fresh start. By the fall of the year he did, indeed, have all his arrangements made, except for one essential step. It was to negotiate a contract with the Associated Press, so that the *Herald* would have as good news service as any West coast paper, that Nugent employed Henry George to represent him in New York.

The difficulty was that Nugent was being cold-shouldered in San Francisco once more. California had a new monopoly. A decade earlier the San Francisco *Bulletin*, supported by the organized and agitated business community, had edged him out, and now that newspaper was consolidated with other newspapers in a state press association. This group alone had present access to the Associated Press dispatches coming across the country by wire. It was made up of the Sacramento *Union*, and of four San Francisco papers which were not in complete competition with one another: the *Evening Bulletin*, and the *Morning Call*, which would soon become the *Bulletin*'s partner; the *Alta California*, which was the senior newspaper in the city and the principal commercial one; and the *Times,* Henry George's old paper, which was soon to sell out and lose identity in the *Alta.* The California press association was a tight organization; the *Chronicle* could not get in, nor any minor papers.

For this biography few missing documents would be more welcome than some undiscovered memoir by Nugent, saying how and why he happened to assign to Henry George the job of negotiating the *Herald's* independent way into the Associated Press in New York. It would seem that Nugent might have preferred to handle that business himself. The negotiator would have to deal with some of the nation's top journalists and businessmen, and he would have to make decisions on which would depend the birth of the San Francisco newspaper. Clearly a great compliment of trust and confidence was paid the twenty-nine-year-old. It was to make an immediate arrangement for the new year, 1869, and to end waste and waiting in San Francisco that hurried George on from Philadelphia to New York, after no longer than a week-end visit with his people.

But he was doubtful from the start about doing business with the Associated Press. Thinking that time would be lost if he went direct to that headquarters, he approached first the people at Western Union. Though Vice-President McAlpine, the official with whom George dealt, refused a written contract, he did allow that for $900 a month the *Herald* could have 500 words a day in San Francisco, to be telegraphed from New York, Philadelphia, or Chicago, at the paper's option. Put off by the Associated Press until a February meeting, George explored at once the other possibilities for getting the news. He reported to Nugent his future rather than immediate hopes: once a new French cable was laid, Reuters could be expected to bring in foreign news; and once an opposition telegraph began real competition with Western Union, domestic news too would loosen up. Such eventualities he thought near enough in the future to give the *Herald* something to count on, and he advised expedients for the present to launch the paper and tide it over. Even when the Associated Press advanced its meeting to mid-January, and shocked him by tabling unanimously the *Herald's* application for membership, George favored going ahead at once. 'The present news monopoly must be broken before long,' he wrote his employer, 'and you are certain ultimately to fight your way into the California association if you deem it desirable.'

His first expedients were rapid, loose-jointed, and ethically dubious, but effective. He returned to Philadelphia; he employed as assistant a boyhood friend, John Hasson; and he established himself in his father's coal office. There he was able to buy the news, as he told Nugent he would. For a couple of days only he got the dispatches from a 'principal editor' in Philadelphia, and one dispatch 'coup de main,' not a reliable practice he admitted. Then Hasson arranged with the Harrisburg *Patriot and Union* to have its AP dispatches as soon as they were received and before printing. A clerk made copies; these were taken to the Atlantic and Pacific Telegraph office right in the *Patriot*'s building; and a generously tipped messenger brought them quickly to Henry George in Philadelphia. Thence on to Western Union, and to San Francisco.

On this basis Nugent launched the new San Francisco *Herald*, 19 January, and made a play of having the transcontinental telegraphic news. The state association was defeated. The expenses of the system ran high, however: besides the $900 a month to the Western Union, George was paying $21 a week to the *Patriot*, $5 a week for copying, a cent a word for telegraphing to Philadelphia, and $35 a week to Hasson. Outside his own pay, which (whatever it was) he had trouble enough to collect, the *Herald* was committed to a monthly outlay of about $1200, by George's quick arranging. George reported the Harrisburg machinery as he contrived it, a matter of days after the paper began. So Nugent knew from the start that his agent was proceeding independently of the AP, and that they were taking chances.

George expected to win, but he did not rate the enemy low or expect him to yield without a fight. In 1869 the Associated Press was a new organization, but neither youth nor small size made it tender; it was a hard-boiled youngster not yet civilized up to its natural responsibilities. Specifically, the AP was a trade association: it pooled equally the cable and telegraph news received by its members, seven leading papers of New York City. It sold those dispatches, transmitted by Western Union, to papers throughout the country. In the person of one correspondent, it had just launched its overseas news gathering services. Events of 1866 had pointed up its character as a business monopoly. In that year strong mid-western voices, those of Murat Halstead of the Cincinnati *Commercial* and Henry White of the Chicago *Tribune*, had demanded better service.

But protest had come to very little; and, according to the AP's friendly historian, that organization, at the time George confronted it, presented a very stony face indeed.

To make things completely difficult, moreover, the AP had recently elected as its general agent the hard-fisted James W. Simonton of San Francisco. No man could have been so utterly the opposite of George; no one else could quite so completely have identified the press associations of the two cities. Ten years earlier Simonton had purchased the share of the San Francisco *Bulletin* which had belonged to the murdered editor; since then he had been a member of the inner group of controlling owners of that paper; and as such he had been a part of the squeeze against the first *Herald*. His background and situation were such that one hardly needs to inquire whether he had read and been needled by George's editorials in the *Times* denouncing the *Bulletin* as inaccurate to the point of dishonesty. Almost assuredly he had, and he was going to hear worse later.

At the start of his mission George learned from a confidant that Simonton was opposing a contract with the *Herald,* and that factor became a part of the report to Nugent. Next the story was that Simonton had learned, by bribing Western Union George guessed, that the *Herald*'s news was being sent from Philadelphia; and then that Simonton had come on from New York 'to lay traps.' But he did not learn about George's Harrisburg arrangement; and George felt that unless he hired detectives he would not discover it. So George continued the operation and planned if necessary to repeat the procedure elsewhere, say from Pittsburgh next time. He felt that he had to stay out of New York City. To a San Francisco friend he wrote, when the operation was two weeks old: 'It is a *big thing* to run full tilt against this Association, a bigger thing than you folks probably appreciate, and I regard success so far as a pretty big feather in my cap.'

George estimated a close understanding between the Associated Press and Western Union; but apparently he expected the telegraph company to stand by the oral contract and do business with him no matter what his relations with the AP. In this he assumed too much. Not detectives but telegraph officials put on the pressure for Simonton. After first merely refusing George the economy of using cypher in his San Francisco dispatches, Western Union gave notice that those dispatches would have to be sent from New York. This was contrary to the original agreement with McAlpine; and George identified the superintendent who served the notice as a friend of both Simonton and the proprietor of the *Alta California.* When the telegraph people went a step farther and pressed for information about his news gathering, George bluntly refused. But the pressure to move to New York he could not overcome. Accordingly, in the middle of February, after a month of jabbing holes through the news associations, George left his family for New York. He still assumed that his arrangements could be continued and stabilized sufficiently for the *Herald*'s need.

And in the lion's den he did succeed in establishing new operating connections. A 'supplier' of dispatches was found, evidently a member of the staff of the New York *Sun;* and the New York *Herald* gave its namesake access to its 'specials' and to the Havana news. Western Union did not balk again for a while, and George planned a forward action and an eye-catching triumph.

The inauguration of General Grant made the occasion. George went down to Washington three days beforehand. Working through Senator Cole of California, he managed a promise from Grant's secretary, General Rawlings, that he would be given a copy of the inaugural address at the AP office, immediately on delivery and as soon as any newspaperman received it. His scheme was to wire the speech direct to San Francisco, and also very early news about cabinet appointments and the like. The *Herald* would scoop all the San Francisco papers. And on 4 March, so far as he could tell, things went very well. Staying away from the inaugural ceremonies and seeing very little of the parade, George received his early copy, and nothing more untoward happened than a ten or twenty minute delay by the telegraph operator. His dispatches hit the wires early, and he was sure that they would reach San Francisco ahead of the AP news which had to clear through New York.

Then came the humiliation of being tricked. The AP papers in San Francisco actually received their news far ahead of the *Herald,* and taunted the challenger. George learned what had happened when the president of Western Union told him that a copy of the inaugural had reached the hands of the Associated Press in Chicago in advance of delivery and was released as General Grant was speaking. George's fury shifted to the managing officials of the AP. For falsely stating that he was getting the release as early as any, George demanded explanations. Lacking satisfaction, he declared he would go with appropriate charges to the President, the Speaker of the House of Representatives, General Rawlings, and the news-reading public, all of whom were affected.

Actually there was very little he could do beyond threatening. This event was the time, and might reasonably be accounted the immediate cause, of George's dissolving whatever attachment he may have had left to the Republican party. In the *Herald* George's correspondence gave Grant no higher credit than for 'the best of intentions.' The new cabinet he called 'astonishing'; and, about the new appointments generally, he said, 'There are many, of whom I confess I am one, who dislike to see enormous wealth and political power joined.' To a friend who twitted him about his old party connection, George declared that he was no longer a Republican.

Back on the job in New York, the Washington episode must have struck him as an evil omen for the future of Nugent's second *Herald*. John Hasson was having less and less success in gathering the news. When pressed by the AP, the New York *Herald* withdrew favors it had granted; and hopes, which George's new friend, John Russell Young, encouraged as managing editor of the *Tribune,* that that paper would lend a hand, were soon destroyed by authorities at high level. Then Simonton discovered the paper, though not the individual, from whom George's AP news had been tapped; and that well dried up. At last resort George turned to what he called 'stealing the news.' This procedure, which the name to the contrary hardly seems less moral than his earlier efforts, meant buying the New York papers as soon as they were out and telegraphing what he selected for the *Herald,* at once. He had to be on the streets between three and four in the morning, but with the advantage of the Pacific coast time differential, the scheme would work as long as the telegraph did.

In the second half of April, after three months of somehow doing the job for the *Herald,* Western Union refused service. Rather, it demanded impossible terms. The company notified George that the present arrangement would terminate in May, that to conform with a new contract with the Associated Press Western Union would in the future charge the San Francisco *Herald* $2000 a month — instead of the old $900. The 122 per cent increase was practically a death sentence. In George's mind, this decision represented the last word in the power, caprice, and injustice of private monopoly.

Yet he was not too frustrated to be enraged, or so utterly helpless as to think the sentence as good as executed. During recent weeks his feeling had become greatly mixed about his employer. Nugent kept him constantly in arrears as to salary and working funds. He sent no instructions or letters; an occasional telegram and payment was all that George's long reports drew from San Francisco. Even so, George now urged carrying on the newspaper and persisting in the fight. He predicted more specifically than he had earlier that a new telegraph would in less than a year open up news selling in competition with the AP. For the immediate present, if Nugent was unable for the waiting period to bear Western Union's extravagant demands, George suggested reducing the size of the *Herald* — just as Nugent had done when the vigilance committee supporters took away his advertising — and sustaining always an editorial barrage against the monopolies. He proposed stealing the news in San Francisco if need be: this would 'terribly torment the combination.' But the main thing was to keep up the fight.

Though George's advice did not set the course for Nugent, or save the *Herald* or even sustain his connection with his employer, the counsels he gave were sound. His prediction that the news gathering he and Hasson had been doing could be maintained proved accurate. Fifteen months later, this associate was to join forces with John Russell Young to found the American Press Association. Exactly as George now said, they were going to be able to give the Associated Press a run for its money and to crack through the California news monopoly.

At the same time he was advising Nugent, George himself, still in New York, practised his own fighting precepts. He took to the president and vice-president of Western Union a written review of the whole affair: he charged the telegraph company with intention to suppress the *Herald* and any opposition to the Associated Press. In George's account of the exciting interview, Vice-President McAlpine complimented him sincerely but cynically on the case he had built up 'as a writer.' Neither McAlpine nor President William Orton made the least effort to justify Western Union. They freely admitted that for a long time the AP had been urging them to do what they had just done. General Orton said that if George did not like it he could go back to California and build a telegraph of his own.

George made free to go to the public. He ordered printed 6000 copies of his history of the case, and he distributed many among New York newspaper people. He raised the moral question of the freedom of the press. But for the most part he presented financial facts: Western Union was demanding $2000 a month for 500 words of news daily. This was its 'conforming' with new rates being given the California press association papers — $3333 total, to be shared by 4 San Francisco dailies, for 2500 words a day. George did the arithmetic. While the *Herald* was being raised from 6.92 cents to 15.28 cents per word per day, the association papers were, pro-rating, being reduced from 2.4 to 1.28 cents per word. Under the old rates the telegraph company would have grossed $40,000 a year from California newspaper business, and under the new, though for more words, $40,000 from the combination alone.

The New York *Herald* printed George's full story in the Sunday edition of 25 April about fifty inches in small print; and it ran an approving editorial. The German-language *Demokrat* chimed in the following Tuesday. But so far as George could discover, no other papers mentioned the affair, and his circular was virtually boycotted. He enclosed a copy with a note to Senator William Sprague of Rhode Island, whose recent anti-monopoly speeches he had written up for the San Francisco *Herald*. He wrote also to the recently elected Senator Eugene Casserly, requesting him — in vain, as he anticipated — to speak as Californian and Democrat against the monopoly. More than this he could not do in New York, and by the first of May he was ready and anxious to leave. Years later he rehearsed the matter before a Senate committee; and still later, forgetting editorials of 1867 in the San Francisco *Times,* he said that the events of 1869 had swung him to believe in a publicly owned telegraph system; he had been convinced 'when General Orton forcibly presented . . . the *argumentum ad hominem* in its favor.'

So ended Henry George's battle against the Goliath of contemporary journalism. The defeat confronted him with questions — they appear in his letters of spring and summer — about what he should do next. Continue in New York in some effort to beat the Associated Press? But, saying he did not wish to be a 'purveyor' or 'sender' of news any longer, he effectively gave up that choice by surrendering the New York work to John Hasson. Should he return to journalism or try other writing? Stay east or go west? In the end, though he had once said that of all possible jobs he would enjoy most being a correspondent in Washington, it was natural that he decided to go back to San Francisco for a while at least. Corresponding with Mayor McCoppin he let on that he might be a candidate for the legislature in the fall. And to his friend Sumner, on the staff of the *Herald,* he said that should Nugent withdraw the two of them could make the paper 'spin.' He also had other ideas: possibly a paper of his own in the mining town of White Pine, Nevada, and just perhaps an evening paper in San Francisco to match the *Herald* and oppose the *Bulletin.*

David had not succeeded, but his missiles had stung, and he was ready to deliver more from a western angle of firing.

-3-

The fight with the monopolies does not tell the whole story of Henry George's half-year in Philadelphia and New York; nor does that fight compounded with the newspaper writing we have noticed and with the obligations and anxieties which attended his visits with the family in the Third Street house tell all. Yet the total excitement of these things together does seem to go far in explaining the climactic personal event of the sojourn. This was the famous vision and dedication of his life which occurred on a sidewalk of New York — much like the call to Saul of Tarsus on the road to Damascus, Father McGlynn would say after George had become an international leader.

There is a disappointing lack of testimonial about how George held up psychologically under the pressures of 1869. Thirty years later John Russell Young retained an impression that his friend had been breezy, openhanded, and western, and also unusually thoughtful and serious, and anxious to make friends among fellow journalists, during the long battle. The only contemporary indication we have, aside from George's own letters already drawn upon, is a phrenological chart, the second and last in the book, which was recorded in humor by 'Professor John Hasson.' But it tells about a physical and nervous condition which was not amusing, and accords with the strains to which George had been subjected. He was very light, down to 113 pounds, and so tense he could sit at table no longer than fifteen or twenty minutes. It is hard to endorse Hasson's finding that George lacked self-confidence, but perhaps the friend had perceived doubts or hesitations which do not appear in the letters to San Francisco.

We know, from George's own retrospect of the vision, that part of the background lay in an emotional reaction against the cities he visited. Of course he had not been in Philadelphia since 1858, nor in New York since 1856. One recalls Henry Adams' recoil, at precisely this time, when he returned to the United States and commented on New York especially, after spending the war years in Britain. The home city Henry George remembered from before his California days had been to him a decent place in which to live, and the New York he visited had seemed neat and lovely. But now New York confronted him, as it did the patrician from Quincy, with a terrible and an incredible social order. George never forgot the shock. Years afterward, when he was running for the city's highest office, he described the distress of seeing and realizing; and still later he told a Chicago audience that in 1869 New York's 'conjunction of wealth and want' had been 'absolutely appalling to a man from the Far West.'

When in 1883 he did put into writing his memory of the vision, he made it very private. 'Because you are not only my friend but a priest and a religious,' he wrote to Father Thomas Dawson, an Irish brother in reform, 'I shall say something I don't like to speak of — that I never before told anyone. Once in daylight, and in a city street, there came to me a thought, a vision, a call — give it what name you please. But every nerve quivered. And there and then I made a vow. Through evil and through good, whatever I have done, and whatever I have left undone, to that have I been true.' He spoke less as a mystic, more as a pledged reformer, when he told the story to the people of New York who wanted him to be their mayor. 'Years ago I came to this city from the West, unknown, knowing nobody, and I saw and recognized for the first time the shocking contrast between monstrous wealth and debasing want. And here I made a vow from which I have never faltered, to seek out, and remedy if I could, the cause that condemned little children to lead such a life as you know them to lead in the squalid districts.' These words were spoken on an especially stirring occasion, but even late in life George did not many times choose to mention the spiritual event.

The occurrence is not to be doubted, yet from tardy testimony there is little opportunity to examine it. Remembering the Millennial Letter of 1861, and recalling the Lincoln editorials of 1865, it is best to observe simply how capable George was of intense social feeling, of intense identification of himself with public situations. In this sequence the vision of 1869 becomes the culminating event of a series — there was to be only one more, and that one soon and a kind of supplement to this.

In another man, the vision and dedication might have led to drafting blueprints for a new utopia. But escape to alabaster cities was not George's way. Typical of his own realism, he set himself rather, while still in New York, to solve the California problem that seemed at the time most likely to reduce laboring men there to the world's low level. As we have anticipated, California's Chinese question posed problems especially knotty for a moralist. Those who favored the immigration had available the arguments of human equality and international opportunity, and they had also the interest of the employing classes, as Hittell and the *Alta* illustrated in California. To oppose Chinese admission involved drawing the color line into politics, and tangling with Negro problems. George had to select his premises carefully as he now went all the way with labor in saying that the Chinese could not be assimilated into American life.

Evidently he found time to do the thinking during his weeks in Philadelphia. At any rate it was in one of the libraries of his home city that he searched and borrowed from John Stuart Mill's *Principles of Political Economy* — the first certified occasion of his using that epitome of classical economics, the book that introduced him to the field. And because one particular idea became crucial in his later development, we must notice that at this point George adopted as his own the widely accepted, and highly pro-capitalistic, wages-fund theory of employment. From the conception that wage rates are determined by a ratio between the size of the labor force and the amount of funds which business assigns to wages, George reasoned that Chinese coolies were bound to bring down the normally high rates of the Pacific coast and to have effect across the land. The economic prospect which was meat to Hittell was poison to George. Lower wages he believed to be sure to reduce trade, and to injure everyone by decreasing sales. So explained George in his vein of economy of abundance, much as he had spoken in the San Francisco *Times*.

Arguing this way George succeeded in avoiding a racial opposition to Chinese immigration. He particularly said that individually the Chinese were known to be intelligent and teachable. But from San Francisco he knew also that the coolies really could not be considered as though they were free individual settlers like other immigrants; they were unfree transient laborers transported from and committed to return to a culture which he believed to be 'in petrifaction.' Mainly he conceived the Chinese immigrants, in the Malthusianism of the common mind, to be the advance party of an unlimited labor force, a threat to free workers more terrible than the Negro slave trade had ever been.

The writer submitted his essay in the form of a letter to the editor of the *Tribune,* and on 1 May 1869, within days of George's leaving New York, that paper published it. The historian of anti-Chinese sentiment, Dr. E. C. Sandmeyer, judges that the argument was too involved to become popular or politically influential. But George had done the job in hope that the essay would be circulated for political effect among the 'horny-handed' in San Francisco, and accordingly he sent copies ahead of his return for republication there. Nugent published it with favorable comment, and with gauntlet down to the *Alta* and the *Bulletin.*

The Chinese letter was George's biggest intellectual effort during the hectic half-year in the East, a very limited expression of his spiritual commitment, and yet an important first step in his study of economic processes. It was to influence his coming California career rather more as a student and editor and social critic than as a young man interested in practical politics.

–4–

When arrangements were made and Henry George put his foot on the train for Chicago, he traveled alone once more. Annie was better, but they decided that she and the children should stay on in Philadelphia until things worked themselves out. She was probably not ready to set up a new household in San Francisco, and he cannot have been in shape to pay for one. The *Herald* owed him

$700. He was grim, but not too much so for humor, when he departed: 'I am doing well for a young man . . . I have already got the Central Pacific, Wells Fargo, and Western Union down on me, and it will be just my luck to offend the Bank of California next.'

Yet George left New York fortified with a pass on the Union Pacific and with a contract to correspond for the New York *Tribune*. This was arranged and signed by John Russell Young. During the trip it called for visits to Salt Lake City and White Pine, expenses paid: George was to send elaborate accounts of the mining country. After reaching San Francisco he was to write two letters a month, to be paid for at $5 a column, and Mr. George was to rank as the New York *Tribune*'s 'chief resident and representative correspondent in California.'

His personal papers contain notes he made on the western trip; probably he intended them for rendering into *Tribune* articles. This time — 1869 was the year of completing the transcontinental link — he liked the Union Pacific better than in 1868. Pullman Palace cars went part way; the bridges were being improved; the railroad restaurant meals were good, especially at Laramie, at $1 or $1.25 each. It was a much easier trip than in 1868, and he must have traveled in a mood of relief and rising hopes.

But when he reached San Francisco he learned that he would do no corresponding for the *Tribune* and had no future of any kind with Nugent's *Herald*. Samuel Sinclair, the publisher of the New York paper, had annulled his contract. Behind that event, George learned, his friend was being eased out as managing editor, to be succeeded by Whitelaw Reid.[1] And as for George's money and prospects with the paper which employed him, things were pretty desperate when he reached San Francisco. Nugent accused him of dishonest dealing and refused payment. George had to wire Hasson to hold up the eastern dispatches, and had to start a lawsuit, before he could collect. The San Francisco *Herald* died in the fall.

Even political hopes were disappointed. By August some cam-

---

[1] George encouraged Young to start a new paper and join Hasson in fighting the AP. But, though Young did become president of the American Press Association and did plan a new journal, the *Standard,* he very soon went to Europe on a confidential mission for the government. He returned to journalism, on the staff of the New York *Herald,* three years later.

paigning within the Democratic party proved that George would
not be nominated for the legislature. To be sure this was less than
a defeat. As Annie wisely wrote: it had been too much to expect
that he would be chosen; he had been a Republican; he must keep
courage. Nostalgia and waiting, and catch-as-catch-can, were Henry's
fate for the summer and fall of 1869. 'There is nothing out here
like the old-fashioned farmhouses of the Eastern States,' he wrote
a sister: 'There is some magnificent scenery and beautiful country;
but the people have not been here long enough to make it a country
like the East.' He had an opportunity to eke out an existence when,
for reasons unknown, the *Bulletin* hired him to write a few editorials. But before long he was doing a short turn at the printer's case
again. One compensation, it must have seemed a pathetic one, was
leisure and some chance to read, more than he had had for four or
five years.

Exactly the reverse of the year before, family events now supplied about the only bright spots in Henry George's history. The
politics of the city presently associated him with his Irish uncle-in-
law, Matthew McCloskey, from whom he had been estranged since
the event that forced him and Annie to elope. Their reconciliation
gave joy to all concerned. And in Philadelphia, Annie did not have
to report illness this year. Her hardest words for her husband were
lovers' quarrels: he must, she insisted, omit the 'josh' from his
letters or his family would think that all the McCloskeys were
drunkards. Wifely pride soared as she reported that Hasson had
called, and, saying how much he himself admired Henry, confided
that Young was going to want Henry George on his new $100,000
paper. Young, she wrote, 'thinks there is no one like you, told
Greeley they let the very man go they had been looking for for two
years, when they let you go.' But Annie's new hope for a fresh start
in New York had to die with Mr. Young's stillborn paper; and the
next spring, 1870, she thrilled to return to the West coast.

For the husband, the upturn came when to his amusement he was
appointed for the period of a friend's illness to be acting editor of
the San Francisco *Monitor,* a Catholic weekly. He inserted Irish
items from other papers — news stealing again — and wrote 'miscellaneous' editorials. What fun, he reflected, if he could only edit
simultaneously an anti-Catholic paper. Then he could print the
pieces that did not suit this one and have controversies with him-

self on the two editorial pages. The *Times* and the *Examiner* in pious miniature.

But before long Henry George was voicing on the *Monitor,* as he had in the *Times,* his own preferences. He spoke in behalf of Mayor McCoppin; and he spoke against the *Bulletin,* in which he now discovered a 'Hanglo-Saxon' slant. His reply to that paper, when it deplored the way in which Irishmen were getting into city politics, must be noted, because it gives us his own estimate of the political arena he wished to enter. One-quarter to one-half of San Francisco's population was Irish, he observed. Yet only 5 native Irishmen held elective offices, out of 52 seats of office; and there were only 40 Irish policemen, as against 46 native Americans and 27 born of other nationalities. This was no time, said the *Monitor,* for a San Francisco Know Nothingism, such as the *Bulletin* was encouraging.

In anticipation of Henry George's fight of 1886 and 1887 with Archbishop Corrigan, which almost led to the banning of *Progress and Poverty* to Catholic readers, there is rare irony that George now used a tiny Catholic paper to voice for the first time his proposition that every individual has a natural right to land. Of course this was not new as a general idea: labor reformers and others since Jefferson — as Irish as McClatchy of the *Bee,* many of them — had invoked natural-rights doctrine in favor of the homestead policy. And moral law as grounded in universal principles is of the essence of Catholic thought. Nevertheless *Monitor* editorials were George's first step toward an ultimately radical result — putting philosophical underpinning beneath his protest against land monopolization.

Two editorials in one issue of the *Monitor,* that of 11 September 1869, tell the story. Like many another protest of this period, this one took the grievances of Ireland to demonstrate the grievances of the world. Inevitably Irish landlords would have to show cause why they monopolized the soil occupied and worked by millions, George asserted. Their discomfiture would affect other lands. For 'beneath the Irish land question is the English land question . . . What is there in the laws of entail and primogeniture that should set aside the God-given law, that these who toil shall enjoy the fruits of the earth?' Irish protest was to be read as a sign of class discontent, the world around. 'The masses are beginning to think — beginning to feel their power and demand their rights; beginning to unite to obtain them. And sooner or later their just demands must be granted. Speed the day!'

It sounds almost as though Henry George was already at the point of denying that land should be held as private property. The major premises were laid. But when he came to the second editorial of 11 September, 'The Land Question in California,' he steered, more closely than later, by the local markings. Not that he thought that the state was in a unique position; on the contrary, tragically, he said, California was spiraling down the grooves familiar in the course of time. In place of the old world's military conquests and feudal grants, he saw about him 'Combinations of capitalists who have secured principalities for a nominal sum by the location of scrip, and who now demand extortionate prices or grinding rents of the actual settlers.' California's difference from the ancient past, he said, was political not economic. Though the Mother of Parliaments might probably fail to break up land monopoly in the old world, where the cake of custom was very hard, the California legislature could succeed if it would try. Economics poses the problems, politics can solve them. Henry George was one of the earliest industrial-age radicals to say just that.

Specifically, for the one state, he proposed: first, that big land aggregations should bear 'full taxation'; second, that there be set by constitutional amendment a sliding scale of land taxes, higher rates for large estates and lower for small. The two implements were designed, of course, to cut the same way. By keeping assessments at full value, and by raising rates on large aggregations, George hoped to squeeze out the monopolizers, force the land back into public hands, and open it for proprietor-farmers to take over. This is quite different from his ultimate proposals. Yet in boldness, philosophical assumptions, and faith in the power of government, George had made a sizable step into his future; and his pledge for the poor, made in New York, was getting into the stage of the tool blueprints.

Later George looked back on this period, or rather on the entire two years between his return to California and his important writing of 1871, as the passage of a traveler westward across the high plains. A long course lay behind him, and he was pledged to distant goals. Immediately ahead lay the mountains of thought which were the hazard of his journey.

–5–

In the period since he had left the *Times*, George's San Francisco contemporaries, whom we have called the Hamiltonians of the state, had themselves ventured a little into the highlands of thought. And, just as the first round of proposals in Hittell's book and in the *Alta* had drawn from George his first sustained economic thinking and criticism, so now a second round from the same side drew him forward again. The propaganda of the California Immigrant Union, very similar to the economic regionalism of Hittell and the *Alta*, yet somewhat different, was more specific than anything else so far in proposing policies for California. This organization requires a short digression.

The Immigrant Union was a brand new body, and its principal spokesman was its president *pro tem*, Caspar T. Hopkins, who was also president of the California Insurance Company and something of an intellectual and writer as well. He never reached Hittell's stature in this respect, but he is referred to as the well-educated son of an Episcopalian bishop and the author of a none-too-successful patriotic textbook in civics; he was an occasional lecturer at the University of California, a founder and writer for the Pacific Social Science Association, and the writer of memoirs. His presidency of the Immigrant Union associated him, not for the first time, with men famous in California history. Among the officers or trustees of the union appeared the following: Charles Crocker of the Central Pacific; A. D. Bell, a manufacturer; Charles Lux, of Miller and Lux, the holders of the hugest ranchlands in the state. Besides these there were a dozen or more others who can be identified as important bankers, merchants, or real-estate men; and on the honorary committee sat Governor Henry Haight, who was president *ex officio*, ex-governors Downey and Stanford, ex-senator Milton Latham, more businessmen, and the consuls of Italy and Peru. Just about all the large-property interests of the state, interests not always too friendly among themselves, and both political parties were represented.

A year earlier Henry George had predicted in the *Overland* that 'the railroad and the consequent great increase of business and population, will not be a benefit to all of us, but only to a portion.' Now the Immigrant Union was dealing with actualities much worse

than George had foreseen. In Mr. Hopkins' words, in a principal
piece of propaganda, California was being 'forced to stop and ask
what there is in our civilization that is so shrunken and shrivelled
by the magnetic current setting towards us through the iron con-
ductor from the East. We are led for the first time in our existence
— hitherto isolated — to look beyond the present moment, to
study the past and contemplate the future, in order to derive from
the experience of the remaining ninety-nine and a half per cent of
the world's population the facts and figures wherefrom to work out
our own destiny.'

The Immigrant Union's diagnosis was different from Hittell's,
principally because it was quite a bit more critical than his.
California's paralysis, said Hopkins, was land speculation. When
mining-stock inflation had given way, investors had been 'too impatient to wait the slow gains of mere industry, guiltless of any
knowledge of political economy.' They had turned to another
gamble: 'Homestead associations took the place of mining incorporations.' Though for five months now, 'the iron horse has crossed
the Sierras daily, yet the population, the money, does not come to
sustain these values.' The fact that millions were wrapped up in
the napkin of unproductive real estate — that is, of inflated prices
and established monopolies — was preventing California's growth.
In later publications the Immigrant Union presented statistics on
California immigration from 1862 through 1871 and kept the
diagnosis up to date.

To renew the energies of the state's economy, the writings of
Hopkins and Alexander D. Bell, and other propaganda of the Immigrant Union, all urged the old idea that California needed more
settlers. Hittell himself contributed. The familiar prescription was
altered just a little: not just immigrants *and* capital, but immigrants
with capital. With the adducing of many, many facts and figures,
the union proposed that the state set up an official agency — mid-
western states had done so — to promote and assist from overseas
the right kind of immigration. The best agricultural skills available
for developing California's lands, and men and families, mainly
from northern Europe, with sufficient credit with which to buy in
when they came, were what the Union wanted.

The Immigrant Union thus put itself behind the northern utopia
for the state: its goal a society of owner-farmers at center, a diver-

sified commercial, mining, and manufacturing economy surrounding. Asking for immigrants with cash, it was fair-minded enough, on the home front, to ask also that California landholders subdivide and sell their lands at reasonable low prices. Economically this was logical in the vein of the regional writers: Hittell had asked for low wages and low interest, and this extended the deflationary policy.

There is no need to praise as altruistic the union's exhortation to sell cheap; but a sincere idealism does appear in that part of the propaganda which differed most considerably from the old Hittell and *Alta* line. The Immigrant Union opposed the importation of Chinese laborers. Quite clearly this was President Hopkins' idea, and his feelings resembled Henry George's own. As a Lincoln Republican, and as a writer on civics who believed 'that had the American people, South as well as North, been alike trained in the principles of American government, the Civil War would not have occurred,' Hopkins now pursued a logic like that with which George has made us familiar. He would exclude the Chinese rather than have coolie labor stratified into a permanent peonage in California.

At first survey the program of the Immigrant Union may seem too small-farm-minded to fit comfortably under the designation Hamiltonian, which we applied to the first round of regional economics. But the aim again was a balanced economy, farms *and* industry and commerce. Furthermore the means, which the Immigrant Union proposed to use, involved the action of the state, and of voluntary groups within the state, in an almost neo-mercantilist pattern. In comparison with the earlier solvers of California's crisis, the union relied much more on economic plan and positive action, and much less on the automatic forces of a *laisser faire* economy.

The scheme as a whole — deny as Hopkins did that it represented any conspiracy of land grabbers — conformed perfectly with the general interests of property. Even the plan of holding down the asking prices of farm lands was a means of sales promotion, and a shoring up of basic values. In these features lay the vulnerability of the plan to attack, from Jeffersonian premises. Given the newness of California values, and their dubious respectability not to say morality, *should* those values have been shored up? Was this the time for a mercantilistic state policy to be put into action, in California?

–6–

It was inevitable that Henry George should want to quarrel publicly and prominently with Immigrant Union economics. What apparently was a chance meeting of late summer, 1869, with the governor of the state, led to opportunities for him to do just that.

The Democratic incumbent of California's highest office at this time was Henry H. Haight, a Yale man and lawyer who might today be ranked no lower than second or third in the short list of California's outstanding liberal governors. The occasion of his and George's striking up an acquaintanceship was a San Francisco meeting of the American Free Trade League. We are free to guess what common interests drew the two together: perhaps the inclination of like minds did it, but not unlikely there was prearranging, say by Mayor McCoppin, or Matthew McCloskey, or James Barry of the *Monitor*. However the contact developed, Professor Destler has neatly caught the symbolism of it, in his essays in *American Radicalism*. The Free Trade League as an American movement derived in part from British example, but its domestic lineage traces back to the '30s, and to the radical, pro-labor, Loco Foco wing of Jacksonism, which centered in New York City. For Governor Haight and Henry George to strike up a connection at the meeting was to illustrate the continuity, here in the West, of post-Civil War protest from a pre-war protest which had occurred a generation distant in time, and a continent's span distant in geography.

Shortly after the meeting, a recommendation by Governor Haight secured George a new editorship. Though this one lasted only from September 1869, to the middle of the next February, and the newspaper was suburban and not important, the event was big enough to restore Henry George to a proper job as editor, and moreover to launch him as a Democratic party newsman and as a political thinker into the bargain. Although not every personality of the Oakland *Daily Transcript* pleased him — the proprietors were a colonel on the governor's staff and a real-estate man — George had enormous enthusiasm for supporting the state administration. Haight was now at the middle point of a four-year term;

and the election of 1871 was coming into sight. His claim to a liberal's loyalty was a big one: principally that he and his party had brought about the repeal of certain railroad subsidies, and by doing so had reversed an ominous trend. The governor had also aligned himself with such projects as providing a state board of health and a fish commission and helping the state university. He proposed a special auction sale of valuable lands for the university — a truly Henry George way of securing to the state the actual present value of public lands.

So connected, George the editor tackled the state's Hamiltonians once more. Though he took caution, now as before and always, to acknowledge the good that railroads and all manner of new technology were doing California, he directed editorial after editorial to sounding the alarm. The terms of his anxiety were much like Hopkins' own: California was not getting its rightful share of America's immigration and development. Significant of the degree of radicalism George had *not* yet reached, the *Transcript* underwrote the homestead-farm idea for California. The paper followed a new writer, Dr. John Todd, a New England clergyman, in an editorial of 23 December 1869, saying that such settlers as New England dairymen and farmers, men and families who would be content with 'farms' and not demand 'plantations,' would be ideal for the state.

But beyond these obvious stages of agreement, the *Transcript* differed from the Immigrant Union right down the line. All the means the Union proposed the newspaper called expensive and unnecessary. Immigrant aids, from advertising in Europe to travel assistance, could only end, it said, in high and uneconomic charges sure to fall for the most part on the immigrants themselves. Even when Governor Haight made moderate proposals, the *Transcript* was hardly lukewarm. In George's analysis, all the costs of the private operation of the Immigrant Union would be thrust back into the price of the lands the immigrants would buy, and all public costs would come out of the taxpayers. The economic reasoning, which traced the flow of credit in the state's economy, became pretty abstract.

In editorials of October, November, and December, however, George made his indictment plain and tough. The Immigrant Union would serve as a front for the land aggregators themselves, he said; and its operations would add to California's record of speculation and quick profits. Its machinery, if set up, would present the state with a debt-ridden tenantry and would verge close to bringing contract labor to the country. Lands offered at ten dollars an acre, eight times the federal charge for domain lands, and the Immigrant Union's wanting wage rates to drop the *Transcript* gave as indications that the Union had a strong owning-class bias.

George's own solution was straight anti-monopoly and *laisser faire*. Assess great landholdings at full value, he said as he had said on the *Monitor;* then tax collection would begin the squeeze on aggregators to make them release their holdings at prices low enough to be attractive. Let all taxes except land taxes be reduced. With these charges down the immigrants would come, without state bureaus and outlays, said the *Transcript:* in due time the happy letters of new citizens would supply California's advertising, and the movement of free immigration would flow according to the true drawing power of the state's resources and charms.

The editor of the *Transcript* refused to be appeased by the pro-labor plank of the Immigrant Union. The *Alta* and the *Bulletin* were keeping to their old opinion about coolies. There was no real break in the conservative front. George had thought through the Chinese immigration problem first, and he intended to make political capital of the ideas of exclusion. Now he conceived the notion of asking for a statement from the highest possible authority. Writing to John Stuart Mill, he particularly mentioned the old argument addressed to American working men in behalf of admitting the coolies. It was that this form of labor would affect the economy in the same way as new machinery did: the Chinese would do the work Americans disliked to do and raise the standard of living for all. Would the author of the *Principles of Political Economy* be so good as to comment?

On this particular point most definitely, but also in a general way, Mill's long and generous letter, sent from his hideaway at Avignon, put a feather in George's cap. 'Concerning the purely economic view of the subject,' he wrote, 'I entirely agree with you; and it could hardly be better stated and argued than it is in your article in the New York *Tribune.* That the Chinese immigration, if it attains great dimensions, must be economically injurious to the mass of the present population; that it must diminish their wages and reduce them to a lower state of physical comfort and well being I have no doubt. Nothing can be more fallacious than the attempts to make out that thus to lower wages is the way to raise them, or that there is any compensation in an economical point of view, to those whose labour is displaced, or who are obliged to work for a greatly reduced remuneration.'

On other points Mill's agreement was less complete. Where George could find nothing but faults in the Chinese as a social group, unsavory and unassimilable in California, Mill made distinctions and discriminations. While acknowledging absolutely that coolies, as found in 'a form of compulsory labor, that is of slavery,' should be excluded, he suggested that it was not justifiable to assume that all Chinese were of that order and kind — especially children exposed in the United States to 'the most potent means that have yet existed for spreading the most important element of civilization down to the poorest and most ignorant of the labouring masses.' Mill phrased as moral problems the questions whether or not 'those who have first taken possession of the unoccupied portion of the earth's surface' have a right to exclude later comers, and in what degree 'the more improved branches of the human species [should] protect themselves from being hurtfully encroached upon by those of a lower grade in civilization.' He ended by saying it seemed that a little sharing in California would represent an improvement for the Chinese, those at home as well as the immigrants, which ought not to be withheld.

George printed the letter in full in the *Transcript* of 20 November, and, unlike other editorial writing, he signed his comment. He urged that the 'nine-tenths' predominance of the coolie element among the California Chinese justified labor's anti-Chinese attitudes, by Mill's own standards. He yielded little relevance to Mill's hortatory comments. On the point of the Chinese children, though they had good natural capacity, he thought that their living in a miniature China and a sordid one, right in San Francisco — the ugly beginning of today's Chinatown — would prevent them indefinitely from becoming assimilable into the common social and political life. After stating his reservations about Mill's reservation, George added a grateful tribute to the generous economist.

He had brought off a journalistic *coup*, and more. For the first time Henry George stood as a leader for a cause, in his home community. The San Francisco press took notice. The *Alta* and the *Bulletin* discovered a demagogue in Oakland; and the *Chronicle*, a 'vulgar, self-advertising, showman.' On the other hand, the San Francisco *Call* gave George strong support; and the Sacramento *Union*, qualified support. Though five months of the editorial pages of the *Transcript* show George firming up other specific ideas — the critique of speculation, and his opposition to the national banking policy, for instance — nothing else equals his pushing of the Chinese problem, or comes near to being as important, in his effort to achieve prominence and recognition.

Indeed he had now fixed on an idea of policy which he was to hold for life as peculiarly his own. Up to a quarter century later, even after Chinese exclusion had become national policy by virtue of acts of Congress, George would be arguing the morals of the matter. At this time his friend and follower of illustrious name, William Lloyd Garrison II, opposed him. That he was a racist, George denied. In his words of 1893: 'To your proposition that the right to the use of the earth is not confined to the inhabitants of the United States, I must cordially assent. But when you seem to think it follows that, "the humblest Chinaman has as much natural right to the use of the earth of California as yourself, and it is your inalienable right to change your residence to any land under the sun," I must emphatically deny. Are men merely individuals? Is there no such thing as family, nation, race? Is there not a right of association, and the correlative right of exclusion?' Thus from March 1869, Henry George's thought had essayed the burden of asserting nationality while denying monopoly — surely as awkward a burden as a democratic theorist has ever undertaken.

Still separated from his family, still wrestling the problems he had tackled in New York, George had another moment of clairvoyance in Oakland. Though, as in the case of the vision and dedication on the sidewalks, his telling of the story puts no date upon it, about New Year's 1870, is a likely time. His greeting to the new decade, a New Year's editorial in the *Transcript*, seems to set the psychological stage: 'Into the seventies again. A decade most noticeable in the annals of the Republic. God grant that in the years to come the same spirit that animated the fathers may animate the children, that the heritage they bequeathed may be preserved unimpaired.'

This time George was riding in the lovely foothills where the eye is drawn west, above the flats on which Oakland lies, across San Francisco Bay, to the world's broadest waters beyond the Golden Gate. Especially in the winter season, when the rains let up, distant objects there seem poignantly sharp and near. This day he was absorbed in his own thoughts. Resting his horse, he 'asked a passing teamster, for want of something better to say, what land was worth there. He pointed to some cows grazing off so far that they looked like mice and said: "I don't know exactly, but there is a man over there who will sell land for a thousand dollars an acre." Like a flash it came upon me that there was the reason of advancing poverty with advancing wealth. With the growth of population, land grows in value, and the men who work it must pay for the privilege. I turned back amidst quiet thought, to the perception that then came to me and has been with me ever since.'

'Like a flash the reason seemed to light my brain,' said Henry George again, about a quarter-century after the event. Although the illumination must have been almost as emotional, certainly more hopeful, than the New York experience, the overtones of mysticism were pretty well absent this time. In his posthumous book he says that the occurrence 'crystallized my brooding thoughts into coherency.' He 'there and then recognized — the natural order — one of those experiences which make those that have not had them feel that they can vaguely appreciate what mystics and poets have called the "ecstatic vision." ' In his own judgment, George had not had a vision, but a less intense experience which would justify belief in visions.

With a little exercise of the imagination we can try to recapture the milling ideas of a dissatisfied editor, that day as he sought refreshment in the Oakland foothills. We know that the countryside itself seemed to speak to him, and perhaps he felt the same about the broad horizon of Pacific waters. But what about some possible tingling memory of books? Considering that the recognized treatises and handbooks on economics, of that day as now, specified and named the value of desirable land as producing 'economic rent' — and that none did so more clearly than John Stuart Mill's *Principles* — it is almost incredible that the Oakland perception came to George without benefit of literature.

There is, indeed, no reason to question George's assertions, late in life, that in 1870 he had taken nothing from either Adam Smith or the French Physiocrats, who are known for assigning high place in the economic process to the land and its tillers. And he might as well have included in the denials the writings of David Ricardo, the author of the widely accepted law of rent which he himself would soon accept. George, the Oakland editor, deeply read in local affairs, knew very little general economic literature.

Partly on this account, and partly because of the man's transparent sincerity, we read with sympathy George's defense, in his posthumous work, *The Science of Political Economy,* of the independence of the Oakland illumination. 'It is a mistake to which critics who are themselves mere compilers are liable, to think that men must draw from one another to see the same truths or to fall into the same errors. Truth is, in fact, a relation of things which has to be seen independently because it exists independently.' George was always an idealist in the philosophical as well as in the colloquial sense of the word: to him true ideas were real and permanent entities, available to right thinkers and the private property of none.

Yet the unanswered question persists of a present debt to classical economics, not unlikely to John Stuart Mill. All that is certain is that in the East George had read Mill for wage theory, and found what he could use. Certainly the *Principles,* in the early and current editions, contained the prevailing theory of rent; the book even contained a friendly presentation of the notion of land nationalization, which at this very time Mill was beginning to advocate on the ground that rent ought to be a public, not a private, income.[2] I just hazard the guess that from his reading George had actually picked up some notions of rent theory, that they were in reserve in the back of his mind. He could easily have done this, any reader could, without realizing at first — the British economists

[2] See Mill, *Principles,* 1864 edition, Ch. xvi. How interested George would have been had he known that, in 1868, his senior in land reform, Congressman George W. Julian, had like himself sought Mill's advice. In reply the liberal economist had approved Julian's 'endeavoring to prevent the sale of public lands to mere speculators.' Mill often thought, he said of himself, 'that it would be much better if a new country retained all its lands as state property, giving, as we do in India, leases renewable forever at rents guaranteed against any augmentation except by a general measure . . . According to my own notions, absolute property in land, even when owned by the cultivators, is a prejudice and an abuse.' Mill to Julian, 29 May 1868. Giddings-Julian Collection, LC.

themselves did not — that a rent theory drawn primarily from considering English rural landholding might apply more radically to American land, especially land in the vicinity of a rapidly growing city. George could quite naturally have failed to sense at first acquaintance the moral dynamite that resides in rent theory for Americans who — different from the British economists — reject as wrong any preference for a class-structured society.

If the Oakland perception was what it seems — an intense quick operation of mind — then there is no need to blame George very much for denying that he had stolen ideas. If he did not acknowledge handsomely, as of that date, a debt to Mill, we shall find much quoting and citing of the *Principles* on rent, when he came to write *Progress and Poverty*. But I think he made a contemporary acknowledgment. On 16 July 1870, about half a year after the Oakland vision, George inserted the following clause in a letter to the master himself: 'In an endeavor to account for the continuance of pauperism in England, and the gradual sinking of the working-classes in the older parts of the states, I have come to conclusions which were cleared and strengthened by your works . . .' This is not very definite, but I believe that it is George's thank-you for ideas about rent, concerning which he was not yet ready to say more.

–7–

Henry George had been too big a man for the Oakland *Daily Transcript,* and his enlarging kit of ideas must have made the job in speculator-ridden Oakland doubly incongruous. Fortunately his new friend had another assignment for him. Before spring Governor Haight called him to Sacramento to take charge of the *Reporter,* a Democratic party organ which was being rebuilt out of the *State Capital Reporter,* of which ex-governor Bigler had been editor.

At last after nearly two years, family life could be restored to proper footing. 'My poor darling you have been having a hard time,' wrote Annie, when she received the glorious news. She was inexpressibly glad to be coming back to California; Hasson was helping her plan the trains. This would be their third recourse to Sacramento: the earlier ones had led to happy intervals of their life together. George made this new beginning the occasion of having his brother, John Vallance, come on with Annie and the children.

Though storms loomed ahead, for 1871 would be election year, there were many promising things about the job. George began with a 'fair salary' and a tender of one-fourth of the company's stock. The battle he had first fought for Nugent was now won. Before the end of April the opposition telegraph, which he had predicted, had actually materialized: the Atlantic and Pacific, the system he had used between Harrisburg and Philadelphia, now leased the railroad companies' wires along the transcontinental line. And his friends in New York were more than ready to send the news. Now in the capacity of 'general agent' of the American Press Association, Hasson wrote: 'Oh Harry . . . It's gay. Instead of waiting for the *Sun* to rise, we are beating the Associated Press, especially in foreign news, almost daily.' And when his partner of last year appointed George as California agent of the new association, another friend endorsed the document, 'This appointment is confirmed. Salary sentimental. In time material and practical . . . John Russell Young, President.'

The fun spread to California. The San Francisco *Chronicle* had no choice but to join up with the American Press Association, and this put George's old employer, de Young, not his favorite, on a spot. George could 'laugh loud and long' when he heard that the *Chronicle*'s proprietor objected to his being California agent for the APA; and he must have had even greater pleasure in learning Hasson had upbraided de Young 'for defaming the man who had done more than any other man on the coast to build up the A.P.A.' But the *Chronicle* came in with the *Reporter*, and George corralled several of the small papers of the inland towns as well. He triumphed as he kept down the total charge for the wire services to $800 a month, and triumphed again as he assessed the *Chronicle* for $100. The success of the APA he celebrated in vigorous editorials on the new free trade in news; he savored in irony the complaints of the California AP papers, as they now reduced their prices.

Meanwhile the *Reporter* moved in on a concession, even a monopoly, of its own. The legislature passed a bill — 'your bill,' George's father called it — which authorized the publication 'of certain legal notices in a state paper.' This preference assisted the *Reporter* through and beyond George's term of editorship; later, a Republican legislature repealed it in resentment after a different set of owners and editors had taken over. We do not know how important or unimportant the subsidy was to the paper's income or George's. However low the estimate, it makes an interesting preliminary to the state appointment, in some degree a sinecure, which was to sustain him after 1875, while he was writing *Progress and Poverty*.

On two fronts of his economic thinking especially, the editorship of the Sacramento *Reporter* was just the thing to stimulate George: on the state control of corporate monopolies, and on taxation. Although he had made the vow against poverty in the heat of a personal war on the giant corporation which monopolized transcontinental telegraphy, and the fight had confirmed his ideas about the need to nationalize at least the one monopoly, George had not given much thought to the public regulation of corporate institutions in any general way. He was always — especially by comparison with latter-day socialists and progressives, men like Henry Demarest Lloyd — to be light on that side. But he was not entirely negligent; and in 1870 he could not avoid that class of public business. With his shoulder next to Governor Haight's, he had no choice except to give California's railroads and railroad policy much fresh attention.

The governor's attack denied any hostility to corporations 'in their proper sphere,' but he was old-line Democrat from first to last. 'We object,' he urged a friend, to the corporations' being turned 'into agencies of public plunder, and we object to placing the government into the hands of their managers and making the people their serfs and tributaries.' To Haight it was 'inexplicable that men claiming to be imbued with the democratic principles of the olden time should fail to denounce and resent this monstrous system of taxing out of existence farmers and small property-holders in order to add to the surplus of those already enriched out of the public treasury and the public domain.' In this line Haight set up his case against railroad subsidies.

George went with him. In the *Reporter* the editor made no effort to build on the archaic idea he had ventured in the San Francisco *Times*: the notion of publicly owned roadbeds and privately owned rolling stock. He took the railroads as consolidated enterprises and tried, as the governor did, to think out ways of bringing them to terms with a people's government. Protesting the subsidies, he admitted that new trackage would be put down less rapidly without them but said that slower growth would be better all round.

When a rival paper said that railroads were 'essentially private property as much so as a wagon, a hotel, or steamboat,' George answered with a justification of state regulation which might equally have served to justify state ownership. 'Railroads are a peculiar species of property, exercising peculiar privileges, and in favor of which certain concessions are made . . . No individual can build a railroad without obtaining from the state a grant of rights and powers that do not belong to individuals, and can only be exercised by them by virtue of the authority of the State. And furthermore, there is this difference between a railroad and other kinds of property. A railroad is from its very nature a monopoly, that is, its existence makes competition impossible. A railroad is not only a common carrier, subject to all the duties of a common carrier, but it is a common carrier with a monopoly of the business. Thus to the other titles by virtue of which the state may control and regulate railroads is added the highest right — the right of necessity.'

This 'right of necessity' to regulate corporate monopolies was not theoretically satisfying as a point of rest for a democratic ponderer of the ethics of property. Yet like nearly everything else in George's mental history in 1869 and 1870, it shows an advance in his apprehending industrial-age problems — in this case the role and sphere of public utilities.

As for taxation, except to protest the complexity and costs of California practice and except for the reformist ideas he had voiced in the *Monitor,* George had not previously had much to say. On the *Reporter* he began lightly, at first with little foreshadowing of his life's future, praising certain reductions brought about by the Haight administration. Then in the later spring he began to display a large new interest in taxes and related economic theory. All at once general problems of the tax structure, and of the whole distribution and flow of credit through society, became a field for his editorials to explore and estimate. There were ample reasons for this: the Oakland vision, and his criticism of the Immigrant Union, and perhaps some reconsideration of the matter of his 1867 editorials on money and banking all demanded working ideas about distribution. Also he may well have been affected by Governor Haight's belief that railroad subsidies force money to flow from country to city and from class to class; and perhaps the writings of his San Francisco contemporary, John Alexander Ferris, affected him. Like Ferris, and like many another Westerner in due time, George envisaged the credit of California as being manipulated and exploited by Easterners and foreigners. The policies that impounded gold in San Francisco, or else drained the treasure east in monopoly charges, were actually 'taxes,' said the *Reporter*.

George puzzled and discussed the incidence of taxation on social classes. All citizens are affected by the federal war taxes, he agreed, but the large payers feel them only as a railroad feels a tax which it passes on in larger fares. Taxes really fall where the tax gatherer never visits, the garrets of the cities, the child laborers at the Massachusetts looms, in the eastern slums 'where the man from the fresh new West cannot go without a sinking and a sickening of the heart.' Taxes are our 'main trouble,' the writer was now beginning to think: they were obstacles to economic flow, and barriers enhancing the line between poverty and riches. Though Henry George's own historic prescription of taxes was far from ready, and he had yet to begin a hard study of state taxation, his critical frame of reference was pretty well established.

In certain aspects of economic questing and answering, Henry George on the *Reporter* changed rather the intensity than the direction of his ideas. Sometimes there was a new dogmatism added, for instance this: '*Free trade is the great* NEED *of California,*' and 'We believe in the international law of God as Cobden called free trade.' In regard to labor, over and beyond his familiar assertions for the eight-hour day and against Chinese immigration, on the eve of the Franco-Prussian War and the Paris Commune, the editor hinted about possible social revolution. So different from his later sustained war on socialism and general distrust of all forms of European radicalism, his paper now thought a desirable result would follow if a little of labor's international spirit, purified of 'the wildest notions of the continental mechanics,' were to cross the Atlantic. 'We would wish it God-speed,' he said on 24 May 1870. How much George knew in that year, or did not know, about the Marxist International Workingmen's Association is not clear.

George deserves credit for being able to keep his eyes open and to make important and truthful observations about social conditions. On one crucial point, an editorial of the *Reporter* said that, although the wages paid to American working men had increased of recent years, their real earnings were diverted more to taxes and bought fewer goods and services than in earlier times. This was a hard but not a commonly admitted truth; forty years later a brilliant California-trained academician proved it statistically. And, in another issue, the *Reporter* quarreled with the advice of Greeley's *Tribune,* that unemployed workers should go to the empty lands of the western frontier. Such a step was desirable but not practical, George countered, speaking against assumptions widely held for more than a century in the United States. How could a laborer out of work move his family to a farm and stand the costs and make the adjustments? Only since about 1930, with the help of a revision in historical studies, has the country learned that the West rarely if ever served as a safety valve for city population pressures, but rather that the cities provided a safety valve for the farm lands when times were hard. In very fact the decade from 1865 to 1875, during which George's talent for interpreting the condition of labor flowered, was economically one of the most adverse in history for American working men.

In the summer of 1870 California events and conditions, which illustrated labor's hard times, gave George a chance to return journalistic attention to the Chinese question, and to bring off a newspaper affair much like his coup while he was running the Oakland *Transcript.* While other wage rates in the state, according to George, were declining a bit, in line with the hopes of the regional economists, wages in the shoe and slipper industry dropped suddenly. This occurred immediately after 500 or so Chinese were employed; and at once a spate of bills to exclude Oriental immigration was brought into the legislature. Simultaneously on the political side, the Fifteenth Amendment now promised equal suffrage to all American-born Chinese. Responding to this convergence of events, the *Reporter* waxed alarmist. It advised the shoemaker's union of San Francisco to expel the coolies from that industry; and it predicted that beginning in the next election — twenty-one years after the Gold Rush — Chinese Americans at the polls would begin a new chapter in the history of corruption. With votes at $2 apiece, George foresaw the buying of Oriental votes by American employers and more trouble for working men and the labor movement.

Once more George drew strength from John Stuart Mill. Pro-immigration newspapers were charging him with having garbled or otherwise misrepresented the Mill letter, as he had printed it in the Oakland *Transcript*. George laid the matter, with evidence, before the English economist. Again Mill was very gracious: he acknowledged that George had printed his letter accurately and fully; he neither accepted nor debated correction on their points of difference. At about the same time George had a sympathetic note on the Chinese problem from Horace White. Thus the third round in the issue of exclusion firmed George, gave him an admirable chance to restate his ideas; and, an experienced propagandist now, he identified his case with the Democratic party of California at the official center.

A very large part of the story of George as editor of the *Reporter*, indeed, is his effort to give the party the imprint of his own mind. As we have already seen in the instance of the Immigrant Union, this was partly a business of saying 'No.' The *Reporter* criticized Governor Haight again when the administration showed reluctance to recognize the full force of the Fifteenth Amendment, on ratification. Teaching the Democratic party lessons mainly involved saying 'Yes' to reform, however; and this meant going beyond Governor Haight's own field of fighting the Central Pacific Railroad.

George's central theme of argument in the reform vein of thought was the idea of the unfinished Civil War — the obligation of the country to effect more completely its war ideals. Only the Democratic party could become the vehicle, he said in many an editorial: right ideas of reconstruction should be applied across the land, by no means in the usual terms of Reconstruction in the South. A few lines from the *Reporter* will chart the moral situation as he saw it. 'We have despoiled the South of its state freedoms, now what of our own?' 'Swindle after swindle; corruption after corruption, is constantly coming to light; so tainted has the moral atmosphere in Federal circles become that it is literally thought no harm to steal.' On the Fourth of July only the 'graver thoughts' came to the editorial mind: a present crisis, a 'crucial test of our institutions . . . land dearer . . . class distinctions sharper . . . colossal fortunes . . . mammoth corporations . . . We have lost that high regard for law.' In this condition, the editor pleaded, the country should not belittle political parties; it should recognize that Democrats and Republicans do stand for different principles. To the Democratic party he credited four attitudes as right: a determination to

limit the federal government; a racism (unqualified and acknowledged, this once) 'that this government was instituted by and for
white men and their posterity forever'; faith in free trade and opposition to tariffs; a fixed enmity to all monopolies. Richard Henry
George, now signing himself 'Old Pop,' could hardly have judged
more accurately than he did when he wrote about having shown
the *Reporter* to some good old Jackson Democrats. 'Many worme
congratulations I have received that I have a *son* so bold to stand so
firm for the good old Democratic Principals.'

By all the signs of editorial performance George at midsummer
1870, after half a year, was filling to satisfaction the job for which
Governor Haight had called him to Sacramento. Yet suddenly,
within days of the editorial last quoted, he was out. And very shortly
he and his family moved to San Francisco again, for once with
money to tide them over.

The story came out later. From San Francisco there appeared,
one day, in the office of the *Reporter,* 'an honest old gentleman'
who wanted to buy 'a controlling interest in a good Democratic
paper.' The bidder denied any wish to change policy and offered
good money. George was willing. (What he told Mill, about this
time — that he was working out his ideas about the universal causes
of poverty — is the only sign he gave, that he had other interests
than journalism pressing.) As Governor Haight was out of Sacramento a message was sent; but before his telegram warning against
a fast deal came back delayed, the sale had been made. When the
smoke cleared away it was proved that the ancient gentleman's bag
of twenty-dollar gold pieces had come direct from the Central
Pacific office on K Street. Two days after the sale a change of officers
took place, and the Sacramento *Reporter* became, and was commonly recognized as, 'the obsequious organ of the Railroad Company.'

Though the ex-editor of the *Reporter* and agent of the American
Press Association must have been piqued at being tricked by a railroad henchman, he who had had no money now had some; and no
purchase had bought his lasting silence.

–8–

Two years earlier George's article in the *Overland,* 'What the
Railroad Will Bring Us,' had epitomized his regional criticism and

utopianism, as first conceived in writing for the *Times*. Now he
summed up and moved forward again. This time the product was
two pamphlets: one is today a forgotten piece of state-election campaign literature; the other is a minor classic of American criticism.

The first, entitled *The Subsidy Question and the Democratic
Party,* consolidated into sixteen closely written pages the ideas he
and Governor Haight shared on that bitter question. Written to
support the governor's fight for re-election, it used *laisser faire*
theory against big business, and in behalf of labor and the small
people — the opposite of twentieth-century habits of thought.
George demanded, of course, that the railroad companies rely on
private resources, with little or no staking by the government. His
more doctrinaire ideas he embellished with quotations from the
Democratic Review of 1837; and the practical results of government handouts and politics he illustrated from unappetizing recent
history, especially from the case of the Los Angeles and San Pedro
Railroad. Ideological though the pamphlet was, George's detailed
use of data and figures made it the most assimilative factual piece
of writing in the author's record so far.

Though Governor Haight was defeated by a Republican, Newton Booth, that event did not put the idea of the pamphlet too much
on the losing side. In Sacramento the new governor soon developed
a strong resistance to monopolies, as surprising to George as pleas-
ing. Concerning this there will be more in the next chapter. Simultaneously in Washington, by 1871 the era of Congress's lavish railroad grants was at last yielding to a period of grant forfeitures.
Henry George's policy for railroads must be accounted to have
been part of a national reaction.

In the other pamphlet, *Our Land and Land Policy,* George
reached a new level of intellectual achievement. A 48-page booklet,
as published for 25 cents in San Francisco, 1871, it fills 130-odd
pages in good type and modern book form. We have already caught
the hint that he was working on the problem of poverty as early as
July 1870. He was not yet reading economic literature broadly.
Even so, a year of finding materials and establishing perspective,
thinking, organizing, and writing would not have been too much for
Our Land and Land Policy had he given it all his time. It was a
first book in a virgin field.

The title of it is big enough to be right for the first two-thirds, the remembered portion of the text; it is too modest for the scope of the whole. Beginning with a colored map which indicates by bands across the country the routes of the western railroads and the share of the domain granted them as subsidies — an alarming generosity of the government — George made a Malthusian-minded presentation of America's dwindling land surplus. He reasoned from the assumption, common in his day and based on population history, that the people would multiply at a rate of about 24 per cent each decade, or would double each quarter-century.[3] He took his figures on the domain lands from United States Land Office publications. The two together, population figures *versus* land figures, presented an unfamiliar and an unhappy conjunction.

Though we may bypass his statistics, we must not miss the common sense of his ideas, or the naturalness of his doing what he was doing. He had had an intuition that landholding had everything to do with the distribution of wealth. Very well, he was checking the data and reporting. He wrote in part from his old editorials; he also ventured new vistas of criticism. From the vast totals of Land Office figures, which included desert and waste, he cut down to the size of 450 million acres the actual ungranted and available part of the domain which might still be settled by farmers. This meant 12 acres per American, in 1870; or, according to his population predictions, if distributed among the new Americans of the next decade, 33 acres apiece; or again, 12 acres apiece among the new Americans from 1870 to 1890. Of course his population estimates ran too high. But his essential prophecy was true: America's arable domain land would be dispersed before the beginning of the twentieth century.

In the second chapter George shifted from the general picture of federal resources and federal policy to a detailed analysis of 'The Lands of California.' This was the strongest criticism yet. Where Hittell had been satisfied to find fault mainly with the confusion of titles, George cut deep. In the greatest federal-land state in the union, and a thinly settled one, he found and said that 'a large part

[3] George's Malthusianism here was conventional but not unstudied. He knew the old predictions of Elkanah Wilson and thought they set the right pattern for population study. On this kind of thinking, see Joseph J. Spengler, 'Population Prediction in Nineteenth-Century America,' *American Sociological Review*, 1 (1936): 905–21.

of the farming is done by renters, or by men who cultivate their thousands of acres in a single field.' Remembering his writing for the *Times,* George spoke again of the *pueblo,* and of San Francisco's lost opportunity. It might have been a city of light: 'the size of London, dedicated to the purpose of providing every family with a free homestead,' a city without poverty or crime, he still believed. He reviewed the Mexican-grant problem: he exposed the 'floating grants' and the faked ones; he demonstrated the utter corruption, state government acting as cat's-paw for speculators, in granting away the so-called 'swamp lands' — often the best river-valley arable there was. 'There never was a cat rolled whiter in meal,' was Horace Greeley's opinion of Congress' policy of giving the 'swamp land' over to state-government control.

The recapitulation of the California chapter presented a parvenu class of 'Marquises, Counts, Viscounts, Lords, and Barons,' all elevated to property and power in twenty years of land grabbing. George named companies and men who are still famous in land engrossment. After the railroads and the individual holders preferred by the railroads, he specified a second group whose aggregations ran to the hundreds of thousands of acres apiece: Miller and Lux, the San Francisco butchers, whose cattle-range holdings exceeded all others; Abel Stearns, of Los Angeles, who had 200,000 acres and sold much; William Chapman of San Francisco, a leading scrip speculator; an ex-surveyor-general of the state and an ex-surveyor-general of the United States, each said to have engrossed more than 300,000 acres. Without land monopolization, George reasoned as he had editorialized against the Immigrant Union, California would long since have been heavily populated by farmer-proprietors. But because of it there were instead the speculation, the coolie labor, the tenancy, the empty lands, the California tramps, the 'general stagnation,' the private monopolization of water supplies, and the absentee landlords living so dashingly in San Francisco and Europe.

These two, the first and second, chapters make a devastating indictment of a national policy and a state situation. Except locally, however, the edition caused hardly more than a ripple of policy comment in 1871, no more than the letter against Chinese immigration as printed in the *Tribune.* Major recognition waited for later times; perhaps the first such acceptance was Hubert Howe Ban-

croft's still unequaled history of California, which in a general way
seconded Henry George's findings. Today's experts do likewise.
Professor Fred A. Shannon, a reviser of the frontier theory of American history, says that George's strictures on land policy have never
been refuted; and Professor Gates judges what George said about
the grants to railroads to have been 'the best criticism by a contemporary.' This scholar's own critique of America's 'incongruous
land system' recognizes the same incongruities of democracy and
land distribution as George himself explored. Could we imagine a
Pulitzer Prize committee in General Grant's day, anxious to reward an exposer of corruption and a proponent of reform, we
should be free to imagine also Henry George at thirty-two winning
national kudos a decade ahead of the public excitement about
Progress and Poverty.

Yet for the development of an intellect the third, fourth, and
fifth chapters of *Our Land and Land Policy* — the part of the book
not comprehended by the title and quite naturally not noticed by
students of the domain — are more revealing than is the critical
realism of the earlier chapters. Facts combined with moral indigna-
tion against monopolizers were not enough for this writer. *Why*
fight land engrossment? How phrase, how justify the ideas of the
Oakland perception? Could he blueprint a course of action which
just might make an inspiring and practical land policy for a democracy? These were the problems to which the forgotten one-third of
Our Land and Land Policy was addressed.

To establish a base for logical reasoning, the author set up textbook definitions and assumptions from classical economics: land,
wealth, labor, and so on. Only one of the definitions needs detain
us, it is a little special: land is 'that part of the earth's surface habit-
able by man not merely his habitation but his storehouse upon
which he must draw for all his needs, and the material to which his
labor must be applied for the supply of all his desires . . . On the
land we are born, from it we live, to it we return again — children
of the soil as truly as is the blade of grass or the flower of the field.'
To Henry George, land included *resources and location,* and it had
poetic meaning not separate from the economic. These factors
blended now into an article of lifelong belief.

So also emerges a second idea — not as sharply and freshly as the
wages-fund idea when he was thinking out Chinese immigration,

but with similar, and more lasting, utility for reform purposes —
the labor theory of value, common to classical economics. Perhaps
twentieth-century readers should be warned, as George's contemporaries would not have needed to be. There was nothing unusual
that George should insert in his book, quite interstitially and without self-consciousness, that wealth is 'the equivalent of labor,' and
that private property in goods is justified because it represents accumulated toil, either one's own or someone else's for which value
has been given in exchange. In 1871 more complicated modern
theories of wages and of prices were being developed, but they had
not displaced the old labor theory in the economists' kit of tools;
and likewise, though Marx had by now used the labor theory in
building his system, that system had not been rendered into English-
speaking — and had not reached Henry George's — awareness. In
other words: the labor theory of value was not yet either outmoded
or rendered suspect by having kept company with revolution. Like
that other commonplace of British middle-class thought, the contract theory of government on which the American Revolution
hinged, this theory stated ethical common sense. In the ordinary
parlance of the textbooks it was kept reasonably disinfected and
unexciting to readers; but the germ of social heterodoxy and protest always lurked in it just the same, not for Marx alone but for
any thinker.

In *Our Land and Land Policy* Henry George, putting two and
two together, began to make history with economic ideas. Value
occurs in land, he now said — remember that his definition of land
excluded improvements made by man's labor — by reason of
scarcity. And value in land means power: the 'power which its
ownership gives of appropriating the labor of those who have it
not.' An increase in land values, he pushed on, does not increase the
wealth of a community; an increase affects the distribution of goods,
not their production. It raises social classes. To the owners of land
of heightened value, purchasing power does flow; from the users
of such land, higher payments are demanded. In such terms, a year
and a half or more after the experience, George found formulas
and context for the Oakland perception. Weaving his own thought
into the web of accepted economic theory, George did the most intelligent thing possible to strengthen his case and to persuade other
people of its rightness.

Into the fabric of fact and theory of *Our Land and Land Policy*, moreover, the author assimilated the kind of utopianism he had put into 'What the Railroad Will Bring Us,' and the ideas of the universal rights of men which he had put into the editorials of the *Monitor*. The following will illustrate his blend of religion with economics and politics: 'The right of every human being to himself is the foundation of the right of property. That which a man produces is rightfully his own, to keep, to sell, to give, or to bequeath, and upon this sure title alone can ownership of anything rightfully rest. But man has also another right, declared by the fact of his existence — the right to use so much of the free gifts of nature as may be necessary to supply all the wants of that existence, and as he may use without interfering with the equal rights of anyone else, and to this he has a title as against all the world. The right is natural; it cannot be alienated. It is the free gift of the Creator to every man that comes into the world — a right as sacred, as indefensible as his right to life itself.'

Lengthening his democratic vistas in the directions he had promised, George discovered that inequality of opportunity in England indicated a diagnosis of that country's ills. He had been reading parliamentary papers and did not hesitate to judge. 'Certain it is that the condition of the slaves upon our Southern plantations was not half so bad as that of the monopoly slaves of England.' He made the diagnosis a dogma: 'The Almighty, who created the earth for man and man for the earth has entailed it upon all the generations of the children of men by a decree written upon the constitution of all things — a decree which no human action can bar and no prescription determine. Let the parchments be ever so many, or possession ever so long, in the Courts of Natural Justice there can be but one title to land recognized — the using of it to satisfy reasonable wants . . .

'We are not called on to give to all men equal conditions, but we are called upon to give all men an equal chance. If we do not, our republicanism is a snare and a delusion, our chatter about the rights of men the veriest buncombe in which our people ever indulged.'

Doing *Our Land and Land Policy* had taken the author back to first principles, and it had also taken him far into his future of reasoning, preaching, and reforming. Yet a caveat is required: the little book is not, as some have thought, *Progress and Poverty* in miniature; it is the great book in embryo only if the figure of speech allows for change in embryonic growth. The crucial difference is that in 1871 Henry George affirmed the homestead policy as about adequate for implementing American principles of equality. He did separate himself from the 160-acre tradition: 80 or 40 acres now seemed to him a better norm, more naturally what an owner-farmer could cultivate; and, Westerner that he was, he knew that homesteading did not work for cattle and sheep raising.[4] But the exceptions prove adherence to the homestead rule; and, though George threatened non-conforming theory on one page — saying that there is 'in nature no such thing as fee simple in land' — he said on the next page that 'it is also true that the recognition of private ownership in land is necessary to its proper use — is, in fact, a condition of civilisation.'

Differing from most land reformers, George was already pre-pared — though the 'single-tax,' properly so called, lay sixteen years in the future — to cope with the owners of land already monop-olized. In *Our Land and Land Policy* he first built into extended argument the lesson of history discussed in San Francisco's *pueblo*-land controversy: that the modern world should take from the Middle Ages the practice of fixing the cost of government on charges made on landholders. And in this connection, in a three-page pas-sage, George began his career-long effort to demonstrate — what he now took from Mill's *Principles* [5] — that a tax on land is the most collectable and the most fair of any tax ever devised.

For immediate action at federal level, *Our Land and Land Policy* recommended that grants from the domain be restricted to farms for proprietor-settlers, according to the terms of his judgment. He thought that railroad lands not yet fully transferred could be re-captured for the public. And, broadening his assault on the col-

---

[4] Let the cattlemen and sheepmen have access to the domain as a public com-mons, he recommended, a sound idea, we now know, if backed up with due pay-ments and restrictions against overgrazing. See *Our Land and Land Policy*, 99, 100.

[5] George's increased facility with economic ideas in this pamphlet might suggest a recent large amount of reading. But in a letter to David Ames Wells, 26 October 1871 (Wells Collection, LC), he said that he followed Mill in dis-cussing the land tax. And signs in the text of *Our Land and Land Policy* that his reading did not yet extend much farther are confirmed in a note by his son (*Complete Works*, VIII, 82).

lege grants, he assured his readers that 'the earnings of a self-employ-ing, independent people, upon which the state may at any time draw, contribute the best school fund.'

At state level, *Our Land and Land Policy* proposed cutting down the protection California's 'possessory laws' gave large holdings of dubious title. As before, he urged that the great aggregations be assessed to full value, the same as small. Admitting that these meas-ures would not suffice for his purposes, he declared for an amend-ment to the state constitution; and, as an immediate step, he called for enacting a very high inheritance tax. To protect the weak, he incorporated his proposition that a minimum exemption from land taxes be allowed every holder.

Refocusing in conclusion, George sketched again the narrowing lines with which he had diagramed the domain in the West and placed them on a larger canvas. According to up-to-the-minute statistics, conditions in the industrial East, especially Massachusetts and New York, looked ominous for working men. So too, Great Britain; and, in France there were the rumblings of revolution. Movingly he cited a famous text for pessimism, one that became a favorite with him. This was the historian Macaulay's denial of the opinion of that greater historian, Gibbon, that modern civilization would never go down. As Henry George phrased it, the world's danger had returned to just where Rome had known it, 'in the very heart of our great cities,' where 'poverty and ignorance might pro-duce a race of Huns fiercer than any who followed Attila, and of Vandals more destructive than those led by Genseric.' To the Cal-ifornia writer this forecast for the twentieth century was a picture beside which his own utopia — a free, developing, egalitarian econ-omy, its settlements not constricted or misshapen, its people con-fident — offered a vision infinitely luminous.

Read as a whole, the famous criticism of land policy and the little-noticed passages of theory and reform, George's pamphlet re-veals previously unrealized capacities for gathering and systema-tizing information, and like capacity for setting into pattern his proposals and reasons for economic and social change. It displays also the overwhelming contemporaneousness of the author's mental operations. He had the strength, at this stage, of being up to date; he may possibly have fortified himself from articles of 1871 by the Treasury official, E. T. Peters, some of whose statistics he certainly borrowed from official sources. He had a corresponding weakness: the author who knew so little of Thomas Jefferson and Thomas Paine as to say that the founding fathers of the country had had no ideas like his own about land still had some reading to do to tighten his case.

Yet makers of history are not often writers of it, and George in *Our Land and Land Policy* was arriving as an original thinker. As a critic, as an editor and writer informed on public affairs, as an influence in the Democratic party, as a tractarian he had arrived.

VII

Trying Out Radical Ideas:

The San Francisco *Daily Evening Post*

1871−1874

1

IN THE amazing surges of energy which have always given a special character to California's economy, the decades of the 1860s and 1870s displayed sharper alternations of excitement and depression than often occur in regional growth. As the story of economic criticism has told us, the slowing down of expansion during and following the Civil War caused such a darkening of outlook, in contrast with the 'golden fifties,' as to cast gloom on the long-run prospects of the state.

But many newcomers to California soon showed that the anxieties of the Immigrant Union had occurred too late to be effective in stimulating immigration and an economic upturn. At the end of the '60s and in the early '70s, just as the propaganda began to flow, people came in numbers again, without benefit of the legislation the union had asked, and the state entered a period of flamboyant prosperity. It was not all gaudiness and superficiality. For about five years the diversifying process, which all the economic diagnosticians agreed was necessary, accelerated promisingly: grain production increased, and so did meat raising and vine and fruit culture. Then this was the time of the incredible accumulations and expenditures of the bonanza kings of the Comstock, and of the 'big four' of the Central Pacific, Stanford, Huntington, Hopkins, and Crocker.

With profits flowing into San Francisco, Ralston and his Bank of California had their golden moment; the Palace Hotel was put up with its tier on tier of balconies, and the overstuffed houses were built on Nob Hill. For a breathing interval in 1873, California's boom seemed the brighter by contrast with the horizon of gloom, depression, and unemployment in the East.

Then, with a swifter impact on the state than any reverses of the preceding decade, bankruptcies in 1875 brought on new economic troubles with a vengeance. Hard times raised a cry for deep reform. The legislature did nothing that made a difference. Kearney spoke, and the famous sand-lot riots upset San Francisco as it had not been upset since 1856. Alarm crossed the line from fears for prosperity to fear for the security of the community. A convention was called at last in 1878, and a new constitution was written for the state. At this point the affairs of California became working men's politics as well as farmers', businessmen's, and lawyers' politics. The state is governed today by the instrument, amended time and again, which was drawn up and ratified in 1879.

Henry George's career, as constructive successful newspaperman from 1871 to 1875, and as toiling author of *Progress and Poverty* from 1875 to 1879, corresponds to the phases of California history, precisely. He started his San Francisco life of the 1870s, it will be recalled, with something in the kitty for a change — his share of the gold pieces for which the Sacramento *Reporter* was sold. How far those funds went, and just how otherwise he supported his family is not at all clear. More than likely the coffers of the Democratic party assisted. Not only did George write *The Subsidy Question and the Democratic Party;* he gave considerable time to party business and apparently wrote Governor Haight's Jeffersonian-minded platform for the 1871 campaign.

Indeed George was politician as well as political thinker and writer that year, and his hopes for state office rose higher than in 1869. In February a supporter urged him to be candidate for the secretaryship of state. 'If I run for anything it will be for Congress,' he countered in humor, 'but whether for the upper or lower house I have not decided.' In June he served as secretary for the Democratic state convention, which met in the assembly chamber in the capitol and passed resolutions according to his inclination; and then he did run for a seat in the state legislature. Henry George, Jr., has it, as we may well believe, that the Central Pacific went for the scalp of the man whose opposition to subsidies had not been quieted by purchase money. But until election night George thought he would win. Then, according to the same witness, who should have been in bed at the time, his father came home agitated. 'Why,' he told his family in loud voice, 'we haven't elected a constable.'

Meanwhile George did some magazine writing again. The February 1871 issue of the *Overland* carried the last story he ever wrote from the yarns of his voyages in the '50s. This one, 'How Jack Breeze Missed Being a Pasha,' was an innocent blend of humor and adventure, unlike his earlier stories without even a suspicion of religious or ethical implication. His other *Overland* piece of the year could not have been more different. Since the subject was 'Bribery in Elections,' and in the article George declared for the Australian ballot, which would become the third main reform of his career in reform, we shall need to return to his argument in the proper place. Here the article concerns us because it helped boil the pot, and also because it gives the defeated candidate's second and hot reaction to the state election. San Francisco had been bought, he charged, by a 'more shameless and more extensive' use of bribe money than at any time since the Vigilance Committee had cleansed San Francisco politics by fire; and now a more desperate situation could not be corrected by that 'most hazardous remedy.'

Henry George's situation in the fall of 1871 recalls 1868, before he went to Philadelphia and New York. Then he had broken with newspapers, the *Times* and the *Chronicle,* when their ideas did not please him and had found himself dangling without a proper job. Though he now belonged to the political camp he liked, the enemy had conquered, and for a few months he was at loose ends again. He had no office; he had no journal. Reminiscent too of the most unfortunate event of 1868, moreover, Annie George took ill again; and once more she and the children had to go to Philadelphia where they could have the support of a household of several women.

This time the symptoms suggested cardiac or circulatory difficulties, and most likely something of that kind had been at the bottom of her earlier troubles. Fortunately she did not suffer as much during this visit, and family adjustments were easier in Philadelphia. Mrs. George now exceeded all the others in affectionate attention to Annie; and the family, in a new house on Ninth Street, provided a lavish Christmas and many happinesses for the California members. Even so, Henry George received heartsick and homesick letters and had to live without those who comforted him, during many of the most strenuous months of his life in journalism. Had there been a John Russell Young or anyone else to offer him a job in the fall of 1871, or during a crucial interval early in 1872, Henry George would have had ample reason to go east for good, a decade earlier than he did.

Yet probably he would have decided to remain in California. For we may now understand as a factor in his attachment to the state a responsibility which had not had weight in 1868, and which would not again, in 1880. Call it western mission unfulfilled; and picture it in the obligation of the author's preachment in *Our Land and Land Policy,* especially the chapter on California lands. The reception of the book in California gives the clue to why Henry George preferred to continue in the state where he had discovered his ideas.

Some flattering responses, actually, had come to him from the East, on an intellectual not a political plane. Congressman Julian had skimmed *Our Land and Land Policy* and promised to do more: 'A glance has shown me how well and thoroughly your work has been done,' he wrote, and 'It is timely too.' Better than this was a letter from David A. Wells, who, since George had first known his writings as favorite material for the San Francisco *Times,* had shifted from a federal to a New York state commissionership, and was now getting out his famous reports as Commissioner for the Revision of the Revenue Laws of that state. 'You have enunciated a principle relative to value of land and pauperism which strikes me as original and well put,' Wells wrote; and this led to an exchange of letters in which George admitted that he had not studied taxation very much, but that he now regarded it 'as the most important function of government.'

Perhaps the most ingratiating response of all came from Mr. E. T. Peters, some of whose statistics George had incorporated into his own. Mr. Peters not only wrote in appreciation of *Our Land and Land Policy,* but also in his own writing, as George correctly said to Wells, took 'substantially the same ground in regard to the essentially appropriative nature of land values.' And so it was, in general, with all the response of eastern appreciators of *Our Land*

and Land Policy: they gave him the strength of knowing that, as he tried to apply to land policy the logic of liberal economic thought, he did not march alone.

Only from Chicago, east of the Sierras, came the least suggestion that *Our Land and Land Policy* might have an immediate effect on affairs. Horace White of the *Tribune* — the full control of that paper had not yet shifted to Joseph Medill and his brand of Republicanism — gave space to the booklet and promised more when Congress convened and 'the land jobbers begin their annual raid.' According to all other signs, though, away from home George's manifesto had fallen on unpolitical soil.

In California there was more to work on. Though *Our Land and Land Policy* represents a second failure if George still nourished such hopes as he had allowed himself about the Chinese letter, that his writing would catapult him into prominence in working men's Democratic politics, the book did get a broad newspaper reaction. Conspicuously not a single one of the larger papers challenged either the hard facts about California in chapter two or the general ideas of the whole. Even the *Bulletin* and its new associate, the *Call,* which the Simonton, Pickering, and Fitch partnership had recently bought, managed a few words of approval for George's 'patient research combined with knowledge of subjects treated.'

In both San Francisco and Sacramento, moreover, one strong paper went nearly all-out for *Our Land and Land Policy.* The Democratic *Examiner,* which had recently hired George to do an article on Well's report on New York taxation, acknowledged that he had surpassed its own attacks on the 'greedy speculators.' The paper lavished space; it summarized with approval George's population argument; it recommended 'for earnest reflection' the theory of the chapter on 'Land and Labor'; and, though refusing assent to taxing land exclusively, it ventured so far as to say that 'Mr. George supports his [tax] proposition in the strongest manner and places it in a light which is both novel and attractive.' In Sacramento, McClatchy's independent Republican *Bee* urged all its readers to study *Our Land and Land Policy,* and especially all members of the legislature. The *Bee* believed that George had illuminated 'the leading question of the day — the one which is absorbing all others — and which must remain the leading question until the people in their wisdom have settled it wisely.' Less enthusiastically, but in a friendly way, the Sacramento *Union* went with George; it quoted long passages and agreed that little prospect remained for the homestead farm in California.

Thus newspaper recognition would seem to have compensated for political defeat, for Henry George in 1871. More than that, there occurred at year's end in Sacramento a remarkable harmony of assertion that the land problem, about as George envisaged it, was becoming a focal problem in state affairs. In his final message to the legislature, Governor Haight renewed a charge he had made in his first message: 'Our land system seems to be mainly framed to facilitate the acquisition of large bodies of land by capitalists or corporations, either as donations or at nominal prices.' And Governor Booth's inaugural, three days later, might almost have been written by Henry George himself.

Tackling California's tax problem, the Republican governor observed that 'Among taxpayers the proportion paid by each is in reverse ratio to his ability' — the wealthiest paying the least percentage on the value of their property. Then came the governor's *Plan of Taxation Suggested* — the tax suggested was one on land values. 'If land values (including, of course, village, city, and country) alone were taxed, the revenue of the state would be in the nature of a reserved rent, stipulated for at every transfer, and modifying the consideration at every sale.' Such a tax would cut down speculation, and lands would be more generally cultivated by farmer-owners, the governor said; and, *if* the proper kind of law had only been passed early in the state's history, it would have eliminated the need for other taxes. To be sure the governor admitted no debt to *Our Land and Land Policy* while he hypothesized so boldly; and he spoke to the legislators from behind a very conditional 'if' — for he did not now ask for action so upsetting to private property. Still and again, a joint committee of the legislature soon took the exact position George had taken on the educational land grants; and it also asserted in formal statement that 'the earth which was fixed by irrevocable decree as man's abiding-place was designed as the rightful heritage of the many, not as the privileged allotment of the few.' Though George and his party had been trounced in an election, there was nothing out of date about the author of *Our Land and Land Policy,* in California in 1871.

2

Such a chance as he had dreamed of came at last, late in the year, at the time of the change of administration in Sacramento. More accurately, Henry George made his own chance. A printer friend, William M. Hinton, who admired *Our Land and Land Policy,* asked why he did not launch a San Francisco paper of his own. With enterprise and spirit the venture would win. Though Mr. Hinton did have capital to invest, he spoke disinterestedly: he said later that he had advised his friend as one who needed a job; he had had no thought of becoming involved in any way himself. Yet as George's enthusiasm took over and arrangements shaped up, he did agree to come in as the partner in charge of the printing; and a business associate, Mr. A. H. Rapp, came with him as business manager and equal partner. Together the three men raised something like $1800 in risk capital. They named the paper the San Francisco *Daily Evening Post* — brave echo of William Cullen Bryant, a continent's span away — and started publication on 4 December 1871.

While, pending examination of the editorial page, we must reserve judgment about the appropriateness and rightness of the *Post* in its time and place, we may notice at the outset that, at least as a business venture, the newspaper conformed well with California habits. Certainly nothing else in the economic history of Henry George compares with it. The *Standard,* of fifteen years later, also his personal journal, was to be a weekly, the organ of a reform movement, sustained by that movement. The San Francisco *Post had* to make money! As a printers' paper it meant a living or not for the principal, and perhaps for his partners; and as a commercial venture it meant a chance taken toward capital accumulation and power.

The risks were great; the entrepreneurial spirit ran high. If Henry George had not had sufficient personal experience to warn him, he could have read in the *Call* the business hazards of new journalism. Five years earlier this successful *parvenu,* now the *Post*'s competitor, had estimated the situation: San Francisco's voting population of 15,000 meant that a circulation of 12,000 was maximum and 7000 good. The *Call* believed that a paper would survive with 7000 purchasers, but that if it preferred a policy of low rates — the *Call* itself charged a bit a week, as against the *Alta*'s then four bits and the *Bulletin*'s three — it would be obliged to depend heavily on advertising. From $2000 to $3000 a week were required for normal operating turn-over. This estimate appeared while George was working for the San Francisco *Times,* and in the interval the *Call,* though persisting in its low-price policy, had ominously sold out to the big enterprisers of the *Bulletin* and the Associated Press. Now the same paper brought newspaper economics up to date. To be sure, it pointed out, though California stood twenty-fourth state in population, it was near the top in newspaper publishing; it was producing 129 weeklies, and its 49 dailies were surpassed only by those of New York and Pennsylvania. But except for the San Francisco and Sacramento papers, California's dailies were all either small-town or small-time journals; and the larger papers in the larger towns operated in tightening combination and competition. Fitch of the *Bulletin* currently estimated that the *Alta California* and the Sacramento *Union* were barely getting along with circulations of from 6000 to 10,000. Probably George knew in 1871, as he did later, that the Simonton-Pickering-Fitch combination had paid $125,000 for the *Call*—a symbol of the stakes and the toughness of the battle.

Like the San Francisco *Herald,* then, and the *Call* when it was new, and like the eighteenth-century Pennsylvania *Gazette* in the hands of Henry George's favorite character in home-state history, the *Post* began as a long shot in personal journalism. The first innovation offered by George, Hinton, and Rapp was an eye-catcher: the *Post* hit the streets as a penny paper, the first on the Pacific coast. Of course the symbolism was right and was so intended. One-cent journalism had begun in Jackson's day in the East: news and ideas for the working man at the lowest possible price. But in California, where the copper never circulated, sheer publicity-catching tells most of the story. Somehow the men of the *Post* persuaded the Bank of California to have and to release $1000 in pennies, timed right for 4 December. The first editorial page explained good reasons for welcoming the penny to San Francisco: it would accelerate petty business, such as the selling of fruit in the streets. Meanwhile purchasers of the *Post* had discovered that the newsboys were loaded to make change with the unfamiliar new coins.

For the bargain price, the partners offered a fairly good-looking paper, with all the essentials and some of the trimmings. The telegraphic news, American Press Association service, went in the middle of the front page; and the editorials began in the left column of that page and carried over into two columns of the second. On Saturdays a 'Labor Review of the Week' addressed itself to the main body of citizens the *Post* wanted to catch. For the first few weeks the sheet was pretty small, four pages, 10½ by 14 inches; and the print was tiny, though it was no harder to read than the print of the other San Francisco papers. Certainly the format of the *Post* represented the big improvement of a generation over the earliest penny papers. One of the neatest features was the front-page emblem: a seated female figure, center, bearing helmet and spear and representing the sovereign state; next to her, a California bear; and in the surrounding field appeared, left, mountains, flume, and cottage; and right, railroad and telegraph lines descending a mountain slope.

What were the chances of capturing California for the working man, or capturing the working man for a reform program in California? Henry George had too much honesty and too much mind not to have fears and doubts. Only the preceding summer he had privately expressed his deep anxieties, and his even deeper faith. To David A. Wells he admitted that his old-time 'habitual view of the nation' had turned into an outlook 'far less rose-colored than it once was': he was too appalled by the way in which the working classes were 'deluded with words and led by demagogues' to be very hopeful about their future. And yet, he said soberly, 'the earnest honest man,' the thinker like themselves 'who would do what he can in his day and generation,' had no real choice: he must sustain the effort for true democracy. Perhaps, George said to the learned economist, really questioning him, the time had come for 'a new political organization . . . I am quite certain that in some way co-operation between the liberal, free trade wing of the Republican party and the like wing of the Democratic party should be secured prior to the next election.' Through a union of liberals transcending parties, George now thought, the opportunity approached for 'the patriot, the true philanthropist, the true social reformers . . . to replace bad economic laws with good ones.' Though it was hard in California — 'I am on the outskirts, intellectual as well as geographical' — he pledged himself to make the effort.

As he spoke privately so he performed publicly in the columns of his newspaper. His pilot editorial in the first issue of the *Post*, on the 'Great Work of Reform,' demanded 'a union of the good men of both parties' and a four-point program for the nation. First, 'something like economy in government'; second, lower taxes; third, a reformed civil-service system; and fourth, a reverse of America's trend toward concentrating wealth and power, mainly in industrial and landholding monopolies. George made a class-conscious argument and a region-conscious one: colossal fortunes were being made while 'the masses were growing poorer'; and California was being exploited by a 'steady drain of federal taxes.'

But he nationalized rather than localized his argument; and he never talked down to working-men readers. Nor did he sustain party shibboleths. While he announced that 'in the higher, wider sense of the term we are Democrats, and the *Post* will be Democratic,' he insisted that for 1872 at least, while Reconstruction conditions persisted, the Democrats were fated to lose, and that they should not try a separate ticket. They had everything to gain by joining with liberal and free-trade Republicans. So, eleven months before the election, early enough to be noticeable in the Liberal Republican campaign, George went all-out for a fusion. Win or lose, the campaign would create a greatly needed new party, he believed, an assurance for the future of the Republic.

Although, as we shall need to understand later in some detail, George never abandoned thinking and writing about California's economic problems and their remedy, his editorial focus of 1872 remained where the pilot editorial had put it, on the coming election. On 27 December, when the *Post* was less than a month old it noted with satisfaction that a political convention of organized labor was about to gather in Columbus; and the editor was pleased to predict that George W. Julian would be nominated. Mr. Julian had identified himself with 'the popular side of the greatest of all questions — the land question,' and the paper believed that a fight between him and President Grant 'would be a square fight between labor and capital, and that is the real issue today in the United States.' But the hope for Julian soon proved premature. In voicing it, George may have been too much impressed by the political possibilities of the National Labor Union, which, though it had recently succeeded in setting up new locals in California, was already fading in the national scene. At any rate the *Post* went with the current in looking for a different leader for the proposed fusion movement. For an interval Lincoln's old associate, Judge David Davis, seemed likely; then Horace Greeley. In March the *Post* hailed Greeley's declaration for the fusion as right, and it saluted Greeley himself, one of the principal founders of the Republican party and stalwart egalitarian friend of labor for three decades, as the best man for the nomination for president.

Henry George, the editor and proprietor, who now threw himself as he did his newspaper into the campaign, did so as a man of some power and influence, more than he had ever been before. His paper had already proved solid and strong. In less than its first month it had had to increase in size to allow for the amount of advertising 'now crowding upon us'; and in less than two months it had ventured an occasional eight-page edition. Very soon it made the double-size issue a regular Saturday event. Perhaps success derived from the one-cent policy. The *Post* believed both that it had confirmed what had already been proved for the East, namely, that low price and mass appeal brought in the advertising, and that it could assert 'without egotism' that no other penny paper anywhere had ever carried so much news, or featured such attractive presswork, or depended so little on reprinted material.

The clinching evidence of success followed quickly on a surprise notice, 13 April 1872, when the *Post* was five months old: 'My editorial connection with the *Post* ceases with this issue.' A reshuffle occurred, evidently for the reason that Mr. Rapp, the business manager, wanted to get out. Whether for the sake of quick profits or for other cause, he sold his interest to H. W. Thompson, possibly a creditor of the *Post,* for $2500. Then, according to George's reminiscence of a quarter-century later, 'Mr. Hinton and I concluded that we had better withdraw, and we sold our interests, each getting $2700.' So far, so good. If remembered figures are correct, an $1800 investment had sold for $7900. Even Annie George in Philadelphia, who was distressed about the loss of the

paper and who hoped that her husband might return in a new
partnership to control the editorial page, saw the point of collecting the gain of capital value. It would be nice to furnish a house
without running into debt, she wrote to Henry.

Nor were wifely hopes too high. The *Post* dwindled under
Thompson. Two months after selling, George and Hinton were
given an opportunity to buy back the newspaper at a bargain price.
They took a new third partner, this one on less than equal terms;
and they started again, as they announced on 10 June, happily
convinced that the control of the paper was theirs for as long as
they pleased, and that they could make it succeed in every sense.
The lucky timing of events on the *Post* worked out as neatly as
could be: George took the saddle again just at the moment
when the national-party conventions were becoming immediate
business.

The local Democrats improved the coincidence. Along with ex-
mayor McCoppin, Henry George was chosen a delegate from the
fourth district to the national convention in Baltimore. He traveled
by way of Philadelphia, where he picked up his wife and took her
along. At the convention he became secretary of the California
delegation, and had the satisfaction of casting an editor's vote for
the doughty editor whom the *Post* was saying stood for 'the spirit of
peace' against the 'spirit of war.' And, after the convention and a
trip with his delegation to New York to visit Horace Greeley at his
home, George felt even more satisfied. Every Californian present
had sensed, he told *Post* readers, 'that in this sturdy, benignant
old man we had a candidate round whom we could all rally, and
who fittingly represented the grandest idea of the time — the idea
of reconciliation.'

Restored to his editorial chair, during the summer and fall
George made sage economic comments in the *Post*. That 'the
South has been made the Ireland of America' was one of them.
But the political spirit — which brought him to forecast at mid-
July that Greeley would win, 225 electoral votes to 129 — led
him to repeated extravagances. Though he admitted privately to
Whitelaw Reid that the Liberal party in California was 'utterly
impecunious' and apathetic and 'cut up by our local quarrels,'
and was ineffective by contrast with the energy and bribe money of
the Grant forces, the *Post* put no doubts into print earlier than

October, when defeats in certain state elections required open
pessimism. Then, when the killing 'rout — utter irretrievable'
occurred at the general election and Grant was returned to office,
an editorial soberly questioned whether or not American democracy could ever succeed, given the limits set by the narrowness and
prejudices of party-bound voting.

Within a month, having rendered its tribute to Greeley as martyr,
the *Post* came up with a revision. Not a fusion of elements from the
Civil War and postwar parties but a return to the old parties of the
Jackson period should be tried, to renew the life of politics. The
Whigs and Democrats had once faithfully fought the perennial
issues between capitalistic nationalism and radical democracy; now
let the battle be resumed and be won again, by the right side. Thus
Henry George was ready to be a Democrat once more, so far as
national affairs were concerned, a Democrat and nothing else. This
was the first stage of a new political wisdom which he would distill
in the columns of the *Post* during the middle years of his editorship.

-3-

George's important advance during the early 1870s, as an original
thinker on California affairs and on political and economic affairs
generally, will be better understood if we first take time to notice
his continuing success as a businessman in journalism. During the
election year, and in 1873 and 1874, his first hopes and successes on
the *Post* were more than consolidated. Now that the paper's name
and character was established, it could afford to change from the
one-cent policy. George and his partners put up the price twice
during 1872: at mid-summer to two cents, in October to five, the
second rise 'more to accommodate the price to the currency than
for the sake of the addition.' At the beginning of 1873 the regular
subscription rate was fixed where it stayed, at fifteen cents a week
or five dollars a year. This left the *Post* still the cheapest paper on
the coast, and the owners justified the increase by enlarging content more than in proportion, and by improving and extending
delivery service in the city and in the interior of the state. At the
end of its first year, the paper claimed that it had the largest evening
circulation west of Chicago, and that its 'career so far has been one
of unexampled prosperity.'

With newspapers, as with gold mines, increasing production called for larger outlays and heavier capitalization, and Henry George accepted the necessity with a true Californian alacrity. Six weeks before election he wrote Whitelaw Reid, Young's successor on the *Tribune,* that he wanted more telegraphic news exclusive for the *Post:* 'We have very frequently to counteract the Administration tendencies of Simonton's news and keep up the spirit of the Greeley people by drawing on our own private wire which we keep coiled up in a box.' This overture failed, though without injuring his improved relations with Greeley's paper; and it was only one of several efforts, many of them successful, which George made to expand the scope of the newspaper.

During 1873 the *Post* sped up production by contracting for the afternoon use of the *Chronicle*'s new 'lightning press,' a piece of machinery which would print 30,000 papers as quickly as the old press would 12,000. Before the *Post*'s second birthday, a fifth enlargement increased the size to 17½ by 25 inches. The regular edition now contained four pages of eight very long columns; and, for one of its eight-page issues, the *Post* claimed to have produced the largest daily ever printed in California and, it believed, except for a few issues of the New York *Herald,* the largest ever anywhere in the United States. By the time the paper reached full size it maintained many regular departments: Telegraphic, Police Court, Amusements, Stocks, Mining Notices, Commercial and Financial, and so on. Perhaps the *Post* was a little on the sensational side, as the editor's mother thought, bracketing in that respect with the *Chronicle,* and differing from the *Alta California* and the *Bulletin;* but by twentieth-century standards it seems quite sober. About half the space was taken by advertising.

We have to take from where we can find them the facts about how Henry George in his middle thirties carried the roles of editor and proprietor, and tribune of the people. His last office on the *Post* was a small room piled high with papers, magazines, and *Congressional Records,* and untidy with cigar ashes; he had a baize-covered sofa there, where he slept nights when he could not get away, or caught a cat nap as needed. He made a lively boss, and an interesting one. The male secretary who took his dictation recalls that, temperamentally high-strung, George drove himself incessantly and could be sharp with his associates. But the remembered events speak most of little-disciplined work habits, amusing to behold, and good deeds and generous attitudes, which endeared him to those around him. His editorials arrived habitually late; his door was always open. On one occasion he rescued by a reach from his own balcony a sailor in *delirium tremens* who was hanging from an adjoining one; and another time he tickled his associates by taking a shot of whiskey to buck himself for a temperance address. The stimulant more than worked, and he delivered a speech on land taxation.

A good fellow among journalists, he was elected to the Bohemian Club, becoming not a charter member but a regular one as early as the second week or so of that famous society's life; and very soon he became a trustee. Here he had the association not only, notably, of fellow newspapermen from the journals he attacked, but also of men of future fame — Samuel Clemens, Ambrose Bierce, and the future senator and conservationist leader, Francis G. Newlands. It is pleasant to catch so earnest a man having fun under the motto, 'Weaving spiders come not here'; and to learn that he participated in the 'high jinks' and other foolery at the club's Russian River encampment.

Though the early San Francisco *Post* years were among George's hardest as husband and father, because Annie and the children stayed long in Philadelphia, we do find them all together at last in 1874, as happy as they ever were while the children were young and before George's greatest successes. They lived that year in the Mission District; and George rode to and from work on a bony horse which cost him many jokes and jibes. For him it was a time of pride in the three youngsters: especially in Richard, the child of the poverty of 1865, who now began to anticipate his future as artist and wished to send pictures home to his grandparents in Philadelphia. The most inward peep into family life comes from Annie George's letter to her father-in-law about the celebration of her thirty-first birthday. Her husband and his partner had given her a square grand piano — 'This is from the office, as neither can afford to pay cash for it' — and she had also been given a biographical dictionary, a set of old English poets, a silver pie knife, a gold thimble, a box of candy, and an exquisite bouquet. Safe to say that never before in her life had Annie George had a birthday like that one. Had her husband been asked to explain how so lavish, doubtless he would have said privately what he had said publicly in his issue of 22 October 1873 about the ingredients of the success of the *Post:* it was 'certainly not due to capital, nor yet so much to ability, enterprise, or application, as to the popular appreciation of our desire to deal honestly and justly. If we have struck hard, it has always been on the side of the poor, the wronged, and the oppressed.' Very much like the famous muckrakers in the national magazines of about 1900, who were in a degree his spiritual successors, George made money fighting the good fight.

Crusading spelled success; and success stimulated the brainwork of the crusader. Of George's whole life, the years on the *Post* were the time when his mind ranged the most freely, when he made his decisions and developed his ideas the most independently and pragmatically. His strategy cannot be called simple. Rather than just reasoning forward along lines laid down during his march with the Haight administration, and diagramed in *The Subsidy Question* and *Our Land and Land Policy,* George turned certain sharp corners, as we shall see in the next section of this chapter, and he penetrated new terrain of general economic ideas. But short of these major changes, as liberal editor he advanced also his modes of political thinking, and notably developed a number of policy convictions, as he discussed issues current in the state and in the city.

To his own surprise, the new administration of Republican Governor Booth pleased him, even while his disillusionment about liberal fusionism was still sharp after the Greeley fiasco of 1872. George noticed and praised in the *Post,* for instance, Booth's inaugural address, the plea for taxes on land values which was quoted at the opening of this chapter; and he praised the governor as a man evidently far less committed to the Central Pacific than had seemed likely. These judgments placed George exactly beside James McClatchy, as that editor declared the policy of the independent Republican Sacramento *Bee.* They put him in the position of being less a man of state-party Democratic loyalties — at the very moment of becoming more a man of national-party ones — than he had been since returning to his father's political party. Perhaps the new governor's winning support from Democrats as well as Republicans may be seen as an early illustration of California's present-day special habit of segregating state politics from national-party patterns.

Certainly cross-party reformism was the political method Henry George now made his own, in state affairs. Late in 1873, though he had recently criticized the governor for failing to live up to his inaugural address, he supported Booth when the legislature chose him for the United States Senate, 'as coming nearer to being senator by common consent' than any Californian had ever been. The editor likewise approved and criticized as he pleased the new 'Dolly Vardens' in California politics, the independent Republican followers of Booth who won control of the assembly in 1873. With like freedom, as occasions arose, George supported the intrusion of Grangers in state politics, yet sometimes criticized them sharply; and again, he backed independent fighters of land monopoly, notably John W. Days and Pascal Coggins. We may look far forward to Henry George's own candidacies to be mayor of New York, the most heterodox of all such candidacies in American history, and discover him still true to the conception of local politics which he phrased first as editor of the San Francisco Post. 'Let the people who desire reform vote independently of all parties,' he said on 3 June 1875. 'Where the office is mainly an administrative one, let them vote for the best man. Where the office is a political one, let them vote for the men who are pledged to cut down the number of offices and undue expenditures.' George's permanent conviction, in short, was that parties are instruments. At national level they generalize the broader differences which voters need to distinguish at the biennial and quadrennial elections. At lower level, however, grass-roots reformism, remaking parties by introducing new men and reintroducing right principles, is the essence of party growth and political life.

On the side of economics, regional and other, George withdrew after 1872 from some of the old insistences of his days on the *Times*, the *Transcript*, and the *Reporter*. He gave the figures, and rejoiced, along with his old opponents in the debate on immigration policy, when trainloads and shiploads of newcomers poured into California. Though one-sixth to one-fourth of the immigrants, according to the *Post* of 11 October 1873, were Chinese (and the editor never changed his mind on that subject), he did not voice so much alarm about any phase of immigration as he had put into the Oakland and Sacramento papers.

He even softened his comment on the railroad monopoly. True, Stanford and his associates had by now consolidated and expanded their control of California transport, and the *Post* said so bluntly. Their monopoly was *fait accompli,* and the paper acknowledged that the state should 'be thankful that [Stanford] is not a worse man.' The transcontinental railroads were still leasing their wires to the American Press Association, on which the *Post* depended; and a brief editorial gave 'the devil his due.' Following a declaration by Stanford that the Central Pacific had broken pre-existing monopolies, the *Post* of 13 September 1873 admitted that the old steamship lines to Panama had been 'meaner and more oppressive, though smaller, monopolies' and that four years after the railroad had been put through the state flourished better than when it had been robbed by them and by Wells Fargo and the California Stage Company — 'It is the difference between one despot and a host of tyrants.' George's attitude toward Stanford in the *Post* probably echoes impressions he got in Sacramento in 1862 and 1863, and it conforms also with his lifelong habit of critical admiration for constructive capitalists. He had now arrived as a capitalist himself. He had been guilty of an election-year inconsistency in 1872, when he said that capital and labor are inevitably at war with each other.

So far as concerned industry or business, not landholding, Henry George's anti-monopolism concentrated now on the objections to consolidating too much power in the hands of too few people, and most of all on the evils of absentee ownership and control. Be it remembered that his reading clientele was largely Irish. When the question came up of Vanderbilt control possibly extending to the West coast railroads, George preferred Stanford; and when there arose a likelihood that capitalists of St. Louis and San Francisco (this group under the lead of Caspar Hopkins, of the Immigrant Union) would combine to put through the Atlantic and Pacific railroad to compete with the Union Pacific and Central Pacific, the *Post* balanced judgment. For a while it presented advantages that might be gained from this competition of roads; then it considered a second possible new road. But throughout it feared the debts and burdens of an unnecessary installation. The several San Francisco papers went their separate ways on this problem, the *Bulletin* being strong for Caspar Hopkins' A and P.

Without coming to clear-cut opinions on the immediate and practical problem, the *Post* took a turn at analyzing the more general and underlying issues of railroad economics and regulation. Accepting a lead from an *Atlantic Monthly* article, George endorsed the opinion that a cut in federal tariffs and taxes would do more to save the public's money than would rate regulating by states, Granger style. Then George renewed his earlier probing toward public ownership. 'Irresistibly' railroad monopolism was forcing the country 'on the horns of a dilemma,' he said, 'one of which we must choose — either the government must own the railroads, or the railroads must own the government.' But this dilemma he evidently envisaged as still at some distance in the future, and not yet clear-cut; at any rate he allowed himself editorial leeway to go afield again and reconsider his old Pennsylvania notion, of the government owning the roadbeds and private companies running the trains. He never became dogmatic in the *Post* about public versus private railroads.

Indeed George editorialized with force and determination in favor of the government ownership of only one public service — the one indicated to him by General William Orton in 1869. With wire communication he unquestionably had experience on which to draw,„ and recently he had had stunning good luck. Because his American Press Association had the use of the railroad wires, it had grown from Sacramento days to combine some interestingly opposite bedfellows. In addition to the *Post* and *Chronicle* in San Francisco, the *Alta California* had abandoned the AP and joined; and in Sacramento the *Record,* and then the *Record-Union* belonged when the railroad paper which succeeded George's *Reporter* combined with the old *Union*. This meant that half the big papers in the state, and some of the minor ones, associated and depended on the anti-monopoly press service, and needed the telegraph service, which George had been the first to make available.

Yet, although the *Post* lived and profited by this success, and occasionally took advantage of it by printing words of self-congratulation for having defeated the Western Union-Associated Press combination, and although, perhaps more than George knew, the American Press Association was cutting sharply the profits of the *Bulletin* and the *Call,* the paper's own situation was precarious. In spite of firm assertions that the telegraphic news came through freely and completely, there remained cause for embarrassment when the AP papers charged that Henry George, San Francisco's attacker of railroad subsidies and monopolies, was himself depending on a railroad monopoly and was receiving a subsidy — all this by the simple compromising fact of receiving news from the wires of the Central Pacific Railroad.

Under these circumstances, George declared strongly for public ownership. He was not alone, and the position he took is not at all to be thought of as indicating socialistic doctrines. In the second issue, and in one of the *Post*'s few editorials ever to praise Ulysses S. Grant, that of 5 December 1871, it commended the President for asking Congress to establish telegraph service within the operations of the United States Post Office. Then and thereafter the Henry George argument for a postal telegraph was simple and obvious: telegraphy indicates a national monopoly; the competitive duplication of wires is wasteful; government operation promises low and reasonable rates and assures access to the wires, without discrimination or favoritism, to any and all.

This policy of the *Post* was 'academic' only in the sense that the United States government did not change, or come near changing, the system of private telegraph communications. The issue represented actual and acute affairs in California, and it signified the *Post*'s participation in a nation-wide debate. When the *Alta* dropped out of the Associated Press group, the *Post* said that the senior paper had actually been pushed out, for the reason that its editorials favored a postal telegraph. Stanford's 'oppressions' grow dim, compared George, before the infamy of such an abuse to the freedom of the press. Though not feeling that nationalization could become a practical issue, the Sacramento *Bee* believed that there prevailed 'almost a unanimous public sentiment in favor of a Postal Telegraph'; and eastward across the country similar ideas appeared.

The *Post* took it as a body blow to nationalization, when David A. Wells wrote at length on the other side. Henry George's editorial reply to this recently sympathetic correspondent gives the pattern of his own lasting conviction, not about the telegraph alone but more generally about whatever monopolies are produced by industrial technology. According to the *Post:* 'The government should be restricted as nearly as possible to the preservation of order and the administration of justice, leaving everything else to private enterprise — in a word it should only do for the people what they cannot do for themselves . . . The progress of invention has created certain great and necessary businesses which are in their very nature monopolies, in which competition does not operate to secure good service at a fair price.' Besides a national postal telegraph, this editorial recommended the municipal distribution of water and gas; and, a little waveringly, as in other editorials, it spoke for the public ownership of railroads.

Henry George's comment, here, makes him one of the earliest observers in the United States to recognize the economic phenomenon of the natural monopoly.

-4-

The policy ideas so far presented from the history of the *Post,* mainly from 1872 and 1873 but some of them from later years, probably go far toward accounting for the success of the paper. Had the editor been willing and content to operate mainly in such directions, and had he not ventured into salients of his own, the *Post* might well have turned out to be for Henry George the way into a long San Francisco career in liberal journalism. With the sagacious and practical idealism he was displaying in matters of national and regional politics, such a career, which perhaps in the end would have had much in common with the careers of Horace Greeley and David A. Wells, would seem to have been a reasonable possibility.

But the moderate and sagacious side of Henry George was only half. And, as the *Post* up to the national election displayed mainly that side, so the *Post* in 1873 and after evoked the other side. This was the more individual and inspired Henry George, the man of the visions of 1869 and 1870, the man of ideas not yet fully comprehended and expressed, and the man of special intensity. This emergence — which now led George to assert the economic proposition of his lifetime — was bound to come. But its occurring when it did was a response to criticisms which hit him, first right and then left, during the election year.

Just a month after the *Post* had been started a new trade journal had been launched in San Francisco, *Green's Land Paper*. It was a weekly, published and edited by Will S. Green, former editor of the Colusa *Sun* and now the head of a real-estate company in the Pacific Bank Building. Mr. Green was that *rara avis*, a real-estate operator with ideas; and he made his paper every inch a defender of the kind of policy the Immigrant Union, and earlier the *Alta California*, had stood for. Particularly like the Union, he asserted belief in a small-farm economy, and he rejoiced at the arrival of German immigrants who wanted farms and had money to buy. 'Divide up your estates!' he urged his readers.

To editor Will Green as to Caspar Hopkins, land withholding represented an injury to California. But naturally Green defended the dealer and speculator in real estate: they were merely business-men doing useful jobs, and 'any talk about discriminating laws against [the speculators] is the sheerest nonsense — the most disgusting demagoguery.' In his first issue, Mr. Green acknowledged his number-one enemy in opinion making. Calling the *Post* the 'spiciest' paper ever to appear in California, he warned that the reforms it wanted would be unconstitutional under the instrument of 1849: the doctrines of equal taxation incorporated there would not permit of sliding tax rates on different sizes of holdings. Admitting that 'Harry George has both talent and industry,' Mr. Green promised to get after Harry sometimes on some of his 'Commune' notions.

To call a man a sympathizer with the 'Commune,' in the early 1870s, amounted to less than calling a man a communist eighty years later, but it was not a matter for Henry George to take lightly. Not unlikely the touch carried extra annoyance, because in actual fact George in recent issues of the *Post* had spoken favorably of giving the working men 'internationalists' a hearing.

His reply to Green shows the point charged against him: was not his paper actually propagandizing for the public ownership of land, while dishonestly pretending to believe in private ownership? The *Post* said on 2 January 1872 what George had said in *Our Land and Land Policy*, that private property in land must be understood and accepted as necessary, even though it cannot be called logical. This time, putting the crux of the matter in italics, George focused the paradox more sharply than in *Our Land and Land Policy*. '*That the land of a country rightfully belongs to all the people of that country; that there is no justification for private property in land except the general convenience and benefit; and that private rights in land should always be held subordinate to the general good.'* At a meeting held the next month under the auspices of the 'Internationalists' of San Francisco — which probably signifies a branch of the Marxist International Workingmen's Association — George in the opening address criticized strongly the principle of the nationalization of land and developed an argument that private property is necessary to have full production from the soil. Foretaste of much to come, he assailed 'Internationalist' ideology and commended rigorous land taxes as the best means to harmonize large private holdings with democratic rights and interests.

Interestingly, it was a friendly critic, well to the left of Will Green to be sure but not at all of the Marxist complexion, who drew George along the hard road of judgment and doctrine. Assemblyman John R. Days of Nevada County, a reader and admirer of *Our Land and Land Policy,* was distinguishing himself in 1872 by sponsoring measures of the kind Green opposed and called unconstitutional. Early in the year he introduced in Sacramento a bill 'to reserve all lands within the state belonging to the state of California for sale to actual settlers only.' He had proposed also what was, according to the *Post,* 'the best bill ever introduced in the legislature.' This one scheduled a graduated license tax on holders of vacant — unoccupied, uncultivated, unfenced — land; it was scaled from 25 cents an acre on small blocks of land, up to a dollar an acre on blocks of 5000 acres or more withheld. Such a law, once enforced, the *Post* said, would pay the debts of the state in a short time and would cause the population to double; especially would San Francisco gain from the stimulus to port activity.

Of course the Days bill closely resembled George's own earlier proposals, and George now gave a great deal of space and favor to the assemblyman and his ideas. The *Post* printed the news — and observed that no other paper did so — when the graduated license tax got 19 ayes to 46 nays on the question to engross. In Henry George's opinion this was encouragement and warning: 'Let the friends of land reform labor and wait. Who would have thought a few years ago slavery would now be a thing of the past?'

In May 1872, George met Mr. Days, and political affinity led to personal friendship. Mr. Days lent George books on English and Irish social discontent; and, before long, apparently late that summer, he persuaded George to give a Sunday-afternoon address before a San Francisco lyceum of which he was president.

George brought up the nagging problem that afternoon. He phrased his paradox negatively, though, and apologetically. At least according to Mr. Days's impression, he said that although the logic of men's equal rights to the gift of the Creator indicated that landed institutions should be different from present private hold-ing, not until the millennium destroyed 'the old savage, selfish instincts' in man would the common ownership of land come into being. But the chairman thought that the speaker was contradicting himself. In his closing remarks Mr. Days put it to the audience that 'every argument' George made showed that he ought to disbelieve in private property in land. The afternoon ended without a con-clusion of the matter. But Mr. Days's reminiscence closes with a debater's triumph and a friend's tribute: 'From that day to the day of his death Mr. George openly opposed by word as well as argu-ment private property in land.'

True, but not the whole significant truth about the author of *Progress and Poverty*. George never again spoke of private property in land as a necessity of civilization or agriculture; he never again assigned common property in land to the millennium, as some-thing not to be achieved in practice. Yet neither did he now speak dogmatically, or even loudly, about this radical doctrine. One searches the *Post* in vain for a clear-cut recognition of land na-tionalization as unreservedly right in principle, or as a practical alternative to private property, as John Stuart Mill was now begin-ning to preach, or as George himself was going to say in *Progress and Poverty*, half a decade later. Rather one finds oblique criticisms. For instance this *obiter dictum* in an editorial: 'A false treatment of land ownership is putting into the hands of one class the wealth that belongs to all.'

As for what the new belief fostered in the way of policy thinking, George pondered harder than before, and somewhat differently, the role of land taxation in economic reform. This problem is so special that it must be deferred a few pages, to the final section of this chapter. The new belief encompassed also a great effort, by the

Post, to expose the facts of California landholding, and a great interest in supporting land reform of the familiar, though in California unsuccessful, kinds.

Specifically, the newspaper always made a business of reporting, in almost 'believe it or not' spirit, spectacular cases of land engrossment. Typical was a report from the Chico *Enterprise,* of a Colusa County farmer who seeded his lands in fields of two thousand acres. When the *Post* picked up a case of land monopolization below Los Angeles, Henry George observed mildly enough that this was 'the style in which a great deal of farming is done . . . No land can ever be prosperous when the land is held and ruled this way.' There was nothing especially radical about this reporting; the *Post* carried such items both before and after the editor's 1872 increment of radicalism. But, on the editorial page certainly, there was an intensification of the policy of exposing engrossment and land withholding. For instance, in 1875 the eye that loved the Pennsylvania countryside noted that beautiful Marin County, on the peninsula north of San Francisco, though it 'ought to be covered with comfortable farms and dotted with thriving little villages, is condemned to semi-solitude by the curse of these large landed estates.'

As to policy specifically, George continued from *Our Land and Land Policy* his old habit of condemning the agricultural-college grants; and he named and smote with words the big speculators in federal scrip. As in the case of railroads, so with landholding he condemned the most vigorously the abuses of absentee ownership. On the other hand, he was not too single-minded to give the wiser speculators their due: for example, when Miller and Lux provided irrigation on certain lands and offered it for sale in small farms at reasonable prices, the *Post* had a word of praise.

Likewise when new legislation came up for review and comment, George was not restrained from speaking for measures that would increase homestead farming in the historic Jeffersonian pattern. During the first month of the *Post* George praised, as a measure that 'would be worth more in securing the liberties of the people and the perpetuity of our institutions than all the rest of the constitution,' the amendment to the United States Constitution wanted by California Congressman Coghlan: 'The public land of the United States shall not be disposed of except to actual settlers thereon, for homestead purposes only, and in quantities limited by general laws.' And during 1872 and after, when his mind was quite made up on the issue of principle, the *Post* spoke, as proposals came before the state legislature, for such reforms as limiting a holder's 'possessory rights' to 160 acres and requiring purchasers to pay cash for state lands. These were just such reforms as the Sacramento *Bee,* and even the *Union* and the *Bulletin,* were simultaneously advancing.

Had the homestead policy really worked, truly and broadly distributing the resources of the country among the people, without flagrant privilege, George would have had little excuse in America, outside the cities at any rate, to push the moral logic he believed in against the private ownership of land. By the signs he would not have tried to do so. But, in California more flagrantly than in any of the other domain states, the homestead policy was not working broadly or achieving the Jeffersonian results its philosophy contemplated; and fresh measures were not being taken to make it effective. The state and federal reforms George favored, in this pattern, remained bills and got nowhere; they were not enacted either into statutes or constitutional amendments. This being so, and George being George, the editor had every reason to ponder his own logic and observations, and to write as he pleased in favor of a different, more universal, program for equality of benefit from America's domain.

–5–

In 1888, when Henry George had become a world figure, a learned and friendly critic explained in the *Harvard Law Review* that the famous single-tax doctrine really comprised two ideas and that the two were separable. First, it contained the contention of egalitarian logic, that all men have a natural right of access to the gifts of the Creator's bounty. And second, the proposition, which the critic thought less well grounded and certainly separable, that economic rent was just the right flow of credit which ought to be captured, in this case by taxing land values, for the sole or principal financial support of the state, with generous welfare services included.

There is no reason to be forward and to try prematurely to match wits with a New York lawyer on the merits of the case for the single tax. But 1873 is the point in the Henry George story to notice that historically Mr. Clarke was correct: two different propositions — the proposition of principle and the proposition of operation — are joined in Henry George's reform proposal. And, though there had been signs of the affinity of the two in *Our Land and Land Policy* and earlier, they finally became linked on the pages of the San Francisco *Post*. George's decision against private property in land — because it involved the question: if private owners ought not to have economic rent, where should economic rent be directed? — practically forced the ideas into partnership. This means that, just as George could not, we cannot any longer postpone attention to the heavy business of taxation.

The years of the *Post* happened to be important years in state and national tax history. In 1872 and 1874 were published Wells's thoughtful New York state reports — pilot studies of local taxation for the country as a whole they proved to be. Then also, in California, as the learned monograph of Dr. William C. Fankhauser points out, part of the work of reform during the Haight administration had been the acts of 1868 and 1870 which required (what Governor Stanford, too, had recommended, years earlier) that the whole body of California law be revised and codified. The codifying commission reported in 1872; and the adoption of its report included a job of tax rewriting, the repeal of certain laws, and a bit of tax reform. This amounted to an inspection of the tax machinery set up since 1849, with a certain tightening of bolts and minor repairs, but not a new or even a rebuilt mechanism.

In those days, before the income tax had become anything more than a war-emergency measure, or else a threat of socialism, property taxes were the main source of revenue everywhere. They were levied on nearly everything. In California this meant not only real estate, land and buildings being treated alike, but also personal property; and personal property included both visible property in goods and capital equipment, and invisible property, such as mortgage notes — which multiplied the tax burden on real estate — and other commercial paper. A common rate was enacted by the legislature: it had risen to a high of $1.25 per $100 valuation in 1864 and had tapered under $1.00 in 1870 and 1871,

Besides the property taxes California had a poll tax and a congeries of license taxes — taxes on auctions, on gambling, on billiards, on foreign miners, and many others. An *Overland Monthly* writer in 1875, E. A. Waite estimated the charges of all taxes to average $40 per individual Californian, or $200 for each family of five. George told Wells that probably the California tax structure was more confused and wrong-headed even than the New York one.

From Dr. Fankhauser's record of condition and complaint, it is easy to judge, as George judged, that real-estate taxes involved the biggest stakes and the most sizeable abuses in the California system. The legislature's setting up a new state Board of Equalization, a fact-finding body intended to review and to help smooth out tax discrepancies from county to county, in a way confirms this opinion. But, not for George alone but for all who shared the thought that property in land always and everywhere carries special public responsibilities, there lay, over and beyond the questions of the quantity and the collection of land taxes, a political and moral question: did not the fundamental tax law of California specifically protect the land monopolizers in their engrossments, and specifically exempt them from public obligations?

This thought impinged on Section 13 of Article XI of the constitution of 1849, a clause that had been designed by southern members of the Monterey convention who were known to be plantation-class sympathizers. It was the clause on which Will Green relied to render void any such sliding-scale taxes, should they be enacted, as Assemblyman Days and Henry George proposed for California. The clause had a good and conventional sound, as follows: 'Taxation shall be equal and uniform throughout the state. All property in this state shall be taxed in proportion to its value,' and assessing and collecting officers shall be elected by the voters of the district in which the tax is collected.[1]

These provisions meant two very substantial barricades to protect property in land from being distributed. Land taxes must always be low, or at any rate no higher than the assembly would impose on any and every kind of property; and, second, the provision about

[1] Concerning the southern influence on the taxation provisions of the 1849 constitution, Senator William A. Gwin, former Mississippian and leader at the Monterey convention, said that delegates 'from settled portions of the State, who had great land grants and represented those who had vast grants of land from Spain and Mexico, would not listen to any proposition that would subject their real estate to taxation and the onus of supporting the state, while the great bulk of the population, the newcomers, had no real estate, in fact nothing that could be taxed, and nothing could be collected from them except a poll tax.' Gwin called the local election of tax officers a guaranty against oppressive taxation on large landholders. *Gwin Memoirs*, MS, 28–9, UCBL.

assessors and collectors prevented any officials unsympathetic to landholders, say from the mining districts or from the cities, from intruding into the agricultural or ranching areas of California's most valuable land aggregations. In actual operation, landed property was assessed at 88 per cent of cash value in the mining counties, and much lower on the coast, for example, at 15 per cent of cash value in San Mateo County on San Francisco peninsula. The *Post* was right when it said that California taxes were 'neither simple nor equal,' for the 'burden falls most heavily on those least able to sustain it — upon the borrowing classes and the laboring classes. It is true that under our present Constitution, or at least under our present Constitution as interpreted by the courts, it is impossible to make a good revenue system; but a much better one might have been made than the present.'

In this passage the *Second Report of the Commissioners to Revise the Laws for the Assessment and Collection of Taxes in the State of New York,* published in 1872, came through with incomparable support for tax reformers. Now George and George's kind had a firm point from which to depart, for writing new editorials and designing sharper programs. The New York commission reasoned from propositions like those of Adam Smith that any taxes anywhere should have the three qualities of being equal, or just, in, incidence; and 'certain,' or plain and aboveboard in operation; and economical to administer. It condemned forcefully personal-property taxes, and especially those on negotiable instruments of indebtedness. Wells and his colleagues favored instead, first, taxes on real estate, 'lands and buildings, at a full and fair market valuation'; second and third, they recommended corporation taxes and a building-occupancy tax. Their whole design favored simplification and reduction of structure. As if addressed to Article XI of the California constitution, the Wells report condemned, as 'one of the greatest obstacles which stands in the way of a reform of local taxation in the United States . . . the theory that in order to tax equitably and uniformly it is necessary to subject all property to assessment.'

Wells sent George a copy of the *Second Report* soon after its release. Though not accepting it whole hog — there was too much argument, to suit George, in favor of taxing capital improvements on land; and Wells opposed tax rates scaled according to ability to pay — George quickly absorbed the main ideas into his own arsenal. An early editorial note in the *Post* fired the report at the *Call*, because that paper favored taxing all kinds of property; and the *Post* praised Wells for distinguished service to the country.

In the New York report, economic reasoning based on the classical economists had slashed at American tax practices; and now an old hand at applying John Stuart Mill to California affairs was ready to follow suit. So, on 2 January 1873, in exact coincidence with the editor's finding his ideas against private property in land, the *Post* turned tax conscious and tax active, as had no Henry George paper before this. There should be *three taxes,* it announced, on the second day of the year: (1) a tax on the value of land, not counting improvements, above a minimum exemption; (2) a tax on the estates of deceased persons; and (3) license taxes on such businesses as require regulation, liquor and gambling houses for instance.

Like the New York report, the *Post* justified its proposals by exhibiting them alongside the classical canons of taxation. Its own simple, three-point program, it reasoned, would unburden both capital and labor from present charges and annoyances and make for much freer flow in the economy. Assessments on values that could not be hidden would be accurate and fair; and tax collecting would be rendered economical and easy. *Per contra,* George estimated a 'mob' of 100 to 150 'assessors' deputies, license collectors, fee and tax gatherers' in San Francisco alone, under the present system.

As George was to do for the rest of his life, and as the Wells report had just done, the *Post* speaking for reform made much of the question of the incidence of taxation. Who pays the collector, and who really pays the taxes? Doubtless the nature of this problem was not as universally apprehended in George's day as in ours. But nothing could be plainer than that the *Post's* second main tax proposal could not be passed on to others; and as now there was then a powerful argument that the paper's first proposal, land-value taxation, deprives the first payer and no one else. Beginning at once, and never changing his mind, George made and remade that argument — that economic rent regardless of tax policy always and everywhere flows automatically from producers to landholders, and to capture it from the owners is to take from them alone. When they pay, the credit has already reached its point of accumulation, and it cannot be demanded again from other members of the economy. So the Henry George line, which may be qualified a little but can hardly be upset.

The *Post*'s announcement of a three-point scheme started much, not quite all, the discussion an editor could have wanted. Among his neighbors in San Francisco, the *Examiner* and the *Chronicle* met him halfway. The Democratic paper understood the program as simple anti-monopoly; and the *Post* replied that, pleased as it would be to break monopoly, land-value taxation actually contemplated more: it would prevent the recurrence of monopoly once broken, and it would present the community with a generous and easily collected income. Perhaps the *Chronicle* was the first paper to object to the singleness of George's program. Why tax land without taxing capital, it demanded, making illustration of taxing the Central Pacific's strips of land without taxing its strips of steel and its rolling stock? Because, George replied, the idea is precisely not to burden labor or to penalize capital accumulation. Over and over the *Post* reiterated that land values do not represent wealth in action, as capital values do, but represent the power to collect from someone else. Within the year, the paper was claiming that the *Chronicle* was half converted to its plan.

There was reminder of the past and there was unanticipated future, both, for Henry George in the objections now raised by the little Catholic journal in which he had first tried to be very philosophical about the land problem. The *Monitor* said that land-value taxation would make land a drug on the market. No, replied George on 26 February 1873: only speculative land would become a drug, and no need to object to that. Furthermore, the editorial added, the *Post*'s scheme contemplated an exemption of $500 for every city landholder, intended to favor the homestead-lot man and to encourage home building; and doubtless the *Post* had the *Monitor* in mind when it added, in another connection, that land-value taxation would not affect church buildings at all and would affect only a little the land on which they stood. Of course, though, the lands which San Francisco's Bishop Alemany held, in expectation of the city's growth, would not return him increments. For Irish readers, George had made a skillful and anti-hierarchical rejoinder — interesting preparation for New York City politics, and Archbishop Corrigan, in 1886 and 1887.

The debate that George's tax ideas might have stirred in San Francisco never quite came off, however, for the reason that the Fitch-Pickering papers brushed aside, rather than considered, the *Post*'s editorials. Not until the end of 1873, after considerable goading by George, did the *Call* get around to saying that the due-process clause of the Fourteenth Amendment would render unconstitutional any such scheme as George proposed — not a very responsible argument, and not a sound one, as we now know. Yet George did stir up sufficient San Francisco protest to get a first hearing on a question that was to bedevil him the rest of his days. This was the counter-proposition that to shift all taxes to land values would place extravagant and unjust burdens on farmers, to the advantage of city people.

When the *Chronicle* and *Examiner,* and later certain inland papers, raised that objection, the *Post* answered by running two lines of distinction, the first between the farmer who owns and operates land and improvements of the size a family can manage, and his neighbor, the speculator-owner of unimproved arable land; and the second, between the owners of rural land and the owners of city land. The working owner of a family-size farm, the *Post* told the Stockton *Independent,* might or might not be obliged, under land-value taxation, to pay more real-estate taxes than at present. If his farm was small, he would pay less, and certainly would do so if he was allowed the $1000 exemption which the *Post* now proposed. Even if his farm was large and well favored, and his tax was as high or higher than before, he would be free from taxes on his house and all improvements, and he would be encouraged to raise his income by purchasing more equipment and improving his techniques. And beyond all that he would live in the satisfaction of knowing that his neighbor of equal acres would share evenly with him the tax burden of the community, whether or not he had invested equally and worked as hard. Taxation according to *opportunity* to produce.

When the same delta-area journal protested that George's plan would do 'little to persuade men to seek homes in the unpeopled solitude,' the *Post* agreed, with a twist and a difference from the usual American complacence about going to the frontier. Men take their families into the solitude only when they cannot get lands that they can use and afford near their neighbors, and that will be available to the schools and churches which people everywhere want. When another paper objected that all farmers want more land, whether or not they cultivate it decently, the *Post* observed that land value taxation would change all that, to make living more compact. 'Settlement would be closer, cultivation would be better, the cost of transportation and exchange would be less, and the farmers and the state at large would be richer.'

While George's editorials were explaining to farmers the advantages of eliminating buildings and all improvements from the tax-collector's schedule, he was saying also that land-value taxation would fall more heavily, and make for more social and economic reconstruction, in the cities than in the country — in two ways. First, it would take away from the urbanite absentee owners of farmlands the rents they were accustomed to receive from the country. George believed that as many members of this class would yield ownership — that is, permit themselves to be expropriated — as would find it worth while to retain title for the sake of the return from whatever capital they might have put into improvements. Second, land-value taxation would capture for the public the economic rent of urban sites. To be sure the *Post* predicted little in the way of owners' yielding ownership here. Rather it foresaw proprietors' being compelled to use capital to build on vacant lots and to improve their buildings when sites increased in value: all in order to collect the surplus with which to pay the new tax, and at the same time have interest and profit on money invested and risked.

Here the prospect was painted rosy. The early gainers from land-value tax, the *Post* said, would be laboring men. There would be much new work for the building trades, and a general stimulation to industry and commerce. Figuring that an ordinary house lot cost more than the house built upon it — roughly $1000 to $1500 for the lot, $1000 to $1200 for the house (a radically different ratio, as well as different figures, from today) — George believed a building boom to be implicit in his plan for a tax-free home lot for every city family.

George invited his San Francisco readers to calculate for themselves. In 1873 a $2.00 rate on land, improvements, and personal property would raise the needed funds; so also would a $3.25 rate on land alone, exempting other forms of property. Which would the citizens prefer? Even at present assessments, and even disregarding the enlargement of a city's social services which should follow capturing for the community the full product of urban site rent, George believed that the answer of his San Francisco readers should be obvious.

In all this reasonableness, conceived as pro-labor and pro-capitalist both, Henry George did not lose sight of the fact, nor was he less than candid, that his plan would radically alter property relationships and change the structure of society. In an editorial of 8 November 1873, 'How To Tax the Rich,' he explained: Land values are the source of most of our greatest fortunes. 'With one or two exceptions, perhaps, there is hardly a rich man in San Francisco, or in California, who does not owe the largest part of his fortune to this source . . . The proposition to put all taxes on land is a proposition not to exempt the rich and tax the poor, but to exempt the poor and tax the rich.' Looking backward the *Post* remembered the *pueblo* lands — which could have provided free homesteads for two or three million people but had instead created a few millionaires — and said that land-value taxation could now correct that wrong. Pursuing this vein when the *Alta* observed that San Francisco like other cities would in the future have to expect chronic pauperism, the *Post* gave an explanation. Because, 'estimating roughly, it is certain that at least one-eighth, and probably one-sixth, of the aggregate earnings of San Francisco is paid in the various forms of rent to the owners of the land on which San Francisco is built,' some would always lack. 'As the city increases in population this proportion becomes greater and greater, as is shown in the increase of real-estate values.' George's mind's eye had already reached the point where progress and poverty seemed fated to dwell together, especially in modern cities, as long as property rights in land remained unreformed.

In San Francisco the unwillingness of some papers to give space to debate his program, the part-way acceptance of others, and the rejection of most were all reactions he might have expected, according to the record. But Sacramento, where George had always fared more comfortably, promised to be different. To be sure the three papers there were all Republican, not one of George's party; but two of them as we know had historic records against monopoly. As a current sign of Republican feeling, moreover, Governor Booth's biennial message, delivered at the close of 1873, had expressed again his anxieties about land and land policy. Though the governor specifically refused to recommend laws that would change much the institutions and usages of ownership, he urged the legislature that, 'It still remains true that a large portion of the lands of California are held "on speculation" for the advance in value, to the detriment of the growth and prosperity of the state, and in contravention of the "natural right of everyone born on the earth to so much of its soil as is necessary to his subsistence." ' In making these observations the governor referred to the recently created state Board of Equalization, as a moderate first step of reform already taken.

Of any element in Sacramento politics and opinion, the *Bee* was of course the nearest to the *Post*. There was no chance, though, that it would go all the way with the new George program, and George understood the reason perfectly. McClatchy, as an old member of the New York group of reformers, had given his mind permanently to the homestead principle. Unlike his earlier self, when he wrote *Our Land and Land Policy,* George no longer cared for the theory of limited-size holdings. 'Restriction would be useful to break up some of the large holdings of agricultural lands, until we can do better,' was the best he could say for that reform now. But even though the *Post*'s shift to a tax reform scheme might have offended McClatchy, and even though George pointed sharp comment directly against that paper, McClatchy gave the *Post* claps on the back and reprinted certain strong editorials. Picking up the argument that land-value taxation would accelerate immigration, the *Bee* said: 'That ought to be the law of every land, but more especially this one . . . [Land monopoly] is the curse, the blight, the dark cloud upon California.' In the same editorial, early in 1873, the *Bee* went with the *Post* in calling for the repeal of all license taxes except those on saloons, and abolishing all property taxes except on land, 'so that the soil shall pay the expense of government.'

As for the other Sacramento papers, the *Union* gave the *Post* a degree of satisfaction. 'The people are aroused,' was George's comment when the paper for which he had worked responded to his ideas with an editorial for a sliding scale of land-tax rates. On the other hand, the *Union* had recently condemned Henry George's idea of doing away with taxes on capital, particularly the railroad; and there was very little community of thought between the old and dying paper and the new one.

George's recent acknowledgment of virtue in Leland Stanford to the contrary, he must have been surprised as well as stimulated when the Central Pacific's Sacramento *Record*, once his own *Reporter*, came out, while discussion about land policy was heaviest, with a diagnosis and interpretation of the situation very much like his own. Under the general title, 'The Farms of California,' the railroad newspaper brought out fourteen heavily statistical articles between 27 October and 14 November 1873, which had been worked up from the tax figures of the state Board of Equalization. Each article surveyed landholding in three or four counties, forty-eight in all. Farms were classified according to size, average holdings were calculated for each classification, and the name of every holder of more than 500 acres was listed. Editorial comments along the way pointed up the more particular findings. Examples are: there was much land engrossment in Los Angeles County, but not as much in that area of Mexican grants as in some other places; Colusa County in the north, where the Bidwell estate was situated, and Kern County in the south, where 13 persons owned 487,908 acres, were the counties where aggregation created the highest-average holdings; and there was one holding — it must have been the Jacks estate, which had also caught Henry George's eye — of 334,100 acres in Monterey County. At mid-series the *Record* printed a table of recapitulation which was printed also by the *Union* and the *Bee,* and gave a round-number survey of the state as a whole.

Because these findings give much the best control point from which to view objectively the land situation in California, it is reproduced in part, below. This is done especially for the benefit of skeptical readers who may still think that Henry George was imagining things. The immediate source is the Sacramento *Record*, as that paper took the figures, accurately, from the official tax statistics of the Board of Equalization.

The Sacramento *Record*'s moral judgment of the whole situation, rendered on 26 October, sounds like Henry George: 'California

Number of Farms	Class by Acreage	Total Acres This Class
23,315	100–499	4,663,000
2,383	500–999	1,787,250
1,126	1,000–1,999	1,689,000
363	2,000–2,999	834,000
189	3,000–3,999	?
104	4,000–4,999	458,000
236	5,000–9,999	1,852,000
158	10,000–19,999	2,670,000
122	20,000 or over	8,782,000

stands today in the singular position of a state which was admitted into the Union on the express principle of opposition to slavery yet which has contrived to blunder into a line of action which could not have been better calculated to build up a slave state had it been the carefully matured plan of some far-seeing Southern politician.' Again like the *Post,* the railroad newspaper blamed land monopolization for the slow settlement of California: a 65,000 acre farm in Alameda County across the bay from San Francisco, it said, which actually supported 20 or 30 people, could well support 1000; the census found only 6165 inhabitants in Colusa County, where there could be 8000 farms and 100,000 people. Naturally Henry George called attention to the *Record*'s revelation. He took up again his old refrain, that land engrossment breeds slavery — no longer a monopolized idea.

At the point of recommending action, 5 November, the *Record* retained the role of broad investigator and judicious selector. It considered and dismissed the *Union*'s policy of a graduated land tax, for which that paper was probably indebted to John R. Days. It presented an adequate and accurate summary of the San Francisco *Post*'s plan. Finding that full-value land taxation would mean that 'the property aspect of land ought to be abolished' and something like leasehold title instituted, the *Record* rejected that plan also. 'Custom, prescription, and vested rights' all oppose it, the paper said, and furthermore there exists no 'natural right' to land — no man creates land of his own mind and effort. This fell far short of a sympathetic understanding of George's underlying ethics. Yet in the future we shall look in vain to discover an equally appreciative discussion of George among the great newspapers, and we shall certainly not find it in the conservative New York press during his days of mightiest influence.

The *Record*'s own proposal — which it called the one 'feasible plan' because no amendment to the constitution was required — began with a voluntary convention of all the principal landholders of the state. Let them agree on a scale of low prices, none to be higher than $5 an acre and preferably not higher than $2.50; and let them bind themselves to sell a given proportion of their lands at the low prices, say one-fourth, or one-half, or two-thirds of their total holdings. Then let the legislature set up a commission to dispose of the land in parcels. The landholders should be willing to act, the *Record* concluded, because nothing less than the filling up of the state waited their decision; prompt action would ease tensions and advance the interests of all Californians.

The fact that the railroad newspaper stepped ahead of the *Post* and did a journalistic 'first' by systematically exposing California land monopolism is rendered yet more piquant by that paper's political conclusions. It advised the forces of protest in the state to put the pressure on the monopolists. Yet the game is perfectly plain: it conforms with the *Record*'s opposition to the telegraph monopoly; and it represents the shrewd, not to say Machiavellian, public relations of a railroad which, having consolidated its own monopoly, was now trying at once to build protective political connections in the state and yet keep protest disinfected of much radicalism. The *Record*'s 'feasible plan' amounted, of course, to a renewal of Immigrant Union tactics, though with more bite than earlier, to put speculative land cheaply on the market. The Sacramento *Bee* was fair when it described the *Record*'s plan of a convention of landholders as a mechanism calculated to defend and perpetuate all the 'customs, prescriptions, and vested rights' of landholding. And the *Post* spoke the obvious truth about the *Record*, saying that the railroad had everything to gain from speeding up settlement in California.

The *Record* articles and the comment of the other papers, coming to a climax of discussion during the first week of November 1873, raised to the highest intensity of any time during Henry George's California years the public debate on land monopolism. Four solutions had been presented: in San Francisco the *Post*'s; in

Sacramento the *Union*'s and the *Record*'s, and also the *Bee*'s old policy of acreage limitation on the homestead principle. No one of the proposed reforms ever carried the day; California is today as it was in Henry George's day very much, though not completely, a state of excessively large landholdings, and of a farm-labor problem that has been widely recognized — most famously in John Steinbeck's *Grapes of Wrath* — as akin to slavery. But though the problem has persisted it has never been quite dismissed as unconquerable; and after the attack of 1873 some little headway was made in land reform. Though in February 1874 the *Post* bemoaned that not even such first and immediate steps were being taken as requiring assessors never to assess below government minimum price, it did acknowledge gains in process, when a bill came up to limit holdings of timberland and grazing land. It saw hope when the author of that bill, Assemblyman James Murphy of Del Norte County, was appointed chairman of a session committee on land.

As events developed, the report of that committee in the spring, at the close of the biennial session of 1873–4 — the last during George's career as a big newspaper editor in California — supplies one of the best indications we have of the reach, and the limits of the reach, of Henry George's ideas in the region where they were first proposed. In a passage of opening eloquence, which Henry George approved, the committee used words that might as well have been his own: 'Those who own the soil of any country make all others who live therein pay tribute for living in their native land.' The committee took perspectives on history which sound like the later Henry George: in the Old World landholders have always been men of power as well as of wealth; in the New World we have no right to think the situation very different. Except that primogeniture and entail have been abolished, American land law remains like Europe's; and America, California climaxing the development, has monopolies as great as the greatest in Western civilization. Here the committee took statistics from the Sacramento *Record*: one group of 2,325 Californians owned an average, each, of 7,265 acres, an estate four times that of the average British landlord, the assemblymen reported. Thus far, as for the premises of action, the committee and Henry George were of one mind.

For the plan of action, however, the committee followed the Sacramento *Bee*. As they were instructed, the committeemen con-

sidered the program of the *Union* and the program of the *Post;*
they had no reason to consider the *Record*'s plan, because it began
with voluntary, non-political action. But they were governed,
nevertheless, by the obstacles to graduated taxation and land-value
taxation argued by the *Record:* either plan demanded an amendment to the state constitution, and this meant at least a three-year
wait. So the report called for a homestead system to be brought
about by what was, in effect, a death duty. Present holders, it said,
should be undisturbed, but their inheritors should be required to
distribute whatever land might come to them in surplus over and
beyond a homestead-size estate, which they might retain. Four times
the 160-acre unit was suggested for timberland; eight times the
unit for grazing lands. The committee estimated that a quarter-
century of such a law would end monopoly. From all this the *Post*
took such comfort as it had taken from the preceding session, when
a sizable minority had voted for the Days land-licensing scheme.
Things would happen in the future, Henry George asserted; and he
urged readers to remember at the next election the questions
formulated but not solved in 1873 and 1874.

Besides being out front in the general direction of the legislature's
attention, the *Post* could and did claim that the governor thought
about as it did — his biennial message followed the *Record*'s report by only a month. And plainly Henry George enjoyed the association of ideas when the Colusa *Sun,* Will Green's old paper,
bracketed him with Governor Booth, the two as leaders in California of a group of political economists in the style of John Stuart
Mill. Being associated with Mill was as timely as it was flattering to
George. Early in 1873 he knew and reported to his readers when
the Englishman made a speech at the Land Tenure Reform Association to oppose 'the treatment of land as private property, like
things which are the product of labor.' This principle, observed
George, had inhered in British economic thought from Adam
Smith, but only recently had Mill drawn the full and formal deduction; the great economist was now on the right track, and so
was the English land reform movement in which he participated.

The sum and structure of George's writing on land institutions
and land taxation, his identifying himself and the *Post* with the
two connected but different reform-ideas — no private property in
principle, land-value taxation in practice — all amounted to a far

more deeply considered position in 1874 than in 1871, when he brought out *Our Land and Land Policy* and launched the *Post*. When the *Sun* made fun of his ethic that 'land belongs to him who will use it,' George reduced to the irreducible his new-found dogmas: 'The foundation of all property rights is the right of man to himself . . . The great principle for which we are contending is the right of the producer to the full fruits of his labor. But rent (for land, not improvements) is legalized robbery; to demand a price for unused land is legalized blackmail; and the land-grabber is a worse enemy of the state than the horse thief or footpad.'

The *Post* never quailed, late in 1874, when the Yreka *Union,* which belonged to Democratic State Senator William Irwin — who was to become governor the next year and was to do Henry George a great favor — said that the *Post's* tax scheme would lead to the public ownership of land. This time George admitted openly the equivalence of full land-value taxation with landholding by the state. Said the *Post:* 'We only propose taxation instead of state landlordism, because it is more consistent with the ideas and habits of our people, and could be more easily carried out.' Citing John Stuart Mill and Adam Smith to testify that a land tax cannot be shifted from the owner, and asserting as moral principle that the value of land 'belongs to the whole community' because the community creates that value, Henry George had now carried the *Post* as far in this direction of theory as he could possibly go. Once he even proposed practical state landlordism as the right solution for a particular abuse. When General Bidwell's 23,000-acre holding in Butte County appeared to be a fraud, George recommended that the United States, as reversionary owner, assign the estate to California, and then that the state rent the lands, the proceeds to go to the public schools.

The Oakland illumination he had now thought through, and the New York pledge he had rendered into concrete ideas and procedures. The refinement of radical ideas, and still more the task of adjusting them to other ideas — to philosophy and politics — were the more proper undertakings of a book than a newspaper. But he tried them first in the *Post*. Then more years at hard labor would be needed, as we shall see, before *Progress and Poverty* could be born.

VIII

Rounding Out an Editor's Thought:

The *Post*'s Utopia

1872–1875

DURING the '80s and the '90s, Henry George's decades of world recognition and wide influence, the author of *Progress and Poverty* was saluted sometimes as *the* American economist, the one man who better than any other summed up the condition and the spirit of his country. Sometimes also, too frequently for comfort, he was greeted with contempt. The Duke of Argyll tagged him the 'Prophet of San Francisco,' and writers in the British quarterlies and American professors of economics were the ones who habitually snubbed him. Of course George's ideas were the principal reason for their rejecting him. But in the eyes of such people, George's background and training, and his evangelical fervor, helped justify distaste and distrust. Why respect a man preaching the reconstruction of society whose school of economics had been California newspaper experience and little else?

The irreducible truth was, of course, that at no stage of his career did George achieve just the same reassuring kind of recognition as a professional economist may claim. He had no membership in the guilds of scholars — in the social-science associations which were formed in the '70s, or the professors' organizations in the '80s and '90s — the connections that give kudos and some security to men of learning. He had no university certificate or attachment. Nor did time and place fall right for him to be a member of one of those rare fraternities of mind which now and again join creative men into epoch-marking circles. Nothing was ever available to him like Franklin's Junto or the Transcendental Club of earlier generations, or the Metaphysical Club to which belonged his younger contemporaries in thought, the early pragmatists of Cambridge and Harvard, or like the Bloomsbury set which meant so much to John Maynard Keynes before the Second World War. The Bohemian Club was as near as Henry George of San Francisco could come to that kind of thing.

Yet the American newspaper has been a mighty institution of education and intellectual achievement, famously so for Philadelphians and New Yorkers — for the Franklins, the Careys, the Greeleys, the Danas, the Raymonds of American mind and leadership. The history of the development of Henry George's mind may be read fairly as a case in point. Between 1872 and 1875, especially, on the *Post*, his writing broadened and deepened and strengthened. We have already seen him as a student of government documents and of the leading journals; so likewise in a broader reading of the *Post* we discover a thinker taking sides on books and general ideas. Philosophy, in the sense of the main thought currents of his age, was not too weighty for him to tackle. So also economics, going beyond the range of California's immediate concerns; so politics, conceived as institutions as well as party conflicts; and so again the links of ideas which cross-connect the main chains of social thinking.

–2–

From the beginning, George had as an editor always coupled his critiques of land monopoly with the plea for free trade, the very first article of his personal economic faith. In his own *Post* he enlarged upon the free-trade idea exactly at the time when he was changing his opinion about private property in land. The staples of California, gold and wheat, naturally seek a world market, George said in editorials; and likewise the major imports, textiles and metal goods, were more economically purchased from British sources, specifically in the overseas markets of Australia and British Columbia. Why should Congress put up obstacles to this natural give-and-take?

The editor did not hesitate to drop from the general to the concrete, and to fight questions where local interests were concerned. He ridiculed the early orange growers of Los Angeles, who wanted a customs duty on foreign citrus fruit; he denied that a tariff would assist the new wineries of the upper state, and he had a heated exchange on the issue with a Petaluma newspaper. This was his attitude toward agricultural tariffs.

On the industrial side, he explained with satisfaction that the San Francisco *Post* was printed on California-made stock, which was manufactured with San Joaquin straw and Nevada soda, without benefit of tariff preferences. And, paying his disrespects to the elite of the city, he pronounced to be incomprehensible the attitude of the merchants of San Francisco who accepted the pro-tariff argument, when they should have been able to see that business would double if only the city were a free port. Henry George's argument was much the same, and just as good, as the case made by the free-traders of the cotton-producing South during the generation before the Civil War. Right national policy, he was saying, would allow a region — any region — to sell and buy in the markets of the world without paying tariff tribute to the manufacturers of the northeastern United States.

But George did not permit anti-tariff to be degraded to a purely regional level. The *Post* always presented free trade as a universally desirable policy, and as a cause with a meaning and a theoretical justification. By this time the studying editor understood that America's school of nationalistic economics — which Henry C. Carey had been maturing in book and newspaper writing for four decades — was his enemy set of ideas. And a *Post* review of an anti-tariff book by a Rochester journalist, Isaac Butts's *Protection and Free Trade,* shows that in addition to Wells's reports he knew at least a few books on his own side of the argument. In contrast to what he would think a decade later, when he himself brought out a book with a title almost the same as Butts's, George at this stage forced no great meaning into the distinction between the two degrees of opposition to the protective tariff: 'The battle of *free trade,* or a *revenue tariff,* is a battle for the whole; the battle of protection is not a battle, but a robbery of the many on the part of the few.' Tariff reduction *and* freedom of trade, both impulses promised a paring down of economic monopolies, to the editor's way of thinking; and at this early and less doctrinaire stage of his writing either was a good cause.

By reason of his taking up certain problems directly, and of the implications of what he said about industry and trade, writing for the *Post* carried George far toward rounding out his conception of the roles of capital and the capitalist, and of those of labor and the trade-union movement, in the economy. No need to recapitulate how his crisis thinking of 1869 and 1873 had brought him through the rough-hewing stage of this phase of his ideas. As of the key year, 1873, his prime loyalty to working men — whom he practically identified with the citizenry at large — remained as always the anchor of his thought; and also by now he had decided that there was no contradiction in believing that great virtues and great faults were interwoven in the going practices of the private ownership and operation of capital. Though at this time the large swing of his thought favored the individual free enterpriser — and asserted that the businessman as much as anyone would gain from land-value taxation — one or two local matters turned him toward public utilities again, and toward new exceptions to the rule of private ownership.

Both illuminating gas and water distribution came into San Francisco affairs and *Post* editorials, and as was natural the water problem led to a fight. George would have agreed with the recent, authoritative word of Professor Paul Taylor, who says that water control ranks with land policy and immigration as one of the top few decisive influences which have shaped social growth in California over an entire century. Though as city man he did not write very much about the famous water needs of the semi-arid valleys of the state, he was aware of them, and sometimes made very modern and conservationist-sounding proposals in favor of impounding and distributing the mountain waters for irrigation.[1] But he could not have avoided the policy questions posed by the Spring Valley Water Company, the private-monopoly firm which supplied San Francisco. At the time when George started the *Post*, that company's fourteen-year-old contract was expiring; and the company's high rates raised the issue whether a new contract should be written, or

[1] As when he proposed building dams in the Sierras, from which water could be released to the farmlands below. 'Make the land benefited pay the expense, and give the people interested the management.' SF *Post*, 6 May 1875.

whether San Francisco should declare independence and set up a
public system.

George took on the role of the muckraker, and his findings were
startling. Water cost one-seventh to one-sixth as much as the rent of
an unfurnished house in San Francisco; the city was obliged to have
its sewers cleaned by hand at 50 cents a barrel, instead of by flushing; the operating costs of hydraulic elevators ran much too high.
Comparing San Francisco with the East and the Middle West, the
newspaper called attention to the fact that several cities now owned
and operated their own water works at rates a fraction of San Francisco's; and contrasting itself with other papers, the *Post* noticed
that the others criticized San Francisco's water situation when the
legislature was not in session, but kept quiet while it was meeting.
An editorial said that the *Post* could produce proof that the Spring
Valley Company had 'fixed' the *Call* and the *Bulletin* in friendly
editorial attitudes. 'There is not in the world so outrageous, so
exacting, so soulless a monopoly, as the Spring Valley Water Company.'

At first the *Post* did not want San Francisco to take over the water
business. The reason was more a fear of paying extortionate prices
for the old capital equipment than anything else; the paper had
perhaps some hope that a new private company would save the day.
But in the course of a long newspaper debate it switched completely
to a municipal system. The paper proposed that the state authorize
a bond issue, the proceeds to go either to purchase the old water
works or to build a new one, whichever might prove more advantageous. It would be hard to think that other and greater editorial decisions did not have something to do with this one, for the
Post's recommendation for city ownership was made to the 1873–4
session of the legislature, the one to which the *Post,* the *Bee,* and the
Union addressed their solutions of the land-monopoly problem —
the *Post* now opposed in principle to the private ownership of land.

At the showdown in Sacramento, San Francisco's delegation failed
to unite and pull for reform, and finally an act was passed too
friendly to the Spring Valley Company. But for George as thinker,
something had been gained. Certainly he had developed and recorded his disposition in favor of a city's owning its essential utilities. And, as he now spoke for free water for city residents — much

as he was to speak a dozen years later, amid fame and ridicule, for free in-city transportation in New York City — we may judge it likely that he had already thought through to his later theory, that the collective economic gain created by urban living should be drawn upon, by collective not individual charge, to support the extra services required by people who live and work in cities.

As in the matter of land monopoly, so in that of water monopoly, George marched with other reformers. It is not too much to call him an early municipal socialist. That is, he was a leader of the one, very limited, type of socialism which has been widely and willingly assimilated into American life, as today's situation of city utilities across the land — considerable public ownership and much control — indicates.

As for Henry George's thought on the labor movement, his writing in the Sacramento *Reporter* and some of it in the *Post* has already given us the timing and the essence of the most class-conscious thinking he ever did. A quotation will show how near he verged, for a minute, to the spirit of European socialism. On 8 December 1871, that is when the paper was new, the *Post* said that, though 'not prepared to take our stand squarely upon the principles of the European Internationals,' it would endorse their general proposition that the existing constitution of society is radically wrong and vicious, and that what the world needs far more than any mere reform in government or a reform of any special abuse is 'a REORGANIZATION under which every man's interest will not be, as it now is, opposed to his neighbor's.' Such an idea is nothing to be brushed aside by calling it names — socialism, communism, or agrarianism. It is simply 'an attempt to set aside the principle of *competition* on which society is now based, and to substitute for it a system of the state as in the main a family, in which the weaker brother shall not be pressed to the wall.' America's 'exaggerated individualism' demanded change, the editor was certain.

This is George's maximum Marxism. The mild flirtation lasted for two or three editorials, no longer, and took place shortly before the International Workingmen's Association moved from Europe to America, to die in peace and isolation. But no love affair ever developed, quite the contrary; and as early as June 1872, George's reaction had begun. At that time, while speaking strongly for trade unions, the *Post* urged that the strike be reserved as an emergency weapon, to be wielded only at last resort, when it becomes 'the only means left to the workingman for the amelioration of evils fastened upon him by centuries of injustice.' George's *Post*, like George's earlier papers, pleaded for milder methods: for the eight-hour day, for instance, not as a revolutionary idea as some insisted, but as the moderate democratically inspired proposition it really was. In 1874 George built an editorial around an amusing news story concerning a meeting between William Sharon, a mining entrepreneur, and a committee of his employees. First serving the laborers sherry, Sharon had lectured them against the eight-hour idea, taking as text the iron law of wages. Quoth the capitalist: 'Labor is a commodity which will not keep'; wages follow supply and demand just like the price of grain. Not so, retorted the *Post:* labor can affect the supply of labor, by the eight-hour day, and it can affect demand for labor by its own purchasing power for goods and services. Again George's early perception of the economy-of-abundance idea had cropped out, not a prominent thread but one of the longest in his editorial writing.

The stand of the *Post* was for labor rather than of the labor movement, and against abuses rather than against capitalism or capitalists. This is dramatized by its role in what it called the '*Sunrise* Horror,' in the fall of 1873. The *Sunrise,* a merchant ship, put into San Francisco out of New York, burdened with hate. During the voyage the discipline or torturings by captain and mate had caused three seamen, who had been kidnaped in the first place, to fling themselves overboard to drown. Word got around San Francisco, but no United States marshal or other official made a move. Then Henry George swore a complaint in federal court; he retained W. H. L. Barnes as attorney. His editorials pleaded that the American sailor's grievances were unique; that his discipline was more cruel than the Negro slave's had been, his condition harder than a British seaman's. His hardship lay in the sanctions of law which kept him bound according to his articles for long voyages. Simple repeal would make the difference, the paper said. Let all the special statutes lapse. Then seamen would be 'free to claim their wages and leave the ship whenever the anchor was down.' This would set up a bargaining situation to persuade owners to provide decent conditions and food aboard ship, and it would give sailors equal footing with other workers in a free society, to keep or change their jobs.

While its editorial page discussed general questions of maritime labor policy, the *Post*, abetted by the protests of the *Alta California* and the *Bulletin*, fought the present fight. When the mate of the *Sunrise* disappeared, the paper offered a reward of $400 for his capture. Meanwhile the court action went on: Captain Clarke was convicted, fined $5000, and sent to jail for fourteen months. This was much too light, the *Post* said, but the paper took pride in having started the wheels of federal justice. The *Sunrise* dropped from the columns with an appeal for starting a Society for the Protection of Seamen. The *Sunrise* affair, according to the San Francisco *Chronicle*'s historian of the city's journalism, made Henry George heard across the land and around the world. It was the second event of that kind, for about the same thing can be said of the fight with the Associated Press and Western Union.

We have now gone far enough to see that the editor of the *Post* envisaged the economy as divided by a boundary. In front lay the area of competitive business. In general he regarded conditions there as sound, and, in the tug and pull of capital and labor, he believed private enterprise capable of producing abundant goods for all. Behind the boundary line, in the area of monopolism, George pictured a predatory situation. Of course his several reform proposals had a single strategy, which was to put an end to private operation there. He counted on two of his tactics, free trade and land-value taxation, to push back the boundary. Then, where the boundary could not be moved and natural monopolies could not be denied, he made his proposals for public ownership at appropriate national or local levels.

If present-day readers feel that George's total picture of the economy as it was working was pretty dark, and his means for brightening it quite extreme — even disregarding the Marxist coloration of 1871 and 1872 — they may be assured that contemporaries other than Will Green sometimes thought so too. Picking up one of the *Post*'s *obiter dicta* on the distribution of wealth, for instance, the Sacramento *Record* called Henry George a communist. The furious editor replied in an editorial of 10 June 1874 *'that everyone has a right to the wealth he produces or earns,'* but that the *Post* had never spoken for an equal division. 'Until we could guarantee to all equal intelligence, equal industry and equal prudence it would be as foolish to ask that as to ask that water should run up a hill as well as down.'

One understands that George's critics thought him radical. And yet on fair and complete reading of the *Post* there can be no doubt of his sincere belief in business and capitalism. Commenting on something Herbert Spencer had said, George was able to agree, 5 September 1873, that modern industrial organization was really 'about as good as present human nature allows,' and to say that a change of social spirit and policy, not an altered social structure, was what he wanted. To avoid depressions he believed that high wages, which he was sure accounted for California's staving off hard times a year and more after the East collapsed, were the right preventative; and that a program of public works, instead of doled-out food as in New York, offered a reasonable restorative. We should have our economic 'New Declaration of Independence,' he said, when America stood for the right of every man to have a job, and to earn according to the product of his labor.

As for the ordinary operations of the business system, George had ideas which followed a middle lane, or rather moved in dual lanes, of reform and high-powered entrepreneurial activity. In 1875, the year of specie resumption, the old critic of the national banking system reverted to policies he had put into the San Francisco *Times*. Resumption he still as always wanted; a system of hard money 'that cannot fluctuate in value' was his fixed idea. But the policy of restoring coin to circulation by withdrawing federal greenbacks, which cost the government no interest, while retaining the system of the national bank notes, which required interest payments at two levels and which involved high costs and private monopolism, drew his fire. Acknowledging as he had in 1868 some debt to Ohio leadership in ideas of finance (Democratic leadership this time), he wrote again in behalf of an expansible and contractable money system. Properly set up such a system would operate automatically, he said, 'by the demands of trade, which may easily be done by making currency convertible into bonds, and bonds reconvertible into currency.'

Though long an opponent of the San Francisco Hamiltonians for deflation, George now admitted — while the national depression was growing but before the California crisis of 1875 — that the time had come for the interest rate to fall. But, always the resister, he wanted no 'jackass bill' passed by the legislature to hurry the process. Fencing with the *Call*, the *Post* said that, 'The legislature can no more regulate the rate of interest than it can regulate the winds, the rains, or the tides.' George's main proposal for providing financial service for the people was postal savings banks. This idea is related to his case for interconvertible bonds and money: a slight extension of federal policy — postal savings were actually to be made the law of the land among the mild reforms of the Taft administration — would bring the resources of banking closer to the grass roots of the economy. In like vein he compared the presence of *one* building and loan society in San Francisco with 2000 reported in London; and, taking up a reform which had been a quarter-century agitating in eastern labor circles, he urged the advantages of purchasing homes on the co-operative principle by means of small installments. He welcomed as suggestive some schemes of the Grangers for going into banking; but he questioned the merit of preferential interest rates, and suggested that the Grangers ought to separate, not combine, the functions of investment and commercial banking.

While he thus asked for more spread and democracy in the policies and institutions of banking and credit, George also admired the going machinery of free private banking. He never boggled at mere bigness of operation. The suspicious may better be told, ahead of the story, that the *Post* was booming on a loan which had bought a wonderful new printing press. But, before this, in 1872 the paper compared the mighty enterprise of Chicago businessmen with that of San Francisco's cautious ones: if the capitalists would wake up, pull together as they should, and be more liberal about it, the city would go ahead, he said. As occasion invited, George scolded the local moneybags, for instance, when they denied credit to a promising glassmaker, or when they themselves speculated in foods; and he praised them when they financed the Palace Hotel, or moved toward a new telegraph line.

William C. Ralston, the head of the Bank of California, and speculator of speculators, entranced him. When, the day after his bank had been forced to close by the run introduced by the crash of the Comstock bonanza, the body of that handsome man was found in San Francisco Bay, the *Post* believed that the death stirred

San Francisco like none since Lincoln's. Though odor of scandal
was rising, George defended Ralston as a businessman, against the
charges in the *Bulletin* and the *Call*. He limned him as 'pre-emi-
nently a Californian. He possessed in excess the qualities which
gave special character to the men who gathered here from all parts
of the world and made this state what it is — the energy and dash,
the generosity and extravagance, the propensity to bold movements
and great enterprises, rather than to slower and more cautious
methods.' Less than three weeks after the collapse, the *Post* cited
the quick reopening of the Bank of California as signifying the
recuperative power of private banks operating in a system of hard
money.

As equal to an Olympian, George loved a generous capitalist.
While few in early California were minded to make great gifts to
the community, the *Post* praised Edward Tompkins, who in 1872
made the first endowment to the University of California. The
paper compared him to W. W. Corcoran of Washington, founder
of an art gallery, and asked readers to consider what it would mean
for California if the richest men gave for the public good. When,
before long, James Lick did just that (we may disregard certain
shortages of fulfillment, and remember the great observatory on
Mount Hamilton), the *Post* praised him warmly. This was the kind
of spirit that had thrived better in the Greek city-states than in
America's republic so far, Henry George observed.

–3–

Henry George's very earliest ideas had been Christian, and his
first teen-age resistance to these ideas had been directed at evangelicalism's intensity. In California we have discovered him making assertions that he believed in immortality and spinning stories
about occult experiences at sea. But for a period of years nothing
markedly Christian appears in the record. The dedication in New
York and the Oakland vision seem to have focused his moral intensity. Apparently he let wither his membership in the Bethel
Methodist Church where he was converted and married, and in his
San Francisco life he sought no substitute for that, or for old St.
Paul's.

From the middle years with the *Post*, however, we have his son's
word that Henry George experienced a deep renewal of religious

feeling. Parenthood was part of it. The father who took the boys out on the bay and read poetry and discussed affairs in the family circle now insisted on morning and night prayers for the children and encouraged hymn singing at home. New faith, Henry George, Jr., says, was born of his finding himself, stabilizing his ideas. 'He had turned from a religion that taught either of a Special Providence on the one hand or of a merciless fate on the other. Now all the fervour of his spirit went forth in the belief that social progress is governed by unchanging and beneficial law.'

While the *Post* confirms in a large way the son's impression, it suggests also a good deal more: a complicated mind and conscience; a mood not always optimistic; and an inclination to move, explore, judge, and choose among the crowding thought currents of the decade. Editorial comment on books and ideas, and occasional book reviews which, though not signed, were almost certainly written by George, supply the evidence that his mind was reaching out in philosophic and religious, as well as in economic and political, directions.

What the later *Post* had to say, for instance, about the man of intellect George had once praised without stint, tells much of the arrival of an almost absolutistic philosophical point of view. Though still pleased to speak of John Stuart Mill's activities in behalf of land reform, to say that the English libertarian 'endorsed the principles upon which to tax nothing but land is based,' Henry George discovered a failure of nerve in Mill. He could not understand a reformer's logic which carried so far with his own, yet stopped short of speaking for an actual taking over of the income of land for the community. George was wise enough to acknowledge the rightness of a certain amount of moral relativism. Mill's saying that private property in England had so long assimilated land with capital and other forms of wealth that to reduce private values in land alone would be capricious and unjust, George understood and reported. He said freely, too, that the newness of property rights in California land rendered them more available to capture. 'Our state is young, our lands but partially occupied, and whatever injustice we might do in this way [of appropriating land values] will be less than we would do at any future time.' Yet, with all differences admitted, the editor likened Mill to those Americans before the Civil War who, hating slavery, nevertheless opposed the anti-slavery crusade — the kind of people he had known at St. Paul's in Philadelphia.

Mill's death, and the posthumous appearance of an American edition of his *Three Essays on Religion*, widened the gap of thought. The *Post*'s review, which was a kind of summing-up of the old master, described the book's skepticism as something which fell short of either atheism or faith, a state of mind too condescending and too reserved to be inspiring or even very interesting. For George, the noblest British lion had left the stage a mouse. The human and moral qualities he now admired he stated in a review of Senator Charles Sumner's collected volume of prophecies, *Prophetic Voices about America;* he praised the abolitionist's 'manliness,' his 'Miltonic intensity,' and his capacity for combining with 'severe public virtue and eminent legislative capacity, a genius for art and letters.'

In reviews of the two huge histories by the two able and patriotic historians of the same surname, George displayed appreciations appropriate to the writings. It was not the old neighbor of Independence Hall in him alone but also the patriotic idealist who was stirred by George Bancroft on the American Revolution. And the Californian in him responded to Hubert Howe Bancroft's record-making achievements as writer of Hispanic American and Pacific coast history. That a San Franciscan could now produce and publish such monuments of learning elicited from George a statement of the ideal which we know he had cherished as a personal ambition, at least since *Our Land and Land Policy:* 'There is no work so great as a great book . . . And a book like this, which brings to a condensation and a summary any branch of human knowledge, which focuses, as it were, into a grand intelligible picture the scattered rays of experience and research, has the strongest promise of immortality.'

While current history writing gratified George, current popular science and scientific philosophy troubled and challenged him. Under the editorial heading, 'Scientific Materialism,' on 11 September 1874, the *Post* discussed in detail Professor John Tyndall's presidential address before the British Association for the Advancement of Science. Perhaps this is the first, surely it is the earliest clear signal that George at maturity realized he would have to go to war with a major thought current of his age. He credited Tyndall with frankness, said that the great physicist had made a 'candid but repulsive' affirmation that science knows no need to find God in the universe. Quote the San Francisco *Post:* 'The sufficient answer to any materialistic theory is involved in its very statement — it springs spontaneously from the consciousness of man. The investigator who concentrates his gaze on one drop of the infinite ocean of existence may become so involved in the machinery of creation and life as to lose all sight of its purpose and aim.'

Along with asserting his own idealism — a theistic kind which might be spelled with a capital 'I' — George rediscovered and asserted also some of the more particular values of his religious upbringing. The recurring pessimism, which was a part of his new maturity, he first conceived in quite material terms: that America was ruining its future by wasting the domain. But even in that discovery his language echoed the Christian sense of sin and responsibility in which St. Paul's had trained him. And especially when he discussed the more purely moral problems, the old presumptions came out. On the matter of how the federal government was behaving, for instance: 'The American people punish honesty and reward corruption. Get money, get power — get it no matter how it is got — that is the lesson we are teaching our children, even while we are teaching them to repeat old phrases we have robbed of all their meaning.' Though he once made occasion, as will be recalled, to express his loyal fondness for the service and the prayer-book of Protestant Episcopalianism, most of what he said about churches was contemptuous. He could not abide the low-grade moral concerns of the ones he saw about him in the city. They thought they were doing their duty, the *Post* said, when the preachers declaimed against Sabbath-breaking and drunkenness. Most of all he protested the property-class loyalties of the Protestant clergymen. According to the *Post,* they made apologies for Chinese immigration; they speculated — the paper gave names — in land and shares; they prostituted good talents for pulpit oratory in making 'shallow attempt' to reply to 'Darwin or Huxley, or to get rid of such historic facts as are damaging to their sect or profession.'

Entertaining such a picture of the ordained of Christ in the community, George had to enlarge his own philosophic dimensions to find an answer he believed in, against materialism of the type voiced by Tyndall. Not Charles Darwin, not the first-class thinkers were colored by it, he said in an editorial of 6 March 1875. But many were. From some reading or acquaintanceship — Thomas Starr King, the Unitarian, is the present writer's guess — George found reason to believe that, while scientists of his day were becoming more dogmatic, men of true religion were becoming less so. What light could science throw on the truly grand questions of life, he wanted to know, better than the wisdom of Job, or Socrates? Angered at the moment by San Francisco revivals carried on by Protestants and Paulists, he inquired also: Was Jesus joking when he said, 'Sell all thou hast, and give to the poor?' The so-called Religion of Humanity of that day seems to have impressed him.

His new breadth and depth involved more world awareness than at any stage of his career so far. Reaching out from the comparisons between California and Ireland, which he had been making frequently since 1869, the editorial mind discovered events of interest around the world. The *Post* was up-to-date when it notified its readers of the rise of the land-reform movement in Melbourne, with a plan to have land nationalization in Australia. And, a couple of times as in his earlier papers, he waxed prophetic and hopeful about Russia in its similarity to the United States. 'Opposite in many things, they still have much in common.' Predicting the twentieth century — and probably borrowing from Tocqueville to do so — George foresaw two 'colossi, each a continental power, which might, if they chose, divide the world between them.' When, as he was about to quit the *Post,* he learned that in Russia the Tsar was ordering certain Polish landlords to sell out at fixed prices to the tenants, he ventured that, if this kind of thing persisted, Russia, 'with the forms of an unlimited monarchy will soon in reality become the most democratic of civilized nations.' *If emancipations persist!*

International goodwill sometimes fostered deeds of kindness. In 1874 the offices of the *Post* were used by a committee — promoted also by the *Examiner* — which raised $300 for the relief of striking agricultural workers in England. Henry George contributed $5. And, close at home, when a local problem popped up — which flags to display on the Fourth of July — the editor called for those of many nations, the Union Jack included. This annoyed the *Call;* and that paper's saying that Henry George's flag was 'English' not American gave the *Post* a chance to render a bit of biography and idealism. 'By birth and parentage,' Henry George was pure American. 'If [he] could never have gotten beyond the prejudices of early association, he would probably be an intense Native American, and would hate everything British with a hatred only understood by those who know what bitterness the personal tradition of two wars left on the Eastern seaboard. But he is enough citizen of the world to know that that which is good and beautiful and admirable in manhood is monopolized by no country or religion, and utterly to despise that miserable, narrow-minded prejudice which thinks a man is either better or worse because of his birthplace or faith.'

'Citizen of the world' — his daughter's favorite phrase for him. Truly George's mind had adopted such a sentiment while he edited the San Francisco *Post*.

-4-

It would be a formula which overlooked facts already presented in detail to say that the political ideas of Henry George of the *Post* were equal to the sum of his economics and his religion. Yet, outside the area of party loyalties, inherited and acquired, there would be truth in the proposition. In George's own words, written for the Fourth of July 1874: 'The great American Republic must be a republic in fact as well as form; a Christian republic in the full grand meaning of the words . . . till time shall come when warships, and standing armies, and paupers and prisons, and men toiling from sunrise to dusk, and women brutalized by want, and children robbed of their childhood shall be things of the dark past.'

There is utopianism but no fully developed conception of government explicit in the *Post*. All governments, European and American, the editor eyed with suspicion. The comment just quoted followed an editorial of a few days earlier, one that had been inspired by a German report telling of six million men under arms in Europe, 'kept in a state of idleness at the expense of producers that they may be ready to cut each other's throats.' Though not at all a pacifist, George always thought that men put at arms, and held in readiness when not needed, represented incredible waste and immorality. In 1874 he condemned the army of the United States as too large, and as undemocratic and extravagant. He called for reduction to 2000 or 3000 well-paid, picked men, all treated and imbued with a spirit of equal opportunity, like the old French army.

Next to an inflated military, a civilian bureaucracy disturbed him most. He criticized customs houses everywhere, especially the San Francisco one; and, in the same bracket, the Navy Yard at Mare Island.

Yet the anxieties of a Jeffersonian failed to move George to the last ditch of opposition to the machinery of government. He had a bit of Thoreau in him, not a great deal. As political philosopher, he spoke on the *Post* in established dual character, that of visionary combined with patriot, in the old Manifest Destiny style. As a reformer he believed always that government must be ready to make mighty changes in society, and as Manifest Destiny man he asserted confidence that the American federal system could be extended almost indefinitely. The constitution of 1787 was so designed as to be right, he said, for any population, into the 'hundreds and perhaps thousands of millions,' and right for any land mass up to 'a grand federation of the whole continent and perhaps the world, bringing into reality the long dream of peace and brotherhood.'

To be elastic but not overburdened was George's idea of how a large government in Washington, or anywhere, should be. What he said about the income tax, when a congressman proposed renewing the Civil War measure, is a case in point: 'Theoretically the income tax is next to the land tax, the best and fairest which can be levied, but in practice it becomes a tax on conscience, and a large part of it is consumed in collection.' Thus the dilemma of the *Post:* government had to be assigned unprecedented tasks of social reconstruction yet doubts about the human race demanded that power locations be few and little concentrated, and that men at the controls be kept not too long, and not too available to temptation. In George's own words: 'Our representative system is a failure . . . We tax too many things. We elect too many officers . . . The preventible evils which affect this country are owing to the attempt to do too much by means of government and convert it into a sort of Special Providence.'

Though moral generalizations came spontaneously from Henry George, much blueprinting of what government ought and ought not do, Jefferson and John Adams style, would hardly have been applicable to editorial writing. To be a newspaperman, George had to indicate practical choices. Thus the *Post* affirmed belief in states rights: 'It believes in local self-government as the only means by which the unity of so great a country and so numerous and diverse a people can be permanently maintained.' The paper asked for new strength on both the executive and the legislative sides of state government.

With correct history the *Post* remarked that the period of the American Revolution had meant a reaction against one-man power, but that in the nineteenth century the pendulum had swung back. It cited Governors Haight and Booth to show that a responsible man's high authority protects the people, Andrew Jackson style, and his veto gives security from the anonymous corruption of legislators. In that vein the paper preferred to have the state pay well for good administration, and it picked a little quarrel with the *Bee* to demonstrate the point. When the Sacramento paper congratulated California on having less expensive public servants than Great Britain, the *Post* estimated contrariwise that, though under the English system California might pay the governor $40,000 or $50,000 (a fancy estimate), and San Francisco pay the mayor $10,000 or $20,000, the sheriffs in every county would not be collecting $40,000 over and above their small salaries, and city supervisors would not be spending $20,000 to be elected to an office with a $100-a-month salary. One fears that George was more correct in his California than his British figures. He could not have pled a better cause with a less accurate comparison, for in his time the British paid their public servants, especially those in local government, very little.

As improvement for San Francisco, the editor prescribed legislation to fix large executive and policy-making responsibility in the office of mayor, as had recently been done in Chicago. And, for specific state economies, he suggested — of course not forgetting his most-wanted reduction of tax-collecting costs — the following: abolishing the offices of the state and county treasurers and assigning their jobs to the banks; combining the California offices of secretary of state and controller; reducing prison costs by developing prison industries; and other smaller items. The *Post* also proposed simplifications and reductions in the state judicial system.

Governmental efficiency and responsibility meant much to George, but more important to him were the politics of economic legislation and the effectiveness of public opinion. Six months before the *Post* was started, it will be remembered, he had been beaten in the election in which Haight went down; and his article on 'Bribery in Elections' was his response to that defeat. Here for the first time he took up the final major reform idea of his lifetime, the Australian ballot. Later, at full tide of his public leadership, he would make this reform the third corner of his triangle of reform: he would urge secret voting as the needful political leverage by which to lift the economic reforms, land-value taxation and free trade, into high politics.

In the *Overland* article of 1871 he was not ready to be so schematic. Thinking his way against corruption, he reasonably dismissed as unpromising any possible legislation to make criminals of the offerers of bribes. He urged instead a reform of procedure that would give the voter real freedom at the moment of voting. The Crown Colony of Victoria had done better than the great republic. If Americans would only follow suit — instead of the old-style party ballots handed out by party workers, give the voters a general ballot and a chance to mark it unwatched and uncompelled — direct bribery would be eliminated. The Australian procedure would have the extra advantage, George foresaw accurately, of encouraging independent, split-ticket, voting. As Anna George de Mille notes with pride, her father's *Overland* article preceded by more than a decade the American reform movement — to which he then contributed — that actually placed the Australian ballot in the statute books of the several states.

His stand was taken. But George did not assign much space in the *Post* to ballot reform; and he was selective, as many kinds of proposals were offered, about strengthening democracy by extending or refining political machinery. He approved, but only mildly, the notion of primary elections, intended to reduce the power of insiders in the parties. At this stage he was cool to votes for women. 'We are not advocates of female suffrage, nor particular admirers of the strong minded.' But he did hope that the feminist movement 'with all its froth and all its absurdities' — these were the days of Lucy Stone, as well as of Elizabeth Cady Stanton and Clara Barton — would promote the cause of equal pay for equal work. Economic improvement for women he really wanted, then perhaps political rights. Let women be cashiers, bookkeepers, and store clerks, the *Post* said — let them even be barbers, since the *Chronicle* wanted them. At top level, George recommended that women be chosen for seats on the school boards and for superintending positions in the school system. And in 1874, when George W. Julian and John Stuart Mill made news as friends of woman suffrage, the San Francisco *Post* softened to say that 'we care very little' whether they vote or not.

The new device of democracy which intrigued George most at this period was proportional representation. He argued that in California such a system would help reach desirable goals: the bypassing of the city political machines, and the giving of voice and weight to minorities in the state capitol. At this point George was doubtless thinking of the considerable minority that supported John Days's land reform bills, even when a Republican majority was dominating Sacramento. Whether or not land reform would have gotten farther, had the voting system been different, it is difficult to estimate.

Once a legislature was elected, George, in his role of editor and utopian, would have had it meet in almost constant session. The California arrangement could hardly have been more discontinuous: meeting for 120 days, every other year, each session shortly following the biennial election, but each election long after the last session. George proposed to have the legislature convened every month or every quarter. Continuing service, he believed, would lead assemblymen and senators to become acquainted with one another and to much better knowledge of the state, and so to such thoughtful legislation as would restore their branch of the government to its rightful first place.

Such tenets doubled and redoubled — over and above the necessity posed by the land-value taxation idea — the reasons the *Post* had for desiring a new constitution for the state. Here George's thought was far from unique; for constitutional reform was in the air. During the session of 1873–4, for instance, the *Alta California* wanted the legislature to initiate the two-year process of amendment. The *Post* called for a total rewriting. When a committee of the bar association, headed by ex-governor Haight, moved toward a constitutional convention, George's paper seconded; and, though his editorial page was not one to make much of the common plea that a voter's simple duty is to choose the best man, it did now make that plea. A constitutional convention, it very well said, ought to bring public opinion to a focus and draw the state's best minds into high public service. After this effort failed in Sacramento in 1874, along with land reform, the *Post* urged a convention again, in what was the last opportunity of George's editorship, during the state campaign of 1875. Again a failure; but just three years later, when in crisis conditions a convention was actually called, George would be ready to abandon work on *Progress and Poverty* to campaign and speak for a reform constitution.

-5-

The characteristic ideas of what we have been explaining as the *Post*'s utopia have all been reported: free enterprise without private monopolism, free trade, equal opportunity, an economy of abundant production for all, a Christian state, an idealistic culture, an efficient government, a democracy uncorrupt and sensitive to the people's needs. What George wanted was remote enough from things as they were in California. The mere statement of visionary goals forces a present day reader of the *Post* to ask: of what practical use was it to assert such aims in daily journalism? Was George politically effective as a reforming Democrat in a city run mainly by Democratic politicians? Was he morally effective as an idealist addressing himself to a particularly materialistic sector of a materialistic culture, California in the age of Grant?

Part of the explanation lies in the *Post*'s financial success. Readers must have liked what they were getting. Another part is the influence moral imagination may command in a community, even though it fails to reach its ultimate goals. The *Sunrise* affair is a case in point: the *Post* put a tyrannical sea captain in jail, when no other paper took the initiative. So also editor and paper got results in half a dozen cases, in all but one of which they must have been overwhelmingly right. It does seem that Henry George was fated — say by the inner logic of his concern with land and labor in industrial areas — to be an urban reformer, concerned with all manner of things, whether or not relevant to land-value taxation and free trade, for about a quarter of a century.

In the first month of the existence of the paper, the *Post* smelled out corruption in the San Francisco police department. A strong editorial charged that policemen were conniving with gambling in the city. But the matter only simmered in the editorial pages until 1873, which was in so many ways George's year of decision, when investigating the facts led him and his partner to go to the infamous Mint Saloon on Commercial Street. John Vallance George, who was working for the *Post* at the time, tells the story, apparently from the principal's first-hand account. 'As they entered, James Gannon, an ex-detective and supporter of [Chief of Police] Crowley, tapped my brother on the shoulder, saying that he wanted to speak to him privately. My brother stepped inside with him, when Gannon said, "Let up on Crowley or there will be trouble," and when asked what he meant, the ex-detective seized my brother by the neck with one hand and slapped him in the face with the other. My brother tried to strike back, when Gannon reached down and drew a revolver.' Two city supervisors protected the little editor. Stuart Menzies, 'a very strong man' who accompanied George and Hinton, seized Gannon's shooting arm; and with the help of Supervisor McCarthy, 'pulled Gannon away.'

George did not prosecute, and perhaps considered himself the winner at the moment. He was described as a hero in the other papers; and there followed some kind of a police investigation of gambling and a degree of improvement in the situation. But reform did not cut deep enough to outlast a change of department administration. In the winter of 1874–5 the *Post* moved again, this time concentrating on the new chief of police, whose name was Cockrill. In the *Post*'s own words and specifications: 'We have a plain duty to perform in exposing a Chief of Police who has disgraced his office and his constituents.' It is common knowledge that faro playing 'is conducted by friends of the Chief or his friends' friends, and that he fails to prosecute.'

Such a comment invited a suit for libel. But evidently court action was just what George wanted, as an opportunity to display the facts. At any rate he was ready, when Cockrill sued, to print a facsimile of a receipt which connected the chief's liquor business with the operator of a well-known faro table; and he also printed a facsimile of a promise, put in writing by Cockrill before election but not made good, that if elected he would appoint a certain Negro to a position as detective — a trafficking in offices which alone, George said, should put the chief in jail.

According to the *Chronicle*'s news story, when this 'rare and racy' case came up, Cockrill, the plaintiff, acted 'slightly nervous and anxious,' and his counsel 'continually interposed objection to the testimony offered.' Meanwhile George, as defendant, 'amid considerable commotion among the sporting part of the spectators,' carried his role as if he himself were plaintiff. Apparently the reforming editor had an easy time. Though the judge ruled that the *Post* had not proved to be fact the exact phrases of its editorial, the court allowed that there could be 'no moral doubt that Cockrill was paid for conniving at gambling' in San Francisco. Further, the action brought evidence of 'dozens' of Chinese gambling houses in operation, the *Post* said; and the paper welcomed the next step, an investigation by a grand jury. This kept up the fact finding for an extra three weeks. Then, as an 'ignored bill,' the case of 'Henry George and W. M. Hinton, misdemeanor, libel,' was finally disposed of.

The grand jury commended to its successor a fresh review of the evidence of gambling, and of possible connections of the police with that gambling. This fell short of full victory, yet the *Post* was fairly satisfied. The 'grand jury expresses the sentiment and belief of the whole community,' it said. Wheels within wheels, the *Post* had connected Chief Cockrill with the Fitch-Pickering-Simonton papers; and the editorial silence of those two, the *Call* and *Bulletin,* is tacit acknowledgment of a score by George.

Meanwhile, during the year 1872 especially, George displayed a commando-type of attack on other widely dispersed areas of civic wrong. Late in October, on the eve of the national election, less than a year after the 'Bribery in Elections' article, the *Post* condemned out of hand the newly compiled Great Register of the voters of San Francisco. It estimated 10,000 voters listed who had left the city, and 15,000 more listed in the wrong wards; and said that unless a voluntary organization would send challengers to every voting place, any amount of repeat voting would be possible. Within a month the *Post* blasted at the city hospital for bad food, bad nursing, and stealing from the patients; and very soon it renewed with force an old demand that the city's Industrial School, the boys' reformatory, be reorganized.

The *Post's* original charges against the school had been incompetent management, waste and graft, and an average cost of $263.50 a year to keep each boy in a school which was a crime breeder. During the first ten days of December, on the occasion of an inspection by the city supervisors, the newspaper ran a new series of revelations. It also produced some very liberal suggestions. Developing a reform idea from Wisconsin, it proposed running a school on the cottage plan, with resident couples in charge of each group of boys. From a colleague who witnessed the event, we learn that Henry George went personally to the Industrial School, and, much as at the Mint Saloon, was threatened with a pointed pistol. In this effort the *Post* succeeded completely, by driving the school director out of office and out of the city.

Most of George's campaigns to clear out nests of civic corruption are self-recommending, and favorable judgment need not be withheld because the bulk of the evidence, though with occasional flashes of confirmation, comes from the *Post*. But one case at least is more complex. In this instance the institution where he alleged graft was the University of California, and George's opposite number, far from being a minor politician, was on the way to becoming one of the great statesmen of American education, Daniel Coit Gilman. Yet the *Post* moved in on university criticism from the side of George's strength, his expert knowledge of federal land policy; his total lack of academic experience had little bearing on his effort. Doubtless, too, the editor was somewhat influenced by a member of the faculty, Professor William Swinton, with whom he had established a friendship while living in Oakland.

The professor, who was a brother of John Swinton, the New York labor leader and journalist, had a considerable record of accomplishments. Though short on teaching background, he was long on writing experience, as he had been a *New York Times* correspondent, and later an historian of the Civil War. He taught literature, and was something of a malcontent on the faculty. It is easy to guess that he encouraged George to criticize the university. At any rate, many months before Gilman came, the *Post* complained that the regents were laggard in developing the agricultural and mechanical studies to which their having accepted the benefits of the Morrill Act committed them. But the *Post* was not wholly critical. And it might well have been at the suggestion of a professor of literature that George paid warm respects to the great opportunities the state university had for developing a people's culture. For, though the *Post* was minded to fear that an old-fashioned 'college of polite learning' might emerge, it declared that the very existence of the institution ought to refute the supercilious who said that California was altogether materialist in spirit. The paper neatly made the point that Edward Sill, the gifted poet (whom Gilman soon appointed professor of English), was already producing verse across the bay.

Ideally a liberal editor would have recognized that Gilman, who arrived in the fall of 1872 from the Sheffield Scientific School, which was the new and practical branch of Yale, might become just the man to nurse along together in tender transplantation the scientific and the humanistic vines of learning in the new California environment. (He was presently to do just this, with famous success, at Johns Hopkins.) An editor who perceived this possibility would have been slow to anger and would have erred on the side of patience with the new project. On the other side, ideally the new president would have refrained from comment on social and political questions not relevant to his office, and would have been extra careful about press reactions to university policy and expenditure.

Unfortunately, there was no ideality in these respects on either the San Francisco or the Berkeley side of the bay. On 1 July 1873, the *Post* pronounced in favor of certain public statements about land policy made by E. S. Carr, the university's professor of agriculture, an individual whose truculence perhaps surpassed Professor Swinton's, and who was also leader and historian of the Granger movement in the state. By legislature time the next winter, being on Carr's side meant being against Gilman, for the Grange was turning on pressure in Sacramento to have more practical subjects — the Morrill Act again — in the curriculum, contrary to the president's policy. The Grange wished also to transform the university regents from appointive to elective officials. Within university walls the mounting tensions drove William Swinton, now Carr's associate, to resign his chair. It seems to have been almost foreordained that the *Post* would fight the university administration.

A crescendo of editorials, early in 1874, sounded the battle. The main thing was the *Post*'s allegation that the state had been swindled and the eight-hour law broken, in the building of North Hall, on the new Berkeley campus. The paper also said that the faculty had suffered serious loss when Swinton quit, and that the operations of the university were defeating the good intentions of Congress and the state legislature. The new university was charged with ignoring 'the idea of bringing science to minister to the daily wants and lighten the daily labors of the people; to marry as closely as might be the educated brain with the toiling hand.' George caught Gilman in a vunerable opening, moreover, when, according to the *Post*, the president released an essay 'in which he presumes to give an intelligent account of various phases of civilization in the state,' and concluded with an opinion in favor of Chinese immigration.

George came face-to-face with university problems, and perhaps confronted Gilman and some of the regents personally, in February 1875, when an assembly committee investigated his charge of fraud. His contention was that Regent Merritt had unfairly arranged for business associates of his own to have the building contract, and that they had profited mightily. There are of record nearly 500 pages of assertion and counter-assertion before the committee, but even so it is not clear how right or wrong George was in charging dishonesty to the Board of Regents. Yet it is certain that his article opened the investigation; and that, though the investigators refused to sustain him, the obstreperousness of the San Francisco *Post* helped decide President Gilman to leave California, even before he was called to the new Johns Hopkins.

The antagonism in California between the future greatest reformer and the future most creative university president of an epoch, both men in the preliminary stages of their careers, shows neither personality at his best. The academic man fell short of comprehending the moral worth of George's pro-labor protest, and the editor made no suitable effort to be patient and keep hands off while a young university wobbled in its first steps toward larger life.

–6–

The one instance in which the *Post*'s reformism did not pay, so far as the evidence tells, occurred in July 1874, not without drollery. In Alameda, across the bay, a Miss Sally Hart and companion, workers in the local-option movement, ran into obstructions while they were campaigning for a no-license vote in a local election. Rowdies threw firecrackers at them, and lifted skirts on seventy-year-old legs, and enacted a mock funeral of the ladies' cause. The *Post* blamed these bad manners on the encouragement of San Francisco German liquor dealers, and it came forward with a gallantry toward Miss Hart which no other San Francisco paper equaled. If the first local-option election could be swung by bribery and ruffianism, it queried, would not all local option be doomed?

The affair proved not too trivial. The *Post* printed 'a little secret history' which revealed that an intermediary had made it known that if the paper would oppose local option it would receive material benefits from the liquor dealers. Doing the opposite, the *Post* was boycotted in places where it hurt: saloon and grocery-store sales stopped, and many Germans dropped their subscriptions. In one week 1101 subscribers were lost and 959 new ones taken, and the *Post* started printing lists of stopping and beginning subscribers. After a week of this the Methodist *Christian Advocate* saluted the *Post* as the only San Francisco paper 'not ruled by the liquor interests,' and Henry George's paper became known as being for temperance. Not a prohibitionist journal, it did print an estimate that the city of San Francisco had one saloon for each 100 inhabitants, and did demand a reduction. Quite consistent with its tax principles it proposed a very high license law, a tax for social control.

Thirty-odd years later a friend of Henry George said that the attack on the liquor interests marked the beginning of the end of George's regime on the San Francisco *Post*. This is possible but doubtful; and certainly the boycott of the saloons and stores was no more than a contributing cause to his withdrawal in 1875. Just before the Sally Hart episode the paper announced a circulation of 30,000. This may or may not be an entirely reliable figure, but it is three or four times what newspapers seem to have required to stay in business; and the *Post* presently decided to make a huge investment and expansion in basic equipment.

At the time the *Post* was being printed on the *Chronicle*'s press, the fastest in San Francisco, and could hardly supply its customers. It announced its decision to purchase an up-to-the-minute Bullock press, which would print 26,000 copies an hour. An editorial thanked the public for the patronage 'which, in so short a time, has enabled the one-cent *Post* to place itself, so far as machinery is concerned, ahead even of the New York *Herald* and the London *Times* and *Telegraph*. With the new facilities it will be our aim to make the *Post* more than ever the people's paper of the Pacific Coast.' The *Post* reported in pride a transcontinental pat on the back recently given by *Leslie's Weekly*. Though a writer on that paper discovered more to condemn than to praise in the newspapers of San Francisco, and called the lot inferior to the better papers of the Middle West, he gave his best commendation to the *Post* — 'a smaller paper, which is bright, intelligent, and paragraphical, not entirely local.' When he suggested for the city an 'improved typographical newspaper,' the *Post* promised happily to supply just that need.

How did George and Hinton swing the deal? Twenty-four years later the business manager and partner testified that John Percival Jones, mining operator and speculator, who had not very long before moved from California to Nevada, and in 1873 was elected to the United States Senate from that state, had supplied the cash. For $30,000 he was tendered three-fifths of the stock of the company, and $18,000 more comprised a loan for which he received notes.

Just exactly why the senator, a Republican, should have ventured so much in the *Post* there is no evidence to tell us. George's editorial praise for his hard-money principles does not seem to explain such an interest. If he bought in so that he might later take over the paper, he acted slowly; and if he bought to promote George's main ideas, he acted disloyally in the end. The San Francisco *Bulletin* had a Machiavellian explanation, that Jones merely 'wanted a paper to throw mud.' When that newspaper observed that if such was the senator's purpose, he had selected well, the *Post* simply denied that Senator Jones had a controlling interest, and denied also that he exerted or tried to exert any influence on policy.

On George's side, over and above the business connection, there appears a feeling, like his old attitude toward Governor Haight, that Senator Jones was a man of power who could be led into paths of righteousness. Shortly after the new press had been installed, the *Post* said that it believed that Senator Jones thought as it did on the points of free trade, land-value taxation, and the functions of government; and it saluted him as the senator who could, if he would, make himself the Cobden or Bright of the United States. So far as meets the eye it was the editor advising the senator, rather than the politician using the newspaper, which describes the relationship between Henry George and J. P. Jones for the remainder of George's editorship.

No more in private than in public, so far as the record goes, did
George intimate that there was any limit on his enthusiasm for
what the new investment had bought. The summer and fall of 1874
were full of excitement for a naturally impatient man. Only in
October, after three months of hopes deferred, did the telegram
come which announced completion and shipment of the press. It
had been built in Henry George's native city by the firm that only
a decade earlier had constructed the first press which would print
in one operation both sides of the sheet as it came off the roller —
the web-perfecting press. Meanwhile, as George wrote his mother,
there was a plant to get ready and business expansion to manage.
He had 'fire engine and boilers built and a new class of type made,'
and anticipated that very soon the *Post* as enterprise would 'either
burst up or get rich.'

The climax came at the turn of the year. On 28 December the
Post moved along Montgomery Street to the corner of Sacramento.
Three and a half weeks later a champagne party in the new offices,
and the production of an eight-page Saturday edition by the press,
celebrated the new installation. It was complete. A new lamppost
specially decorated with a gilded eagle was set in the sidewalk outside; the business offices, the press, and tables for folding and mail-
ing occupied the first floor; and the whole upper floor was arranged
for editorial work and composition. Speaking tubes, dumb-waiters,
and steam elevator connected all parts of the plant; there were
stands for twenty-three compositors, and the 'most airy and comfortable' working space for newsmen in California. All this had
been achieved, said the *Post*, by the strength of its own efforts and
principles.

The expansion took place at a time of readjustment in journalism in the state. The Sacramento *Union* was about to sell out and
consolidate with the *Record;* in San Francisco the cheaper papers
were gaining, the *Chronicle* and the *Call*, while the older and more
expensive *Alta* and the *Bulletin* were slipping. At least so the *Post*
interpreted events, and everything confirms its judgment except
about the *Bulletin*, which, much as George would have liked otherwise, was still making money. With steam up, and the new press
rolling, the editor started a new weekly edition of the *Post* —
weekly and 'steamer' editions were an old habit in San Francisco
newspaper production — at the incredible price of $1 a year. Ac-

cording to George: 'We have put its price at the mere cost of white paper and press work with the intention of gathering a larger circulation than that of all the Republican papers combined, and think that at One Dollar a year you will find many persons who will wish to subscribe.' To the public the *Post* offered the weekly in terms appropriate to Henry George's economy-of-abundance ideas. Savings in presswork, in distribution, and in the mass purchase of supplies were said to make the offer possible. Seven months after starting George told a friend that things were working out well. The *Weekly Post* in October 1875 had more subscribers than any other newspaper weekly, and it was reaching the market it sought, the miners, farmers, and valley merchants of the state.

Meanwhile in late summer the Post Publishing Company, as the business was now styled, ventured the ultimate move into competition with the Fitch, Pickering, and Simonton group. On 20 August, one week before the crash of the Bank of California, it launched the San Francisco *Morning Ledger,* a seven-days-a-week paper. George's hopes soared. Acknowledging as he had before that an evening paper could reach only so far, he fascinatedly believed that the new morning paper with the old Philadelphia name would soon overshadow the *Post* and become, it might be, *the* great paper of the Pacific coast. This time again, George ventured one-cent journalism. On the first day he printed 60,000 copies, the biggest edition ever put out on the coast. He announced that he would rely more on readers than on advertisers for support, and that he wanted the paper to be for everyone — for laborers to read on the way to work, and for businessmen and housewives.

Though naturally there was a conformity of ideas with those of the *Post,* yet by announcements made and by areas of affairs omitted from the editorial page, it is plain that a more general and less opinionated paper than the *Post* was intended. Begun a week before a state election, the *Ledger* purposely omitted taking a party stand. Although operating painfully close to the promise of little advertising, the *Ledger* put up a good front. In October, after only two months of life, the page size was doubled to 25 inches by 17 inches, a bigger sheet than the *Post.* Like the *Post* it surrendered early the one-cent bargain, its price being raised to fifteen cents (a California bit) a week.

Imagination went into the paper, and particularly into the Sunday edition — Sunday journalism was still new and little developed in the age of Grant. Before the Bullock press, the *Post* had made a regular feature of its double-size Saturday editions: it included a bit of fiction and several departments of general appeal, such as the theater, for week-end reading. Now it turned that enlargement into the Sunday *Ledger,* and that edition was included in the subscription arrangements of both the *Post* and *Ledger.*

Pictures were the exciting thing about the new Sunday paper. Possibly taking a hint from a recent attempt in San Francisco to publish an illustrated weekly — a failure which the *Leslies* article said indicated an open area for journalism — George and his associates spread across the front page pictures which were a vast improvement over the blurred little cuts then familiar in newspapers. San Francisco was treated to a mirror of itself, as the paper carried, for instance, large clear pictures of the Palace Hotel, and of banks and other buildings. The *Ledger* varied the fare with interesting cartoons, too, some by Jules Tavernier, formerly of *La Vie Parisienne* and the London *Graphic.* The claim is made for George that this was a world innovation, that the *Ledger* was the first Sunday paper anywhere to include pictures. Different from the *Post,* the morning paper carried an unusual amount of foreign correspondence, from Dublin, London, Paris, and Peru, for instance.

Not forgetting his principal stock in trade, Henry George solicited and received — too late for publication — from John Swinton of the New York *Sun,* a series of letters with a radical pro-labor interest. The journalist Swinton was probably a more brilliant writer than his brother, recently of Berkeley. George had known him in New York, during the mission for the San Francisco *Herald.* (Without a shred of direct evidence, it is easy to suspect, from this familiarity of 1875, that John Swinton had been the *Sun* man who, that spring six years before, supplied the Associated Press dispatches which George relayed to Nugent across the continent.) On 26 October, in behalf of the *Ledger,* George wrote his kindred mind: 'I know that you and I think alike on important subjects, and that our religion is the same. New York is not only the grand center of the country; but it is also the type of all growing American cities of the future, and I believe a letter from there written by a man who thinks as you do will be not only extremely interesting but would do something to make people think. If you do conclude to write something, sign your name, not only that it would attract more attention to the letters, but would give them more weight. Our literary men are so universally the apologists and defenders of the House of Have, that what are dubbed agrarian sentiments are generally set down either to idlers too lazy to earn a living or to demagogues.' This was George's request. A little later, when the paper had failed, he explained to Swinton that, 'The special thing I referred to in writing you was your "communism." I wanted you to chuck in a little of that.'

The expansion of the Post Publishing Company outran Henry George in November 1875. The Bullock press had gone into operation half a year ahead of the closing of the Bank of California, and the *Ledger* had been started one week ahead. Perhaps the large general factors of financial crisis are sufficient explanation of failure; more than likely some fault lay in George's individual decisions to expand, and yet again expand. Four years later, summing up his California career, he admitted remorse. In his own words: 'tempted by the idea of a fine building and press we let in John P. Jones,' and, at the same time, thinking that 'the leadership of journalism on this coast' was truly within reach, we started the *Ledger* 'on a more expensive scale than ever attempted in San Francisco before or since,' and 'We strained our credit.' According to this reminiscence, George's wrong decisions had made all the difference in his own affairs. He had had a chance to sell earlier in 1875 for 'what to me was a fortune,' but at the end of the year had gone 'out without a cent.' Characteristically he concluded, 'Sometimes I wonder at myself for giving up so easily what I had won so hardly, but I suppose I was utterly worked down. However, it was good fortune in the guise of evil.'

At the moment he lacked this much philosophy. A woman visitor at the *Post*'s office discovered Henry George in tears. Senator Jones, when he bought the new press, had promised, George told her, never to ask the editor to advocate a measure he did not believe in; but now 'he has asked me to do that very thing and I will not do it.' Retribution may have been possible. George considered himself free to insert in the *Post* such an *exposé* of the senator's bad faith as 'would have ended all hopes of his getting anything' from the property. Mr. Hinton persuaded him not to try this, for the sake of the working staff, and in the end George wrote a sportsmanlike editorial, 27 November, which began, 'Circumstances which I cannot control . . .'

In San Francisco the rival papers did not grieve. Conspicuously, the *Bulletin* gave no notice, editorial or news item, to George's going. The *Alta California* merely said that George's and Hinton's work had given the *Post* 'the respectable position in journalism which it has obtained, and their withdrawal will be regretted by very many.' The Sacramento *Bee* of course spoke warmly, crediting George with having made 'the most brilliant paper yet on the Coast.' The Colusa *Sun,* Will Green's old paper, had a twisting series of compliments to pay on 4 December: 'Harry George, the founder of the San Francisco *Post,* who built it up and made it a power in the land, has been ousted from editorial control . . . The change is, of course, the effect of some wheel within some wheel . . . George maintained many notions that were not our notions, but we always believed that he was actuated by an honesty of purpose . . . We maintain, while we do not consent to his doctrine, that such men are absolutely essential.' The *Sun* endorsed every word of George's valedictory of good faith.

Joseph T. Goodman, appropriately from Virginia City in Senator Jones' state, and appropriately a liberal Republican, took over the editorship of the *Post.* After this change the paper survived under its own name nearly forty years, until Hearst bought it and submerged it in the *Call.* Later the *Call* was merged with its old partner to make the *Call-Bulletin,* the present-day paper which combines the two names George hated most.

At the moment of his exit, the Sacramento *Bee* hoped that George would continue to contribute to the *Post* — and in fact the paper did carry on an anti-monopoly line of fire — and even George himself was not sure how deeply policy would be changed. Writing to Swinton a month later, on 27 December, he expressed uncertainty about Goodman's taking the letters which he himself had invited: 'How much radicalism they would print I cannot tell. They look on me as a pestilential agrarian and communist, and will avoid what they call my hobbies. But though they do not know it, the very aggressiveness and radicalism of the *Post* was its strength. In making a paper that will not offend gunnybags they will kill it, as you will in time see . . .'

This letter, and one other to the same man, are George's real

valedictory on a passage of his life. It will not hurt to put together
sections from the two: 'Since I last wrote you a change has come
over the spirit of my dreams. From running two dailies and two
weeklies I am down to none. It is the old story, so I won't weary
you with it, and in fact have not much heart to repeat it. The
Ledger under ordinary circumstances would have been a success.
Its reception was all that could be asked — but the extraordinary
stringency induced by the failure of the Bank and intensified by
the Virginia fire cut to nothing the advertising which a new paper
can get, while depriving us of all aid. So we went down. And then
while credit was strained and resources exhausted, the big fish in
the Post company, John P. Jones — reached out — and took it in.
A couple of months ago I reluctantly consented to put the price
of $36000 on the interest held by myself and partner. Now I just
take a walk . . .

'If I never do anything more I have the satisfaction of knowing
that I perceptibly affected public thought, and planted ideas which
will some day [change ?] into action . . .

'As for being depressed I am not — twenty four hours is enough
to cry over spilt milk . . .

'It is all in a lifetime, and I have seen too much to think I can
certainly tell what is good and what is evil fortune . . .'

IX

From Isolation:

Speaking and Writing in Time of Crisis

1876–1879

—1—

TWICE before he had the *Post,* George did pieces of writing by which he intended to raise himself into public prominence and leadership. Yet, though both the New York *Tribune* letter on Chinese immigration and *Our Land and Land Policy* retain significance today, neither one so much as made an assemblyman of Henry George in the state elections. His immediate thought, in 1871, that he would try a greater manifesto sometime, was for the next few years crowded out of the realm of practical possibilities by the demands of running a newspaper.

But intimations along the way tell us that no stage of pressure of work or of the enjoyment of success ever quite banished from his mind the urge to do a bigger, more developed and philosophical, presentation of the ideas in *Our Land and Land Policy.* If Hubert Howe Bancroft, ally of the California regionalists could bring off a monumental work of knowledge and thought, and publish it in San Francisco, Henry George could do the same. So George's own appreciation of Bancroft seems to read. Certainly he was determined to communicate his dedication, and his program, to people whom the San Francisco *Post* could never reach.

It is one thing to plan a noble book, and to envisage fondly, but at a comfortable distance in the working future, the ideas it will develop. It is altogether a different thing, many an author has found, to abandon accustomed routines and sources of income, to find the necessary books, to isolate one's self, to face the blank pages, and chapter by chapter to fill them with the symbols of persuasive thought. In this case more than a year and a half went by, after George lost the *Post,* before he concentrated heavily, and about two years and a half before he concentrated exclusively, on undertaking the full austerities of authorship. Though, within all the circumstances we know, it is easiest to think that he considered himself committed, from the moment when Senator Jones let him down, to go ahead early with the major effort, we have no absolute evidence on the point. Doing several other things briefly, he was perhaps trying alternatives to composition, or was making up his mind. But it seems more likely that he was fortifying himself for the task.

In the spring of 1876 he wrote his father that he was going to try a new method of self-expression. He had done enough writing for the moment, he said, and enjoyed a good reputation for what he had done. He would not return to journalism for some little while. 'Now I propose to see if I cannot do a little speaking.' He intended to focus his intellectual energies. 'Now I want to concentrate, get fixed easily as to money, and study and think, and then when I get ready I will come prominently before the public again in some way or other.' Half a year after leaving the *Post* he was already reading law, and he hoped to be admitted to the bar sometime, though he might never practice.

In the season of finding himself, his family seemed especially dear. Annie and he were now more than ever lovers, he said in the letter just quoted, and together they took infinite pride in the three children. Little Jane was turning out the brightest of the lot; the boys they believed to have the makings of 'noted men'; all had bank accounts in their own names. 'God has been too good . . . There has never been a point in my life when I have been so happy.' To Annie herself, Henry wrote a letter about Abélard and Héloise. Abélard's way was the way he loved her, he confessed, with passion blended with a wish to lead his darling into knowledge of truth.

Even the money side seemed smooth. To Philadelphia the somewhat vague word went that he 'was doing very well,' paying his debts and promising himself never to go into the red again. 'I have never, though, been an improvident or reckless man. I have always had some main object in view and have always worked my way steadily nearer and nearer to it. Money has never been my main object — but position which was to me capital.'

Certainly he now discovered a very satisfactory way to pay his bills. On losing the *Post,* he had immediately gone up the river to Sacramento, his old recourse; and doubtless that was the occasion of making the arrangements. The new Democratic governor whom the *Post* had helped elect, William S. Irwin, at once appointed him state inspector of gas meters. 'The appointment was more than anything else a tribute to intellect,' testifies the governor's private secretary, recollecting his own astonishment. He himself, as secretary of the state Board of Equalization, had known George as investigator and thinker, and had admired him; but he was nonplused when his 'cold, unimpassioned' chief expressed enormous admiration for the ex-editor's 'elegant and brilliant style,' and gave him a plum. Perhaps the fact that, early in election year, the *Post* had commended a British act which required food to be sold as represented and water and gas to be tested for purity and quality, diminishes a little the mystery of George's appointment. A critic of monopolies was now set up to check the performance of a natural monopoly which, according to his ideas, should be publicly not privately owned.

Henry George himself tagged the inspectorship a sinecure intended to give him leisure for study and writing. But this was the long view taken many years after the event. At least at first there were arrangements to be made, duties to be learned, jobs to be deputized; and for a little while the new office holder worked hard, politically and otherwise. After taking charge, 15 January, and setting up an office at 531 Mission Street, San Francisco, he went back to the state capital to see the knots tied. If we can trust the impressions of a woman friend who sat in the Senate gallery on the crucial day, all went smoothly. 'To his appointment there was not a dissenting vote, and more than one senator spoke of the choice of the governor in terms of warm approval. After the adjournment of the Senate I heard Henry George thank those men, and his voice trembled with feeling, and his small hand shook as he held it out to receive the warm grip of men then so prominent.'

But George was not simply the honored man of thought, and

soon his own letters reveal a very human mixture of motives. In one of these he begged a friend, an assemblyman from San Francisco, to support a bill which would plug holes in the meter-inspection law; in another, to his Annie, he confided distress when a Mr. Donohoe, calling him a scoundrel, said that he was lobbying to make his job worth a hundred thousand a year. 'I am sorry I attempted the grab, as if I have to go back I will have the name without the game.'

Yet even on the unimproved original terms the new job pleased and intrigued him. The California *Political Code,* which was excerpted at length in small print on the margins of his new office stationery, set forth his duties. On request the state inspector was to test any gas meter any time; if he found it correct he was to seal it with an official seal; if not correct, he was to require the company to make it so, and then seal it on first satisfactory test. As the law required the gas companies to have all new meters inspected and set a fee of $2.50 for the job, it would seem that George had a very good thing. 'My office is in truth about the best in the gift of the Governor,' he wrote his mother. He was bonded for $5000 and had the right to appoint and act through deputies.

During the first year he gave considerable attention to the job. This meant learning the operation of the testing devices as well as the operation of the law, and gathering from far and near what information he could about the most successful mechanisms and procedures. His brother Val often traveled with him and, it seems, very largely took over the mechanical operations George himself might have given much time to.

Of course the money was the first delight. He made $52.50 one early day in the field and wrote Annie that surely he would average out $500 a month for the first year. Pleasant ideas burgeoned with the spontaneity of the spring: he would learn to dance, as much for his own sake as his wife's; they would take a little vacation together; the family would visit Philadelphia and see the Centennial Exposition; they would buy the little house they wanted, even if they did have to pay by installments.

Not one of these dreams came true. Even so they represent a short intense period of relaxation between two big efforts. We catch him breaking his rule against writing only once during this time. In a long letter to the editor of the *Bee,* later printed as an eleven-page pamphlet, George made an interesting case for personal journalism. A state senator had introduced a bill which would have required newspaper articles to be signed. Entirely correct, reasoned Henry George: in present American practice the editorial 'we' signifies not the thinking writers but the interests of the proprietors. Moral questions aside, proprietary journalism lessens the energy of the journalist and deprives him of kudos. Everybody knew Starr King, wrote George, but nobody knew Henry Watson, his old boss, the editor of the Sacramento *Union,* who had been just as great a wartime patriot. George listened to debate on the bill from the Senate gallery, where it passed; and he regretted its failure in the Assembly.

But even this mild degree of personal participation in affairs was unusual for about a year. Next to the job, Henry George's studies took right of way, though not too strenuously at first. 'I am converting the august position I hold into a sort of state Perambulator,' he wrote the new dear friend, Dr. Edward Taylor, who had recommended books. 'What I read now is on the wing.' He had bought Oliver Wendell Holmes' new edition of Kent's *Commentaries,* and Austin's *Lectures* on sovereignty, also a recent work. From an inspection stop in Marysville, where Val was able to do the work, George reported to his wife on what may have been a representative free day. He went to his hotel room 'and took a tussle with Kent . . . I was making fine progress until all of a sudden he threw me . . . I feel encouraged by my progress in law, and really interested, though it does put me to sleep, and I think I can in a year make as much progress as ordinary students do in three or four.'

Release from pressure and being away from home afforded rare opportunities to notice little things, and to write of whatever came to mind. There was time to be amused while he and Val were driving a two-horse buggy on an inspection trip inland, in the direction of Grass Valley. They arranged to spend the night at a farmhouse, where they heard the farmer say that his bedbugs were as bad as anyone's — and only after an interval did they understand that they were being ribbed. This part of the state George thought specially beautiful, and he loved the 'piney odor.' But the bay-region towns appealed, too, especially Napa and San José. He wrote his mother about the charm of the little wooden Episcopal church, and the 'perfect garden' that was San José in May.

To Annie he had intimate things to say, often. After listening to a debate in Sacramento he wrote her sadly, for instance, that one divorce was now being granted for every three marriages in the city where they lived. 'If ever I had any leanings toward the modern doctrine in this matter I have entirely got over it.' And, a few letters later, he tried to balance in words the 'pride and pleasure in feeling that I am really your "lord and master" ' against the joy of acknowledging that, 'if my darling is mine I am also hers.' He missed her dreadfully, he wrote. 'How much delight there is in our love. From the time I first saw you and was captivated by that something in face and voice and manner, which I never could explain in words, it has gone on increasing and increasing . . . And this love is the great thing with me. All outside ups and downs are trivial compared with that.'

–2–

The national event of November 1876 as naturally turned George toward his plan to develop himself as speaker as it drew him away from his aloofness to political affairs. Before the nomination of Tilden, he preferred the Democratic candidate Senator Allen Thurman of Ohio, a strict-constructionist 'Old Roman' of Virginia birth. Very different from his role four years earlier, George went as delegate to no Democratic conventions this time. 'I think as a general rule that state conventions are good things to keep out of,' he wrote his father. When the national party nominated for president the prosecutor of the Tweed ring, a lawyer who had made a fortune in the service of railroad and mining interests, Henry George was willing, but understandably he lacked enthusiasm.

He had to do some hard thinking, accordingly, when the Tilden and Hendricks Central Club of San Francisco, an organization of young men of advanced opinions, invited him to make 'the keynote of the canvass of California' in a great meeting to be held in Dashaway Hall. It was an invitation not to be turned down: his first formal speech before a large audience, and a chance to shape a little the ideas of resurgent Democracy — even though the party had already chosen a Wall Street candidate.

George proceeded a hard way. In a 12,000-word address he stated a persistent issue of American politics, in the perspective he had taken on the editorial page of the *Post*. 'The question involved in this election is not as between two men; it is not as between two parties. It is between two great policies of government, and your vote, or even your refusal to vote, must be its answer. Between the policy of Alexander Hamilton and the policy of Thomas Jefferson you are called on to decide. You have tried the one . . . Will you continue it, or will you try the other?' Back of Hamiltonianism and Jeffersonianism George pictured the eternities of 'Have' and 'Want'; and, in the same rough-hewn way, he identified the great political divisions of history — from 'the Right and Left of the French Assembly, the Cavalier and Roundhead of the England of Charles I' to present-day party alignments.

One passage through which passion still glows denied that the Civil War should be blamed for the country's present moral predicament. 'Many things the war may teach us, but not to distrust the manly qualities of our people. Many are the lessons we may read in its million graves, but not the lesson that the virtues of our blood have run out . . . The object of telling you that these things are due to the war is to induce you to quietly rest in the belief that they will remedy themselves in time . . . No; it is not the war that is responsible for all this . . . Our public service is corrupt because the natural result of our laws has been to engender corruption; our industry [particularly our shipping] is oppressed because our laws have prevented its natural development; the masses are becoming poorer and the few richer, because the whole tendency of our system of finance and taxation is to make $100,000 more profitable in the hands of one man than in the hands of a hundred.'

It was a writer's speech, and George was to need a long time to learn not to take too many risks of chilling his audience with perspective and morality. And another episode of about this time tells us that as a speaker he had other frailties to conquer. Called to the platform from a seat on the floor by the audience at a Democratic rally, he held back at first, then ran across the rostrum, hat in hand, and said what came to mind — without good voice control, and with awkward stance and gesture.

Yet his prepared address caught on. The original audience had ordered it printed and circulated, and the Democratic State Committee asked him to stump the state. There is every indication that he loosened up and performed with flare and effect. He was able to simplify his ideas for delivery from the wayside platform. A newspaper from San Luis Obispo etches him at an outdoor meeting, one October evening in that town. The speaker stood on a hotel balcony; in near foreground listened a sizable crowd, many ladies present; and the background was marked with bonfires. Lights and flags were everywhere.

At campaign's end George received the compliment of being invited to give the principal address at the closing Democratic rally in San Francisco, at Platt's Hall. It would be interesting to know whether he understood the irony, that evening, that the party official who introduced him, a medical doctor, was a member of the Wilson-Shorb family of enormous landed estate in what is now the Pasadena-San Marino area. And finally, when the vote was in, though distressed about the result, he wrote his mother with a sound of personal triumph: 'I have shown that I could make myself felt without a newspaper. I have always felt that I possessed the requisites for a first-class speaker, and that I would make one if I could get the practice; and I started this campaign with the deliberate purpose of breaking myself in. It was like jumping overboard to learn to swim, but I succeeded. I think no man in the state made such a reputation as I have made . . . I wanted to do this, not as a matter of vanity or for the mere pleasure of the thing; but to increase my power and usefulness . . . And so it will — whether I go into politics, into the law, or into the newspaper business again. I do not intend to rest here, but to go ahead step by step.'

The Democrats had given George his first experience as a speaker, and the next speech has the look of the San Francisco party wanting to take advantage of his powers. Whatever the story behind the event, six months after the Hayes-Tilden campaign appropriate officials invited George to be orator of the day for the Fourth of July celebration in the city. The year before, Horatio Stebbins had been orator for the national centennial, and the magnificent celebration had included a parade which brought 200,000 people to the streets. This year there was less to expect, for the depression was closing in, and a one-hundred-first birthday is less exciting than a one-hundredth. Still and again, the honor of being orator was immense and cherished; the Fourth was the glorious day; and then as now San Francisco was a brilliant place for a civic celebration.

According to the *Alta,* 'myriads of small flags were thrown across the principal streets,' thousands turned out on the evening of July third, and the next morning everyone was up early for the ten o'clock parade. Color marched as well as fluttered. A brigadier general stood in the reviewing stand. Among the military, besides the regulars from the Presidio, appeared the City Guard and certain independent companies, the most visible of all the Franco-Americans of the Lafayette Guard and the troop of Zouaves. These last two escorted the civilian dignitaries. Henry George was present, in morning dress, seated in a barouche. He kept company that day with the mayor, the president of the day, the poet of the day, the chief-justice of the state, an ex-senator of the United States, and an ex-governor. French and Russian naval officers from vessels in the harbor also rode in open carriages. The Sons of the Emerald and the Knights of Pythias and the like followed on foot.

The California Theater, the place of the main event, was decorated in keeping. Outside a huge transparency of George Washington and inside a magnificent state seal were made the centers of the festooning. Three thousand people jam-packed the auditorium, and an orchestra played at intervals. No occasion could have been more to the speaker's inclination at the time and he spoke of his childhood love for Independence Hall, the words with which this book opens.

Though the oration is as much too long for a twentieth-century reader as hints suggest that it was for the afternoon crowd in the theater, and though the periods of the speech were rounded off in the rococo of the Victorian age, its structure and its ideas do command attention, the more so because they indicate Henry George's near future as both speaker and writer. Whether or not he so intended, the address took the same broad form as the great syllogism of politics set forth in the Declaration of Independence. In 1776 Jefferson and his colleagues had made the natural rights of man their major premise. In the oration, George began with human liberty — so had preacher Stebbins the year before. 'It is meet that on this day the flags of all nations should mingle above our processions . . . In keeping this day to liberty, we honour all her sacred days . . . From every land have been gathered the gleams of light that unite in her beacon fire.' At Philadelphia the fathers had put down as second premise George III's violation of their rights: he had taxed unjustly, denied fair trial, and had done many wrongs, contrary to contract. In San Francisco the orator of the day likewise spelled out abuses. For the first time, perhaps, he made analogy between the condition of California and the land enclosures famous in the history of British anguish. 'We have repeated *the* sin of the sin-swollen Henry VIII.' Technological progress, said the speaker, had been unfavorable to workers so far: 'The tendency of all modern machinery is to give capital an overpowering advantage, and make labour helpless.' And finally: 'Land monopolized; water monopolized; a race of cheap workers crowding in, whose effect on our own labouring classes is precisely that of slavery; all the avenues of trade under one control, all wealth and power tending more and more to concentrate in a few hands.'

The Declaration comes to a climax with the assertion that when a tyrant abuses the natural rights of his subjects, his true authority is dissolved by the wrongdoing. The patriots of 1776 believed that they were merely taking what belonged to them. Henry George asserted that modern America had inherited this morality, rather possessed it of inherent right, as all men do; and now, in Darwin's day, he confirmed natural rights with the powerful idea of political growth. The more because evolution never became a favorite conception with him — he certainly cannot be connected with the young American pragmatists who were about this time beginning to build heavily on Darwin — it is striking that he now used evolutionary- and pragmatic-sounding argument. 'For life is growth, and growth is change, and political progress consists in getting rid of institutions we have outgrown.'

Through these channels of reason George arrived at his conclusion: the American revolution must be completed in economic life. 'The assertion of the equal rights of all men to life, liberty, and the pursuit of happiness is the assertion of the right of each to the fullest freest exercise of all his faculties, limited only by the equal right of every other. It includes freedom of person and security of earnings, freedom of trade and capital, freedom of conscience and speech and the press. It is the declaration of the same equal rights of all human beings to the enjoyment of the bounty of the Creator — to light and to air, to water and to land. It asserts these rights as inalienable — as the direct grant of the Creator to each human being, of which he can be rightfully deprived neither by kings nor congresses, neither by parchments nor prescriptions —

neither by the compacts of past generations nor by majority votes.'

'The American Republic' — for so George entitled his address — must have required sixty or seventy minutes to deliver, and perhaps more. Its fancy dress suited the occasion, and so did its mood of patriotism. But its weighty argument made no compromise with the ceremonial state of mind, or with the festival spirit; and for that George paid a price. One newspaper observed that the gas measurer 'kindly spoke for several hours on the Goddess of Liberty and other school-reader topics.' Likely a representative reaction was the one printed in San Francisco's new weekly, the *Argonaut*, on 7 July: 'His oration was an able one and eloquent. His peculiar views upon labor and land tenure are greatly in advance of the opinions of that intelligent and not unselfish portion of our community, and do not work.' Even the *Examiner* groped to find congratulatory phrases.

Wry comments at this point accurately suggest the serious problems Henry George had to solve if he was going to become more than a campaign speaker. Merely stating what listeners want to hear, and doing it better than they themselves do, would not suffice for George's larger intention. Nor was his handicap simply that of being heterodox. As an economist in the making, an economic proposer always, he had still to train himself to speak familiarly and interestingly in the elucidation of fairly complicated ideas. One might exaggerate to say that his problem was unique; America for a century had had its more than generous share of elucidators of principle and spokesmen for social reconstruction. The age of Jackson had been rich in them. But to combine in public oratory any such amount of abstract economic reasoning as George did was unusual, and perhaps unprecedented in our national history.

Earlier in 1877 he had tried his skill, just once, at lecturing on economics. The invitation had come from the University of California, where John Le Conte, physicist and brother of the famous geologist, had succeeded Gilman as president. Professors of economics had not yet become standard personnel in American universities, and there was none at Berkeley. Something of the lack was made up by an occasional guest lecturer; George was preceded by half a year by Caspar T. Hopkins, his old opponent in debate about immigration policy, who about this time founded a Social Science Association in the region. When his own invitation came,

George understood that a chair of economics was about to be set up, and that he was mentioned for the place. Perhaps also some appeasement was intended to remove irritations remaining from the battle with President Gilman. On this occasion Henry told Annie George that he wished for no title in the world, unless it was that of 'Professor.'

Perspective on George's own lecture is gained by noticing that Mr. Hopkins had chosen to speak on 'The Relations of Commercial Speculation to Legitimate Business.' Rarely has the Protestant ethic of dedication to work been more tightly joined to the spirit of capitalism than by this son of a bishop. 'Build a railroad or write a book,' he admonished the young people, selecting two activities he himself had tried; avoid 'stock-gambling' and 'note-shaving' as no more worth while than games of chance. Since right thinking according to this lecturer amounted so largely to accepting the standards of business and property, it seems not unreasonable that in his turn George chose to speak for labor.

But by no means exclusively so. A title could hardly have been more neutral than the one at the top of his manuscript, 'The Study of Political Economy.' And, whether or not there really was a professorship hanging in the balance, the lecturer proceeded as formally as if there were. He crossed the bay with his good friend Assemblyman James V. Coffey. President Le Conte entertained them with other distinguished guests at lunch, and then introduced the lecturer. The audience included members of the faculty and students, perhaps forty of whom were women.

With *Progress and Poverty* still two years in the future, it would have required an informed listener indeed to sense the full meaning of the discontent George voiced, that afternoon, against economic ideas all but universally accepted in the Anglo-American world. Present readers may recall that he had once put second thoughts about John Stuart Mill, far less admiring than first thoughts, into an editorial. Now he spoke still more sharply. He said that political economy must be viewed as a laggard study, and that it had made 'no substantial improvement' since Ricardo. (Americans had not yet learned of William Jevons.) In the larger history of economic thought, this Berkeley address may be put down as one of many signposts that classical economics was failing to meet needs which were becoming urgent during the 1870s. On the American side, the Carey school of economics, and, overseas, Karl Marx's writing *Das Kapital* are among the plainest indications that theory was changing; but such ideas had little standing in university classrooms.

The main trouble with economics, specified George, lay in the fact that theory fell short of the natural usefulness of the subject. For 'the science which investigates the laws of production and the distribution of wealth concerns itself with matters which among us occupy more than nine-tenths of human effort and perhaps nine-tenths of human thought.' More than that, the study of economics goes far to explain the rise and fall of nations, and even 'the mental and moral as well as the physical states of humanity.' (A number of remarks indicate that during the early authorship of *Progress and Poverty* George was more nearly an economic determinist than before or after.) What a study, what a tool for the welfare of state and nation, mused George, political economy ought to become.

He assured the students that it was not a dismal science at all, but truly a 'simple and beneficent study' available to everyone. The old writers had indeed gone in for needless hair-splitting; they had neglected the most important of all economic questions, the recurrent phenomenon of depression. Worst of all, economics had arrayed its *laisser faire* ideas against improvement and reforms in behalf of the working classes.

All this could be changed, and must be. Though economics demands 'the habit of careful thought,' it is perfectly available to those who need it most. Let working men study, demanded George, and be deluded no longer, either by too much *laisser faire* or by 'the absurdities of protection and the crazy theories usually designated by the name of socialism.' The lecturer concluded where the author of *Progress and Poverty* would conclude, with a plea that economic truths be studied and laid to heart as continuous with the other truths of human life. 'You will see that the true law of social life is the law of love, the law of liberty, the law of each for all and all for each: that the golden rule of morals is also the golden rule of the science of wealth; that the highest expressions of religious truth include the widest generalizations of political economy.'

George had given a splendid lecture, and one which three years later his publishers did well to have printed in *Popular Science Monthly,* as a kind of advertisement for *Progress and Poverty.* He had ranged a broad field, yet kept focus and direction; he had been critical without limit, yet also idealistic. The address must have been much better geared to his audience than the Fourth of July oration. It is easy to credit the lecturer's own two-way impression 'that his utterances had been well received by the students, but by the authorities with a polite and dignified quietness that made him think that he might not be invited to lecture again.' After the event his connection at Berkeley tapered down to continuing social visits with President Le Conte and his brother. The rest of this biography would be much shorter had Henry George been fixed on the Pacific coast by being seated in a chair of political economy.

From the historical angle of vision which seeks out the gathering ideas of *Progress and Poverty*, the two addresses of this year become luminously important. Henry George, Jr., applies to them a figure of speech from oratory, which confirms a reader's impression that the ideas of the two ought to be read consecutively. The university lecture he calls an 'exordium,' proposing a change in economic thinking, and the Fourth of July speech a 'peroration,' demanding practical measures. It may be seen too, that, though neither address specified as concretely as the *Post* had done just what practical measures George recommended, the two together prefigured, in a rough sketch more natural in the form of lectures than in that of editorials, the total pattern of the coming book.

–3–

But this makes George's advancing work as author seem easier, and his total course seem plainer, than they really were. The summer of 1877 he did spend in the way a writer likes to do. He took his family across the Golden Gate to Sausalito, a lovely place between sea and mountains, where he studied and loafed. By fall he was writing hard on the analyses of economic ideas which are an essential part of *Progress and Poverty*. For nine months after the Fourth of July address he made no more public speeches; and one may guess whether this was altogether a matter of his wishing to drop out of circulation, or whether, as he had twice spoken his radicalism beyond the welcome of his hearers, he may have received no more invitations.

But in the latter part of 1877 occurred the famous Sand Lot riots in San Francisco, the most shocking phase of the labor insurgency led by Dennis Kearney. Events occurred to make a prophet of Henry George. Ten years earlier, in the 'What the Railroad Will Bring Us' article in the *Overland,* he had predicted labor's degradation in California, and a rising of Huns within the cities, fighting to have a share of the wealth of the community. Now the riots outdid the prediction; and almost at once the organized working men of Kearney's new political party sought George's interest and help. His old friend, Assemblyman Days, approached him in their behalf; and, in August, only a month after violence broke out, he was offered a nomination for the state Senate by the People's Reform and anti-Chinese Legislative Convention.

George refused to go along. He detested Kearney as a labor boss and a demagogue and a misleader of the working people. His duty as the first secretary of the board of San Francisco's new public library was, over and above the meter inspectorship, the only public business George did during that fall and winter. He continued with his study and his writing.

Before long, nevertheless, events drew him into affairs. The clamor in San Francisco, the threats of outbreak and the pressures of vigilantism, seems in large degree to explain the gathering, early in 1878, of the earnest men who set up the first organization in the world to advance the social ideas of Henry George.

Among the leaders were two good friends: James Maguire, recently George's colleague in the Tilden campaign, a future judge and congressman; and John M. Days, the same who had recently tried to connect George with Kearneyism and who in 1872 had been midwife to his formal declarations against private property in land. There were also John Swett, school superintendent for years, at the moment a high-school principal, and John Vallance George. Altogether a group of twenty or thirty came together on Sunday afternoons to talk seriously. As in later days in the New York history of Henry George organizations, serious, religious-minded lawyers were the most prominent members.

The group seems to have been in the first instance a study and discussion group exclusively. They read and debated, we are told, 'the economic parts of *Our Land and Land Policy,*' which of course comprised the only presentation in book form, so far, of Henry George's theory. Doubtless the questions and answers helped clear the mind of the working author. But only a short time passed before the members wanted more than just talk among themselves; and one meeting, when about thirty were convened in one of the city court-rooms, decided to set up a formal organization. They elected an Irish-born lawyer to be president; and one Patrick J. Murphy, a newspaperman trained on the *Post*, became secretary. Thus was born the Land Reform League of California, the first of hundreds, perhaps thousands, of its kind the world around.

Organization meant an appeal to the troubled public, and a meeting; and, for Henry George, having a following meant the obligations of leadership and a return to public speaking. He was obliged to put manuscript aside to prepare a keynote address. There was no need, this time, to diagnose without prescription, as in Berkeley. If there was ever an occasion to come to the heart of the matter, this was the time. The title George chose, 'Why Work Is Scarce, Wages Low, and Labor Restless,' expressed his sense of the situation; and naturally he incorporated the more concrete and practical notions he was distilling into *Progress and Poverty*.

Where he had blamed the great economists for refusing to go, he himself now ventured. 'Why Work Is Scarce' anticipated in detail the chapter on 'The primary cause of recurring paroxysms of in-dustrial depression,' in the coming book; and it set the pattern of analysis he was to hold for life and to apply in the depression of the 1890s, with very little change. He began with the proposition that the time had come for economists to look for general and under-lying causes of economic upset. He phrased as current history very nearly the same thought he had phrased as prophecy before the railroad had been finished: 'Under our very eyes, a highly civilized community has risen on virgin soil. From a social condition that was nearer equality than anywhere else existed, we have seen the rich and the poor separate.' What common cause explains, he wanted to know, the tragic conditions in new California, in the industrial East, in old Britain — in the whole Western capitalistic world?

The speaker worked toward his solution, 'The Great Cause' of depression and poverty, through a series of negations. Anyone's talk about an imbalance between supply and demand for labor, or an oversupply or underconsumption of goods, he dismissed as high-sounding cant. (The 'disequilibrium' known to present-day econ-omists was not his problem.) Nature provides two hands for every

mouth, he noticed; and on a desert island a man can provide for
his own. *Robinson Crusoe* had become favorite reading with
George, and he used it effectively. Reverting to his old observation
that the greatest wealth, the highest technology, and the largest
populations appear together in the same areas of the modern world,
he argued that in the correct relation those factors should produce
the highest standards of living in history. George refused on the
platform, as at other times since 1872, to blame different results on
any inherent struggle between capital and labor. Those two together 'represent the human elements in production'; the only
other element is the world's God-given fertility, the annual cycle of
the seasons, the universal burgeoning of life. 'There is no conflict
between capital and labor — and that there is popularly supposed
to be arises from a want of exactness in the use of words.'

George managed eloquence of argument — but we cannot imagine surprise for any listener — as he asserted at climax that 'The
Great Cause' of depression was monopoly. Mainly, not exclusively,
land monopoly, he said: resource monopoly, without mention of
industrial monopoly, is what he chose to stress, in this oratorical
simplification of his ideas. 'All history shows that the fact which
ultimately determines the social, the political, and consequently
the intellectual and moral condition of a people, is the tenure of the
land . . . Truly the earth is our mother.' He pleaded, as in the
Post, that the only correct policy was to reassert the natural right
of the people of California to the land of California, to reapply to
the land and water, in even more positive form, 'the equitable
doctrine that in earlier days we applied to the land . . . the doctrine that no one can hold more than he can reasonably use, and
for no longer time than he does use it . . . This is called agrarianism. Do not be frightened at the word . . . It does not mean warfare against society . . . Agrarianism is the true conservatism.'
Late in the lecture, answering a question, he spoke of confiscating
land values: 'Nay, the confiscation is in the present system.'

On a rostrum, economic diagnosis, akin to accusation, comes easy,
but the doctor's prescription is hard to deliver. Once again George
thought and spoke in three's, but this time he made his program
more consolidated than in the *Post.* First, he said, addressing himself to California's old problem of security, let any occupant's peaceable *bona fide* use of a parcel of land for a year or longer be under-

stood as 'conclusive evidence' of ownership. Second, he wanted all taxes abolished save land taxation, of course the buildings and other improvements not counted. This simplified to one point the three-pronged tax program of the *Post*. Third and last, George recommended a summary process under which any land not in use could be condemned and assigned to any citizen who wished to use it and would pay the assessment.

In this address, as always in the future, George's analysis of depression came up with institutional and moral failure. That is, he believed that job opportunities were withheld and poverty induced by reason of wrong-headed policies and exploitative institutions, rather than because of mechanical flaws in the operation of capitalism. Actually he was ahead of his time and with the future in making the general proposition that depressions are a natural product of the going system and should be anticipated. But also he was different from the future main line of business-cycle analysts who would find depressions inherent in the frictions of *economic* operations narrowly regarded. 'Why Work Is Scarce' should be read, George wrote John Swinton, 'as an attempt to put into popular form a great truth which marries political economy with common sense, and which once appreciated is the key to all the social evils of our time. Of course the exigencies of a popular lecture prevent the exhibition of truth in its full form, but the truth is there which can be worked out by anyone who will catch it . . . The seed that I have for years been sowing is springing up on every hand . . . I can see what I never expected to see, the result of my work. Where I stood alone thousands now stand with me. The leaven is at work. And there can be but one result. But the struggle will be long and fierce. It is now only opening.'

Besides making the advance he mentioned to Swinton, that of connecting his economic analysis with a political program, George's 'Why Work Is Scarce' address marks a step also in his shifting from mainly regional to more generalized habits of social thought. To be sure he said many things that only Californians would have understood. His observations about land titles, for instance, sound like a page from the debates of 1867; and one fellow journalist, E. A. Waite, who held a friendly judgment about the speaker — 'Henry George writes a very vigorous article . . . has some motive about him' — complained at this point that George had borrowed without due acknowledgment ideas he himself had put in a San Francisco magazine article. On the other hand, George was compelled by his distaste for Kearney to separate himself from California's race antagonism. Though the anti-Chinese issue was still as accessible to him as it had been in 1868 and thereafter, he touched it now only in a way to be different from Kearney; and the moral contrast between the famous California radicals may be measured by George's refusal to join in the clamor that the Chinese must go.

In political essence, Henry George and the Land Reform League of California were making that most difficult of all democratic efforts: they were making the appeal of reason and dispassion to men already inflamed. The nature of the effort put enormous strain on George's powers as a speaker, and a story, from the day of his first delivering 'Why Work Is Scarce,' indicates that he was a little overwhelmed by the task. He went with Mrs. George to the hall to rehearse, and he met a clergyman there. When this experienced speaker told him that his speech would go over the heads of a working-class audience, George took offense. But that evening there was a very small turnout, and he was upset. According to a witness 'he kept his eyes on the paper and seemed to be so nervous he was almost frightened.'

Nevertheless the address did catch on, and one of Henry George's hardest years, 1878, does mark his first success — dimly prophetic of the decade of the 1880s — in using the spoken word to render his ideas into general currency. He repeated 'Why Wages Are Low' in San Francisco; and, under title of 'The Coming Struggle,' he gave it again in Sacramento and received a fair notice in the *Record-Union*. Five months after first delivery, the *Argonaut* in two issues reprinted the essential argument. And, up to the present time, followers of Henry George still distribute copies as a concise introduction to his economic thought.

Not until his next speech, however, the fourth and last one of the series between the campaign addresses of 1876 and his completing *Progress and Poverty*, did George strike just such an appealing vein of eloquence as promised a successful future on the rostrum. In June 1878, though he was at the one-third-of-the-way stage of drafting his book, George accepted the invitation of the new Young Men's Hebrew Association in San Francisco to deliver a prominent

address. By announcing the title, 'Moses or Leader of the Exodus,'
he chose to jolt a little his hosts' expectations, for they were a liberal
group and wanted to hear George on a public issue. We may suppose that in writing the speech he drew on childhood accumulations of Bible knowledge, and we may be sure that he read freshly,
too, from Exodus and Leviticus.

The appeal he made lay in his rendering into the language of
tradition and emotion his own enlarging social thought. 'Everywhere in the Mosaic institutions is the land treated as the gift of
the Creator to his common creatures, which no one has the right
to monopolize. Everywhere it is, not your estate, or your property,
not the land which you bought, or the land which you conquered,
but "the land which the Lord Thy God giveth thee" — "the land
which the Lord lendeth thee" . . . [Moses] not only provided for
the fair division of the land among the people, and for making it
fallow and common every seventh year, but by the institution of
the jubilee he provided for a redistribution of the land every fifty
years, and made monopoly impossible.'

George made the quality of leadership the main theme of the
address. His mind had sprung to that problem when Lincoln died;
today a reader of 'Moses' will hardly need the suggestion of his
daughter to understand that George's 'enthusiasm for the Biblical
leader arose from a feeling of kinship with him.' Unobliged in this
speech to compress much economic and political argument, George
let his mind rove freely in areas of morality and the interpretation
of human events. He had a word for any enthusiastic materialists
in the audience who might be inclined to think of 'the prominent
characters of history as resultants rather than as initiatory forces
. . . It is true that "institutions make men," but it is also true that
in the beginnings "men make institutions." ' The new Bible criticism, he said, while placing Moses the lawgiver later in time than
the prophets, was also recognizing him as at 'the beginning of that
growth which flowed after centuries in the humanities of Jewish
law, and in the sublime conception of one God, universal and
eternal, the Almighty Father.' George estimated the character of
Moses from the work he did. 'Habits of thought are even more
tyrannous than habits of the body. Hebrew freedom must be seen
as reaction against Egyptian tyranny.'

In lines of thought which run strikingly in the same direction as certain ideas of Reinhold Niebuhr's modern commentary, George praised the Jews for their religious practicality, for having 'sternly repressed' any too abstract 'tendency to take the type for the reality,' and for refusing to make too much of the comforting idea of immortality. After their sojourn in Egypt — for which the members of the Y.M.H.A. were free to substitute 'California' — the Jews who followed Moses had found power to assert 'a God of the living as well as of the dead; a God whose inimitable decrees will, in this life, give happiness to the people that hold them and bring misery among the people that forget them.'

With an intensity that moved his audience, George built up the proposition that the concern of Moses — and of Puritan and Covenanter — had been to lay the foundation of a social state in which deep poverty and degrading want should be unknown. George's final word praised Moses' calling — and obliquely his own. 'Of something more real than matter; of something higher than the stars; of a light which will endure when suns are dead and dark; of a purpose of which the physical universe is but a passing phase, such lives tell.'

So combining in one speech the qualities of sermon and oration, George hit at last a vein of emotion that could lift men's hearts. In due time, six years or so, 'Moses' would become a favorite address. We shall find Henry George giving it again and again, a kind of sustaining piece, especially good for Sundays, and particularly acceptable in Scotland and England, where Bible formulas had more appeal than formulas from America's Declaration of 1776.

But this was not for California in 1878 and 1879. Dr. Taylor, whose literary assistance to Henry George was deepening their friendship, urged no more speeches now. Perhaps he saw that without the finished book George's power would soon run down; and perhaps George himself needed little persuasion. But the inner circle of the Land Reform League must have felt enormous regret that, during California's deepest crisis and her period of constitution making, Henry George lived in retirement, that he was not personally on the political front, as powerful as in 1873 or more so, constructing institutions or policies out of the ideas he had now matured.

-4-

Yet George did make one more try for practical influence. In March 1878, a short time before the legislature passed the act which made the constitutional convention possible, he wrote Assembly-man Coffey how anxious he was for the convention to be called at once. The ex-editor of the *Post* could not have thought otherwise; and, book or no book, he was only being true to old principles when, a month later, he brought out a broadside 'To the Voters of San Francisco.' In that way he announced candidacy for the convention.

Though he built his platform in somewhat more specific terms than the Fourth of July oration, as a whole he made his manifesto general, more like that speech than like the heavy argument in 'Why Work Is Scarce.' On taxation he declared simply for shifting the burden 'from those who have little to those who have much, from those who produce wealth to those who merely appropriate it, so that the monopoly of land and water may be destroyed . . . and an end put to the shameful state of things which compels men to beg who are willing to work.' Appropriately in political more than in economic language, he favored a 'dignified' resistance to Chinese immigration, and the designing of a 'symmetrical and re-sponsible' government for San Francisco. Broadly he declared him-self for the philosophy of the Declaration and for loyalty to the 'Republicanism of Jefferson and the Democracy of Jackson.'

Yet, having stepped forward, a man of principle for the con-stitutional convention, George soon decided that he did not really care whether he was elected or not. Mainly, not entirely, the candi-dates for seats lined up either for the Workingmen's party, or against it, the conservative opposition fusing Democrats and Re-publicans into a big 'Nonpartisan' bloc. George could not go with the fusion. And when the Workingmen offered him a nomina-tion he made issue with the stipulation they required, that their nominees pledge themselves to follow the party line in every re-spect, and even agree beforehand to resign, should occasion arise and party 'constituents' so demand. Nettled by this, George went before the appropriate meeting and answered with a resounding 'No.' Reporting to John Swinton in New York, he said that if elected he was sure to be flanked by monopoly on two sides, and the success or failure of his candidacy would mean very little.

The nomination he did accept came from a Democratic Nominating Convention, an element not absorbed in the state's polarization of politics. But even here George entered an exception. He told the convention that a certain clause of their platform, which favored a long period for redeeming real estate taken by the state for delinquent taxes, would not help homesteaders and would favor land withholders. He would not pledge that plank. 'Upon the land grabbers who have carved up the soil of California into baronial estates, I wish to bring to bear the power of taxation with remorseless vigor.'

The short story of George's candidacy for the constitutional convention, then, adds definition to the longer story of his having made himself a solitary, a cynic about present politics, an idealist for the principles he would not compromise. The story's end discovers the voters letting him retain his solitude. Henry George, Jr., has it that 'the whole Democratic ticket was beaten at the polls,' which is literally true of San Francisco. The Workingmen's party captured the entire delegation from the city; and from the state as a whole, 81 Nonpartisans, 51 Workingmen, 11 Republicans, 7 Democrats, and 2 independents were chosen. The morning after the election Assemblyman Coffey, who also ran, put a card on the gas-meter inspector's door: 'Accept congratulations on leading the Democratic Party to the Devil.' George had received more votes than any other Democratic nominee in the city.

So, while others wrote a new fundamental law for the state, Henry George worked on his manuscript. For two and a half years his activities had been narrowing; now, for the third and fourth quarters of 1878 and the first of 1879, the exact period of the convention, he concentrated completely. Apparently with embarrassingly little to distract him at the inspector's office, and with not a single speech to write, and no editorials, he forged ahead to his conclusion.

George worked mainly at home, in surroundings he would remember with nostalgia during New York years. After the lovely summer in Sausalito, where he had warmed up for the task, the family moved to the Rincon Hill district of San Francisco, not far from his office on Mission Street and near the bay. They took a house on Second Street, late in 1877, and then moved to one on First Street near Harrison, remembered as the place where *Progress and Poverty* was written. The houses were shabby and, in the President Lincoln style, already a bit old-fashioned: a visitor remembers scrollwork decoration on Henry George's gables. But there was comfort enough; and the large second-floor workroom in the First Street house, the three windows of which commanded San Francisco Bay and the hills surrounding, gave resource and joy to the writer.

Within doors the caller just cited, a bibliophile come to see George's library, gives us a glimpse of such domestic turmoil as many a writer at the age of forty has had to live with. There were four children now, from Henry, Jr., at sixteen, down to Annie Angela, the baby named for her mother and the Feast of Angels, the day of her birth in 1877. The visitor found nothing special among the library's 300 books, except the owner. Working in a saffron-colored dressing gown, George babbled with comment, criticism, and appreciation of the books around him. General dishevelment far from obscured the sweet good-feeling in the household.

For the time being a kind of puritan Bohemian, Henry George took to his sofa for reading. He wrote whenever he could, frequently at night when sleep refused to come. When he could not work he took his troubles to the bay, where wind and water relaxed him. He kept notebooks, he rough-drafted, he rewrote and revised. Under the slogan, 'Hard writing makes easy reading,' he took the most time for the analytical passages. More than would seem possible, he used the inexperienced help of his wife and oldest child. Mrs. George checked the manuscript, and Henry, who had finished school now and was studying shorthand on the side, acted as amanuensis. But the final manuscript copy of *Progress and Poverty*, now deposited in the Library of Congress, is every line done in Henry George's own hand, very neat and clear and with few emendations, a huge piece of painstaking. Nerves must have been tight sometimes in the home which produced the book, but the children record a good and happy time during the months of composition.

No isolation is quite complete, and even during this interval George depended on his friends, most especially Edward Taylor. Their acquaintanceship dated from George's days on the Sacramento *Reporter,* when Dr. Taylor had been Governor Haight's secretary. He was a man with connections. Presently he was practising law, a member of the ex-governor's firm in San Francisco. He had some family tie with Leland Stanford; and a few years later it was he who transmitted to the author of *Progress and Poverty* the not quite incredible story that the railroad president had read the book and said that he had become 'a disciple of Henry George.' While *Progress and Poverty* was in process, Dr. Taylor extended the hospitality of his firm's law library, and George did a great deal of work there.

Dr. Taylor did much more. With a quick appreciation of the size of George's task, he urged the writer to think big. From a mind that knew and treasured literature and suffered because his own poetry seemed not equal to the cry within, he helped George with leads and ideas. His one certified specific contribution to *Progress and Poverty* is the stirring poem of exhortation at the opening of Book VIII, wherein George sets forth his alternative proposals for doing away with private property in land. Dr. Taylor asks:

> *Shall we in the presence of this previous wrong,*
> *In this supremest moment of all time,*
> *Stand trembling, cowering, when with one bold stroke*
> *These groaning millions might be ever free?*

In the first edition of *Progress and Poverty* the poem was made anonymous, apparently at the author's request; later George insisted on entering a credit line. To suggest what other passages in *Progress and Poverty* may be due to Dr. Taylor would be guesswork. Yet any reader of *all* Henry George's works who senses how much richer than the others this book is, in quoted passages of poetry and prose, is likely to credit this intellectual friend with a considerable contribution. George's lifetime gratitude to him accords better with such a debt than with a minor one.

In San Francisco George had the benefit also of expert help from one or two other associates, of whom John Swett, the principal of the Girls' High School, is least anonymous. Mr. Swett may have been the member of the Land Reform League who sometimes brought John Muir to the meetings: at any rate the two were friends, and the great naturalist and conservationist knew and was much stirred by Henry George at this period. At the stage of proofreading Mr. Swett combed over *Progress and Poverty* for errors in expression and grammar — needlessly, he says. Not completely convinced by George's ideas, this friend understood the book as a product of the time and place. 'It really seemed as if the foundations of society were breaking up. A part of George's book took its tone from these hard times.' Another member of the league remembers talking with George about how it had taken Herbert Spencer twenty-five years to get a respectable hearing, and recalls George agreeing that *Progress and Poverty* had better be directed to influencing the twentieth century.

Outside San Francisco lay a personal debt perhaps not much smaller than the one to Dr. Taylor. This is the debt to James McClatchy, which, being of dateless origin in the past, is hard to evaluate. According to a story more than twice told, the editor of the *Bee* deserves credit for first suggesting that George write the big book. This claim depends on a remembered conversation: on the story that George once told McClatchy that *he* ought to state his philosophy about land in a book; and that McClatchy replied, no, he was too old, but George should do it. If this advice was given early enough, say just following *Our Land and Land Policy* in 1871, then McClatchy is probably due the credit that the *Bee* later claimed for him. If the conversation took place much later than 1871 — a question not to be determined — then the story implies more dependence on McClatchy than can have been true and indicates good will between the two but nothing more than this. Whatever the fact of the suggestion, George sent chapters of *Progress and Poverty* to the old editor for comment and revision, and had his help that way.

According to recent standards of biographical procedure, there should now be some description and exposition of George's library, some analysis of the books he is known to have worked with, as determinants or conditioners of *Progress and Poverty* in gestation. Unfortunately George's own collection of books was dispersed and we have no list of it. His son says that he had about 600 volumes, twice as many as the estimate cited above; and we know that, in addition to it and the Taylor library, he drew on the State Library in Sacramento and used four libraries in San Francisco — the Odd Fellows, the Mercantile, the Mechanics, and the Free. (What Cheer House is not mentioned at this time.) Lacking much evidence about

George's borrowings, the reader is referred back to chapters III
and VIII, especially, for some account of his earlier reading, and
forward to chapter X, where he will find a little detective work on
what George read while he was composing, based on evidence
within *Progress and Poverty* itself.

–5–

We have seen how George was affected by the rise of the Kearney
movement. Yet the influences on him were pretty negative at that
stage. He refused to go with the party; he made some effort to
launch a rival reform; he blamed Kearneyism as much as anything
for his having been defeated for the constitutional convention; he
retired from affairs.

But during the early months of 1879, when *Progress and Poverty*
was finished and the new constitution was submitted for ratification, George undertook a more active role. For this reason the
political background now requires a little further sketching in.
By 1879, emotions had been thoroughly aroused, anti-labor de-
fenses had been marshaled, and what a recent scholar calls California's 'Big Red Scare' had seized the state.

Readers of a generation more familiar than Henry George's was
with the phenomenon we call fascism will not need long explanations. Behind California's tensions were the national and international conditions of a prolonged depression. The railroad strikes
of 1877, originating many miles away, had been the event that set
off the riots. On the Pacific coast itself, a serious drought aggravated
economic hardship. Laboring men knew that there had been a
huge immigration of Chinese in 1876, about 22,000 of them; and
the news-reading world soon learned that Kearney's followers were
dramatizing their poverty, with an effectiveness hardly possible
elsewhere in the world, by assembling very near the recently built
palaces of railroad kings and silver princes on Nob Hill.

While Henry George's energies drained off in the Land Reform
League, Dennis Kearney's organization succeeded in drawing together trade-union elements and locals of the national Workingmen's party, and it became a large and potent thing. Not only in
the San Francisco Bay area, but throughout the state, clubs were
formed and an impressive number of local elections won. Not since
Jackson's day, nor in that day, had the country seen anything quite

comparable: a working-men's party overwhelming an election in a major city, and threatening to take control of city and state.

Hence the red scare. Largely thanks to the new biography of John S. Hittell by Professor Claude W. Petty, it is possible to visualize how the psychology of fear transformed conservatives into suppressors. Hittell's employer, Frederick MacCrellish, proprietor of the *Alta California,* joined the vigilantes in 1877, at the moment of organization. And the old editorial writer, the man whose ideas had been George's departing point for dissent and difference during the '60s, became a regular red-baiter. One can imagine Henry George's feeling about Hittell's editorials, say the following propositions: 'Reform is a word familiar to every political villain . . . Civilization and intelligence are most active where individuals have been enabled to accumulate great wealth . . . Equality is not enviable when it is the dead level of intellectual and industrial stagnation.'

Hittell attached the name of 'Kearneyism' to every brand of California protest, and completed the smear by tagging, in the title phrase of one of his editorials, 'Kearneyism Another Name for Communists.' The irresponsibility of the *Alta*'s procedure becomes clearest in the case of the Grangers, who were more conservative in California than in their principal locations in the Middle West. Three years earlier, ahead of the strikes and the sharpest crisis, ex-professor Carr had found time to bring out his *Patrons of Husbandry on the Pacific Coast,* more a manifesto than a history. He acknowledged some debt to Henry George. He made his most theoretical chapter a rendering of the ideas of John Hiram Lathrop, midwestern agrarian, son of Yale, and president, successively, of the universities of Missouri, Wisconsin, and Indiana. Yet the Granger movement too, the farmers' baby, the *Alta* would have thrown out with the radical bath.

A part of the price paid by the state was, naturally, the stifling of moderate and liberal opinion. As a kind of control point, for observing the ineffectiveness of Henry George's voice in state affairs, we have the effort of a new weekly newspaper, *Hall's Land Journal,* to represent, in a more progressive variation, the middle-of-the-road conservatism that Caspar T. Hopkins had expressed a decade earlier. (President Hopkins at this time was cultivating the California Social Science Association, but would return to the

printed discussion of state affairs in the *Overland,* in the early '80s.)
The new journal was edited by Charles Victor Hall, who had recently been a student in the state university and would presently
become a wealthy promoter. Engagingly the editor applauded
Henry George's Fourth of July address, and quarreled with the
low-interest and low-wages policy of the *Alta,* while he also printed
more conservative editorials. The paper did not last; and its significance in the Henry George story is that its young editor produced
a lonely flash of the Greeley-like, or McClatchy-like, spirit which
we have caught earlier in San Francisco journalism. But that spirit
is conspicuous by its infrequency during the 'Big Red Scare'; and
it never had been present in the now dominant *Alta California*
and the Fitch-Pickering-Simonton newspapers.

In the face of this kind of situation, Henry George decided to
launch a new newspaper. The immediate occasion was the adjournment of the constitutional convention in Sacramento, in March
1879, and the impending contest over ratifying the new instrument.
George was free to act because his book was written; and he was the
readier to do so because his gas-meter job was about to terminate.
Where he found the funds for even a very small paper is not clear;
it is perfectly plain that he needed a job once more.

For the first time George's political goal coincided with those of
the majority of San Francisco newspapers. In the city, only the
Chronicle, among the established journals, wanted the new constitution ratified. The common reason, not George's reason, for
opposing it was that the new frame of government was radical and
would discourage businessmen. 'No one in this country can be induced to invest a dollar in any California enterprise until this communistic constitution is broken down by the common sense of the
people,' wrote an ex-Californian, E. F. Beale, from the nation's
capital. But on his side, Henry George believed that the constitution was too conservative, and that it should be defeated on that
account. Not fearing the Kearneyites as upsetters of the social order,
but rather as being politically ignorant and corrupt, George had a
distaste, equal to that of the *Alta California,* for the labor party's
growing force. Dennis Kearney took the stump for ratification;
and we may glance forward to see that at fall elections his party
would actually achieve its maximum strength — it would elect six
Supreme Court judges to a bench of seven, and seat sizable minor-

ities, eleven senators and sixteen assemblymen, in the two houses of
the legislature. Kearney's power was a part of the challenge that
brought George back into state affairs.

But the heart of the matter was the constitution itself. The
plainest thing about it was its extreme length; in this respect it
differed utterly from the principles of simplicity and flexibility advanced by George in the *Post*. Concerning real-estate taxation, it
contained a procedural requirement, Article XIII, Section 2, which
has pleased twentieth-century single-taxers, indeed, because it prescribed an arrangement they have had to fight for elsewhere, for
instance in New York and recently in Pennsylvania. 'Land and improvements thereon shall be separately assessed . . . [and] land,
of the same quality and similarly situated shall be assessed at equal
value.' But this did not make Henry George a friend for the constitution. To him another provision about land, Article XVII, Section 2, was the crucial thing: 'The holding of large tracts of land,
uncultivated and unimproved, by individuals or corporations is
against the public interest and should be discouraged by all means
not inconsistent with the rights of private property.' *'Not inconsistent with the rights of private property'* — this clause, conserva-
tively interpreted, could protect the speculator and withholder
against the policies George desired, even more effectively than the
equality-of-taxation clause in the constitution of 1849.

On 5 April, Henry George's new paper, a weekly, *The State*,
began to appear. Perhaps Sir William Jones' poem, 'The State,'
suggested the name. George seems to have loved this poem, for he
had inserted it in his very first printed piece, in the *Journal of Labor
and Workmen*, fourteen years earlier; and now he printed it again,
on the front page of the first issue. A few lines are worth quoting,
for they will help capture George's own mood:

> *What Constitutes a State?*
> *Not high raised battlement or labored mound,*
> *Thick wall or moated gate;*
> *Not cities proud with spires and turrets crowned . . .*
> *No: — Men, high-minded men*
> *With powers as far above dull brutes endured*
> *In forest brake or den*
> *As heart excel cold rocks and brambles rude . . .*

> *These constitute a State;*
> *And sovereign Law, that State's collected will . . .*
> *Sits empress, crowning good, suppressing ill.*

George's editorial 'Salutatory,' hard by the poem, announced 'a Democratic paper' but denied that the *State* started with any backers, partisan or financial. 'It will not shrink from supporting the right because it is unpopular, nor cringe to wrong because it is strong.' The editor sounded as though he meant to stay in business, whether or not the constitution was ratified. Though 'not as big or as good a paper as many would want to see . . . it is as good and as big as I can now make it. If it succeeds it will grow.' George promised to proceed according to the lessons he had learned on the *Post* and had tried to preach. He would run signed articles. He would not regret the lack of outside funds: $200,000 not earned in journalism would spoil the independence of the *State,* he said. This first issue won a flicker of recognition from his old critic, the Colusa *Sun:* 'We have been growing stupid of late,' that paper admitted, from lack of fire and originality in the California press.

While the *Alta* called the *State* communistic, George swung into editorial sympathy with the Sacramento *Bee.* McClatchy's paper, which had accused the convention at mid-session of being managed by land and water monopolies, said on 29 April that, 'Land reform will be set back fifteen to twenty years if this new instrument shall be adopted, and water monopoly by it is protected and perpetuated.' In his second issue George attacked the clause in the constitution about private property in land, which is quoted above. Nine months later, in the *Bee* of 24 December, he said even more forcefully that that clause could be read by judges to render unconstitutional any future legislation intended to appropriate economic rent.

There is no need to comb the editorials of the *State,* as we did the *Post,* for ideas which often reformulated the convictions of the earlier paper, or which drew on the arsenal of the unpublished book manuscript. Amply and strongly against ratification, George argued the merits of having a short constitution and a short ballot, as in the interest of working men most particularly. At points of greatest difference from Kearney, he ran a series on the economics of the working class, and he took a more moderate attitude than ever before toward the Chinese — this last in perfect contrast with the exclusions in Article XIX of the new constitution. He exposed a fresh instance of civic corruption.

Most of this poured out in the five issues of the weekly that preceded the ratification vote. It is fair to suppose that San Francisco's majority of about 1600 against the constitution, in a vote of some 38,000, owed something to George's radical opposition. And we may suppose also that, although George continued some six weeks longer, his quitting the *State* in June was in part due to his general discouragement about politics under the new frame of government. Though his children say that the little paper was breaking even, and that he dropped it in order to give full attention to publishing *Progress and Poverty,* we have his own more complicated story in a letter which is really a testament, dated 6 May, the day before the ratification.

Writing to John Swinton, he pretty much summed up the issue of a dozen years of trying to influence California. The fight against the constitution, he said, had been *'very, very* lonely'; and now he was pained to discover 'that we differ, when we ought to be together, and that you who ought to applaud it, regret my course.' The newspapers which Swinton had been reading in New York, George said — the *Bulletin,* the *Alta,* the *Argonaut,* and the *News Letter* in opposition, and the *Chronicle* in behalf of the constitution — would naturally make it seem 'that here is a closely drawn struggle between the monopolysing [sic] classes on the one part, and popular right on the other. But it is not so.'

George admitted nothing except coincidence in common between himself and the 'capitalists who are fighting this constitution . . . They fear and dislike me. They look on me, as the man who is the head of the anti-constitution committee expressed it — as a man more dangerous in the long run than a hundred Kearneys . . . I make no friends with them; but on the other hand I am losing the confidence of the men who ought to be my friends. If I were a demagogue all I would have to do would be to go in and shout, and I could be popular with the only men I can be popular with. But I would be false to my firmest convictions.'

Contrary to the charges of the red-baiters, George denied the least 'glimpse or gleam of communism or socialism' in the document. 'Vacquerel, the only real communist in the convention, is fighting it; the real and thoughtful socialists . . . are opposing it;

men like Chas. A. Sumner [the old friend on Nugent's *Herald*],
Jim Lane, and others who have fought the railroad monopoly inch
by inch, are opposing it. Men like John M. Days, John A. Collins,
who have steadily fought land monopoly are opposing it. I do not
know a single man who believe[s] as I do that land is not rightfully
private property who is supporting this new Constitution. But men
like these have no voice that you hear.'

As for the winners, George emphasized that the great strength
of the new constitution belonged to the Grangers, 'a class which as
you know is the one least likely to accept radical ideas. It is warmly
supported by men who hold five, twenty, fifty thousand acres of
land.' George spoke of the Grangers in almost the same way as
liberals speak of the Associated Farmers in California today, and
for his eastern reader he carefully differentiated them from the
discontented farmers of the Middle West — 'for we have not in
California in any considerable proportion that class of small farmers
who settled the West side by side in quarter sections.' Politically
and for the moment only, George agreed that the Kearneyites stood
with the Grangers. But, he went on, 'The so called workingmen in
the convention did not make a single point — in fact they had no
intelligent idea of what a constitution should be or what would
benefit the working classes; they simply fell in with the Grangers
because by this combination they thought to make a party which
would carry the next election and give them the offices. That is
their highest idea.'

Beside the working men, among those who said yes to the Grangers' constitution, George placed 'the great railroad monopoly,'
which also expected to have its own way. 'They made the Commission section,' he told Swinton, with reference to a board of railroad commissioners to whom the constitution assigned broad but
toothless powers to supervise the railroads of the state. In the *State*
he had been even more specific: 'Astute lobbyists and manipulators
are kept in the constant pay of the Central Pacific Railroad, which
has organized corruption into a perfect system,' and which succeeded in placing friends of monopoly in the convention.

A more unrelieved picture of the politics of self-interest and
jobbery than George's would be hard to turn up. 'The constitution
is repugnant to the business classes on account of its scheme of
taxation; to the corporations on account of the d—d fool clauses

regarding corporations; and to all the more intelligent classes because of its want of coherency, precision, and every quality which should be shown in a Constitution; to me and men like me it is chiefly repugnant because giving no real reform it will if adopted but block the way to reform . . . The very rich class have nothing whatever to fear from it. Though they have to a great extent got themselves worked up by the shadow of that bugbear which they call "communism." The men who have most to fear are men who want reform which will go to the very foundation of the social structure, and who have an intelligent idea of what they want.'

For George personally, all this amounted to more than a mood of discouragement and defeat, and more even than a sense of being at the moment displaced in a community where he had risen high and gone down. It represented his permanent judgment of affairs in California, and the fear which was deepening within him for the safety of the republic as a whole. A year later, when Professor Youmans invited an account of Kearneyism, done in the spirit of scientific inquiry, George generalized. 'Given universal suffrage, a vague blind bitter feeling of discontent on the one side and of practical political impotence, producing indifference and recklessness on the part of the great mass of voters — and any incident may start a series of the most dangerous actions and reactions.' In a still later comment he noted that the railroad had been the real winner — that, though Californians had voted 'against the railroad time and again, or rather imagined they did,' the great corporation, 'of whose domain California, with an area greater than twice that of Great Britain, is but one of the provinces, absolutely dominates the State.' This would in fact be a valid estimate for the coming three decades of California politics.

To the younger Henry George, in days on the *Post* and the *Reporter,* the railroad monopoly had seemed dangerous but not overwhelming. It might have appeared tyrannous, or Machiavellian, on many occasions, but the leadership had seemed admirable on others; and the system had proved almost benevolent to the American Press Association. Likewise only short years before 1879 the land monopoly had seemed not impossible to break, and the water monopoly had appeared to be subject to the democratic process. But now all the monopolies had entrenched themselves, and at the age of forty George saw no hope of change.

At this point, friends far and near told George that he had better leave California. John Swett said so. John Russell Young, who presently came to San Francisco with General Grant on the ex-president's round-the-world tour, sensed that his old friend was deeply troubled. Though in intimate conversations George would spell out few of his perplexities, Young testifies, he seemed to be 'swimming in heavy seas . . . He spoke as a stranger with his abiding place in a strange land.' He appeared to be a square peg in a round hole: 'San Francisco did not appreciate him.' The visitor helped make the decision that the author of *Progress and Poverty* go to New York for a fresh start.

In November 1876, when Samuel J. Tilden missed clear-cut victory at the polls, and the California Democrats were routed, Henry George had written his mother that political defeat was as good as victory for such as he. 'In fact, I think better, as a man of my mind has a better chance of coming forward more rapidly in a minority than in a majority party. However, about all such things, I am disposed to think that whatever happens is for the best. Talent and energy can nearly always convert defeats into victories.'

In 1879 George was reduced close to being a one-man minority with a program, in California. But *Progress and Poverty* he now addressed to the world, and he had uncommon faith in the rightness of his thought.

X

Before the World:

Progress and Poverty

1879

THE very size of *Progress and Poverty* — 563 pages in the standard edition — demanded qualities of authorship which Henry George had had no earlier occasion to exercise. Even the many chapters that drew on the thought and phrases of old editorials and recent speeches required him to make associations of ideas hitherto unmade, and to weld structures of logic at culminating heights above any he had ventured before. There were also new areas to fill in, weak spots to strengthen and develop. This is especially true of the first, second, and third 'books,' and the tenth and final one, where he made his great dissents from classical economic doctrines, offered a revision of the theory of economic distribution, and made the strongest affirmations of his own social faith.

In a true sense, accordingly, the total argument came out new. Though George's reform contentions remained the same as in the *Post* in 1873 and after, and the same as in the addresses, his new completeness and definiteness, and the fresh assimilations of scholarship — the infrequent miracle that a living book had been born — put the author's ideas on a new footing altogether.

Readers of this biography, who may pick up *Progress and Poverty* still bearing in mind George's fifteen years of writing and speaking about California affairs, will sense, more completely than his contemporaries did, how intimately the book bears the marks of the region of its birth. To be sure the text is strewn with California illustrations. There are some fifty of them, picked up from Sierra mining camps to seal hunting in the Santa Barbara channel; and they are more numerous than illustrations from all other places. But all illustrations are incidental only, in a treatment mainly logical, abstract, and moral. It took Dr. Edward Taylor's inside perceptions to say, on publication: 'It is not merely an American book, but a California book. We do not mean merely that it is a book written in California by a Californian, but that it is distinctively and peculiarly Californian, for not only are its illustrations drawn from this coast, but the freshness of its views bespeak the novel and suggestive circumstances that have been presented in California.'

In California and of California, but not especially for California, nor even for the United States, was the book executed. George found literary devices, over and above the logic of argument, to sustain the note of universal meaning. Systems of thought which are fused by the 'imagination,' says Isaiah Berlin, a wise man of our day, 'if they are filled with sufficient energy and force of will — and it may be added, fantasy, which is less frightened by the facts and creates models in terms of which the facts are ordered by the mind — sometimes transform the whole outlook of an entire generation.'

In *Progress and Poverty*, fantasy takes the form of incorporating Mrs. Browning's sonnet of the working children, rather than statistics, to convey a situation; it takes the form of quoting a bit of Hindu lore, and recurring to the quotation as a leitmotiv in a music drama, to renew for the reader the author's main diagnosis of social evil. 'To whomsoever the soil at any time belongs, to him belong the fruits of it. White parasols and elephants mad with pride are the flowers of a grant of land.' No exercise of the author's imagination worked more effectively than the decision to abandon a humdrum title — he had announced before publication a forthcoming work on the 'Political Economy of the Social Problem' — for the famous one. To twentieth-century readers, the Victorian oratorical quality of *Progress and Poverty* at certain climaxes is likely to be distasteful; but this is a simple reflection of George's age, and of his own public speaking during the period of writing.

The work makes many levies on social thinkers not previously tapped by George, or certainly not marshaled in force. Where in newspaper days he drew on John Stuart Mill's text, and we can be sure of little else in economics, *Progress and Poverty* shows, as we shall see in some detail, knowledge and use of Ricardo, and in some degree of Adam Smith (though not a thorough knowledge yet, if ever), and of Malthus, Cairnes, Fawcett, Herbert Spencer, and others. In the less economic and more historical and sociological passages, the book indicates interesting leads or borrowings taken, notably, from Sir Henry Maine and Walter Bagehot and Sir William Jones, contemporary British lions of social research and theory, two of them students of India. Like many a Californian in business, to make his borrowings George went straight to the resources of the mother country. A few American economists, like Perry of Williams and, most notably, Francis Amasa Walker, did offer him something usable. But in the main it was the famous English thinkers, contributors to the ideas and policies of liberalism, asserters of laws and uniformities in society comparable to the laws of physics and biology, who gave him intellectual capital to draw on. He sought no farther than the English Channel. The famous similarities between Henry George's economics and Physiocracy to the contrary notwithstanding, the author of *Progress and Poverty* up to this point had no effective knowledge of French thought, either from Turgot's century or August Comte's.

For reasons of analogy at least, and because just possibly a philosophical writer may have influenced him profoundly, a chapter from Thomas Henry Buckle's already famous *History of Civilization in England* demands mention. This was Buckle's brilliant 'Examination of the Scotch Intellect during the Eighteenth Century,' which we know George pondered carefully. Commenting on Adam Smith, the historian noted that the great economist had written his two treatises from quite separate premises about human nature, and had never reconciled them. 'In his *Moral Sentiments*, he ascribes our actions to sympathy; in his *Wealth of Nations*, he ascribes them to selfishness.' Buckle explains that Smith wrote with one hand as though men lived in great and religious concern with affairs outside themselves, and so evoked the highest principles and the deepest emotions; with the other hand he wrote as though self-seeking were the only motive in the world.

We would have to disregard much in Henry George's life to suppose that the reading of Buckle's *History of Civilization* taught
him for the first time that the poles of human action are far apart,
and that a philosopher needs to relate them to one another. Even
when he was a youngster, he alternated between cool description
and intense exhortation; and the letters and editorials and speeches
of the California printer, editor, and reformer had often voiced
romantic utopianism in one vein and muckraking and near-de-
terminism in another. For years he had managed a balance between
the two without advice from a great historian. But George's native
capacity to see life both ways — to consider the economic man and
remember also the Christian — does not exclude the possibility
that Buckle's observation posed him an issue and gave him food for
self-consciousness, while he was writing *Progress and Poverty*.

Whether this be true or not, certainly the 'Scotch Intellect'
chapter expresses the central philosophical problem which every
economist who rejects materialism must in some way face, and
which was present and immediate with George while he was writing. The strictly economic reasoning in *Progress and Poverty* rests
squarely on the nineteenth century's common, hedonistic and
selfish pleasure-pain psychology.[1] And the reform reasoning rests
on the vastly different Christian and democratic presumptions of
the author's life of faith. George's dual role as economist and as
reformer makes acute the tension between the two assumptions
about the nature of man, in the pages of the book.

The whole architecture of *Progress and Poverty*, indeed, is arranged to accommodate this duality. In the large the book may be
envisaged somewhat on the order of the Berkeley and the Fourth of
July addresses of 1877, as offering the reader two sequences of
thought, distinct and separable but each dependent on the other.
The major sequence begins in the introduction, with a concise
statement of 'The Problem' of the book. This is Henry George's
old paradox of fifteen years of articles, editorials, and speeches: that
modern material progress actually increases poverty and insecurity,
that under industrial conditions depressions strike, Huns rise in
the cities, and wars threaten, all in increasing terror. The opening
section of the book presents the author's moral vision of the social

---

[1] *P and P*, 204, 217.

question completely: it presents the question of the failure of modern men to deal justly with one another.

George's moral question is suspended here, without the solution his moral faith had to offer, while the succeeding 450 pages take up what we shall call *Progress and Poverty*'s 'economic syllogism.' This is the well-remembered core of the book, the part which criticizes and tries to amend accepted economic theory, which reviews and finds to be lacking all current programs of social reconstruction, and which offers George's own program. Though the economic syllogism occupies the larger part of the text, it is really the minor one of the two sequences of thought. It particularizes the nature of the social question posed in the introduction, and it names a *possible economic procedure* to solve that question. But it has no reach of thought to assure the reader that humanity has the power to follow through, to make good its economic insights and actually replace moral evil with moral good.

In entirely specific terms, the essential argument of the economic syllogism begins in Book III, where George for the first time systematized his ideas on 'The Laws of Distribution' in economic life. The place of this elaborate and important piece of writing, in the syllogism, is that of first premise. The essential proposition is that rent — an increment of monopoly not earned by individuals — always and everywhere opposes and reduces wages and interest, the returns which the economy makes for labor's toil and for the investment of capital. The second premise of the economic syllogism, in Books IV and V, is historical rather than theoretical like the first. It incorporates the depression ideas of the address, 'Why Work Is Scarce,' and asserts that the forces of industrial economy operate observably to enlarge the take of land ownership, and that that creates unbalance, poverty, and depression. The conclusion of the syllogism appears in Book VI, 'The Remedy,' and is justified in Books VII, VIII, and IX, the 'Justice of the Remedy,' the 'Application of the Remedy,' and the 'Effects of the Remedy.' In this long passage Henry George made his classic presentation of the necessity to do away with private property in land; and he suggested his alternatives to private property and painted the utopia that would follow if economic rent were taken for the public benefit.

Had Henry George been an ordinary nineteenth-century believer in the idea of social progress as a nearly automatic process, he could reasonably have submitted the argument of Book III through Book IX, the economic syllogism, and could have spared himself bothering with the rest. Then the reform would have been proposed and argued within the limits of economics, and the tacit assumption would have been made that the simple common sense of mankind could be counted upon to provide adequately for mankind's betterment.

But any such optimistic presumption would, as we know, have been quite false to Henry George's feeling. *Progress and Poverty*'s introductory statement fairly represents his judgment that the world's morality had fallen short. Accordingly the book would have fallen short, also, if the opening presentation of the social question had not been followed somewhere by social assurance — by something more than a technical answer to the question of poverty. The economic syllogism itself produces a program far more drastic than reformers ordinarily contemplated, and one that would have been more upsetting to the economic order than any reform ever adopted by a modern government at peace. This indicates the purpose served by Book X and the Conclusion of *Progress and Poverty*: the completion of the primary sequence of the book's thought. Hereafter, to distinguish it from the economic syllogism, we shall call this sequence — comprising the opening and the closing sections — *Progress and Poverty*'s 'moral sequence.'

Like the economic one, the moral sequence is stated in three parts. The premise at the beginning is social injustice, asserted not as theory but as plain fact. The second premise, withheld until after the *economic* case for reform has been fully argued, is pure theory, unadulterated democratic idea. 'Association in equality is the law of progress,' is Henry George's irreducible formula in this passage; he phrases the doctrine of equal opportunity for all men as a datum of universal moral law. The antithesis he discovers between social fact and social theory he presents as a tragic contradiction, and very nearly a complete one.

His resolution of the problem indicates why *Progress and Poverty*'s moral sequence of thought may not be called a 'moral syllogism' instead. A syllogism leads to a sure conclusion, or synthesis, of the premises. Henry George is not sure that mankind will solve the question of poverty: he says only that we have the power to try to solve it. No historical necessity compels the fulfillment of the moral law; and this argument makes him entirely different from Marx, and makes *Progress and Poverty* a book opposed to all materialistic and deterministic social ideas. The conclusion, we may anticipate, is a conditional one. *If* men will but turn to God, and seek His help, the moral law *may* be made to rule. On condition of God-given righteousness, and only on that condition, equal economic justice will prevail in industrial society, or anywhere.

In a passage near the end of *Progress and Poverty* the ancient battle of Ormuzd and Ahriman is woven into the fabric, a splendid touch of design. For the struggle of good with evil, present in all history, was to Henry George the process that reduces economics and religion to common terms.

−2−

Books I and II of *Progress and Poverty*, George's ground-clearing preliminary, develop in strength the criticism of classical economics he had ventured in Berkeley, and had anticipated a little in the *Post*. He regarded this as important enough to give it one-quarter of his text; and in time it caught his reviewers' eyes, especially those on the far side of the Atlantic.

The matter of the two books is much less controversial today. It is a refutation of ideas he himself had once accepted, first, the old wages-fund theory of employment and, second, Malthusian population theory. These two were the main components, of course, of the 'iron law of wages' — the name socialists gave to the hard presumption of classical economics, that wages tend always to be depressed to subsistence level. The 'dismal science' was dismal because its doctrines of employment denied hope to the masses of men.

In his newspaper criticism of the wages fund, George had said that that theory, since it made employment depend on a special reserve of capital accumulation, attributed too much authority to the capitalist. He now developed this thought into a series of counterpropositions. According to *Progress and Poverty:* wages are paid *after* labor has been rendered and value has already been added to the materials being prepared or moved to market, whether or not the product has been sold. Not so much a capitalist's reserves — money in the bank — as current labor, for instance the labor applied in food production, sustains working men while their product is in process. And, ultimately, the *people's needs* are what keep the economy in motion: '*The demand for consumption determines the direction in which labor will be expended in production.*' [2] This prepares for George's important labor-employs-capital argument in Book v, on distribution.

Stating his criticism of the wages fund was much easier in *Progress and Poverty* than in the *Post,* because during the interval, in 1876, Francis Amasa Walker, already the distinguished director of the census and a professor at Yale, had brought out a first-class monograph on *The Wages Question.* Time has recognized Walker's book as a kind of classic because it gave the crushing blow, at least so far as American academic economics was concerned, to the wages-fund idea. *Progress and Poverty* credits it as a 'most vital attack,' even though George disliked the residue of Malthusianism contained within its thought. More than he had any way of knowing while he was writing, George was in line with the protest that was rising in both Britain and America, as he thus early condemned the wages-fund idea.

The standing of Thomas Robert Malthus's population doctrine, four score years old in 1879, has always been debatable in America; the broad domain, the uncrowded population, the shortage of labor, the nation's mood of optimism, the doctrine's unfriendliness to democracy all held against it. It is still being debated. Before *Progress and Poverty,* the nationalistic economists of the Carey school, notably Henry C. Carey himself, had been the chief spokesmen for the opposition; and the writing of a member of that school, Professor Francis Bowen of Harvard, came out in powerful criticism at the same time that George's book was published. But this represented minority resistance. The more because classical economics was accepted so universally, American professors, for instance, had no united front of resistance to Malthusian theory; rather the opposite. No one better represents the fear and dread the doctrine could inculcate among those who accepted it than Henry George himself, up to about 1872. His argument in the letter on Chinese immigration, and his correspondence with John Stuart Mill, in 1869 and 1870, will recall that stage of his thought.

Now he wrote at length with the ardency of a man who has changed his mind. George answered Malthus mainly by drawing

[2] See *P and P,* 58, 74, 75.

on the American treasury of belief in the power of enterprise, know-how, and freedom to provide for the masses. His argument resembles today's national attitude toward the underdeveloped economies of the non-industrial areas of the world, but George was more dogmatic. In his own words: 'There is not a single case in which the vice and misery can be traced to an actual increase in the number of mouths over the power of the accompanying hands to feed them . . . Nowhere can want be properly attributed to the pressure of population against the power to procure subsistence in the then existing degree of human knowledge . . . everywhere the vice and misery attributed to overpopulation can be traced to the warfare, tyranny, and oppression which prevent knowledge from being utilized, and deny the security essential to production.' [3]

In the grand strategy of *Progress and Poverty*, the need to drive Malthus from the temple of accepted ideas amounts to more than just clearing the way for the coming proposal of economic reform. It concerns the sequence of moral thought as well. As in the *Post*, the author envisages in Malthusian ideas a phase of materialism and determinism. To George this seemed the more serious because he sensed (accurately, as Professor Richard Hofstadter's report on *Social Darwinism in America* shows) that people's increasing acceptance of evolution was at the moment fortifying the anti-democratic population doctrine he attacked. In his own warning: 'The support which is given to Malthusian theory by the new philosophy of development, now rapidly spreading in every direction, must be noted in any estimate of the sources from which this theory derives its present strength.'

With the start, then, of having laid a barrage at the Singapore and Gibraltar of classical economics, George entered the third book, a seventy-five-page invasion of the empire of the theory of economic distribution. As the first premise of *Progress and Poverty*'s economic syllogism, Book III may fairly be called the crucial passage of analysis in the work, and of the author's life. In all conscience he chose his ground carefully and proceeded with caution.

First a paragraph is in order concerning the method of economic reasoning available to George. In his day statistics had hardly entered general economics. Accordingly there is nothing surprising in the fact that, even in his treatment of rent, and with all the com-

[3] *P and P*, 106, 123.

pleteness George intended for *Progress and Poverty,* he said nothing quite so empirical as he had said years earlier in the *Post:* that in San Francisco the product of land values equaled about one-sixth of the community's income. 'It is unnecessary to refer to the facts,' he wrote in a passage of the book which concerned the relation of rent taking to poverty, for facts 'would suggest themselves to the reader.' [4] On the model of the deductive reasoning common in the treatises he knew, he wrote his own study of how the product of the economy is distributed.

He was able to open the third book's argument at good pace, because he had inserted in Book I his critical definitions of the economic terms that were fundamental to all he had to say. There, in the manner of a textbook writer, he elucidated the three factors in production — land, labor, and capital — to which he assigned the three elements of distribution — rent, wages, and interest. (Other writers had more than he to say about profits; George said more than many did about interest, but not entirely to the neglect of profits, as we shall see.) In the same place the author rejected with contempt the economists of the chair, especially the American ones, who confused in their writings the distinction, so plain and necessary to him, that prevents land from being classified as capital. Labor, with or without the assistance of capital, combines with land — the term defined to include site and resources, and to exclude improvements — to create wealth, George said once more; and capital is that portion of man-made wealth which is returned to production or exchange with a purpose to procure more wealth. In setting up his primary definitions, the author sieved and examined the ways in which Smith, Ricardo, McCulloch, Mill, Wayland, H. C. Carey, and F. A. Walker used the terms, and he declared himself essentially a follower of Adam Smith.

Coming to the center of the problem of how the current product of the economy is distributed, George stated, more amply and formally than ever before, the image he had held, since the Oakland vision, of economic rent as an entity separate from interest and wages. In *Progress and Poverty* he forces the separation by hypothetical illustrations of labor applied to land without capital. In Book I, against the wages fund, there is a good deal about the self-employing laborer, who operates almost without capital goods, a

[4] *P and P,* 222.

type found more frequently in America than in England. Even under primitive conditions, George reasoned, as in mining country, wherever benefit of site or natural resource conveys an advantage to one producer above another, that advantage, which is by definition monopolistic, should be understood as rent to owner rather than as wage to workman. 'Or to put it in algebraic form:

As Produce = Rent + Wages + Interest
Therefore, Produce − Rent = Wages + Interest.'

In the author's own recapitulation: 'Wages and interest do not depend upon the produce of labor and capital, but upon what is left after rent is taken out . . . And hence, no matter what be the increase in productive power, if the increase in rent keeps pace with it, neither wages nor interest can increase.' [5]

In this passage George exercised an author's prerogative of turning his reader's attention in the direction he wanted it to go. In the bit of algebraic formalizing just reported, he could, had he chosen, have set up an opposition between wages and rent-plus-interest, as a Marxist would have done. This would have changed the equation to:

Produce − (Rent + Interest) = Wages.

The reasons *why* he chose the opposition he did, between rent and wages-plus-interest, and thus pitted workers and investors together against landholders, not workers against landholders and capitalists, he did not explain until the next book, on the 'dynamics,' or the social phenomena which affect distribution. At this point concerned only with 'statics,' or mechanical operations of the flow of wages, rent, and interest, he simply arranged the argument in such a way as to bring to the reader's attention the opposition he would later make the very center of his protest and his program.

Familiarity with the childhood of George's ideas will excuse us from paraphrasing the chapters on 'Rent and the Law of Rent' and 'Wages and the Law of Wages.' Besides saying that those two elements are separate from one another in economic thought, and are separate from interest, George set down, quite concisely, his understanding of their derivation and nature. Quite naturally the new thing about the treatment of rent and wages, in *Progress and Pov-*

[5] *P and P,* 171.

erty, is the author's enlarged scholarship, rather than any revision of his main concepts. Now for the first time he developed his own perceptions from the most famous of all sources of rent theory. The law of rent, set forth sixty years ahead of *Progress and Poverty* in David Ricardo's *Principles of Political Economy and Taxation,* has proved the most durable idea of classical economics, able not only to hold its own into Henry George's day but to survive even into ours. Though George did not find Ricardo as quotable as John Stuart Mill, his own phrasing of the law of rent, with the surrounding text, catches the essential doctrine. Quote *Progress and Poverty:* 'The ownership of a natural agent of production will give the power of appropriating so much of the wealth produced by the exertion of labor and capital upon it as exceeds the return which the same application of labor and capital could secure in the least productive occupation in which they freely engage.' [6]

Not the first or last radical to take something of Ricardo's hard-headed businessman's analysis as a base from which to make an un-Ricardian leftward departure, George was just the man to appreciate the law of rent. He, who had a decade earlier perceived economic rent in an almost visionary way, while he contemplated the growth of a new city, now made his own the ideas of the British economist whose findings had been mainly a commentary on Britain's rural landholding. In the words of *Progress and Poverty,* Ricardo's law has the rightness of 'a geometrical axiom,' and 'authority here coincides with common sense.' Ricardo had instructed Mill; and Mill had assisted George, early in his economic education. Now, as George assimilated Ricardo, the linking-up of the nineteenth century's principal rent theorists was well accomplished.

Into the discussion of rent, George introduced the conception of the margin of productivity. Marginalism was a piece of economic sophistication at which he had only hinted earlier, and one a little too technical to have been incorporated effectively in editorials or in platform speaking. Ricardo had reasoned that the differentials of higher and lower rent are set by the differing advantages of pieces of land. But the British economist had conceived a hierarchy of land values governed sometimes by mineral values but usually by the fertility or non-fertility of the soil (the British milords becom-

[6] *P and P,* 169.

ing the richer, according to the agricultural productivity of their estates, as demand for foodstuffs increased in the cities). *Progress and Poverty's* conception is broader. It contemplates natural resources as creating different land values, but, true to George's perception, it includes also urban-site values. George's conception of the margin of productivity, moreover, placed a movable floor under his hierarchy of values; or rather, it made an escalator of the steps. As population increases, reasoned the author, later-choice lands are drawn from idleness into use, at the new margin of productivity. This process enhances the value, that is to say the rent, of the more advantageous earlier-choice lands, whether those lands be in the country or in the city.

A later section of the present chapter will be a more convenient place than this is to explain a little how George's use of the idea of the economic margin placed him in the advance guard of English and American economic theory in 1879. Here it is necessary simply to see the strength that marginalism adds to *Progress and Poverty's* opposition between rent and wages-plus-interest. A crucial passage must now be quoted, from the chapter on rent: 'To say that rent will be the excess in productiveness over the yield at the margin, or lowest point, of cultivation, is the same thing as to say that it will be the excess of produce over what the same amount of labor and capital obtains in the least remunerative occupation.

'The law of rent is, in fact, but a deduction from the law of competition, and amounts simply to the assertion that as wages and interest tend to a common level, all that part of the general production of wealth which exceeds what the labor and capital employed could have secured for themselves, if applied to the poorest natural agent in use, will go to land owners in the shape of rent. It rests in the last analysis upon the fundamental principle, which is to political economy what the attraction of gravitation is to physics — that men will seek to gratify their desires with the least exertion.' [7]

The idea of the margin, indeed, becomes the unifying theme which runs through the several chapters on distribution. As regards wages, the writer's only other new important thought is the development of a comparison — a fairly autobiographical one — between wage earners and capitalists, stating first their similarities. Workers such as the superintendents of new ventures earn the highest wages

[7] *P and P,* 170.

278 HENRY GEORGE

because they like capitalists are risk takers, George put down, and like them deserve their winnings within reason. The wages of ordinary crafts largely affect others, because movement from like job to like job is easy — not different from the flow of credit. All wages are affected by employment at the lowest level. But, in a poignant passage which calls to mind 1865 and 1866 in Henry George's life, the author speaks of the unhappy rigidities of society which make the position of a laborer so different, and so much more painful than a capitalist's. There is no average of well-being, no basic wage rate always available on the job market, comparable to the interest rate. And the author who rejected the components of the iron law of wages nevertheless added that even favorable conditions in the labor market have no capacity to increase labor's total take from production, as compared with rent or interest. He wryly objected 'that both Smith and Ricardo use the term "natural wages" to express the minimum on which labor can live; whereas, unless injustice is natural, all that the laborer produces should rather be held as his natural wages.'

This line of thought brought George back to the margin of productivity, as he phrased his none too cheerful 'law of wages.' '*Wages,*' says *Progress and Poverty* in italics, '*depend upon the margin of production, or upon the produce which labor can obtain at the highest point of natural productiveness open to it without the payment of rent.*' [8] In less formal terms: those workers who go in and out of jobs, and whose last resort is the use of unoccupied land, comprise the group on the margin — the peripheral group in the whole picture of economic distribution. Before the Civil War, Henry George's predecessors in land-and-labor reform had demanded homestead land free, as an escape from unemployment in the cities. They had believed, mistakenly, the scholarship of today asserts, that the vacant land of the frontier offered a practical solution of their problem. But, in *Progress and Poverty,* George, who had never thought very well of the American West as an escape from trouble, now pictured the very difficulty of going to marginal land as the measure of the general predicament of labor.

The return to capital, which is the remaining one-third of the distributing system, as Henry George examined it, gave him the most trouble to explain. He took three chapters to do so, instead

[8] *P and P,* 213.

of one, as in the cases of rent and wages. Part of the author's difficulty was due, to be sure, as the text correctly notes, to the unsolved confusions of the subject. Economics books were full of subdivisions but lacking in agreement about the return to capital of interest and profits, about the overlappings of those two with rent and the wages of superintendence, and about the replacement and increase of capital goods from produce. These were practical problems, though with implications of theory about which nineteenth-century economics was much less concerned than is modern, especially Keynesian, economics.

But over and above the technical difficulties, George's effort to formulate a 'law of interest' was a doubly crucial operation. Though in the wages fund he had rejected a major doctrine about capitalism, he remained always an ex-capitalist and a believer in capitalism; and this required of him, if not a conventional rationalization, then a fresh and independent one in favor of interest taking. Again, though his historic bouts with Marxists lay in the future, he had already reacted against socialism; and accordingly he had special reason, when speaking about interest, to justify it morally against the socialistic idea that interest is a steal from labor. All this adds up to a necessity for George to be as sharp and definite as possible, in this passage of the book.

George began with another round of rejecting classical doctrine. What Nassau Senior had said, and Mill had adopted for his own, the absurd proposition that 'the profits of the capitalists are properly the remuneration of abstinence,' particularly annoyed him. Regarding the characterization as untrue of the capitalists of his own knowledge, and one which in general assigned the capitalist an inappropriately passive role — guarding portfolios instead of doing things — George himself took off in an opposite direction. Referring to the high interest rates of California, he reasoned again as he had against Hittell that the variations of the rate in time and place must respond to factors of risk and productivity. His question narrowed to about this: What is the usefulness, and what are the operating habits, of the investor in the expanding sectors, the Californias of the world?

Suggestively enough another San Franciscan was commenting on the point, at just the time George was writing. Alexander del Mar, who ten years earlier had been director of the United States Bureau of Statistics, whose career had embraced an international education, editorial positions on the national magazines, and insurance-company work investigating and predicting the interest rate, and who at this time was making himself the active leader of Caspar Hopkins' Pacific Social Science Association, early in 1879 gave a lecture on 'Usury and the Jews.' The coincidences are remarkable. Mr. del Mar addressed the same Y.M.H.A. that had invited George's lecture on 'Moses'; the date was 11 February 1879, a matter of weeks before the completion of *Progress and Poverty;* and the lecture reviewed the whole history of thought about interest — Biblical ideas, medieval opposition to usury, and the modern acceptance of interest, including also the lecturer's own theory.

Mr. del Mar came up with a proposition which, though it sounds a little bizarre today, was not out of line with old doctrine, had a special appropriateness in California, and contained a suggestive echo of Old Testament ideas. He said that the generative powers of nature supply the justification of a basic return of interest to invested capital. Capital accumulation, most particularly when put into food production — the planting of a stand of olive trees say, or the introduction of new strains of livestock — increases and wins a return to the investor by reason of the cycle of life. Del Mar's thought separates this return, though it depends on land and labor, from the flow of rent and wages. It makes the investor a planner and a collaborator with nature.

Progress and Poverty incorporates this idea, not as the whole but as part of its theory of interest. In 1885, when Henry George's fame had soared to international height, Mr. del Mar charged — while denying any other likeness of thought to George — that in *Progress and Poverty* George had 'adopted the author's postulate with reference to the origin of interest, but has nowhere given him credit for it.' The charge is very plausible; the blame for pillaging which it attaches to George is nevertheless conjectural. Is it a plagiarism to pick up a public lecturer's idea, especially if the idea is kin to one's own thinking? And even to ask this question assumes that George attended the lecture or heard about it; and it assumes that February 1879 — or the later date at which the lecture was published — was not too late to incorporate a borrowed idea into a text all but ready for the printer. The other possibilities of borrowing are two: the first, that George knew del Mar's ideas from earlier writings in obscure places; and the second, and perhaps more likely, that del

Mar's theory of interest had entered the domain of general discussion in San Francisco, perhaps filtering out through the members of the Social Science Association. Neither pure coincidence nor straight-out plagiarism, but some point indeterminable between, seems the nearest possible answer to the question of the relation of Alexander del Mar to the section on interest in *Progress and Poverty*.

At any rate the book's explanation and justification of interest begins on the rural side and speaks of the passage of time during which wines mature and irrigation ditches multiply the productivity of a piece of land. This kind of planning and investment deserves reward, says Henry George. Then, in continuous reasoning and illustration with reference to phenomena almost equally typical of California, capital makes a gain also, *Progress and Poverty* asserts, when it is invested in commerce and manufactures. This accrues, at bottom, from 'the utilization of the variations in the powers of nature and of man which is affected by exchange, an increase which somewhat resembles that produced by the vital forces of nature.' One may guess that George was thinking, as he wrote this, of the *Post*'s wonderful Bullock press — of Philadelphia technology, once applied through him to California, the application arranged by investment capital. The passage concludes with the observation, good for farm, railroad, or factory, that interest 'is not properly a payment made for the use of capital, but a return accruing from the increase of capital . . . It is not an arbitrary but a natural thing; it is not the result of a particular social organization, but of the laws of the universe which underlie society. It is therefore, just.' [9]

But not to let capital and capitalism go free, and seem to be justified outside their desirable orbit, by *Progress and Poverty*, George troubled to do an extra chapter, 'Of spurious capital and of profits often mistaken for interest.' He would not permit readers of his book any possible chance to misunderstand his saying Yes to interest and capital, as signifying approval of private monopoly or monopoly gains, of whatever kind. Some called those profits interest, but he called them monopoly thieving. *Progress and Poverty* affirms George's old proposition in the *Post*, though it does not develop it, that the monopolies created by technology, such as railroads and communications, should be transformed into govern-

[9] *P and P*, 186, 187.

ment-owned and operated businesses; and it even ventures to propose that government go in for railroad building.[10] In this line of thinking, George condemned by name contemporaries presently under Kearneyite attack, the Stanfords and Floods, as men who operated beyond the pale of sound policy, and contrary to proper moral and capitalistic usage.

Though the chapters on interest make *Progress and Poverty* an aggressively pro-capitalist book, it is a limited, principled, truly free, and competitive capitalism which he here justifies, and one which acknowledges the primacy of labor. 'It is not capital which employs labor, but labor which employs capital.' We may bring alongside a sentence from a near-by portion of the book: 'Capital is, as is often said, but stored up labor, it is but a form of labor, a subdivision of the general term labor; and its law must subordinate to and independently correlate with, the law of wages so as to fit cases in which the whole produce is divided between labor and capital without any deduction for rent.' George is not here talking about utopia but proposing a rationale for the large part of the business economy which seemed to him sound and durable. For the rest he was as ready as with the system of landholding to contemplate far-reaching change, to substitute public for private monopoly.

But this anticipates. To round out distributive theory, he drew up a 'law of interest' to stand alongside his laws of rent and wages. 'To sum up, the law of interest is this: *The relationship between wages and interest is determined by the average power of increase which attaches to capital from its use in reproductive modes. As rent arises, interest will fall as wages fall, or will be determined by the margin of cultivation.*'[11] It will be noticed that this generalization covers both the agriculture side, from which del Mar justified interest, and the commercial and industrial sides, to which George extended the justification.

In drawing Book III to a conclusion, the author undertook confidently the obligation of his logic, to fit into a pattern covering the whole of distribution the three laws — of rent, wages, and interest — he had offered. Yet, before we follow him in this piece of mosaic fitting, a final preliminary is still required. To comprehend George on distribution we must bear in mind explicitly what has been

[10] *P and P,* 410, 454.
[11] *P and P,* 202.

implicit in the report above, and what he makes explicit at the end. This: that as he discusses the return to land, labor, and capital, he is talking about the *proportions of the total economic product as they are channeled into total rent, total wages, and total interest.* Absolute amounts (whether money wages or real wages or interest payments) and market rates (whether an annual *per centum* on capital or an hourly sum for a given type of labor) are not the object of the inquiry. That is to say, when George contemplates a rising 'rent line' pressing against interest and wages, he does not assume that when land ownership receives more than earlier, wage earners must certainly receive either less money or fewer goods or a lower rate of pay per hour, or that capitalists must lose out on interest. *Progress and Poverty* specifically allows the possibility — not, George might have said, an actuality in California, 1879 — that wages and interest can rise absolutely, in a period when rent rises faster than they.[12] George's fearful conviction was that the operations of our economic institutions even in good days were denying the workers and the investors equal justice; this to him was a greater anxiety, ultimately more dangerous, than the hazards of rate adjustments.

In his own words, then: 'The harmony and correlation of the laws of distribution as we have now apprehended them are in striking contrast with the want of harmony which characterizes these laws as presented by the current political economy. Let us state them side by side: [13]

The Current Statement	*The True Statement*
RENT depends on the margin of cultivation, rising as it falls and falling as it rises.	RENT depends on the margin of cultivation, rising as it falls and falling as it rises.
WAGES depend upon the ratio between the number of laborers and the amount of capital devoted to their employment.	WAGES depend on the margin of cultivation, falling as it falls and rising as it rises.
INTEREST depends upon the equation between the supply of and demand for capital; or, as is stated of profits, upon wages (or the cost of labor), rising as wages fall, and falling as wages rise.	INTEREST (its ratio with wages being fixed by the net power of increase which attaches to capital) depends upon the margin of cultivation, falling as it falls and rising as it rises.'

[12] *P and P,* 216.
[13] *P and P,* 218.

The 'margin of cultivation,' the base of George's whole thought about distribution, is a moving boundary line across the world's resources, separating the used from the unused. As he had now shown the importance of that boundary he was ready to proceed, in grander style than in any earlier writing, to land economics and land institutions, the favorite fields of his thought.

–3–

Book III, which the present chapter envisages as the first premise of an economic syllogism, asserts a natural opposition between rent on one side, and wages and interest on the other. It assumes, but does not examine the nature of, a relentless war between the two. For making clear the syllogism, the first premise may be stated as follows: Right economic theory sees an eternal tension, not localized in time or place, between rent and the other forms of economic distribution.

Books IV and V, here grouped as stating the second premise, assert that increasing pressure makes that tension ever more acute. That is, they argue that in the industrial economy land ownership naturally and irresistibly takes from non-owners more and more rent (in pace with the retreat of the margin of cultivation to later-choice lands). To establish a perspective of approach to the matter of the two books, we may formulate tentatively in advance the second premise of the economic syllogism: Correct observation and opinion attribute the deprivations of society, and its spasms of unemployment, to the power of one class of ownership to draw unto itself society's mounting surplus in the form of rent.

This new phase of the argument is opened under the signpost, 'The dynamics of the problem yet to seek.' 'I have displayed the special, unearned and automatic nature of economic rent,' observes the author with a glance back at Book III, and 'without farther ado moral sense calls for confiscating it as public revenue.' Yet moral decision he let wait upon a full description, not of the blueprint drawn by lines of theory alone, but also of the fires that drive the mechanism and the result that occurs. 'To say that wages remain low because rent advances is like saying that a steamboat moves because the wheels turn around. The farther question is, What causes rent to advance? What is the force or necessity that, as productive power increases, distributes a greater and greater *proportion* of its produce as rent?'

This is the point at which the twentieth-century reader, accustomed to connect closely the how with the why of social phenomena, notices especially the lack of statistics in *Progress and Poverty*. Surely, the thought is natural as we turn the pages today, the next section will come up with great columns of figures — perhaps taken from something over and beyond the Sacramento *Record*'s exposé of California landholding — a cold record of the landlords' marching privilege. But instead this is the passage of the book in which George relies perhaps more heavily than anywhere else on the sheer intensity of a decade of reflection and analysis. Here he inserts Mrs. Browning's eloquence of the children's weeping, and John Stuart Mill's startling doubt that any mechanical inventions had ever yet 'lightened the day's toil of any human being.' In the words of the book, 'the universal fact' was too tragic and too obvious to want elaboration, 'that where the value of land is highest, civilization exhibits the greatest luxury side by side with the most piteous destitution. To see human beings in the most abject, the most helpless and hopeless condition, you must go, not to the unfenced prairies and the log cabins of new clearings in the backwoods, where man single-handed is commencing the struggle against nature, and land is yet worth nothing, but to the great cities where the ownership of a little patch of ground is a fortune.' The margin below the margin of cultivation, in the cities — the memory of New York in 1869!

In the first cycle of presenting this phase of his argument, the author spoke in a quieter tone than he had in the *Post*. Whereas in the newspaper he had denounced the Millers and Lux's and the Jacks's by name, in the book he spoke of villainy, rather than of personal villains, in land engrossment. Looking across the seas, he took testimony from the sober historians, Henry Hallam and Thorold Rogers, and from the Cambridge economist, Henry Fawcett, M.P., that changes in wage rates had raised the standard of living of British labor little, if at all, since the Middle Ages. He borrowed also those scholars' round estimates of land values and rental incomes multiplied many fold in recent times — a fact about nineteenth-century Britain which will be endorsed presently by important new scholarship. In a few lines, *Progress and Poverty* is more statistical about Britain than about the author's own state or nation.

George does seem justified in presuming that people believed quite generally that rents were rising. A glance stolen forward to the reviews of *Progress and Poverty,* many of them mentioned in the next chapter, would show that this principal assertion was little questioned when all else was challenged. To be sure, critic after critic would deny what George said about wages, or rather would deny what it was easy to mistake him as saying, for it proved more natural and easy to argue that real wages were rising under industrialization than to discuss precisely George's argument that wages and interest were losing proportionately to rent. But there was hardly a handful of reviewers in the world-wide lot who chose to deny that rent was increasing by leaps and bounds.

Meanwhile George named population growth and the cities' concentrations of technology and skill as the dynamics which were forcing up rent, and in his belief would always do so. Of course to the fighter of Malthus these were potentially, and in some degree, actually benevolent forces. As always a good San Franciscan, George put in the book his patriot's vision of cities rising from the bare earth, each city 'the heart, the brain of the vast social organism which has grown up from the first settlement' of each region. For all that George said about the warping and blighting effects of overcrowded cities and underdeveloped countryside, and about how speculation and land withholding twists and unnaturally compresses the processes of land occupation, he had perfect faith in the essentials of city growth. Though he admired the Christian achievements of the Middle Ages, he had nothing in common with the neo-medievalism of Ruskin and Morris, and never wished to escape into a pre-industrial past. For him there was hardly such a thing as diminishing returns from having more and more labor available in a modern city, given an increasing accumulation of technology. Not just ideally, but as a present goal within society's grasp, George envisaged, here with special eloquence, an economy of abundance made possible by the growth of society and science.

This drawing together in economic thought of ideas first stated in the preface, accumulated poverty *versus* accumulated progress, swings the logic of the book very close to making reform proposals. George could, in his own phrase, 'without more ado' have delivered his formulas. But instead the reader is carried forward once more, with the discussion of the city factors that enhance rent to assist him, into Book v's presentation of George's depression-and-poverty analysis. Here the propositions of the lecture, 'Why Work Is Scarce,' are given again, in ample treatment.

As we saw in the last chapter, those propositions, considered by themselves, seem dated and a little crude when compared with the twentieth century's elaborate scholarship on business cycles. But in the book's context, of a vigorous author attacking a subject neglected by earlier economists, this chapter, entitled 'The primary cause of recurring paroxysms of industrial depression,' has great force. The argument is restated that poverty and hard times flow, not from *rent* as an economic phenomenon, for that is set forth as inevitable in any society, but from *rent as captured by private landholders,* in a stratified society. With copious California illustration, George once more displays depression as capital and labor wrongfully deprived of economic use; and once more he dismisses current explanations of overproduction and underconsumption as so much pretense. The author inserts his old epigram effectively: 'The supply of labor is everywhere the same — two hands always come into the world with one mouth, twenty-one boys to every twenty girls; and the demand for labor must always exist as long as men want things which labor alone can procure.' We may notice here, ahead of the report of the reviews, that the depression analysis in *Progress and Poverty* receives more respectful modern comment in several European histories of the theory of the economic cycle than it does in the comparable American history.

In summary, Book IV of *Progress and Poverty* matches Book III's theory with some examination of actual conditions, and opinion about conditions; and Book V draws condition and theory to common focus. This completes the second premise of the economic syllogism. To repeat the first premise: Rent opposes interest and wages, always and inevitably in the logic of economics. The second premise may now be rephrased, as follows: The actual observable compulsions and sufferings of society confirm theory, and show land monopolization — supplemented by monopoly in other forms — to be the bottom cause of the inequities of modern society.

−4−

In a reformer's mind, when theory and fact of abuse coincide, the need to propose and to act becomes compulsive. But even in Book VI, 'The Remedy,' *Progress and Poverty* mounts slowly to its climax. First there is a side tour of observations, calculated to clear vistas for the big proposal. Selecting a vein of thought much like the one which occurred prominently in the United States in the years before the New Deal, when certain intellectuals, journalists among them, bade farewell to reform, the author argued that the crisis of his day demanded deeper change than current reforms even contemplated, much less could be expected to bring into effect. As in the *Post*, he reviewed the going proposals for government economy, for more and better education, for the co-operative movement, for 'governmental direction and interference' in economic affairs, and found them all to have their points of strength, yet each and all to fall short of need.

Though conceding that 'the ideal of socialism is grand and noble; and it is, I am convinced possible of realization,' he objected that such a state of society cannot be manufactured — 'it must grow. Society is an organism, not a machine.' Not unlikely following the thought of his friend Charles Nordhoff, he said that 'the only force that has ever proved competent for [socialism] — a strong and definite religious faith — is wanting and daily growing less.' Again, while George was drafting *Progress and Proverty*, an old National Reform Association man, Lewis Masquerier, had renewed in a book the pre-Civil War plea of organized labor for a national policy of inalienable homestead lots, a method of economic security. *Progress and Poverty* refutes this reform also, in George's old way; [14] and so it rounds off in style the author's long but friendly debate with the Sacramento *Bee* and Editor McClatchy.

Commenting on two possibilities for economic amelioration which were before the public in 1879 — the two which between then and now have apparently done more than other efforts of policy to level the distribution of income in America — George achieved no great success as prophet. Reviewing once more the *pros* and *cons* of the income tax, he dismissed that reform as too inquisitorial and too discouraging to accumulation, for the United States. [15] About trade unions, his judgment conforms better with the future. He acknowledged that great combinations of working men might actually increase wages at the expense of rent. 'The advance of wages in particular trades by combinations of workmen,' he wrote,

[14] *P and P,* 319–25.
[15] *P and P,* 318.

'has nowhere shown any effect in lowering wages in other trades or in reducing the rate of profits.' [16]

Yet, opposite to Marx, George contended that working men, as they succeed in raising particular wage rates, advance into ever greater difficulties as they reach for higher successes. He thought, truthfully for his own day — and a generalization about American labor that perhaps held up until the New Deal — that the kind of union which can demand and win large wage gains is a small and exclusive union, and that such gains do not extend to unskilled labor; and he argued that only a 'general combination,' such as the 'Internationals' proposed, could press back the rent line to make great and general differences in labor's income. But he believed that 'such a combination may be set down as practically impossible, for the difficulties of combination, great enough in the most highly paid and smallest trades, become greater and greater as we descend the industrial scale.' Doubtless thinking of Dennis Kearney, George stated a matter still important in the days of John L. Lewis: 'As even the man who would fight for freedom, must, when he enters an army, give up his personal freedom and become a mere part in a great machine, so must it be with workmen who organize for a strike. These combinations are, therefore, necessarily destructive of the very things which workmen seek to gain through them — wealth and freedom.' [17] George hated strikes and he hated bosses, and he wrote in certainty that he had a better plan than unionism for solving labor's most important problem.

After all the preliminaries, the author took only a two-page chapter to present 'The True Remedy' — which is the conclusion of the economic syllogism — and he required only six words for the formula, '*We must make land common property.*'

Wherein lay the compulsion? 'We have traced the unequal distribution of wealth which is the curse and menace of modern civilization to the institution of private property in land . . . There is but one way to remove an evil — and that is, to remove its cause . . . Every step has been proved and secured . . . Deduction and induction have brought us to the same truth . . . I [now] propose to show that the laws of the universe do not deny the natural aspirations of the human heart; that the progress of society might be, and,

[16] *P and P*, 308.
[17] *P and P*, 311, 313–14.

if it is to continue, must be, toward equality, not toward inequality;
and that the economic harmonies prove the truth perceived by the
Stoic Emperor —

> *"We are made for coöperation — like feet, like hands, like
> eyelids, like the rows of the upper and lower teeth." '* [18]

Now almost ready for his reform proposal, George circled once
more. He asserted again everyman's equality with respect to the
Creator's work: 'The equal right of all men to the use of land is as
clear as their equal right to breathe the air — it is a right proclaimed by the fact of their existence.' For we cannot suppose that
some men have a right to be in this world, and others no right.'
Also *Progress and Poverty* repeats the author's old contempt for
the facing-both-ways people of British land reform. John Stuart
Mill as land nationalizer is classified, as in the *Post*, along with the
soft anti-slavery reformers in America, among the weak who would
compensate owners for a type of property which they had no moral
right to hold.

To strengthen this passage of the book, the author now exhibited
knowledge, and knowledge of scholarship, concerning primitive
peoples, which the editor of the *Post* had not displayed. No admirer
he, said George about himself, of the myth of the noble savage.
Yet he preferred, to the justice rendered at the seat of the British
Empire, the Maori justice of New Zealanders, who would not sell
title to certain lands because they would not surrender the rights of
children not yet born.

In support of his own standards of morality, he found useful the
writings of Sir Henry Maine and Emile Laveleye, and a Cobden
Club volume on *Systems of Land Tenure in Various Lands* which
was slanted toward the Irish question. From these sources he gar-
nered the propositions that primitive societies hold their lands in
common, and that private property in land, like private property
in slaves, derives from conquests. As George summed up the history
lesson: 'Historically, as ethically, private property in land is robbery. It nowhere springs from contract; it can nowhere be traced to
perceptions of justice or expediency; it has everywhere had its birth
in war and conquest, and in the selfish use which the cunning have
made of superstition and law.'

[18] *P and P*, 326, 327, 328.

While twentieth-century criticism would not permit a land reformer today quite such glibness as this, about the origins of tenure, George cannot be called anything worse than glib for having made these generalizations. And, following an opinion he had put in the *Post,* on one point of the contemporary history of land tenure he shows superiority of insight. Contrary to frequent assertion, in his day and since, he said that the South now, after Emancipation and Reconstruction, was actually and tragically not very different from before: the planters' 'ownership of the land upon which the freedmen must live gives them practically as much command of labor as before, while they are relieved of responsibility, sometimes very expensive.' The most recent and realistic scholarship about landholding in the post-Civil War South reverses older interpretations, and agrees in substance with those of Henry George. A new serfdom, growing from land and resource monopolization, sums up George's anxiety for the whole of Western, and particularly British and American, civilization.

No reader should be surprised to be told that when, after 403 pages, *Progress and Poverty* proposes a 'simple yet sovereign remedy' for poverty, the remedy is not the single tax by name, and that it is only in some degree the future single tax in spirit. (The phrase, 'one single tax,' does slip into the book in glancing allusion to the physiocrats of France.) *Progress and Poverty* recommends a tax policy as the best means to a social end; but it is less of a tax-reform book than the *Post* was a tax-reform paper. Addressing a world audience, the author naturally gave ends not means the greater emphasis, and came circuitously toward confiscatory taxation.

At the crucial point of telling readers how a revolution in property holding could be brought off by a people's representative government, George called first for land nationalization. 'We should satisfy the law of justice, we should meet all economic requirements, by at one stroke abolishing all private titles, declaring all land public property, and letting it out to the highest bidders in lots to suit, under such conditions as would sacredly guard the private rights to improvement.' Doubtless the author was thinking of the nationalization movement in England when he mentioned this possible policy; at any rate to assure readers that he was guilty of no vagary he called on Herbert Spencer, the popular philosopher then, for support.

Because of the events of a dozen years following, especially because of George's book against Spencer in 1892, there is no other passage in *Progress and Poverty* so crammed with the human comedy as the sober quotation from *Social Statics*. Though it is not often noticed about him, Herbert Spencer in 1850 had declared for owner-compensated land nationalization in the little book which had since become famous. Now, not knowing that he had caught his authority napping, or that he would bite if disturbed, George quoted in accurate fullness as follows: 'Instead of being in the possession of individuals, the country would be held by the great corporate body — society . . . Instead of paying his rent to the agent of Sir John or His Grace, [the farmer] would pay it to an agent or deputy agent of the community. Stewards would be public officials instead of private ones, and tenancy the only land tenure. A state of things so ordered would be in perfect harmony with the moral law.' George reluctantly admitted that Spencer wanted the landowners paid, whenever the state might take over, but he predicted that the English philosopher would presumably not stick to this, as it was 'undoubtedly a careless conclusion which he upon reflection would reconsider.' [19] A prophecy could hardly have been more mistaken.

Only after offering the alternative of land nationalization, and doing so as a kind of hedge against any possible charge of idiosyncrasy, does George renew from the *Post* and the lectures his own preferred solution: *'It is not necessary to confiscate land; it is only necessary to confiscate rent* . . . We already take some rent in taxation. We have only to make some changes in our mode of taxation to take it all.' The book does not quite say that *all* rent, or nearly all rent, ought to be taken, though it presents that choice, the position which became George's own in the later controversy; it does say that *'all taxation save that on land values'* should be abolished.[20]

No doubt existed in the author's mind that all or most of the annual value of a community's land would provide handsomely for public needs, even though all other revenues were abolished. To the author of the scheme, such a reallotment of funds, and added to that the shift of balance in society which the reallotment would

[19] *P and P*, 401, 402. See Spencer, *Social Statics*, New York, 1873 ed., 141–2.
[20] *P and P*, 403–4.

bring about, would suffice to achieve the goals of socialism without the growing pains. The appropriation of rent would 'raise wages, increase the earnings of capital, extirpate pauperism, abolish poverty, give remunerative employment to whoever wishes it, afford free scope to human powers, lessen crime, elevate morals, and taste, and intelligence, purify government, and carry civilization to yet nobler heights.'

Though many were to disagree with George's proposal, his contemporaries were not to say that its enactment would fail to provide lavishly for any government's expenditures. The probability of the present day, that the cost of twentieth-century wars and social services exceeds the amount of economic rent which arises in the economy, measures one of the great differences between Henry George's time and our own.

—5—

Rapidly, once the economic syllogism — of theory, abuse, and reform — had been rounded, *Progress and Poverty* turned the corner into ways and means, and the transit to utopia was short. This leads to George's inquiry, appropriate for all seekers and questers to pursue: What are the laws of civilization? To what goals may humanity reasonably aspire? That is to say, *Progress and Poverty*'s economic syllogism reaches to join the moral sequence; and the two connect in the affinity without which neither one would have much life.

Naturally George had to draw on imagination, not British scholarship, to round out from the ideas of the *Post* his design for freedom. Now strengthened by Book III's analysis of distribution, he said that taxation which took all rent would eliminate speculative pressure on land and would permit the rent line to drop somewhat; this in turn would increase the earnings of labor and of capital. But the main thing in this passage was to illustrate the many, many gains the people could expect. In one shining paragraph a new community splendor is suggested: not common dining rooms, according to the family man who was writing, but libraries, universities, and parks and other civic improvements beyond anything conceivable in the present order — the city as *pueblo* imagined once more. As we read we visualize economic rent flowing past and beyond the reach of the mansion dwellers on Nob Hill and on Fifth Avenue, and being channeled at last into reservoirs of public capital for public investment, or being distributed in community consumption. Democracy's possible beautiful city — avenues of cottages, with ample space and trees, with books in the libraries and service in the hospitals, and light and heat for all — has nowhere in American literature gleamed more brightly than in Henry George's package of promises of what a transformation of property rights could make possible.

Does it make sense, *Progress and Poverty* now asks, a utopia trying to be practical, a republic of democracy and economic justice some time soon? Not perfect love but justice among men George chose as his goal. Could a fair balance between economic collectivity and security, and individualism, be enacted? Such are the inquiries that underlie the book's last roundup of the informed opinion of the age.

The key ideas here are the two broadest conceptions of common parlance in nineteenth-century social thought, the twin concepts of progress and civilization. In *Progress and Poverty* they are connected with a third, possibly following Tocqueville, the concept of association. In George's rendering, civilization is the sum, progress is the process, and association the method of social improvement. The terms are used to draw together all manner of human achievements: social and individual ones, material and intellectual, practical and aesthetic. 'All these improvements, therefore, in man's powers and condition, we summarize in the term civilization. Men improve as they become civilized, or learn to coöperate in society.' George's definitions win the highest praise from the distinguished scholars — otherwise no admirers of his — who are the principal historians of the idea of civilization in the United States. Charles and Mary Beard find in George's writings a weaving together of economic with non-economic matters that for comprehensiveness surpasses the work of all other American economists.

Once more *Progress and Poverty* moves carefully, and keeps a little apart from English thought, and especially from moral tones of social Darwinism. The book goes a certain distance again, indeed, with the age's most prominent social thinker, then qualifies as follows: 'That civilization is an evolution — that it is in the language of Herbert Spencer, a progress from indefinite, incoherent homogeneity to a definite, coherent, heterogeneity — there is no doubt;

but to say this is not to explain or identify the causes which forward or retard it.' In complete moral dissent from dominant British and German habits of thought, George entered the opinion that the age's inclination to justify overseas expansion, as though the name of evolution and the science of Darwin made right the exploiting of weak peoples, had encouraged a hateful racism and nationalism. The 'sort of hopeful fatalism' assumed by imperialists he condemned as ethically wrong and intellectually dishonest. He condemned also the indifference to human suffering, and the complacence about science and technology, which he discovered in Winwood Reade's *Martyrdom of Man,* one of the most popular writings of the time.

True progress, *Progress and Poverty* asserts, is neither automatic nor exclusive. Remarking a phenomenon of history greatly developed by Arnold Toynbee of the present day, George observed that many of the world's civilizations are interrupted ones, like those of India and China, which have gone so far but then stand still, uncreative, oppressive, and decadent. In this passage retrogression or standstill becomes altogether as sober a thought and quite as tragic as in the more famous pessimism of Henry George's younger contemporaries, Henry and Brooks Adams. But George did not let the mood persist; and, again like Toynbee, he believed that a leap forward in civilization is possible, sufficient even to encompass the hazards of the modern world.

To justify confidence, George resorted to his heritage of democratic and Christian faith. 'Association in equality is the law of progress,' and in this axiom the author found sufficient interpretation to explain the failure of some civilizations, and the power of others to advance. In later Egypt, he reasoned, human 'mind' or power of creativity had been too tightly contained in the social hierarchy; and in a broad way he found that wars and the conflicts and frustrations of social classes explain the case when progress stops. On the other hand, he said in affirmation of faith, the occurrence of freedom and equality explains sufficiently the historic occasions of moral progress; and keeping these conditions fresh and productive is the obligation of modern man. In this frame *Progress and Poverty* makes a final restatement of the necessity to make land common property. That step alone would ensure association in equality to future generations.

The eloquent Book x, 'The Law of Human Progress,' from which some of the ultimates of George's thought have just been drawn, brings to a logical conclusion the moral sequence. The Introduction had stated, in advance of demonstration, that material progress in present society creates poverty; and Book x now added that the longer history of man shows that a better outcome is possible.

Near the end, Book x affirms also that God's law rightfully belongs in human affairs. Through the book, the ancient concept of unwritten, immutable law — embedded everywhere in American thought, up to and including George's day — appears variously as economic law, moral law, the law of nature, and the law of God. In the final fusing of Book x, Henry George reaffirmed the faith which he had proclaimed in Berkeley, and doubtless many times less formally, that there is to be realized in man's affairs a uniformity, 'a law,' which connects even the operations of political economy with Christ's teachings by Galilee. 'Political economy and social science cannot teach any lessons that are not embraced in the simple truths that were taught to poor fishermen and Jewish peasants by One who eighteen hundred years ago was crucified — the simple truths which beneath the warpings of selfishness and the distortions of superstition, seem to underlie every religion that has ever striven to formulate the spiritual yearnings of man.'

The closing lines of the book, as George took it for printing to his friend, Hinton, reached a similar climax.[21] Some years later George wrote his father about completing the manuscript, in the dead of a March night. The letter says that faith flooded him then. As he put down his pen, he dropped to his knees, weeping. He had done all he could: 'the rest lay in the Master's hands.'

–6–

How good a book had Henry George written? Because the present biography could be described as a historical review of *Progress and Poverty,* and because Part Two will discuss the reception of George's ideas in a way I believe proportionate to Part One's discussion of origin and development, I feel no need to follow the delineation just completed with a clause of simple praise or dis-

[21] Compare *P and P,* 549, the point at which George first closed the manuscript, with 523, the passage quoted.

praise. But there are certain aspects of the work which, though the reviews missed them, seem important; and certain omissions from the book, which, being omissions, could not affect his contemporaries in a positive way, yet invite designation in the vein of might-have-been.

I have nothing left over to add to what I have already said about the evolution of George's economic ideas between his little first book and his big second one. But from the change of his reform ideas there are consequences to be noted. In *Our Land and Land Policy* he had regarded as roughly equivalent the old land reform and his new one: either a full application of the homestead policy, or land-value taxation, or the two combined, comprised his recommendation for democracy in 1871. In 1879 George's full and final shift to the logically more perfect system — or systems, if we regard the choice between land-value taxation and land nationalization as equivalent — had an implication which renders *Progress and Poverty* less a political tract, at least for the United States, and more exclusively a piece of social criticism and universal prophecy, than it might otherwise have been, or needs to have been.

In *Progress and Poverty* the main line of reasoning, to justify the strategy of land-value taxation, is the proposition (in Book VIII, 'The Application of the Remedy') that 'great changes can best be brought about by old forms.' This is a general idea not to be taken for granted. And in this case 'old forms' mean that Henry George was proposing that local government undertake the burden of a social and economic transformation in America. For in habit, though not in any constitutional limitation, land taxation in the United States is local taxation. To be sure, George the California Jeffersonian, believer in decentralized government, had inserted earlier in the book certain memories and opinions, brought forward from his journalism of the '60s, about how miners in the Sierras had devised on their own a system of tenure wiser, by the writer's standards, then freehold tenure; and he drew also on San Francisco's lost opportunity, which need not have been lost, to become a community-owned city. Such knowledge of what communities could do, put together with a powerful belief in Adam Smith's canons of taxation, which were of course pointed toward land taxation, gives more strength than a twentieth-century mind readily grasps to *Progress and Poverty*'s thought that a revolution in property rights might be brought about by America's acting purposefully through the mechanisms of local government.

Yet the difficulties of such a thought confuse even George's text. The paradox, not to say contradiction, of passages on adjoining pages in Book IX, 'The Effects of the Remedy,' will illustrate. Here *Progress and Poverty* says, first, that under land-value taxation, 'Society would thus approach the ideal of Jeffersonian democracy, the promised land of Herbert Spencer, *the abolition of government*.' Then, after explaining a bit, appears the equally strong hope that, 'Government would change its character, and would become the administration of a great cooperative society. It would become *merely the agency by which the common property was administered for the common benefit*.' [22]

'Does this seem practical?' George asks. The present writer thinks that, where practicality rather than theory is the question, by comparison with *Our Land and Land Policy, Progress and Poverty* comes off second-best. Had the author retained in *Progress and Poverty* his inclination of eight years earlier to classify land according to availability and location and economic potential, and had he admitted the rough-hewn rightness of the 160-acre — or 80-acre — homestead as democratic policy for the well-watered farming regions, George would likely have avoided some of the indifference and opposition of farmers, which were so much more frequent than displays of sympathy, during his later years. Again, had he permitted his driving mind to range freely once more into land classification, he might have named certain residues of domain land for which a developmental policy of nationalization — the lands were already federal property — would have been best. America's conservationists would very soon be making such classifications — the famous Donaldson report was already in the works — and Henry George might have led the way.

In sum, had *Progress and Poverty* produced multiform applications of 'the remedy' in Book VIII, instead of making such a complete commitment to land-value taxation, one can imagine the later George supplying ideological support for the practical but none-too-philosophical-minded Roosevelts and Pinchots of the actual conservationist movement. And plainly, if *Progress and Poverty*

[22] *P and P,* 453, 454, italics mine.

had proposed such compromises, or rather such variant applications of the same reform, there would have remained room enough for attempts at land-value taxation: all the cities, and any rural areas so inclined, would have been as available as ever, to tax reform by the state legislatures. Altogether *Progress and Poverty*'s willful concentration on land-value taxation displays an astonishing blindspot toward American conditions George knew well — a blindspot toward domain policy, and toward the federal-and-state-and-local distribution of tax power and practice.

While my estimate is that the political science of the book invites pragmatic criticism, I venture also that its economics was stronger, and more up-to-the-minute, than economists frequently admit. Apart from the critical handling of the wages-fund and Malthusian theories, and the extension of Ricardo's law, judgment on this point turns on George's use of the concept of the margin — 'the margin of cultivation,' on which he hinged his general ideas of distribution.

The history of the marginal idea has not been written. As has been indicated, Ricardo has gradations of fertility as the influence controlling rent, in the chapter Henry George studied; but this is the idea without the word 'margin.' Not unlikely George took the phrase 'margin of cultivation' — he also spoke of a 'margin of productivity,' and at least once of the 'margin of building' on the edge of a city — from Henry Fawcett's text; but this is uncertain, for the same phrase appears in John Stuart Mill, who atributes it to Dr. Thomas Chalmers, the Scottish theologian. We can rule out as unavailable to George the French and German scholars who seem to have been the earliest to wield the idea; and there is no sign that George had even heard of William Jevons' fundamental and mathematically reasoned-out work in marginal economics, *Theory of Political Economy*, which was published in England in 1871.

This accumulating background considered together with the well-known development of marginal conceptions during the decade or so after *Progress and Poverty*, makes the more important George's decisive use of the word and idea, in 1879. Moreover John Bates Clark, who two decades later at Columbia became the leader of the neo-classical group of economists in the country, himself acknowledged that George's point 'that wages are fixed by the product which a man can create by tilling rentless land' caught his eye, and suggested to him that he 'seek a method by which the product of labor everywhere may be disentangled from the product of co-operating agents, and separately identified.' For the reasons that academic economists have mostly opposed or disregarded George (Clark opposed him in a debate at Saratoga, 1890), and that George made no effort to develop further the line of theory he used so early and so strikingly, Clark's acknowledgment of debt to *Progress and Poverty* is the more suggestive. For the moment at least, George took a front position in America in the rough-hewing, non-mathematical stage of applying the marginal type of economic analysis.

In the history of American academic ideas, the next-door neighbor, or rather twin, of the marginal concept in economics is the frontier interpretation of American history. Like Ricardo's law of rent, Frederick Jackson Turner's frontier idea, first stated in 1893, survives criticism and lives on from one generation to the next, though at present in reduced circumstances. Here again, *Progress and Poverty* anticipated a master idea in social science. Though the book as a whole argues against much reliance on frontier settlement as an economic safety valve for America's underprivileged, it contains eloquent passages on the influence of the West on American life and character, passages which, like those in earlier *Post* editorials, were very Turnerian before Turner. For example: 'The general intelligence, the general comfort, the active invention, the power of adaptation and assimilation, the free, independent spirit, the energy and hopefulness that have marked our people are not causes, but results — they have sprung from unfenced land. This public domain . . . has given a consciousness of freedom even to the dweller in crowded cities, and has been a wellspring of hope even to those who have never thought of taking refuge upon it . . . In America, whatever [a man's] condition, there has always been the consciousness that the public domain lay behind him; and the knowledge of this fact, acting and reacting, has penetrated our whole national life, giving to it generosity and independence, elasticity and ambition.' [23] In the judgment of F. L. Paxson, one of Turner's most distinguished disciples, 'the "hither edge of free land" became the magic element in the Turner hypothesis'; and, as all know who read history, that hypothesis in a degree

[23] *P and P*, 387–8.

governed America's understanding of America for a long generation.

Discovering predecessors of Turner, and tracing the lineage of
his ideas, has become a too frequently repeated operation to render
very interesting the observation that George preceded him. So did
many others. But a recent scholarly finding, that the Italian land
economist, Achille Loria, segments of whose thinking much re-
semble George's, largely contributed to the Turner hypothesis,
sharpened in the present writer's mind the natural question: Could
Turner have distilled a historical theory out of the air of commonly
held ideas and not owe a debt, heretofore not noticed, to the most
popular and exciting book on economic life and policy, published
during the period of the distilling? Other indications to the contrary, Professor Turner's biographer, Dr. Fulmer Mood of the University of Texas, finds he probably did owe something to George.
Dr. Mood generously shares the discovery, made from Turner's
own copy of *Progress and Poverty,* that the young historian read
and marked the book in 1888-9 while a graduate student at Johns
Hopkins; and Turner took part in a seminar discussion of the book
that year. For Henry George in 1879, this later evidence means
simply that his mind had seized and incorporated one of the great
insights into the national character and history, and this, with the
marginal idea, adds power and authority to the book.

Having ventured criticism of certain points of the political
science and the economics of *Progress and Poverty,* the writer may
review briefly one or two other things. Somewhat akin to George's
blindspot, in 1879, with respect to the special character of American government, there is a conspicuous absence, still, of the claim
he might have made that certain of the fathers of the American Republic could reasonably be counted on his side. Despite his fondness for saying that he sought only to fulfill the Declaration of Independence, he seems not yet to have discovered Jefferson's now
famous phrase, graven large on the walls of the Library of Congress
and of the Jefferson Memorial, that the land belongs in usufruct to
the living; and still less to have known that Thomas Jefferson contemplated using the power of the state to reallocate land privately
held to the landless, if necessary. 'If for the encouragement of industry we allow [the land] to be appropriated,' wrote the author of

the great Declaration, 'we must take care that other employment be provided for those excluded from the appropriation. If we do not, the fundamental right to labour the earth returns to the unemployed.' Other reinforcements for his idea, which George might have borrowed from Thomas Paine's *Agrarian Justice,* or from Ralph Waldo Emerson — 'Whilst another man has no land my title to mine, and your title to yours, is vitiated' — the author of *Progress and Poverty* evidently did not know to be available to him.

Again related to the shortcomings of *Progress and Poverty* as a political tract, George failed to notice the awkwardness of saying that the land belongs to all the Creator's children, without also recognizing that this argues for the *internationalization* rather than the *nationalization* of land, and without observing that land-value taxation in, say San Francisco, if imposed by city or state government, would appropriate values created by all the peoples of the Pacific, not to say of Europe and the United States east of the Sierras. The economic advantage of great cities derives from the whole area of their trade. To be sure George's dedication to free trade relieves him a little at this point. But the point is more than a quibble; and the author who explored so many lines of ethical logic ought to have noticed that only a world organization with power to tax, or at least to distribute the proceeds of land-value taxation, would fit well his ideal scheme.

Yet the present writer believes that these practical or detailed shortcomings, as they are omissions rendered visible by the moral standards of *Progress and Poverty* itself, have one effect of displaying the ethical magnitude and elevation of the work as a whole. If the book is a devastating attack on land monopoly, as intended, it is also a moral Mount Whitney in American protest. It is a signal, good for any place and any time where freedom and equality have meaning, against monopolism in any form, unless that monopolism be truly necessary in economics and truly public in administration. Still more than this, *Progress and Poverty*'s fusion of economics and ethics, its passionate blend of love of God with comprehension of the entrenchment of selfishness, give it — despite the long and winding Victorian argument — an intensity which places it at once high in letters, and yet at the threshold of the common man.

-7-

While the manuscript was at Hinton's print shop — and the writer himself was setting some of the type — George became discontented to end *Progress and Poverty* as he had brought it in, with a final appeal to Christian ethics. The death of his Aunt Ann, in Philadelphia, had turned his mind again to immortality, though that alone could hardly have impelled him to make an addition to the book. At white heat, to Book x he now added the Conclusion, 'The Problem of Individual Life,' his justly famous statement. More definitely than any part of the moral sequence which precedes it, this section attaches *Progress and Poverty* to a religious metaphysic, to a deeper intimation of philosophical idealism than appears in any of his other books. Henry George knew about Socrates, and it is entirely possible that this concluding impulse to attach the idea of immortality to the book's plea for justice was in some degree an imitation.

Only his own words, which are richly autobiographical, will do to convey the thought. 'My task is done . . . Yet the thought still mounts . . . Behind the problems of social life lies the problem of individual life . . . Out of this inquiry has come to me something I did not think to find, and a faith that was dead revives.

'The yearning for a further life is natural and deep. It grows with intellectual growth, and perhaps none really feel it more than those who have begun to see how great is the universe and how infinite are the vistas which every advance in knowledge opens before us — vistas which would require nothing short of eternity to explore . . .

'When we see that social development is governed neither by a Special Providence nor by a merciless fate, but by law, at once unchangeable and beneficent; when we see that human will is the great factor, and that taking men in the aggregate, their condition is as they make it; when we see that economic law and moral law are essentially one, and that the truth which the intellect grasps by toilsome effort is but that which the moral sense reaches by quick intuition, a flood of light breaks in upon the problem of individual life. These countless millions like ourselves . . . do not seem so much like meaningless waste.

'What then, is the meaning of life — of life absolutely and in-evitably bounded by death? To me it seems intelligible only as an avenue and vestibule to another life. And its facts seem explainable only upon a theory which cannot be expressed but in myth and sym-bol, and which, everywhere and at all times, the myths and symbols in which men have tried to portray their deepest perceptions do in some form express.' [24]

Two pages later there is the superb selection from Plutarch with which *Progress and Poverty* closes. Dr. Taylor may have helped George find it, but this is a kind of passage he himself might well have discovered: '*Men's souls, encompassed here with bodies and passions, have no communication with God, except what they can reach to in conception only, as by a kind of obscure dream. But when they are loosed from the body, and removed into the unseen, invisible, impassable, and pure region, this God is then their leader and king; they there, as it were, hanging on him wholly, and be-holding without weariness and passionately affecting that beauty which cannot be expressed or uttered by men.*'

Pleading immortality Henry George was neither instructing his readers in an article of faith, nor was he speaking — as certain critics would say — in a way not related to the text preceding. He was asserting an idealism bigger than that of most reformers. He was saying in the most intense language he knew that this is God's world and we are His children, and that those who believe, with passion and without fear, have a resource to overcome even the resources of selfishness and evil.

On that assumption Henry George made his appeal. Within two decades incredible numbers of Irishmen and Scots, Englishmen and Americans, and representatives of every civilization would under-stand him, and would respond.

[24] *P and P*, 553, 555, 557–8, 561.

PART **II** 1880–1897

A CHRISTIAN EFFORT

XI

In the Tide of Idea and Opportunity

1880–1881

–1–

THERE are tides and currents in man's awareness of mankind's affairs, and in today's retrospect we can see that 1879, the year of *Progress and Poverty,* marks as well as a date can the beginning of a mighty flow. 'That was when the civic conscience awoke in 1879,' wrote Jacob Riis twenty years later, in remembrance of the war on the New York slums.

To see the matter in a national perspective, we may glance backward and forward, half a century each way. Of the hundred years beginning with the age of Jackson and coming down to present times, the '80s were a flood time of resentment and criticism of the industrial order. The first New York printings of Henry George's great book came early among the freshets of that protest; and, during the ten years which followed, the new editions and translations of *Progress and Poverty,* the writing and publication of Henry George's next three books, and all but one of his famous campaigns for office and reform contributed more than did the work of any other individual to the awakening of conscience in the United States of the modern period. The decade 1880 to 1890 included also: the early critiques of business monopoly by Henry Demarest Lloyd; Edward Bellamy's famous utopian novel, and a many-faceted revival of socialism in the country; America's first large advance of social-gospel Christianity, kin to a movement in England; the labor insurgency of 1886 which brought on the near-

est thing to a general strike in our history; the rapid growth and
rapid decline of the Knights of Labor, and the emergence of the
American Federation of Labor; agrarian protest in South and West
more organized and effective than in any earlier day; immigration
on a scale and of a type unprecedented in history; and Congress's
first round of monopoly regulation, the famous railroad and anti-
trust legislation of 1887 and 1890. Assimilating strains and anxieties, Americans were seized by incredible fears that the country
had come to the brink of disaster; and yet most national leaders
asserted that economic individualism contained all the wisdom
needed to guide us toward the good life Andrew Carnegie ex-
tolled. It was a disturbing time for reflective minds.

Every one of the events just listed represents a development
in an area of life or thought with which Henry George had long
been familiar; and we shall have to return to them all, because
his activities of the '80s either influenced or were influenced by
every one. But George had not written *Progress and Poverty* for
Americans alone, and, as quickly as the book was recognized at
home, in a few cases more quickly, it was recognized overseas as
well. Early in the '80s it reached British, Continental, and
antipodean horizons. In its own day perhaps more readily than
now, readers and reviewers understood that *Progress and Poverty*
belonged in a context of thought and theory not confined by national boundaries, though the ideas were characteristically American, and belonged in a time sequence longer than that of the usual
problem book of a depression era, though *Progress and Poverty*
was that as well.

To estimate the career of the book at all proportionately, 1864
is not too early to begin, on the American side, with the little-
remembered great book of a New England scholar. In the year
of Henry George's very earliest printed writing, George Perkins
Marsh brought out *Man and Nature,* a powerful work of cumulated
scientific, historical, and moral insight into mankind's dependence
on the resources of the earth. About the time George was laboring
on his own manuscript, the Marsh volume was beginning, Gifford
Pinchot tells us, to do its effective work of supplying inspiration
and resource to the makers of the conservation movement in
America.

And simultaneously, just two years ahead of *Progress and Poverty,*

Lewis Henry Morgan of upstate New York summed up three decades of investigation and thought about Indian anthropology, and related it to the history of all mankind. His *Ancient Society, or Researches in the Lines of Human Progress* attaches rather to the Whiggish than to the Jeffersonian branch of American thought; and it is worth noticing that by a not too incongruous marriage of ideas it was taken into the family of Marxism by Friedrich Engels in his book on the *Origin of the Family, Private Property, and the State,* which appeared in 1884. The Marsh and Morgan volumes can be considered efforts of social thought as profound as George's, but they are books which, in contrast to *Progress and Poverty,* emphasize the organizational, rather than the emancipating, needs of society. To put the matter in a second genealogical figure of speech: these books represent the birth, into the large family of American social thought, of new ideas from the Hamiltonian side, cousins of the theories from the Jeffersonian side which George had sired on the West coast.

The fact that neither Marsh nor Morgan ever approached a popularity comparable to George's does not mean that ideals of organization or conservation were remote from public questions in their day. Related to *Man and Nature* in purpose, the famous report on the *Public Domain* by Thomas Donaldson was published as a congressional document in 1879; and almost simultaneously John Wesley Powell's like-minded *Report on the Lands of the Arid Region* made its appearance, also in Washington. More closely kin than followers of Henry George have often recognized, there was intellectual and political coincidence, both, between his land-and-labor movement and the save-our-forests movement at the national capital.

While Congress was investigating and the United States Geological Survey beginning its work, moreover, the universities were staking out wide new interests in the condition of the land and the economy. Harvard and Cornell were unusual in having professors interested in forestry. But the land-grant colleges with their agricultural and mining studies were building up, and government experimental farms were being started. And whereas the University of California had been typical, lacking a professor of economics when Henry George lectured, the decade of the '80s dates the appearance of a specialized and organized profession of economics in

American higher learning. That profession, in fact, probably did more than the other new professions in the social sciences — those in history, sociology, and political science — to begin in earnest during the '80s the modern-age practice of colleges: the cultivation of professorial experts in the affairs of the Republic, as well as of experts in the humanities and in the natural sciences.

From many and diverse directions poured the writings which made the decade as great in the history of the social mind as in the history of the social conscience. Parkman brought out *Montcalm and Wolfe,* a climax in his study of rival empires; George Bancroft concluded his half a century task of writing an idealistic history of the United States; and Hubert Howe Bancroft completed the seventh and final volume of his *History of California,* economic life included — these last two histories known and appreciated by George. While veterans rounded off their studies, men in their forties asserted themselves. Oliver Wendell Holmes, Jr., still a professor and about to become a judge, ventured in his lectures on the *Common Law* the new pragmatic doctrine; Henry Adams launched his incomparable nine volumes on the *History of the United States during the Administrations of Jefferson and Madison;* and a visitor from Oxford, James Bryce, composed his famous treatise on the *American Commonwealth* — for the California chapter of which he acknowledged a large debt to Henry George. In this same decade able young men stepped forward, also. Woodrow Wilson did his parliament-minded doctoral dissertation on *Congressional Government;* and John Bates Clark pushed steadily ahead with his articles, and brought out the book, *The Philosophy of Wealth,* which marked his young leadership among academic economists. In a fullness not yet sufficiently studied or understood, the '80s mark a formative and creative decade in social scholarship in America; and a doubt may be ventured that Darwinian evolution is as surely the key to unlock its secrets as sometimes appears.

Concerning Britain and Europe, no more is required in anticipation than simply to recollect that transformations had been reached not different from those in the United States. For the destruction of slavery in the United States, substitute the crumbling of the hierarchical order in Britain, just as it was defended so brilliantly by Bagehot in 1867; in lieu of agrarian protest here, substitute

Ireland and the Irish land problem, and falling prices for farm products, there; and in place of our labor insurgency of 1886, substitute the more successful dock strike in the mother country. The greater British John Bates Clark was Alfred Marshall his contemporary; and during the '70s their Stubbs, their Gardiner, their Green, their Lecky, and their Acton set models for our own vigorous new historical scholarship.

At the line where social thought challenged social condition, Britain of course knew Karl Marx a little, as his long-time London host. More frequently than in America, critics and menders of society were ready to study his ideas and adapt them to national need. But the Christian Socialists and the Fabians rejected Marx; and a real analogy exists between such people as Sidney Webb and Bernard Shaw and their contemporaries in this country, such collectivist-minded wielders of the pen as Henry Demarest Lloyd, Edward Bellamy, William Dean Howells, and Hamlin Garland. How British architects of the positive state owed more, or at any rate acknowledged greater debt, to George than did their American brothers in spirit is a considerable part of the coming story.

Of course the international coincidences of the awakening of social conscience were no coincidences at all. They were variants, rather, of the social and intellectual transformations that followed on the industrialism, the empire building, and the democratic assertions in some degree common to all the nations of Western civilization. Yet no individual case of similarity is more arresting than the parallel between Henry George and his future most distinguished convert. Exactly in 1879, halfway round the world from George, Leo Tolstoy put down in his *Confession* that he had found a way out of spiritual inadequacy — that he had discovered something better than the common beliefs in natural progress and human perfectibility which had beset his thought so far. Except for Tolstoy's turning to Christian love and non-violence, and the international social Christianity his change represents, the Henry George story after 1879 would have been a far less broad and interesting one, and the two decades which remained to him would have been much less effective than they were.

Of some of the great books, great men, and changing ideas of his mature career, Henry George became aware about as soon as anyone could. Of others — Tolstoy among them for some years —

he knew as little as a man from Mars. Yet, Platonist who knew little Plato, from before 1879 the author of *Progress and Poverty* believed the ideas he apprehended to be universal truths of unlimited validity and dawning light; and this idealism had present meaning for him. It is wiser to read as practical belief on his part, rather than as airy peroration, those late words in his book: 'The truth that I have tried to make clear will not find easy acceptance. If that could be it would have been accepted long ago. If that could be, it would never have been obscured. But it will find friends — those who will toil for it; suffer for it; if need be, die for it. This is the power of Truth.'

As if to confirm the sincerity of this we have a letter of 1879 to George W. Julian, the elder statesman of anti-slavery and land reform whom George admired most. The letter follows their becoming acquainted while Julian visited California, and it follows also Julian's article in the *Atlantic* which demanded classification of the lands of the federal domain. Responding to his compliments on receiving a gift copy of *Progress and Poverty*, George wrote a letter which the Indiana statesman chose to preserve: 'I thank you for the good words you tell me you will speak for the book . . . You can in this way do it great service.' It is, 'as you say, profoundly religious . . . I of course do not know your inner life, but I know that to every man who tries to do his duty there come trials and bitterness in which he needs all the faith he can hold to.'

–2–

Immediately on completing his manuscript, George had sent a copy to Appleton and Company. Appleton was the immensely successful publisher of the American editions of Herbert Spencer's writings, and the publisher also of the International Science Series, and *Popular Science Monthly,* which promoted the doctrines of Spencer and Darwin in America as no other journal did. The firm's acknowledgment of manuscript must have reached Henry George a few days after the first issue of his little newspaper, the *State,* came out; and their declination must have reached him about eight days later. The book 'has the merit of being written with great clearness and force,' the letter said, 'but it is very aggressive. There is very little to encourage the publication of any such work at this time and we feel we must decline it.'

Thus began the author's two-and-a-half-year struggle for recognition. The first step was taken for him by one of his brothers. Advised by William Swinton, Thomas George peddled the manuscript in New York — at Harper's and Scribner's, and until he had no choice but to telegraph San Francisco that 'it seems impossible to get a publisher without plates.'

We know already the second step. William Hinton, George's old partner, now back in the printing business, offered the credit and facilities of his shop, so that George could go ahead with a small author's edition. Beginning in mid-May, both Henry Georges, senior and junior, set type; so did printer friends; and even Dr. Edward Taylor, who also read proof, joined them at the case. Hinton's generosity amounted to risking $1000 to $1500, whatever the cost of the plates, which the New York firms were unwilling to venture. This arrangement was rendered more hopeful — more in the nature of an advance than a charity — when a friend of Henry George who was in New York as agent and trustee of the San Francisco Free Library interceded with William H. Appleton, the head of the firm, and found him, though still making no promises, somewhat disposed to change his mind.

Though altogether the summer of 1879 must have been an anxious one for George — he had now dropped his newspaper, and his state job was bringing in little — there must also have been compensation and excitement in the work of every day. Besides enriching *Progress and Poverty* by adding the conclusion on immortality, the author loosened up the tight mid-section of the book. He subdivided 'The Remedy' into the 'Justice of the Remedy,' the 'Application of the Remedy,' and so on as we have seen. He entered new mottoes and revised details as the typesetting progressed; and he had the solace of friends around him and the encouragement of their faith. Typographically, and as a total piece of manufacture, the result of the summer's work was very impressive: 500 beautifully printed copies solidly bound in dark cloth covers. 'It will not be recognized at first,' George wrote his father as he sent an early gift, 'maybe not for some time — but it will ultimately be considered a great book, will be published in both hemispheres, and will be translated into different languages.'

Appreciation of the book grew in Mr. Appleton also. Reading the manuscript had kept him awake at night, he confessed to a friend of Henry George, but because *Progress and Poverty* tore to pieces 'all the recognized authorities on political economy,' he had not at first dared to publish. But now, with the plates all made, his fears diminished. 'It appears to me it will create some sort of a sensation anyway, and I don't think we shall lose anything by publishing it.' Accordingly within a couple of weeks of the time when copies of the San Francisco edition crossed the continent, the proposition went back to George, that if he would supply the plates, Appleton's would bring out a New York edition in January. No other publisher so much as nibbled at the bait.

During the fall of waiting — and George had an anxious time about the delayed safe arrival of the plates — a few responses to gift copies came in. With the exceptions of George W. Julian and Sir George Grey, the land reformer who was the first statesman of New Zealand, the general statement would hold that the bigger the public reputation of the recipient, the smaller the comment rendered on the free copies sent out. Sir George made an interesting advance on future sympathy and correspondence. The new book he regarded as one that surely 'would be of great use' to him. 'It has cheered me much to find that there is so able a man working in California, upon subjects on which I believe the whole future of mankind now mainly hangs.' But while this came from the fighting outer edge, the responses from the center of the British system, those from Gladstone and the Liberal Duke of Argyll, in whom George thought he had discovered sympathetic ideas, amounted to courteous dismissals. Joseph Chamberlain wrote much more cautiously than his future attitude would suggest.

Probably the most encouraging word out of the British Isles came from the distinguished Professor T. E. Cliffe Leslie, of Queens College, Belfast, a strong scholar who had made himself an early critic of the wages fund, and who wrote on land systems and on interest and profit. His first letter assured George that the Manchester School was already more shaken than the journals would indicate; and that though he differed from *Progress and Poverty* on some points, he shared the author's criticism of economic orthodoxy. A year later, when this scholar had an article in the *Fortnightly Review* on 'Political Economy in the United States,' he chose the word 'imagination' for Henry George's work, and he nominated *Progress and Poverty* and the writings of the nationalistic school as the best economics the United States had produced, each in special ways superior to the textbooks of America's professors. At the time of writing the article he invited George to correct his facts before publication, and urged him to write on political economy in America, say in the *North American Review*.

From nearer home George received the encouraging private comments he might have expected from John Swinton of the New York *Sun* and Charles Nordhoff of the New York *Herald*. The friend who only five months earlier had differed so sharply about the new constitution of California, wrote on 30 October with complete enthusiasm of the delight he discovered in a work of economics dedicated to 'Truth, Nature, and Man,' and strong with the juice of earth. A great relief, observed Swinton, after a bout with the writings of William Graham Sumner.

Nordhoff's tribute, received in December when time was running short on the position of gas-meter inspector, led George to write back about his present troubles and his brighter hopes. 'You speak of the intellectual poverty of this coast. You can hardly understand how deep it is, for of course you came into contact with the highest people, and they must have seemed to you relatively far more numerous than they really are. This is bad enough; but what is worse is the moral atmosphere — at least in the circles in which I have moved and lived.' By this George meant California's materialism, and he confessed that if *Progress and Poverty* should succeed and opportunity come to him, he would choose to do two more books: the first 'a brief political economy,' and the second 'a dissection of this materialistic philosophy which, with its false assumption of science, passes current with so many.' The chapters he had done on civilization, he said, amounted to no better than the skeleton of an argument, and he had much more to say.

A month later, in a kind of postscript to these reflections, George told Nordhoff of the anxieties he suffered at the time of the New York publication of *Progress and Poverty*. 'Perhaps it is the deep faith which in Christian faith is expressed in the incarnation; but it is certain that successful efforts for the amelioration of the condition of the lowest class can come from the class above, not below . . . And I am anything but sanguine — sometimes this amounts to utter hopelessness of carrying out any real reform.' Would people read the book? Most especially would it influence those who had the power to affect the common lot? George must have been thinking of the great newspapers, as he shared his worries with this friend. How would metropolitan journalism respond to what he had written?

First indications were anything but cheerful. Though he expected much of the eastern reviewing to wait on the Appleton edition, the New York *Tribune* and *Herald,* papers with editors who had once been his friends, did comment. Greeley's old paper, now managed by Whitelaw Reid, took a moderate tone in describing the tax remedy, but then pretty much washed its hands of the book by saying that the general thesis — the wrongness of private property in land — must be dismissed because it was quite as speculative as squaring the circle. The *Herald* at mid-December, shortly after the *Tribune,* was wise enough to say that *Progress and Poverty* belongs between the conservative and radical poles of social thought. But its mild opinion could hardly have reassured an author that his effort of analysis was going to command attention and debate.

To be sure Horace White, who as editor of the Chicago *Tribune* had applauded *Our Land and Land Policy,* now called *Progress and Poverty* 'very impressive.' In a private letter he agreed that the state might eventually be compelled to confiscate economic rent; but at the same time he rejected George's analysis of depressions and said that to him it was 'not quite clear' that Malthus had been overthrown. While he half promised to say something favorable in print, he was for the time being out of journalism. George would have been less than encouraged, when he received White's letter, had he been able to foresee White's later review and the kind of treatment he was going to get from the New York *Evening Post* and the *Nation* after White had become one of the editors of those distinguished journals.

The California reviews of *Progress and Poverty* have the quality of the predetermined. Friendly newspapers spoke first, the Democratic San Francisco *Examiner* and the land-reformist Sacramento *Bee,* the two papers which had gone almost all-out for *Our Land and Land Policy* eight years earlier. Quite properly the writer in the *Examiner* called his piece an 'announcement' rather than a review: he made the regional uniqueness of the book his principal theme. *Progress and Poverty* surpassed all earlier California writing, the paper said; it was 'a product of deep, painstaking, and honest' thought, and would surely command wide reading and response. The Sacramento *Bee* quoted and took the same line, though its net judgment came closer to being an endorsement. 'The most wonderful production in its line — political economy — that has been presented to the public since the days of Malthus,' the review said. 'In diction it is equal to Macaulay's purest and best.'

By stroke of either luck or arrangement, Dr. Edward Taylor, the author's consultant and great friend, did the review for the *Californian*, the new monthly with an old name which now succeeded to the *Overland*. In some ways Dr. Taylor's review was as it should have been the most perceptive comment of the lot — the passage on the California-mindedness of *Progress and Poverty* has been quoted in the preceding chapter. But a review that would match wits with the book's central themes and purposes Dr. Taylor was hardly the man to undertake. Other favorable reviewers might have done substantial analyses, but did not; and in this respect Henry George's friends let him down. In California his book was deeply discussed only a few times, never from a favorable point of view.

The friendly California papers commented on the San Francisco edition; but the adverse reviews all followed Appleton's publication, and one may reasonably interpret the delay to mean that the author's old enemies would have disregarded *Progress and Poverty* pretty unanimously had not New York recognition forced their attention. Yet in all reasonableness some sympathy is due the reviewers for the conservative newspapers on the coast. They could hardly be expected to salute a future classic as delivered from the pen of a gadfly editor; and the argument went over their heads. Thirty odd years later Dr. Arthur N. Young recovered in interviews some of the San Francisco climate of feeling about George as a new author. His brothers in the Bohemian Club pooh-poohed the book; many printers who knew about the venture at Hinton's scoffed at it; and a friend of George, the bookstore keeper who was chief distributor of *Progress and Poverty* in the city, gave away more than he sold of his stock of 200 copies. In this context the *Alta California* took no more trouble than to print the curtest of dismissals, in the spirit of the red scare. *Progress and Poverty* was simply 'land communism,' it said.

Other newspapers, not nearly as friendly as the *Examiner,* disposed of the need for judgment in the way that paper did, by praising Henry George as a Californian of achievement and by omitting real comment. Yet from the side of Republican journalism, in the columns of the Central Pacific's *Record-Union* of 21 March 1880, there did appear the one serious early review done in California, a performance reminiscent of the *Record*'s full treatment of land monopoly and of the proposed reforms of land monopoly in 1873. The Sacramento paper argued at length, as many later reviews would, that George was wrong about Malthus. But it gave him an opportunity, which he relished, to reply — he took eight and a half columns for rebuttal. This proved the nearest he came, before leaving California, to taking up his cause in new strength, in debate with those who held influence and affected policy.

Yet the troubled author must have had a moment of glee in February when a Dr. Montague Leverson, who announced himself an old student of John Stuart Mill and a writer of economics, and who was being obstreperous in the discussions of the Pacific Social Science Association, caused a ripple through the press by a splash in the weekly *Argonaut.* Leverson himself saluted *Progress and Poverty* as '*the* book of the half-century'; and then proved his sincerity by withholding a primer of economics he was writing until he could assimilate the ideas he now accepted. His piece in the *Argonaut* led to an open letter from one who signed himself 'Ex Rebel.' What are you Republicans and ex-abolitionists going to say now, demanded the Southerner, with an irony made possible by the moral of *Progress and Poverty.* 'You scoffed at vested rights, you preached human equality . . . Now the spirit you have fostered turns on you in turn. And I am curious to see whether men of your class are going to join in the march, or are going to make a stand against it.'

At about the same time George received another California

tribute which in the end came to mean more. The person was C. D. F. Gütschow, a German San Franciscan previously unknown to him, who picked up a copy of the author's edition and was captivated. In December, before the reviews had accumulated, he began to translate into his native language. Years were to pass before George would have reason to learn how good a friend had discovered him, in Gütschow. Of their relationship now we know only that the author gave permission for the translation on single condition of a faithful rendering, and that the translator worked at a pace to complete the job in eight or nine months. It was published in Berlin in 1881 and sold in Europe and America, the first foreign-language version of *Progress and Poverty* and, of ultimately three German translations, it was the only one that ran to more than one edition. The translator knew what he was about. His preface estimated the book more accurately than any California review: a system of economics and sociology, Herr Gütschow announced, which defies the ancient defeatism of economics, a work at once radical and also conservative and religious, individualistic and democratic, yet fearless to expose the evils of democracy, a book neither optimistic nor pessimistic, exactly, a creation of the spirit which defies classification.

But this anticipates and reaches afield. The sum of Henry George's situation, in late winter and as 1880 advanced to spring and summer, was pretty discouraging in San Francisco. In January the new Republican state administration put him out of office. (This seemed right to him even though, since 1878 at odds with his own state party, he had voted for Governor Perkins.) He was in debt again, to Hinton in some amount not paid off by the sale of the San Francisco edition, and perhaps to others. And locally the publication of his book had netted him just one solid review, the adverse one in the *Record-Union,* one friendly essay, and perhaps ten other — whether favorable or unfavorable, always superficial — notices. The score was no better than that. No wonder the memory stuck when a wealthy landowner, General Beale of Tejon Ranch, sought him out to congratulate him on *Progress and Poverty* as an intellectual performance, and yet assured him that the book would not be read by those it was intended to affect. And equally no wonder he felt dispirited and half ill, and that he wrote

Dr. Taylor, who had gone to Washington, please in his behalf to
call on 'Redpath or some other of the Lecture Bureau people.'

He felt that he must go east somehow.

–3–

Though George remained in California until midsummer 1880,
his real center of gravity, his thought-life of hope and planning,
shifted across the continent in January. Indeed the temptation is
to say that before year's end, 1879, it had made a quick crossing
of the Atlantic, two years ahead of his first visit in Europe. He
accepted an invitation, at any rate, to contribute an article about
'The Irish Land Question' to the Christmas issue of the Sacramento
Bee. The article has so much in common with the little book of the
same title, 1881, and in turn that book connected him so directly
with overseas affairs, that it is easy to think he wrote for the *Bee* less
to inform the people of Sacramento and to earn a fee, than to call
the attention of Irish radicals to his own ideas. More roundly than
ever in the *Monitor* or the *Post* he applied his perception to
the homeland of many Californians; and comparatively from the
two places he read again the lessons of land monopolization. He
said that in California rents rose sometimes to one-third or even
one-half of the land's product; he offered Buckle's opinion that
in Ireland they came to one-fourth or so; and comparing the politics
of protest he described Parnell as an 'educated Dennis Kearney.'
He left his readers with one impression: inadequacy of land-
reform leadership in both Ireland and California — and the world
around. Very shortly he sent twenty-five copies of the Appleton
Progress and Poverty to John Russell Young to pass on 'to the
radicals or the leaders of the Irish movement' in New York.

Publication in New York, which came off according to schedule
in January 1880, shifted the question of George's future from
whether *Progress and Poverty* would be published to whether or
not publication would succeed before the wider world. And also,
though the writer's anxieties were many, it brought the comfort of
new allies. Appleton publicized Henry George by way of promot-
ing the book. The March issue of *Popular Science Monthly* carried,
besides a friendly — though unsigned and undistinguished — review of *Progress and Poverty*, George's 1877 University of California lecture on 'The Science of Political Economy.' Four months

later the same magazine brought out his article on Kearney. And the March number was hardly distributed before Professor E. L. Youmans, the famous editor, proposed certain more complicated strategy.

The newspapers that should be reviewing *Progress and Poverty,* he wrote, were 'afraid of it, and would do it no justice.' So at Mr. Appleton's request he had engaged a writer to do an essay on the book, and the result so pleased him that he was going to make it the lead article for April. George of course acceded, though his twenty-five dollar half-payment of the writer's fee hurt at the moment; and the result was a handsome survey article in the most appropriate journal in the country. Four appearances within six months in *Popular Science Monthly* — two articles of his own, two about his book — may be accounted generous publicity for a previously unknown writer.

And in fact the first resistance against *Progress and Poverty* did begin to yield. In February Appleton reported that reviews 'very good generally' were coming in, but sales were few; and in March, that the first edition of 1000 copies was nearly exhausted and 500 more would be printed. By the end of that month, A. J. Steers, a youthful employee of the firm, succeeded in persuading Mr. Appleton that a cheap edition — to be issued at $1, half the regular price — would be appropriate and successful. Naturally this delighted Henry George, the more because young Steers wrote that his mind had been fired by the principles of the book.

Meanwhile on 14 March *Progress and Poverty* had had its best newspaper criticism so far, ten and a half columns by M. W. Hazeltine in the New York *Sun*. Receiving that newspaper's recommendation that the country take *Progress and Poverty* as a very serious book prompted George to share with a friend a flash of hope, on the anniversary of sending the manuscript to New York. 'After the toil and pains of the writing came the anxiety, the rebuff, the weary waiting; and I have longed that by this day at least there might be some sign that the seed I had tried to plant there had not fallen by the wayside. This review is that sign; it secures for my book that attention which is all I ask.' Just a bit earlier the New York *Critic* had noticed his Berkeley lecture as printed in the *Popular Science Monthly*, a pleasant pat on the back from an exacting journal.

Later spring and early summer brought mixed voices but a growing response. Patrick Ford's *Irish World,* the leading Irish newspaper in America and one with a rather radical slant, naturally liked *Progress and Poverty* but grumbled with a socialistic sound at the way George condoned interest taking. To George's great satisfaction the same paper revised and printed in April his Christmas article on 'The Irish Land Question.' This suited him better, he said, than going ahead as he had planned with a similar article in the *North American Review.* On the other side, the *New York Times* — which was then a Republican paper and had not yet built up the special authority it voices today — spoke in utter condemnation. This reviewer's method was simply to blast at the heterodox first quarter of *Progress and Poverty,* the book's rejection of accepted economic ideas, and to pay little attention to the rest. George had had that kind of review in California, and would have it again, many times, in Britain.

The difference between the *New York Times* and the *Irish World* indicates the completely unsettled standing of *Progress and Poverty* half a year after New York publication. So far there had not been, any more than in California, any serious intellectual discussion of the book. But there was real encouragement in the way in which important national newspapers had indicated interest. This much was better than the West coast; and, though the New York response to his book had not quickly given him any such salute as he craved, at least he was still free to hope for that salute — the doors were open and not closed.

This was the eastern situation when George made up his mind to leave San Francisco, and leave his family awhile, and venture alone the move to New York City. John Russell Young made good on the advice he had given. He lent George money, and gave specific suggestions about how to cross the continent. Unless he could afford the best accommodations, this globe-trotter suggested, he had better take the immigrant cars. He would have to sit up anyway, and he would do well to have the experience from which he could write up immigrant travel. This was tactful advice, for apparently George had had no more than $250 advanced from his publishers, and no other income since December. For whatever solace of pride, he traveled as California member of a commission recently set up by President Hayes (Governor Perkins had nominated him), for a fair to be held in New York to celebrate the centennial of the peace treaty with Great Britain.

From Winnemucca George wrote back to San Francisco: 'I am enjoying the trip and am full of hope. The spell is broken and I have taken a new start.' Yet this mood had to yield to stoicism when he reached New York, in August. He found that sales were going poorly. Young was out of town, and the employment Young had thought he might have on the *Herald* never materialized. Nor were the recent criticisms, which amounted to a kind of rounding off of first journalistic reaction to *Progress and Poverty*, anything too favorable.

Probably the New York *Nation*'s two-issue review, which has been attributed to Horace White and which George likely understood to have been written by the recent writer of encouraging letters, hit him first when he reached the city. The honor of the review lay in the way it took *Progress and Poverty* seriously, and allotted it precious space. But the reviewer rejected the book three ways: in a shaded and scholarly criticism of George's anti-Malthusianism and his total dismissal of wages-fund doctrine; in direct attacks on his interest theory and depression theory (White also made himself one of the few to assert that rents in England were probably declining); and in a silent refusal to consider more of the book than what we have called its economic syllogism. The review did admit a certain expediency — not related to George's logic of principle — in the case for land nationalization with owners compensated; it nowhere suggested that *Progress and Poverty* so much as contained what this biography names the moral sequence of its thought.

Quite likely Henry George's being alone in New York was the occasion of starting the scrapbook collection, later kept by other hands, in which are gathered together hundreds of reviews of his books and notices of his public addresses. The collection helps us to perceive a regional pattern which was quick to develop in the reviewing of *Progress and Poverty*. Most of the early reviews came from the industrial northeast, and occasional ones came from the South, while journals in the Middle West were pretty silent. From the heart of the old Confederacy, for instance, the Charleston *News and Courier*, printing a very long summary of the book, commented that though few Southerners would

be likely to accept Henry George's remedy, his book demanded
consideration, and that readers would be persuaded to tolerate
no longer the squandering of the public lands. Why, questioned
the Brooklyn *Eagle* (perhaps with this very review in mind) did
the agrarian South sometimes take to Henry George? Because,
it answered, *Progress and Poverty* shows that serfdom is quite
as unjust as chattel slavery. Never frequently, but beginning
now (and more often later, we shall see, after George had made
himself powerful spokesman for free trade), the question that
'Ex Rebel' had asked in San Francisco was repeated in the South:
How far will Henry George's applications of Yankee notions be
accepted, in attack broader than the anti-slavery crusade?

At the same time, the newspapers and magazines of New England
were beginning to enter the discussion. In the Boston *Christian
Register,* the leading Unitarian journal, the Reverend George A.
Thayer recorded the religious spirit of *Progress and Poverty* as
completely as almost all the other reviewers were omitting it. 'It
is so full of the milk of human kindness, so sympathetic with the
world's misery and so religious in temper while withal so bright
and unhackneyed in its comparisons and illustrations, that it is
one of the most wholesome and stimulating books . . . that has
been provided for many a day.' Suggestive of the line he would
trace in the not distant future, Edward Atkinson, layman and
liberal businessman of Boston, fired back at this review, asserting
that in America industry helps everyone. But the reverend critic
had the final word, answering correctly that George did not blame
industrial technology for poverty.

Authentic secular voices of New England were heard when the
Springfield Republican in June and the *Atlantic Monthly* in the
fall printed reviews. The famous inland paper, which had been
strong against the extension of slavery and yet moderate toward
the South during Reconstruction, compared George's book with
Blanqui's critical *History of Political Economy* in Europe, and
agreed that *Progress and Poverty* had struck at 'the current conceptions of political economy with much vigor and some success.'
The reviewer doubted that the end of private property in land
would come in his day. The *Atlantic Monthly* — among the major
magazines early to comment — assigned the task to two reviewers,
side by side, with an eight-page result. First William B. Weeden,

manufacturer and writer, and future economic historian of New England, quarreled with George's technical procedures, with his distrust of current notions of progress, and particularly with his labor-employs-capital idea. He allowed some virtues to the book's thought and expression but he believed that 'to revert to a common property in land would be a backward course,' and that to go backward means decay. Not so Mr. Weeden's associate in reviewing, Mr. Willard Brown, who barely quibbled with *Progress and Poverty*'s analysis. Though admitting that the reform would 'rob the landholders,' he was willing to 'confess we see no other means by which the laborers can ultimately better their condition, and Mr. George's plan is one of the least objectionable means of that character.'

Private comment rather than public gives a hint that the year 1880 contained just a beginning of George's career of winning, more than readers and friends, real converts to his ideas — and that sometimes the opposite happened. We learn from certain letters that George was in contact, again, with David Ames Wells, and that the economist who had once been a kind of mentor sent some criticism of *Progress and Poverty*, and discussed the 'moral inertia' which prevents reform ideas from doing their logical work. Though George's trying to see Wells in New York indicates a continuing friendly relationship, it becomes clear that the new book drew lines of separation, rather than affinity, between them. On the other hand, as the cases of A. J. Steers of Appleton's and the translator, Herr Gütschow, indicate, occasional individuals were already beginning to announce that *Progress and Poverty* had changed their lives. George says that there were others. 'Youmans says I don't make converts,' he wrote Dr. Taylor, but 'I find them in all directions. Every day I get letters.'

Confidence was growing, at least by fits and starts.

-4-

On first arrival in New York George had the excitement and pleasure of meeting people who wanted to see him, and to whom he was important. Professor Youmans and Patrick Ford, the two editors most concerned, both treated him warmly, and he liked them both. He learned at once that though he might be disappointed in sales so far, Appleton's was willing to go ahead with the

cheap edition; and very soon the word came that part of the
German edition — the translation was to appear first in install-
ments, according to German habit — would be out in September.
At Youmans' suggestion, George ran up to Boston to see William
Swinton, his old friend from Oakland days and after.

But in the nature of the case it was a grim situation he had to
ride out. Back in San Francisco Annie was having a hard time.
Within less than a month she moved from the First Street house
to something that cost less, and before long she had changed to
boarding as less expensive than housekeeping. George agreed to
both moves, yet the decision hurt to sell his books and abandon 'my
pleasant little house — that I was so comfortable in.' It hurt also
that his wife had to borrow from his friends in San Francisco:
'It is at such a time as this a man feels the burden of a family.
It is like swimming with heavy clothes on.'

He could not protect the boys from the strain, and given the
situation it is characteristic of him that he did not try — rather
used the situation for education in the school of life. To fifteen-
year-old Richard, who was doing undistinguished work at school,
he made the same recommendation his father had made to him
after the trip to India; learn to set type, he suggested. And he told
the boys — Henry was at work — that they would have to support
their mother and sisters should anything befall him. In the same
season he confessed to Dr. Taylor that he felt crowded near the
limit of spiritual strength. 'I did feel depressed when I wrote
you,' he said at Thanksgiving time, 'but it was not so much on
account of circumstances. I am in the way of being a good deal of
a Stoic. Adverse fortune does not depress me — what always
worries me is the thought I might have done better, that it is
myself that is to blame, and it seemed to me then as if I had been
fooling my time away very largely.' And the next spring, when he
paid back a twenty-dollar loan from the same friend, he admitted
that at the time of borrowing — 'my darkest hour' — he had been
morbid, quite able to understand why men kill themselves.

In New York George lived in as inexpensive a way as possible.
We have the testimony of a new acquaintance, Poultney Bigelow,
a young lawyer, who was the son of a prominent family and who,
recently graduated from Yale, had studied economics under
William Graham Sumner. Lending George books, and absorbing

an influence which would affect his future writing, Bigelow gained an indelible memory. Living in the slums, he says, Henry George had to pick his way along sidewalks crowded with ashcans and refuse; neglected streets with abominable pavements; children with no place to play save the gutters.' The irresistible thing was the man's conviction that he could change all that. 'He was a saintly man; he walked with angels.'

But George's most reassuring friendship at this time was with John Russell Young — the one intimate, according to Anna George de Mille, who never fully adopted her father's ideas. In the latter months of 1880 Young lost both child and wife; and the two lonely men took midnight walks on the Battery, and sometimes went to the park or to Westchester for companionship and talk. Young admired as Bigelow did Henry George's incredible courage: 'It was a daring experiment — this unknown gentleman with no aid but his own high spirit, nothing in his carpet-bag but one book of gospel, coming at 42 to make his way into the heart of mighty Babylon. The more I studied George under heavy conditions the more I admired him. His ability and his courage; his honesty, independence, and intellectual power were those of a leader of men . . . It was the courage which, as has been written, makes one a majority.'

The first invitations George received to appear in public in New York were requests appropriate to his record as a Tilden orator and campaigner in 1876. Youmans asked for a political article to come out just before election, in the *Popular Science Monthly;* and a Democratic committee asked him to address a whole series of working men's meetings. George was particularly ready to renew his speaking career, and he chose to talk about the tariff. But as luck fell his first appearance followed a speaker who sounded to him more like a Republican than a Democrat, and he could not resist the opportunity to counter with full free-trade doctrine. The son of a customhouse clerk demanded that all customhouses be abolished! The audience applauded; but the speaker received an immediate wire from party headquarters to make no more speeches. For him the one good outcome of the event was that he captured the admiration of Andrew McLean, the managing editor of the *Brooklyn Eagle.* This led to another speech, and in the long run to an affinity and a cluster of Brooklyn admirers. But

George's grand reaction to the campaign and the campaigning took him back to his mood of 1871 and 1872, in a fresh disillusionment about political parties. 'Yes; look at the Republican Party, and look at the Democratic Party. It is pot and kettle. I am done.'

He fared no better as an election-time journalist than as campaign speaker. Youmans turned down the article he had asked for, and George regarded the event as a not very big 'stumble' but a disturbing one.

Real relief for a man at sixes and sevens seemed to come just after the election, when Appleton arranged for him a chance to do some economic writing. Congressman Abram S. Hewitt, who had just returned home from Europe, needed help, which today would be called research assistance and ghost-writing, for a Congressional investigation of labor conditions. Though George had promised himself no hack writing, this opportunity he could not refuse, and it was as attractive as such a thing could be. Hewitt had much in his favor as employer: as son-in-law and partner of Peter Cooper in iron and steel, he was a wealthy man; as first lieutenant to Governor Tilden, he belonged at the center of the reformist wing of the New York Democracy; as a public benefactor, he had become the kind of capitalist for which George had expressed admiration in the *Post*. Best of all, George learned from Appleton that Hewitt admired *Progress and Poverty;* and such a feeling seems to be corroborated by the ideas about labor and poverty which Hewitt voiced in his speeches.

The agreement between employer and employee pledged George to anonymity and secrecy, and gave Hewitt freedom to use as his own whatever data George's investigations might produce. George asked, and understood that he was promised, $50 a week for three hours a day — he thought that he should be paid a journalist's wages — 'till the thing is done or either of us is dissatisfied.' For a fortnight at least George worked in the Hewitt house on Gramercy Park; and this prosperity led him to rent a comfortable bedroom and to buy some new clothes. His research involved going through a pile of Congressional documents. Very soon he had a first draft, and he was sure that Hewitt was '*much* pleased' with the work. But when he requested a payment of $100 — he had already had one hundred, and apparently was asking for an advance — Hewitt balked. Hard feeling ended the connection.

This little event demands attention, though it can be told from George's side only, as more than just a disappointing episode in his period of difficult adjustment in the East. Memory was to carry over six years and to intrude a personal element when George and Hewitt became opposing candidates for the mayoralty of New York. And the event would become the story behind the story of 1897, when George accused Hewitt of saying falsely that he had once hired George as secretary and had discharged him for bringing into his writing everywhere the idea of the single tax. As of 1880 the break between George and Hewitt is good also for a might-have-been, a bit of irony, in Henry George's personal history. Had George's campaign speeches before working men come off to the satisfaction of Democratic party officials, and had he and Hewitt become friends, the author of *Progress and Poverty* might conceivably have risen to some such place in the New York party as the ex-editor of the Sacramento *Reporter* had reached, in the California party. The possibilities of George's being party brains man might have been great.

Actual events were different. Year's end 1880 marked a low point in George's personal condition; and presently when the situation did improve the change occurred to George as author not as Democrat. First he was invited in a very engaging way to do an article for the Christmas *Bee* again. McClatchy's specifications called for an essay as good as anything Henry George had ever done. Though he chose an awkward title, 'Political Economy the Framework of Political Science, Brains not Muscle Rule the World,' George wrote a philosophical piece. The idea was anti-materialism again. He condemned all such economic determinism as he himself had verged on, before *Progress and Poverty*. He asserted that politics is a bigger and more inclusive part of life than economics, but that economics sets the problems of politics. Immigration, canals, railroads, taxes, and so on, he specified from the current scene. The essay illustrates an economic interpretation of political issues, and a non-materialistic understanding of economics. As he liked to do, he placed on the working men the responsibility for bringing into being the Golden Age — a thought especially appropriate to this period of Henry George's life.

At about the same time George realized a little money by public lecturing, a hope long deferred. He was proud to be invited to perform in a 'star course' at Hudson, New York, as the starter of a series which included Parke Godwin and David A. Wells. Best of all, *Progress and Poverty,* which despite widening horizons of publication had sold very poorly through election time, now began to move. About Christmas, in the author's own words, 'a movement began, and on the last day of the year every copy of the previous editions and every copy of the 1000 cheap edition were gone, and orders and inquiries came piling in from every quarter. Appleton and Company began to realize for the first time that I had been telling them the truth, and that they have got hold of a book capable of enormous sale and now they are beginning to open out.' There was relief and assurance in noticing that the papers which had reviewed him favorably, the *Sun* and *Herald,* were now given first-class advertisements; and satisfaction in saying that no other American work in political economy had ever sold more than 1000 copies during the first year.

Accident or incident or improvement, the early winter brought George an invitation to an elegant dinner of New York *Sun* people. Dana was host, and John Swinton and Hazeltine, the reviewer of *Progress and Poverty,* were there. George was pleased by the event and only a little embarrassed at being the only one not in dinner dress. Then there was another dinner with Albert J. Bolles, liberal journalist of Norwich and writer about capital and labor, who stood on the then advanced position that trade unions are necessary and that capital should share business direction with labor. Simultaneously with these courtesies came word of agreeable developments abroad. A Canadian economist warmly invited George to 'campaign' in Canada; and, the news the author wanted, Kegan Paul, head of the important London firm which published the *Nineteenth Century,* ordered an edition of *Progress and Poverty* for British sale to begin early in 1881.

To be sure these threads of hope spun much more rapidly than they wove. John Russell Young, who had to go abroad, took a dozen copies of *Progress and Poverty* and placed them in 'a smoky little bookstore' in Haymarket, where he knew the proprietor and knew that the great men of England would see the display. The unwell Disraeli and others did see the book, we are told, but none bought; and before leaving, George's friend withdrew the copies and gave them to the men he hoped would read them — some of these men were the same as those to whom the author had sent copies of the San Francisco edition. From this distribution, which included Tyndall and Huxley and Spencer, Young claims the credit for inciting the Duke of Argyll's savage article, 'The Prophet of San Francisco,' which later helped George's cause immensely.

In New York the acceleration of recognition brought with it an exciting diversity as well. Sometimes George was confronted with demands and challenges, occasionally he was offered discipleship or assistance generous in the extreme. For an example which counted, late in March he received a letter from a stranger, Thomas G. Shearman, a Nassau Street lawyer, a member of a famous firm. A resident of Brooklyn and a member of Plymouth congregation, Mr. Shearman had been Henry Ward Beecher's counselor when scandal brought the famous minister to account. In Shearman's first communication he said a good deal: he was distributing *Progress and Poverty* among his friends; he agreed heartily with George about Malthus; and though he admitted he could not reach an absolute conclusion about the land question, he was thoroughly favorable to land-value taxation. (The 'single tax, limited,' Shearman's side, *versus* 'single tax, unlimited,' George's side, the issue of the end of the decade, lay aborning in this letter.) Shearman's one direct challenge of 1881 called George utterly mistaken to have said that professional men lack interest in reform; they are as interested as anyone, he declared.

The lawyer's initiative led to a couple of lectures by George in Brooklyn at mid-April, one of them before the Revenue Reform Club of which Beecher was president. During the same month, on the near side of the East River, Henry George's upper-crust lawyer friend, Poultney Bigelow, got him into the New York Free Trade Club — along with Theodore Roosevelt. And in May George gave his earliest well-paid lectures. The first occurred in Chickering Hall — a place to become famous in his New York career — and the second in Historical Hall, Brooklyn. Altogether George made about $225; and the rise in his position was enormous.

Meanwhile he had recovered from the writing 'stumble' with Youmans, and if not in the *Popular Science Monthly* at least in *Appleton's Journal* he had an article in June, and one, 'The Common Sense of Taxation,' in the *North American Review* for July.

This marks the beginning of his long and happy connection with
the country's oldest and most authentic national magazine. With
all this going on he achieved sufficient momentum to be gay when
William Graham Sumner wrote a demolition review of *Progress
and Poverty* and *The Irish Land Question* in *Scribner's*. 'The thing
begins to draw fire,' he gleefully wrote Taylor.

With a little money at last he completely and definitely disconnected from San Francisco. Annie and the children came on;
and the family found a pleasant house, once the porter's lodge of an
estate on Kingsbridge Road, in the Fort Washington area above
One-Hundred Fifty-fifth Street. At midsummer he himself crossed
the continent, just a year after leaving, to settle some business,
probably unpleasant business with creditors. But he saw friends,
and made a speech before a large audience in Metropolitan
Temple, and was given a dinner at one of San Francisco's Italian
restaurants on the eve of departing for New York.

Doubtless all this good will connected in his mind with a compliment he had just received in Sacramento. Warren Chase and
James C. Gorman nominated him in the State Senate for United
States senator from California. The vote had read 27 for the winner,
10 for another candidate, and 2 for George. 'I presume that that
is about as near as I shall ever come to being elected to anything,'
the low candidate wrote, not without satisfaction, to his old friend
and fellow Democrat, James Coffey.

–5–

The story of Henry George's reception and adjustment in New
York City, so far, has bypassed one main area of his interest. Of
course this is Europe — the reaction to *Progress and Poverty* there,
and the possibilities George envisaged for making converts in the
Old World. His interest by no means stopped with Ireland. In
San Francisco he selected 'The Next Great Struggle' as the subject
of his lecture: he predicted a great battle for political and economic
reform about to occur in the British Isles and across Europe
generally.

Actually the first year and a half of *Progress and Poverty*'s life
failed to raise any great amount of response overseas. But what
reaction did come is the more worth noticing because it displays
a quality of attitude on the European side which would prove

consistently different from the American. Over there first-rate minds more quickly took *Progress and Poverty* seriously and judiciously; and high-level journals, once they noticed George, more frequently estimated him to be important, however much they rejected his ideas. From George's own point of view, one of the best reviews he ever had came from Paris, a criticism of the San Francisco edition in *La Revue scientifique* as early as January 1880, an event which the Sacramento *Bee* reported with enthusiasm.

The writer was Emile de Laveleye, the distinguished Belgian scholar and socialist of the chair, whose studies included history and law and philology as well as economics, and from whose writing on the history of property George had drawn for passages in *Progress and Poverty*. Laveleye gave no full endorsement; his important specific reservations — offered in context of saying how different American affairs were from European — were that rent is a passive rather than active cause of poverty; that George had overlooked national debts and armaments as main causes of labor's hardships; and that George failed to express the exploitative power of capital, as for instance French investment in Africa. Even so, the tenor of the review was friendly, and it specifically underwrote the main thesis of George's economic syllogism. In Laveleye's own word: 'All economists admit that rent increases in proportion to the progress of civilization, so that on the other hand wages and interest tend to the minimum.' The new book had instructed him and caused him to reflect, the professor graciously acknowledged. He advised George to fight for an American policy of granting public lands in no more than temporary tenure with reversion to the domain written into the deed, as sounder than permanent-freehold policy.

In Britain one of the very few important 1880 reviews of *Progress and Poverty* appeared in the *Economist*, three months in the wake of the Appleton edition. (The *Statist* reviewed also, an unsparing condemnation.) As would be expected, though the *Economist* had a middle-class reformist attitude toward land policy, it disliked *Progress and Poverty*. The review objected that George had said things that were much too extreme about Ireland and India, and it ridiculed his diagnosis of, and prescription for, depressions. Yet the critic reported in interested detail George's argument that wages are determined by the margin of production; and he called 'powerful, graphic, and instructive' the chapter on the evil done by the inequalities of society, a large concession from a British reviewer.

On the German side, comment on *Fortschritt und Armuth* began in 1881, following on the Gütschow translation. Staude, the publisher, did what he could to force attention: he distributed free copies to members of the Reichstag, the Economic Council, and to many newspapers. Sales were small, and the total number of reviews apparently not great. But the kind of response characteristic of German learning *Progress and Poverty* did receive. In 1881, long, scholarly, and balanced criticisms appeared in two of the most learned journals. One of them was by Adolph Wagner, the famous University of Berlin proponent of the welfare state: he was ironic and adverse, and yet appreciative of George's effort. During the next year Gustav Schmoller, the leader of Germany's historical economists, criticized *Progress and Poverty* in his own 'Schmoller's *Jahrbuch*.' While he thought George pretty uninformed about Europe, and guilty of gross exaggerations (as Professor Wagner had said), he would not deny that land might have to be nationalized some day. He had picked up the book depressed at having to go through one more reweaving of the threads of British economics, he said. But when he had finished, Schmoller, who spoke always for broad social studies, acknowledged in George a writer of large heart and sharp vision who had penetrated the American situation and the American character, and who drawing from life had woven new woof across the old warp of classical economics. 'The author is an uncommonly gifted thinker,' he said, and *Progress and Poverty* 'eine nicht zu verachtende Leistung' — 'a not half-bad work.'

Again we have run ahead of Henry George's own story, and yet only far enough to understand that in looking overseas George was not merely searching out a terrain of conflict but was also taking a direction in which he had achieved some appreciation and could expect a fighter's chance to speak and be heard.

We have no way to trace in close detail how George became involved in the Irish struggle of 1881. In a sense this involvement had been written into his future by his past: by his marriage, by his participation in Democratic politics, and most compulsively by the Irish associations in California — with James McClatchy and

John Barry and the rest — which had brought him to understand the land troubles of the new state and old Ireland as parts of one universal exploitation. For about a year, from the Christmas *Bee* essay of 1879, we know nothing (except that he met Patrick Ford on arrival in the city) about whether George was aggressive or indifferent in keeping his Irish contacts.

But just after election the current did flow. One of the events of the end of 1880 that helped lift George from the pit of his troubles was the arrival in New York of Michael Davitt, the fiery Fenian leader of the Irish Land League. This new organization was driving Anglo-Irish affairs into such tension as never before; and on his visit Davitt made what the historian of the movement designates as a most memorable address. Working out from the slogan, 'The land for the people,' Davitt told a Cooper Union audience that, 'We have declared on a hundred platforms that it is our intention to shoot Irish landlordism, and not the landlords.' Davitt was a man of tremendous pressure and power but little theory, and he led that kind of movement. The Irish situation in 1880, like the California one earlier, could reasonably be read as calling for fresh understanding and theory, and for a new leader to specify valid aims and possible goals.

George turned Davitt's way as needle to near-by lodestone. He called on the visitor and was pleased to win a promise that Davitt would push *Progress and Poverty* in Ireland. But evidently George decided at once that the big book might be too heavy a dose. In order to do 'what will hereafter tell,' as he explained to McClatchy, he wrote within three months 'a little book, or rather pamphlet' developed from the year-old article in the *Bee*, and with the same title. Though it was really a very long pamphlet — divided into seventeen chapters, and eighty-five pages at first appearance, and over one hundred pages in more modern dress — Appleton published at once. We may assume that there was not even a demur this time. Disciples of Henry George sometimes still offer *The Land Problem*, as the booklet was before long renamed, as the easiest approach for first readers of his ideas.

No richer in factual data about Ireland than *Progress and Poverty* was, the new book was more able to have immediate effect because George concentrated the argument completely *ad hoc*. In his chapter IV, 'Proposed Remedies,' he pointed out that such debated reforms as legalizing and extending tenant rights, or having the government buy out the landlords and then sell to peasant owners, could produce only narrow and limited results, and would subject the economy to strains too heavy to bear. Irish affairs gave George the opportunity to argue within the premises of action that economic rent should be taken by the state and returned to the community in the form of benefits and services. Thus the headlong issue of confiscating property outright would be avoided. George drew on the old arsenals of argument, including Herbert Spencer's passage in favor of land nationalization; and he urged the Irish not to be too narrowly Irish-minded in their struggle. Make common cause with the landless of England, he proposed: the laws and traditions of tenancy are essentially the same everywhere, he said, and in detail a little more severe, actually, in England and the United States than in Ireland.

The New York newspapers seized on his treatment of the hot issue, and mentioned the little book 'magnificently,' he wrote Taylor during the first week. A column and a half in the *Times*, two and a half in the *Sun*, one in the *Express*, one and a quarter in the *Star*, and two and a half in the Charleston *News and Courier* pleased him immensely. 'And the astonishing thing is the goodness of the comments. Nothing like the back action of the early notices of *P & P*. I am getting famous if I ain't making money.' The reaction extended up the scale. Scribner's now had Sumner criticize *Progress and Poverty* and *The Irish Land Problem* together, the gratifying counterblast already mentioned; and, approaching George the other way, the New York *Critic* gave him flattering notice.

The next stage of George's identification with the Irish problem came on the crest of this wave of reviews. During the winter he had done a piece or two for the *Irish World;* and this developed his connection with the explosive and sensational editor, Patrick Ford, who had made himself the principal organizer of some 2500 American branches of the Irish Land League, and had raised hundreds of thousands of dollars. To George, writing in January to another Irishman, Ford had become a hero: 'not a politician but a single-hearted devotee to principle.' And it must have been Ford who secured for George the invitation that presently took him on his first speaking tours in the East. During March he went to Boston to address a Land League branch; and in May to Montreal, with stops at Rutland and St. Alban's on the way north, and at Ottawa and Toronto and towns in upstate New York, returning. Making $25 or $50 a night he was sometimes satisfied and sometimes dissatisfied with his performances. He knew that lecturing was not the best thing for him, he confessed to Taylor who had opposed much speaking in California, but it was 'infinitely better than hacking — and worrying.' Actually he loved the travel and excitement, and it is hard to believe that anything could have held him back.

This rounds out the story to the summer of 1881, a little beyond the time of George's other big audiences, not Land League meetings at all, in New York and Brooklyn and San Francisco. With the record of speech making, and with his reputation as author and member of the Irish movement, his fame was waxing. Very quickly George became a public personage, a man with many friends and connections. Not unlikely he was the one who made the motion to renew friendship with his childhood playmate, Heber Newton, who was now a prominent rector in New York. In turn Mr. Newton took the platform and introduced Henry George to the Chickering Hall meeting, the first of many such services he rendered.

In July a man who was presently to be about as influential in George's life as Dr. Taylor, and who ranks among the first four or five associates of his lifetime, sought him out. The elderly Francis G. Shaw of Staten Island was a member of a well-to-do and well-connected Boston family. His turning to the author of *Progress and Poverty* was the more moving because he was the father of a famous son, the gallant Colonel Robert Gould Shaw who died leading the first Negro troops to go into action against the Confederacy. Confessing to George that until he read the book he had despaired of true moral progress these latter days, Mr. Shaw proposed to buy space to 'cause' certain newspapers to print extracts from the book.

Naturally George responded with emotion. He was deeply touched at being taken for what he wished to be, a transmitter of the old anti-slavery spirit to new needs and new times. But he suggested that instead of purchasing newspaper space Mr. Shaw subsidize distributing 1000 copies of *Progress and Poverty* to the public libraries. The author persuaded his patron, also, that if

the gift to the libraries must be anonymous there ought to be
cards acknowledging that the books came from someone other than
author or publisher. 'It is the moral refinement,' George urged,
'an answer to those who have stigmatized the book as incendiary
and communistic.' Making the necessary arrangements led to one
of the most affectionate and delightful friendships of George's lifetime — presently to high-minded talk about the Hindu *Gita* and
other literature of India, and later to good correspondence and
further subsidy as we shall see.

Almost simultaneously, but not early enough to have affected
George's opposition to Mr. Shaw's purchasing newspaper space,
another way opened to get *Progress and Poverty* into newsprint.
By a decision made by members of the staff, the mass-circulation
newspaper *Truth* asked the author's permission to serialize the
book. Louis Freeland Post, the editor who conducted the negotiations, tells the story; and he etches a sharp portrait of George on
the day they met. He noticed that the economist was wearing a
long-tailed coat which enhanced his shortness of leg and breadth
of torso, and that black cloth made prominent his brick-red beard
and circle of hair. There might be a little strangeness in Henry
George's manner, Mr. Post decided, but the man had confidence,
and a personality not to be resisted. An important conversion was
being made at the interview, but George did not know this until
later.

Back of the invitation to serialize *Progress and Poverty* lay personal enthusiasms which the book and the author had stirred. A
writer of short stories for *Truth,* who had heard and met George,
urged the step; and he was seconded by a composing-room foreman,
a New Zealander of Irish and Maori blood, who had perhaps known
George in San Francisco. These two persuaded Post to read *The
Irish Land Question* and more, and Post was fired as Mr. Shaw was
by the recrudescence of the abolitionist spirit he thought now
dead. The editor maneuvered *Truth's* proprietor into a wish to
publish *Progress and Poverty* in several installments. That was the
proposal — permission asked but no money paid or promised —
when the author came in. Of course George acceded: it meant
that during months when he would be out of the country a newspaper sympathetic with labor would spread his doctrine. *Truth,*
with a circulation of from 75,000 to 100,000, would carry *Progress*

and Poverty beyond the normal reach of public libraries, to a clientele his hopes embraced.

Meanwhile had come just the recognition of talent and opportunity George was most ready to seize. In September the *Irish World* invited him to go at once as correspondent to Ireland. The proposition was fair not bountiful: passage both ways for himself and Mrs. George and the two girls, and $60 a week salary for a period of three months. He was to write a weekly letter for publication in the *World*. George would not have been wrong if he included in his calculations the fact that this paper exercised as much or more power than any other Irish newspaper in the world, for besides its readership in New York it carried as much weight as any in the old country. To his best friend George wrote: 'The chance I have long waited for opens. It will be a big thing for me. I think the biggest thing I have had yet.' And to the Irish editor of the *Bee:* 'When next we dine with you in Sacramento which I hope we will do again we will be able to tell you all about the kings and queens and dukes and that sort of thing we see on the other side.'

The surrounding circumstances could hardly have been more favorable. Word was just arriving that, after months of being 'dead as a log,' the sale of the Kegan Paul edition of *Progress and Poverty* was picking up. And Henry George had heard too that Alfred Russel Wallace, the great geologist and evolutionist nearly equal to Darwin, who had almost completed his own book on *Land Nationalisation* before he heard of Henry George, had endorsed *Progress and Poverty* as 'undoubtedly the most remarkable and important book of the present century.' This was the first of the handsome salutes from high place which encouraged Henry George's later life.

Family arrangements had to be made. School was the decision for Richard this time. For Henry there was a chance to go to Harvard, but his father favored a job on the *Brooklyn Eagle*. We think back to the Episcopal Academy of Philadelphia, as we read the advice he gave: 'Going to college, you will make life friendships, but you will come out filled with much that will have to be unlearned. Going to newspaper work, you will come in touch with the practical world, will be getting a profession and learning to make yourself useful.'

To make his farewells, Henry George went down to Philadelphia to see his parents. Traveling with the boys he confessed surprise that *Progress and Poverty* had succeeded so fast: 'Men are rising up everywhere to hail it!' he meditated. He visited Staten Island also. Without fresh help from Mr. Shaw, money to pay some outstanding debts, he might not have been able to go at all.

On 15 October, a Saturday, the correspondent and his ladies were ready. They sailed that day on the steamship *Spain,* bound for Liverpool.

XII

Prophet in the Old Country:

Ireland and England

1881–1882

—1—

THE Ireland toward which the liner *Spain* bore Henry George in late October 1881, was suffering from the worst festering of social and political sores during the nineteenth-century history of the British system. There were of course larger areas of economic anguish in the eastern reaches of empire, but in Ireland the poison and the danger lay close to Britain's heart. The infection was deep and so old that some could say the system tolerated it. It had broken out last in the politics of Physical Force, which had been organized in the Fenian Brotherhood during the late '50s, and which aimed for Irish independence to be achieved by revolution.

As of the '70s, on the economic side the Irish situation compares with California, in even more ways than Henry George had said. The opening years of the decade had been prosperous, and, with a mild land reform enacted by Parliament in 1870, political tensions had decreased. The brotherhood by no means broke up. But where the recent hottest Irish nationalism had disbelieved in Parliament and reform had seemed a mirage, now both Home Rule and ideas of economic amelioration were taken to Westminster in hope that wrongs could be made right after all by constitutional processes. New Irish leadership, notably in the persons of Charles Stewart Parnell and Michael Davitt, represented the new situation.

Parnell, the acknowledged Irish leader in Parliament after 1875, was a Protestant and a property holder and never a Fenian. But always a patriot he associated somewhat with laboring-class elements and with persons more radical than himself, and presently he was identified with the Irish Land League.

If Parnell represented the upper-class side of Irish protest, and much of the fascination of leadership, Michael Davitt, who was still more of the heart and center of the Land League, represented the common substance. Davitt derived from working-class origins (as a child he lost an arm in a textile factory), he had been for years a Fenian, and in 1880 he had been elected to Parliament—in a membership, sometimes interrupted by jail sentences, which would last for nineteen years. This man better than anyone else exhibits the paradoxes of 1881. He voiced Ireland's protest in the Commons according to ancient rules of order, and also he associated with out-of-doors protest where violence merged into crime; he embraced a radicalism compounded of despair and nationalism, and yet he was constrained by Catholic loyalty and faith.

In the large, though the Irish Sea had not been bridged solidly either by political institutions or by good faith and mutual understanding, and never has been even yet, the situation of the '80s tells no story of complete frustration. This passage of history offers, rather, the annals of solutions proposed and compromised, of imperfect successes, incomplete failures, and continuing hopes. As things stood when George drew near, Ireland may be estimated to have been half-assimilated into the British system. Though the smaller island had its members in Parliament and its justices of the peace across the counties, it had developed no such full habits of political participation as Britain had. Underlying the incidents of protest the question always remained: Was Irish resistance outside the channels of loyalty and constitutionality a necessary recourse? Or would cabinets and parliaments, mainly British and heavily Protestant and always conservative on property rights, actually achieve the vision to understand Irish problems deeply and act forthrightly? Under Victoria, would government have the capacity to solve Irish questions as it had not solved American ones, during the age of George III eleven decades earlier?

In all truth the prospect in 1881 could not be called promising. In the last four years agricultural prices had brought Ireland to a stage of deprivation to be compared with the potato famine of the '40s; in the western counties during 1879 there had been a 75 per cent failure of that crop. Agrarian suffering was due in part to competition from the American West. The very moderate provisions of agricultural credit which had been set up by Parliament's Land Act of 1870—the law which Henry George must have had in mind when he said that tenants' rights were more amply protected in Ireland than in Britain and America — supplied no reservoir sufficiently available or sizable for the tenants' needs. Evictions rose in four years from an ordinary 2400 or 2500 to more than 10,000 in 1880, out of about 600,000 tenants on the land and perhaps 100,000 vulnerable. As farmers simply could not pay their rents, Ireland's recurrent *jacquerie* broke out into more appalling violence than for 200 years. This was the human urgency behind the Land League's slogans, 'Down with landlordism!' and 'The land for the people!' This was the condition of affairs that justified the 'New Departure' which the league represented in Irish politics: a unifying shift of emphasis from Home Rule to radical land reform.

Unfortunately the stand of British politics in late 1881 was as little encouraging as the economic situation. The Irish pressures had built up while Disraeli was still in power. But the six-year Conservative government ran out in 1880 (and the extraordinary leader died the next spring), and the Conservative party's impulse for humanitarian legislation did not include the urge to change the institutions of land, in Ireland or anywhere. The time for practical hopes that parliamentary action would accomplish substantial relief for the peasants of Ireland occurred between April 1880, when Gladstone won a huge victory at the polls, and the summer of 1881, when the prime minister put through a famous land act.

But the painful months of decision — which coincided with Henry George's first year in New York — ground out a checkered record. The auspices of 1880 were good. The great Liberal carried from his first government of a decade earlier the record not only of land reform but also of having disestablished the Church of England in Ireland. And recently he had associated with young Radicals of intelligence and strength, Joseph Chamberlain, Charles Dilke, and others; and the Radical element was the most friendly in England to lenient treatment for Ireland. But when Gladstone assembled his second government he drew principally from the Whigs, and brought in only two Radicals, Joseph Chamberlain, whom he made president of the Board of Trade, and John Bright, who served in a limited, consultative capacity. Thus the inner conflicts of the Liberal party became stumbling blocks to Irish relief and reform. When a bill to assist Irish tenants was introduced it passed the Commons, but the vote was less than three-to-two. A number of Liberals opposed it; and it failed in the House of Lords.

Meanwhile anguish piled on anguish in Ireland. During late 1880 and early 1881 evictions mounted to perhaps 1000 a month, and violence increased across the land. This was the time when peasants in the Land League country created the verb 'boycott' in our language. By reducing Captain Boycott to isolation on his acres — denying him field labor and household servants, preventing him from receiving mail and telegrams — they worked out a technique of social pressure. The reaction in England was to strengthen the elements in Parliament that demanded a new act to coerce Ireland. With the premier in the minority of his own cabinet, a force bill was passed, and *habeas corpus* was suspended before the Liberal government accomplished any relief measures.

Then at mid-1881 Gladstone came forward with his new land act. It reduced the freedom of Irish landlords, in exercising their property rights, to sterner control by the state than that to which recent labor legislation under Disraeli had reduced industrial employers. A judicial commission was established with power to fix rents, on the application of either tenant or landlord. Based on the 'three F's' which had marked the maximum demands of Irish land reform before the Land League, the new law made practical provisions for the tenants to have Fair Rents, Fixity of Tenure, and the Free Sale of whatever improvements they might put upon the land they occupied. By the standards of the '80s this was an astonishing law: 'The most revolutionary measure that passed through Parliament in the nineteenth century,' according to J. L. Hammond, and the 'beginning of the end' of Ireland's underlying problem, in the observation of Joseph Chamberlain's biographer. Never before had a government in the Anglo-American tradition in time of peace so forcefully asserted the general interest over property rights; and the House of Lords which enacted the reduction of rents spelled out the doom of its own class elsewhere than just in Ireland.

Had Irish politics, both parliamentary and outdoor varieties, followed amiably in the logic of Parliament's strong action, Henry George might have had the happy but inappropriate task of reporting for the *Irish World* a deep improvement in the land to which he was assigned. Indeed the Irish members of Parliament had been surprised at Gladstone's bill. But a little familiarity with it bred contempt in Parnell; and of course by the standards of Land League ideology the land act conceded too little and came too late. In Parliament the Irish leader and his men withheld and gave their votes in the shrewdest way to extract gains, and when the law was passed advised against much use of the tribunals it instituted. In short the Parnellites played to keep the agitation going and American funds coming. Parnell's political convenience was not disserved when he was thrown in Kilmainham Jail, a martyr, 11 October. Davitt had already been in Portland Prison in England for eight months.

We know now that a turning point in Irish social history had been reached. In due course the peasants were going to assimilate gradual land reform and abandon more revolutionary goals. By November 1881, in fact, the new land courts were clogged with thousands of applicants, even in the regions where the Land League was strongest. Henry George's arithmetic for the *Irish World,* estimating that if sixty-five decisions were reached a day, the business would be complete by A.D. 2154, pictures the situation. Before long, however, the Irish Land League was going to disintegrate, more because reforms were removing the need for it to survive, than because the government had prosecuted it.

But this state of affairs had not arrived when Henry George reached Ireland. Not peasant proprietorships nor Home Rule, both reserved for the twentieth century; nor harmony of any kind. The old want and suffering had come to no abatement; the griefs of three years of bloodshed were mounting, not diminishing; coercion was waxing ever more stern. While the *Spain* was in mid-ocean, Parnell and his brothers in Kilmainham Jail had composed their famous 'No Rent Manifesto.' In reduced form it follows: 'Fellow-countrymen, the hour to try your souls and to redeem your pledges has arrived. The Executive of the National Land League, forced to abandon the policy of testing the Land Act, feels bound to advise the tenant farmers of Ireland . . . to pay no rents under any circumstances to their landlords until the Government relinquishes the existing system of terrorism and restores the constitutional rights of the people . . . You have to choose . . . between the Land for the Landlords and the Land for the People.'

To the No Rent Manifesto Henry George's employer in New York quickly responded in a cablegram: 'A thousand cheers for the glorious manifesto. It is the bravest act of the Land War.' And, in the columns of the *Irish World:* 'We believe that the No-Rent manifesto is the initiation of a mighty revolution that is destined not to end till the disinherited, not only of Ireland but of all lands, are restored to the inheritance of which they have been robbed . . . The present is big with hope.'

Had he still been in New York, say consulting with Ford about *Irish World* politics, Henry George would have argued with the editor we may be sure. 'No rent' was the opposite of his economic belief; he wanted rent to be socialized. Yet against Ford's accepting the present tactics of the men of Kilmainham, George would have made no protest. And as things were George would, we may believe, have wished to change places with no other journalist in the world.

—2—

George's tickets read for Liverpool, but when the *Spain* put into Cork he quickly changed his mind. An agent who identified himself as a Land Leaguer advised him to adopt another name and change the markings on his trunks, for he was sure to be 'dogged' whenever his presence became known. The prophecy proved true; but the advice was not accepted. The American newspaperman settled his ladies in a Cork hotel, and at once went on alone to Dublin.

No one interfered directly while he searched for bearings. He took in the sights, and his first letter for publication in the *Irish World* mentioned the impressive houses of Dublin. He reported the many redcoats everywhere, and the trouble he was put to to meet Land Leaguers during the day of arrival in Cork, until he discovered a priest who trusted him and talked freely. In private to Ford on 10 November he expressed his full reaction: 'I got indignant as soon as I landed and I have not got over it yet. This is the most damnable government that exists today outside Russia.' Even Ford, he thought, could have no idea of the reign of terror; and with the Land League outlawed and people afraid to talk, he could not see how he was going to get his feet down.

At first he concentrated all efforts to visit the famous prisoners in Kilmainham. Three days of waiting seemed interminable; and he wished he could alternate the irony of Dickens (in the manner of the description of the 'circumlocution office') with the eloquence of Mill on liberty, to convey his feeling of how the jail was operated and to what purpose. At last he was permitted a few minutes with the prisoners, political talk forbidden, out of their daily ration of a quarter-hour for visiting. He and Parnell managed to communicate about present politics by seeming to discuss the persecution of the early church and the triumph of Christianity. Perhaps, as George believed, they deceived 'the gold-banded chief warden.' The correspondent came out deeply impressed with the quality of Parnell — not a durable impression as we shall see; and he was gratified a little later, on visiting the Parnell country home, to realize the privileges the leader had risked for his country.

Immediately on arrival in Ireland, George had discovered that as the Land League faded the women of the movement took over, operating partly for the men and in contact with the underground, and partly above board in their own new Ladies Land League. Miss Anna Parnell, the jailed man's sister, was the most prominent; and associated with her was Miss Helen Taylor, the stepdaughter and literary executor of John Stuart Mill. This wonderful lady — Henry George thought her the most intelligent woman he ever knew — came from England to persuade Miss Parnell to go there and avoid arrest, while she herself at less risk should undertake direction of affairs in Ireland.

Even Annie George, a non-political woman thus far, caught the spirit. In December, when her husband had gone off to London, she was invited to take the chair of a Dublin meeting. The Ladies Land League was not proscribed, but Miss Parnell had been warned not to appear this time. One may readily believe that Mrs. George was quite as nervous as her daughter says, but she was nevertheless able on the morning of the meeting to write her sons, as though about equal events, of Jennie's having a hotel beau, and of her own plan for the afternoon. She might be arrested, she said. 'Of course they can't keep me — so I'm going to see if they try it — this is the most strangely governed place ever heard of I think. Dreadful as matters are one can't help laughing — they are so funny. All speak of being arrested as an honor. So if I am honored don't get alarmed. It will sell Papa's book like hotcakes . . . By the way we all went to the theater . . . and some man in the balcony hollowed three cheers for Mrs. George. So you see I share Papa's popularity.'

Meanwhile George himself, greatly admiring the women and their work, had cut to the inner operations of the resistance. His findings could not be put in the paper, he wrote Ford after three weeks in Ireland, but the men of Kilmainham 'still keep direction,' though prison portals were becoming increasingly difficult to pass. Out of jail one leader, Patrick Egan, had gone to Paris to receive and distribute money — mainly the funds coming from America. At home, 'Maloney is a sort of head center outside jail,' with Clancy as a kind of lieutenant. Sixteen men and ten or so women, members of the Ladies Land League, were traveling the counties, he said, and 'communications are received under cover and destroyed when read.' Under Miss Parnell, the 'ladies run the whole business of relief and its support.'

The writer expressed no repugnance for the conspiratorial procedures of the Irish. He seems to have had none to express, except for the crime and terror which the Land League disavowed and at least on the surface discouraged. But he did become very critical of the looseness of the underground's organization and the waste in its handling of funds. 'Sometimes it seems to me,' he wrote Ford with respect to his impressions of both Irish radicals and a group of British socialists, 'as though a lot of small men had found themselves in the lead of a tremendous movement, and finding themselves being lifted into importance and power they never dreamed of are jealous of anybody else sharing the honor.'

To see the root of the matter, George traveled west into King's County to witness a group eviction. He described it eloquently for the *Irish World:* a miserable group of tenants were driven from their hovels, then readmitted as caretakers, while a land agent, a sub-sheriff, three priests, 150 police, and a company of soldiers stood by to see that nothing went amiss. Such was the testimony of continuing land crisis and of coercion as George reported them. Yet his political comments show that within a couple of months he pretty well realized that the Land League movement was just about collapsing, and that the No Rent Manifesto was a failure.

In the nature of the case George's assignment involved more than ordinary reporting, it involved what naturally accompanies an exportation of American funds and American interest. 'Radicalization' is the word George selected to express Ford's and his own intention to influence events. Yet there were many limitations on how much he could say. It was not simply that detectives followed his every move always with the threat of more than watching, but there was also the sense which grew on him that the *Irish World* represented an American influence not altogether wanted in Ireland even by Land Leaguers, an outside interference in inside affairs. The matter came up in practical form very soon after George's arrival in Dublin.

Ford had wanted immediate arrangements made for him to lecture in the city. But among those in charge doubts occurred, and hesitations postponed the event about a week. Yet when the lecture did come off, at mid-November in the Rotunda, it was a personal triumph. According to the speaker, the affair gave Dubliners the first opportunity in a long time to show their feelings, and at the end they went 'wild with enthusiasm.' Leaving the building he fought off men who wanted to unhitch his carriage and draw him through the streets. Tribute in such a form seemed undemocratic to George. But when the affair was over he feared that he had brushed aside a demonstration which would have won him much attention in the papers.

Though he gave no other speech in Ireland for nearly a year, and he was aware always of the weakening of the resistance, George let himself become more and more involved emotionally in the movement. His sympathies, he told Ford at year's end, were 'so strongly aroused in this fight against such tremendous odds that it is impossible for me not to find myself in it.' His letters at this time take over from his associates the phrase 'Spread the Light,' a slogan common among socialists. There was urgency in the air wherever he went.

The most interesting ideological discovery of George's first few weeks in Ireland was the existence there of an ancient critique of private property in land. This tradition had not been rendered into high theory, yet it was an idea better designed to please George than simple anti-rent talk. I have caught no mention to indicate that he ever heard of James Fintan Lawlor, a journalist like himself who a generation earlier had put the idea into eloquent words for the incitement of the Physical Force party. George tells us that the critique came to him from a Catholic bishop; and of course a Christian source of social protest was the kind to please him best. Certainly he was delighted when the politically active Bishop of Clonfert saluted him, 'God bless you, my son,' as the author of *Progress and Poverty*. 'Your doctrines are the old belief of our race . . . Our people have bowed to might; but they never have acknowledged the right of making land private property. In the old tongue they have cherished the old truth, and now in the providence of God the time has come for that faith to be asserted . . . There is no earthly power that can ever stop this movement.'

Hardly less interesting to George than the fact of the tradition was a second discovery, namely, that besides Clonfert a sizable and important number of the clergymen of the island, rather than the Land League or any other secular group, were making themselves the present-day disseminators of the idea. Not long before he landed in Ireland another bishop, Dr. Thomas Nulty, had addressed his diocese of Meath. 'The system of land tenure in Ireland,' this churchman had said, 'has created a state of human existence which in strict truth and justice can be characterized as the twin sister of slavery.' Very like the distributive economics of *Progress and Poverty*, Nulty's argument derived from labor theory: labor creates and justifies private property in things, and opportunity for labor demands common property in land. Every child of God, the reverend bishop told his flock, has an equal original right in what God has given; only the improvers of land have a right to hold it; and usufruct should be the highest form of tenure. Rent belongs to the community.

Bishop Nulty especially gratified George because he spoke publicly and independently, making his own application of Christian conscience to affairs. On this point the diocesan letter was very specific. In a passage which George chose to remember —

and to use in his later conflicts with an American archbishop — Nulty asserted that he exercised as bishop no divine right to direct his flock in their conceptions of civil rights and political economy. Rather he advised them in paternal concern for their temporal welfare. To the visiting American believer in a commonwealth based on Christian principles, the Bishop of Meath represented the best influence at work in Ireland.

A little awkwardly, however, this warm appreciation on George's side led to embarrassments. When his reports about Dr. Nulty, or more strictly when garbled versions of those reports were printed in the *Irish World,* the bishop was seriously put out. Yet George felt free to use the bishop's ideas, when he decided from something heard at an interview that Dr. Nulty really favored the No Rent movement. George took the liberty of having the diocesan letter distributed by the Ladies Land League; and before Christmas it was printed and posted, all over the land. Doubtless George regarded this cross-connecting of ideas and politics in Ireland as an errand in 'radicalizing' the resistance, but it definitely displeased the bishop, and imposed a new strain on all concerned.

The episode ended some weeks later. When Nulty had finished reading *Progress and Poverty,* he wrote handsomely that he believed it to be 'the best book ever written on political economy since the *Wealth of Nations.*' Yet there was dismissal in his comment that George's strength lay in 'scientific writing,' and that his thinking ran too deep for great success in journalism. In retrospect of his connection with the Bishop of Meath, George felt that he had learned, from one of the best and strongest, something about the 'timorousness of prominent men' and the unfreedom of churchmen.

In this vein, after three months of observing in Ireland, the correspondent writing privately to his editor added a trial balance of impressions. He recognized that, like the Catholics of England, most of the upper members of the church hierarchy in Ireland stood on the side opposed to Nulty. He blamed Rome, principally, for this economic conservatism; and in general he felt obliged to qualify his original hopes that the clergymen of Ireland would emerge in time as the true leaders of a social reconstruction.

Even so, George retained the impression that the parish priests were not complacent, and that they served the cause of resistance and in a degree offset the conservatism of the majority of bishops — an opinion sustained by modern historical research. In the history of George's opinions, about how reform may be achieved, though the Catholic Church in Ireland failed to come up to his conception of what Christian performance should be, what he saw on this visit represented his first interest since childhood in church efforts of size and consequence. Henceforward we shall find him, so different from during the California years, always ready to regard the commitment and vitality of the churches, both Protestant and Catholic, as containing an enormous potential for social justice, a potential that should be able to be put to practical effect.

–3–

By the end of January 1882, George's three-month contract with the *Irish World* had run out. Lacking notice he continued and was paid for his weekly letters. His relationship with his employer and editor remained satisfactory, even though his $60 a week was not enough. Hotels and travel, though Mrs. George and the girls did not move about as much as he did, took all he earned. His greatest discouragement, he confessed to Francis Shaw, was with his own performance. 'I have never felt so dissatisfied with myself as since I have been here.' He was swamped with people to see, things to do, and letters to write. He would have given much to have Harry to take his dictation and act as general secretary. 'Nor have my letters to the *World* satisfied me. In short I have felt to use one of our expressive Americanisms "all up in a heap" ever since I have been here.' The constant strain on the 'perceptive faculties' was the heart of the trouble, he decided, and he regretted that his mental habits were not good for quick work of a large sort.

This did not mean that he wanted to hurry home. He preferred to return no sooner than the fall lecture season — early for the season, he decided, as a wave of Irishmen could be expected to cross the ocean to explain Ireland to listening Americans. He hoped that he would be able to earn enough quick money on the platform to afford time later on for writing the handbook of political economy he planned, to be done according to the governing ideas of *Progress and Poverty*.

For all his doubts about himself in a foreign land, George's confidence increased that events in the British Isles were actually developing according to the diagnoses and prognosis in *Progress and Poverty*. 'Things are moving so fast that ere long they may want a series from you for the *Nineteenth Century*,' he heard from a new socialist acquaintance, H. M. Hyndman, whom he had not yet come to distrust. He himself made a series of predictions about Britain, negative and positive. On the negative side, he was more pessimistic than the events of the next few years would justify. He said, two years before the Fabian Society drew together, that he 'had little hope of the literary class here,' and, four years before Gladstone rounded out Liberal policy for Ireland, he added that he had no hope 'at all of the men who have made their reputations.' But on the affirmative side he foresaw accurately what he believed in, the rise of labor in public affairs. Tell Youmans, he instructed A. J. Steers, that far from encountering difficulty in discovering friends with a common mind, he was having an easy time. Not in Ireland alone, where he sensed 'a great blind groping forward,' but in Great Britain too he believed that 'the beginning of *the revolution* sure' was on.

Naturally he liked to go to London whenever he could. This was not hard to arrange, for the capital city fell within the natural area of his assignment from the *Irish World*. He managed a short visit in December and a good deal of time there during the later winter and spring. But in London he was mainly concerned with publishing, and only secondarily with letters for his newspaper. Kegan Paul had consistently good news now; and George's sense that the times were justifying his social analysis enlivened his hope that *Progress and Poverty* would rapidly catch on. Once the first indifference had vanished, in the autumn, according to Mr. Paul, 'purely on its own strength the book began to make its own way.' The first English edition ran out in December, and a second was issued, and by spring a third was needed. The author had hardly dreamed of better.

What he now wanted was a cheap English edition, parallel to the Appleton one. George found encouragement from the fact that the Glasgow and London edition of *The Irish Land Question* was selling well, better than *Progress and Poverty;* he believed that the popularity of the tract would lead readers to the treatise. But Mr. Paul was not easily persuaded to go ahead. So George investigated on his own the publishing arrangements which distributed standard novels in cheap editions by way of the newsstands everywhere in Britain. It took until June to win his point. Mr. Paul's final decision for a cheap edition, unprecedented for a work on political economy, George believed to be forced by his own threat to go to another publisher.

About every phase of publishing Henry George kept in constant communication with his wealthy patron on Staten Island. As early as April Mr. Shaw, to whom he had written something about the tension and strain of what he was doing, had sent a subsidy of £100 simply to strengthen George's position and enable him to work without anxiety. On George's own motion half of this money was assigned toward paying the cost of the cheap edition. The gift seemed 'like a fulcrum for a lever that will move the world,' he wrote the giver.

But Mr. Shaw was ready to do still more for *Progress and Poverty*. The £100 had hardly gotten across the Atlantic when he sent further word that he had from an anonymous source $3000 more for the distribution of the book. Though he maintained secrecy at first, he soon acknowledged that his brother was the giver. The Shaws originally planned to use this money in the United States, but when George asked they readily assigned half to Britain. 'Even from an American standpoint,' George said, the immediate thing should be 'a cheap edition here, and force the question into discussion, as England reacts on America.'

So when late in June he received £300, the author concluded very special publishing arrangements. A sympathetic new friend and a Radical, James C. Durant, undertook to print an 88-page quarto edition of *Progress and Poverty*, bound in paper; and Kegan Paul, Trench and Company agreed to act as the distributors. The price was fixed at sixpence. At the same time George managed to buy in the plates of *The Irish Land Question,* and at an extra outlay of fifteen pounds to have 15,000 copies printed, with a four-page tract by Mr. Shaw himself included, for distribution at threepence.

Free copies of both *Progress and Poverty* and *The Irish Land Question* were sent to every member of Parliament, and to Land League organizations, working-men's clubs, and newspapers in long lists — the last intended to bring out reviews in the provincial press and so to force the attention of the metropolitan newspapers.

George wished that there had been enough money to send copies to the libraries also, as in America, but he was grateful and well satisfied. With your help the movement *has* begun, he wrote Shaw, and discussion is the next essential. 'When that point is reached the movement takes care of itself.'

Mass-scale publication was the one piece of essential business, over and beyond his work for the *Irish World,* that George had planned for the trip. But to his present satisfaction, as the year before in New York, he was invited to do a certain amount of circulating and speaking. In February he gave an address at Liverpool. He made a St. Patrick's Day speech in Glasgow for an Irish audience, and a second appearance in that city; there was also an appearance in Manchester, about which more later; and in June he was back in Dublin, speaking in the Rotunda for the benefit of the political prisoners. As occasion made it possible, he used his public appearances to announce his program and ideas as his own, apart from the Irish crisis.

Again as in New York, he was sought out occasionally by interesting individuals. Indeed, on his first day in London, he encountered, on Fleet Street, Mr. J. Morrison Davidson of the Middle Temple, who as writer was later to propagate single-tax ideas. The two had dinner together at the Old Cheshire Cheese. To Mr. Davidson that day Henry George communicated a great feeling of vitality, and of events about to occur. That the 'Hour had brought the Man,' that the Irish question had made Henry George, that this American possessed more color than did his book — such were the impressions he caught from George.

The earliest important new connection George struck up in London was one with that curious rich man of the left, Henry Myers Hyndman. At this time a strong friend of Irish resistance, Hyndman is remembered principally as the chief leader, a colleague of William Morris, in the Social Democratic Federation, and as the author of a socialist book, *England for All.* Both were new in 1882; and organization and book represent the first serious effort to adapt and apply Marxian doctrines for the practical political guidance of Englishmen. There is high irony in the likelihood that Henry George and Henry Hyndman were brought together, each hoping to convert the other to his own way of thinking, by Miss Helen Taylor — two naturally opposed spokesmen for social recon-

struction introduced by the literary heir of the late historic read-
juster of classical economics, John Stuart Mill.

Circumstance forbade George's ever knowing Karl Marx personally, nor could he ever have known *Das Kapital* well had he had the
inclination. In 1882 the great author of modern socialism was out
of England, though he was to die there the next year. Only one
volume of the big treatise had been published at that time, and
years were still to pass before it would be put into English; the posthumous second and third volumes would not be translated during
George's lifetime. But Marx had formed a judgment about George
at least as early as 1881, and, partly because Hyndman knew what
it was and followed it, it must be inserted here. It is expressed in
full in a letter to Friedrich A. Sorge, dated 30 June 1881. 'Theoretically the man is utterly backward!' said Karl Marx. 'He understands
nothing about the nature of *surplus value* . . . We ourselves, as
I have already mentioned, adopted this appropriation of ground
rent by the state among numerous other *transitional measures*
which . . . are and must be contradictory in themselves . . . The
whole thing is therefore simply an attempt, decked out with socialism, to *save capitalist domination* and indeed to *establish it afresh
on an even wider basis* than its present one . . . On the other hand
George's book, like the sensation it has made with you, is significant
because it is a first if unsuccessful, attempt at emancipation from
the orthodox political economy . . . He is a talented writer (with
a talent for Yankee advertisement too) as his article on California in
the *Atlantic* proves, for instance. He also has the repulsive presumption and arrogance which is displayed by all panacea mongers without exception.'

As a guest in the Hyndman house on Portland Place, where he
experienced for the first time a very expensive way of living, Henry
George confronted, also for the first time, a strong spokesman for
Marxist ideas. Not improbably he recalled his first intimation of
those ideas, which had come by way of the immigrant International
during the early months of editing the *Post*. Certainly Hyndman
did much to please the Georges, and communication between the
two men must have been made easier because the Englishman had
traveled in America, and knew persons and places on both coasts
familiar to George. But from the host's own account we are assured
that he invited the Georges to stay with him, 'because I hoped, quite

mistakenly as it afterwards appeared, to convert him to the truth as it is in Socialist economics.'

Hyndman soon discovered the nature of George's resistance. The guest proved 'as exasperating as Kropotkin' to the socialist by reason of his 'bump of reverence . . . of cathedral proportions,' and because he could not be induced 'to admit that he only captivated his audience by clever manipulations agreeably put.' This estimate of George's mental operations is retrospective. As of the moment, George tried and persisted in a counter-offensive. Though he observed and was amused by Hyndman's humorless formal manners, and though he understood the man's surrender to Marxist 'mental influence' — ample signs of a stiff-necked personality — George did not have the capacity to give up arguing his own case. He even persuaded himself that he was winning a little against his host's materialistic philosophy.

The skirmish for ascendancy does not mean that either man foresaw that one day they must break. Certainly they maintained common fronts in several different directions. Their minds met when Hyndman showed George a discovery he had made in the British Museum, a lecture by Thomas Spence, dated 1775, 'The Real Rights of Man,' which declared for common rights in land and for land-value taxation. George turned it over to the *Irish World* for publication; and he made an effort to have an article by Hyndman published in America. Hyndman it was who took the Georges to an elegant London reception, where they had the satisfaction of seeing Tennyson and Browning. This was rather like George's playful notion of travel and mingling with the mighty. But at the same party George met Herbert Spencer and had his first disillusionment from that philosopher. The great man astonished and angered him by discussing Irish land problems from an entirely conservative point of view.

There was intellectual drama in the drawing-room event. Three years earlier, working on his manuscript in San Francisco, it will be recalled, George had reinforced his argument for common property in land by discussing English land nationalization, and by attributing to it merit almost equal to land-value taxation. By borrowing the authority of the British social theorist most appreciated in America — by quoting *Social Statics* — he had assured his readers that *Progress and Poverty* accorded with acknowledged leaders and ideas. In view of what followed presently and in 1892, Herbert Spencer's snubbing Henry George at a party is to be understood as more than a snub. It was a real rejection of the American reformer. On the other side of the situation, Henry Hyndman's playing host signifies the sponsorship of one pro-labor theorist by another. As Dr. Elwood Lawrence has neatly pointed out, George during this first visit to Britain, very different from after 1886, made no effort to prevent people from connecting him with socialism, and none to prevent them from identifying him with land nationalization. Though not at all overwhelmed by Hyndman, he did go a certain distance with him politically as well as personally. On the speaking trip to Scotland, George and Miss Taylor stood on the same platform with the Marxian socialist on behalf of the Social Democratic Federation, in an effort to establish a new branch.

During the London visits George developed other connections, and other signs of recognition appeared. From one direction, Mr. Thomas Briggs, a future patron, befriended George and entertained him — in a 'magnificent house' in West Dulwich, according to the guest's appreciation. At about the same time, a number of agreeable letters came in from Germany. The news did not include the word George wanted most, that sales of *Fortschritt und Armuth* were good; but with benefit of Mr. Shaw's bounty the author was able to pay off a debt to Gütschow, and he was pleased to receive a request for biographical data to appear in an article in *Die Illustrierte Zeitung*. From close at hand came the most flattering compliment of all. After three months of acquaintanceship Miss Taylor told the Georges that she believed that, had John Stuart Mill lived, he would have accepted *Progress and Poverty* as she herself now did.

In the spring, journalistic duty led to a trip to Paris, to visit Irish Land League officials in exile. There George met Patrick Egan and liked him personally. He made a critical report, nevertheless, to Patrick Ford. The treasurer, whose funds came for the most part if not all through the offices of the *Irish World*, was disbursing them too much for relief and too little for reform propaganda, George believed. The journalist saw at least something of Paris in April, outside the sphere of duty; and so too did Mrs. George and the girls, who crossed the channel with Miss Taylor.

One suspects that the costs of this expedition were borne in part by Mr. Shaw's subsidy, which certainly helped purchase some English outfitting for the family at about the same time.

Six weeks or so after returning from Paris, George made what must have been his earliest contact with land nationalization as a practical movement with a leadership worthy of that of John Stuart Mill. This reform stood on its own feet, quite distinct from any variety of socialism; and the present leader was Alfred Russel Wallace, the scientist whose good opinion of his own work George had learned, just before leaving home for Ireland. As of the spring of 1882, we know that Wallace sought George's help in getting a reputable New York paper to review his new book on *Land Nationalisation*, and that he said in another letter that he must not be understood as endorsing Michael Davitt's ideas. He preferred for himself no such close association with Irish protest as George had ventured.

Yet for future understanding, and because *Land Nationalisation* was a considerable event in the cross-connecting of Henry George's ideas, and because Alfred Russel Wallace was a very special person, the exchange between scientist-reformer and journalist-reformer demands a filling-in of background. George would have been exhilarated to know that a year earlier letters had passed between Wallace and Charles Darwin about *Progress and Poverty*. Wallace had explained to the senior scientist that the book's anti-Malthusianism involved no rejection of such use of population doctrine as they both had made in their scientific writing. 'Mr. George, while admitting the main principle [of Malthus] as self-evident and as actually operating in the case of animals and plants, denies that it ever has operated or can operate in the case of man, still less that it has any bearing whatever on the vast social and political questions which have been supported by a reference to it.' To which Darwin replied: 'I will certainly order "Progress and Poverty" for the subject is a most interesting one. But I read many years ago some books on political economy, and they produced a disastrous effect on my mind, viz. utterly to distrust my own judgment on the subject and to doubt much everyone else's judgment! So I feel pretty sure that Mr. George's book will only make my mind worse confounded than it is at present.'

Beginning with the persuasion that George's anti-Malthusianism did not offend science, Wallace let *Progress and Poverty* affect his

Land Nationalisation considerably. He quoted at length, and he wrote an extra chapter: 'Chapter VII. Low Wages and Pauperism the Direct Consequences of Unrestricted Private Property in Land.' One of Wallace's interesting findings was that during the '70s Professor J. E. Cairnes, an Irish follower of Mill whom George had cited on interest, had published ideas in 'quite independent accordance with the special views of Mr. George — an accordance which must add greatly to the weight of their teaching.' Wallace had been more acute than George in noticing this support.

As his own goal the naturalist announced that he would set forth conclusions 'reached by an examination of the actual condition of the people' of the British Isles; and he asserted that in comparison *Progress and Poverty* set forth general theory. He believed that the two books reinforced one another. For, 'if, as I maintain, [my] conclusions have now been demonstrated by induction from the facts, that demonstration acquires the force of absolute proof when exactly the same conclusion is reached by a totally distinct line of deductive reasoning founded on the admitted principles of political economy and the general facts of social and industrial development.' Though it is possible to say of Wallace that he was too much of a humanitarian to be a fully effective scientist, and too much of a naturalist to be a great expert in social questions, there can be no doubt that his book's endorsement strengthened George's intellectual credit in England.

Meanwhile George had had an invitation and spent an evening which indicates that in England he had established the capacity to interest men nearer to power and less extreme in persuasion than either Land League Irishmen or rich socialists or scientist philosophers. The invitation came from Walter Wren, an Oxford man and intellectual of means who had previously entertained Mr. and Mrs. George in his London home. He gave a dinner for four at the Reform Club. The other guests were John Bright, the ancient leader for free trade and political reform who at present enjoyed the distinction of a thirty-five-year record of speaking for justice and mercy in Ireland, and Joseph Chamberlain the rising Radical star in Gladstone's cabinet.

'We started on Irish affairs with the soup,' the guest of honor wrote Patrick Ford, 'for Bright asked me point blank what I thought of what I had seen in Ireland, and I had to tell him, though it was not very flattering. We kept it up to half past ten, when Bright had to go down to the House, having left his daughter in the gallery. Mr. Chamberlain remained until nearly twelve.' From certain allusions George gathered that the cabinet member had some familiarity with his letters in the *Irish World;* and Chamberlain's reply when George hinted that he would like permission to visit Michael Davitt in Portland Prison seemed to indicate that before long the Irish radical would be released — as he was not too long after this conversation. Chamberlain laughingly told George 'to look out when I went back to Ireland that I did not get reasonably "suspected." '

Altogether George was entranced by the personable statesman and was ready as many were to see in him the man of Britain's future. He wished that he could repeat the confidences heard at the Wren dinner, he told Ford. During the following summer George must have felt confirmed in his good opinion when an Irish nationalist made that dinner public, as though the news were sensational. Chamberlain wrote then that he had no objection to its being known that they had spent such an evening together.

In the same area of intellect as the conversation with the distinguished Radicals, George found his first opportunity for magazine writing in England. Occasion offered in the *Fortnightly Review,* which was edited by John Morley, the liberal lawyer, essayist, and biographer. This brilliant man was already closely connected with Chamberlain, and the next year would enter Parliament as a strong Gladstone supporter. When the *Fortnightly* wanted George to do an article on Ireland, he was naturally more than willing. He took time off from the *Irish World,* in order to do the work.

When the article appeared, by chance a month after the horrifying Phoenix Park murders in Dublin, it could be read as support for the Gladstone government's first bold refusal to be stampeded into deeper coercion. George wove together a great deal about local and general government in Ireland; he demonstrated the actual dominance of the landlords at every level; he pictured the lord lieutenant in the castle as no true ruler — 'The machine runs him.' The article analyzed Irish society to show the factors that prevented the growth of vigorous commercial and industrial classes, and most effectively it argued the wrong-headedness of Englishmen who attributed mischief in Ireland to some inherent racial or national characteristics. The article was as tough and sinewy as any George ever did, and it is reminiscent of his analyses and exposures of economic and political abuse in California.

The summer of 1882, when George returned to Ireland for most of the remainder of this visit, would be too early in his career in England to attempt a summing up of all the directions of his influence there — on labor, on land nationalization, on the socialist movement, and so on. But his approach toward the young Radical element demands a final word. Though there is nothing to indicate, up to the time when George talked with Joseph Chamberlain and corresponded with John Morley, that either man had read *Progress and Poverty,* it is clear that very soon thereafter both did read it, and that the book caught on in their group.

According to J. L. Garvin, Chamberlain's masterful biographer, speaking of the end of the calendar year 1882, *Progress and Poverty* 'electrified' the cabinet member. And 'the effect on Morley was the same. They both read likewise the simultaneous plea of Alfred Russel Wallace for nationalisation of the land, and they compared ideas from time to time. They believed that the whole English land question, with its urban aspects of housing, overcrowding, ground rents, and the rest, may have to be "the great business." Chamberlain was against nationalisation; he thought it predatory; but he was keener than ever for multiplying small owners on the soil, for breaking up big estates to the extent required, and began to meditate on taxing urban property to abolish the slums. To promote social reform in general, he aimed especially at taxing wealth automatically increased in towns by the growth of the community without effort to the owner . . . He would levy on all "unearned increment" and bear hard upon comfortable possessors of slum property.'

'A book had been born' is this same writer's phrasing for what occurred. 'Reborn, in England,' would of course be a more accurate statement.

–4–

According to George's letters in the *Irish World,* not very much happened in Ireland from the end of 1881 until the following May. The journalist wrote his dispatches about coercion; and in fact he was doubly obliged to do so because a number of Americans had been thrown into the Irish jails. The *Irish World* itself was now excluded from Ireland.

George knew in detail also, what he could say only privately, that with the disintegration of the Irish Land League and the No Rent impulse, new dangers were confronting the cause of amelioration in Ireland. He understood that, with the more responsible leadership in jail, the less responsible elements were rising. With the passing months, terror broke out in many places. To Francis Shaw, George wrote no more cheerfully than to pledge that 'We must "spread the light" without [the Leaguers]. But sure as we live, the light is spreading.'

Secretly at top level meanwhile, the Liberal government was taking steps along lines not inconsistent with what George had heard at the Reform Club dinner. Though the cabinet was still divided, and the prime minister himself was immersed in the budget, Gladstone permitted the Radical president of the Board of Trade to go ahead with what became this government's last effort for a general settlement in Ireland — the Liberals' last effort prior to the climactic decision of Gladstone's third government, in favor of Irish Home Rule. Though ill-starred from the beginning, the scheme that Joseph Chamberlain now arranged scarcely deserves the bad reputation it has gathered under the dark misnomer of the treaty of Kilmainham.

It was no more nor less than a political bargain between the government and the Parnellites in jail. The crown would release the Irish leaders from Kilmainham; and they would pledge themselves to support, instead of No Rent and the destruction of landlordism, such moderate reforms as had already been enacted or might in the future be worked out along lines of law and order. For the jailed leaders this meant accepting the program of the Land Act of 1881, which was precisely what great numbers of their countrymen were doing in practice; and for Britain it meant a policy of reduced coercion, a step in the direction Radicals and prime minister alike wanted.

So much outlines what may be called the practical side of the matter. Before considering other aspects, it should be stated that later, in midsummer, though the treaty of Kilmainham still distressed him, Henry George had the fairness to say that the government's land reforms were actually taking hold and doing good.

Conceding this much, he did not retract his deeper criticism. For Ireland as for California he believed that piecemeal reform would finally prove insufficient, and he argued that land nationalization could accomplish far more good than shoring up peasant tenures. Impatience toward Gladstone, whom he thought greatly lacking in imagination, and criticism of rent reduction and estate subdivision, indicate Henry George's final estimate of British economic statesmanship toward Ireland in 1882.

For a man of his sympathies the appalling thing about Kilmainham was what it did to Irish politics. The Irish leaders' accepting the bargain, their acting individually in such a way as to demoralize more radical associates and to undermine 'radicalization' upset Henry George extremely. As early as January he had begun to revise downward his admiration of Parnell. Now he suffered a real disillusionment, and when the Bishop of Meath said that by acquiescing in the treaty of Kilmainham the parliamentary leader had become an apostate, George bitterly concurred. He had reverted to his earliest, long-distance impression about Parnell, the estimate he had put in the *Bee* in 1879: 'an educated Dennis Kearney.'

The treaty of Kilmainham was an event of policy, and the better-remembered tragedy which coincided with it, the Phoenix Park murders, was an act of crime. But during the first week in May the two events rolled into one, a combination of horror and defeat for men with the sympathies of Henry George.

On the fourth of the month, two days after the cabinet decided to release the prisoners, Lord Frederick Cavendish, a moderate, and a relative and favorite of the prime minister, was appointed chief secretary of state for Ireland. He crossed at once to Dublin. On the sixth he went with the undersecretary to walk in Phoenix Park, in sight of Dublin Castle. There the two were murdered in cold blood. It appeared later to have been the work of a murder club, and the undersecretary had been the particular object of wild Irish vengeance. The horror of the event revolted the public, and even certain of the Fenians. The result was pure loss for every cause except coercion.

Henry George had been in Dublin, and save for orders from New York he would have been present to report firsthand the scene and situation of the crime. But much interested in the news of the cabinet change, and learning that Davitt was about to be released from Portland, Patrick Ford cabled him to go at once to England and to interview certain members of Parliament. So George was traveling on the fateful day, a Saturday. He met Davitt, whom he had not seen since November 1880 in New York, in a London railroad station. The hour was too late for talk, and they made an appointment for Sunday. Perhaps no one in the capital city, outside top government circles and the men in certain clubs, heard of the assassinations that night.

The news came to George by telegram from Dr. James Kelly, the medical man and patriot at whose home he had been staying in Dublin. Under burden of emotion and with great trouble to get conveyance, he went as rapidly as possible to the Westminster Palace Hotel, and at five o'clock he found and wakened Davitt. The Irishman remembered the American as coming in with open telegram and 'a scared look in his kindly big blue eyes. "Get up, old man," were his words. "One of the worst things that has ever happened for Ireland has occured." ' And, according to George, Davitt reacted in the same way as he scanned the message: 'My God, have I got out of Portland to hear this? For the first time in my life I despair. It seems like the curse that has always followed Ireland.' George broke the news to Dillon, who was in the same hotel; and Dillon went for Parnell.

According to George's reports of Sunday's events, Davitt was the writer of the manifesto to the Irish people which the three leaders issued that day. They denounced the murders and called for due punishment of the criminals; once the manifesto was written it was submitted to the Parnellite members of Parliament; then it was signed by the three — Davitt, Parnell, and Dillon — and released for publication. Only much later was it suggested that George had been the real author.

The purpose of writing and publishing the manifesto was of course to persuade the public to disassociate the politics of Irish protest from the assassination, a purpose toward which George was peculiarly sympathetic. His news report suggests rather than specifies that the three leaders took for granted that the murder had been committed by a secret society, and that that society was not the Fenian brotherhood but some organization unknown to them. Not by reason of any intimation from George himself, but because of a letter written a full half a century later by a priest who remembered the event, did Anna George de Mille recently make public the suggestion that the manifesto was really her father's idea and phrasing. She offers the possibility but refuses to endorse it, in her biography. I am inclined to think the suggestion quite probable. As Father Dawson said, phrases in the manifesto do sound like George; and it certainly would have been natural for him to act as a sort of public-relations man for the group that day. Indeed the role would have been practically prescribed for him, by his job as *Irish World* correspondent. According to Davitt, moreover, George presently went so far in the same vein as to embarrass him toward fellow Fenians, by attributing to him a more complete repudiation than he liked of the idea of some necessity for physical force in a revolutionary movement.

Speaking in another instance for moral coherence between ends and means, George pleaded that Parliament should exercise forbearance. In the *Irish World,* he made himself one of the first to say that the English reaction was not vindictive; and he chose to hope, as Lady Cavendish was the noblest to do, that the deaths in the park would become martyrdoms for reconciliation — the Lincoln theme again — not acts for which one nation would try to punish another.

At first there was room for hope; the government refused to be stampeded. But by early summer cabinet and Parliament took the old course of tightening the screws. A Prevention of Crimes Act was passed, the effect of which George himself was soon to feel. Hopes sank for any early or rational solution of the Irish problem. 'I never felt more like celebrating the Fourth of July than this year,' he commented in the columns of the *Irish World.*

Under these circumstances, George's appreciation of Michael Davitt increased. He liked the fact that this leader was not sold out of his old Land League-ism as the men of Kilmainham were; and he was more attracted as he sensed that Davitt might make up his mind for a program very like, possibly exactly like, his own. He was delighted, before May was out, to report that the Irishman would promote the coming cheap edition of *Progress and Poverty* — he had read the book four times, twice in Portland Prison. And George was gratified also that Davitt was willing to take the chair at the meeting he himself was scheduled to address in Manchester. 'I think in that historic place I'll make a good speech.'

As the affair turned out, teamwork proved to George's disadvantage for once. Davitt arrived late, and when he came on the platform received an ovation and took time for a stirring pronouncement on Kilmainham — the event which sliced down to paper thinness his already none-too-stout connection with Parnell. All this stole Henry George's show. The principal speaker of the evening was left with only fifteen minutes, and with injured feelings about an opportunity lost in Liberalism's home city.

But he was compensated within a fortnight. In a much noticed speech at Liverpool, Davitt announced for land nationalization. The procedures he advocated sound more like Alfred Russel Wallace than like Henry George's preferred reform, but George was credited with having made a great convert, and he professed not to care about procedures this time. To Francis Shaw George wrote on 8 June: 'Now by St. Paul, the work goes bravely on! I think that we may fairly say that we have done something, and that our theory is at last forced into discussion . . . I have gained the point I have been quietly working for, and now those who oppose us most bitterly will help us most. Well, after all the toil and worry and the heartsickness, when the devil comes to whisper, "You are doing nothing!" there are some half-hours that pay for all.' And to Ford: 'At last the banner of principle is thrown to the breeze, so that all men can see it, and the real, world-wide fight begun . . . Davitt proposes compensation. Of course neither you, nor I, nor Bishop Nulty agree to anything of that sort; but that makes no difference . . . I don't care what plan any one proposes, so that he goes on the right line.'

George's excitement and, this once, his uncommon indifference about compensation for landholders are both easy to understand. He believed that his full ideas would prevail in time, anyway; and he saw in Davitt a great and dynamic leader to bring the essentials forward in discussion and thought. When Davitt went very soon to New York, George wrote ahead urging that he be given money and backing, and yet warned Ford to play down the idea that he had become 'disciple' or 'trumpet' of Henry George.

George foresaw American events but could not control them. Before Davitt landed, Parnellites in New York reached and persuaded him to deny the impression that he had been captured by George or anyone else. But this only fired a spokesman for the op-

posite side. At the first Davitt meeting in New York, Father Edward
McGlynn, Irish American priest in charge of St. Stephen's huge
downtown parish, an earlier pro-Negro spokesman, rose up to chide
his visting countryman. Why apologize, or explain away Henry
George? he demanded. 'I quite agree with Michael Davitt to the
full and with Henry George to the full,' pronounced this orator,
'and lest any timid scrupulous soul might fear that I was falling into
the arms of Henry George, I say that I stand on the same platform
with Bishop Nulty, of Meath, Ireland. But for that matter — to let
you into a secret — my private opinion is, that if I had to fall into
the arms of anybody, I don't know a man into whose arms I should
be more willing to fall than into the arms of Henry George.' Reports of such words, spoken at three separate appearances from the
same platform with Davitt during his short tour and thunderously
applauded, were the first knowledge George ever had of his coming
gifted lieutenant, the pastor of St. Stephen's.

Naturally this event turned him toward America. Was the time
peculiarly right to go home again? He was worn out, and Mr. Shaw
was begging him to come. On the other hand there was no practical
reason for hurry; rather the contrary. The *Irish World* was still
taking his letters, and he thought the family could enjoy the summer in Ireland. Why not forget any notion of going to Avignon
with Miss Taylor, he suggested to Annie, and instead take the children to some convenient Irish watering place for the summer.
He proposed that on the way the four do a little sight-seeing in
central England. This much went according to plan. They stopped
at Stratford, Warwick, and Coventry and a few other places, as
Americans have always liked to do.

Henry George's course as journalist was meanwhile changed by
an invitation which attracted him. Bishop Duggan of Clonfert proposed that he visit the Carmelite priory at Loughrea in Galway.
This would take him into an area of Ireland where coercion was
operating in force, and he would see many things firsthand. George
hoped that his publisher Kegan Paul, who as an ex-clergyman and
a Radical was interested, would go with him and meet some of the
Land Leaguers and others with whom George would be able to
make contact. Though Mr. Paul declined, he sent in his place a
young Eton master, Mr. J. L. Joynes, who was interested in observing economic and political problems firsthand.

The two men met in Dublin. Joynes made it his first business to interview people in the city. He talked to Davitt, who had returned from America, and to members of the Ladies Land League; and, on the other side, to a sufficient number of men in the landlord connection to get a vivid impression — a little different from George's emphasis — that they all hated Gladstone and believed that his one purpose under the law of 1881 was to reduce rents, under the name of fair rents. Traveling west, George and his companion went first by rail third-class. On the train they talked with a laborer who had come miles from home to make four shillings, in harvest wages, and who had suffered a bad scythe cut in earning them. He would spare no money for treatment, nor would he buy tobacco; and the sympathetic travelers helped him on both scores. It amused them to watch the poor man struggle with one of Henry George's cigars.

After detraining at Ballinsloe, they hired a cart to take them cross-country to Loughrea. But they paused first to call on Matthew Harris, a Land League man who had been arrested when Parnell was, and they watched the police watch them. The next fifteen miles struck them as beautiful but depressing. The soil looked wonderfully rich, but it was little occupied, and they noticed where old farmsteads had once made it fruitful. Now cattle and sheep, not men, occupied the land; they talked with a sheepherder along the way about his work and wages. Coming into the village at last, they noticed the relief huts put up by the Land League, and counted seven police 'fortresses' or huts placed in interesting nearness to one another. They drove to the one hotel in Loughrea.

But they were given no chance to enter. 'I arrest you under the Crimes Act as a suspicious stranger,' was the police officer's formula. The two men had to remount. Preceded, flanked, and followed by police, they drove to headquarters like a military funeral, Joynes said, 'a sight for all beholders.' George felt that the schoolmaster was unbearably embarrassed, but he himself was more amused than anything else. 'The whole thing struck me as infinitely ridiculous.' He wished that Mr. Paul had come with him to Loughrea.

The sight-seers were detained three hours. Their bags were searched and copies of the *Irish World, The Irish Land Question,* and Mr. Shaw's *A Piece of Land* were turned out; Joynes squirmed while the officers spelled their way through a bit of doggerel he had written. They were allowed no dinner, nor given prison bread and water when they asked for it; but a policeman brought glasses of milk at his own expense, against the rules George assumed. When at last a resident magistrate came, Mr. Joynes' statement of who he was turned the trick for release, actually too fast to suit Henry George, who enjoyed dramatizing the American factor in his own case. When asked whether he was a subject of the United States, he responded 'No, Sir! . . . A citizen!' He used all the formality he could as he demanded of Magistrate Byrne why they had not been allowed to identify themselves and state their business, before the indignities of detention and search. 'Going through everything like a parcel of monkeys' was his phrasing of the matter, for Annie.

At last the couple had their night's sleep in the hotel; and the next morning they visited the priory. This gave opportunity for reflection as they saw the sandaled Carmelites, vegetarians by rule, leading their ancient life of Christian communism on Irish soil. During the course of the day they noticed how the soldiers and policemen 'savarmed' about, and they estimated that Loughrea was supporting about the equal of its population in this kind of law and order. They visited little shops that belonged to some resident 'suspects' who had been thrown in jail. They chose the cool of the evening for the next leg of their journey, the short distance to Athenry where they planned to take the train. 'Had a very pleasant drive,' Henry George wrote his wife, 'and didn't get arrested, much to my disgust — for I want to see this Englishman in jail again — though the police dogged us pretty well.'

In Athenry the sight-seeing was permitted first, but they did not escape 'the Bastille.' Looking around, George counted one water pump, which was adequate for the population, and twenty-six constables and at least fifty-six soldiers, to keep order. The two men called on the village priest and visited the abbey. Before going to the station George bought a collar button, as it chanced in a store operated by a lady Land Leaguer. Minutes later, as they were about to board the train, George was approached by a sub-inspector, a polite man with hair parted in the middle (the victim noted), and was arrested under the Crimes Act for the second time in three days. Though Joynes was not picked up, he stayed with George by his own choice.

This time the police took George direct to the magistrate's own residence. The writer on Irish social controls noticed that the judge was a gentleman landlord, living in the midst of rural beauty but not ready for duty. He was away from home when the prisoner arrived, and on return not free for court business. The party was obliged to go back to town. Magistrate Byrne was brought over from Loughrea, and at George's suggestion he called the session in the railway hotel. The officer charged association with suspicious characters, and offered evidence that the prisoner had had some connection with Parnell and Davitt. Some of George's notes on the Land League were read in court. George laughed aloud at certain charges.

After the judge had lectured and discharged him, George handed around copies of *The Irish Land Question* to judge, sub-inspector, and constables. He had two copies of the *Irish World* with him, the issue that told how the priest of New York's largest Catholic parish had welcomed Davitt with the proposition that he ought to be proud to be a disciple of Henry George, but he could not persuade himself to give those away. Later, when he made his complaints to newspapermen and to government at highest level, George made a good deal of the fact that the delay in Athenry had set his schedule back a full day. Still later, when he had been told some things he could not know while in Ireland, he acknowledged that telegrams sent to local officials in Athenry from the new chief secretary for Ireland, George Otto Trevelyan, perhaps better accounted for his quick discharge than did his own remarks, or Magistrate Byrne's common sense, in court.

Because Henry George's arrests made international news, James Russell Lowell, then the American minister in London, was obliged to act with such promptness and force as many earlier arrests of Americans in Ireland had failed to command. George in due time heard a story that indicates what the Boston Brahmin diplomat's attitude toward him and his book was — it came to him from Francis Shaw, whose daughter was married to Lowell's son. 'Why, who in the world buys such a book as that?' Lowell had asked one of the Appletons. 'Well, one man who buys it is a friend of yours — Francis G. Shaw. He bought a thousand, and then came back and bought another thousand.' To which Lowell replied: 'Goodness: He is a dear, good friend of mine — but he must be getting eccentric.'

Whatever his disrelish for Henry George and *Progress and Poverty*, Lowell detested the Prevention of Crimes Act of 1882. Stimulated by pressure from Washington, he acted in George's behalf before he had any information except what was in the newspapers. He made connection with the American consul in Dublin, and, short-cutting the British foreign office for the moment, he wrote direct to the secretary for Ireland. Secretary Trevelyan conveyed immediate assurances that the law would not move very far or very hard against the *Irish World*'s correspondent in Ireland.

Naturally George, who had managed to get just about what he wanted, did what he could to keep the matter alive. Within days after his release he wrote President Arthur reciting the events of his arrests, and he urged that other innocent Americans had been much more harassed. With intention to criticize Lowell — that is, of saying to the highest authority what he had already said in the *Irish World* — George asked that the government be more forward than in the past to watch and speak for the rights and freedoms of American citizens. George's following-up kept the events of Loughrea and Athenry active as state-department and foreign-office business, and kept them reappearing in the journals through September and into October — that is, until after he reached home. In the end he received by way of Washington an official apology from Her Majesty's government. The Foreign Office believed that George had actually been guilty under the Crimes Act, yet regretted that he had been disturbed.

As the dramatization of an idea is an essential part of presenting it, the Irish arrests must be rated as a real triumph of Henry George's visit to Ireland and England. It was the third great success. The earlier two had also been successes of propaganda, namely, the arrangements for mass publication of *Progress and Poverty* and *The Irish Land Question,* and the conversion, or near-conversion, of Michael Davitt to his way of thinking. A fourth was coming, in the month which remained, a success of a different order.

−5−

After the adventure in western Ireland, George made a couple of crossings to London before he sailed for home. He traveled now without his family, for Jennie, the older girl, had taken desperately ill of typhoid and needed such time to convalesce as delayed departure. George's first business in London concerned publication; and already the news was wonderfully encouraging. Twelve thousand copies of the cheap edition of *Progress and Poverty* had been printed, he wrote Shaw on 12 September, at a cost of no more than £100 in excess of the subsidy; 2000 copies had been distributed to newspapers and men and organizations according to plan. He hoped that sales at sixpence would pay off the printing debt. Very soon that kind of question vanished. Within a week he was able to write that 5000 copies had sold, or 7000 in all 'gone out,' and by the first of October that the edition was almost exhausted and a new run of 20,000 was being prepared. There was no precedent in economic literature, said the happy author. A dealer in Melbourne took 1300 copies and 300 were sent to New Zealand. 'Thanks to you, and to your Boston friend,' George told his patron, 'I think I have this year done a bigger work (or rather started bigger forces) than any American who ever crossed to the old country. I say this freely to you . . . ' There was no comparison to make.

Up to the middle of September, however, the major British newspapers and magazines had made a record of neglecting to review *Progress and Poverty* which exceeded that of the papers and magazines of the eastern United States after the earliest editions. Kegan Paul had no Professor Youmans or *Popular Science Monthly* with which to force attention. So it was pressure from the Irish excitement, and response to the subsidized edition, that must have brought the wanted change. The Irish factor was acknowledged in the review in the most important newspaper in the English-speaking world.

On 6 September the London *Times* printed a letter submitted by George, and made editorial comment. George pleaded for moderation in Ireland: his own case proved how inept coercion was, he said, and how incompetent to achieve the purposes of Parliament. *The Times'* editorial comment ran long. It acknowledged George to be a force in agitation and politics, but it had no word of toleration for his ideas. It classified him and all land nationalizers as essentially the same as socialists and communists. They were less sound reasoners even, the paper said, because they failed to perceive that having denied private property in land they were obliged to deny the rightness of any private property. The editorial gave George more space, and credited him with more importance, than the San Francisco *Alta* had done, but the judgment of ideas was identical.

George must have been astonished, therefore, at the event of 14 September, the full-size review in the same newspaper. Though the reviewer began with the comment that George would have 'no reason to regret the temporary inconvenience which he has suffered' in Ireland, he then shifted focus completely from the American as agitator to his books as argument. One column on *The Irish Land Question* stressed the universalism of the argument. It credited George with assessing blame for violence in Ireland on both landlords and tenants, and it noticed that he represented landownership as everywhere the result of conquest, and as often the privilege of persons absent from the soil. 'We gladly recognize the large amount of sound sense his appeal contains, and we should be still more glad if his appeal bore good fruit.'

The columns devoted to *Progress and Poverty* were mostly summary, and loaded with quotation. There was friendly, or at least neutral, explication of the critique of wages-fund and Malthusian doctrines; and George was praised as an American who refused alike to take the road of a Carey toward a special economics for the United States, and to blame poverty on the political institutions of the old world. George's Ricardian assumptions, and his logic of economic distribution, the review passed lightly by. It acknowledged the community between *Progress and Poverty* and *Social Statics* on land nationalization; and its one sharply adverse comment was to place George's work in line with the utopian tradition, and to say that despite Thomas More and Brook Farm the world spins on unaltered.

The conclusion of *The Times* review requires quoting: 'Mr. George's idea will long be found in the book only; nevertheless, *Progress and Poverty* well merits perusal. It contains many shrewd suggestions and some criticisms of economic doctrines which future writers on political economy must either refute or accept. Mr. George's reading has evidently been wide; he has reflected deeply; he is an acute reasoner, and he is the master of an excellent style. The readers of his book may dissent from his statements and conclusions without regretting the time they have spent over it, and, if conversant with economic doctrines and interested in the problems of social science, they will find in its pages much to ponder with ease and much that is highly suggestive.'

Naturally the author was transported. He cabled at once to Francis Shaw, saying that the great paper had been 'exceedingly appreciative' and that the review would lead the provincial press to give the book attention; and he sent a copy to Dr. Taylor, as concerning the book the *Alta* had said would not be read. Probably John Russell Young, now United States minister in Peking, phrased Henry George's feeling as well as his own. 'A review like that is the blue ribbon of critical approbation, whether bad or good. The spirit of the review did not interest me. The fact was all — it ranks you among the thinkers of the age, whose words are worth hearing in England.' It was 'an achievement,' Young assured his friend, 'of which you may feel proud — no one of your friends feels more pride in it than I.' His own expectations were increased, Young went on. 'I have so much faith in your courage and sincerity and integrity, that without having the least comprehension of your philosophy, I am sure it will have a following and make its mark on the age.' The friend had troubled to reread the book in China. 'It grows,' he confessed. 'God bless you.'

Besides *The Times* review, which was the fourth and final public triumph of the visit, George won victories of the spoken word during the month before he sailed, and one of them was to produce enormous reverberations. This was his address, 'Land Nationalisation,' before the Land Nationalisation Society, which invited him to make his first platform appearance in London. Alfred Russel Wallace took the chair; and the speaker had the blessing also of Professor F. N. Newman, who had thirty years earlier written a little book with a solution much like George's, and now sent a letter which commended both *Progress and Poverty* and *Land Nationalisation,* and welcomed George as coadjutor in a great work. There was a good audience and discussion at the end. The house passed appropriate resolutions offered by Sir John Bennett and by the Reverend Stewart T. Headlam, who was the founder of the Guild of St. Matthew, a Christian socialist organization within the Church of England.

But the inner interest of the meeting derives from a listener, a twenty-five-year-old critic, who dropped in late. Since the critic was

George Bernard Shaw, he must tell the story himself. As he wrote Hamlin Garland a quarter of a century later, he knew at once that the speaker must be an American, for four reasons: 'Because he pronounced "necessarily" — a favorite word of his — with the accent on the third syllable instead of the first; because he was deliberately and intentionally oratorical, which is not customary among shy people like the English; because he spoke of Liberty, Justice, Truth, Natural Law, and other strange eighteenth-century superstitions; and because he explained with great simplicity and sincerity the views of the Creator, who had gone completely out of fashion in London in the previous decade and had not been heard of there since. I noticed also that he was a born orator, and that he had small plump and pretty hands.'

But Shaw's mind caught unquenchable fire that evening. He listened while George spoke about the rents of London, and linked the land question with the labor question. Some magic of personality and mind, says Shaw, enlisted him then 'a soldier in the Liberative War of Humanity.' George's logic of the law of rent captured him for life. 'The result of my hearing the speech, and buying from one of the stewards of the meeting a copy of *Progress and Poverty* for sixpence (Heaven only knows where I got that sixpence!) was that I plunged into a course of economic study, and at a very early stage of it became a Socialist and spoke from that very platform on the same great subject, and from hundreds of others as well . . . And that all the work was not mere gas, let the feats and pamphlets of the Fabian Society attest. When I was thus swept into the great Socialist revival of 1883, I found that five-sixths of those who were swept in with me had been converted by Henry George.'

George certainly did not know of Bernard Shaw in 1882 and perhaps never learned of him, and he was never to love the socialist revival when it came. Yet this meeting and one or two others in September — a working men's two-shilling banquet in his honor, a three-hour conference with a group of clergymen — were undoubtedly what he had in mind when he wrote friends that he had discovered those locations in English society where he thought he could plant his ideas with excellent prospects of growth. The working class, he specified, and the clerical profession both Protestant and Catholic, and some spots where wealth and education were blended together with conscience were ready for the best he had to give. Scotland, he sensed, was readier than England; and Great Britain, the governing island, readier than Ireland after all.

When George at last got his family in health aboard ship, 4 October at Queenstown, he had a warm invitation he had not been able to accept from Thomas Walker, a manufacturer, to visit him at his home in Birmingham. By a small subsidy of the popular edition of *Progress and Poverty*, Mr. Walker had already indicated that he might become a second Francis Shaw to Henry George. George had an invitation also from Professor F. Max Müller, the great Orientalist, to come to Oxford. In a sense the business which had brought him across the Atlantic was done. But in the sense that concerned him most, it seemed as he turned home to have just begun.

XIII

Prophet in the Old Country:
England and Scotland
1884–1885

–1–

FOURTEEN months in the United States, from October 1882 to Christmas the next year, thrust upon Henry George a succession of events and recognitions that added up to a vast elevation of his position at home. His personal history in 1883 confirms handsomely the opinion he had used to persuade Mr. Shaw to subsidize the low-cost English edition of *Progress and Poverty* — that Britain reacts on America, and that a British hearing would advance his book and his cause in the United States.

Yet, again in agreement with his foresight, American gains did not affect his standing in Britain with equal force. Accordingly we may best reserve for a later chapter the hero's reception on returning to New York, and the mounting events and circumstances which made the name of Henry George a household word across the continent. The period in the United States closing with the calendar year 1883 prepared in a way for the campaign for mayor of New York in 1886, but had little bearing on building up his reform movement in England and Scotland, in 1884. Except for one achievement at home, there is no reason to think that he might not as well have chosen a long vacation in California as to work hard in and out of New York, so far as his influence overseas is concerned. The exception is the magazine articles he wrote for *Leslie's* in the spring of 1883. These were published as a book later the same year, and then on his return published again in England. *Social Problems* is George's most socialistic sounding book, no greater or more influential than one or two other of his minor works, but very timely.

Rather than American gains giving his reputation new force in England, it was the movement he had started in 1882 which with accumulating momentum now carried forward there. *Progress and Poverty* was being bought and read and discussed, and his friends were searching for ways and means to put his ideas into practical effect.

He had left the British Isles warmly invited, and wanting and expecting to return. But he had left also without a single line of commitment from anyone which would make return a practicable thing. Yet October 1882 had not passed before James Durant, the printer of the cheap editions, was telling him that with Gladstone he was one of the two most talked-of men in England. In the same month William Saunders, who wrote on land questions and who was the head of the British Central News Agency, sent him a proposal to start a newspaper in London. And before long an invitation to lecture offered also.

Except that in Britain lecturing was less well paid and less organized than in the United States, that was the kind of invitation now the best for Henry George. Accepting the newspaper would have required him to settle in England more or less permanently; and neither this offer nor later invitations that would have expatriated him ever really engaged his mind. Lecturing involved the fewest difficulties and the most of what he wanted: a temporary commitment, a chance to meet people of all kinds, above all a personal opportunity to start discussions and make converts to his ideas.

The source of the invitation he accepted was the new Land Reform Union, an organization set up in London during the spring or summer of 1883. As the union was explained to George it signified an addition, not an opposition, to the work of the Land Nationalisation Society. The people in it whose names are mentioned make practically a roster of his English friends; and the Land Reform Union seems to have been very much like the California Land Reform League in San Francisco five years earlier. It was the second organized movement to promote the ideas of Henry George.

Probably the most distinguished members were Miss Helen Taylor and two clergymen, the Anglican Stewart Headlam, he who spoke for the motion at the Land Nationalisation Society meeting just before George left London, and Philip Wicksteed, the scholarly Unitarian, about whom more presently. The Land Reform Union contained also sympathetic journalists and publishing-house people: William Saunders and James Durant, and William Reeves who was soon to bring out another cheap edition of *Progress and Poverty*. Two members are recognizable as men of wealth, George's admirers Thomas Briggs of London and Thomas Walker the manufacturer of Birmingham. James Joynes belonged. His letters during the winter of 1882–3 told Henry George that their Irish adventure together had cost him his mastership at Eton and turned him toward a career of writing about social problems — a career which would lead to Marxist socialism.

With the advantage of present hindsight on the making of modern Britain, Henry George's rising influence will be plainer if we notice a couple of younger members of the Land Reform Union about whom he could have known very little, much less have suspected their distinguished futures. One of these, who may or may not have been an early joiner, was Sidney Olivier, a recent graduate of Oxford who within a few years would be a Fabian tractarian on 'Capital and Land,' and four decades later secretary of state for India in Ramsay MacDonald's first Labour government. During the late autumn of 1882 this young civil servant wrote a letter which supplies a rare insight into how a very sophisticated and intellectual Britisher could react both to *Progress and Poverty* and to his own class's ordinary reaction.

'I would remark with respect to the main thesis of the book,' he said to Graham Wallas, 'that it is all very well to poke fun at Henry George and his deduction of the immortality of the soul from the sound theory of property in land, in which I do not think you will have any fear that I shall follow him — indeed he does not himself point out the connection, but I am anxious to see, what I have never yet seen, some other argument than the pooh-pooh one, which is all one is generally treated to except when the "whatever is, is best" is assumed . . . I have no wish to champion George, who has a rhapsodical and unchastened style, strongly suggestive of the pulpit, and who starts with ideas of the Divine Purpose and Final

Causes exceedingly incongruous in such a treatise, but inasmuch as his book has brought the question into general notice of others than readers of Mill and Spencer, I think he is to be thanked.'

If George had any way at all of sensing that *Progress and Poverty* was beginning to disturb the young, the able, and the heterodox among Britain's intellectuals, the instance known to him was Philip Wicksteed. At the age of thirty-nine, Mr. Wicksteed was already a distinguished man, the vigorous minister of the important Little Portland Street Unitarian chapel. But he had yet written no book to indicate that he would achieve fame as one of Britain's most brilliant economists, and none to indicate his coming distinction as Dante scholar. A decade later he would begin to produce the works which made him a leader in modern value-theory, and one to influence academicians and Fabian socialists, both. Reading *Progress and Poverty* at a time when he needed help, Mr. Wicksteed wrote the author, the book fell 'on old and deep lines of thought in my mind, and has given me the light I vainly sought for myself.' He thanked George for exposing the wages fund, and for designating political economy's weakness in explaining depressions. Meeting George on a more thoughtful level than most of the reviewers did, Wicksteed offered some suggestive comments about *Progress and Poverty*. He thought George to be right in assuming increasing returns from an ever denser labor supply only in respect of those places where more and more food was available; and, while he agreed that Malthus had been substantially refuted, he countered that population pressure, and sometimes diminishing returns, could not always be gainsaid. The minister's large judgment, however, was unqualified: you have opened 'a new heaven and a new earth,' he told George, and thanked him for a 'freshly kindled enthusiasm.'

Though they met once or twice, there is no evidence that Henry George ever learned much more about his influence on Philip Wicksteed than this first response indicates. Yet at the very time when George was making his second visit in England, the minister was leading discussions of his ideas before the Economic Circle of Manchester College in London. In time this group came to meet at the Belsize Square home of Henry R. Beeton, a member of the London Stock Exchange who strongly sympathized with George; and it grew in size and distinction. Two London professors of political economy attended, H. S. Foxwell of University College and F. Y. Edgeworth of King's College; and Sidney Webb came, and Bernard Shaw. The play of mind between Shaw and the Unitarian minister was particularly exciting.

This runs ahead of the story, for the Economic Circle lasted from 1884 to 1888; and it is not to be suggested that the members' debt to Henry George meant mortgaged minds. Yet though in the end Wicksteed's technical economics stemmed rather from Stanley Jevons than from Henry George, he remained always loyal to *Progress and Poverty*'s central idea. Land nationalization, to be achieved gradually by way of taxation and with special attention to mineral lands, remained a conviction to the end, with Philip Wicksteed.

Though George could no more know all the present than foresee the future impulses that would stem from his books in Britain, the signs did accumulate rapidly. Surely compliment and challenge both were intended by Miss Taylor when, writing from Avignon, 7 January 1883, she said that she deeply deplored the way in which Gladstone's mild reformism was making little gains seem larger than they were, and then declared that *Progress and Poverty* was selling well even on the newsstands, and that England's need was leadership of vision and power. Challenge came from Hyndman too, who wrote that the anarchists were gaining in the international race to bring laboring men into politics and power. Davitt could do much, the wily socialist suggested in a line of thought already George's own, to bridge the gap between the Irish resistance and the British working classes, but that would not be enough. If he would only do so, Henry George could make himself the uniter of the British and American labor movements, Hydman urged most warmly.

Meanwhile the less pretentious recognitions, and very reassuring ones, multiplied also. Mr. Walker wrote in the spring of 1883 that he had distributed about 100 copies of *Progress and Poverty* among Liberal party workers in Birmingham, and that he had taken the chair at a couple of meetings to discuss the book. He asked permission to have a summary made for working men. 'Anything for the cause,' Henry George replied. A few months later, Mr. A. C. Swinton, who was particularly generous in writing George about how his books were being received, reported that the London Society of Positivists was assigning their fortnightly discussion time to

Progress and Poverty for as long a period as they might need to do a thorough study.

This was notable company, though not exactly Henry George's own kind. It included Professor Beesly and Frederic Harrison, leaders of the cult, the latter a speaker and writer on social problems and one to be more forceful than logical when he praised and dispraised George. John Morley's *Fortnightly Review,* which it will be remembered had displayed a real interest in Henry George in 1882, still retained much of its old Positivist flavor.

According to the many indications that came to him, the time was right for George to return to England. When the invitation to lecture was matched by a personal invitation, that he use Mr. Walker's home in Birmingham as his headquarters, and when adequate funds were assured, Henry George had no choice except to say that he would come.

–2–

The hospitality of admirers gave George a speaking role in Britain's social drama, but other people and many minds set the stage. No question was more important to him, after the low-cost editions and after *The Times* review, than the natural one: How would critical opinion respond?

Much more now in England than three years earlier in New York, the expected reviews promised a valuation to be regarded as in a sense ultimate. There existed no critical court of appeals beyond the judgments presently rendered. There would be no higher authority to upset these decisions, should they be unfavorable, in any such way as, say, the *Alta California*'s dismissal had been rendered silly by the judgments even of the unsympathetic New York *Nation,* or as the *New York Times* had in a way been overruled by the London *Times'* thoughtful opinion. The historic British reviews of the nineteenth century — the *Edinburgh Review,* the *Quarterly Review,* the *Contemporary Review,* the *Nineteenth Century* — represented the international as well as the national arbitrament of ideas in the English language. Far more than any journalism in the United States except possibly that of the *North American,* their opinions signified judgment weighted with authority — with the authority of the main traditions of British politics and intellect.

Much the same was true of criticism from the universities. In England's more consolidated culture, the dons of Oxford and Cambridge were more natural speakers on public affairs than professors in American colleges and universities, and they carried more prestige. At this time Sir Henry Fawcett, the blind Cambridge economist and member of Parliament, had a very high standing; and soon Alfred Marshall and later John Maynard Keynes would represent the same kind of authority. At Oxford the brilliant young Arnold Toynbee, protégé of Jowett, who poured amazing energy into working-class causes, indicated most engagingly the contact point of conscience between social scholarship and social amelioration — the point at which *Progress and Poverty* was sure to be tested.

As the London *Times* review may fairly be understood to have been a quick response to George's prominence in Ireland, so the wave of reviews and discussion meetings during the fall and winter of 1882–3 is to be understood as reaction to the popular editions. Long before George undertook the lecture tour, the sales of the Durant-Kegan Paul paper-bound *Progress and Poverty* were mounting spectacularly toward the ultimate record-breaking total of 109,000 copies; these sales were well advanced before the Reeves edition was even started. While, from the author's point of view, successful distribution vindicated his own strategy and Mr. Shaw's subsidy, from the reviewers' point of view, it indicated a change of situation. After 1882 *Progress and Poverty* could never again be reasonably dismissed as mere utopianism, or as a book mainly useful for understanding Ireland, or California.

George himself understood very well that the measurements of his book and of himself being taken principally in London meant much, and that favorable or unfavorable they signified — as John Russell Young had told him — a day of his own in the highest court of public opinion. By early March the hearing had gone so far that there was no reason why he should not boast a little when writing to an intimate. 'The animals are getting stirred up' over there, he said to Dr. Taylor.

In November the *Contemporary Review* led off the series of criticisms. Though this monthly lacked the antiquity and the associations of power of some of the other journals, it was rising into liberal influence and prestige. The November issue contained a twenty-page critique of *Progress and Poverty* by Emile de Laveleye, who had done the review in *La Revue scientifique* more than two years previously. This time the Belgian scholar shifted the weight of his comment away from the earlier degree of approval; he made a pretty evenly balanced series of observations, *pro* and *con*. The socialist in him found many faults with George's pro-capitalist ideas: with the book's justification of interest and other rewards to investment, with what Laveleye called George's exaggeration of the increment of land values (even in California), and with his under-appreciation of the profits taken in the mining lands by reason of capital monopoly (apart from site monopolization). Laveleye criticized as insufficient George's answer to the wages fund; and he repeated his original counter-proposition, that the best land reform would be lease tenures from the state.

The professor pretty well restricted his praise to specific points this time. He applauded George for adopting Ricardo's law — 'which may be looked upon as a demonstrated truth'; he seconded *Progress and Poverty*'s anti-Malthusianism; and he agreed that George had a right to claim Herbert Spencer on his side of the argument, and even suggested that John Locke and others could be claimed also. Not a materialist, Laveleye approved George's attaching social protest to the ideas of religion. How else, he queried, could the good society be brought to being?

Except for a private communication which this reviewer presently sent the author, it would be hard to say to which side his judgment leaned. But he assured George that in his net opinion *Progress and Poverty* was a book to be admired, and he offered compliments on the huge success of the English editions.

In January, two months after the *Contemporary*, the *Quarterly Review*, the *Edinburgh Review*, and the *Modern Review* all had their say. With complete fidelity to the loyalties of their journals, the reviewers in the *Quarterly* and the *Edinburgh* spoke their respective Tory condemnations and Whig objections to *Progress and Poverty*. The *Modern* of course was different. It assigned the criticism to George Sarson, M.A., who endorsed the book as timely for England, and in a moderate way — which seems to identify the reviewer as a Radical — recommended land-value taxation as sound policy. In 1884 the Land Reform Union reprinted the Sarson review as a pamphlet.

Unfortunately for the quality of the result, the *Quarterly Review* elected a very brash young writer to answer Henry George. Though its contributors had included Tories of the highest talent, ranging from Sir Walter Scott to the Earl of Salisbury, this time it let William Hurrell Mallock speak the Conservative mind. The son of a rector and a graduate of Oxford, Mr. Mallock's own memoirs identify him as a frequenter of country-house and drawing-room society, and they display him in unconscious caricature as dilettante and snob. He was concerned at the time of this review, he says, to show 'that "social equality" was a radically erroneous formula'; and his demonstrations led him into literary free-swinging at radicals of sundry Liberal and socialistic types. But Henry George must have been this writer's special antipathy, for including the review in the *Quarterly*, he shortly piled up more than 250 pages of refutation of *Progress and Poverty*.

The *Quarterly Review* essay — for 'criticism' is hardly the word for forty immoderate pages — presumed that British institutions were at stake. To Henry George, Mallock granted no element of truth, but only surface brilliance of writing and a demagogue's appeal. The writer nevertheless took trouble to assure readers of the *Quarterly* that *Progress and Poverty* was wrong, point by point along the whole line, the critical passages and the utopian ones the same. The suggestive thing about the review is the incitement in its tone, and the apprehension it voiced in fear of England's safety. Because Mallock represents what was in some degree a national attitude which George was going to be obliged to confront, a quotation to illustrate is in order.

'False theories, when they bear directly upon action, do not claim our attention in proportion to the talent they are supported by, but in proportion to the extent to which action is likely to be influenced by them; and since action in modern politics so largely depends on the people, the wildest errors are grave, if they are only sufficiently popular. How they strike the wise is a matter of small moment; the great question is, how they will strike the ignorant.' Mallock believed that the recent visitor had excited the discontented of Britain far more than he had his own people. 'In America the author, so far as we have been able to learn, has failed hitherto to make any practical converts. He has been more fortunate on this side of the Atlantic . . . Mr. George's London publishers have lately reissued his book in an ultra-popular form. It is at this moment selling by thousands in the alleys and back streets of England, and is being audibly welcomed there as a glorious gospel of justice. If we may credit a leading Radical journal, it is fast forming a new public opinion. The opinion we here allude to is no doubt that of the half-educated; but this makes the matter in some ways more serious. No classes are so dangerous, at once to themselves and to others, as those which have learned to reason, but not to reason rightly . . . They will fall victims to it, as though to an intellectual pestilence. Mr. George's book is full of this kind of contagion. A ploughman might snore, or a country gentleman smile over it, but it is well calculated to turn the head of an artizan . . . It is not the poor, it is not the seditious only, who have thus been affected by Mr. George's doctrines . . . they have been gravely listened to by a conclave of English clergymen. Scotch ministers and nonconformist professors have done more than listen — they have received them with marked approval; they have even held meetings and given lectures to disseminate them. Finally, certain trained economic thinkers, or men who pass for such in at least one of our Universities, are reported to have said that they see no means of refuting them, and that they probably mark the beginning of a new political epoch.'

The *Edinburgh Review*, historic carrier of the Whig tradition, recorded less anxiety and included more in the way of actual criticism. In a combination which must have given ironic satisfaction to Henry George, this quarterly reviewed together *Progress and Poverty* and Herbert Spencer's *Social Statics*, published as far back as 1850, the two under the heading, 'The Nationalisation of Land.' Taking George's ideas to be sufficiently valid to speak of the good and the bad, the reviewer praised the passage against Malthus as excellent, the best in the book; and he acknowledged as common truth George's basis in Ricardo's law of rent, and quoted a recent version of that law by Professor Thorold Rogers. He rejected George's theory of distribution, however, and, not stopping to quarrel with the analysis of margins, he counter-proposed that British law and practice recognized sufficiently the difference between property in land and property in things. He said that land nationalization would lift no burden of rent from the land occupiers, and would likely be harder to bear than present landlordism. 'The payment, instead of going into the pocket of the proprietor, is diverted into the coffers of the State. The *dramatis personae* only are changed; the plot and the outcome of the drama are the same. It is only a new way to pay old rents.'

This comment meant, of course, either that the reviewer had not caught, or that he chose to dismiss, the public benefits George asserted would follow from transferring economic rent into the coffers of the community. To the Edinburgh reviewer, *Progress and Poverty*'s remedy seemed 'plunder,' quite as immoral as Mr. Mallock judged it.

In defense of all property rights he rendered his general judgment of the book. Again a quotation is required, for these concluding comments supply a special revelation of the anxieties which knowledge that *Progress and Poverty* was being read stirred up in England during 1882 and 1883. 'Writers like Mr. George and Mr. Herbert Spencer are at war not only with the first principles of political economy and of law, of social order, and of domestic life, but with the elements of human nature . . . The strongest incentive to industry, economy, and good living is the desire to provide for the future, and to hand down to our children some results of our own lives . . . Land has hitherto been regarded as the most secure of all property . . . We can only regard Mr. George's work and Mr. Davitt's speeches as a part of the revolutionary warfare now waged by certain Americans, or Hiberno-Americans, against the institutions of this country, which degrades them to the level of the Socialists of Germany, the Nihilists of Russia, and the Communards of Paris.'

Though the *Edinburgh Review*'s criticism sounded again the opinion of the *Alta California* — and many others papers — it was rendered in the context of a serious study of the book and its ideas. A decade later Henry George with the magazine open before him was able to say that this reviewer had written 'as fairly, it seemed to me, as could be expected, though of course adversely.'

An immediate by-product of the review appeared in the conservative *St. James Gazette,* to which Herbert Spencer addressed an angry letter. The philosopher utterly repudiated the association of his name and ideas with Henry George's, and he asserted that *Social Statics* had only pointed out a difference between the 'purely ethical' and the practical views of property in land. Reserved for nearly a decade later was the debate that Henry George would make of that highly arguable distinction. At the time the ruction in the *St. James Gazette* publicly knocked a weak support from under George's argument in *Progress and Poverty,* and it perhaps diminished the connection between land nationalization and land-vaue taxation. The letter was widely reprinted in America, and certainly it distressed some of George's admirers at home — as was natural, for this was the time of Spencer's greatest American vogue. But George himself had discounted Spencer since meeting him in London; and in the direction of the support he now wanted — among the clergymen, working men, and intellectuals of England — it is not likely that repudiation by Herbert Spencer injured his cause.

Along with the reviewing came the public discussions of *Progress and Poverty.* The way in which some of these discussions were reported to George, and how they encouraged him to return to England, has already been related. But there were others. Some were friendly, such as the debates of the Trade Union Congress in 1882, and later. Other meetings were not friendly, and in outstanding cases they fed the stream of serious criticism.

For an important example, early in 1883, Alfred Marshall gave a series of three lectures in the city of Bristol. The future distinguished economist, who was a little younger than George, was still a professor at University College in that city; within a year he was to move to Oxford, and very soon to go on to Cambridge, the scene of his influential career. In the first and second lectures Marshall criticized severely George's ideas about wages: he submitted as his own finding the fact that the product of the British economy divided into a low share to rent (£75 millions, less than 7 per cent) and high shares to interest and wages (£250 millions and £800 millions, respectively). He said that the real wages of the laboring class were constantly improving. These statements did not literally contradict *Progress and Poverty,* and perhaps Marshall did not think they did. But they were intended to deflate the book; for in presenting them, Marshall, whose inclination was toward mathematical economics rather than the methods of general logic and hypothesis which survived in George, characterized *Progress and Poverty* as altogether unscientific.

The one 'real value' which the university man acknowledged in

George was his 'freshness and earnestness' — 'he is by nature a poet,
not a scientific thinker.' Professor Marshall concluded the series by
calling himself a 'more moderate defender' of property in land,
and making a number of recommendations. For the elevation of
living standards he proposed late marriages and universal education; and he thought that new countries would gain by some application of Laveleye's plan of fixed-term land tenures, held from
the sovereign state. This was a rejection of Henry George ideas,
quite completely, and yet another act that admitted the American
radical to high debate in England.

Ten years later pronouncements by Alfred Marshall would have
been the weightiest of their kind, but in February 1883 the London
lectures of Arnold Toynbee — an uncle of the present-day phil-
osopher-historian — caught far more attention. A tutor and bursar
at Oxford, Toynbee at thirty had distinguished himself by dedication and quality of personality rather than by any known achievement of original thought. Yet the suggestive little book by which
his permanent reputation is made secure, *The Industrial Revolution,* is made up of lectures which he had already delivered at the
university. As director at Oxford of the studies of young men preparing for the civil service in India, and as generous participator
in social causes, his career brought him into public affairs; and for
reasons of conscience he had chosen to live awhile in Whitechapel
slums, and to travel in insurgent Ireland.

Altogether naturally he was an early reader of *Progress and Poverty,* and one who, though he discovered 'fallacies and crude conceptions,' would take it seriously. We gain a peep into opinion
making about Henry George as we learn that Professor Henry
Fawcett, visiting at Professor Jowett's, asked Toynbee about *Progress and Poverty,* confessing that he himself had not read it. One
would like to know the young man's brief reply; and one would
like to know also how much attention Oxford gave to two lectures
he delivered, the last of his teaching career, in criticism of the book.

He was invited to repeat those lectures in London. Someone suggested that the Social Democratic Federation sponsor the appearance, Hyndman wrote George, 'but we declined as I disapprove of
attacking allies and Toynbee calls himself a Radical Socialist.' The
lectures were given, 11 and 18 January 1883, in St. Andrews Hall
on Norman Street. The audience must have been thoroughly

mixed. Among known admirers of both the speaker and the author under discussion, Sidney Olivier and Philip Wicksteed were present; and there seems to have been a large element of working men, some of whom were pretty rowdy and shouted for revolution. Between a disturbed audience and a lecturer who, especially at second appearance, was plainly suffering from illness and exhaustion, the occasion proved as emotional as possible.

Toynbee himself very largely defeated the critical purpose of the lectures. He spoke extemporaneously and overlong. Although an economist's learning shines through the text, his objections to *Progress and Poverty*'s analysis — which largely assert inconsistencies in the book's wage theory — are complicated and difficult even as printed, and must have been nearly impossible to understand from the platform. On the other hand, the disturbed conscience of the speaker, and his leaning backward to be sympathetic with Henry George's ends, and to do no more than oppose his means were transparently clear. The first lecture, 'Mr. George in California,' was I think the first commentary since Dr. Taylor's to picture George adequately against his proper background, and to present *Progress and Poverty* as thought developed from *Our Land and Land Policy*. Toynbee concluded less with counterblast than with alternative reforms. Workers' insurance, city-subsidized housing, and so on, he said, would be sounder for England than nationalization of any kind.

The record of these very exciting meetings, and the comment made about them, combine to create an impression of remarkable tribute rather than resistance offered *Progress and Poverty* by Toynbee. In his peroration the speaker admonished the well-to-do members of the audience not to resist democracy. 'It is violent, I know; it is stormy at times, but it is only violent and stormy like a sea — it cleanses the shores of human life.' To the working men present he admitted the guilt of England's social conscience. 'We — the middle classes, I mean, not the very rich — we have neglected you; instead of justice we have offered you charity, and instead of sympathy we have offered you hard and unreal advice; but I think we are changing . . . But we students, we would help you if we could. We are willing to give up something much dearer than fame or social position. We are willing to give up the life we care for, the life with books and with those we love . . . If you will only keep to the love of your fellow-men and to great ideals, then we shall find our happiness in helping you, but if you do not then our reparation will be in vain.'

Shortly after the lectures, Philip Wicksteed wrote George in happy irony that the Toynbee lectures had been a huge success: they had cleared out the publisher's stock of *Progress and Poverty*. Toynbee's 'concessions,' according to this expert witness, were 'large and significant, and his defense of private property in land half-hearted and feeble.' Kegan Paul followed up with a form letter, widely distributed, which referred to the lectures and invited readers of *Progress and Poverty* to organize reading and discussion groups in every town, to diffuse Henry George's ideas.

Presently the news went out that Toynbee's exhaustion of the lecture day had not been due to the one exertion, but that that effort had been too much for a chronic condition. He died in March of 'brain fever.' The *Economist* of 17 March 1883 recalled the hollow cheeks and the nervous manner of the lecturer, and how he had 'actually blazed up in defense of Michael Davitt and succeeded in producing the impression . . . that he would be prepared with a panacea more didactic than the changes which form a part of the Radical programme.' Toynbee had not been the man for the occasion, the *Economist* believed.

Exhaustive work in the historical sociology of ideas would be required to trace, from the January of the criticisms in the major reviews, and of the Toynbee lectures, until the next December, when George returned to Britain, the assimilation of *Progress and Poverty* in the kingdom. Yet there is little reason to think that any amount of investigating the labor press and the provincial press, or of searching out records of organizations and meetings, would alter very much the observation of J. L. Garvin at this point in his biography of Joseph Chamberlain. By 1883, Mr. Garvin says, Henry George's ideas had 'awakened new imaginings and aspirations among Radical working men; they thought they saw a great light.'

Only a lengthening and spreading public interest in George could explain the many efforts made, month after month, to refute his writings. In *Macmillan's Magazine* for July, for example, Sir Henry Fawcett had an article, 'State Socialism and Land Nationalisation,' which he had designed as a chapter for a new edition of his textbook *Manual of Political Economy,* and which was presently issued as such. Taking a moderate position, Sir Henry inveighed against George for proposing to confiscate land values without compensating the landlords. This was a Liberal point of view. A second denunciation from the pen of Mr. Mallock appeared in the October *Quarterly Review.* In form this was a criticism of Hyndman's *England for All,* but in the main it amounted to a fresh attack — and a less flashy and a more considered piece of writing than the January review — on *Progress and Poverty.* This article Mr. Mallock soon combined with others to make a book, *Property and Progress,* the most elaborate answer to Henry George ever written. When the *Quarterly* article appeared, unsigned according to usage, an English friend of Henry George attributed it to the Marquis of Salisbury and was worried about the effect.

Even from journals in which more favorable things had been said, signs appeared, in late 1883, of rising resistance to George. In December, the month of his arrival, the *Contemporary Review,* which had published the Laveleye criticism, perhaps compensated a little by carrying an article by Samuel Smith, a Liberal M.P. Writing on 'The Nationalisation of Land,' this earnest man asserted that the time had now come when 'leading statesmen can no longer keep quiet on the subject,' for the George and Wallace movement was really 'as absurd as a South Sea Bubble.' And the *Fortnightly,* in midcourse of a series of articles intended to blueprint a program for the Radicals, denied that the proponents of land nationalization had shown adequately that their surgery would produce gains to justify their operating on the economy. 'The only difference would be that the increase in the value of the land would go to the new holders.' The Radicals should work toward the principle of 'the right and duty of the state to fix within certain broad limits the extent, and to control the conditions, of private ownership.' Parliament should vest in local authorities 'the power of expropriating for public purposes, on payment of fair compensation, and adequate securities being taken against the possibility of extortionate demands.' So qualified the *Fortnightly.*

In sum: the Irish journey had won George his first sizable recognition in Great Britain, and the low-cost editions of *Progress and Poverty* had brought unprecedented attention to book and man. The major round of reviewing, from *The Times* in September

1882 through the *Contemporary Review,* the *Edinburgh Review,* and the *Quarterly Review* of January 1883, all indicated serious discussion. As discussion waxed, however, disagreement and astonishment, and anxiety if not panic, grew that *Progress and Poverty* had reached too far.

Before the end of 1883, moreover, a more definite reaction occurred than just a cooling off among Liberal journals. A backfire started. Printed materials were circulated and public meetings called, answers in kind to the propaganda efforts on the Henry George side. A Liberty and Property Defense League circulated gratis a fifteen-page pamphlet by Baron Bramwell, 'The Nationalisation of Land: a review of Mr. Henry George's "Progress and Poverty." ' This was republished two years later. And another pamphlet, four times as long, by Francis D. Longe, 'A Critical Examination of Mr. George's "Progress and Poverty" and Mr. Mill's Theory of Wages,' was issued also. Money and effort were being spent against the American egalitarian.

So negative reasons, as well as the positive ones urged by his friends, made late 1883 an appropriate time for Henry George to speak for himself again in Great Britain.

–3–

He traveled this time with his older son. The winter voyage, and the hardship and expense of lecture traveling, suggested that Mrs. George and the girls stay home. The three and Richard went to Philadelphia, to live with Kate George Chapman, Henry George's sister married to an actor-turned-farmer, at their place in Haddonfield. Both father and mother George had died only weeks before; but their natural time had come, and Henry thought of brothers, sisters, and cousins as very happy together on Christmas Day. On shipboard he wrote directing that while he was away Jennie should have dancing lessons and piano too, while Dick, the indifferent student of the family, was to go to the same Mr. Lauderbach under whom he himself had tutored.

For the voyagers all went pleasantly. Harry who had been unwell suffered only one difficulty — to satisfy a huge appetite. He reached England in good shape for his duties as secretary, assistant, and companion to his father. George himself had a perfect rest. He enjoyed four volumes of Macaulay's *England* better than the novel he had brought for shipboard reading. Though his letters told of a traveler's mind reaching back home, he had also much to look forward to; and it is hardly too risky to guess that returning to England he relived the day he had had in Thomas Walker's home, and anticipated return there. And how could he have helped anticipating Oxford? Max Müller had followed his overtures of 1882 with letters, once begging George to write about economic solutions for India; and, though he mentioned Toynbee and other Oxonian objectors to *Progress and Poverty,* he renewed the invitation to visit the university. There was a similar letter from a faculty member at Nottingham College.

The English visit began at high speed and in good running order. Landing in Liverpool, the two Georges were met by Michael Davitt and Richard McGhee, a Glasgow member of Parliament and the future most prominent organizer of the Henry George movement in Scotland. The visitors went on at once to Birmingham, where Mr. Walker received them warmly, and then proceeded to London. Kegan Paul snapped at a chance to publish *Social Problems.*

After being in the metropolis only a few days, George was able to write his wife and Dr. Taylor that he had sold his British rights in the book for £400, and that with the advance from his American publishers he had had $3600 from the book before a copy had been sold — 'considerable difference from *P & P.*' He had been paid £50 royalties from earlier British publications too. It was happiness to send $200 home at once, half for Annie to draw on and half for himself, and to tell her to regard $100 as her 'own personal private money to use as you may choose.' He could say now that he would pay all his debts, whether in California or New York, and have a surplus too. Even more thrilling to add, a kind of New Year's message: 'Here I am in London and at last begin to realize that I am a very important man.'

At the request of a working men's association, Henry George went out of London on his first Sunday to return on an afternoon train as if just arriving in the city. The stunt brought out a crowd. Two or three thousand men turned up; a committee of the Land Reform Union gave the official welcome; a fife and drum corps played; and policemen directed the crowd. Though not able to conceal embarrassment about the fake arrival, George warmed to the reception after he had made his explanations. From the top of a cab he saluted the working men as members of the Republic of Man destined to federate the world. His phrases may or may not represent a response to Hyndman's proposal.

Lecturing started under a heavy schedule. Beginning in London, a cold-weather trip loomed ahead, all the way to Wick and Skye and back, not an easy undertaking. But the pressure at the outset was of an ideological kind. George's first few days of contact with the Land Reform Union indicated that the group harbored confusions which if allowed to continue would obscure the message he intended to deliver. On the left (as it seems fair to describe the divisions of sentiment), the union, like the Land Nationalisation Society, contained an element inclined to say that interest charges exploit labor in the same way as rent taking. This avenue would lead the Land Reform Union to socialism, George believed. Simultaneously on the right, the Land Reform Union included another element which counseled him to withhold the argument of *Progress and Poverty* that proposed abolishing the private-property values of land without compensation to the landlords.

Objection to his anti-compensationist argument was of course familiar to George at home, in California and elsewhere, and the question had come up in a critical way when he and Davitt closed ranks in 1882. But during this second visit, anti-compensationism emerged as a routine characteristic of resistance in Britain, not among his enemies exclusively, but often among his friends. A decade earlier, finding his bearings and criticizing Mill, George had acknowledged that in the nation where since Henry VIII landholding had been intimately blended with other property holding, the case against property in land would be harder to present than in California. Now confronted with the actual British situation, George needed such a leverage of ideas as he had in America — the still-remembered moral logic of anti-slavery.

To adjust effectively the internal divisions of the Land Reform Union required, if not new theory, at least fresh tactical thinking and a pronouncement from Henry George. This need made the first lecture a doubly important event. Contrary to recent habits of preparation, George gave up the couch and took to the writing desk, as in the days of first platform appearances in California. He dictated and revised drafts for two days and a night; and when the hour came he scrambled into evening clothes and was rushed by a committee to St. James Hall, which was jam-packed with an audience of four thousand.

John Ruskin had been scheduled to introduce the speaker. This arrangement followed shortly on a report to George that the famous essayist and art professor had called *Progress and Poverty* 'an admirable book' — which may have been George's first knowledge of the existence of a somewhat kindred spirit. But illness prevented Ruskin's coming, and the chair was occupied by Henry Labouchere, who was the wittiest Radical in Parliament and one of London's most successful journalists. Davitt, Stewart Headlam, Frederic Harrison, Philip Wicksteed, and others sat on the platform. At the moment Labouchere had an article forthcoming in the *Fortnightly* which said that all Radicals wanted land reform, and that some went all the way with George, though the wiser ones were moderate. Making the introduction, he said that four Georges had muddled the affairs of Great Britain, but that now an uncrowned fifth came with sympathy for the poor.

Taking the rostrum the speaker abandoned his manuscript and whispered to Thomas Walker to pull his coattails if he talked too long. With American directness Henry George urged the moral logic of equal opportunity; and as in the Land Nationalisation Society speech he illustrated landlordism from the city about him. Quite as dogmatically as in San Francisco he denied moral justice to any owner's taking for private use the rent created by urban growth. The helpless-widow argument he answered by Queen Victoria's pension: she and every other widow deserved a pension by right, but widows deserve no rents — not even queens, the American asserted. When a questioner demanded to know who brought the slum dwellers into the world, George answered that it was God Almighty, 'and whom God Almighty brings into the world who shall Man put out?' Before the meeting closed Michael Davitt gave a short benedictory address.

The London *Standard* went into high irony about George's speech; and a *Times* editorial voiced alarm that the popular American was appealing to the 'shiftless' — people who should blame their own deficiencies for their poverty. But in the speaker's estimate the evening turned out a grand success, and the unfriendly reactions really gave the measure of his influence. 'I satisfied them,' he wrote Annie about the huge audience, 'I certainly have attained

fame at last.' Years later Henry George, Jr., remembered being in
the hotel room the next morning when his father came in, not
noticing anyone present. Turning over *The Times* and other newspapers, Henry George's face lighted up. 'At last,' he said aloud, 'at
last I am famous.'

After the opening lecture, he swung west to Plymouth and Cardiff and Bristol first, before the big trip through the Midlands and
the length of Scotland. A packed hall pleased George in the Pil-
grims' port city, and father and son took time to see the sights.
There and at Cardiff, he believed that he had '*telling* successes,'
and presently, following a phrase he chanced in a lecture, began to
visualize himself as a 'missionary' overseas. He hit a regular stride
as platform performer. He used no notes; he concentrated beforehand and relied on inspiration at the rostrum to find the best
phrasing for each audience, of the central ideas which he repeated
time after time.

There could be no doubt of instant excitement in the smaller
cities. Even before reaching Birmingham George was writing Annie
about how wonderfully he was being received. He sent money again,
and promised more, and let his mind race to the pleasantest conclusions: at home time free for writing, a summer's trip to California for the family, an early return to Britain. In his own words to
his wife: 'I can't begin to send you the papers in which I am discussed, attacked, and commented on — for I would have to send
all the English, Scotch, and Irish papers. I am getting advertised to
my heart's content and I shall have crowds wherever I go . . . I
could be a social lion if I would permit it. But I won't fool with
that sort of thing.' Once again he thought of launching a paper of
his own — he meant in New York this time — but not before election, 'so as to arouse no political antagonisms.'

As he crossed the country, lines of comment followed him. The
new Social Democratic paper *Justice* applauded warmly and consistently; and when *Social Problems* was published that paper carried an entirely approving review. According to Dr. Lawrence, this
trip marked the 'height of socialist enthusiasm for his cause.' The
other side of the coin was represented by an event of harsh rebuke
for academic people fond of *Progress and Poverty*. Before January
was out, Lord Fortescue exposed in *The Times* the fact that Henry
George's book was being used in the City of London College

as a textbook, with the result that the book was withdrawn from use.

About the time the lecturer reached the Midlands, the British re-sistance to confiscationism caught up with him, in the reaction of his audiences. In Birmingham, though he had the satisfaction of hear-ing Miss Helen Taylor give a twist of irony to the compensationist side, he himself was heckled rather sharply. And in Liverpool his own address had been preceded by one from Samuel Smith, the M.P. who had recently made a point of compensationism in his article against George in the *Contemporary*. On arrival Henry George dis-covered that this had had a telling effect. The Reform Club which had sponsored his coming now withdrew sponsorship; and only one man, the M.P. who had agreed to preside, would accompany him to the stage.

Henry George the public speaker of 1877 or 1878, and perhaps of any time earlier than this visit, might well have failed. He tells the story well. 'The consciousness of opposition which always arouses me,' he wrote to Mr. Walker, 'gave me the stimulus I needed to overcome physical weakness, for I was in bad trim from loss of sleep, and I carried the audience with me, step by step, till you never saw a more enthusiastic crowd.' At the end he used a platform device which he had tried before and was beginning to make habitual. He called for a vote on compensation, and the whole audience except three went with him. 'Of the effects at the time there could be no doubt, and I hear of the most gratifying effects upon those who did not go.'

But audiences are more suggestible than individuals of mind and experience, and George learned immediately that his unwillingness to compensate landlords was cutting off sympathies which were both useful and dear to him. Immediately after the Birmingham address — at the same time *Punch* went after him — Max Müller wrote, mentioning that his students had hissed at the name of George. 'There is in every branch of human knowledge a kind of religion,' advised this scholar as to one who demanded too much too soon, 'something which we believe, desire, [strive (?)] for, but still we know to be unattainable in this short life . . . To do evil that good may come is the excuse of Jesuits not honest men.'

Perhaps George was affected by the learned man. At any rate he had sympathy and humor to draw upon when his Birmingham

host, Thomas Walker, added new and affectionate protest to the
accumulation. 'The thing for you to do,' replied the author of
Progress and Poverty, 'is to pose as a compensationist and me as a
confiscationist, just as Snap and Go join different churches. With
you and Miss Taylor representing the Conservative Wing the landlords may well ask to be preserved from their friends.'

Flexibility was George's virtue under this pressure, and he held
up well. He did not mind too much being told, as he worked his
way north, that John Bright and Frederic Harrison had spoken
against him. They were not the kind he much hoped to affect. But
he was grateful to learn that Joseph Chamberlain had recently announced for land-value taxation in the cities, in order to have
capital for public investment in housing for working men.

Chamberlain he still regarded as Britain's coming leader. And,
as he moved through the industrial heart of the island, he conceived not without good cause that he himself was at the point of
changing deeply the social conscience and mind of the greatest industrial nation of the world.

–4–

Crossing into Scotland as the month of February arrived, George
invaded an area of the British economy where both feudal-style
landholding and aggravated conditions of industrial-working-class
poverty were present; and, along with both, Presbyterianism's stern
legacy of faith, and obligation.

The first part of the trip, which bypassed the major cities, revealed much. The chairman at one of George's meetings was a
minister, named Macrae, who told of having lost his kirk by reason
of a landlord's power. At the conclusion of an address in Skye, a
member of the audience arose to ask what the visitor proposed to do
with the landlords. George had no knowledge of the questioner
as landlord, absolutely no notion of his fame for having deprived
his tenants of oystering in certain waters near by. The reply, which
brought the house down, was pure chance: George proposed to do
what one does with an oyster — open it, take out the fish, and throw
away the shell. The trip through the Highlands wore him down,
the hard-working lecturer wrote home; he earned little and slept
little but learned much. 'But we are waking the animal,' he assured
Walker, 'there is no use talking, my audiences don't want any com-

pensation. They nearly mobbed the provost in Wick for insinuating it.'

The outlying places revealed characteristic signs of social discontent, but it was the return trip, the last ten days of February and the early days of March when George was in Glasgow and Edinburgh and the smaller cities of the industrial Lowlands, which utterly confirmed in his own mind the accuracy of his two-year-old prophecy, that Scotland was readier to receive his ideas than either Ireland or England. The actual economic situation there still awaits a scholarly investigator, but there is little reason to think either that James Joynes and other associates of Henry George were wrong in saying that the condition of the crofter was particularly bad, or that statistics would fail to support the proposition that rents were huge in both country and city, and were largely monopolized among the Scottish gentry. Glasgow and the whole Clydeside area suffered especially the ravages of industrialism; an early growth of trade unionism had recently been almost eliminated by hard times and bankruptcies. Professor Clarence Gohdes's observation, that the Scots have habitually taken more quickly than Englishmen to American literature and American radical ideas — a characteristic traceable as far back as their interest in Jonathan Edwards — is suggestive.

George's schedule called for an initial appearance in the region in Glasgow, then he was to go to Aberdeen, Edinburgh, and Paisley. His first address he ventured to call 'Scotland and Scotsmen.' Reminiscent of his speech to the San Francisco Y.M.H.A., he intended to sting into new thought the bearers of a moral tradition. Not confining himself to the conditions of economic hardship he had seen, he attacked also the extravagances of the established church. He asked Presbyterians to be missionaries at home rather than to the heathen — it was a characteristically American speech.

The challenge evoked a unique response. Five hundred persons remained in the hall to form a society to propagate Henry George's ideas; and a week later, 25 February, George returned to Glasgow for the meeting which organized with enthusiasm the Scottish Land Restoration League. Mr. McGhee suggested the name; 1940 signatures were enrolled in the first membership list; and George drew up a manifesto to the people. The organization gave him a farewell dinner on March first.

A chain of development had been started. The Scottish Land Restoration League spread rapidly to the cities where George had just lectured — to Edinburgh, Aberdeen, and Inverness — and into Dundee and Greenock and other towns as well. About six weeks later the English Land Restoration League was set up in imitation. This absorbed the year-old Land Reform Union; and in due time it led, through stages of organizational turnover, to the English League for the Taxation of Land Values, and to today's International League for Land Value Taxation and Free Trade.

In the descending lineage of Henry George ideas, two developments are indicated. First, the Land Restoration League marks some definition, in action, of Henry George's preference for destroying private property in land by means other than land nationalization and by a method clearly different from socialism. But for 1884 this was a clarification rather than a separation, and there appeared as yet no serious conflict of these related ideas. Second, the Land Restoration League indicates that the three impulses — land-value taxation, land nationalization, and socialism — at that time definitely continued to march abreast, as they were going to do until 1887.

Indeed two of the most memorable events of the Scottish Land League's first decade are that it launched the pilot career of Keir Hardie in labor politics and supported him in making his 1892 candidacy the first to put a socialist in Parliament. That is to say, Henry George's British mission signifies an American impulse behind the Scottish labor movement, which became historic in making the modern Labour party, and in forging the character of twentieth-century Britain.

−5−

There were two or three ordinary public meetings before George reached London again, at Leeds and Hull, but nothing counted in George's anticipation like the second week end in March, when he was scheduled for a Friday lecture before a university audience at Oxford and a Monday one at Cambridge. For the first event Max Müller had made detailed arrangements; for the second, George had been invited by a group of students.

Though in their recent correspondence Professor Müller had mentioned, in writing of opinion at Oxford, that his colleague,

Bonamy Price, an economist, had been very critical of *Progress and Poverty,* he had said also that this kind of expert opinion did not change his own mind. And the professor could hardly have been more generous in honoring his American guest. He insisted that father and son would find his guest rooms more pleasant than a hotel; he would have as additional house guest, Mr. George E. Buckle, the new editor of *The Times* (and future biographer of Disraeli); he would provide an opportunity for the visiting Americans to see Oxford; he would have a group for dinner before the lecture, at which he expected a large attendance.

Perhaps George would have been more comfortable had his host tried less hard. Tired for weeks beforehand, he could not sleep the night before the lecture. Thanks to this ordeal we have, from a letter to Annie, an extra insight into the strains and tensions of the situation. 'Here we are at Max Müller's: a beautiful place, splendid man, nice family, everything charming only I am suffering from my old enemy sleeplessness. I hardly got any sleep last night; have been like a drowned rat all today and now tonight it is as bad as ever until in desperation I have got up and started to write . . . I am to lecture before a magnificent audience of University people tomorrow night. The only thing I fear is my condition. Well, good night.'

In the Clarendon assembly hall the next evening George made no effort to present new learning or new criticism, such as had given body to his one earlier university lecture at Berkeley seven years before. He tried a simple inspirational address, in moral challenge not different from the 'Scotland and Scotsmen' lecture in Glasgow. He told the students that it cost £250 a year to attend Oxford; he contrasted the situation of the poor; he proposed that educated men work through land reform for England's social betterment. Possibly no choice of subject and no tone of presentation could have been right to engage this particular audience. Certainly he chose with little understanding, and he made a tactical blunder when, cutting his remarks short at twenty minutes or so, he asked for questions from the floor. To Oxford men this meant debate and a chance for heckling.

First Alfred Marshall, who had come to Balliol College that year, and then an undergraduate son-in-law of Max Müller each in his own way made the speaker miserable. Marshall's serious questions, and those of others, attacked the depression theory of *Progress and Poverty*. For whatever reasons of exhaustion, or not unlikely because he was annoyed by patronizing phrases the don chose to direct toward him, George answered the questions all too captiously. The undergraduates roared and heckled and moaned; and the worst occurred when the son-in-law called George's remedy a 'nostrum' and the visitor lectured the young man on his manners.[1] The affair ended with Henry George telling the students that it was 'the most disorderly meeting he had ever addressed,' and with the undergraduates giving groans for 'land robbery.'

Though Professor Müller apologized, and a tutor wrote at once how sorry he was 'for the personal rude treatment you had to endure by being baited by a mass of howling simpletons,' George must have felt pretty grim about going next to Cambridge. His undergraduate hosts had been honest to warn him that everyone was 'so disgustingly cautious' that they had trouble to get permission — from 'an autocrat most supreme' — to have the meeting. On the other hand, they had persuaded the Reverend Mr. Caldecott, 'an economist of the new school' who was understood to go a great way with *Progress and Poverty*, to take the chair. Mr. Keynes, the father of the future economist, and others would sit on the platform, and the inviting committee believed that 'the great majority among the undergraduates and younger and more progressive dons are in favor of land nationalisation.'

We are lucky to be able to see the visit through the bright eyes of Mary Gladstone, the prime minister's daughter. She had been well prepared for the week end. She had read *Progress and Poverty* the previous summer and had discussed it in the family. The reputation she had heard of it, as 'the most upsetting, revolutionary book of the age,' had not put her off. While reading she had agreed with it 'at present,' and when she finished she confessed to her diary 'feelings of deep admiration — felt desperately impressed, and he is a Christian.'

The young woman met Henry George at a Trinity College tea.

---

[1] In his autobiography (*Life, Journalism and Politics*, New York, n.d., I, 21), J. A. Spender, apparently writing from memory, says that the questioner's word 'nostrum' provoked George to demand, 'Sir, are you a member of this University?' All unconsciously he had used the words an Oxford proctor always put to undergraduates caught doing mischief. The roars of the audience, the sympathetic members included, further miffed the visitor.

At the more liberal university he had regained his composure. Professor James Stuart was in charge, a friendly host who knew *Progress and Poverty* well enough to differentiate between the morality of the book, with which he agreed, and the economics of it, with which he frequently disagreed. At this Sunday afternoon social event he was taking the critical line, making an effort to 'convert' Henry George, according to our witness. 'But, alas, [George] far more nearly converted us. He deeply impressed us with his earnestness, conviction and singleness and height of aim. I don't think we made the faintest impression on him and he was very quick and clear in argument. Helen and Mr. Sedley Taylor and Mr. Butler and the son of George sat mum throughout. I made 2 or 3 desperate ventures and got red as my gown, but felt crushed. Perhaps Prof. Stuart hardly stood quite to his guns. Walked to chapel with the man and he told me of his horrid Oxford meeting.' Later Miss Gladstone enjoyed the 'long and earnest' dinner discussion of George, at Professor Stuart's. Writing home that night, George mentioned 'chatter' with the prime minister's daughter.

At the Monday evening lecture Miss Gladstone sat with her host and with Arthur Lyttelton, her father's secretary. All three, she says, 'were struck . . . At first it seemed very doubtful whether he would be heard, and he was not well or up to the mark. Still on the whole, considering that the audience disagreed with him and were undergraduates, his fate was better than was expected, and certainly he has a good deal of the genius of oratory about him, and sometimes the divine spark — he is a man possessed and he often carried one away. Questions were asked him of all kinds at the end. He did not flinch and had a wonderful way of leaping to his feet and answering with great spirit and manliness.'

The immediate observation of another woman, the sister of William Clarke of Fabian history, confirms Miss Gladstone and makes additions. 'Confronting what promised to be a very hostile audience he stood like a lion at bay,' this lady felt, 'and fairly cowed his opponents. Evidently he carried a great part of his audience with him, for I think Cambridge has been undergoing a great awakening lately, with regard to the working section of society.' Already societies for the discussion of social questions were rising in the university.

Poor George went on to London played out. But after seeing a doctor and getting a bromide of potassium to break the chronic sleeplessness, he rushed back to Glasgow for an extra meeting or two. At this point of moving ahead with the Land Restoration League, he received a letter from Davitt which put a kind of Irish blessing on concentrating for the present in Scotland. 'We Irish people are too prone to man worship to lead a movement of ideas,' he said, and predicted that the new Land Restoration League would 'become a big movement, and in my opinion the Land Reform Union people should have thrown their lot with it and have one great movement for Great Britain.' Davitt's approval of what was actually happening was all that George could want, for the present, from the Irish side.

He had planned to have a free month for a trip to the Continent before going home, but under pressure the time melted away. Harry went to France alone. George's last month, after the flying return to Glasgow at mid-March, went into more lectures at Hull and Birmingham, with about a fortnight at the end in London. He needed to see people and conclude business, and there was much to do.

The last week in London was like no other in his life up until then. He went to Parliament one day and found himself 'treated with distinguished consideration,' as he told Annie. Mr. Walter Wren had him to dinner again at the Liberal Club. He called on Philip Wicksteed, and another day on Hyndman, and on still another day lunched with General Booth of the Salvation Army, whom he enjoyed more than he expected. We have no date, but this seems to have been the time when he was introduced to Cardinal Manning. It was an emotional event. 'I loved the people, and that love brought me to Christ as their best friend and teacher,' George is remembered as saying. And the churchman reformer had replied, 'I loved Christ, and so learned to love the people for whom he died.'

At top level of London Society, Lady Stepney, who had been Mary Gladstone's companion in reading *Progress and Poverty,* had George to tea. She gathered again the Cambridge group, Miss Gladstone, Professor Stuart, Arthur Lyttelton, and this time Herbert Gladstone also. Again Miss Gladstone, who by her own story had very recently tackled her father 'on female suffrage and nationalisation of land,' and had talked Henry George with Alfred Milner, gives a lively account of British behavior vis-à-vis the American. 'Herbert and Prof. Stuart chief questioners and examiners, Alfred L listening and putting in much sympathizing with Mr. George. A great success for they much liked and softened towards the good little man, and as to Maggie [the hostess] she was converted.' By next day the guest of honor had forgotten Lady Stepney's name, but was not so wrong, it seems, in writing Annie that the younger Gladstone group was 'at least three-quarters with me.'

In a few days before 6 April, George made the concluding speeches of the visit. At a large meeting in Shoreditch Hall and at a hotel meeting of London Scots, he urged that Scotland was now as ready for leadership in reform as ever in the past; and at a farewell banquet by the Land Restoration League, in Piccadilly, he heard Stewart Headlam praise him for having applied religion and the moral sense to public affairs.

Acting on an invitation arranged by Michael Davitt, he went off to Dublin for his one appearance in Ireland. On 13 April he sailed from Queenstown for home.

–6–

Without affecting the British story we may withhold until a later chapter, as we did George's American months between the Irish trip and the trip just accounted for, the narrative of home events from April until November 1884. George's third British visit, made in the service of the Land Restoration League and spent all, except for a few days, wholly in Scotland, makes a two-month codicil to the history of the second visit rather than a separate story. Thereafter a break does occur, and the later visits in Britain — of 1888, 1889, and 1891, two of them very brief and incidental — belong to a different period of George's career and influence.

At the moment of departure, and during the months of his absence from Britain, he was treated to a cross fire of criticism such as he had never before received on either side of the water. Whereas the biggest guns of British criticism had blasted at him, or rather at *Progress and Poverty*, during the year 1883 while George was in the United States, now the firing was more closely aimed and quite as difficult to take. Partly this occurred in the reviews of *Social Problems,* and partly the fusillades were simply the old effort to thrust his ideas out of Britain. The *Saturday Review* in a series of editorials piled up peculiarly strong invective; the article against

land nationalization by Samuel Smith of Liverpool — who had refused George's challenge to a public debate — was reprinted from
the *Contemporary Review* and distributed; Mr. Mallock's writings
in the *Quarterly Review* and *National Review* were gathered
into the book of counterblast, *Property and Progress,* as already
mentioned. In 1885 appeared Robert Scott Moffat's shorter but
stronger book-size criticism.

Meanwhile the friendly publishing house, Reeves, in some sense
replied by bringing out a hundred-page biography, the first ever
written of Henry George. Dedicated 'In Remembrance of the Campaign of 1884,' and saluting him as a 'Columbus in Social Science,'
the book did a fair job of telling George's personal history. It made
bitter point of how London halls had been closed to him during the
latter part of the 1884 visit; and it classified him as Christian socialist
and gradual land nationalizer.

Henry George made a general policy of refusing to reply to criticisms. But the April 1884 issue of the *Nineteenth Century,* which
thus far had paid no attention to his work, reached him on the eve
of sailing for America, and it contained a unique challenge. The
lead article on 'The Prophet of San Francisco' was as packed with
irony as its title; and the author, the Duke of Argyll, was one of the
greatest of the great landholders of Scotland. In San Francisco days
George had known of the duke as social theorist and had admired
his *Reign of Law;* and by 1884 he must have known of him also as
an intimate of Gladstone, a holder of the highest offices, and as the
mighty Whig who had resigned from the Liberal cabinet in 1881
when the advanced Irish land law went through. Argyll had made
himself spokesman for his class at that time, saying that the act
which would reduce Irish landlords threatened landholding in
both kingdoms.

George's followers of the Scottish Land Restoration League
begged him to reply to the article. They were pretty practical advisers: the duke was titular chief of the clan of Campbell; his peer-
age stood close to royalty; he offered a perfect symbol of what
George attacked — a debate with him would carry the question of
the land into every household in Scotland. George agreed. He
worked at his reply late the night before he sailed, and then decided
to 'take it to New York and polish it like a steel shot.' Under the
title 'The "Reduction of Iniquity" ' one envisages George's pride

as author quite as much as one recognizes his sense of the timing and tactics of publicity. The reply was published in the July issue of the *Nineteenth Century.*

Yet, though the opposed articles of noblemen and visitor to Scotland made the most telling exchange of George's lifetime of controversy, it would not be correct to report them as a debate. Using the vehicle of irony, Argyll discovered contradictions in George's two books: Malthus rejected, yet much argument based on a presumption of surplus population; the corruption of democracy asserted, yet a policy of vesting huge properties in a people's government. Inveighing against the American's wish to confiscate property rights in land as truly communistic, the duke — in his final 'reduction to iniquity' — condemned all George wrote as contrary to moral sense. Argyll asserted throughout the superiority of private over public ownership; and he envisaged, as he illustrated from his own estates, the beneficial necessity of large owners making improvements, and of unpropertied workers cultivating the soil — the familiar hierarchical order of society approved. If not a national it was a class attitude which Argyll brilliantly, condescendingly, and yet attractively displayed.

George equaled his opponent's brilliance. To contradict the peer's assertion of what landlords do to improve soil and village, capital and community, George asserted his personal observations of poverty in Skye, the terror of landlords across Scotland, and the degradation of workers — all of them ultimate payers of rents — in Glasgow and Edinburgh. The reformer had his own vein of irony which might be considered of the Jacksonian variety. Stating the presumption of equality, he asked his Scottish adversary as mental exercise to 'put the bodies of a duke and a peasant on a dissecting-table, and bring, if you can, the surgeon who by laying bare the brain or examining the viscera, can tell which is duke and which is peasant.'

George's friends at least thought that he had won handsomely the exchange of fire. They reprinted the two articles together, 'Property in Land' or 'The Peer and the Prophet,' in a half a dozen or so editions in London, New York, and Copenhagen; and they happily adopted 'The Prophet of San Francisco' as a favorite designation of their own. For years we shall find the author discovering people, William Lloyd Garrison II among them, who were first attracted to Henry George when they happened to read the *Nineteenth Century* article.

In the United States during October, two months after the article appeared, the author received two summonses from Britain, and he accepted both. When Michael Davitt asked, George cabled an article for the first issue of the London *Democrat,* a half-penny paper the Irish leader was starting with Miss Taylor and Saunders and Durant. Simultaneously he accepted the invitation of the Land Restoration League for a second series of public appearances in Scotland.

Another winter trip confronted him. George sailed in November, again taking Harry and leaving the ladies of the family behind, with arrangements too hastily made and too incomplete to be very satisfactory. When he went aboard the *Germanic* details of his speaking schedule, payment, and even the question whether or not he would go first to Glasgow or run down to London were all unsettled. But he departed in confidence. He had written no lectures, he wrote Annie, but was ready to improvise according to the occasion. On the voyage he enjoyed especially the electric light over his berth, apparently his first experience of the new invention.

From Liverpool he did go first to London. He discovered to his anxiety that his first address would be in St. James Hall, the scene of his initial triumph the year before. He wanted no small audience now, no anti-climax, and he worried that the management had not done enough about publicity. But the worst that occurred was a thin attendance in the expensive seats. Miss Taylor spoke especially well, he thought, and Davitt and the president of the Scottish Land Restoration League the same; and he believed that his own address set off the campaign with enthusiasm. Presently he was able to send home $220, but he warned Annie to go slow in paying for new furniture. 'How would you like to have me take charge of a first-class paper in Glasgow or London?' he asked his wife. That question was up again, momentarily.

The trip through Scotland, involving nearly thirty stops, only two of them in Edinburgh and only three in Glasgow, lacked the exhilaration of the previous year's schedule. The pace was hard again. Working north through the smaller cities, he had to speak from seventy-five minutes to two hours and a half each night; and he was annoyed by the thought that his management had done a slovenly job of publicizing and arranging. He had to accept as inevitable the fact that his kind of lecture might fill the cheap seats, but the expensive ones almost never. He noticed and resented that the newspapers and news agencies pretty well disregarded him — boycotted him, rather — during this trip.

On the brighter side he had the satisfaction of understanding his audiences better and of improving his acquaintanceship with the conditions of the country. He remembered a lesson learned in embarrassment the year before, that political talks were not acceptable on Sundays. This time he made a custom of his lecture on 'Moses' for Sunday-evening and other appropriate occasions — and he was now ready to speak on 'The Eighth Commandment' and two or three other Biblical topics in addition. In Glasgow he was pleased to have 'intelligent working class' people in his audience, and in the capital city, an 'aristocratic element.' There was a very special satisfaction in lecturing in Argyll's domain. He had a glimpse of agrarian rioting in the west country; and he did some pleasant sight-seeing in Abbotsford and Melrose in the south.

Back in London by the tenth of January, George turned painfully anxious and homesick. He yearned for old days in California. He felt pride in his achievement, yet doubted that it was substantial; and he worried about his future as breadwinner. 'I have at last attained what I have always believed was in my power. This trip has aided in my development and I think that I am now a *first-class* speaker,' he wrote his wife. 'But I don't believe that the time has come when I can utilize this on the lecture platform. The people who make the paying audiences want to be amused. I feel as though I cannot count on lecturing.' He was worried not for the propaganda success of the trip but for the security of his family.

During the week before 24 January, his last abroad, George spoke at important places: London, Manchester, Liverpool, Glasgow, and Belfast. 'I expect that in spite of the boycott you'll hear something of this by telegram,' he wrote home in renewed excitement.

In respect of social drama the last appearance in London outdid all others. The lord mayor refused the Guildhall, but a mass meeting was arranged for a Saturday afternoon, in front of the Royal Exchange. According to estimate 7000 workmen, perhaps most of them unemployed, turned out. Stewart Headlam and two other clergymen spoke; so did William Saunders and three representatives of labor — a tailor, a shoemaker, and a joiner. George himself brought a roar from the crowd when he pointed to the inscription carved in the granite of the Exchange, 'The Earth is the Lord's.' 'Aye, the landlords',' Henry George went on.

That same afternoon, in what seems to have been staging for effect and symbol, socialists of the Hyndman-Morris inclination held a meeting of their own near by. They so distributed their literature, and so arranged their speakers as not to compete with George, but to increase the size of the day's demonstration. Thus George's departure from the London scene exhibited his idea and the Marxist idea carrying on together, the one stimulating the other. The socialist paper, *Justice,* wished the visitor Godspeed.

In Belfast, the capital of Protestant Ulster, perhaps 4000 crowded the hall to hear George address the new Irish Land Restoration League. The affair proved somewhat disgraceful, however, with a chair-throwing episode at the end.

But the important thing — in Belfast, London, Glasgow, and the other cities the same — was mass participation. With new ideas of social justice, new practices of social politics, too, were being born in the British Isles. Henry George's role was shifting to that of midwife to social democracy.

–7–

One more event, which occupied one of his very last hours in London, exhibits in intellectual light George's still continuing sense of parallelism between himself and his leading Marxist contemporary. On invitation from the *Nineteenth Century,* George and Henry Hyndman met to do a dialogue on 'Socialism and Rent Appropriation,' for publication in that magazine. They had no time to do more than dictate to a stenographer.

Of course they diverged somewhat. Hyndman charged George with relying too much on land nationalization, and asserted in socialist style that truly the landlord plays the humble role of sleeping partner, in contrast to the aggressiveness of capitalists. Hyndman denied the validity of the idea of 'natural rights.' Henry George countered according to his opposite ideas. And yet he accepted still the identification of land nationalization with his own cause; and he agreed — as he had said in the San Francisco newspapers, and less clearly in *Progress and Poverty* but very clearly in *Social Problems* — that certain industries ought to be socialized. Thus the dialogue ended in a sizable and practical concurrence between two men who knew their moral ideas to be far apart. George credited the socialists with helping to break down complacency about poverty, much as Marx and Hyndman from their side credited him.

Yet there is considerable paradox that the author of *Progress and Poverty* should have maintained a common front with the Social Democratic Federation people, through his first three visits to England, while he failed to make substantial, if any, connection with other socialists whose deeper ideas were much more like his own. By the time of his second visit the Fabian Society had begun to gather — Shaw and Olivier among them. Probably George knew of their group. The evidence is slight and seems to represent a tenuous connection.

But of his enormous influence among them there can be no doubt. To add to Bernard Shaw's impression, we have the authoritative testimony, first, of Sidney Webb. That scholarly leader's little book of 1890, *Socialism in England,* credits the 'optimistic and confident tone' of George's writing, and 'the irresistible force of its popularization of Ricardo's law of Rent' with having 'sounded the dominant "note" ' of Fabianism. Webb credits George with having reached also Britain's none too easily indoctrinated trade unionists. 'Instead of the Chartist cry of "Back to the Land," still adhered to by rural laborers and belated politicians,' said Sidney and Beatrice Webb in 1894, 'the town artisan is thinking of his claim to the unearned increment of urban land values, which he now watches falling into the coffers of great landlords.'

As Webb estimated the influence of George's Ricardianism, Edward R. Pease, the member of the Fabian Society who became its historian, asserted the power that George's political philosophy gave to reform in England. It was the American's gift to British social thought, testifies Mr. Pease, to insist that a 'tremendous revolution was to be accomplished by a political method, applicable by a majority of the voters, and capable of being drafted as an Act of Parliament by any competent lawyer. To George belongs the extraordinary merit of recognizing the right way of social salvation . . . From Henry George I think it may be taken that the early Fabians learned to associate the new gospel with the old political methods.'

In other words: *Progress and Poverty*'s moral sequence and its economic syllogism, both, took hold in non-Marxian circles favorable to labor.

The most immediate practical results occurred, as was natural in the structure of British politics, not as a result of trade-union or Fabian efforts but through the pro-labor 'Lib Lab' movement among the Radicals of the Liberal party. Shortly after George's third visit a parliamentary commission on housing for the working classes reported the economic and public-health conditions of the industrial cities. It was a two-party commission. Sir Charles Dilke, Joseph Chamberlain's associate in Radical leadership, was chairman; from the Conservatives, Salisbury was a member, and two or three others voted with him in dissent from the commission's more radical recommendations. Cardinal Manning was the one member who almost surely had had personal and sympathetic contact with Henry George. But the memorandum of Mr. Jesse Collings — an associate of Chamberlain, and future writer in favor of 'three acres and a cow' — contains a strong plea which indicates more plainly than anything else in the report that George's ideas had been assimilated by parliamentary Radicals.

In the main report itself the crucial evidence of Georgism was the recommendation, urged by Mr. Collings and supported by a majority, that vacant city funds be taxed at a rate of say 4 per cent on capital value, and that the proceeds be used as capital to be invested in public housing. This proposal to shift taxes from the income of land to the capital value of land, known as the American system, would have been an innovation in Britain; and to propose a tax rate at a level at all near the interest rate on capital was of course to enter entirely within the premises and expectations of land-value taxation.

For 1885 the report signifies that Henry George's ideas had reached farther into the policy making of Parliament than they ever had into the policy of the legislature of California. And a few years later, when high urban-land taxes were actually imposed to finance slum improvement in London (though rating-levels were not put up to what Henry George asked), Herbert Spencer cried that the American radical had quietly conquered Parliament.

Twelve years after George's third British visit, in the year of his death but written in no expectation of that event, J. A. Hobson, the distinguished liberal economist and journalist, never a socialist, wrote for the *Fortnightly Review* an appraisal of 'The Influence of Henry George in England.' The article's sweep of course includes the later visits which identified George with British Radicalism, opposed him to Hyndman socialism, and built some bridges of light traffic with the Fabians. But nearly everything that Hobson said could have been said of the influence of the author of *Progress and Poverty* and *Social Problems* without regard for his later books, and of the public speaker of 1882, 1884, and 1885. After more than half a century Hobson's authority is still good, and his findings command endorsement.

'The real importance of Henry George,' wrote Hobson, 'is derived from the fact that he was able to drive an abstract notion, that of economic rent, into the minds of "practical" men, and generate therefrom a social movement . . . Keenly intelligent, generous and sympathetic, his nature contained that obstinacy which borders on fascination, and which is rightly recognized as essential to the missionary . . .

'Although the thinking members of the working classes had never thoroughly accepted [the] *laisser faire* theory of the doctrinaire radical and the political free trader, they had unconsciously absorbed some of its complacency and its disbelief in the need for governmental action. Henry George shook this complacency, and, what is more, he gave definiteness to the feeling of discontent by assigning an easily intelligible economic cause . . . years of gradually deepening depression brought rural land questions more and more to the front and that divorcement of the people from the soil, which formed the kernel of the social problem according to George, assumed increasing prominence . . . Moreover, George's ability enabled him to fully utilise that advantage which land grievances possess over most other economic issues, their susceptibility to powerful concrete local illustration . . .

'But George's true influence is not rightly measured by the small following of theorists who impute to landlords their supreme power of monopoly. Large numbers who would not press this extreme contention are disciples of Henry George because they regard unqualified private ownership of land to be the most obviously unjust and burdensome feature in our present social economy. The spirit of humanitarian and religious appeal which suffuses *Progress and*

Poverty wrought powerfully upon a large section of what I may call typical English moralists. In my lectures upon Political Economy about the country, I have found in almost every centre a certain little knot of men of the lower-middle or upper-working class, men of grit and character, largely self-educated, keen citizens, mostly noncomformists in religion, to whom Land Nationalisation, taxation of unearned increment, or other radical reforms of land tenure, are doctrines resting on plain moral sanction. These free-trading Radical dissenters regard common ownership of and equal access to the land as a "natural right," essential to individual freedom. It is this attitude of mind which serves to explain why, when both theoretic students of society and the man in the street regard Land Nationalisation as a first and a large step in the direction of Socialism, organized Socialists regard the followers of Henry George with undisguised hostility and contempt . . .

'No doubt it is easy to impute excessive influence to the mouthpiece of a rising popular sentiment. George, like other prophets, cooperated with the "spirit of the age." But after this first allowance has been made, Henry George may be considered to have exercised a more directly powerful formative and educative influence over English radicalism of the last fifteen years than any other man.'

XIV

Not Without Honor in His Own Land

1882–1886

AFTER each of his three visits to the British Isles in the early '80s, Henry George came home convinced that he had started a movement of ideas and politics that would change history. He was naturally proud that *Progress and Poverty* had now broken all records as the most widely distributed and read book in economic literature, and he believed it to be the most influential one since the *Wealth of Nations*. In retrospect George thought that he had succeeded in bringing to his own point of view every lecture audience he had addressed in Britain, excepting only the two at Oxford and Cambridge. His fondest memories of public speaking overseas were the first meeting in St. James Hall, at the opening of the great tour of 1884, and the meeting at Liverpool, when he conquered the resistance that had been specifically prepared against him. As he entered and re-entered the life of opinion making in the United States of James G. Blaine and Grover Cleveland, he had the reassurance of knowing that the England of Gladstone and Joseph Chamberlain in some degree belonged to him.

His first British success, however, did not prepare him for the welcome he received when he returned to New York from Ireland in October 1882. At the moment he was two months out of the Irish 'bastille,' those few hours of detention, and a month or more past the thrilling review of *Progress and Poverty* and *The Irish Land Question* in *The Times*. Certain elements in the greeting may

417

fairly be attributed to a change in the climate of American opinion, to some new awareness in the country of underlying tensions and economic injustices. Perhaps there is no better symbol of this, apart from George himself, than the emerging voice of Henry Demarest Lloyd. During the summer of 1882 a famous article in the *Atlantic Monthly*, 'The Political Economy of Seventy Three Million Dollars,' advanced that lawyer a sizable step toward his powerful book of the next decade, *Wealth versus Commonwealth*. Plainly a conscience-stricken state of mind was represented by certain educated-class elements which helped celebrate Henry George's return in 1882.

The lead in celebration was taken by Irish partisans. People in the office of the *Irish World* assumed charge but were careful to include non-Irish elements. Felix Adler and one or two others from the Ethical Culture Society shared in the planning; and, in the name of all that he considered appropriate, Mr. Adler urged against extravagance. 'Why waste all that money on a banquet? Why not use it to buy a library for Mr. George?' But others wanted a splash; and Louis Post favored such an event as would make publicity for Henry George.

The group finally agreed on a banquet at Delmonico's. This proved to be the second but principal event of the welcome home. The first was managed by the Central Labor Union of New York, of which Mr. Post was the legal counselor, and which four years later would be the instrument of bringing Henry George into his greatest political campaign. On 20 October the CLU gave its own reception in Cooper Union's somewhat church-like auditorium. Banners for 'Land, the Common Property of the People,' were hung on the walls; a trades-union man spoke; and the returning hero replied that the flame had been lighted, 'the fire is burning on, and in a few months there will be a great movement all over the civilized world.'

Nothing was spared for the banquet next evening. Many prominent men signed the invitation. Besides Patrick Ford, Louis Post, and Thomas Shearman, who must have been the moving spirits, Henry Ward Beecher and Thomas Kinsella, preacher and editor, both from Brooklyn, and R. A. Pryor, then a lawyer and later a judge, were on the committee. So were Heber Newton, George van Slyck, Cameron King, and David C. Croly. The last named was an editor and leading American Positivist, and was the husband of a better-known social radical, and the father of the later editor and writer, Herbert Croly. The invitation announced that the sponsors did not all endorse George's remedy for a social evil, but that all did wish to give testimonial to his 'personal worth,' to his sympathy for mankind, and to the intellectual vigor of his book.

As Louis Post had feared would happen, the guest of honor arrived late, nearly an hour late, and his shoes lacked polish. The guests were lined up, 170 strong, and were presented to him by Algernon Sullivan, lawyer and wit of the city. 'How did you get them to come?' George hissed at Louis Post, when opportunity offered. When at last the company was seated they were rewarded with twenty-eight items of food and drink, according to the menu card in French. It was a Delmonico's party done in the style of that day, and the charge was $10 a person.

Stories are told of the evening's cross-purposes and confusions. 'What part of Ireland does this man George come from?' one guest was heard to inquire. Mr. Post himself believed that of the several speakers only a minority, William Saunders over from London, and Thomas Shearman and Thomas Kinsella, had any comprehension of the man they praised. Post thought that Henry Ward Beecher did not, nor did Representative Perry Belmont, or two justices of the Supreme Court of New York state, or others.

Happily the event did not frighten George out of enjoying the situation in more ways than one. There is suspicion of irony blended with the flow of conviction in the speech in which the hero of Loughrea admonished this particular circle to consider, 'gentlemen, how this city would grow, how enormously wealth would increase, if all taxes were abolished which now bear on the production and accumulation and exchange of wealth. Consider how the vacant spaces on the island would fill up, could land not improved be improved by him who wanted to improve it, without the payment of prices now demanded.'

It was 'a good deal like going to sleep and waking up famous,' George wrote Dr. Taylor about the double-headed reception. He felt greatly reassured for the future. He expected to pay his debts and live well, he confessed to this most intimate friend. He planned to settle in New York but travel much, and to keep Harry as secretary and general assistant.

George had known before leaving Ireland that the channels for distributing *Progress and Poverty,* which had opened just before he left the States, had actually carried much traffic in 1882. The New York *Truth* had made good its commitment to publish serially; and in May of that year the Chicago *Express,* with a circulation he was told of 100,000, undertook the same thing. Meanwhile, over and above Mr. Francis Shaw's first free distribution of *Progress and Poverty* to the libraries, and beyond the subsidy he and his brother had given for English publication, the Shaws were making further contributions. Quincy Adams Shaw paid for 1382 copies of *The Irish Land Question* and for the same number of copies of *Progress and Poverty,* put into a special binding, to be sent gratis to members of the rather elite Society for Political Education.

Overseas George had demurred at first, at this last allocation. He considered the society too much a Professor Sumner and David Ames Wells kind of organization; and the only comfort he could derive was to think how 'very annoying' the gift would be to Sumner, whom George of course knew to be the one who had 'sat down on the book in an anonymous diatribe in *Scribner's.*' But in the month of Loughrea and Athenry the result proved more desirable than a professor's irritation: a Boston paper reported the quiet fact that the Shaw family was subsidizing *Progress and Poverty.*

Excellent, wrote George. 'You have kicked up a row. And of all the things we want to do, to kick up a row is first and foremost. For when the row begins those who most bitterly oppose us serve the cause the most.' He chuckled at the thought that the people at home should know that the ' "Socialistic seducer" of the Society for the Propagation of Sumnerian Political Economy is of the bluest Boston blood.' 'Yes,' agreed Francis Shaw at last, 'Yes, nothing could have been more fortunate than the Boston *Daily Advertiser* episode. It has set a good many people reading *Progress and Poverty,* and opened an entrance into New England much wider.'

Presently the death of Francis Shaw affected Henry George in much the same way his life had. George received a legacy of $1000 early in 1883. It was the first such event in his life, and very timely. For, contrary to hopes that had mounted while he was in Ireland and had seemed to be encouraged by the welcome home, neither book royalties nor lecture fees amounted to much that winter. The legacy 'puts me at ease,' George wrote Dr. Taylor, on 17 January. 'I shall use it in the way I know he intended it — to give me some leisure to do some writing — and hope that before that time is gone I shall have my feet well under me. What a curious life mine is — literally from hand to mouth; and yet always a way seems to open.'

After his benefactor's death, ways kept opening for George's ideas, partly on Mr. Shaw's account. Among many letters of early 1883, none can have stirred Henry George more deeply than one from Elizabeth Peabody, who was then nearly eighty. This associate of Channing and Parker, Emerson and Alcott, one who had had a distinguished career of her own in educational reform and thought, wrote that though she had studied political economy all her life, 'I never obtained satisfaction until I read your *Progress and Poverty* recently, incited to it by learning that Francis G. Shaw died happy because the book was in the world . . . But I am almost afraid to say how it has cleared up my mind, how clear has become what has ever appeared to me a muddy science, for it seems almost too good to be true that the tremendous conundrum of poverty increasing with the progress of civilization is solved.'

While there are no other letters to compare with the historical interest of Miss Peabody's, many either had personal meaning or else indicated the spread of George's ideas on the wave fanning out from Britain and Ireland. There were several from California. James McClatchy, disregarding the fact that George still owed him money, sent $20 with an order for as many copies of *Progress and Poverty* as that amount would buy; and an anonymous buyer ordered 100 copies sent to a certain labor leader in San Francisco. Others in his old home city wanted him to return to California for a lecture tour; but now as earlier, Dr. Taylor advised him to stick to his desk. Requests from California always stirred and tempted George, but evidently the way in which he had been rejected in that state, at the time of the constitutional convention and when *Progress and Poverty* was published, affected him permanently, for after 1881 he did not return until a decade had passed and it precisely suited his convenience to do so.

The Middle West, which had been the region of weakest response to George's book before the British missions, now showed signs of stirring interest. A Presbyterian clergyman of Toledo wrote that there were 'few earnest men' in that city who had not read *Progress and Poverty;* and he was sure that the same could be said of all five states of the old Northwest — Ohio, Indiana, Illinois, Michigan, and Wisconsin. From Detroit, Joseph Labadie, the philosophical anarchist, inquired whether George would come to attend some meetings and to give some speeches. From St. Louis, after George had gone there for an address, came back word that the *Post-Dispatch* had called *Progress and Poverty* the most remarkable work ever published in political economy.

On the eastern side of the hemisphere, from places as widely separated as Lake Ontario and the valley of the La Plata, George received communications which stated appreciation, in the lift of the wave from Britain, and which sometimes hinted possibilities for future action. A number of congratulations came from Canada: one was from Professor Le Seuer of Ottawa, who invited a second lecture visit. And, far away, an Irish medical man, Dr. John Creagher of Buenos Aires, launched a correspondence in which he urged that *Progress and Poverty* be translated into Spanish, and said that the book would surely have a great effect in Argentina. From near home, George received greetings that told him of interest in every area of society. For example, he heard from E. T. Peters, the sympathetic economist and statistician; he had an invitation to Bridgeport from a barely literate member of the Knights of Labor; and he received a prim invitation to attend a Sunday *soirée* in Farmington and to see the sights of that lovely town.

The letter from farthest afield, from the old friend in the legation at Peking, was the one that carried the most specific — and ultimately acceptable — career advice. 'What you want for your views is *light*,' said John Russell Young. The *Irish World* might represent 'a passion,' but it was not a proper vehicle for George in the future, this adviser believed. He suggested that the author of *Progress and Poverty* start a weekly of his own. Young admitted that he could make no confident predictions. He guessed humorously that by the time of coming home in 1885 he might discover Henry George jailed or hanged as a revolutionary, or else seated in the United States Senate. He would do what he could, he promised not very hopefully, to have *Progress and Poverty* translated into Chinese.

Though in one sense Henry George's actual position was about as wide open as it looked from China, the radical-at-home did of course have certain attachments and certain practical things to do, which gave his life a degree of continuity. Here as in Great Britain there were always publishers in the forefront of his planning; and as of this year it would be hard to say which was more pressing, the business he had to do to keep *Progress and Poverty* moving, or the work of new writing he wanted most of all to tackle. Even before he undertook a one-week speaking tour in December, less than two months after arrival home, he received a fresh offer for new low-cost editions.

This came from John W. Lovell, who headed the publishing house bearing his own name, and who wanted to bring out a twenty-cent *Progress and Poverty* in the paper-bound Lovell's Library. He himself sympathized with the working-class movement and was personally interested in the socialist community at Sinaloa, Mexico. His proposal would not reduce the American price quite as low as the English one; but, like the English cheap edition, it involved a simultaneous publication of *The Irish Land Question* — to which George now gave its permanent title, *The Land Question.*

There is a suggestion that George was the readier to go ahead with Lovell because he felt that Appleton was not energetic, or not successful enough, in pushing sales. The result appeared in February 1883 as number fifty-two in the Lovell series, a *Progress and Poverty* in very plain dress. Sales did prove large we are told; but there are no records of whether this edition reached the quarter-million mark Lovell predicted, and of how much the author received in the way of royalties, at the 10 per cent agreed upon.

In the spring the question of more translations of *Progress and Poverty* came up. When the editor of the New York Swedish paper, *Svenska Arbitaren,* wanted to publish as a booklet the Henry George articles he had recently run, translated from the weekly *Leslie's,* the author tried to negotiate a Swedish translation of his principal work. Perhaps these exchanges explain the edition that was actually published in Upsala in 1884. Meanwhile George's old friend and first translator urged an American German-language edition. It should be done in Roman characters, Gütschow advised, echoing Lovell, and it could be made to undersell the imported Staude edition. Gütschow argued that the election of 1880 had proved the importance of the German vote, and that George should not be discouraged that German socialists did not like him, for the

socialists represented no more than a small minority of the immigrant Germans. Sound advice or unsound, the German-language
edition of *Progress and Poverty* was never published in America.

–2–

The situations and developments described above may be characterized, all of them, as the passive side of Henry George's history
after the tour in Ireland and England. They tell of recent events
making the man: a man more recognized, more in demand, than
ever before in his life in the United States. But they tell nothing
of his own reaction to the reaction, or of the active intellect and
strategist of social reconstruction. How was he envisaging his obligations and opportunities, now that he was world famous?

Part of the answer is to be found in the persons and groups he
chose as followers, from among those who came forward to befriend
him or seek his help. Another part is to be discovered in his new
writing — in the ideas and policies he felt most ready and anxious
to advance. Immediately, and apparently without benefit of invitation from any publisher, he set to work on the book he had long
intended, an attack on industrial monopoly and a defense of free-
trade policy. Three years later he would develop from this beginning a powerful manifesto, his second or third most important writing, *Protection or Free Trade*. But from first to last this effort was
bedeviled by obstacles and misfortunes, and the first difficulty was
the not unpleasant one of being requested to do other things. Before year's end, 1882, magazines on both sides of the Atlantic were
asking for special articles. In close succession the *Contemporary
Review*, the *North American Review*, and the weekly *Frank Leslie's
Illustrated Newspaper* all made requests.

For the *North American*, to which it will be recalled he had
contributed in 1881, he did two articles. The first, which was published in March, concerned 'Money in Elections'; it broadened out,
from decade-old editorials in the San Francisco *Post* and from his
similar article in the *Overland Monthly*, the writer's argument that
the Australian secret ballot was needed in America to help defeat
the political machines. Eastern cities were the worst seats of political corruption, he now asserted, but state governments in the West
were about as bad. 'Sparsely settled Nevada is notoriously a rotten
borough,' observed this old associate of Senator Jones, 'and Kansas,

Nebraska, Colorado, and other new states are little better.' In respect of political ethics, old Britain was more truly democratic than America, George now believed.

The second *North American* article of 1883, 'Overproduction,' was published in December. It renewed from *Progress and Poverty* his stern criticism of those who would use that idea as the explanation — and the explaining away — of depressions, and of course renewed also his proposition of land-value taxation as the answer. The two articles together may be thought of as bridging the gap between George's first writing for this magazine and his several articles of 1885 and 1886, when the *North American* began to look surprisingly much like a regular outlet for Henry George.

While in the *North American* the reformer of 1883 seems to be a man gaining in strength and acceptability, in *Leslie's,* a more popular magazine, he appears in the role of insurgent. During the early months of the year, *Harper's Weekly,* the rival of *Leslie's,* ran a series by William Graham Sumner — connected essays on contemporary history. Immediately gathered and reprinted under the still-remembered book title, *What Social Classes Owe to Each Other,* Sumner's commentary is well described by his biographer as setting forth 'with extraordinary coldness' the professor's full conception of *laisser faire;* and Professor Hofstadter characterizes Sumner's ideas at this stage as the most uncompromising example of Social Darwinism in the history of that movement.

The Yale sociologist named few books or persons whose ideas he opposed, but from first to last he condemned any and all who wanted the government to regulate social conditions; and many passages indicate that he bore *Progress and Poverty* specifically in mind. Entirely in line with the *Scribner's* review in 1881, Sumner's ideas on the nature of civilization differed completely from the egalitarianism and from the plea for religion as an influence toward co-operation that are voiced in *Progress and Poverty.* In quite as extreme a degree as William Mallock, though of course from the roots of a more individualistic defense of property, Professor Sumner represented the rejection of Henry George by the mind which all but officially spoke for America's prevailing current of social thought.

Henry George's invitation from *Leslie's* did not contemplate a debate with Sumner, nor did he try such a thing. He was asked simply to prepare a series of articles on general questions related to capital and labor, and to the condition of the people. A competitive venture rather than a controversy was the proposition, and naturally it appealed to him. When he learned that Sumner was being paid $50 apiece for his articles, George demanded and received $100 for his own. *Leslie's* contracted for thirteen essays.

As a preliminary the magazine gave him a good announcement on 31 March and printed a striking portrait. *Leslie's* even endorsed *Progress and Poverty* to the point of saying that it had 'not merely shaken to their very foundation theories previously accepted, but it has popularized, and is popularizing, political economy as previous to its publication would not have been possible.' George's essays would be called 'Problems of the Times.' With such a send-off, the series appeared in late spring. Then, like Sumner's, the essays were published as a book, early the following winter. Belford, Clarke and Company, a Chicago house, brought it out, under the title *Social Problems;* and, as we have seen, Kegan Paul followed suit. On both sides of the water the book made money for the author.

Although a British reviewer was not wrong in observing that *Social Problems* presented again the main ideas of *Progress and Poverty,* the more important fact in the context of 1883 is that this book marked a shift in the author's emphasis which accorded with his present location in the industrial Northeast, and with his interest and connections in Great Britain. For the first time since working out his larger economic ideas in the San Francisco *Post,* he made a strong statement of his opposition to private industrial monopoly, and of his belief in public ownership. In the autobiography of Henry Hyndman, where the ultimate judgments of George are very adverse, the socialist was nevertheless pleased to claim part of the credit for George's having written *Social Problems,* and pleased to say that in this one book there exists a certain beginning of socialistic wisdom never quite fulfilled by the writer. What Hyndman did not know, of course, and what few readers of Henry George's books have known, is that, though the emphasis on the socialization of industry is light in *Progress and Poverty,* the author had actually been consistent for sixteen years in asserting that natural industrial monopolies ought to be publicly owned and operated. In that degree George had long been a state socialist; and now, as he considered private corporations becoming larger and mightier than sovereign states, he stated the possibility that 'a revolutionary uprising might be necessary to turn out the praetorians who were doing the corporations' bidding in government office.'

To his notion of California days, of what the nation-size natural monopolies actually were, the telegraph system and the railroads, he added the telephone; and, discussing the local monopolies natural in the economy of the modern city, he added electricity to the items previously specified, which were water, heat, and gas. In these areas George was as ready as anyone for socialization. Though he defended the policy by saying that government ownership involves fewer risks of corruption than private monopolism, he did not abandon his old belief that the number of public enterprises ought to be kept at a minimum. In this line of thought he urged again that lowering the tariff would reduce monopolism and increase competition — an argument which made *Social Problems* a preparation for the book already in process, *Protection or Free Trade.*

In answer to Sumner, whose ideas concerning the tariff were startlingly like his own, the writer in *Leslie's* turned irony on the Yale professor's defense of a social 'elite' in America. Though always qualified about social theory derived from Darwin, George did insert in *Social Problems* the thought — which Professor Eric Goldman calls Reform Darwinism — that biological and social evolution means eternal change; and he observed that in the present hour ancient creeds were dissolving and 'old forces of conservatism' were 'melting away.' He renewed his charge that the churches were too complacent about modern poverty. *Social Problems* was a fighting book. However critical of aggrandizers, professors, clergymen, and others, it was written with confidence that forces powerful in the world were on the author's side.

Not directly with Sumner, but tangentially with a still more imposing economist of Yale derivation, the articles in *Leslie's* stirred up controversy and took a measure of Henry George. It was the fifth essay, on 'The March of Concentration,' which challenged the authority, even the integrity, of General Francis A. Walker, who of course held as high a rank as any American economist. In *Progress and Poverty* he was the admired author of *The Wages Question;* in the academic world he had just become president of the Massachusetts Institute of Technology, and he was president also of the American Statistical Association and would soon be first president of the American Economics Association. A large part of his distinction derived from the service he rendered as director of the United States Census; and it was on account of certain data in the Census of 1880 that the argument between Walker and Henry George began. George did not necessarily try to provoke a fight, but he must have known that he was taking chances when he denounced certain statistics about landholding which had just appeared in the *Compendium* of the recent census.

A parallel-column statement there indicated that the average size of all farms in the United States had dropped from 153 acres in 1870 to 134 acres in 1880. In George's condemnation this piece of information was 'not only inconsistent with facts obvious all over the United States and with the tendencies of agriculture in other countries, such as Great Britain, but it is inconsistent with the returns furnished by the Census Bureau itself.' Whether he knew it or not, George was criticizing General Walker's own personal interpretation of the data, as well as the data themselves. In an article in the *Princeton Review*, which presently was to be reprinted in the census volume on the *Statistics of Agriculture*, the academic man asserted that landholding in the United States was in cold numerical fact 'highly popular,' or democratic according to Jeffersonian aspiration. In criticizing the *Compendium*, George said that it was the more blameworthy because the official averages would be interpreted as confirming popular belief that America was making progress away from land aggregation and toward the goal of the family farm. The census should be doubly careful not to misinform the people in a sensitive area of policy, the critic said.

In the columns of *Leslie's*, General Walker replied in unveiled contempt. Paying no attention to the disparities in the tables of figures to which George referred, he gave a short lesson in how averages are computed, which included the following blundering sentence: 'There has been a greater increase, on the whole, in the number of farms below 153 acres than in the number above 153 acres. And, consequently the average size has been reduced.' He said he would be 'happy to resort to a more elementary statement, illustrated with diagrams, if desired.'

George allowed himself more relish than he might have, in demolishing the census director's careless principles of arithmetic; and then took more space still to elaborate the inconsistencies in the census figures. This reply, and Walker's rebuttal, and Henry George's final word amount to twenty-five book pages. But, half a year later, in the preface of a new census volume, General Walker, not retracting his judgments about landholding, admitted that the earlier figures had contained disparity and error. The *Compendium* placed in parallel columns, as comparable, acreage figures for 1870 and 1880 which should not have been compared — in one instance the cultivated lands of the farms were represented, and in the other the farms' full size. Elsewhere the new volume admitted that the earlier one had not counted fully the large-acreage holdings in the West.

The controversy with Walker ended a clear success for George, but the victory did not lie in any invincible formulations of the trend of American landholding. George's best work in that field lay twelve years buried and forgotten in *Our Land and Land Policy;* and he would venture the subject again, three years later, in an article in the *North American Review*. At that time, though admitting that great holdings were being subdivided, he would insist that increases in land values were more and more favoring the owners, to the disadvantage of the community. Henry George's success in the duel in *Leslie's Magazine* was that he had at last confounded the attitude of contempt and disregard with which scholars in the United States had quite consistently treated him.

Very soon the general himself indicated the change. In May, just coincidentally with the beginning of the argument in *Leslie's,* he was lecturing at Harvard, giving the talks he soon revised into the little book, *Land and Its Rent*. In August — exactly parallel with Sir Henry Fawcett's similar article in the *Macmillan's Magazine* in England — he brought out an article, very nearly the same as a chapter in his forthcoming book, 'Henry George's Social Fallacies.' Really reviewing *Progress and Poverty* this time, General Walker described himself as 'Ricardian of Ricardians' who thought that 'under perfect competition the labourer would become the residual claimant on industry.' The worker and not the landlord. Even considering the actual economic world, where competition is less than perfect, Walker said that the radicals, George most especially because he had been too much influenced by California conditions, had pushed beyond reason the idea that the landholder takes a great share of the product of the economy. Also he made a critical parry against George's general proposition that technological progress raises rent. He answered that modern transport sometimes decreases rents, as when a railroad brings to city market the product of distant fields, and so reduces the value of less fertile agricultural land not so far from the city. On the other hand, at a point where he might have been captious, he acknowledged truth in George's rejection of the wages fund, though it was stated in language much more dogmatic than his own; and he made no serious objection to George's case against Malthusian doctrine.

For the decade of the '80s, the article and chapter could be called the official American academic review of Henry George's main ideas. Not only did Walker state his own objections, but he also cumulated the overseas reviews. Quoting the condemnations of the *Quarterly Review* and the *Edinburgh,* he rejected without sympathy George's affirmation of all men's right to the economic product of land — the moral sequence of *Progress and Poverty.* Comparing recent treatments of rent, he reported a rising scale of radical protest. Leroy-Beaulieu envisaged rent 'as no more than the merest mole on the industrial body,' Walker said; Mill diagnosed 'an open sore, a real, appreciable, and considerable drain on the vitality of the state, which should be checked by stringent surgery and cautery'; while George indicated rent to be 'a cancerous evil . . . with only one possible result and that in no very distant future.' By implication General Walker's own position lay between those of Leroy-Beaulieu and Mill — closer to Mill's but nevertheless far from that of *Progress and Poverty.* Seven years would pass, and the first successes of the single-tax movement be achieved, before George's ideas would again receive such close scrutiny and estimation by any American scholar.

A letter in Henry George's own papers, written by a member of the assembly of Rhode Island and a future governor of that state, suggests a personal reason why Walker changed his attitude toward George. Early in 1883 this reformer, apparently speaking as a friend, told the census director that some economist ought to give *Progress and Poverty* a serious review. So perhaps conscience, or love of controversy, or both effected the change. Dr. Garvin, the Rhode

Islander, wanted George, in turn, to reply to Walker's critique; but Henry George refused.

With so much lightning playing about him, there is no wonder that George felt he must put the *Leslie's* articles into book form without delay. During the run of the contracted series, moreover, the magazine's editorial page had turned savagely against him; and he was notified that the proprietor, Mrs. Leslie, would allow him to make no contributions to the journal beyond the thirteen agreed upon, and that she would not permit him to publish a book under the title of the series, 'Problems of the Times.' Fortunately he was able to talk amicably with the representative of the firm who had negotiated the contract, and he escaped any danger that *Leslie's* would block publication under the other title.

To the end *Social Problems* was hard to produce, though it became profitable. The author worked until the very eve of his big lecture tour in England and Scotland to complete the revision and enlargement of the manuscript.

–3–

The report on Henry George in the States during 1883 has indicated, so far, the signs that came to him of new recognition at home, and the ideas that came to his mind as the most important ones to express in new articles and books. As it seems fair to call *Social Problems* socialistic within certain boundaries, and fair also to discover in the free-trade manuscript an intention to educate readers into major doctrines of free enterprise, George was at this stage confirmed in his earlier character of prophet of the mixed economy. But these data fall short of formulating adequately George's own notion of where he stood, and where he thought he should go, in his developing career.

As we know, he interpreted the welcome home in October 1882 to indicate that he would have no more trouble making money to support his family. Though the small audiences he had and the low fees he collected during an immediate, short lecture tour in the Middle West were disappointing, he did not let himself be discouraged. After the $1000 legacy from Mr. Shaw, about the year's income we know only that *Leslie's* paid him $1300 and that he must have received something useful, perhaps in three figures, perhaps in four, from royalties on *Progress and Poverty* and *The Land Question*. The fact that money received from previous writing came in, probably his principal source of income, while he was doing his fourth book, must have been encouraging to him and have lessened his regrets that work on the free-trade manuscript had to be deferred.

During the spring he made a major decision which indicates, as well as continuing optimism, an unusual degree of freedom of action. He was approached in March by Allen Thorndike Rice, of the *North American*. Would Henry George launch a new weekly, a political and economic journal? The proposition was that an investor would put up $25,000 and hold 55 shares of stock; George would be given 45 shares and would be made editor at a salary of $75 a week to start and $100 as soon as the paper began to make expenses. He would be given full editorial control; and, as George himself noted, the job promised to solve his 'bread and butter question for good.'

Yet he refused the offer for reasons that seem shallow: the *Leslie's* articles had to be done, the free-trade book was on his mind, he was not ready to take charge of the new office. The refusing mood was on him. A little later the same spring he made up his mind not to try to lecture in California during the summer. And presently he refused to consider at a low salary an otherwise attractive appointment as commissioner of the new New York Bureau of Labor Statistics, which at the moment was pending before the state legislature. Whether or not he had a right to be so certain, he believed that if he were to nod Governor Grover Cleveland would nominate him. 'I could make something of the place,' he pondered, and added that at $5000 he would have taken it. But when $2500 was indicated he lost interest.

Why did he turn away from New York opportunities in the kinds of work that had sustained him in California — journalism and state office? If they had not quite satisfied him there, and if he had learned the perfidy of a journal's creditors in San Francisco, at least the present offers were made in terms that honored him, and a job in New York would have assured him a long season of being prominent before the nation. A very important reason for refusing doubtless was just what he said, because he was overburdened and needed freedom for thought. And another lay in his interest in

Britain, though the invitation to return there had not become compelling when he turned down Mr. Rice.

To these I add the guess that possibly the controlling reason for his not taking important jobs was that for the first time he was making promising contacts with the American labor-union movement. This was the sector of society that was the most important of all, in his scale of values. And now labor unions, Henry George, Jr., says, urged him for the New York commissionership; and presently the veteran member of the California printers' union became a new member of the Knights of Labor in New York. Very soon he opened a correspondence with Terence Powderly, who as grand master workman was the famous international leader of that order. This proved to be the beginning of a long association between union leader and intellectual-for-labor.

Here an analogy suggests itself. George's concerning himself in 1883 with labor-union leadership and ideology, while he was finding his way into influence in the United States, is reminiscent of his situation a year earlier overseas, when his being concerned in Irish protest led directly to influence in English and Scottish affairs. Terence Powderly himself derived from Irish origins, and so also did great numbers of the Knights of Labor; and Michael Davitt had become a knight while in the United States, and had transplanted a bit of the organization to his own side of the water. Why should George not travel an Irish route to prominence in the United States as well as in Britain? If foresight had not suggested this tactic, then an event of April 1883 certainly did so. As Davitt had done, in 1882, Terence Powderly now said things which half-promised that he would become a follower of Henry George. Delighted with a public statement the grand master workman made, which went beyond the agrarian plank in the Knights of Labor platform, George wrote congratulations: 'I need hardly say how thoroughly [your statement] accords with my own earnest belief.' George happily sent clippings to Thomas Walker in Birmingham.

To Powderly himself he sent further advice and counsel. 'I believe that the promulgation by you of those views marks an epoch in the labor movement. They will powerfully aid in bringing about, among the working classes, that discussion of fundamental principles so much needed, and without which nothing else can be accomplished.' George went on to criticize the little newspaper of the Knights of Labor; and he urged such new editorial boldness as would attract attention and build up the union. 'There is a widespread consciousness among the masses that there is something *radically* wrong in the present social organization. All that is needed to weld this feeling into a power which will at length become irresistible is concentration and enlightenment.' Very delicately George led along into the tariff question. Identifying himself to a Pennsylvanian as a native of that state and as a one-time protectionist, but one who had been converted, he begged Powderly not to tie up with high-tariff doctrine. 'The great injury done by the protective theory seems to me to be that it sets workingmen to barking up the wrong tree.' George ended with assurances that the area of agreement between them far exceeded their differences, and that he had no wish to press those differences.

Powderly did his share in the *rapprochement*. He agreed that his union's journal needed improvement; and, about the tariff, he believed that their two positions were very much closer than George understood. Within a week or so of hearing from George, Powderly tried to call in New York; and failing he invited a visit at his own home in Scranton.

The connection thus begun bore most of its fruit in the later '8os rather than in 1883, but it produced certain results immediately. At midsummer George refused an invitation to speak before the now renamed Irish National League; and to Powderly he explained his reasons, at the same time sounding out the depth of their agreement. Dropping the word 'land' signified a loss of nerve among Irishmen, George believed, an accent on nationalism and a withdrawal from old ideas of economic transformation. 'I regret to say that among the Irish leaders there have been none able enough and strong enough to stand firm.'

Not nationalism but internationalism of protest was the thing, urged George — protest from all who suffer. In this direction his track of thought closely paralleled the socialist one, yet did not do so exactly. 'The only class in my opinion worth considering in any country is the class which these proposed measures [of the Irish National League] totally ignore — the laborers. Not that they are the only class worth thinking about, but until they are affected nothing general or permanent can be obtained . . . While I sympathize with the Irish people in their political oppressions I have no faith in mere political movements of any kind. When I see how much misery and degradation there is in our own country I cannot think that any mere political change would do anything to improve the condition of those classes of the Irish people who most desire our sympathy and need our aid.'

Powderly perhaps failed to answer this letter, but a couple of weeks later, in August, he and George met and talked, probably for the first time. The occasion was a Knights of Labor picnic in Baltimore, where they spoke together before a festive gathering of 3000 persons, colored and white in one audience. Powderly urged that the unions must grow; and George pleaded that working men and the women of their families must get into politics. Eight-hour and other strategy would raise the level of the unskilled worker, he said: raise the marginal worker and you raise all. How ideas do take hold was his satisfied impression after the meeting.

Incidentally the Maryland excursion included personal as well as political satisfactions. Henry and Annie George ran up to Emmitsburg to visit the sister who was located temporarily in the mother house of the Sisters of Charity. Annie had not seen her for nearly twenty-five years, and Henry had never seen her. But after this brother and sister-in-law corresponded occasionally; and he sent presents, and in due course even asked the nun's advice, when he was having his famous trouble with the hierarchy of the Catholic Church.

Before August had passed, Henry George, back in New York, had the opportunity to make his ideas public when a committee of the United States Senate held hearings there on labor conditions and affairs. On the day he testified, the room in the Post Office building was crowded 'with the disciples and admirers of the witness,' according to the *Tribune;* and indeed many of the questions asked him were more than respectful, almost deferential in tone. Several witnesses — Louis Post, Charles Frederic Adams, a lawyer, Robert Blissert, a tailor, and Heber Newton, and there may have been others — expressed ideas very like his own.

Asked at the beginning of his testimony whether or not labor was actually being reduced to a worse condition, he replied cautiously that it was not possible to judge. But he said that discontentment was on the increase, and that social catastrophe might come soon — a not inaccurate prophecy just three years before 1886.

When questioned what he would do to improve things if he were made 'dictator of the universe, or at least of the world,' George said that he would not do much — dictators could not go far ahead of the people. He agreed that the constitutional powers of Congress would have to be enlarged to enact on a national scale the program he believed in; he acknowledged that a general land-value tax could not be reconciled with the circumscribed powers of Congress to enact direct taxes. But he thought the federal government would do much if it eliminated tariffs and established a government-owned telegraph as in England. He told the committee his story of fighting the Associated Press and Western Union in 1869.

Pressed rather hard on public ownership, he agreed, yes, that his 'idea of communal ownership of land,' as the question was phrased, was in some degree a socialistic proposition. Specifying less particularly than at other times what industries should be community-owned, he spoke perhaps more dogmatically than ever before, on that subject. 'Practically I think the progress of events is towards the extension and enlargement of businesses that are in their nature monopolies, and that the State must add to its functions continually.' About this hearing, the New York *Tribune* observed sourly that the federal government had no business concerning itself with such problems, and that, anyway, each senator could have a copy of *Progress and Poverty* at lower expense than a traveling investigation. But the committee members themselves accepted George's recommendation that they hear from Mr. Heber Newton, which of course meant they would be confronted by a clergyman testifying in the same vein.

As in England during that very season — the Land Reform Union gathered in 1883 — so in America the followers of Henry George began to draw together, even on a national scale. Borrowing a name from the history of the pro-labor and anti-slavery movement thirty-five years earlier, Louis Post and others set up the American Free Soil Society. A year later the *Free Soiler,* newly started as an organ of the society, looked back to 1883 and admitted that first progress had been slow. But the members had become acquainted, and the work would catch on. 'We aim to elevate the working poor and to save the middle class from destruction.'

However modest were the early numbers, the fellowship of the Free Soil Society involved a pleasant savor of the Bohemian, a taste none too frequent in Henry George history after his earlier San Francisco days. A group of New Yorkers who had been gathering for dinner and talk at 'Dirty Dick's,' or Pedro de Beraza's at 29 Center Street, decided to do more. In a place which acquired its charm, according to reminiscence, from excellent spaghetti and a cobwebby appearance, and the presence of rats, a noble document was drawn. The group pledged themselves to work 'by peaceable methods' to achieve the remedy of Henry George; and they invited new members to join the Free Soil Society without 'distinction of race, sex, nationality or creed.' Heber Newton became treasurer; Charles Frederic Adams, secretary; and A. J. Steers, George's first New York disciple and the person who had told Father McGlynn about *Progress and Poverty,* was a charter member. There were other lawyers, and members of the *Irish World* staff; and the entire George family down to Jennie Teresa, who was hardly sixteen, belonged.

The organization had some igniting power from the start. From San Francisco, where the first Henry George organization, the Land Reform League, still carried on, George's old friend, Judge Maguire, wrote that the league would reorganize into twelve ward groups of the Free Soil Society. William Hinton, John M. Days, and M. R. Leverson, names to stir George's nostalgia and loyalty, were on the move, the judge reported. By the next spring the *Free Soiler* could list eighteen vice-presidents, each from a different state, the future distinguished Judge Jackson H. Ralston of Maryland among them. George must have been referring to the Free Soil Society when he wrote 'Dear Comrade' Joseph Labadie that what was 'most needed is the propagation of ideas, and for that we want an organization which will serve as a standard and rallying point, rather than numbers. This organization will I hope serve at least as a beginning.'

Besides his principal writings and organizational activities, many incidentals of George's life in 1883 indicate the priority of his concern with labor. Somehow he learned, for instance, about Laurence Gronlund; George was told that this socialist immigrant was living on $5 a week while earning $10, and was saving $3 a week toward publishing a book of social protest. This was the later important *Co-operative Commonwealth,* which actually came out in 1884. George certainly did not anticipate that Gronlund would become a severe critic of his own work, nor was he warned against Gronlund by the uneasiness he felt concerning Hyndman. He simply spoke warmly of the man and expected that his book would be 'a rendition of German Socialism' — as indeed it was — 'a needed thing.'

From a quite different direction, that is, from the papers of Professor Richard Ely, who was still on the Johns Hopkins faculty and still at an early stage of his famous career, we learn that at this time Gronlund was speaking just as warmly of Henry George — as a friend whom he grouped with Heber Newton and John Swinton. And Mr. Newton, who was, as we have just seen, a leading member of the Free Soil Society, was also interested in a new New York journal of a new movement, the *Christian Socialist*. These threads weave into common design. The Henry George impulse, like many if not all native American protests, interfiliated with other impulses, some of them of foreign origin. Such a cross-connecting, to be expected in any period, was never more natural than during the early stages of the 'new immigration' of the last quarter of the nineteenth century.

Yet, as the fall of the year came on, though many admired him, and though he had made some money and refused opportunities to make more, Henry George had not yet really got his 'feet down' in a practical way. And then a series of distressing events occurred. He lost his parents — his father in his eighties and his mother in her sixties. Simultaneously he ran out of funds and felt terribly at loose ends for a period of weeks.

At midsummer he had taken a resort vacation, at Budd's Lake, New Jersey. He had the best rest in years — the first vacation since the studying summer of 1877 in Sausalito. For money he meant to sell his free-trade manuscript for newspaper serializing before book publication, hoping to repeat the financial success of 'Topics of the Times' in *Leslie's*. But unaccountably the manuscript disappeared when it was about half done; and all at once he found himself down to his last $25. He regretted intensely that he had no newspaper to edit and wished from the heart that he had not refused Mr. Rice's invitation.

Personal distress made the invitation of the Land Reform Union, to lecture in England and Scotland, seem doubly important; it meant earnings and the chance that succeeded so well, to sell *Social Problems* to a second publisher. But it also meant more than money.

It meant reputation and authority and power. In late 1883 the question with Henry George was: How great might his influence become in the world? In the United States he had hit upon the element he wished to affect first, which was organized labor. But he had by no means achieved influence equal to that which he had reached in England.

–4–

As the scheduling of the second and third visits to Britain worked out, the summer-and-autumn interval at home in 1884 proved too short for George to determine how new successes in England and Scotland had affected his standing in the United States. There can be no doubt about the longer run. The British tour of 1884 did build up George toward his spectacular entrance into politics. But the intermediate steps were by no means clear-cut; and warning signals again went up that mounting popularity overseas did not promise immediate acceptance at home.

While abroad he had been heard lecturing by one of the partners of Brooks and Dickson, the lecture agency. To George's enormous satisfaction the firm proposed a handsome contract for a six-months tour in the United States. The agency offered to bear all expenses for Mr. and Mrs. George and a secretary; and George could choose to take either $800 a week or 60 per cent of the net receipts. The decision demanded pondering. He was elated to be offered what Ingersoll was paid — $200 per lecture — and he admitted that he would have taken less. But he thought also that the agents must be anticipating a real 'George boom'; and he considered how miserable Annie would be, so he wrote her, should she soon discover '$1000 a night coming in and me getting only a paltry $200.'

So, while he was still abroad and riding the excitement of the meetings that gave birth to the Land Restoration League, he chose the option of 60 per cent. His mind rushed forward to visiting California again, to hoping that Harry would continue as his secretary. He even let himself be sad that the time had passed when he could put a carriage at the disposal of his parents and do other things to give them pleasure. At any rate Jennie could have a pony, he said.

But after a fortnight back in America such hopes were cruelly disappointed. He was welcomed home again at a working men's meeting in Cooper Union, and once more given a dinner on the second night — this time not such an affair as the one at Delmonico's. But the opening Brooks and Dickson lecture, delivered at the New York Academy of Music on 'The Eighth Commandment,' turned out a miserable fiasco — the first and last lecture under that marvelous contract. The audience hardly sufficed to pay the incidental costs.

George did make about ten speeches during the spring and summer, but he made only one during the fall before sailing; and this meant that he gave up lecturing, for 1884, as a method of supporting his family. By the testimony of American admirers and contemporaries — Messrs. Post, Newton, and Charles Frederic Adams — his method of extemporizing produced irregular results at this stage, sometimes ineffective and sometimes inspired. To San Francisco George wrote, immediately after the Academy of Music failure, that the tide had turned quickly against him, and that certain debts he had expected to pay would have to stand awhile longer.

George's metaphor would have been more accurate had he said that no tide had risen. His method of speaking was best adapted, and brilliantly adapted, to audiences already in emotional rapport and willing to be swayed. In this respect America was not as ready to receive Henry George and assure him success on the platform as Britain was. Much the most significant audience he addressed, during the lean summer and fall of 1884, was a congress of the Episcopal Church, in Detroit. Heber Newton, who was becoming a kind of American Stewart Headlam, invited him. There, as a man of faith addressing men of faith on the question, 'Is Our Civilisation Just to Workingmen?' Henry George succeeded well. The speech was reported in the *Churchman* and was generously received. But there were not many audiences of that kind and intensity in the United States — or if there were, George was slow to discover them.

With few opportunities to speak, the other choice must have been completely obvious, that he now return to work at his desk. Anxiety or struggle about the decision was happily removed by Thomas Walker, his British Francis Shaw, who presently advanced him money. First George finished off the reply to the Duke of Argyll and then returned to work on *Protection or Free Trade*.

By the arrangement of Mr. Walter Cranford, a new friend and follower of the Brooklyn group, the writer and his family spent the summer on a Long Island farm near Jamaica, three miles from a railway. The season served the same purpose as the summer in Sausalito. George did some reading and hard thinking. Doubtless governed by experiences in Britain, he decided that he deeply opposed Marxism, and that some day he would have to write an answer to that brand of doctrine. But for the time being he concentrated on the manuscript. By fall it was about finished, he said, and once more he entertained hopes of serial publication and of profits in the not too distant future. For the winter he returned to Brooklyn, taking the house at 267 Macon Street. 'I wish I had a pension or some bonds,' he said.

This was the season of the Cleveland-Blaine campaign, the one that stirred the Irish immigrant element more deeply than perhaps any other election in our history. Ultimately 1884 would mean much to George, for after a quarter of a century the party of his inheritance and loyalty, once again a reform party, returned to power. But at the time he was completely bored, and completely inactive, even more remote from campaign activities than he had been in 1880. The *Irish World* went for Blaine, fully protectionist in the Irish way; and the Republican inclinations of certain of his associates may have been the principal factor that kept George quiet. But at least one friend thought he ought to seek office himself. To Nordhoff of the *Herald* on 24 October 1884, Henry George replied, 'I think I can be quite as useful outside of Congress as in and I would not now seek a nomination in any way . . . But I quite as fully appreciate your kindness and esteem as though I wanted [to run].'

Though he was not to feel the same way in the campaigns of 1888 and 1892, George was not satisfied with Grover Cleveland as candidate and leader this first time. General Butler he regarded as quite an insincere leader of the Greenbackers. Not since childhood had he felt so little personal stake in the quadrennial decision. Sailing for Liverpool the day before election, he did take the trouble to pair with a Blaine man, so in a sense he voted for Cleveland; and in Britain he wrote an article saying that the Democratic victory must ultimately bring the realities of the tariff question back into politics.

But this was all. For Henry George the third trip to Britain, in behalf of the Scottish Land Restoration League, was an escape into political reality.

−5−

About that trip we need to recall only a few points. Not at all an occasion of recession in Henry George's influence in Britain, it was nevertheless a less exciting tour than the one preceding. It was a time for consolidating gains rather than adventuring first thrusts into the world of ideas and politics; and though he did not break the connections of 1882, George was already abandoning fusion tactics with socialists and Irish nationalists. More precisely, he was inviting social protest under his own banner, that of the Land Restoration League; and, outside that movement, he now preferred to accompany rather than to combine with radicals whose philosophy or lack of philosophy he disapproved.

At home to stay in 1885, George followed the same policy as in Scotland. His being in a less class-conscious state of mind than earlier placed no obstacles on his picking up threads, again, with the Knights of Labor. But this did not lead to much before 1886, George's political year; and his first tactic was to return to the lecture platform. This time immediate results were better than in 1884, and perhaps another twelve months of the recession of the middle '80s helped account for increased interest in his ideas. But he retained the doubts which had assailed his courage in England, about whether or not public speaking would do as a way for him to earn his living.

Thanks to a little series of letters, we are able at this stage to look behind the scenes at one of Henry George's more important lecture appearances in inner America. The host who entertained him at Burlington, Iowa, in April 1885, tells us that a year earlier a sizable number of Henry George men, not of the laboring classes, were known to one another. In the group there were a judge, a lawyer, an Episcopal rector, and 'myself a lifetime student of political economy,' according to Mr. David Love. When George came to town, however, he lectured under the auspices of the Knights of Labor. Because he gave 'The Crime of Poverty,' one of his reprinted addresses, it is possible to say that he treated a small-city audience to the same kind of eloquence he used in London and Glasgow. He utilized his most telling platform devices: he illustrated low wages from a fresh report of Michigan statistics; he mentioned child labor as he had seen it within a short distance of Burlington; he retold the story of the degradation of working men in England, and made comparison with Crusoe's island. In the end he reflected on the 'utter absurdity of this thing of private property in land,' and invited his audience to consider what would happen in their 'little town' should land-value taxation be instituted. 'You could have a great free library; you could have an art gallery; you could get yourselves a public park.' The speaker was disappointed that only 400 people turned out, on a Saturday, at 50 cents apiece; but he was appeased to find the Congregational Church crowded, the next night, to hear the 'Moses' address.

Mr. Love himself rounds out the story of Henry George's impact on Burlington. Perhaps a dozen men were now confirmed, 'with more or less clearness,' as followers of the recent speaker; about fifty others followed at a greater distance. In widening circles among the Knights of Labor and among sympathizers with Irish protest, George was being 'constantly discussed.' A newspaper at Mt. Pleasant and a German one at Keokuk were advocating *Progress and Poverty;* and a clergyman near by had been presenting the book at the meetings of a reading society. Mr. Love said that in his own second thinking he preferred George because, unlike the socialists and unlike the churchmen, George made no effort to change men's natures but only to change the operation of the laws of economics. His own group was abandoning their Free Soil Society affiliation, he reported, and was joining with the Knights of Labor instead.

It seems fair to assume that Burlington represents the impact of Henry George in many towns. On the other hand, as he himself discovered, a growing curiosity about his ideas did not mean any such wave of interest as overseas. On this trip he would have welcomed opportunities to go to Minnesota and Michigan, but he was not invited. He did stop at Indianapolis. A not very large audience which paid 50 cents a seat raised the question whether he was charging too much; and, as he had to stay over a day, on invitation to address the state legislature, he decided to experiment. He announced a second public lecture at a 10-cent charge, but he drew in few more hearers than at the regular rate. 'I will do good even if I don't make money,' he wrote Annie at this time. But he said also, 'That will be my policy in the future in lecturing — to have big audiences and to produce an effect.' And in final judgment he added: 'This trip is conclusive to my mind. There are everywhere people who want to hear me; but they do not anywhere amount to enough to make good lecture audiences.' So he would not go to Canada or lecture at all unless circumstances indicated big audiences. 'I will try something else. All the books sent here were sold.'

At home on Macon Street, George headed into several months of quiet work. His prior commitment was to the unfinished *Protection and Free Trade* manuscript, and by fall it was so far revised that he was able to sell parts for installment publication in newspapers. Meanwhile he had a lead article in the July issue of the *North American Review*. This was a dialogue with David Dudley Field, a lawyer and reformer of the law, who was not too opposed to George to draw out his ideas considerably. The article stated clearly Henry George's intention to create both opportunities for labor and opportunities for investment. As definitely as anything in print, it showed that his scheme of taxation was economically equivalent to the public ownership of land; and a passage included the words, 'the single tax upon land values.' This I believe to be his first use of the phrase in print, with the definite article included. Though the phrase of course lacked any of the political connotations it would gather in 1887 and 1888, its appearance in the *North American* is one of several signs that George was now particularizing his program and being careful to make clear its differences from other reforms.

Though he wished when he could to tackle a new book, on money, George did a great deal of writing for the *North American* later in 1885 and in 1886. One of the articles was a potboiler purely, on 'England and Ireland,' for which he drew on his experiences abroad. But another, printed in April 1886, seems doubly important as it indicated, over and beyond his own effort, an effort by Mr. Rice to give unusual prominence to Henry George's ideas. In each issue beginning in January, the *North American* carried articles about American landholding. The first, by Thomas P. Gill, was as severe as George. The 'landlord and tenant laws' of the states, according to the investigator, were 'implements for extracting rent as simple, terrible, and brutally candid in their design as a revolver in the hand of a peremptory road agent.' The February article listed the federal land grants which had been made to corporations since 1862, and let the figures speak; and in the March *North American* two writers replied, making an argument much like General Walker's *versus* Henry George, three years earlier. This remarkable series — four articles in January, February, and March — gave the writer of the concluding article a splendid chance for a climax.

For the occasion George wrote 'More about American Landlordism,' the article mentioned above as the place where he conceded something to General Walker's argument, that the average size of American farm holdings was falling rather than increasing. But he allowed this to be no more than a technical concession. Visualizing the process of land acquirement as a Californian who had seen New York and London, George returned to his original point that concentration and monopoly in landholding was becoming an ever more universal truth. That speculators and railroads disgorged and distributed to settlers he admitted, and those changes brought the acreage figures down. 'But while this division is going on, the ownership of land may be in reality concentrating and landlordism increasing . . . What would be a small market garden would be a very large city lot . . . Where each house was once surrounded by a garden and orchard, a lot of twenty feet front now carries family upon family, living, on top of each other, in tiers . . . The ownership of square feet now enables [one] to live in luxurious idleness on the toil of his fellow citizens.'

Turning from urban landlordism to rural, George made a powerful criticism, not his first but an early one, of the American theory of the agricultural ladder — the idea, more prevailing then than now, 'that tenant-farming is, in the natural order of things, the intermediary stage through which "agricultural laborers" are enabled to pass into a condition of landowners.' George condemned the agricultural ladder as 'just the reverse' of truth. Following his old thought about the South since the Civil War, the article presents farm-tenancy as a form of labor's bondage rather than an emancipation into ownership. 'More about American Landlordism' was Henry George's final piece of writing about land policy and land problems in the United States.

At about the time the article appeared, the author abandoned his desk for a short period of travel in the Middle West and in Pennsylvania. In Ohio he made several addresses, which included a debate on free trade against a labor-union man. But this was not a lecture tour of the kind which had recently baffled him, and all the speaking seems to have been incidental.

During this trip he visited a famous brownstone mansion in Cleveland for the first time, in what seems to have been a response to a call made not long before in his own home in Brooklyn. The caller had been Tom Loftin Johnson, who had made up his mind by then to be a complete follower of Henry George. The story of his decision resembles that of many others: he had read first *Social Problems,* which was sold to him by a railway vendor, and had gone on to *Progress and Poverty.* But Johnson was no ordinary convert. Thirty-one in 1885, and entirely inexperienced in politics, he was an American industrial monopolist, in the historic age of the monopolists. He had already behind him enough of his career as inventor, entrepreneur, and owner, in street railways and steel, to have become a man of wealth and power. When he read George's books he instructed a lawyer to refute them if he could; and, when that effort failed, he decided that no refutation was possible. We are free to imagine the satisfaction the traveler had, by reason of the distinguished hospitality of Mr. and Mrs. Johnson, and of the dedication and promise of Tom Johnson's commitment.

Before he moved from private life to public, in the amazing summer of 1886, George did one more notable job. It combined the activities of the field with those of the study. He was commissioned by the *North American Review* to do a series of articles on 'Labor in Pennsylvania.' Naturally the assignment suited him: a study in his home state, and in a segment of the economy where subsoil resources were monopolized, and where the labor force was drawn from remote parts of the world. Invading Pennsylvania was a little like invading the Duke of Argyll's lands, and a little like studying again California's regional economy. Going in the month of May, he was thrilled by the beauty of the countryside, and he wished that Annie were with him.

But he went to see economic realities, and he observed and talked his way through industrial parts of the state he had not seen before — through Hazelton, Pottsville, Harrisburg, Altoona, Johnstown, and Pittsburgh. The timing meant that he collected his data during the very month of the historic wave of strikes, the biggest and most spontaneous in American history, which was punctuated by the bomb burst in Chicago's Haymarket Square. But George seems not to have been much affected by the emotion of the movement; he enjoyed the assignment and reached an over-all judgment that the condition of the state was bad but not at all hopeless.

His economic findings he took to Brooklyn to write up at his convenience, and the resulting articles were published during the fall and winter. He kept to the tone of objective study and moderate recommendation. Though America's anti-radical panic after Haymarket was represented, even in the journal for which he was writing, by articles telling readers that revolution was breeding in the heavy air, Henry George reverted to the fact-finding phase of his mental operations which had governed his economic reporting on the West coast. Rather than the man with a reform, he became for the most part the student of conditions. He wrote in cold statistics about many facets of the state's economy. Drawing from publications of the state Bureau of Labor Statistics, he indicated how labor's low wages were rendered the more inadequate by unemployment in the mine fields. But he discovered few danger signals of radicalism. He reported that while working men were concerned about their situation they were not rabid, and he thought them cautious about using or approving the strike as a weapon of economic advantage.

Of course the writer's dispassion meant no abandonment of his habitual moral judgments or of his formulas. In these articles, as he had not done in *Progress and Poverty,* he incorporated figures on child labor, and he displayed pages of affidavits by miners whose real wages had either declined or not improved by having immigrated from Great Britain. He compared company-owned houses in Pennsylvania with the huts he had seen in Ireland, mine owners' mansions with Irish manor houses, and the coal and iron police with the Irish constabulary. He raised the question whether or not bringing the 'Huns' to the coalfields involved the same danger as allowing the Chinese in California, but decided not, for he noticed that Hungarian immigrants had already organized effective unions. He urged the necessity for laboring men to take the initiative and think and act with care.

Free-trade policy was his first advice this time. He castigated the state's tariff tradition as superstition, a bondage of ideas which the unions must learn to cast off. Wages were brought low, he said, not by reason of imports but by the competition of laborers for jobs.

He returned to his familiar land-monopoly diagnosis, but did so with uncommon brevity and force.

In contrast with his predecessors in the *North American,* the panicky contributors on the labor crisis in the June issue, George was analytical and restrained. In contrast with aggressive trade unionists, and in completest contrast of all with the country's fringe of Marxists, Henry George's preference in 1886 as always was for political methods, rather than non-political, to bring about changes in society.

–6–

Meanwhile George had actually completed *Protection or Free Trade.* His negotiations of the fall of 1885 led to a fairly satisfactory result. Though some newspapers, which he hoped would serialize certain chapters, refused entirely, and others insisted on price reduction or on cutting down the size of the installments, half a dozen papers did contract to print. They stretched across the continent: the Brooklyn *Eagle,* the New York *Star,* the San Francisco *Examiner,* the Louisville *Courier,* the Charleston *News and Courier,* and the Toronto *Globe.* A little later the London *Star,* run by George's friends, carried parts of the book also.

Because, to the shame of American liberalism, there has been no strong habit in the United States of writing and working in behalf of international freedom of trade, certainly nothing to compare with the vigor of the protectionist tradition from Alexander Hamilton through the Carey school of economists, it is worth while to notice that peddling *Protection or Free Trade* brought in to George agreeable testimony of good will. In San Francisco William Hinton acted for his ex-partner; and when he had sold the rights to publish he wrote also that Judge Maguire and others of the city were busy 'propagating the faith as handed down to them from Henry George with true apostolic fervor.' From the South, Henry Watterson, accepting for the *Courier,* wrote in a friendly way; and the editor of the Charleston paper, the remarkable F. W. Dawson, asking for a price reduction, quite pleaded to have the serialization, for the good of the region. George was pleased to have about $3000 coming from the newspapers. And of course he believed, as he did about *Progress and Poverty,* that publication would help mightily to force a great question on the political parties, and on the attention of the people.

Book publication waited on revision, however, and was delayed until about the time of George's visit to Ohio during the spring.

A new firm, Henry George and Company, was the publisher. By family and friends this organization was understood to represent a partnership between the author and his younger son, for Richard was all there was of the 'and Company.' The timing of events, and future events, suggest the possibility that Tom Johnson had some quiet role as guarantor; but perhaps George's recent take from the newspapers explains all that needs explaining about how capital was obtained. The purpose of the firm was to bring under George's own personal control all present and future questions of profits, propaganda, and the subsidization of his writings.

For the book which was the first to come out under the new auspices, the author chose the opposite of the inductive procedure he had used in the Pennsylvania labor articles. He was entirely conscious of doing this. A letter of 14 September 1884 in which he rejected a suggestion from Dr. Taylor, his old intimate, expresses the decision completely. 'My view of the matter is the reverse of yours,' wrote George. 'I do not think induction employed in such questions as the tariff is of any use. What the people want is theory: and until they get a correct theory into their heads, all citing of facts is useless.'

For the actual text, the author-publisher relied heavily on propositions, reminiscent of the San Francisco *Post,* such as protection is 'repugnant to moral perceptions and inconsistent with the simplicity and harmony which we everywhere discover in natural law.' In an autobiographical passage he alluded to his conversion to free trade, in the Sacramento lyceum meeting of 1866. As earlier — in *Progress and Poverty* and in many places — he represented free trade and land-value taxation as the two sides of one true coin of right policy. Together not separately, he said with an argument more fully developed than before, they could be used to open the resources of the world to all who would invest or work.

At first glance, the middle '80s would seem to have been an unlikely time for so doctrinaire and uncompromising a book. Not only had a quarter of a century of Republicanism built a whole series of tariff walls into the structure of national legislation, but one year of Democratic control had shown no wish to take them down. More than that, for a writer to be for labor and against protection amounted almost to a contradiction in political terms. George could have wanted no alliances with such free-trade econo- mists as his old opponent, William Graham Sumner, if only because the professor opposed labor unions — as an issue of freedom — from first to last. Nor was there comfort from old friends of Liberal Republican days. David Ames Wells is remembered as saying in frustration, of the work of the tariff lobbies in the '80s: 'This is the revolution. It will take another revolution to overthrow the leader- ship now established by business men.'

Yet in a closer view, the timing of *Protection or Free Trade,* even the dogmatism which announced for the principles of the Physio- crats as more thoroughgoing than those of the house of Adam Smith, seems not so strange after all. Though so far as the world knew in 1886, Grover Cleveland possessed no impulse to return to first Democratic principles, against the tariff, there is a possibility that George had a notion that inclinations were actually different at the White House. Not unlikely the working author learned from Thomas Shearman about an interview as early as 1883, in which Cleveland made a confidential statement of distaste for the national tariff policy. And from another direction of encouragement, though he himself was not involved, George must have known when George Haven Putnam, the publisher, called a meeting of free traders and revenue reformers in 1883. As we have already seen, though George regarded the New York Free Trade Club as not his kind, he had accepted membership when Poultney Bigelow got him in. In sum, a certain gathering of anti-tariff sentiment had occurred; and now, as in California against the land monopolizers, he was not entirely isolated in his thinking. Once again, Henry George was simply more vigorous, more articulate and doctrinaire, than others were.

When the book appeared, reviewers made just about such a com- ment as the one above, but they did so with an adverse twist of meaning. In the new *Political Science Quarterly,* George B. New- comb said that George attached free trade too closely to land-value taxation, and the two were set forth as too complete a panacea for readers with intellectual tastes. Though Newcomb was not alto- gether unfriendly, he protested George's 'rhetorical method' and said, much as German scholars had said of *Progress and Poverty,* that a larger use of historical data would have made a more effective argument. In the Chicago *Dial,* Albert Shaw pooh-poohed the book, but the New York *Critic,* a somewhat similar paper which had been friendly to *Progress and Poverty,* gave a favorable notice and selected for praise George's stand for the international copyright. Quite naturally the newspapers were for the most part adverse and spoke in accordance with their editorial policies.

Yet this book, next to *Progress and Poverty,* is the one of George's writings least to be judged by immediate reactions and momentary standards. If its ideological quality offended early readers, the book showed long-run strength which seems to have drawn from that very quality. There appeared an immediate German translation, and there were later Danish and Spanish ones; and though disappointingly no early edition was published in England, Kegan Paul did bring one out in 1903, when the sands were running low on a period of Conservative government. *Protection or Free Trade* is the George book which has the unique history of being printed entire in the *Congressional Record,* and being distributed gratis by the hundreds of thousands through the United States mails. By then, when the book was six years old, some 200,000 copies had gone out from Henry George and Company.

Protection or Free Trade is the climax of the effort of Henry George to find a place for himself on the national stage, before he was drawn into politics. Britain had received him and considered him, and partly adopted him, as the author of *Progress and Poverty.* But his native land had required an apprenticeship longer by three or four years.

As he now emerged to real prominence, the record made the man of 1886 a man of paradoxes indeed: a radical land theorist, but one who denied the homestead farm as a safety valve for working men; a spokesman for labor, but one who protested more strongly than anyone else the national policy commonly believed to protect American working men; a local-government Jeffersonian, but one who spoke for government's playing a strong role in economic affairs, and sometimes for the federal government's doing so. His course in politics would not be easy.

Yet he was quite as ready for recognition at home now, as he had been for recognition in the British Isles a little earlier. His mind had tackled the acknowledged realities of the nation's economic life; he had been accepted in the highest places of journalism; he had forced the attention of a few ranking academic men; he had been heard a little in the forums across the land. He had established durable connections in the labor movement; and he had acquired loyal friends among the upper middle class. No one else in the United States would have filled quite the same specifications.

XV

Conquest in New York City:
Labor Leader and Almost Mayor

1886

–1–

HENRY GEORGE never acted more exactly in accord with his idealistic conceptions of history than he did in late 1885 and during 1886. One day, not too far in the future, he was saying over and over again, Americans will be affected by *Progress and Poverty* and *Protection or Free Trade* and right theory will bring about changes in national policy. Simply realize the hard facts about the condition of labor was the assertion between the lines of the Pennsylvania articles; then hysteria will pass and justice be done.

If George could be optimistic and idealistic about the United States, he could feel that way about Great Britain also. To be sure the British election of 1885 proved to be hard on the Radicals. And presently, as Gladstone in his third government came out for Irish Home Rule, and as this created the occasion of Joseph Chamberlain's famous exit from Liberalism into Unionism, two tendencies in British politics which George approved — generosity toward Ireland and generosity toward the laboring classes — separated themselves from one another. In time the process strengthened such pro-tariff impulses and such Conservatism as George heartily opposed. Yet even while new and strong currents of politics were beginning to eddy in unwelcome directions, he distilled hope from news across the sea.

'A little knot of thorough-going "Land Restorationists" have been elected to the new Parliament,' he wrote triumphantly, late in 1885, to Josephine Shaw Lowell — his patron's daughter, and James Russell Lowell's daughter-in-law. He correctly envisaged in the handful of members, and in like-minded land nationalizers and about twenty others who would go with them, a concentration of energy that would impel British opinion and affect legislation.

Particularly James Durant, his London friend and publisher, encouraged optimism. During his last tour in Britain, Durant had told him that among circles of young men where George had previously been scorned, he was now respected. Would he consider coming to live in England? He might well assume leadership in a new parliamentary party, the publisher said; and he might become editor of a big new paper, at a salary of, say, £1000 a year.

This preceded the election of 1885. After it, early in 1886, Durant again offered enticements to bring George across the ocean and give him an established role. If he would come to London, he could count on time free for a certain amount of writing; a £300 guaranty-fund would be set up, as a kind of re-insurance; he would be free to go outside the city for occasional lecturing, on subjects to his taste. Durant even suggested titles, old and new: 'Why do men starve?' 'Why work is scarce and wages are low,' 'Free Trade and Fair Trade,' 'The Coming Revolution,' and 'Christian Socialism.' In the old country, the invitation pleaded, Henry George could assume at once a certain leadership and power.

This was a little overwhelming. But as the Ohio tour indicated, George's fortunes were picking up at home, and writing for the *North American* must have been profitable in money as well as prestige. George quickly decided that he could not go immediately to Britain, or ever go to stay very long; but he did not easily say no to another visit. Even in midsummer, when the possibility of his becoming mayor of New York had dawned, he reverted to Durant's invitation and seriously considered a trip that very autumn.

To his more intimate British friend, Thomas Walker, George explained his strategy a little, as matters developed. The real reason for bringing out *Protection or Free Trade* in the way he did, setting himself up as publisher, he wrote, was to prepare the way for starting a completely independent paper in New York. He intended something much bigger than the *Free Soiler* of 1884, or the quite similar little *Spread the Light, a Journal of Social Progress and Tax*

Reform, which lasted a few monthly issues in 1886. (This journal used the phrase, 'the single tax reform,' in the September number.) Now he was anxious to be ready in force, whenever his hope of Cleveland's victory might be realized — the hope that a new era of political discussion would open, and advanced economic ideas could be considered once again, in a climate friendly to growth. *Protection or Free Trade* was 'a part of my scheme for the U.S.,' he told Walker. 'Then comes the paper . . . Then I think I can show you that the good seed has been growing here.'

To one of his British correspondents, Richard McGhee, who as leader of the Scottish Land Restoration League and a member of Parliament ranks as the first consistent follower of Henry George to achieve a role in a national legislature, George gave just a hint, in early June 1886, that his 'scheme for the U.S.' might include something practical, over and beyond the ideological effort. The time would soon be ripe for entering politics at home, he wrote, as though that vague statement were sufficient to explain his not accepting the invitations to England.

This was a month before the idea of a great mayoralty campaign arose in labor-union circles in New York. There is no sign earlier than midsummer that George made any practical political moves at all, or even discussed such possibilities among his immediate colleagues. Then, when overtures were made to him, he did go to Tom Johnson and a very few others, by that time with a perfectly concrete situation in mind.

–2–

Apparently there is no document to date the day on which the spark flashed between the cathode of the Central Labor Union and the anode of George's own political charge. Joseph Jackson, a reporter for the *Herald,* claims to have made the original alignment between the two. At a meeting in a hat store in the Bowery, he advised a group of trades-union men that they should concentrate all political energies to elect a mayor. The name of George came up. After someone objected that the reformer was disqualified because he resided in Brooklyn, Mr. Jackson made an inquiry. 'By the way, Mr. George, where are you living?' he asked the question as casually as he could. 'In Harlem, on Pleasant Avenue.' 'You'll do.' 'Do for what?' 'You'll find out later,' Jackson answered, 'it's a little secret just now.' As Louis Post is the recorder of the conversation, the story seems entirely plausible.

The fluid situation in which the contact occurred we have glimpsed in the preceding chapter. It would be difficult to exaggerate the complexities of labor's situation in the United States in 1886. The factors of grievance, accumulating in strikes; the factors of ambition, exhibited as the Knights of Labor expanded and the Federation of Labor was born; and the surrounding anxieties and tensions, drawn to focus by the Haymarket affair — all denoted a condition of energy, hope, cross-purposes, and fear. It may fairly be said that an impulse to political action was as natural in trade-union history in 1886 as Henry George had always believed it to be. But not since Jackson's day had independent labor parties in the East accomplished anything significant at the polls; and, if George had in mind Joseph Chamberlain's success as pro-labor humanitarian mayor of Birmingham, he must have known also that his old friend John Swinton represented the hazard of labor politics in New York. In 1874 that maverick of radical thought, Presbyterian and socialist, had run for mayor as candidate of the Industrial Political Party and had received a mere handful of votes.

The obvious similarity of what was occurring in New York and the nation in 1886, to what had been so bitter to George in San Francisco and California during 1877 and after, must have struck the prophet of depression and reform. There was hunger in the streets, and fear of revolution in the newspapers. For days after the bombing and the bloodshed in Chicago, 4 May, the metropolitan papers carried stories of the event and the consequences of it. Quite naturally the prosecution of the anarchists and the decisions of the Illinois courts became a particularly touchy matter in New York City, and they remained so through the executions of November 1887, and afterward — and were a recurring tragic leitmotiv during the whole period of George's political emergence.

Though the dominant reaction to all this was so generally like the California red scare of 1877, there were also, of course, more liberal reactions. As Professor Henry May has observed in his study of Protestant social thought, the year 1886 designates one of the three social 'earthquakes' of the final quarter of the nineteenth century, which had the effect of arousing numbers of American Christians to the horrid conditions of labor around them. (The earlier 'earthquake' occurred in 1877, the later one from 1892 to 1894.) In the crisis of 1886, spiritual leaders of the quality of Washington Gladden and Edward McGlynn rose in their pulpits to lament and prophesy.

Other literature was converging with pulpit literature in this stream. Journals of religion gave increased attention to social problems; novelists turned again, after the lull that followed antislavery, to writing about social issues. And in the universities likewise, occasional conspicuous scholars, such as Ely of Johns Hopkins, who in 1886 brought out a book on American socialism, and young Professor Edmund James of the Wharton School, addressed themselves to the problems and patterns of industrial poverty.

Organized labor itself had a real role, not only as the object but as a creator and participator in the new social sympathy. This is nowhere better indicated than in the sizable, intelligent, and informing collaborative volume, *The Labor Movement the Problem of the Day*, which, published in 1887, estimated the large situation of 1886 precisely. The editor and compiler was George E. McNeill of Massachusetts, who had been brought up a shoemaker and an abolitionist, and who had reached fame as a trade-unionist spokesman for the eight-hour day. Of recent years he had been an active Knight of Labor, and at present was doing all he could to reconcile the new AF of L with the older K of L. During the coming fall, exactly parallel with George, he would run an unsuccessful campaign to be mayor of Boston. It is a little surprising that, though the Fabian tracts which were just appearing in England have been so much appreciated, the volume McNeill edited is now a forgotten piece of American social literature.

Henry George's assignment in this manifesto was the twenty-third chapter, 'The Land Question.' Of course he did a condensation rather than any revision of his ideas; and the significance of the chapter is that, after American labor had for half a century entertained the homestead idea as its one theory about land policy, following the ideas of George Henry Evans and the *Working Man's Advocate*, George at this stage of his history was permitted to strike for his own particular scheme. He was being admitted not only to trade-union thinking but into distinguished independent company as well. In chapters surrounding his own, for instance: Mr. McNeill himself spoke for restricting the hours of women's and children's labor, a familiar line of trade-union policy; Professor James did an essay on the need to reform the conspiracy laws to prevent their operating against the unions; Franklin H. Giddings — who was still on the *Springfield Republican* but would soon launch his distinguished career in sociology — had an excellent chapter on labor history; and Heber Newton contributed 'Industrial Education.' In this circle, George's chapter, the most theoretical one in the book, may be read as one sign of his arrival at a point he had been aiming for when he began correspondence with Powderly in 1883 — a position of recognition and influence in molding labor thought.

In New York City the Central Labor Union of course represented labor's capacity to combine; and questions of loyalty and attachment counted heavily in that circle. Mr. Jackson tells us that as soon as Henry George's name came up at the hat-store meeting, questions were asked. But the quarter-century-old membership in the printer's union put him in the record as a craft-union man, and his membership in the Knights of Labor certified him as belonging to the still more numerous, and more political, branch of the labor movement. It is easy to understand that George suited the CLU well when a political leader was needed.

From George's own side the *rapprochement* would not be as easy. An Irish element had assisted him into the Knights of Labor, though; and the history of the Central Labor Union showed that the organization had been established, only four years earlier, by an Irish refugee tailor 'for the purpose of sending greetings to the workers of Ireland in their struggle against English landlordism.' (The timing permits conjecturing whether an *Irish World* article by Henry George incited the gathering.) But during the years since 1882 elements less acceptable to George had entered the CLU. Marxist members of the Socialist Labor party sometimes gave addresses; and a class-conscious goal was written into the official appeal. In the organization's own words: 'The concentration of all unions into one solid body for the purpose of assisting each other in all struggles — political or industrial — to resist every attempt of the ruling classes directed against our liberties, and to extend our fraternal hand to the wage-earners of our land and to all nations of the globe.'

From the beginning the organization had matched vigor of words with forwardness in action. It was the first in the United States to use the boycott in a large way, the new Irish weapon of economic coercion; it made itself the central-strategy body of the New York strikes in 1886; it interfiliated with craft unions, with independent bodies, and with assemblies of the Knights of Labor. It made a rule that none but working men were eligible to join; and, apparently at the suggestion of Louis Post, its legal counsel, it was first to adopt and promote Labor Day as an annual holiday. When a new constitution was drawn up in 1886, the CLU brought together 207 unions, and it represented about 50,000 working men in New York, Brooklyn, and Jersey City.

Politics had been the CLU's unsuccessful department, so far. In its year of birth, 1882, candidates had been nominated for Congress, Louis Post among them. But after that election seemed to prove that members of trades unions voted for the nominees of the major parties according to individual preferences, the union withheld in 1884. Thus the nomination of Henry George in 1886 represents a strand of personal succession from the candidacy of Louis Post, the author of Labor Day, to the candidacy of Post's friend, the author of *Progress and Poverty*.

–3–

On 2 July 1886, occurred the event which swung the Central Labor Union back to political activity. The place was the law court of Judge George C. Barrett.

During the spring the union had won a remarkable victory over a keeper of a music and beer garden. This was George Theiss, an employer whom the waiters and bartenders unions by themselves had at first been unable to bring to terms. But the CLU's boycott had worked; and part of the settlement to which the proprietor acceded obliged him to pay the union $1000 as costs.

The matter came to law when Mr. Theiss denounced the commitment as an extortion and illegal. A grand jury acted first, then the criminal court, presided over by Judge Barrett. Mr. Post represented the working men. But the lawyer for the employer, using the rhetoric of the freedom of capital, won the case and won a devastating decision. The judge sentenced five CLU men to terms in Sing Sing, none shorter than eighteen months. To be sure clemency was exercised after 100 days by Governor Hill, who commuted the sentences on the ground that Mr. Theiss's payment 'seemed to lack many of the elements necessary to constitute "extortion" as it had been previously interpreted in the courts.' But by that time, in October, the Central Labor Union had returned to politics in force.

Labor's first response to the Barrett decision was a Cooper Union mass meeting on 7 July. Addresses were made by John McMackin, the union leader who would soon take direction of the mayoral campaign, and by John Swinton, who for four years now had been bringing out a labor weekly under his own name. Four days later the Central Labor Union set up a committee on political ways and means, and that committee in turn proposed a conference to take place in August. The committee envisaged what the twentieth century has known as 'united front' politics. Specifically, it proposed a meeting of delegates — one delegate for each 100 members of the supporting organizations — from all the unions in town and from such friendly political bodies as the Anti-Monopolists, the Greenback party, and the Socialist Labor party. Presumably the hat-store episode occurred at some stage of the warming-up for the conference, during the month of July.

In February 1884, while George was making speeches in Scotland, *John Swinton's Paper* had nominated him for President of the United States, and Louis Post for Vice-president, on a platform of the principles of *Progress and Poverty*. Now on 1 August, Swinton again spoke first. 'It May Be a Boom,' the editor headed his pronouncement. 'A fitter candidate could not be found. He is as true as steel. He embodies the aspirations of the masses. He is a worker, a printer, a unionist, a Knight of Labor, a man of business experience; and it will not be held against him that he is a native of the country, and the most renowned living American author. IT MAY BE A BOOM.' *John Swinton's* must have been the paper which Henry George, Jr., says his father refused to take seriously when Richard interrupted an office conference to bring in the exciting forecast.

But very rapidly the nomination ceased to be at all unlikely. The Central Labor Union called for a clean sweep of the city's offices: 'Honest men can be elected to administer the affairs of government and the laws can be enforced by the rich and poor alike.' On the scheduled day the convention met in Clarendon Hall, more than 400 strong; and it voted, 362 to 40, to fight an independent political campaign. Within two weeks an organization had been blue-printed. A platform was drawn. Planks announced for 'freesoil ideas' and for labor's more familiar and less doctrinaire demands: an effective eight-hour system, the abolition of child labor, and the like. There was no loud sound of socialism, and up until 20 August, no names were announced. On that day a committee called. Would Henry George accept a labor nomination for the office of mayor of New York?

George took a week to answer. To say yes he would have to put behind him for the time being all thought of going to England, and of course would have to defer still longer the writing of his primer of economics. But there is in the Henry George collection a memorandum in his own handwriting entitled 'John Swinton and His Friends' which gives an uncomfortable modern-sounding reason for his hesitating about united-front politics. Would he become a front-man merely, less than a true leader, possibly the puppet of forces which denied his own ideals?

Henry George's anxieties are voiced in comment on a little book of political travels, which Swinton had brought out in 1880 — that is, after the intimacy of their correspondence between California and New York. Swinton, he noted, is 'widely known as a thorough-going communist, in full affiliation with all those European destructives who come to New York when they find their own countries too hot to hold them, and who are plotting to bring about the destruction of society.' The memorandum is undated, but it represents George's attitude of 1883 and after, as we have seen it.

The invited candidate's reply to the labor convention naturally avoided phrasing any such issue. First of all George stated his general convictions broadly, along lines straight from his earliest California-based thinking. Labor should be active in politics, he said, and there ought to be a political party democratic in the fullest meaning of the word. His second proposition was at least as old with him as the *Post*, but one senses reinforcement from his British experiences. Municipalities are the place to start reform, he asserted, for we must 'address ourselves to what is nearest at hand.' One point, of seven in his message, went to land-value taxation. Applying that idea in New York, taking the 'immense values created by the growth of the population,' could bring into existence the most beautiful and healthful of cities. Defeat held no fears for him,

George said, in concluding, but he would not be involved in a movement that might prove to have little popular support at the polls. So he fixed a condition which was then unique in the history of American vote-getting. Yes, he would accept candidacy for mayor if and when the new political organization would present petitions signed by 30,000 men who would pledge themselves to work and vote in his behalf.

As he doubtless wanted, the immediate effect was to slow down and to intensify the labor effort. In September there had to be meetings at every level of organization. To bring funds to the CLU an assessment was placed on all participating organizations, at the rate of twenty-five cents for each individual member. The petition rolls had to be prepared, circulated, and signed. Time was required, and dedication by a great number of people.

But even while energies were being tested and gathered, there were ample signs that George had not demanded too much. On Labor Day he reviewed a parade and received an ovation — the first American demonstration for him to outdo the reception home from Ireland four years earlier. Perhaps the most convincing testimony of labor's mounting political spirit is that of Samuel Gompers. Writing after almost forty years of opposing the American Federation of Labor's entering politics, Gompers recalls 1886 in his autobiography. At first he resisted even this political impulse, he says, but on second thought, 'I appreciated the movement as a demonstration of protest. The campaign was notable in that it united people of unusual abilities from many walks of life and that it proved a sort of vestibule for many who later undertook practical work for human betterment. Many leaders in the constructive work of the following years were recruits of the Henry George campaign.' Presently Gompers became chairman of the city organization of Henry George Clubs and took charge of the speakers bureau. By October he was making speeches every day, convinced in spite of himself that he was marching toward a great victory.

On 23 September occurred a major step in the consolidation between candidate and party. A second general conference at Clarendon Hall made the nomination formal, and it endorsed a new platform written by Henry George himself. Frank Ferrell, a Negro prominent in the Knights of Labor, presented it; and the New York *World* caught the spirit of the document in saying that it was an epitome of *Progress and Poverty*. The new party — some months were required to establish its name as the United Labor party — now departed altogether from the eclecticism of the original platform. On the economic side, there was a denunciation of monopoly in the old and eloquent way. The new platform demanded that values created by urban growth — land values and the monopoly values of utilities alike — should be channeled to the people. As in San Francisco, George called for the reconstruction of city government, and especially for simplifying court procedures. Again as in California he spoke for a constitutional convention, in order to open the avenues for reforms not to be made in any other way. Asserting as always the principle of equality implicit in the Declaration, George reduced the first platform's emphasis on social class; and he appealed for the support of all citizens.

Though formality and finality of acceptance still waited on the great number of signatures, the Clarendon Hall platform brought the union of man and movement close to completion. George may have intended real reservation in an *if* clause he inserted in an interview, which the New York *Sun* printed on 24 September just after the convention. 'I have not sought any nomination, and if I accept one it will be only for the sake of advancing principles I believe in.' But a *Tribune* reporter described him as entirely at ease in his office, dressed in a Prince Albert coat and surrounded by friends, and in an optimistic frame of mind. Would he be able to put his theories into practice, if elected, the reporter inquired. No, not very well as mayor. But election would greatly advance his ideas, George said, and he would not be surprised to receive 90,000 votes. He was counting on the support not of labor alone, but also of men of independent mind, such as Father McGlynn, James Redpath (now of the *North American,* later of lecture-bureau fame), and Poultney Bigelow, all of whom were already committed.

In private fact George made his own irrevocable commitment in a conference with an enemy. Here we have his own account which, though he did not render it until 1897, and then it was objected to, seems to tell the essential truth. While still free to withdraw from the campaign George was sought out by William Ivins, the city chamberlain and a personal friend of the Democratic mayor in office, William R. Grace. As a man of wealth, education, and interest in reform, Mr. Ivins represented the more civilized branch of New York's Democrats, as well as the party in a general way.

The two men met for dinner in a German restaurant in Lafayette Place. 'We sat down in a private room, unattended, and smoked some cigars together.' According to the candidate's memory eleven years later, Mr. Ivins spoke entirely to the point: Henry George could never become mayor of New York, no matter how many votes were cast for him — he 'could not possibly be counted in.' So the Democrats proposed a deal. If George would refuse the nomination, Tammany and the County Democrats would have him elected to Congress from a district they controlled — perhaps this meant Congressman Hewitt's — and, in the interval, George could visit Europe. Mr. Ivins' denials of 1897 said that he could have offered no seat in Congress, because he had no such party authority; that he went to George not to bribe but to befriend; and that he told him that he would be snowed under if he ran, not counted out.

The common area of the two stories is that the two did meet, that Mr. Ivins did suggest that George run for Congress, and that a representative of Mayor Grace did say that George would surely lose if he persisted as candidate. This supplies sufficient agreement as to fact to make it unnecessary to question George's story of his own reply. 'You tell me I cannot possibly get the office. Why if I cannot get the office, do you want me to withdraw?' To which Mr. Ivins did not deny answering: 'You cannot be elected but your running will raise hell.' Then Henry George ended the interview. 'You have relieved me of embarrassment. I do not want the responsibility and the work of the Mayor of New York, but I do want to raise hell! I am decided and I will run.'

By September's end, at war with the country's most powerful machine, George tried a tactic from the fight of 1882 in Ireland. He sounded out the new archbishop of New York. Himself an intimate now of the powerful Father McGlynn, George had every opportunity to understand the interfiliations which, to his advantage, tied his old friends of New York's Catholic and Irish element with his new friends of the labor movement. Likewise he must have understood equally well the loyalties which, to his disadvantage, cross-connected both sets of friends with his new enemy, Tammany Hall. At the moment Father McGlynn was still forbidden, under a ruling given by Archbishop McCloskey, to speak on Irish land affairs. But he had announced for Cleveland in 1884, and he was anything but a cowed or politically indifferent man. If he were free for politics, George would have an incomparably valuable political ally.

The new archbishop, Michael Corrigan, had had as yet no reason for fresh action within the premises. Yet surely, when Father McGlynn supplied George with a letter of introduction, both of them must have understood that they were approaching the most authoritarian kind of archbishop, different in ideas from the Bishop of Meath, and in temperament from a McCloskey or a Cardinal Gibbons. Archbishop Corrigan belonged, as definitely as Bishop McQuaid of Rochester, to a type of churchman frequent in Ireland and traditional in French Canada. On the other hand, he and McGlynn had been collegemates together in Rome; and it is just conceivable that George made his call actually believing that the archbishop could be brought to say that he would not interfere if McGlynn chose to participate in labor politics.

Certainly George proceeded as though he believed in such a possibility. But, while Corrigan received him courteously, he refused to discuss any phase of the coming campaign except the problem of Edward McGlynn. Thus George learned at once that if the preacher were to enter the campaign he would be suppressed. George tried to explain that the ideas he held about property involved no conflict with church doctrine. But here he confronted a closed mind; through all that followed, Corrigan never comprehended, and apparently did not try to comprehend, George's distinctions between property in land and property in things. George fared no better when he tried to persuade the archbishop that priests as citizens should exercise the same right to speak in behalf of a labor candidate as in behalf of a Democrat. Whatever success the meeting had for George lay in its plain revelation of a rough road ahead.

Acting as though their business were not closed, George sent Corrigan a copy of the diocesan letter of the Bishop of Meath, which he himself had distributed in Ireland. (The archbishop's father had come from County Meath.) 'By its incidental allusions,' George explained, the day after the interview, the letter showed that the Irish bishop 'fully shares the views I hold with respect to property in land.' George also sent copies of all his books. 'If you will do me the honor to look over them you will see clearly that there is nothing in them inconsistent with any of the teachings of religion and I think you will agree with Cardinal Manning, who declared to me that there was nothing in the principles I have advocated in regard to the treatment of the land that the Church has ever condemned.'

Before he closed George switched his letter from persuasion to threat. 'If you should step in now, and prevent [Father McGlynn] from expressing his sympathy with the organized labor associations of this city, it will seem to that great body of citizens as if you use your ecclesiastical authority for the purpose of breaking up a movement which has for its aim the destruction of political corruption and the assertion of popular rights.' Very soon John Mc-Mackin, the Catholic chairman of the Clarendon Hall conference, clinched the threat with a protest of his own, that Father McGlynn should not be forbidden to campaign.

By the early days of October the lines of political division were pretty clear, and the forces were gathering in mass. On the second of the month, days ahead of George's formal acceptance, he was nominated by non-labor people, some 2300 who crowded into Chickering Hall. Two Episcopalian clergymen took the front: John Kramer, who presided, and Heber Newton, who made a speech. Three intellectuals, all professors at least in name, gave addresses: David Scott, of City College; Daniel de Leon, future socialist leader who at this time was a lecturer at Columbia; and Thomas Davidson, the wandering philosopher who had been one of the founders of Fabianism in Britain, and who would later assume a role as transmitter of moderate socialist ideas to this country. But the great climax of the evening came when Father McGlynn took the platform. Although already forbidden to speak, he had told no one, not even Henry George. He poured out his feeling 'as if he expected that night to be his last.' The Chickering Hall meeting voted through the nomination with a roar.

The formal consequences of the many beginnings, Henry George's acceptance on 5 October, had the character of a dedication and a festival. Again the place was the somber, be-pillared meeting room on the basement floor of Cooper Union. The huge petitions, tied in blue ribbons and displayed on the platform, looked like gifts of some overwhelming kind. The Reverend Mr. Kramer presented the Chickering Hall resolution. The chairman, Mr. McMackin, said briefly that Henry George had received such a nomination as had never been made anywhere before.

Replying, George offered a line of personal history. Once earlier he had had political ambitions, he admitted; but another career had come to him, 'that of pioneer — that of men who go in advance of politics.' He did not want to be mayor, but he had been told that he alone could unite the forces of labor. He would fight uncompromised as he had been nominated without restriction. The speech voiced the same civics he had made his own in San Francisco. He would not be corrupt; in office he would enforce the laws equally for all; he would work to have the mayor's office transformed into a seat of powerful and responsible leadership. At peroration he spoke, I think for the first time in public, about the New York vision and dedication of 1869. He renewed the pledge: he would do all that lay in him to improve the life of such people as he had noticed for the first time when he was far from home, a visitor from a land of aspirations tramping the incredible streets of America's great city.

George had made a moving address, its thought entirely consistent with his past. If there had been any August danger that he might fall into being a captive candidate, dominated by unions or used as cover man for ideologies not his own, the danger was now passed. By October he had made himself the captor — the writer of the platform, the leader of 30,000 by their pledges, the establisher of tone and feeling. In whatever way he might choose, he could now raise hell as he had told Mr. Ivins he would do, in the politics of New York City.

–4–

For two months and more the initiative had all lain with the labor party; and that situation did not change at once, or change much, after 5 October. As of the end of September, hopes had soared fastest and highest in *John Swinton's Paper*. Henry George would capture the mayoralty this year. Would he not go right up the ladder, as van Buren and Cleveland had done, that paper queried, and take the governorship next, and then the Presidency? As the campaign got under way *Swinton's* saluted the George movement as the bringer of new forces, and said that a New York victory would lead to a great uprising of the masses. Meanwhile the nominee himself had accepted as real the possibility that he might discover in the end that he had done more than fight an educational campaign, and had actually become the mayor of New York.

It is safe to interpret as a sign of the control of the huge city's politics by the machines that neither Democrats nor Republicans nominated a candidate earlier than the middle of October. As late as 7 October, Congressman Abram S. Hewitt, the distinguished man of business and philanthropy who six years earlier had hired Henry George as ghost writer, wrote to Tammany Hall's new boss, Richard Croker, that he preferred not to be re-elected to the house, because he felt 'old and weary' (he was sixty-three), and that he would change his mind only if he were persuaded that 'in the judgment of your organization the public interest will best be served this way.' Two days later Hewitt believed that Tammany's decision for him was another term in Washington. But a week afterward Croker's insistence had made him the Democratic party's choice for mayor; and in his speech of acceptance he claimed for his candidacy the one real alternative to socialism, anarchism, and nihilism — New York's escape from scenes like Paris under the Terror.

At the middle of the month precisely, the Republicans nominated Theodore Roosevelt. The future Progressive was now twenty-eight and six years out of Harvard — since graduation he had lived awhile in the Bad Lands, written three books, and served three years in the state legislature. As opponent of George he offered, in more aristocratic, youthful, and brighter version, many of Hewitt's qualities — wealth, distinction of background, education, a record free of corruption. True, the directions of his reformism in Albany were less promising for labor than Hewitt's record in state and nation. But Roosevelt now as later brought special charm into popular politics. Though from first to last the campaign tended to become a duel between George and Hewitt, the *Times* and the *Tribune* as Republican papers remained loyal to their young man; and Roosevelt's attack kept doubly alive the doubt whether enough votes would go to Hewitt to prevent George from winning a stunning victory.

Republican efforts and motions for the three short weeks of the mayoralty campaign provide some of the most telling illustrations we have, of New York's loyalties, anxieties and needs. In a way quite comparable to George's experience with the San Francisco *Alta* and its editors Hittell and McCrellish during the red scare of 1877 and after, the New York *Nation* and *Evening Post,* dominated by the fiery reformist Republican, E. L. Godkin, swung entirely to Hewitt and against political labor. Using words calculated for incitement, the *Nation* wondered, in the last October issue, what the result would be should Henry George bring 'the Anarchists and Socialists and Strikers and Deadbeats of every description within 10,000 or 20,000' of victory. To Roosevelt's mind this was party perfidy, which he described in his own way: 'Godkin, White, and various others of the better element have acted with unscrupulous meanness and a low, partisan dishonesty which would disgrace the veriest machine heelers.'

But the young candidate had no illusions about his capacity to win back Republican turncoats. Confessing his most private expectations to Henry Cabot Lodge and one or two others, Roosevelt foresaw that he would lose thousands of votes to the Democrats; and he refused to estimate how many to the labor party. Even now there is little evidence from which to guess about the number of Republicans who wanted Henry George, and voted for him. We know simply that some interesting members of the party did do so.

There were echoes of anti-slavery, for instance, surely welcome to the recipient, in a letter written on the stationery of a post of the Grand Army of the Republic. This assured George that a lot of the 'old boys' were on his side. There must have been Republicans among such groups as the Columbia College Alumni for Henry George Club; and nowhere is incidence and connection of Republicanism more likely than among the sixty or so Protestant clergymen — compared to about forty Catholic priests — known to have been favorable. These ministers represented many denominations, spaced as far apart as Universalist and Episcopalian. From a different corner of the religious field, Robert Ingersoll declared that Republicans particularly ought to vote for Henry George.

The simultaneous candidacy of Allen Thorndike Rice, proprietor and editor of the *North American Review,* for a seat in Congress, gave George his best chance to say that Republicans and labor men could be allies. One remembers the root of George's loyalty to Mr. Rice, and he expressed it openly in a letter to the *Tribune,* which was intended as endorsement. 'Mr. Rice in throwing open the pages of the *North American Review* to the full expression of radical thought on social subjects has done more to bring moral support to the cause of the downtrodden than all our members of Congress put together.'

From a most unlikely source we have a revealing peepsight into an area of sympathy, not followership, for Henry George, at very high level. Coincidentally with the heat of the campaign, Rutherford B. Hayes had come from Ohio for a meeting of the trustees of the Peabody Fund for education in the South. As the ex-president tells the story, he buttonholed his fellow trustees, and inquired what they thought. Robert C. Winthrop, of the first family of Massachusetts, ex-congressman and ex-senator but always scholar and orator, replied that the labor candidacy had his 'hearty sympathy . . . it is a protest against the wrongs that have been growing up, and are now threatening the life of the Republic.' Chief Justice Waite approved the comment, and so did Bishop Whipple; and Dr. Samuel Green, one-time mayor of Boston, 'wished success to Henry George, whom he believed to be a thoroughly sincere, honest man, with the welfare of his fellow men at heart.' So at least four of the twelve Peabody trustees, five if we count the Republican ex-president, presumably not one of them an accepter of *Progress and Poverty,* were favorable to George's candidacy. No such Olympian attitude would have been natural in any group predominantly Democratic.

Certainly so far as local Democrats were concerned, whether of the Tammany Hall or of New York's County Democracy variety, there was increasing cause for panic. During late October the labor campaign moved with amazing vigor. Party headquarters were set up at the Colonnade Hotel. John McMackin, the Knight of Labor, and Catholic, who had taken the chair at the principal preliminary meetings when the CLU had charge, became campaign manager; and Samuel Gompers took charge of uniting the efforts of the Henry George Clubs, which sprang up in great unlisted numbers. On 20 October the George organization was reported to have set up twenty-four districts, each with its leaders and workers, some of them having meetings every night.

At that point labor had a windfall. A minor Democratic machine, Irving Hall, abandoned Hewitt and, out of hatred for Tammany, dropped into George's basket. To Henry George it was an apple none too sweet. But when the formal nomination was tendered he was present, and he delivered an address which promised reform — and denied any other commitment. Though never departing from his principal role as intellectual and moral standard-bearer, George himself did succeed in making a number of sizable contributions to the practical and organizational effort. He channeled money into the campaign treasury from as far as San Francisco, in the touching case of his devoted translator, Herr Gütschow; and he tapped purses as fat as those of Tom L. Johnson and August Lewis, a New York trader and manufacturer recently converted to his ideas.

Campaign time also brought in such return payments from Britain as visitors could make — from people whom George had aided or counseled during his missions overseas. On 25 October, for instance, according to a newspaper account, 'a venerable, white-bearded gentleman in spectacles,' whom George introduced as 'the most eminent British naturalist,' spoke for the candidate. He was glad to do so, Alfred Russel Wallace said later, somewhat ruefully: 'I tried my best to be forcible, praised George, and said a few words about what we were doing in England, but I could see that I did not impress them much.'

Even before the campaign proper began, by ironic coincidence on the day on which he called on Archbishop Corrigan, George met Eleanor and Edward Aveling, daughter and son-in-law of Karl Marx, who were over from England and at the moment house guests of George's publisher, John Lovell. Though entertaining reservations about him as thinker, they liked George, and reasoned from *Social Problems* that he was almost the right kind. In speeches before socialist groups they favored and supported the labor candidacy. Apparently a little later than the Avelings, George met Sidney Webb, and the two established a durable, not intimate, friendly connection.

How welcome or unwelcome such socialist attention was, even when it was Fabian, George does not say. But plainly his feelings were hurt when Michael Davitt, in America on one of his many visits, passed him by. The veteran of the Land League wrote that he could not interfere in an American election, nor did he really think that George should win. Thus cropped out again the old touchy problem of international radical politics, and perhaps also an Irishman's persuasion that power corrupts. But George would have liked more generous treatment — it would have diminished the effect of the opposition of Archbishop Corrigan and the hierarchy generally. Though there was no lack of endorsement by the heterodox — in rapid succession by Terence Powderly, Felix Adler, and Robert Ingersoll, for assorted examples — none could have seemed more natural or just than the one he wanted and was denied, from the fighting old Land Leaguer.

The most heartening thing was the volunteering of the masses. Building on the September success in getting the 30,000 signatures, the October campaign rapidly became a new phenomenon of crowds and excitement. One is reminded of the age of Jackson; but this surpassed the rallies and marches of 1828 and 1840, as the industrial age — big-city life and the new immigration — now made possible. An illustration in *Leslie's Weekly* of 30 October gives a good idea of what occurred on many nights. George is portrayed speaking outdoors, center; he stands with three other men in an uncovered, unhorsed tailcart; the four are shown knee-deep in a horizonless sea of standing working men. There are signs raised aloft: 'An Injury to One is the Concern of All.' 'No More Rings No More Halls.' 'Vote for George.' The picture's feeling of disturbance is heightened by torches flaming and smoking in the background. Until the end, even the weather seemed friendly to labor, dry and mild and favorable to meetings and marchings. The campaign history says that many able speakers stood up on carts as George did, on the East Side, night after night, not infrequently several times an evening.

At the moment of the Democratic and Republican nominations, the labor leaders decided that they had to have a daily paper. The Central Labor Union had felt such a need since July; and in the interval the George movement had had the backing of the *Irish World, John Swinton's Paper,* and the socialistic *Volkeszeitung,* weeklies all three. Not a single metropolitan daily came out for George. In response, the New York *Leader* was thrown together in just five days. The *Volkeszeitung* lent physical facilities; the Central Labor Union subscribed $1000, and the paper became known as its organ. But financially the *Leader* was no unilateral effort: the carpenters' union subscribed $1500, and other unions $100 apiece.

There was no trouble either, about gathering the necessary manpower. Louis Post, the most appropriate person, both because of his experience with *Truth* and his old connections with CLU and Henry George, and because he had defended the Theiss boycotters, took charge. But he had the help of many volunteer journalists, some of them from the conservative papers. From the first issue on 19 October, the paper achieved good character, not a sensational one, as news purveyor — at about the intellectual level of the San Francisco *Post* under George. During the two weeks before election, circulation zoomed to 50,000 or more, and perhaps held that number for a few days. To the reader of today, the *Leader* offers an amazing display of high energy and quality of talent placed at the service of the labor party.

Just as the paper began to appear, Abram Hewitt dutifully took up the outpouring challenge. In accepting the nomination he at first made efforts to be disarming: he acknowledged great need for reform in the city, and he drew on his record in Congress to recommend himself for labor's votes. But from justifiable claims for past performance, the Democratic candidate moved immediately into the name-calling for which Roosevelt censured him. Under pressure, we are told, from Croker, whose new career hinged on winning this campaign, Hewitt descended through vulgarism to malice, as he described himself as a son of poverty and as the only present choice for New York to avoid revolution, 'nihilism' (a particularly strong fear-word in 1886), and terror.

George thought he knew how to deal with this kind of procedure. Let us do what Lincoln and Douglas did, he proposed: meet in face-to-face debate. We can acknowledge at the start that the mayor's office does not control tax policy. This would render us the freer to discuss whether land-value taxation signifies what you say it does, the destruction of society, or what I say, its democratization. On what basis, George inquired in an open letter, would Mr. Hewitt meet him? Several times, or once or twice in the city's largest halls? The challenge was printed in the *Leader* and everywhere noticed in the press of city and nation.

Hewitt declined without regrets. The public discussion of public issues had never before been so considerable, he dryly observed, and the voters knew well enough the differences between Henry George and Abram S. Hewitt. Then the Democratic candidate pressed a question of his own, a little hard to answer: If Mr. George sincerely means to put into effect his ideas about property, why does he not contest my seat in Congress? Hewitt commended Andrew Carnegie's recent book, *Triumphant Democracy,* to those who believed that present methods of government had failed. He returned to the proposition that the Democratic party must save New York from anarchy and chaos.

George answered, and challenged a second reply, in the newspapers. Hewitt's practical question he let go with the observation that he could never afford to undertake the costs of a campaign for a seat in Congress. George did not need to say that the present campaign came to him self-generating and largely self-financing; and perhaps he did not wish to spell out for criticism his idea that any campaign in which he participated would be primarily educational and symbolic, and only secondarily a fight to win office. He concentrated now on Hewitt's proposition which infuriated him. Tammany save society from what, he demanded. Did Mr. Hewitt understand how city officers buy votes, and at the moment were doing so, by the old bribery of hiring men for public works, on the eve of an election?

This brought out Hewitt's final statement. The Democrat denied, first, that his voters were being influenced corruptly; and he demanded second, that George elucidate certain questions of his social theory. Why tax a poor man's land? Why relieve from taxation a rich man's capital investments? These were the same old questions as those put by the outlying newspapers of California in 1873, the same ones put by the Sacramento *Record-Union* in reviewing *Progress and Poverty.* At this stage Hewitt's part in the exchange of question and answer ended. He ignored George's final challenge, to appear at a meeting in Chickering Hall, where he would be given half the time if he wanted, to counter a statement of George's ideas. In a third letter and in many speeches, George willingly elucidated the economics of his proposals.

Henry George had been unable to bring his opponent onto a public platform, and yet he had succeeded in having a debate. So his contemporaries, at least, understood the open letters in the newspapers. The New York *Tribune,* for one, assumed a judicial air in sizing up results. 'Mr. George's [second] letter is not quite parliamentary in tone but it is terribly severe because so much of it is true,' that paper editorialized. *Leslie's,* though it could say in one issue that 'what all crime is in practice, Georgism is in theory,' retreated now to a position of balancing judgments. George had proved himself the 'hardest hitter,' Hewitt 'the most skillful fencer,' it estimated. George was right about corruption in New York, and Hewitt correct in saying that present political institutions would be adequate to solve social problems; George had justly ridiculed Hewitt's partnership in reform with Tammany, but Hewitt was as right in denouncing George's theories. Thus a philistine editorial page at bay. The sixty or so relevant excerpts, which were reprinted in *Public Opinion* from newspapers across the land, at least suggest that the panic reaction to George was pretty well limited to the city where the campaign was fought.

After the open letters Hewitt carried on his campaign quietly. He addressed half a dozen or so meetings, none of them very large. His real work was done by Tammany and its allies.

George made everything possible of his forensic opportunities. He took the occasion of the Chickering Hall meeting, to which he had dared Hewitt to come, to speak as he had in London about the community's right in the land. Illustrating concretely from well-known local conditions, he called New York the most crowded city in the world, and deplored with eloquence the space held empty by private owners. 'We want all the buildings we can get. I think that every American citizen ought to have a separate house . . . We are all creatures of the Creator . . . I say that the right to land is one of our inalienable rights.' Perhaps more perfectly than any other event in his American career, this Chickering Hall address represents the battle as Henry George loved to wage it — his mind at play, his audience sympathetic, his major ideas being visibly drunk in with emotion by thousands as he performed.

From five to ten meetings a day, as October came to a close, was almost a routine performance for Henry George. Speeches before labor unions, immigrant groups, and clubs; noontime appearances at factory gates; and evening addresses out of doors — these were the characteristic events. On 16 October, for example, he addressed: a meeting of French Americans, a group in Abingdon Square, an assembly of Broadway railroad workers, and, at eleven in the evening, a crowd in Sulzer's Harlem River Park. On 25, 26, and 27 October he addressed at least seventeen meetings: four were meetings of cigar workers, two were other unions, one was an immigrant group, one a Columbia College Alumni club, and one a meeting of spiritualists. Strenuously courting the support of groups or organizations of Frenchmen, Germans, Bohemians, Irishmen, and Jews, George made himself the exception to the rule, recently stated by Professor Oscar Handlin, that reformers of this period did not much appeal to the new immigrants, or get their interest and votes. At a meeting of the Uptown Bohemian Henry George Club, the candidate said that he was very proud to be endorsed by 'Germans, Austrians, Russians, Polanders, Scandinavians, and Irish.'

At campaign's close, the arrival in the city of Terence Powderly brought into focus the most disturbing issue of loyalty then at stake, the one George had discussed with Archbishop Corrigan. The Grand Master Workman arrived at a stage of being intensely burdened with his dual role as labor leader and Catholic layman. He was fresh from the conferences with Cardinal Gibbons in Baltimore which had decided that, as Catholic scholarship now makes perfectly plain, American Catholics need not be excluded from the Knights of Labor, as French Canadians were. In New York, Powderly met Father McGlynn. Since the one speech, this most dedicated of all Henry George men had kept silence under discipline, except for a single interview. He was quoted then as having declared that Henry George was inspired 'by the same love of justice as was taught by Christ,' and that he believed the candidate to be 'peculiarly a man of destiny . . . Destined to be President of the United States.'

What would Catholics do who felt the least bit the same way as Father McGlynn? How would the Irish voters perform, on 2 November? The *Irish World* continued for George; the *Irish Herald* went for Hewitt. Several times during the last days of the campaign, Powderly spoke for Henry George. He literally took a seat beside the dynamic priest. He and Father McGlynn rode in a barouche together, shortly before the poll, an open and purposeful symbol of Catholics for the labor party. On election day he went about with Henry George, from polling place to polling place, to observe how things were going.

Meanwhile, however, Archbishop Corrigan's side had acted, not altogether quietly. After Father McGlynn had given his interview, a Tammany Hall official had turned in alarm to the vicar-general, Monsignor Thomas S. Preston. What would he say to the question whether the Catholic clergy favored Henry George for mayor? The reply was as definite as the archbishop's discipline: 'The great majority of the clergy in this city are opposed to the candidacy of Mr. George. They think his principles unsound and unsafe, and contrary to the teachings of the church . . . His principles, logically carried out, would prove the ruin of the workingmen he professes to befriend.' The vicar-general's letter was widely circulated by Tammany Hall, and was even passed out to the congregations leaving the churches on the last Sunday or two before the election.

For the final Saturday night of the campaign, 31 October, labor planned a vast demonstration. Samuel Gompers was placed in charge. The hope for Tuesday was 90,000 votes to win; and the plan called for a parade of 88,775 to pass before Henry George in a reviewing stand in Union Square. But the weather changed that night: a cold downpour set in, and the police failed to prevent traffic snarls. Estimates of actual participation vary from 25,000 to 70,000, as the number of men and women who did march — 'intrepidly, a very real symbol of the spirit in back of the campaign.' Perhaps the campaign history's figures are as accurate as any: 30,000 in the ranks, 10,000 watchers in Union Square, two hours required to pass the reviewing stand.

At a rally afterward, the Knights of Labor cheered Powderly on the platform; and the trades-union men shouted for Gompers. Gompers relishes remembering how he answered Hewitt's charge that labor was fighting a class battle. Class warfare was not the goal, but true democracy, he told the crowd.

Confidence prevailed on Saturday night — after the storm, after the parade, and after the vicar-general's letter. The very last words were said on Monday evening, at Cooper Union. Powderly made a speech then, a kind of ultimate endorsement by a Catholic. Though not scheduled, the crowd demanded George, and the candidate spoke briefly, full of hope for victory.

−5−

At the close of the campaign's labors, George's party had its peculiar difficulties to provide the machinery which parties had to provide for election day — ballots and boxes, in that period before the Australian ballot was adopted. Watchers and inspectors had to be organized in numbers. Labor suffered its greatest disadvantages, opposite Tammany, in this part of the effort; but, thanks partly to

Irving Hall, arrangements were ready in time. The election-eve advice of speakers for George, and the last editorials of the *Leader*, urged working men to be sure to vote. Be careful to get your ballots, and allow no dishonest tactics, they were counseled. In case of being ruled out as disqualified, or of being offered a bribe, they were to report and protest the offenders through regular channels of the law.

The recorded vote of 2 November follows: Hewitt, 90,552, a figure just the size of labor's highest hope for George. George, 68,110, a figure just about equal to Godkin's worst fears — a labor vote so large as to come within 10,000 or 20,000 of winning. Roosevelt, 60,435.

Tuesday at midnight George conceded defeat — admitted a setback rather. 'This is the Bunker Hill,' he told disappointed campaign workers. 'We have hit a fire that will never go out . . . This has been but a skirmish that prepares our forces for the battles that are to follow.' He blamed for labor's loss 'the perverted and unscrupulous press,' and said that if there had been a fair vote 'I would be elected mayor tonight.' The campaigners gave him round on round of cheers.

George would have more to say later, and, more bitterly than he, others would speak for him, about having been cheated of victory. But immediately there were more hopeful things to concern him. Less than a week after the vote a labor meeting was called, to take place in a hall which would seat 1600. But 4000 people appeared, and the crowd shouted for five minutes when George came to the front of the platform to speak. The meeting endorsed the principles of the campaign platform and set up a temporary committee to carry on. Thus the United Labor party was born. A brass band and a body of marchers escorted George back to his hotel.

The enthusiasm was by no means limited to those recently first drawn into politics. Ninety men turned out for a post-election meeting of the Henry George Journalist Club; and that organization transformed itself into the Henry George Press Club, for permanent operations. A Social Reform Club of New York was founded also. About half the members were trades-union men, remembers Samuel Gompers, who himself sat on the advisory board. But the memorable names are Lyman Abbot, Felix Adler, Hamilton Holt, William Dean Howells, Mary E. J. Kelly, Josephine

Shaw Lowell, Albert Shaw, E. R. A. Seligman, and the Reverend W. S. Rainsford. Though 'not a believer in everything Henry George advocates,' this famous clergyman said in a Thanksgiving sermon at St. George's, still he was grateful for the campaign, 'because it stirred the people up to a true sense of citizenship, and the movement has just begun.' Commenting on some of this carry-over, *John Swinton's Paper* spoke in pride of having been the first paper ever to nominate Henry George for President. The *Leader* professed contempt when the New York *Herald,* recently for Hewitt, proposed Henry George for Congress. 'Mr. George has more important work in hand.'

As for the retrospect, the bitterness and the blame for losing out to Tammany, the most that came from party headquarters about possible cheating was an announcement that a law committee wished to receive 'complaints of bribery, intimidation, or other illegal conduct.' Apparently only a handful of cases were reported. Henry George himself waited until 1897, until his second mayoralty campaign, before he said much more in public than he had said on the evening of his defeat. At that time he made it plain that when he spoke about unfairness he was speaking about such crimes as stuffing ballot boxes with illegal votes, and stealing legal ones from them. But, as of 2 November 1886, it is necessary to consider that he may have been thinking of the Roman Catholic hierarchy when he spoke of unfairness in the election. 'On a square vote I would undoubtedly have been elected,' he wrote his dear friend Gütschow, without explanations, two months after the election.

Certainly Poultney Bigelow, the literary friend who will be remembered as belonging to New York's highest and most informed circles, put the blame for George's defeat squarely on the church. Henry George Mr. Bigelow estimated to have been 'too credulous and kindly to detect the machinery by which he had been defeated,' but he himself was unqualified in saying that George's 'noisy Land League supporters howled themselves red in the face until the Sunday before election day, and then from every pulpit came a soft whisper more potent on the Tuesday after than Moses on Mount Sinai.'

Bad consciences and resentments among Catholics themselves go some distance to confirm Mr. Bigelow's hard judgment. Michael Davitt, though he had held his distance from George, took home to Archbishop Walsh of Dublin such a picture of cross-purposes and defiance of authority within the archdiocese of New York as he hardly dared to put into words. The messages he bore, from the most venerable clergymen and from laymen worthy of respect, he said, were intended to enlist the sympathy of Cardinal Manning and others, in hope that Rome would be moderate toward Father McGlynn. Davitt's sense that the George campaign had created great moral trouble within American Catholicism was later confirmed by Thomas Sugrue, a Catholic independent. In 1886 many Irish Americans learned, according to this writer, that Catholic loyalty and American citizenship require a different reconciling from the one offered — in the form of clerical bossism — by Archbishop Corrigan and his colleagues.

Concerning the kind of misuse of power first suggested by George in his after-election complaint, the perversion of the press, neither the journalist ex-candidate nor any other participator in the campaign, so far as I know, ever followed up with a specification of changes. But criminality at the polling places has been charged to Tammany by the biographers closest to George — by Louis Post, and by Henry George, Jr., who was twenty-four in 1886; and the assertion has gained rather than diminished with the years. Father McGlynn's biographer says that the beloved priest's appearance at one polling place caused that set of election officials not to manipulate the vote, as they had expected to do. And, a few years ago, relying on a witness who had spoken in detail, Anna George de Mille enlarged the indictment.

Mrs. de Mille's star witness is Charles Edward Russell, well-known social novelist and journalist and occasionally a public servant. He had been a reporter in 1886, and he recalled George as a 'Little Red Rooster,' because of his appearance and temperament. He remembered also his own opinion of 1886, shared by 'skilled observers,' that the labor party was 'impelled irresistibly by the revolt of the workers and the propertyless,' and that it would win. With such recollections, and with a persisting strong economic interpretation of events, Mr. Russell accepted, and placed in his own autobiography as an important truth, a remark that came to him from Richard Croker: 'They could not allow a man like Henry George to be mayor of New York. It would upset all their arrangements.' Mr. Russell puts down, as his own opinion, that, 'When the last vote had been deposited that day, Henry George was elected mayor of New York. In the next three hours he was deprived of his victory by the simple process of manipulating the returns.'

Other students of Tammany Hall hold the same, or very similar, opinions. According to Gustavus Myers: 'if the reiterated statements of reputable eye witnesses are to be believed,' frauds occurred in the mayoralty election of 1886 to surpass all other occasions. Lothrop Stoddard believed that the Tammany machine had to put on 'the last ounce of pressure' in the precints, and had to bring in repeat voters and illegal voters from Philadelphia and Jersey City, in order to win. More recently Professor Allan Nevins, as scholarly biographer of Hewitt, has taken the more moderate, but it seems to me not more logical, position, that, yes, there may have been vote switching by the tabulators, but, no, there could not have been enough switching to cause a difference of result. Professor Selig Perlman, as historian of labor, is much more suspicious.

There remains, of course, no heap of yellowed ballots for the present writer to count, to settle the doubt forever. I have uncovered no new testimony, nor discovered secret confessions of wrong-doing. My own judgment, I should say inclination, is that the big cheat could have occurred and probably did. But we shall never know certainly whether George or Hewitt received the larger number of legal votes.

At this distance in time certain characteristics of New York's mentality, morality, and politics of 1886 seem more memorable than the issue — the two-year term as mayor which ended Abram Hewitt's political career. The city's voters clearly were in no condition, and most especially the Catholic voters were not, to give the hearing of reason and fair judgment to Henry George as candidate for office. Yet, despite the mentality of panic, and despite the possible cheat, George the loser achieved a triumph which was both numerical and moral. Seventy thousand votes for labor were unprecedented.

The triumph justified hopes for a further effort.

XVI

No National Labor Party To Lead

1887

SHORTLY after the mayoralty election Henry George told a newspaper reporter that his own plan was to buy some ink and pens,
and get back to his writing.

In a certain sense he had no choice. He was a defeated candidate,
an ex-journalist, and a free-lance writer. What came next, except
by his pen, depended first of all on invitations he might receive,
on organizations which might volunteer — not very much on himself alone. In a way it was like 1881, when, the author of a new
book, he was waiting opportunities to match his ideas. Now he
rested a moment on a high platform of history, known the world
around, but waiting nevertheless for situations to arise that would
decide his course.

They were not slow to appear. Shortly after the New York City
vote he went to Boston to speak for the mayoral candidacy of
George McNeill, his recent editor as compiler of *The Labor Movement the Problem of the Day,* who presently polled 3000 votes.
Before Christmas George had many invitations to speak, many
more than he could accept if he were going 'to keep our ranks
firm' at home, he explained to Thomas Walker.

He did leave New York for an immediate brief speaking tour
in the province of Ontario, however; and three months later he
took another trip, going through the small cities of northern Ohio,
lower Michigan, and Wisconsin, and on to Burlington and Kansas

City and return. This second effort was both encouraging and discouraging. He had three or four college audiences, including those at Ann Arbor and Madison (which a candidate for the master's degree in history, Frederick Jackson Turner, attended); and he made about $1000, the best yet. On the other hand, he faced some thinly occupied halls and his performances did not always satisfy himself. He enjoyed being celebrated and being offered pleasures along the way. In Boston it gratified him to make his appearance in Faneuil Hall, and in Montreal there was the fun of a sleigh-ride, and of wearing fur cap, gloves, and coat provided by the hotel manager. A little change of scene, some compliments, and relaxation were just in order.

But the ex-candidate could not escape a winter of high pressures. After 2 November the talk about George for President increased mightily; and, far from being confined to *John Swinton's* and other papers which had campaigned for him, it was conceived more frequently in fear of his running than in hope. *Leslie's Weekly*, which may be drawn on again for a sampling of ordinary sentiment, said that the recent elections demanded to be understood, for the country as a whole, as more important than most between-presidential contests. Whereas the usual thing, as in 1874 and in 1882, was for the dominant party's control of Congress to give way to the other party, this time the voters had indicated a deeper change: they had shown that the labor movement exerted a greater pull over its members than did loyalty to the old parties. City politics in New York was not unique, thought *Leslie's:* anywhere in the United States, or throughout the country had he been candidate for President, Henry George would have received a proportionate vote. The New York *Sun, World,* and *Times,* and the *Boston Post,* the *Springfield Republican,* and the Macon *Telegraph* were only the ranking newspapers among those prompted by the vote of 68,000 to speculate on the chances of the Henry George wave rising to presidential force by 1888.

George himself must have known beforehand, must have approved, and must have felt committed when Father McGlynn contributed 'The Labor Party View' of the situation to a *North American* series on the 'Lessons of the New York City Election.' Henceforth there would be a 'new Land and Labor Party,' the priest declared, and it would remain 'utterly distinct from all other parties.' Moreover it would advance 'on the same platform and under the same leader to repeat, at the earliest possible moment, in the State and in the Nation, this magnificent canvass, and to more than repeat the moral victory of the late municipal election in New York.' Not since 1872 had Henry George had anything to do with party irregularity at national level.

McGlynn's article appeared in December. For the time being no more aggressive political role was required of the leader than trying to keep 'our ranks firm'; and he had included in his valedictory to his campaigners the most natural advice about how to carry on. Education was the essence, he said: 'Thought precedes action and controls action . . . [We need] little societies, little branches, little clubs that shall educate, that shall discuss, that shall rouse and stimulate thought. That is the power.' The ex-candidate urged that social reform be fused with political, and that the Australian secret ballot be part of labor's demand. His suggestions amounted to saying that New York's recent excitement would be transformed into a durable movement if New Yorkers would now do what Britishers had done in 1882 and 1883 — organize and discuss the ideas of *Progress and Poverty*. This led to the Land and Labor Clubs.

An early sign that all elements would not consolidate easily, however, appeared before November was out, in the tame-spirited little organ of the Knights of Labor. In the *Journal of United Labor,* published in Philadelphia, Terence Powderly praised George's vote as 'a triumph unparalleled in our history,' and he claimed credit for the Knights as having made a great contribution. But for himself he declined membership in any continuing labor party and said that he would make no more partisan speeches; and, for the order, he declared that the Knights of Labor should now revert to the old principle of staying out of politics altogether.

To a twentieth-century reader it is a little surprising to discover the recent mayor of Scranton making such anti-political pronouncements, and doing so months before Samuel Gompers began his well-known iteration of the same idea. But doubtless George and his colleagues in New York discounted the influence of an out-of-state leader who lacked the capacity for firm control over the rank and file of his order; and surely they understood also that, as the church hierarchy was now sustaining its attack on George, the Roman Catholic Grand Master Workman would need to be extra cautious.

At the close of 1886, about the time Henry George himself was making speeches in Canada, the continuing party organization lay in the hands of a small committee. Father McGlynn was chairman, and John McMackin and Professor David B. Scott, whose place was presently taken by James Redpath, were the other members. Early in January a county convention, 340 present, met in Clarendon Hall. It gathered the representatives of local supporting organizations; and, in three sessions spaced a week apart, it produced an organization intended to be permanent and designed for national expansion, the now definitely named United Labor party. The platform committee worked under the chairmanship of Daniel de Leon. In this capacity the Columbia lecturer introduced as program a reaffirmation of Henry George's own Clarendon Hall platform of the preceding September. Perhaps there is a suggestion of socialist influence in some new phrases and tones of the platform, and the party name does seem to represent a concession made to that side of Henry George's support. But at the moment of launching the new party, as at the moment of George's taking over the mayoralty campaign, ideological dominance as well as political force lay with Henry George. Despite the discomfort which we have perceived in George's attitude toward socialists, and uneasiness which can be seen on the other side in the attitudes of the Marxist *Workingmen's Advocate* of New Haven, as in England the followers of Henry George and the socialists continued to march alongside in reasonable peace.

Soon George's old plan to have a newspaper of his own involved him critically in just this relationship. Immediately after the election he turned to old friends for aid and advice about launching the paper. He corresponded with John Russell Young, who had been the first to suggest his undertaking a journal in New York; and from that friend he took the idea of calling it the *Standard* — the name Mr. Young had intended for the paper which had not materialized, after he quit the *Tribune* in 1869. George also consulted Thomas Briggs of London; and from that source received a loan of $1000, the money with which to start operations. This presented a question of business procedure. Briggs would rather have been a stockholder than a creditor. But George preferred the more old-fashioned, independent, and personal way of doing business — journalistic business at least — and so he stuck to Henry George and Company, and Mr. Briggs accepted the arrangement. The decision put Henry George in debt, but otherwise assured him independence, and he was ready to take the chance. The first issue of the *Standard* appeared on 8 January 1887, two days after the ULP convention gathered in Clarendon Hall.

Though the *Standard* was a weekly, it threw Henry George into some degree of competition, and necessarily into a delicate relationship, with the daily *Leader,* which had now outlived its original campaign function by a full two months. To this situation has been traced the ultimate break between New York Georgism and New York Marxism: the story has been told that the socialists captured the *Leader* away from the recent candidate, and that this led to the founding of the *Standard.* But, as well as disregarding the previousness of George's commitment to a new paper, the story as told overlooks the fact that after the election there occurred a period of active co-operation between George and the *Leader.*

Certainly, as will presently appear, George used the *Leader* during the month of December to return Archbishop Corrigan's fire. Then, when the *Standard* did begin and George hired away Louis Post to be an editor, he urged that others carry on the daily. This is not to say that the *Leader*'s transition, at this point, to doctrinaire socialist editorship, in the person of Serge Schevitsch, could ever have pleased George greatly. On the other hand, the New York socialists were still riding the labor party's kite; and, in his moment of seeming great strength, George would have had no reason to foresee in the Russian emigré a future opponent of significance. For the early months, nearly the first half, of 1887, the *Standard,* with an economic-reform policy like that of the old San Francisco *Post,* and the *Leader,* with a socialistic one, rubbed along without editorial combat, two highly hopeful journals of social reconstruction, equally the organs of the United Labor party.

–2–

By Henry George's standards, Archbishop Corrigan represented a worse political abuse, even, than Tammany's rumored skullduggery at the polls, and a more subversive influence than a Russian socialist at an editor's desk. During the campaign the archbishop had suspended Father McGlynn from his priestly offices, and a little later he issued a pastoral letter which continued the suspension. More alarming than that, the pastoral letter condemned as morally wrong the ideas about property advanced by Henry George and accepted by the recalcitrant clergyman.

A personal letter from Archbishop Corrigan to Cardinal Manning, now printed, justifies our picturing the New York churchman actually scanning the gift volumes Henry George had sent him. He had read a bit, the archbishop wrote; but what he said confirms the opinion of those contemporaries, Archbishop Walsh especially, who believed that he had not appreciated the general character or gathered the distinctive meanings of *Progress and Poverty*. Corrigan's misunderstanding of the book, indicated in the terms of his pastoral letter, and the presumption of authority in his public censure, both, infuriated George. He replied to the archbishop's letter, as if against all the forces of ignorance and the subversion of religion and freedom, in the *Leader* for 8 December 1886.

This made front-page news. Behind the news (we know now, but Henry George at the time had no way of knowing), upper members of the Catholic hierarchy in the United States and Great Britain were consulting among themselves about the two-in-one problem, the discipline of Edward McGlynn and the ideas of Henry George — and simultaneously they consulted also about whether Catholics should finally be denied, or be permitted, membership in the Knights of Labor. The fact that two new cardinals from this continent, Gibbons and Taschereau, were going to Rome in the spring to receive their birettas, gave extra urgency to these discussions; there would be policy making at ultimate levels. The seniority of Cardinal Manning, his interest in social questions, and the fact that he was a member of the Sacred Congregation of the Inquisition are doubtless the factors that account for his advice and counsel being especially sought concerning American affairs.

The correspondence of ranking churchmen, some of it recently made public, reveals complete agreement among Catholic leaders that Father McGlynn would have to be disciplined seriously for defying his archbishop's orders. On this point Corrigan's decision, if not all his accompanying judgments, may be thought of as final. On the other hand, he and Bishop McQuaid of Rochester definitely lost out on the issue of the Knights of Labor. Cardinal Gibbons' more liberal disposition prevailed here. Estimating correctly that the order was rapidly losing its growing power, and would soon wither, the church decided against an overt policy of excluding Catholics from union membership.

As for the issue which concerns us principally — what the church's ruling would be about the ideas of Henry George — the story is very complex. While as we have noticed Davitt assumed a role of intermediary, on McGlynn's side, between American insurgency and Cardinal Manning, Archbishop Corrigan made his own request that the English cardinal speak publicly against George's philosophy. Manning refused to do just this; and the refusal may be presumed to represent in some degree the personal sympathy for George which had sprung up in 1885 when the two had met in London. Doubtless it represented also a degree of community of thought between Cardinals Manning and Gibbons — for Gibbons now estimated George, as he did the Knights of Labor, as a waning phenomenon more likely to diminish if Catholic authority disregarded it, rather than challenged it, in public.

But while Cardinal Manning held back against Corrigan's request, he was forced to consider more vigorously than he ever had, Henry George's ideas. Only a month after the New York vote he wrote Monsignor Preston a letter which it would have pained George to see. The best the cardinal said for the reformer was a brief passage of personal appreciation. The point of the letter was Cardinal Manning's admission that when he had spoken favorably of Henry George's ideas he had read only *Social Problems* (the book the Marxists liked), and had not realized as he now did the degree of radicalism in *Progress and Poverty*.

The sum of the matter, in the beginning of 1887, was that under the drive of a dynamic but an undiscriminating archbishop, one uncommonly deficient in humility, high Catholic authority was beginning to take serious notice of *Progress and Poverty*, and of Henry George's writings as a whole. It was a late reaction — later than the notice taken by academicians in England and America, and five years after the Irish Land League crisis — but hardly the less serious on that account. If Archbishop Corrigan's pastoral

NO NATIONAL LABOR PARTY

letter actually represented right Catholic thinking, then George's writings ought to be forbidden to all Catholic readers: and that is the issue to which the matter rose before the year was far advanced. On arrival in Rome, Cardinal Gibbons discovered a real likelihood that *Progress and Poverty* would be placed on the Index of Prohibited Books — as completely denied to Catholic readers as the writings of Machiavelli and Rousseau were, or those of Karl Marx, among George's contemporaries.

The cardinal from Maryland, the state which carried the tradition of the famous Toleration Act of 1649 and had America's longest record of a mutually respectful Catholic-and-Protestant adjustment, did what he could to avoid that result. Gibbons spoke for Henry George to the degree of saying that property in land *is* different from property in things; and he rallied resistance to prohibiting *Progress and Poverty*. A year later, after Father McGlynn had been excommunicated and after Henry George's political career had been ruined, the New York *Herald* printed a statement by Cardinal Gibbons against placing Henry George's works on the Index.

Just possibly that publicity is partly responsible, along with the action of 1892 which ultimately restored Father McGlynn to his priestly offices, for today's lack of understanding, especially among George's admirers, that Archbishop Corrigan more nearly had his way than not — that the works of Henry George were actually denounced by the Congregation of the Inquisition. This anticipates by two years. But the transition from unlimited political hopes for Henry George in 1886 to political rejection in 1887 is nevertheless the point to interpolate in the Henry George story the events which illustrate the most determined and effective force against him. They have very recently been stated in the precise and detailed scholarship of historians at the Catholic University.

Early in 1889, as the writings of Fathers John Tracy Ellis and Henry J. Browne now make clear, the question of placing George's writings on the Index came up once more. As we shall see, Terence Powderly, though by that time a leader with a command much smaller than in 1886, was then swinging again into the Henry George orbit of thought. Whether or not on that account, the Holy Office acted. It ruled the American radical's writings to be 'worthy of condemnation' — in principle as complete a censure as placing the work on the Index would have been. Rather than risk publicity and an American reaction, however, the cardinals (in their own words) 'decided to refrain from a published condemnation.' This meant that the bishops were informed of the Inquisition's ruling and could act within the premises according to their individual discretion. Presumably this condemnation, and the possibility of action, holds to the present day. At very lowest estimate, the principles of Archbishop Corrigan's pastoral letter of November 1886 were quietly endorsed by the highest authority.

For 1887, George was confronting this situation in the making. How intensely he felt about the archbishop's censorship is indicated by the fact that he risked the first several issues of his new newspaper — literally its new life or early death — on the most emotional of all public questions: Catholic authority *versus* individual political freedom. In this paper his first-issue 'Salutatory,' a general editorial, seems shriveled and unimportant beside his several-column signed piece on 'The Case of Dr. McGlynn.'

In prose as sober as his emphasis was sensational, Henry George reviewed the background and development of the case. He told of Father McGlynn's service as chaplain in the Civil War; he praised, but did not play up as much as a Protestant controversialist might do today, the priest's fondness for public schools and his indifference to parochial ones; and he reviewed also McGlynn's role in 1882, when he had spoken at 'the darkest hour of the land movement in Ireland.' This led to a Protestant's denunciation. Henry George charged Archbishop Corrigan with a 'barefaced attempt' to use the Catholic Church as a political machine. Clergymen should have political convictions, he repeated. Let McGlynn be for Grover Cleveland, or for whomsoever, let him follow his conscience where it might lead. He quoted — and five months later reprinted in full — the diocesan letter of the Bishop of Meath, the one disavowing any authority in a bishop to control the economic thinking of his flock, yet advising them morally to consider private property in land as exploitative and wrong. Catholic political opinion had been freer in Ireland during the crisis than in New York under Archbishop Corrigan, George taunted.

He sustained into February this kind of heavy assault. In one issue he quoted the *Irish World* as saying that every one of the

35,000 Catholics estimated to have voted for George had done so knowing that he braved the displeasure of the archbishop. The *Standard* carried the attack even onto doctrinal grounds: it argued that the church's historic affirmations of the rights of private property did not correctly extend to land. Like the *Leader* in October, when that paper presented in full Hewitt's replies to George's letters, the *Standard* now printed complete statements from the opponent's side. A front page was spread with documents and statements when Father McGlynn was summoned to Rome to have his case adjudicated, and he refused to go. American politics were being directed by a foreign power, the *Standard* observed. Reminiscent of California days, George mixed irony with argument in his editorial onslaught. Archbishop Corrigan, an official in America, whose residence was called a palace, he mused, whose perquisites came to about $40,000 a year, whose authority was as princely as his title.

Among dozens of newspaper reactions to the *Standard,* few were as friendly as the Sacramento *Bee,* now in the hands of his old friend's heirs — to this day a Catholic family. And few were as practical and accurate as the New York *Commercial Advertiser,* which thought that 'Mr. George had succeeded in giving mortal offense to the one great body of his supporters without gaining fresh accessions.' Though for the first month the circulation of the *Standard* boomed, blowing up to 40,000, it soon became apparent that George's anti-clericalism was going to be expensive. In the spring the paper lost money, and the proprietor blamed low sales on Catholic pressure. Only after midsummer, when George and the United Labor party had entered a new campaign, did the tide turn and the *Standard* make a little profit.

George, nearing fifty, is thus very reminiscent of George at thirty and at forty on the Pacific coast. He first committed himself all-out on a public question involving a principle. He then hitched his newspaper to that judgment, and, not uncheerful in daring, waited for whatever might result.

–3–

Meanwhile during the early months of 1887, Father McGlynn, as if in compensation for being a storm center of disruption and conflict of principles, rendered services which made more cohesive and enthusiastic the New York groups that still chose to follow Henry George.

The most aggressive organizer of the United Labor party, he also founded, and became president of, the Anti-Poverty Society. The occasion of this new beginning was one of the many public meetings held to protest the Church's disciplining of the priest. On 29 March McGlynn delivered an address which became famous, 'The Cross of the New Crusade,' a mighty appeal for social Christianity. The meeting led to consultations in the office of the *Standard;* and one member of the staff, Thomas M'Cready, seems to have taken the initiative. Immediately a New York organization was born, and before long branches were started in the near-by cities. As an effort to combine in individual evangelical fervor and intimacy the seldom-combined moral energies of Catholics, Protestants, and Jews (all others were invited), the Anti-Poverty Society must be accounted a unique phenomena in American religious history.

According to its own announcement, the object of the society was 'to spread by such peaceable and lawful means as may be found most desirable and efficient, a knowledge of the truth that God has made ample provision for the need of all men during their residence upon earth, and that involuntary poverty is the result of the human laws that allow individuals to claim as private property that which the Creator has provided for the use of all.' A membership certificate was devised. It centered, in the background, a Maltese cross set within a six-pointed star; in the foreground a figure of Liberty pointed to those symbols. 'God wills it' became the society's slogan.

Regular meetings began in May. Henry George and Edward McGlynn spoke frequently, sometimes together as at the first meeting, which occurred in Chickering Hall, and sometimes one without the other. George, who became vice-president, gave the society a rousing welcome in the *Standard.* Catholics and Protestants had joined, the first report said, and thousands had turned out for whom no seats were left in the great hall. Campaigners of 1886 as different as McMackin and de Leon, Redpath and Lovell, Post and M'Cready, all appeared; and the announcements offered welcome to men of all faiths — from Spiritualists to Deists,

Buddhists, or Mohammedans. One notable early figure was Hugh O. Pentecost, Congregationalist minister of Newark, who now took the first of his many stations on a winding trail of nonconformity and social Christianity. Pentecost soon assumed a prominent place among Anti-Poverty speakers, and told the society that what the apostle Paul had done to give direction to first-century Christianity, Henry George was doing in the present moment of history.

The president and vice-president both wished to avoid any character of having established a new denomination. The purpose of Anti-Poverty was to arouse conscience and thought, said George, not to do charity or substitute for church. But the meetings were held on Sunday evenings, and they included rousing music directed by a loyal devotee of McGlynn who had followed him from the post of choir director at St. Stephen's. The addresses could as well have been called sermons; and there was something very church-like about the taking of collections, which critics called the anti-poverty program of the collectors. Truly the Anti-Poverty Society contained in its history much of the come-outer element and the home-missionary spirit, both familiar in the record of nineteenth-century evangelicalism in the United States. As the leader of the movement, the excommunicated McGlynn could possibly have brought about a major schism in the Catholic Church had he chosen to do so, so massive and so sympathetic with him was lay opposition to the clericalism of Corrigan and his kind.

As for the social critic around whose ideas of a modern Christianity the cross of the new crusade was conceived, the Anti-Poverty Society was a reassuring thing. Henry George, whose family circle joined Catholic and Protestant in spiritual unison, and who himself had long urged that a common religious faith is needful to sustain deep social purpose and morality, naturally envisaged political results to come from the Anti-Poverty Society. In 1887, more deeply even than during his work as missionary in Britain, and in a more sustained way than during the mayoralty campaign, the religious and the political fused in the Henry George movement. During the next campaign, which as we shall see he fought that fall, upstate and in the city both, he pronounced his second effort in labor politics to be 'deeply religious,' and in fact 'no political movement in the ordinary acceptation of that term.'

–4–

At the present time, when labor thought in this country signifies very little in the way of social doctrine and suggests no connotation at all of evangelical feeling, and when Americans have long since been rendered suspicious of united-front politics, it is easy to say that Henry George's labor party of 1886 and 1887 contained from the outset disparities sure to lead to discussion. There would be tensions among similar groupings today: businessmen with working men, craft-union men with industrial-union men, Christian elements in council with Marxist ones, old-family New Yorkers with new immigrants.

The mayoralty campaign, drowning out the discordancies, perhaps justified the thought in 1886 that a labor party could overcome or override them. At home and in charge of the situation, Henry George himself had much less reason than in Britain, at any rate, to be concerned by the ideological irritations between his neighbors in social thought and himself. As late as June 1887, we have his publicly expressed judgment that labor's common purposes would prevail, and that the new party would surely march in solidarity to the victories it set out to win.

He said these things in the lead article in the *North American Review* that month. Discussing the pragmatism of politics, Henry George chose words much like the now famous ones used a few years earlier by Oliver Wendell Holmes, Jr., to describe the influences that mold the law. Great public issues, said the possible labor candidate for the presidency, naturally follow what men 'are thinking about, and feeling about.' The Republicans had lost the gleam. To George, the recent crop of third parties and protest groups — Greenbackers and Prohibitionists, trade unionists and Grangers — had the merit of new life and morality, but they were short on ideas and were too narrowly based to justify hopes of winning office. Particularism must yield, the writer said, to the broader needs of the economy.

The article as a whole gathered many of the ideas of George's old political editorial writing, especially those he had put into the *Post* during the early stages of the 1872 campaign. In very general terms he now proposed for the nation such large and broad acceptance of his own social ideas as he had been able to command from those who wanted him to be mayor in 1886. Henry George could hardly have made a plea less particularly concerned with land-value taxation than he did in this *North American* article — it was really a labor manifesto for 1888.

Possibly one reason for the absence of particularism was the recent appearance in the Ohio River valley — where Liberal Republicanism had once flourished, and where anti-slavery Republicanism had for the most part risen — of a rival labor party. This was the Union Labor party, a new national organization, which gathered in late winter in Cincinnati. It was an assortment of Grangers, Knights of Labor, Greenbackers, and others. At that time, the *Standard* estimated the new party as having low potential, and George's editorial page was only slightly discomfited by the competition it offered — a first judgment amply justified by later events. But the Union Labor party did not die at once, and by summer a skeleton organization had been set up even in New York City, and *John Swinton's Paper* shifted loyalty to it. Despite the differences between them, there must have been personal hurt for George in Swinton's action, and cold comfort that *John Swinton's Paper* presently expired.

During the very month in which the *North American* pronouncement appeared, moreover, signs of disharmony cropped out within the United Labor party's own ranks. It was a crucial time. The party's state convention was looming up for midsummer, and that was the occasion when, according to Father McGlynn's best planning, the George party must take a critical forward step. The nominations to be made for state office would signify United Labor's going outside the one-city area of the party's beginnings into statewide operations, without which there could be no national campaign — Henry George for President — in 1888.

As might have been considered almost inevitable, the disintegration began at the seams between the Socialists and the party leaders. For an early indication, an editorial in the *Leader* of 28 June, presumably by Schevitsch, disparaged Henry George's ideas in favor of Laurence Gronlund's. That Danish-born writer, once admired and encouraged by George, had brought out *Cooperative Commonwealth* in 1884. There he had said about the same thing as *Progress and Poverty* said about land, but the author went on into a pretty definite Marxism; and in 1887 he enlarged the difference between himself and George by publishing a pamphlet entitled *The Insufficiency of Henry George's Theory*. Even as the *Leader* endorsed this line, however, it acknowledged its own debt and loyalty to George the thinker and the leader of the United Labor party. The *Standard* made no response, but we have Henry George's word of five months later that the early efforts of the socialists of New York City to make the labor party their own had seemed to him beyond all bearing.

The showdown came late, in August, less than two weeks before the state convention assembled in Syracuse. John McMackin, as chairman of a meeting of the county general committee, took the initiative. The Manhattan socialists, as members of the Socialist Labor party, were vulnerable under the rule of the United Labor party which excluded from membership any who belonged to other parties, though that rule had been waived for the SLP up to now. The exception had been justified on the ground that the SLP was no party in the ordinary sense of the word, and this principle had been endorsed by a county executive committee as recently as 24 July. (There was considerable interlocking between SLP and Central Labor Union membership.) In the ruling of Chairman McMackin, on 5 August, however, ULP's toleration of SLP membership could last no longer: 'I shall have to rule that according to the constitution all parties which have nominated and run candidates are political parties, and are comprehended by the letter of the section.' For United Labor party success, he went on, 'we cannot afford to tolerate Greenback, Irish, German, or Socialist factions . . . We must stand for American ideas as American citizens.'

A follower of McGlynn against the archbishop, up to now an asserter of labor's unity, McMackin retained a solid majority of the county committee on his side. But the CLU, where the party had originated a year earlier, was badly shaken; and the ULP's assembly-district organizations, which by now had been extended widely into Brooklyn as well as in Manhattan — and local organizations had been established upstate also, in Albany and Buffalo — were some of them split wide open. It is clear that many hated the break within, and wanted George, or whoever could succeed, to restore the united front. The socialist *Leader* and *Volkeszeitung* felt injured but did not yet abandon loyalty to George or party.

This was the occasion when Samuel Gompers, wearying of the battle of ideas and fearing disturbance in the American Federation of Labor, seceded from labor-party politics, for life. His first impulse, though, was just the opposite. The Jewish president of the AF of L had stood by George in the fight with Archbishop Corrigan; and in the present row within the party he proposed first that the rival ideological elements 'give over the campaign to the trade unions.' For the moment he contended for the merging of labor union and labor party. Then he withdrew. 'The Federation of Labor as an organization is keeping its hands off this fight. The questions involved are purely political, not strictly affecting labor matters and call simply for individual expressions by men constituting the Federation. A great many of them are Socialists and very bitter towards the U.L.P. Personally I have nothing to say about the ticket.'

After this the connection between Henry George and Samuel Gompers narrowed down to a strictly personal basis. The labor man phrased his attitude toward *Progress and Poverty* in a personal letter of a year and a half after the 1887 campaign. 'The reading of Henry George can do you no harm,' he advised a friend. 'Read the works but keep a level head. They are enchantingly written, but — I have no time to enter into an economic discussion in a letter.' Bicycle rides together, and talk and mutual respect, were the vehicles of their later friendship; at no time did the two ever have very much in common with one another.

The party purge evoked George's most definitive ideas about socialism. In a signed front-page editorial of 30 July he told readers of the *Standard* that any who knew his *Protection or Free Trade* were fully acquainted with how he felt. 'I neither claim nor repudiate the name of socialist.' Socialism and individualism are correlative as principles, he said once more; but the Marxian socialism of Hyndman and Gronlund he called incoherent mixtures of truth and fallacy. 'The proper line between government control and individualism is where competition fails to secure liberty of action and freedom of development.' George admitted that in pure abstract principle he preferred anarchism to socialism.

A few days before the Syracuse convention, George justified ditching the SLP. Votes from that party might have committed the United Labor party to the 'abolition of all private property in the instruments of production . . . The truth is that state socialism, with its childish notions of making all capital the property of the state . . . is an exotic born of European conditions that cannot take root or flourish on American soil.' Privately George said that the party purge would have been 'inevitable sooner or later,' and he counted on such a degree of success in the coming state campaign as would carry his own ideas forward — 1887 to be a greater 1886 with respect to educating the people.

−5−

But George was being more optimistic than conditions justified. Parties do not recover quickly from such ordeals as the United Labor party was suffering.

First of all, SLP delegates proceeded upstate from the city, in spite of all that had happened. Schevitsch and Vrooman and others went on the same train as George. In Syracuse, he himself arranged to have Louis Post become temporary chairman, instead of one who might have been soft toward the socialists. On the crucial vote the majority supported the credentials committee, and the SLP men were finally excluded.

At the stage of platform writing, the state party pledged itself to land-value taxation, and it followed Henry George's ideas exactly about socializing the natural monopolies. This committed the ULP to the municipal ownership of water, heat, and light utilities, and to the principle of nationalizing railroads and telegraphs, and of establishing a postal-savings system. Organizationally and ideologically, Syracuse was an unqualified Henry George convention. 'The greatest danger that could befall this party,' George himself said, as Gronlund and Schevitsch and others of the socialist contingent were beaten out, 'would not be the separation of elements — but would be a continuance within its ranks of incongruous elements.'

But these decisions about platform and control only preceded the crucial one for George: should he permit himself to be nominated for the state office which headed the ticket? Had nomination for the governorship been possible — Martin van Buren's line of rise, and Grover Cleveland's — the answer would have been automatic. But the highest office open in 1887 was secretary of state. There was strong reason to place someone more expendable than George at the head of the slate this time, and let the real leader speak through the *Standard* and on the hustings. George saw the issue clearly enough, and, according to current reports confirmed by his son, had the wisdom not to want to run.

But Father McGlynn pushed him. And George himself felt that after the purge he should not put on someone else the responsibility for delivering the doctrine of the party. So he accepted the nomination. Shortly afterward he cheerfully forecasted that the ULP would poll a quarter of a million votes through the state, perhaps 100,000 in the city. It would be hard to judge whether he or the socialists who departed to launch their own campaign were guilty of the blinder hopes, or at least claims, for the future.

The United Labor slate as a whole gave the SLP men an opportunity for ironic comment. A businessman with a Wall Street address accepted the nomination for state comptroller; the remaining candidacies, for treasurer, attorney general, and surveyor, went, respectively, to a merchant, a lawyer, and a farmer. Though the lawyer was Louis Post, a year before the editor of the *Leader,* that paper now asserted that Henry George was heading a pro-business slate; and in the same journal John Swinton presently denied that 'the theory of Henry George' was in any way 'an outgrowth of the evolution of the labor movement.' There must have been comfort for George to learn that the campaign splintered the staff of the *Leader* under Schevitsch, and that many who had volunteered earlier now resigned from that paper.

On the other hand, a new consolidation occurred on the socialist side. Within about a fortnight of Syracuse, the expelled elements set up a new Progressive Labor party, for SLP men and any others who would join. The platform called for the end of private property in land, and declared that there could never be harmony between capital and labor. When John Swinton refused, the party nominated J. Edward Hall, a machinist, to head the slate. In the end the Progressive Labor party received some 5000 votes, not enough to bring remorse to those who had forced the socialists out of the ULP.

Back at home in Manhattan, George set his sights for political aggression outside his party's now shrunken boundaries. Through his newspaper he asked for the votes of all who called themselves socialists in the general meaning of the term; he repudiated only the Marxians and Lasalleans and the Gronlund sort. In an early huge Anti-Poverty Society meeting, George voiced for the campaign the slogan of the society: 'God wills it, God wills it,' he said must ring abroad. Though he now gave less time, naturally, to Anti-Poverty than he had earlier in the year, the society did join in the campaign effort; and just before the vote George addressed an overflow audience, under Anti-Poverty auspices, in the Academy of Music.

As for the welcome George received, and the effectiveness he achieved among working men and immigrants, the story is a mixed one, different from 1886. He and Father McGlynn gave Labor Day addresses before a mass meeting of German workmen. Proceedings ended with a resolution condemning all, especially German Americans, 'who flaunt the red flag.' Later in September the printers and telegraphers spearheaded an effort to line up the unions. But this was an effort to bring the unions abreast of the United Labor party (and the Anti-Poverty Society), instead of one to bring the party into line with the unions — as the more aggressive situation had been the year before. Even allowing that George was campaigning upstate much of the time, there were fewer meetings of new Americans and working men for George to address than during the mayoral campaign. And as for the Catholic Irish, whereas during the mayoralty campaign the *Irish World* stood by him, now that paper joined the *Irish Herald* in opposition. With the *Leader* lost, and only the *Standard* to compensate, George and the ULP had not a single daily behind them in the 1887 campaign.

For the campaign upstate George did two tours west, once to Jamestown and Buffalo and once to Rochester, and he made several excursions out of the city, principally up the Hudson. Two days before a trip north he tried the stratagem he had devised against Hewitt. Governor David Bennett Hill had recently advocated equal taxation on all forms of property. This was the old error, with which George had become thoroughly familiar in California, and which David Ames Wells had attacked in New York fifteen years earlier. A public debate on the question would have been exactly to George's taste: it would have given him a superb opportunity to win a hearing for land-value taxation, and it would also have given him a chance to square accounts with the wing of the Democratic party to which Mayor Hewitt belonged.

Unfortunately for the challenger, Governor Hill's polite refusal yielded no such crop of newspaper comment in George's favor, as Hewitt's refusal the year before had done.

On the first trip clear across the state, a large audience at Buffalo surprised the candidate. But the better trip was the one that turned at Rochester, and from there swung through Canandaigua, Geneva, Ithaca, and Auburn — the ground which Mormons and revivalists had 'burned over' half a century before. This is the only time in his career when he ever campaigned for farm votes. Over and over again he met, as he had met from the farm-valley journals of California, the proposition that farmers would never be persuaded by land-value taxation. Reporting this phase of the tour in the *Standard*, George admitted that his idea had not taken hold in the country; the best he could say was that 'the ground is ready for the seed.'

But at Geneva and Ithaca he had college audiences, and he discovered respect and admiration. Charmed by Cornell, he took time to reflect that, though the university's timberlands, located in Wisconsin, transferred east an increment which belonged in the West, it was better to have the credit flow — under Morrill Act policy — to good education than, as might have happened, to the private uses of parvenu millionaires. He was happy to find a student Land and Labor Club, and to notice a dozen or so faculty men in the audience. Everywhere across the state clergymen took seats on his platforms — for instance in Geneva, Rochester, Marathon, Dunkirk, and Pitcher. At Rochester admirers had started a little land-value taxation weekly, *The Earth*. The number of votes he was winning, even in the cities, was very doubtful; but he enjoyed upstate New York, and perhaps was exhilarated by its protest tradition.

On returning to the city for the last week of the campaign, George himself was challenged to debate, and *he* could not refuse. Serge Schevitsch, who was an able speaker as well as vigorous editor, made the demand; and the meeting was held in an Eighth Avenue theater, with Samuel Gompers in the chair. There was humor as well as necessity in the arrangements. United Labor party people came with white tickets and were seated on one side of the auditorium; and Progressive Labor people with red tickets were on the other side. There is no reason to suspect that new elucidations or conclusions emerged at the meeting; and the report of the *Tribune* is entirely credible, that 'the partisans of each debater were equally certain that their champion had by far the best of it.' For Henry George that occasion must have presented painful differences from his platform dominance and from the make-up of his audiences twelve months earlier.

He ended the campaign saying that the attorney general's office — Louis Post's candidacy — meant the most of any in the campaign, in practical terms. On that office, more than on any other, depended the power of corruption in New York City. George pleaded for a great concentration of labor effort on that vote.

But in 1887 no signs appeared of a Henry George-inspired panic among the middle classes. When the votes were counted, he had 37,316 in New York City, which are to be compared with the 68,000 he received for mayor — about 55 per cent. He had 72,281 votes in all — less than 30 per cent of the quarter of a million campaigned for. The Democratic winner of the office of secretary of state received 480,000 votes, and the Republican loser, 459,000.

A sharp tapering-off of the United Labor party is what confronted the leader of that party; it might survive as a minor party, it could hope no longer to become a major one. A large part of the Catholic element rejoiced. For a moment George put on a brave face once more, and called for greater energies and new growth. But six weeks later on 19 December, under the editorial title 'What Shall We Do,' George revealed the deep perplexity he had no way to escape. 'I have *not* definitely decided not to be a candidate for the presidency next year, in case our friends determine to put up a candidate and demand of me to serve as such.'

Henry George was not one to care too long or too much about the fate of a political party. But he had made an error of judgment, letting himself be nominated for the secretaryship of state. There is little reason to think that political results would have been much different had someone else run for that office, however, and had he himself held off until some later try. Hopes for the Presidency, hopes that he might lead a great new national party, and any hopes which assumed that the Henry George wave would roll as high in America as in Great Britain, and then higher still, were not well timed.

–6–

By the month of New York state vote, Henry George's reputation in the world was being affected by the currents of feeling which flowed from international and national debate over the execution of the Haymarket anarchists, which had recently been ordered by the Supreme Court of Illinois.

It is impossible to measure the influence which 1887's wave of anti-radical passion may have had on the election. Being called a socialist, communist, anarchist, and nihilist had not prevented George from winning a very large vote in 1886. By 1887 it would seem that he must have been practically immune to injury from name-calling. Not only had his radicalism been disinfected by the purge of the ULP, but also the national anxiety, at least the issue of it, had shifted. The question of 1886 had been, 'Shall terror of radicals spread?' In 1887 it was, 'Is it just to execute the Haymarket anarchists?'

Henry George's first answer to the new question was the one natural for critically minded pro-labor people, and the one which historical investigation in our day justifies — 'No, this is not true justice.' The second issue of the *Standard*, 15 January, said that the state of Illinois would sow dragon's teeth if it executed men not proven guilty, for the real reason that they held hateful, immoral, and foreign ideas. 'An opinion more dangerous to society than that men who teach unpopular doctrines may be silenced by illegal convictions of infamous crimes could hardly be conceived.' The editorial was written by Louis Post, but it represented George's own opinion as well as that of George's journal, and did so for many months to come.

But early in September, shortly before George began speaking upstate, the Illinois Supreme Court upheld the verdict of the lower court. George read that court's opinion and was shaken. While others declared themselves, he and his associates pondered. Then, three weeks after the decision, he printed a changed judgment. While he did so, he protested those consequences of the decision which came under his eye and were hateful to him. He objected, against philistine suppressors of free assembly, when the police of Union Hill, New Jersey, broke up a meeting of sympathy for the condemned men. He objected, against the radicals, when speakers he called irresponsible stood up in a Central Labor Union meeting to bless the hand that threw the bomb.

Over his signature, in the 8 October issue of the *Standard* just a month before the election, George announced that he believed the Supreme Court to be correct. To George the unanimity of the judges, rehearing the case at a time and place apart from the event, was impressive. He no longer believed that 'the anarchists were condemned on insufficient evidence.' He specified that it had not been proved that any of the condemned men threw the bomb, but said that it was 'proved beyond a doubt that these men were engaged in a conspiracy as a result of which the bomb was thrown, and were therefore under the laws of Illinois as guilty as though they themselves had done the act.' George ended asking for clemency and commutation of the death sentence — not to make martyrs, not to feed minds with reason to think that America is ruled by violence, he said.

For the switch George was called traitor by working-class partisans in America and Europe. Ten days before the election, the Chicago *Labor Enquirer* reported that, when in Cincinnati for a Fourth of July oration, George had asked to have the jailed men assured that they could count on him 'to do all in my power to set them free.' Now observe, 'the scholar and philanthropist is transformed into a seeker for office,' the Chicago paper said. The New York *Leader,* which expired a week after the election, believed that if he had wanted to, George could have exercised such influence as would have saved the anarchists. To this day the charge of faithlessness is repeated and remade. Emma Goldman renewed it. And in the opinion of Professor Henry David: 'The criticism he received was just. It cannot be argued that Henry George's stand was the product of honest conviction.'

Was dishonesty and corruption really true of George, so immediately in the wake of 1886? The first clear and relevant fact, known at least in his own circle and remembered by troubled admirers, is that before he issued the 8 October editorial about the Illinois statutes and the action of that state's highest court, he sought the opinion of a lawyer friend. One of the compliments paid him during the campaign was that Judge James G. Maguire had come on to New York from San Francisco, resigned from the

Democratic party, and made speeches in his behalf. The judge was a Catholic, and perhaps came east to build a backfire against Archbishop Corrigan. George learned afterward, if he did not know at the time, that Judge Maguire's first opinion had been the same as his own, that the anarchists had not been proved guilty. He had said this to a group of people in San Francisco.

Now in New York George asked him to go over 'the papers' following the Illinois Supreme Court's decision. We know that during the fall Judge Maguire read the briefs, the statements to the press of the convicted men, and the new decision. Just how far he had carried his work when he and George talked over the case, sat up nearly all night on it a friend says, is not clear. We know that any meeting and discussion at this time occurred under campaign pressure, between times during George's upstate effort. There is no way to estimate in what detail the editor and candidate accepted the ideas of the judge, on faith in a friend, as he wrote the editorial. We know simply that George's October change of mind conforms with the judge's opinion, as it was printed in November some six weeks later.

In sum, there is every circumstantial reason to think that George changed his mind under pressure of time, under the influence of an old and trusted friend, and without having or making the opportunity to examine the law and the facts independently. This was a short-sighted procedure but not a corrupt one. If we suppose that Henry George was so human as to recognize that he would get more Catholic and middle-class votes if he endorsed the Illinois Supreme Court action, facts compel us to acknowledge that he had earlier defied these elements repeatedly; and though we might guess him to be not so completely above the recent battle with the SLP as not to transfer, from that experience to this, some distaste for radicals with German names, we are obliged to remember how unreservedly he made friends with Germans. Though events indicate that George changed his mind under pressure, there is no evidence to convict him of any form of corruption.

Doubtless the wisest thing would have been to withhold, or not to have tried to write, the editorial of 8 October. He could still have had his say about the social meaning of Haymarket and the trials, and he could have recommended clemency. His moral intuitions in this case still seem sound. In the present writer's estimation, Henry George seems more than a little tragic: under campaign pressure he did not have the wisdom to acknowledge that he did not know about the law and the facts, and he acted simply according to his best, but not very informed and not independent, judgment.

The anguish stayed with him. The first letter he wrote after the election George directed to Governor Oglesby. He sent a copy of the editorial; he noted that he had signed no petitions questioning the justice of the Illinois courts. He simply developed the plea of the editorial for clemency. He was moved, he told the governor, by his knowledge of social injustice in the republic, and by a sense that many whose ideas deserved consideration believed that the courts had not done right. He did not want martyrs made.

Two weeks later on 19 November, when the men were dead, he printed an editorial on 'The Chicago Tragedy.' He printed it alongside the letter from Judge Maguire which now stated in detail that lawyer's reasons for accepting the verdict. Tragedy to George, reasonable justice to Maguire — that is the way the *Standard* might have presented the two faces of the matter on 8 October, in the first place. George said that he and his friend had agreed always that the sentence should be mitigated.

A year later, to Herr Gütschow, the friend who taxed him most heavily about his reversing himself, Henry George recurred to the hard matter. 'I would like to know whether time has changed your view of my attitude in the anarchist business. I acted then without thought about what was politic, but only of what was right, and looking back I do not see that I was wrong. I do not see that it is worthwhile to reopen that.'

By the end of 1887 doors were closed to Henry George which two years previously had been wide open, and which were still partly open in Great Britain. As Beatrice Webb has said, and the Scottish labor leaders particularly illustrate, evangelicalism — British evangelicalism not so forced and strained as that of the Anti-Poverty Society — offered a main route into labor and radical movements in the United Kingdom. So did moderate socialism and land nationalization and Lib Lab Radicalism. These corridors remained open in the island kingdom.

But in America, labor was flanked on the right by Catholicism in an unusually authoritarian, Irish, form; and on the left it was flanked by an unassimilated fringe of radical immigrants not versed in either democratic or Christian feeling. Both sides blocked George's way, neither one respected his doctrine. The main body and center of labor was of course different. But pressure from the edges, and the strains of reorganization within, served during 1886 and 1887 to make the Knights of Labor and the Federation, both, less hospitable than before to radical ideas. The only sizable movement of moderate socialism in this country, the nationalism of Edward Bellamy, was too new and, as we shall see presently, too different from what George stood for, to serve his cause.

Such considerations make the hopes of 1887 for a great labor party — not to say a presidential victory — seem in today's perspective to have been particularly ill-founded. But since his arrival in New York, in 1880, George had been discovering other men with other interests than those of working men who concerned themselves with his ideas. His future now lay largely among the many open spaces in the American middle classes.

XVII

The Father of the Single Tax

1888–1890

ONE of the revisions of the Henry George story that this biography undertakes is to put into historical perspective the place which the single tax occupied in his life and thought. Today, two full generatons after his death, George is usually remembered as the single-tax man; and the common recollection retains little else about him unless it is an impression that, as the author of *Progress and Poverty*, he gave the single tax to the world in more elevated style than reform ideas are usually delivered.

These estimations by Mr. Everyman are, of course, not altogether mistaken, but they do involve such errors of limited perspective and want of information as grossly misrepresent Henry George — his ideas and his influence on history. The misapprehensions are entirely natural, for the single tax of 1888 and after became the most particular and the most organized phase of George's communication to the public, and the name itself is not readily forgotten. Much scholarship has abetted the common errors, moreover, by a misapprehension of its own. Though economists and historians have recognized that the single tax came late in Henry George's life, and concerned him for just one decade and during that short period occupied only part of his attention, they have been wont to say that the one reform nevertheless distills the meaning of his thought and effort — that the single tax was the essential result toward which all his ideas flowed.

No recapitulation of the Henry George story in California, or in Ireland and Great Britain, or in New York through 1887, would be in order in this chapter. But, against the common errors and against the conforming error of certain scholars, readers may be reminded: that the first large idea of economic policy which George's mind ever seized was free trade in 1866; that, though he was stimulated by San Francisco debates over the possibility of a city's establishing public ownership of a great share of the land it occupied, until 1873 George, the West coast editor, asserted dogmatically that traditional forms of landholding ought to be maintained; and that thereafter he contemplated not one but two or three drastic ways of escaping the harmful effects of land aggregation and monopoly. Readers are reminded also that George did not become seriously interested in taxation as a method of social improvement until his Sacramento editorship in 1870, and that thereafter he proposed three types of taxes as useful and desirable; and that even in *Progress and Poverty* he offered land-value taxation only as strongly as the preferred 'application' of his 'remedy.' The remedy itself was not taxation but the displacing of private property in land, by common property.

Readers should remember in addition: that George became convinced in favor of the public ownership of industrial monopolies, beginning with telegraph and railroads, before he became convinced about land; and that, concurrently with formulating his major economic proposals, he developed kindred eloquent sets of democratic political and social ideas, and of idealistic religious and philosophical ones. One may judge that the single tax, when it was offered, was logically consistent with the many phases of Henry George's thought and effort, but one cannot believe that it assimilated or contained them all.

For envisaging in biographical perspective George's role after 1887, no reminder to the reader is more essential than that from first to last Henry George, with only the slightest waverings of inconsistency, had always been a pro-capitalistic thinker. George was radical but not unusual as an opponent of monopoly, and he was both radical and unusual in wanting to transform the institutions of property in land. But he was always conservative as to capitalism, whenever business was competitive, and conservative as to our institutions of church and state. Such are the crosshatchings of the lines of thought which give moderate tone to the ideological portrait.

Readers of the first part of this biography will remember that by the time *Progress and Poverty* was published George had made himself a spokesman for what this century calls a 'mixed economy' and an 'economy of abundance,' both. And recent chapters have indicated that two books of the '80s, *Social Problems* and *Protection or Free Trade,* made him a mixed-economy man still more completely. The earlier book called for public ownership where natural monopolies exist, the products of certain phases of machine technology; and the later one spoke for free trade and free enterprise, wherever possible. Present readers, who will be representative Americans if they believe that abundance is the principal glory of our industrial economy, and who will also be likely to accept a mixture of free enterprise and public ownership as a desirable way of doing things, will have no difficulty in understanding that when the history of Henry George separated somewhat from the history of labor, he easily discovered new middle-class followers for his ideas.

To say that the single tax was born in 1888, a late fruit in its parent's fiftieth year, is not to say that George had not mentioned the name, more or less definitely, long before the birth. To review once more: the phrase 'single tax,' though without the definite article, does appear in *Progress and Poverty;* and George did put the phrase in print, two or three times at least, before 1887. 'The single tax,' as George used the words, did signify the growing particularity of his reformism after 1882. Not by accident, we may be sure, the phrase appears contemporaneously with his separating from socialism, and from land nationalization as a practical reform movement. Up to 1888 the essential element still lacking to the single tax as history knows it was any political content: there was yet absent any connection of the phrase with organization, propaganda, and vote getting. The Land Restoration Leagues overseas did not speak of the single tax, and, if possibly the Free Soil Society had done so, this was a forgotten whisper.

The change which will be delineated in the third section of this chapter, and which may be called the birth of the single tax, was that land-value taxation now became an organized effort, a new reform movement in America and elsewhere. Henry George had long cherished the idea; and in time he came to cherish the movement. Even so, events beyond his control had more to do with the development of the single tax than any efforts he sought to make.

Not even in the crucial years, 1888, 1889, and 1890 would the single tax occupy a great share of his attention and thought. A derivation from him, it would be less his concern than the concern of his followers, especially lawyers and businessmen.

–2–

'George, do you see the hand of the Lord in this?' asked Louis Post on election night, 1887, as the two took a horsecar to a labor-party meeting originally planned as a celebration. 'No,' replied the candidate whose party had broken into pieces, 'I do not see it, but I know it's there.'

He himself was a shade slower than certain colleagues to acknowledge the completeness of the defeat at the polls. In the first issue of the *Standard* after the election, William Croasdale, who had opposed George's running for secretary of state and who disliked the 'whirling dervishes' of Anti-Poverty, had a signed editorial on 'The Driftwood Washed Away'; and two weeks later he, and then Louis Post, said that the United Labor party should abandon thought of a presidential ticket in 1888. But George himself was still not ready to abandon the plan: 'All that we who are in these early days rallying round the cross of our new crusade care for in politics is the opportunities political action gives for missionary work.'

Still a ULP man at the end of 1887, he replied to those who wanted to know how to help the cause by giving familiar advice. If you can speak or write, do so; establish an Anti-Poverty Society in your community; have a reading club, women as well as men. Study *Progress and Poverty*, or *Social Problems* if the big book seems too difficult; and discuss *Protection or Free Trade*. Or help with the mechanics of propaganda: distribute tracts and recruit subscribers to the *Standard*.

Only to an old friend did he say things which reveal the depths of his confusion and uncertainty. Writing to Gütschow, he blamed the setback on the Catholic opposition. In the same letter, trying to be hopeful, he observed that, if he had won the number of votes he expected, he would now be embarrassed by a following

of 'half-educated men.' 'Now we have only those who know what
they are about, and politics is of course with us not an end but only
a means.' February had come before he admitted publicly that he
'felt as though a sand slide had made impossible the road I hoped
to travel.'

George's political anguish was of course compounded of something in addition to his regrets for the fading of the ULP. His
whole experience in the East with the major party into which he
had been born, and to which he had returned after nine years as a
Lincoln Republican, was unpromising, in the fall of 1887, for one
who might return once more. Even if his own exodus from the
Democratic party for the two labor campaigns could have been
overlooked, he would have discovered, in the party of Governor
Hill and Mayor Hewitt and Boss Croker, little likelihood of having again the satisfactions he had enjoyed from being a Democrat
for Haight and Irwin, during the '70s on the West coast. The one
hope George had recently entertained for the Democratic party,
that Cleveland's election would force the issue of tariff, remained
for three years entirely unfulfilled. Continued disappointment
makes intelligible both George's interest and his wariness when
a new light of economic statesmanship did appear in Washington.

The event, which came at a most effective moment for George,
was President Cleveland's state-of-the-nation address of 6 December
1887. Less than a year before the national election — the one in
which George had dreamed of being himself the man to bring
economic realities into politics — the President called for tariff
reduction. He pictured protectionism as a breeder of monopolies.
His attack was pragmatic, not in the least doctrinaire; in the
address he uttered his best-remembered phrase, 'It is a condition
which confronts us, not a theory.' The speech caught the head-
lines and became the biggest event of the administration's history.

Though, to the theory-minded author of *Protection or Free
Trade,* Cleveland's change gave the signal that practical men would
soon need theory in spite of themselves, George's first comment
was guarded. He said simply that the address was better than expected, a fair presentation of tariff realities; and, quoting his own
book, he observed that the President did not realize how the tariff
connects with underlying economic problems. But a week later,
in the editorial quoted in the last chapter, in which George wove

his way through double negatives to deny that he had decided against running for President, he came out with a fairly positive endorsement of the message. The Republican *Tribune* enjoyed mentioning the dilemma of the doctrinaire free traders at this point, the paradox of being for Cleveland's cause, for reasons different from his own.

A protectionist counterblast to Cleveland from James G. Blaine, who had headed the Republican ticket in 1884 and still held the dominant influence in the party, helped George find his own position. In the first issue of the *Standard* of the election year, he said that American free traders could, if they would, assume the historic role of the Physiocrats a century preceding: they had the power, as leaders in ideas, to speak for the future according to their light.

While national politics opened the road back to the Democratic party for George, hostilities within the United Labor party diminished the reasons for his remaining there. His own insistence had put a free-trade plank in the labor platform, though many members opposed it; but the question was one that could be disregarded while the ULP campaigned for nothing higher than state office. The trouble was that, as 1888 arrived, Father McGlynn and others wanted to continue to let the tariff question sleep. This was treason to all that George believed about the right choice of issues for a presidential year, and in the *Standard* he threatened that the United Labor party might be disbanded.

Besides the immediate question of the life or death of the ULP, and his own decision whether or not to return to the Democratic party, George was dealing with a most difficult personal situation. The priest whom he had championed in his defiance of archbishop and pope had recently blurted out some incredible things. Saying that the pope in politics amounted to no more than 'a bag of skin and bones,' like the rest of mankind, was one of his indiscretions. Now McGlynn turned his scorn on Henry George. The Syracuse convention had charged United Labor's executive committee to prepare for a national campaign, he said. The authority was the committee's, and they would be sidetracked by no one, not even by the party's first leader.

The conflict led first to a little Canossa. Henry George journeyed with a few associates and advisers to Cooper Union, where Father McGlynn and his committee had an office. No reconciliation was possible. Instead of having to make a difficult decision himself, to disband the ULP, Henry George had to accept a decision made for him. Like the socialists five months earlier, George and his associates on the *Standard* were read out of the United Labor party.

After this the political history of Father McGlynn, and the history of the ULP, both, are brief. From proposing to suppress the tariff issue in the party, the excommunicated priest shifted first to announcing for protection; from declaring for the minor party, he shifted second to Harrison and Republicanism; and during the summer he complicated things further by proposing No Rent resistance, Irish Land League style, against the landlords of New York City. Without George and without McGlynn, the United Labor party meanwhile held a national convention in Cincinnati, with delegates from a dozen states; and it nominated a Chicagoan, Robert H. Cowdery, for President. Henry George's final words on labor-party politics in 1888 were to suppress a new third-party movement among his own followers, and to make wry editorial comment on Mr. Cowdery's candidacy. He liked the man, but regarded the effort — Cowdery received 3000 votes in November — as fatuous.

With the United Labor party collapse, the Anti-Poverty Society fell into fragments also. Immediately on breaking with McGlynn, George resigned as vice-president; and the surviving organization turned against him completely. On the heels of this, which must have amounted to a Catholic-and-Protestant separation, Hugh Pentecost set up the Unity Congregation in New York. Going beyond Anti-Poverty to assume the character of a new and separate church, Unity Congregation became the religious home of many George followers, though not of Henry George's own family. After some hesitation, because he preferred a third party, Mr. Pentecost followed George and spoke for Cleveland in the presidential campaign. Unity Congregation proved much less a political phenomenon than Anti-Poverty, but for the time being it did help sustain the evangelical phase of the George movement.

The breakups occurred in New York early in 1888. About ten months later, just before election, Henry George put his intimate, and bitter, reflections on the man who had caused them, in a letter to California. He could in no way have avoided a fight with McGlynn, he told Gütschow. 'The truth is that the Dr. whom I first thought an exception, has all the weaknesses that seem inseparable from the life of the priest. So far from urging him forward [against church discipline] as is generally supposed, I always tried to influence him to prudence; and when I seemed to [urge], as when I advised him in the *Standard* not to go to Rome, it was only to pick ground for what I knew to be his determination.' McGlynn had turned against him, George said, as early as 1887, and had tried machine building within the ULP. 'The whole matter was a great pain and anxiety to me,' he concluded, and it all led to 'a selling out of the movement and our influence, for Republican money.' Four years were to pass before the two men would have anything more to do with each other.

Once his own dazzling ambition for 1888 had been destroyed, George was happy, and generous with space in the *Standard*, first to justify, then to participate in, the campaign for Grover Cleveland. In late winter he said in an editorial that the decision to be made in June, the renomination or not of Cleveland, as a tariff reformer, would be a more important decision than the election in November. The nomination would return the Democratic party to first principles. He wrote an elaborate analysis of the Mills Bill. That this tariff-reduction measure, supported by the administration, would really become 'an entering wedge,' sufficient to open a seam for a great change, was Henry George's endorsement. This was what a theorist could do for a President. When the nomination was actually made, the *Standard* gave unqualified support, and George sent personal assurances to Cleveland that a courageous stand against the tariff would not lose working men's votes.

A series of *Standard* editorials wove and rewove the connections of economic logic between free-trade and land-value taxation. The pattern of ideas resembles that of the old San Francisco *Post,* except that George went out of his way to taunt Terence Powderly when the K of L man spoke in favor of a policy of restricting immigration. The editor stood by his old opinion that Mongolians and any others who might not be assimilated into our culture should be excluded, but he believed that the new immigrants from southern and central Europe should be made welcome, and that the Irishman who wanted American portals closed was a shortsighted protectionist twice over.

George was heartened to notice that men of mind felt as he did about Cleveland, and about tariff reduction. Seth Low, the recent Mugwump mayor of Brooklyn, who was soon to become president of Columbia and who would oppose George for mayor of New York in 1897, the *Standard* saluted especially, because he refused to go for Harrison, and made a public declaration for President Cleveland. 'A foremost representative of what is really the best element in the Republican Party,' said George. A liberal convergence was taking place, he believed. 'To me, this Fourth of July comes with more hope than any I have known. Freedom is not here, but she is coming. It is ours to clear the way.'

His commitment notwithstanding, George had a difficult moment in September when President Cleveland released his letter of acceptance of the Democratic nomination. Though this message developed the idea of tariff duties as effecting a reduction in the hiring of labor, George could not pretend to be satisfied with the President's thought. Accordingly he envisaged his own role much as he had pictured it in earlier days, when he had been adviser to Governor Haight and the Democrats in California, or when he had counseled the Radicals in Britain. He paid Cleveland the tribute of having political sagacity and regarded himself as playing an ideological part. 'My great desire in this campaign,' he said privately, 'is to utilize it for the propagation of radical ideas. I do not think [I] ever will be content to palter with the truth, but I believe in taking every opportunity that offers to push ideas that seem to me essential.'

A month later George was campaigning again upstate, much as he had done the year before. He spoke in many of the same places: Dunkirk, Lockport, Syracuse, and Rochester, and at campaign's end in Binghamton and Ithaca; and he went to Harrisburg, Pennsylvania, as well. Once again combat raised his spirits. As the vote drew near, he felt confident 'beyond peradventure' of Cleveland's re-election, and predicted that the President would carry New York, New Jersey, and Indiana, and also Connecticut, Michigan, and California. He felt equally assured that the right principles had been carried so far into the common awareness that a free-trade party would soon emerge.

Too quickly optimistic, George's judgment oscillated extremely after the election. At first, Cleveland's defeat and Harrison's victory shifted him to dire expectations. But the President's near-victory, with a popular vote larger than Harrison's, justified a recovery of hope. From the perspective of the middle Atlantic, about a fortnight later, Henry George managed to write for publication that the gain of 1888 had been all that single-tax people 'most desired.' That is: 'the opening of the great question of taxation as related not merely to the general prosperity but to the rate of wages, to the distribution as to the production of wealth . . . Our true policy [now] is simply to throw our strength from time to time with the party that comes nearest to going our way.'

Naturally the *Standard* was delighted when on 15 December 1888 the New York *Tribune* discovered 'a good deal of *Progress and Poverty*' in the state-of-the-nation address which President Cleveland delivered not long before he surrendered office. It was an accurate discovery, and a flattering one.

–3–

Readers who have noticed that the Henry George story of 1888, as related so far, lacks the usual amount of his perennial effort to achieve utopia, have envisaged already the place the new single-tax movement occupied in his life that year. It is reasonable to say that he could not have done without it. George could gladly be a Democrat again, as he had been one for more than a decade in California. But he would never, not even for a single year, confine all, or the dearest part, of his political effort into the mold of a national party.

In a way we are dealing with the splitting of a political personality. In New York, and in Ireland and Great Britain, from 1881 through 1887, Henry George's activities had been better integrated than at any other stage of his public life. As writer of books, as missioner overseas, and as ULP leader at home, his principles and his political practices for these seven years pretty well merged into a single and consistent effort. That was the period when a just redistribution of economic opportunity seemed to him — as not before *Progress and Poverty* — to be attainable quite soon. He believed there could be social reconstruction in his day.

But then the old dichotomy reasserted itself. On the West coast, when the practical politics he shared with the Haights, the Booths, and the Irwins failed to satisfy him, he wrote utopian editorials,

developed a system, and produced a book. Now in New York, when
Grover Cleveland's Democratic party satisfied him only in part, he
turned again, but in a new way, to more doctrinaire types of
political endeavor. But at this stage of life and leadership, something over and above writing and speaking was required: his
reform ideas were ready to be put to work in the United States.
Unless action followed speech, George believed, the ideas themselves would surely wither. 'The political art, like the military,
consists in massing the greatest force against the least resistance,'
he had said in *Progress and Poverty*, 'and to bring a principle most
quickly and effectively into practical politics, the measure which
presents it should be so moderate as (while involving the principle)
to secure the largest support and execute the least resistance. For
whether the first step be long or short is of little consequence. When
a start is once made in the right direction, progress is a mere matter
of keeping on.'

Thomas Shearman was the man, rather than George himself, who
transformed 'the single tax' from useful phrase into name and
slogan. The corporation lawyer took the initiative on the occasion
of an address before the Constitution Club of New York, in
January 1887. In the antiphonies of propaganda which followed
George's defeat by Abram Hewitt, the speaker sounded a note that
was just as well keyed to middle-class ears as were Father McGlynn's
proposals to the hearing of Irish working men. But the single-tax
movement did not pick up as quickly, from the single-tax speech,
as the United Labor party did from the efforts of the priest and his
associates. The *Standard*, indeed, did not print the address until
28 May, five months after it was delivered; and though the three
words did appear together sometimes, they seem not to have caught
on immediately. While the ULP was wearing itself out, Shearman
appeared in the role of student rather than leader. In October
he contributed to the *Standard* a series of articles on 'The Distribution of Wealth.' Refuting an attack on George's economics by
Edward Atkinson, the New York lawyer analyzed the flow of tax
money in the United States with such thoroughness as George himself had never equaled.

But, in the last issue of the *Standard* for 1887, just at the time
when he was coming to grips with the situation created by the recent defeat, Henry George wrote an editorial under the notable

heading, 'Socialism vs. the Single Tax.' This seems to have been
the occasion when he definitely adopted the term. In a letter to
William Lloyd Garrison II, moreover, he brought together with
complete self-awareness the difficult double decision: to abandon
labor politics, and to speak his message under the new title. 'I
went into politics reluctantly,' he said, looking back to 1886, 'and
only because circumstances seemed to point to that as the best way,
for the moment, that attention could be drawn to principle. It
seems to me now that circumstances have changed.'

That the single tax was not theoretically perfect, George admitted to his friend. 'You say that you do not see in the single tax
a panacea for poverty. Nor yet do I. The panacea for poverty is
freedom. What I see in the single tax is the means of securing that
industrial freedom which will make possible other triumphs of
freedom . . . It is the old, old battle we are fighting, the same
battle, of which your father in his time led the van. It is this that
makes the sympathy of his son so cheering.'

In the course of about a year George worked out a justification
for the new term. He made his fullest statement in the 2 March
1889 issue of the *Standard*, in which he spoke entirely candidly
about his reservations. 'The term single tax does not really express
all that a perfect term would convey. It only suggests the fiscal side
of our aims . . . Before we adopted this name, people, even intelligent people, insisted on believing we meant to divide land
up . . . Since we have used the term single tax this kind of mis-
representation seems to have almost entirely disappeared . . .
[It links] us to those great Frenchmen, ahead of their time, who,
over a century ago, proposed the "impôt unique" as the great means
for solving social problems and doing away with poverty . . .
Our proper name, if it would not seem too high flown, would be
"freedom men," or "liberty men," or "natural order men," for it
is on establishing liberty, on removing restrictions, on giving
natural order full play, and not on mere fiscal change that we base
our hopes of social reconstruction . . . This idea is more fully
expressed in the term single tax than it would be in land rent tax or
any other such phrase. We want as few taxes as possible, as little
restraint as is conformable to that perfect law of liberty which will
allow each individual to do what he pleases without infringement of
equal rights of others.' In other sentences in the same editorial,

George said what he and his followers were often to say, that
actually the single tax was a tax in name only — that is, that it was
not a levy on something belonging to the payer, but a withholding
of something never rightfully the payer's own. 'The term itself
is a misnomer,' he told a Chicago audience, after seven years, yet
'somehow or other the name stuck.'

While the ULP faded away in 1888, the single-tax movement
gained body and strength. George discouraged a meeting proposed for late spring in Chicago, which would have been the first
national single-tax conference, partly because as we have seen
he feared a new third-party impulse, and partly because he wished
to avoid further subdivision among his followers on the subject of
the tariff. But in August a meeting took place in Cleveland, for
which Louis Post went out to be chairman, and George was delighted that the old-time ardor sprang up again. In the *Standard*
he recommended that other meetings be held on a local basis, but
that fees and anything like a party organization be avoided. During
late summer and early fall a series of meetings were arranged in
Jersey City, Newark, Brooklyn, Elizabeth, and Philadelphia; and
several were held in Cooper Union. At one of them James
Archibald, Irish labor leader who had been prominent when the
Central Labor Union first sought out Henry George in 1886, won
a huge round of applause by a free-trade declaration. But in general
labor leaders were conspicuous by their absence from single-tax
beginnings in New York City. Besides George himself, such men
as Post, lawyer-editor, Pentecost, minister, and William Lloyd
Garrison II, lawyer down from Boston, did most of the speechmaking.

As defeat in the New York state election of 1887 may fairly be
said to have given the signal for the single-tax movement to come
alive, Cleveland's defeat in 1888 may be judged to have given it a
more specific role and function. Up until election time the movement had been as spontaneous as possible, and lack of organization
had seemed to George a virtue. But when Cleveland lost, and the
party of moderate reform was put out of office, solidly constructed
procedures seemed necessary to keep alive the ideas and loyalties
centered on Henry George. When he himself returned, at the
end of 1888, from the quick trip across the Atlantic which he had

intended to be a vacation, he faced up to the problem in the new terms.

Though he remained determined against third-party efforts, he was readier than usual to encourage sizable and durable reform organizations. Presently, out of what in 1887 had been the United Labor Party Association of the Tenth Assembly District, and in 1888 had been the Free Trade Club of the Ninth Congressional District, there emerged the Manhattan Single Tax Club — the first and most important organization of its kind. In this final form the organization developed into a vigorous pressure group; it became a center for civic reform generally, as well as a tax-reform effort. It operated, says Louis Post, as 'a propaganda agent along business lines, in business circles, and by business methods.' Thomas Shearman, Lawson Purdy, and Bolton Hall were probably its most distinguished members.

The second to start, the Chicago Land and Labor Club turned itself into the Chicago Single Tax Club, under the leadership of Warren Worth Bailey, a journalist who later became editor of the Johnstown *Democrat* and a congressman from Pennsylvania. The snowball rolled, and by the end of 1889 the *Standard* could list 131 single-tax organizations in the country. There were 22 in the state of New York, and, in the following states, the numbers of organizations indicated: Ohio, 14; Pennsylvania, 13; Massachusetts, 12; New Jersey, 9; Indiana, 6; and California, Colorado, Illinois, and Iowa, 5 each. The list shows how very largely George's followers were established in the industrial rather than the agrarian states. There were only 12 single-tax organizations in the South, and 23 scattered through the states not mentioned.

In the early stages of growth, the single-taxers had difficulties in reaching agreement about strategy. For years, in the columns of the *Standard* and elsewhere, they discussed whether they ought to concentrate their combined political energies in one small state, or undertake a national campaign. If the first, the procedure would probably be to try to capture the legislature of New Jersey or Delaware, and so establish a beacon to the world, an actual one-state utopia. The other choice would be to circulate a grand national petition, which would pray Congress to raise 'all public revenues by a single tax upon the value of land, irrespective of improvements, to the exclusion of all other taxes.' A New York attorney, Samuel Clarke, had said in the *Harvard Law Review* of January 1888 that Congress had ample authority to do just that, by acting under the welfare clause.

Perhaps in strictest logic there was nothing to prevent the early single-taxers from advancing in both directions at once: toward one or several state legislatures, according to local strength, and toward Capitol Hill. Yet common sense and Henry George's principles, alike, warned against too much dispersing of energies. George himself inclined, according to his Jeffersonian tastes, toward state-government action. But under the chairmanship of William Croasdale of the *Standard,* the national scheme moved faster. About 70,000 names were put on the petition in 1889. The climax of this effort came in September 1890, far ahead of the present story, when the leaders timed the first national single-tax conference to be in session to greet Henry George when he returned to New York after his trip around the world.

Though problems of organization, strategy, and procedure developed, and the father of the single-tax movement had his preferences, he did not try to establish detailed personal control. He preferred always to speak his own thoughts first, and leave the follow-up to others. In January 1889, just as the organizational effort was getting well under way, he went off on a heavy schedule of winter lecturing. He was never a man to be held down by administrative undertakings.

He went to the Middle West this time. Chicago, Des Moines, Minneapolis, St. Paul, Three Rivers, and Columbus were all on the itinerary. The best meetings occurred in Columbus, where he and Tom Johnson and Shearman were invited to address the state legislature one day, and to appear before a ministers' union on the next. Each spoke in his characteristic manner before the legislators. George led off with general theory; Johnson talked in a business-like way about the methods and advantages of land-value taxation; and Shearman discussed the faults in taxing personal property. George saw that his colleagues corrected any impression their hearers might have that the single tax was a device purely in behalf of labor. The ministers' meeting, and a third one in the same city, a conference of Ohio single-tax men, all pleased George a great deal.

In Des Moines, to be sure, things were less satisfactory. He wrote

Annie about circumstances that sound like 1885: a small audience, the price of seats (50 and 75 cents) too high, and too small a return to the lecturer. His principal satisfactions there were the presence of the governor and other public men, and the compliments he received from a priest in the audience. In Minnesota, where he had wanted to go previously, he had a delightful time. He gave a lecture which satisfied him in the Opera House in Minneapolis; then he crossed the river to St. Paul and addressed a joint session of the legislature in the capitol building. Yet Charles A. Pillsbury's showing him the Pillsbury plant seems to have been a greater climax and satisfaction, for after their interview George concluded that the country's greatest miller was friendly to his teaching. He found single-tax groups in both Iowa and Minnesota. 'The good cause' is booming in the Northwest, George wrote Thomas Briggs, 'and the next fight will be on radical free trade lines.'

If as Democrat again he needed the single tax, the single-tax man did not forget his other interests.

–4–

It will be remembered that the New York City campaign had prevented George from going to England in 1886, even for a short visit. Though he kept up an active correspondence, and received favors both political and financial from across the Atlantic, two years passed before the question of another voyage came up in a practical way.

Then it rose suddenly and as a surprise. William Saunders, the newspaper man whom George now regarded as the prime spokesman for his ideas in the British Isles, passed through New York on his way home from Mexico. He persuaded George to cross with him, to be ashore for a couple of weeks, and then return to New York immediately. The campaign of 1888 was just over and George was tired and ready for a change. But he could hardly have refused, for Saunders seems to have paid all expenses. The voyage out was warm and pleasant.

Ashore there was no chance for rest. As the steamship *Eider* put into Southampton, a tender, emblazoned 'Welcome to Henry George,' brought a committee of members of the Radical Association and the Land Restoration League to meet their favorite

American. A crowd greeted him at Waterloo Station. And perhaps the greatest satisfaction of the trip was the attention he discovered his ideas were having when he spent several days visiting Parliament. He heard John Morley say in Commons that the landowners gained from all improvements, and that their taxes should be increased. He noticed that Saunders and Thomas Briggs 'and the most radical of the English single tax men' were willing 'to go a step at a time' with other liberals.

Even during so very short a visit George had several speeches to make, and considerable shuttling about to do. There were four or five appearances in London, and others in Glasgow and Liverpool, and a Knights of Labor meeting near Birmingham. The Liverpool meeting pleased him especially, no doubt because of his tribulation there in 1884. He discovered that the Financial Reform Association of that city, a free-trade body since 1848, was supporting land-value taxation. Introducing the American speaker, President Muspratt said that the association now believed the first reform could not be had fully without the other. Naturally Henry George was elated.

Disappointments did occur. The hurry and haste bothered the traveler, and he was sorry to miss seeing Father Dawson. There was real pain to learn that Thomas Walker, his great and well-to-do friend, of Birmingham, objected to the new single-tax emphases. 'I cannot see finality in the land tax,' the manufacturer wrote; and his objections led to very full, anxious, and argumentative replies from George.

Yet the visitor had no doubt, when the quick trip, his fourth, was over, that men and ideas were swinging his way in Britain. Besides the personal appreciations he received, there was the testimonial of a new textbook in economics, written with a distinct Georgist slant, by his old correspondent, J. E. Symes of University College, Nottingham. There was also the dedication of the daily London *Star*, to the taxing of ground values; and more lecture invitations than he could begin to accept. Before he sailed for home George knew that he was going to be invited to Australia soon; and some of the arrangements must have been completed for his next visit to England. He said in the *Standard* that present appreciations of his ideas could be attributed, in part, to the recent public discussion of mining royalties, and to the falling due of many London leases.

George had Christmas at home with his family, and after that three months in the United States before he recrossed the Atlantic. Besides the speaking trip in the Middle West, which was reported in the last section, he gave at Harrisburg his fourth or fifth lecture before a state legislature. The single-tax effort was moving under its own steam; and to take care of the *Standard* during his absence George gave full power of attorney to Henry George, Jr. He himself promised to contribute a weekly letter, the 1882 kind of arrangement with the *Irish World* repeated. He solved the family problem, also, as he had done during that first trip, by taking his wife and daughters with him. Richard had married and set up independently the year before. George's affairs in early 1889, both public and private, were in tidier shape than usual.

On the British side, William Saunders took the lead again, and there was a large 'Henry George Campaign' committee, predominantly Radical in make-up. Yet people who were a little unhappy about certain prospects of the visit advised him most fully before he sailed. In a letter calculated to forestall the factionalism which he thought the single-tax line might provoke, Thomas Walker warned against being too doctrinaire. Land-value taxation leaves 'a slight twinge of doubt as to whether its very glibness is not deceptive,' he said, and he claimed the support of Charles Wicksteed, the brother of Philip, in preferring land nationalization to Shearman-style taxation — for Britain at any rate. Yet Walker rose above his anxieties to say that George would infuse realism again into British politics. With Gladstone off in trivial matters, Henry George would give a thrust in the right direction.

From the new Fabian side, George received a long letter written by his slight acquaintance, Sidney Webb. Worried lest George carry into British fields his American war on socialists, Webb supplied elaborate information on present currents of leftward ideas and politics in Britain. 'You will find us,' the already famous civil servant wrote, 'making progress in a direction which may generally be called socialistic, and, on the land question in particular, ordinary Liberal opinion is fast ripening. The Radicals and the town wage earners generally hardly need your visit, except always by way of inspiration and encouragement. They are already pushing the party leaders as fast as they can.'

While Webb thus said that George's visit was not quite necessary to those who were arranging it, he had his own ideas about the directions in which the visitor could very profitably turn. 'What holds things back is the great class of the middle class, religious! respectable! cautious, and disliking the Radical artisan. These need your instruction most, and you are of course just the man who can give it to them, without offense or resentment. Your visit will do immense good in stirring up the *bourgeoisie* — especially among the dissenting sects. Pray pay them special attention and remind all your committee to bring you into contact with all the ministers around.'

About the line of disagreement which concerned him most, Webb spoke with real candor. 'I am afraid that you will be denounced by the wilder kind of socialists. Headlam, Pease [who was a member of the Henry George Campaign committee], and others beside myself are doing all we can to induce them to keep *quiet, as it would be fatal to arouse an antagonism between the radical and socialist parties.* Many of us have been working for you to keep the peace between them, and to bring them into line on practical politics. Neither the socialist nor any other party is here as in America, and the real force of the socialist movement works in lines you do not at all disapprove, and which are securing daily more and more recognition. See for instance the enclosed syllabus of lectures now being given at one of the best colleges in Cambridge University. How long will it be before Harvard does this?

'Now I want to implore your forbearance, when you are denounced as a traitor, and what not, by Socialist newspapers; and "heckled" by Socialist questioners, or abused by Socialist orators, it will be difficult not to denounce Socialism in return. But do not do so. They will be only the noisy fringe of the Socialist Party who will do this, and it will be better for the cause which we both serve, if you can avoid accentuating your differences with Socialists.'

The final advice Webb gave, compatible with his famous studies of administration, was that, in England, George could 'safely lay much more stress on the nationalization or "municipalization" of monopolies' than was politically feasible in America. 'Our Civil

Service and municipal government is much better fitted to bear the strain, and the people are quite ready.'

Considering Thomas Walker and Sidney Webb together, George approached this trip with adequate prompting, that he should get ahead with the main business and let argument about procedures lapse. For the most part he acted accordingly. At the close of the tour he did debate Henry Hyndman in St. James Hall, and did permit himself a sense of victory and satisfaction that he had spoken better for the single tax than his old associate had done for socialism. Such a debate can hardly have offended Webb and his colleagues, however, for with the passing years Hyndman's Social Democratic Federation had splintered and had lost much connection with the Fabian Society. It is doubtful that George himself had anything to do with Fabians other than Webb and Pease; certainly he had nothing to say about the group. Yet an article by Frederic Harrison, which appeared in the *Nineteenth Century* for November, speaking of moderate socialism, gave it the character of Henry George's *Social Problems*. There seems to have been still much in common between the American reformer and the British gradualists, though there was no great fondness, especially on George's side.

As to travels and activities, this visit divides into three more or less equal parts. The first four or five weeks, in March and April, Henry George spent, except for a short excursion in Wales, in London and the vicinity. Next came an extended speaking tour in the Midlands and Scotland; and third, a trip to the Continent, principally for an international meeting of land reformers in Paris. The visit rounded off with a brief return to England and a pause in Ireland, before a mid-July passage home. Four months all together made it longer than any other visit since 1882; and of course his efforts then had concentrated on Ireland, and he had been more a journalist at that time, and hardly at all a public adviser on the problems of Great Britain.

The first ten days in London both surprised and pleased the visitor. Out of nine speaking engagements, three were before Radical Club audiences, which seemed to indicate middle-class rather than working-class interest. (A little later, after speaking before a specifically laboring men's audience at Lambeth Baths, George wrote home that socialism had had very little influence on these people.) Five, or more than half, of the first series of speeches were before church meetings; and more often than not they were in dissenters' chapels, just as Sidney Webb had hoped. George's very first address, for instance, was in Camberwell Green Chapel. Two days later he lectured in the Congregational chapel at Wanstead, a suburb which reminded him of Orange, New Jersey; and very shortly he spoke at Westminster Chapel — which he believed to be the largest Congregational church in London. Several members of Parliament took part in the discussion. Thus he was able to write home that he was reaching English Liberals through the avenue of Mr. Shearman's church. This amounted to saying that he was trying an approach to social reform new in Britain, much the same as his approach in America. The time was ripe, he added, because the Conservatives might be expected to be displaced soon, and the Liberals would return to power.

Between speeches he found time, as during the preceding November, to see people in Parliament. Seated at the press table in the House of Lords, George caught the irony of hereditary legislators listening to the testimony of working girls about the conditions of labor. Who were noblemen, the American wondered, to be judges and defendants, both, when social questions came up for decision. The visitor's sympathy for the poor seems to have been widely understood. Letters poured in, addressed to him through campaign headquarters. Communications came from ministers and newspapermen; he received requests for interviews and invitations to write; and there was a pathetic inquiry from a boy who wanted to emigrate to America.

On the intellectual side, George took special satisfaction from conferences with the distinguished economic historian, Thorold Rogers of London and Oxford, who was reading in the British Museum. Professor Rogers told him that one reason why British industry had developed further in the north of England than in the south lay in the history of taxation: taxes on machinery in one region, and exemptions in the other. 'Of all the thieves in the world, Professor Rogers says the landowners of England are the worst and most unscrupulous,' George reported in the *Standard*. This sympathy was the more welcome, because in earlier years George, who admired and borrowed from Rogers' findings, had thought the scholar too cautious in interpretation, and had heard that he sneered at *Progress and Poverty*. Now he was able to say that the professor had spoken of the single tax 'with perfect fairness and evident sympathy.' He pleased George also by an invitation to come to Oxford — an opportunity regretfully foregone, for it might have established a happier association than the one of 1884.

So far as the record tells, Mrs. George and the girls were very inconspicuous during the London stage of this tour. Except for a special invitation to attend a couple of balls in London on St. Patrick's Day, so that they might see how the Irish working classes enjoyed themselves, we can only guess how they fitted in. But later, in the second, northern, stage of the trip, after George had taken nearly two weeks working his way from audience to audience, the whole family appears, having a splendid time. Some hosts arranged a picnic for them along the Roman wall, north of Newcastle-on-Tyne; and the sights of Scotland thrilled them. From the ancient capital city, Irish Annie George wrote her sister that she could not disagree with the Scots, their Edinburgh was the greatest city in the world, 'interesting beyond compare.' A stop at Melrose Abbey and Abbotsford interested her, but she was irritated at all the fee taking, and a little shocked to learn that Sir Walter had lived so luxuriously. As for her husband, 'Henry George is certainly doing great work — holding wonderful meetings in a new place every night.'

George's own excitement in Scotland seems to have been proportionate to place and previous association. Just south of the boundary he was stirred to have a speaking engagement at Alnwick, the seat of the Duke of Northumberland; and, in Campbelltown, during a short excursion into the Highlands, he felt a similar stimulation as he invaded the domain of the Duke of Argyll. 'The Highlands are all right,' he decided. 'The reductions in rent and the sweeping away of arrears by the crofter commission are only whetting the appetite of the crofters for more . . . It is a good thing for the men who have hitherto stood in dread of the power of landlords . . . to sit at the same table with landlord or factor — to tell their story and hear the landlord or factor tell his, and then have the commission decide against the "higher orders" . . . It is a new experience, and one that bodes no good to Highland landlordism.'

The Land Restoration League, he could feel, was yielding a good crop.

During his nearly three weeks in Scotland, George for the most part toured the industrial Lowlands. He made speeches in many towns where he had spoken in 1884 and 1885 and where Land Restoration League units had been formed — in Edinburgh, Dumfries, Greenock, Paisley, and, two appearances each, in Glasgow and Dundee. Again he stressed the Bible accent; a mistake about announcing an address entitled 'Thy Kingdom Come' drew thousands to a hall in Glasgow a week before the actual date. This was one of George's best speeches, and it has been reprinted and distributed from then until now.

Scotland was particularly Henry George's country, and he discovered there vigorous ideological growth from his own previous planting. In the person of Keir Hardie, who very soon would make history as the founder of the Independent Labour party, he met the best representative of the early absorption of the ideas of *Progress and Poverty* into British working-class politics. Mr. Hardie told him that nine-tenths of the miners of Scotland lived in one-room houses. The report to the *Standard* which mentioned this also said that in Scotland the ideas of Henry George had safely passed the first phase, that of seeming alarming and revolutionary. 'These men are nearly all men of influence in the Liberal Party here,' the chairman of a Glasgow banquet explained to Henry George, 'many of them capitalists and some of them landowners. I tell you this to show you how we are gaining influence as well as numbers since you were here last.' The single tax pleased this sort of audience.

In the English Midlands, George also sensed improvement for his cause. An accident of the road, apparently, he fell in with Philip Stanhope, who was the son of an earl and himself a prominent Radical in Commons. The conversation convinced the traveler that here, for once, was a sincere radical from the noble class, one deeply convinced that the land question was the real and burning issue of the time. George enjoyed a stop in Coventry, where the guildhall caught his fancy; from here he wrote home the Lady Godiva story, with its moral about taxation. Among the public meetings, the one at Birmingham greatly pleased him. This was successful partly because Thomas Walker was known to be his champion. But the meeting was held in the great townhall and, just as he liked, a Church of

England clergyman presided, and there were other clergymen on the platform, from Unitarian to Roman Catholic. Symbols of acceptance meant much to George, on this trip especially.

The stop in Birmingham, moreover, set the stage for the third and most unusual phase of the whole tour. At the Walker home George was sought out by Michael Flürscheim, a driving personality who was an ironmaster from Baden Baden, and a writer and reformer in the German *Land Liga* effort. Herr Flürscheim had written to George during the autumn of 1888, to pay tribute to his leadership and to discuss reform procedures. With perhaps no more preliminary than this, the two men joined forces. Traveling a couple of weeks with the George party, Flürscheim made several addresses; and, in his own self-estimate, he succeeded better than the American in replying to socialist hecklers. In his own mind a great partnership had been established: 'It was for me a memorable moment in which I looked for the first time into the noble clear eyes of the man to whom I owe so much, and for the first time pressed the forceful right hand of the hero who as commander in chief in the context of ideas, is leading forward.'

Though there is no indication that Henry George knew, beforehand, very much either about Flürscheim or about the ten-year-old land-reform movement in Germany, his letters do show that he had some knowledge of immediate backgrounds. Less than a week after the symbolic date, 4 July 1886, on which the *Land Liga* was established, Max Scheld, of Berlin, had informed him about the new organization, and told him that it greeted Henry George as its master. And recently he had received a good many letters which indicated that Europeans were interested in his books. During the preceding five years, *Progress and Poverty* had been translated into Swedish, Norwegian, French, and Italian; *Social Problems* had been translated into Dutch and Norwegian, and *Protection or Free Trade* into French and German. George had corresponded with most of the translators.

Sometimes his informants said that his ideas were having an effect on practical politics. About the time the *Land Liga* was founded, for instance, he had had a couple of letters from Norwegians. One of them spoke appealingly about the aid George's works could be expected to render to Norway's young and tender democratic institutions. A Danish correspondent reported that

major newspapers in Copenhagen were arguing free trade in the
Henry George way, and that a little single-tax newspaper was being
imported and read, from Norway. The same writer described a
meeting of Scandinavian economists, at which a Swedish professor,
seconded by a Danish one, spoke in endorsement of George's ideas,
and of land nationalization. This is the kind of appreciation of
George which the distinguished Norwegian historian, Halvdan
Koht, has recently summarized as an important part of the impact
of American ideas in Europe. George had had inquiries also, from
interested people as far distant as Chile, and Turkey, and Siam.

Now in the English spring of 1889, Flürscheim pressed an invitation which in a way drew these threads together. In June there
would be in Paris an international conference of land reformers.
George must have warmed to the promise that a group of Frenchmen would be present, men with ideas very close to his own, who
regarded themselves as descendants of the Physiocrats of the eighteenth century. The invitation promised a Belgian delegation to
be led by Agathon de Potter, already known to George; and
Flürscheim said there would be Germans, Dutch, Swiss, and Austrians as well.

Yet Flürscheim warned George that the conference as a whole
would not agree thoroughly with *Progress and Poverty*. The members would be more like himself, he said, in that they would think
that *rent and interest together,* and not rent alone, deprive the
producing classes and help to cause depressions. (Herr Flürscheim
had put his own theory in a book, *Auf Friedlichen Wege,* which
appeared in 1884.) Though the warning may have been discouraging news, there is no sign of controversy between the two new
colleagues. Flürscheim thought that they got along famously, and
George accepted the invitation.

When Henry George had last seen Paris, seven years earlier, as
observer and participator in Irish Land League activities, his role
had been a somewhat surreptitious one. This time he traveled completely in the open. Besides his wife and daughters, a number of
American and British sympathizers went with him. The London
Times said that 500 Americans had been expected, but that the
small number who arrived did not signify that the republic was
underrepresented, because the man to be chosen president of the
conference was an American. The delegates convened in the Hotel

Continental, about 150 strong, and according to *The Times*, they were seated on gilded chairs.

In due course Henry George was actually elected honorary president. He was introduced with a tribute to his success in Britain; and, speaking with special confidence, George said in a keynote address that 'single-tax men stand today where the anti-slavery men stood in 1856.' Great victories might come first either in the United States or Great Britain, he could not be sure which.

As an indication of certain recognitions, widespread in Europe but limited in their political meaning, the Paris meeting does seem a high point in Henry George's lifetime. Yet he actually attended only one or two sessions. On the second day, Jennie George came down with scarlet fever. The most the father could do, after she recovered a little, was to talk a good deal with French delegates who were especially sympathetic. He found freedom, before he left, to do some sight-seeing in the city.

At the meeting he established a friendly relationship, too, with Jan Stoffels, a follower of Flürscheim and the translator into Dutch of *Social Problems*. This led to a trip to Holland, about which George became quite lyrical in the *Standard*. The canals, the sloping houses, the yachts, the museums, and the pictures fascinated him. But when he made an address, for which a large audience turned out in a splendid hall in Amsterdam, he was not at all satisfied. It was theory which concerned him. He decided that European radicalism, even when as friendly as this, was too much opposed to interest taking to suit his own position. Many think that interest on capital is quite wrong, he wrote home, but none knows how to capture it, except by the state operation of all business.

His own reservations to the contrary notwithstanding, he was given early reason to believe that he had been accepted as *the* man of the movement which the conference represented, and that the international work would go on. Paul Leroy-Beaulieu, the distinguished French writer on economic institutions, though with reservations about many of George's ideas, presently paid tribute to *Progress and Poverty*, and to the author's 'enchanting vigor, his brilliant mind, and the apparent force of his style.' In August the news reached George that a Universal Land Federation was being set up, and that he himself would be its leader. All who had attended the Paris conference would be members, and all single-tax organizations wherever they might be. If Mr. George would contribute the necessary references, his recent Paris friend A. M. Toubeau requested on 22 August, the new federation would prepare a master list, covering the world, and it would include the names of newspapers.

While Jennie convalesced Henry George went back to England, keeping in touch by daily wire. The only important event in London this time was the public debate with Hyndman, which came off to his own satisfaction. Then he went to Ireland to make a couple of appearances. Michael Davitt took the chair at one of them, evidently with old injuries sufficiently mended to make the situation a friendly one. Back in England in July, George was honored by a farewell ceremonial in London, and by a farewell lecture before the Financial Reform Association in Liverpool.

During the last week abroad, the family, united in health, welcomed the voyage home. Part of their delight was anticipation of doing more traveling soon. George had been definitely asked to visit Australia and New Zealand. He would be paid £800; and he expected to bring home half, $2000, to bank in New York in 1890, after a trip around the world.

–5–

This time a crowd was waiting to make him welcome when his vessel came into port; and there was a dinner in a Coney Island hotel. The good news was that throughout the country the single-tax petitions to Congress were lengthening by hundreds and thousands of signers.

But immediately he was confronted with a crucial situation at home. It concerned his newspaper and his doctrines. Though, unlike the San Francisco *Post*, the *Standard* did not represent his whole career and livelihood, it did mean much. He was the proprietor of a good-looking newspaper, a journal of opinion which practiced his old preachment in favor of having the contributors of ideas sign their own writings. And of course the *Standard* was the ideological center of the single-tax movement.

But in the summer of 1889, while the movement was growing, the *Standard* was in danger of its life. A glance at the history of the paper is necessary. It had begun with a debt, as we know, and at first the question of financial success had concerned George deeply. Though he told Gütschow at that time that 'on the day I started the *Standard* I was some thousands poorer than when I left San Francisco,' he entertained grim hopes that the paper would support him, as his books had failed to do. We do not know much about the early financial history of the *Standard,* but it is clear that the pendulum swung several times during 1887 and 1888. Though the McGlynn affair lost subscribers in the long run, and the labor party defeat was a setback for the newspaper, George was able to announce at the close of 1888 that circulation was gaining. A fair number of subscriptions in Great Britain and Australia had raised sales from a low of 15,000 to about 20,000. In January 1888, when the interest was due on the Briggs note, George was able to pay; but two months later, things were very difficult. There were never any profits, yet there was always the belief that the need for the paper justified the effort.

Summing up at the time of the presidential campaign, George admitted that the transit out of labor politics had been 'exceedingly depressing' to the morale of the staff. As for himself, 'the drag and worry have been indescribable, and though pressing myself to the limit of my strength I have felt that my energies have been frittered away and that I was not doing my best work. The strain for the last ten years has been very great, and has I feel made me very much older. But I have told friends that I would go through till this year, or at least until this election was over.'

Yet in the autumn of all these anxieties, the *Standard* was given a new lease, and a new condition, of life. Tom Johnson was just entering politics, in the campaign in which he failed for election to the House of Representatives by about 600 votes. He subscribed $500 to circulate the paper as a campaign effort; and W. J. Atkinson, a rich man in Philadelphia, did the same. The $1000 subsidy was like a shot in the arm. The autobiography of Louis Post makes plain that very soon Johnson and Thomas Shearman and perhaps others were supporting the paper regularly, and that the old day-to-day worries never recurred.

Subsidization transformed the paper into a sort of institution, and changed the nature of Henry George's relation to it somewhat. He still presided in the rank of proprietor and editor; but in fact he was steward rather than risk-bearing capitalist, and he was chairman rather than director of the paper's daily routine. It was a natural time for delegating duties, and for tidying up in many ways. Before the 1889 tour in Great Britain George moved the *Standard*'s offices to Union Square, and his household to East Nineteenth Street, near and convenient to one another. About the time he started for Australia, the essential platform of the paper was reduced to a formula and set forth in a box which appeared in the upper left-hand corner of the front page. A three-point program was announced: (1) *the single tax,* stated to mean land-value taxation, with all taxes on labor or the products of labor abolished; (2) *free trade,* defined as more than tariff reform, as world trade as free as interstate commerce in America; and (3) *ballot reform,* the Australian ballot, to be prepared by public authority, and to be cast by the voter in enforced secrecy.

Though these consolidations produced a less exciting paper than the fighter of 1887, they had the merit of winning approval from contemporaries who otherwise cared very little for the ideas of Henry George. The New York *Tribune,* which had earlier had the generosity to say that the *Standard*'s 'subject matter is far above that in what usually are known as labor papers,' printed a warm endorsement of the journal's ballot-reform idea.

Evidently George felt at ease before he departed for the long absence of 1889, in Europe. But all too soon for peace of mind, while he was lecturing in Scotland, he began to hear of injured feelings and conflicts among the editors; and perhaps he perceived then that important differences of opinion were at the roots of the trouble. The stormiest of the discontented ones was Thomas M'Cready, who had been a leader of the Anti-Poverty Society and now had charge of a 'Men and Things' column of opinion of his own; and he was joined by a friend of Samuel Gompers, James L. Sullivan, who was the labor editor. The two together retained the spirit and intentions of Henry George's campaigns of 1886 and 1887; and when Henry George, Jr., refused to print some of their contributions, they poured out their resentment to the traveling chief, to whom M'Cready was especially devoted.

But the ranking editors in New York, Louis Post and William Croasdale, moved more willingly into the new emphases and strategies of the single tax; and they took the other side. They supported Henry George, Jr., George learned; and Tom Johnson, Shearman, and August Lewis, in the role of advisers and guarantors, in turn supported them. The personal conflict came to a climax during the spring, when the 'two strong masterful men,' as Henry George, Jr., called M'Cready and Sullivan, descended on the George household and moved in, offering some previous invitation as excuse. Before George returned from Europe, however, Sullivan resigned from the *Standard;* and on his return, George fired M'Cready and sent Henry George, Jr., from New York for a vacation and a rest. Annie George's solicitous comment was that two of her husband's 'coworkers have proved treacherous — I wonder how this man retains any confidence in humanity — but he does — and he goes on doing his work to the best of his ability.'

But the necessary remedy of conditions at the office opened to view, and even to public discussion, the conflict of ideas which was the serious part of the affair. In this respect Sullivan's actions had been more decisive than M'Cready's. The labor editor was disposed to be somewhat friendly toward the Bellamy Nationalist movement which had just appeared in the United States, and which had come to New York about the time of George's absence. In the wake of widespread reading of Edward Bellamy's *Looking Backward,* a novel of greater social influence in America, probably, than any other except *Uncle Tom's Cabin,* the new socialism took the form of clubs and journals, all dedicated to preparing for a very utopian kind of American life. The Nationalist Clubs were particularly numerous in Massachusetts, where the movement began, and in New York and California.

Sullivan, as an editor of the *Standard,* identified himself with the Nationalists only so far, he says, as to protest when it seemed to him that Croasdale insulted them needlessly on the editorial page. Why should not the *Standard* in New York take as generous an attitude toward an American brand of socialism as Henry George in England was taking toward the Fabians? Must the whittling down of Georgism go on forever — as McGlynn and Pentecost, the Marxian socialists, the Anti-Poverty Society, and the United Labor party had been pared away? These and more like them were the labor editor's questions, as he took leave of the *Standard,* and of the Georgist movement, for good. His questions had considerable moral force before he weakened his case, as he did after George's return, by issuing an absurd pamphlet, 'Ideo Kleptomania, the Case of Henry George,' in which he set out to prove that *Progress and Poverty* was a plagiarism from Patrick Dove.

Meanwhile M'Cready did his share of spreading and publicizing the controversy. He appealed to ministers who shared with him a loyalty to the evangelical spirit of Anti-Poverty, which the single-tax movement had succeeded in quieting down. By turning to Hugh Pentecost, who was now editing a new journal of social reconstruction, *Twentieth Century*, and by publishing through him articles critical of the *Standard*, while he himself was still a member of the staff, M'Cready infuriated George. But the matter was a little different when he appealed to Father James O. H. Huntington, an Episcopalian priest of the Order of the Holy Cross, and a son of Bishop Frederic Dan Huntington, who had spoken for United Labor in 1887. On Henry George's return to New York, Father Huntington prayed his 'dear friend' to keep the *Standard* open to religious elements it had previously made welcome.

What had begun as an office row, the immediate result of an editor-proprietor leaving his newspaper to go abroad, thus widened into an ordeal for the Georgists of New York. Henry George himself can hardly have needed letters from people he had recently seen in England, moreover, to understand that the troubles at home were similar if not identical with the differences of ideas which had come between him and Flürscheim and Stoffels on the Continent, and between Thomas Walker and himself, in the instance which disturbed him most of all. But Walker did write, in an irony which must have cut, to describe the single-tax antics of 'Dear old Cobdenite Briggs, Henry George worshipper Wood, Politician Saunders, Unpledged Recruit Reeves,' in England. Declaring himself to be still the man who loved and appreciated Henry George better than anyone else did on that side of the Atlantic, the Birmingham patron warned that the single tax was already tending 'to fossilize into a fetish.' He begged George to recall that as the author of *Progress and Poverty* he had been the first to make 'our movement' a matter of religion, and urged that old bearings be not lost, and that in England men like Durant and Wicksteed be kept in council. In similar vein but with lighter touch, Thomas Davidson presently warned that George would soon be known as the 'monotelist.' Why not come north, invited this Fabian, and buy a farm adjoining his own, the highest house in the Adirondacks? From that doorstep he could survey Lake Champlain, and gain balance and new perspective.

Even before George reached New York City, the *Standard* had proceeded in a democratic way to straighten out the snarls of doctrine as it could. Now inviting rather than excluding differences of opinion, space was given to Shearman, Pentecost, M'Cready, and Croasdale, and each summed up his own judgment about the best policy for the newspaper and the movement. Shearman said that he intended to be practical, and that he regarded the single tax as a hedge against anarchism and socialism; he denied that his plan reduced the George movement to being 'soulless, principleless,' and he asserted that it contained the leader's essential ideas. Cold reason was in order, the lawyer insisted, and he specified that he wanted the state to take only that share of economic rent needed for fiscal purposes, he estimated 65 per cent. The only disagreement he would admit existed between Henry George and himself was that George wanted to take nearly all the rent, say 85 or 90 per cent. Between them there would be no difference, said Shearman, if experience ever indicated that the community could use the larger return.

From the dissident side, M'Cready wrote with the greatest emotion. 'Friends . . . I think we may as well leave statistics alone and stick to facts — the eternal facts that God is an equal-loving Father, and that men have equal rights of access to His bounties.' And when the next turn came, the minister of Unity Congregation objected to what he called the *Standard's* shifting to Shearmanism in Henry George's absence. Though he denied wishing 'organic union' with any socialists, Pentecost did advocate such 'sympathetic relations' as might be possible.

Managing editor Croasdale criticized both sides. Shearman missed the philosophy of natural rights in land, he said, and became a mere tax reformer. On the other hand, Henry George men could not go with Christian socialism any more than with other varieties. Whatever socialists might say, and however well they might agree with Georgism concerning land, they could not reconcile their other goals with the individualism which Henry George asserted. Croasdale refused to state a preference between George and Shearman on the question whether 65 or 90 per cent of rent ought to be confiscated. In his opinion, the George movement's first obligation was still as always to teach just principles of economic distribution. Other matters could wait on that.

At last in August, the master called the tune. After finishing with M'Cready, he stated his own judgments in the *Standard*. Toward the dissident side, while he omitted any blanket pronouncement against utopian socialism, he did object to the materialism, or threat of materialism, which he believed lay even in that phase of the socialist movement. He criticized Pentecost, saying that in his leftward course the minister had abandoned belief in immortality and had come to a position which was just about agnostic.

Facing the other side of the controversies, George admitted a difference from Shearman. He applied to the lawyer's 65 per cent the phrase 'Single Tax Limited,' a tag he had used before going to Britain; and he called himself an 'unlimited' single-taxer. Yet he did not press the difference very far. Limited or unlimited, the single tax was one scheme, and he and Shearman could work for it together, George asserted. He acknowledged that Shearman had brought great strength to the movement, from the moment in 1886 when he contributed money to circulate *Protection or Free Trade*.

During the midsummer clarification in the *Standard* office, George wrote a lead article on Bellamy's *Looking Backward*. 'A castle in the air, with clouds for its foundation,' it seemed to him, 'cool and tempting to travellers from afar . . . A popular presentation of the dream of state socialism.' He saw much good in the Nationalist movement. Large numbers of people were learning new and necessary ideas; the clubs were driving them home; and *Dawn* and other journals were communicating them successfully. But George's final word, that *Looking Backward* was giving 'a strong impulse' to 'the idea of effecting social improvement by government paternalism,' was of course an adverse judgment.

Again a month later, commenting on remarks in *Harper's Weekly* which he presumed to be written by George William Curtis, George returned to this theme. Even in such lamb's clothing as Bellamy enclosed it, he said, socialism promoted state power. A revolution in property rights in land was desirable, he specified, but not the state management of land. In his own words in the *Standard:* 'If we do not believe in *laisser faire* as it is generally understood, letting things alone,' we do believe that policy should 'clear the ways, and then let things alone.'

In his recent letters to Walker, in his words and actions toward M'Cready, Pentecost, and Shearman, Henry George had become more completely a single taxer than Thomas Shearman ever was. He had widened his differences from the socialists, and had renewed his dependence on idealistic thought. He had not turned conservative, he had not reduced his loyalty to the broader doctrines of his books, and he had not been governed by the preferences of either branch of his followers. He had become a little more isolated, more lonely in the operations of his mind. Things would go that way for the remainder of his life.

–6–

Having cleared the situation sufficiently at the *Standard*, George was free to undertake some speaking, and to go on the road again. In a couple of appearances in New York, one of them before the Manhattan Single Tax Club, he spoke on tax reform, but he by no means confined himself to that subject. After a swing upstate and to Toronto, and a debate with a congressman in Rochester, he made a party of three with Tom Johnson and William Ivins — the man who as city chamberlain had tried to dissuade him from running for mayor. They went together to Boston as leaders in the Australian ballot reform. They observed the first election in the hub city under the new system, and George wrote to his paper in delight. There had been no soliciting of votes, he said, and the Australian system must become the American one.

North of Boston George lectured in Lewiston, Lynn, Lawrence, and Worcester. In retrospect he acknowledged that single-tax organizations were growing slowly in that part of the country. Hamlin Garland was president of one in Boston, however, and Lloyd Garrison was working; and he discovered that some Brown University men were single taxers. He found people to convince him that the free-trade idea was increasing. He cheerfully reported that *Looking Backward* was popular and that the Nationalist Clubs were doing good work — asking the right questions and forcing discussion in New England.

During the last month of the year, touring this time in Ohio and Pennsylvania, George reported further indications of radicalism rising in the country. He noticed the fact that certain officials of the Knights of Labor and representatives of the Farmers Alliance had met recently in Cincinnati. Today we can see in such gatherings a shadow cast by the coming event of Populism; and George caught something of this meaning. He was grateful when the Knights of Labor, meeting in general assembly, declared for the single tax — he called this the most important labor event in three years. Though his enthusiasm outran his judgment — and the *Journal of the Knights of Labor,* if he had read it, would have indicated to him much resistance to his ideas — he had received a real compliment, and his own responses show that, after all the purges, he still kept heart for organized labor. All things taken together, when the year drew to a close George felt quite content with the achievement of 1889.

By Christmastime the speech making was almost done and he shifted his sights to the long trip, which was to start about four weeks later. Recent news from Australia was altogether encouraging. Nine hundred pounds had been raised for his campaign, and he was invited to speak for the single tax 'in its fullness,' and even — in that country notorious for the protective tariff — to speak for free trade as well. 'Everywhere your name evokes the wildest cheering,' he was told.

During the final month at home George put his affairs, public and private, in order. He paid some debts; he approved plans, suggested by Mr. Jackson Ralston and others of the Washington group, for a national single-tax meeting in 1890; and he may have had something to do with setting up the Single Tax Brotherhood of Religious Teachers, which was announced in January. This effort gathered Episcopalian, Presbyterian, Methodist, Baptist and other Protestant clergymen, and a few Catholic priests, into one organization for reform — a renewal of old procedures. As for the *Standard,* George wrote a new contract. He gave Croasdale full authority on the editorial side, for the period of his absence. He arranged to have Henry George, Jr., go to Washington and contribute a weekly letter.

At the point of departure from New York, Henry George received such a salute from the intellectual, professional, and upper-middle-class elements among his admirers as he had not since the Delmonico banquet of October 1882. At this dinner Lyman Abbot,

Beecher's successor in Plymouth Church, and other clergymen paid tribute; and so did George William Curtis of *Harper's Weekly*. Letters of good wishes were received from Texas Representative Roger Q. Mills and from ex-Speaker of the House John G. Carlisle, the two most prominent men in the recent Democratic effort for tariff reduction. Perhaps for the first time, university presidents joined in acclaiming him. Seth Low and E. Benjamin Andrews, the one just become the head of Columbia and the other, of Brown, joined in the pleasant send-off; and so did Professor Arthur Twining Hadley, who a decade later would be president of Yale. Terence Powderly, who was still grand master workman of the Knights of Labor but would soon begin his new career in law and federal government, more nearly than anyone else represented the kind of greeting Henry George in older days had been accustomed to receive.

This time Mr. and Mrs. George traveled without their daughters, free for a grand adventure. They routed themselves by way of St. Louis, where they visited Sister Teresa, and where Henry George was given a splendid dinner and reception, with many businessmen present. To family and followers at home, stories went back which were intended to sustain interest and morale: a meeting of a group of George enthusiasts at a Harvey restaurant stop in New Mexico; a hotbox and delay at Flagstaff; Mrs. George taking snapshots, and keeping her husband straight as to hats and clothing, typewriter and papers, all the way. At Los Angeles Henry George missed a meeting by reason of the train's delay. He gave one speech, one hour and three-quarters long.

San Francisco warmed the Georges' heart. Dr. Taylor and about twenty friends met the train at Martinez; and, from Tuesday through Saturday of the first week in February, they had a triumph. Standing before a paying audience in Metropolitan Temple, the very hall in which, a dozen years earlier, he had half-failed in the address which began his speaking career, he scored a platform victory. Surrounded by 100 prominent citizens, facing a full house, and greeted with pandemonium, he spoke the thoughts which must have come with the easiest spontaneity. No longer, he said, did the movement depend on one person alone. 'It is sweet to a man long absent to be welcomed home . . . Now so well forward is the cause . . . that it makes no difference who lives or dies . . . At last —

at last, we can say with certainty that it will be only a little while before all over the English-speaking world, and then not long after, over the rest of the civilized world, the great truth will be acknowledged that no human child comes into this world without coming into his equal right with all.' Perhaps this was the occasion on which the speaker was presented with verses which Dr. Taylor had written, and which were printed and distributed to honor the visit.

George addressed a free meeting for working men in the Metropolitan Temple. It was very crowded. He crossed to Oakland for a speech; and he was dined and feted on every available occasion. He had no more than three hours sleep, any of those San Francisco nights, he said. In the press he became 'California's Political Economist,' and 'The Prophet of San Francisco' was used as a designation of honor in this place. As in days gone by the *Examiner* praised him cordially; and his old friends doted on his present recognition and power. A couple of hundred people waved the Georges off when they sailed, westbound, on the *Mariposa* — an American-built ship which the old India sailor found excellent.

California had seemed glorious and bright. During the three remaining weeks of February the tropical seas supplied the rest which the travelers needed. In a one-day stop the Georges saw Honolulu, and Waikiki and the Punch Bowl. Mrs. George thought the island spoiled from four decades earlier. In port a group of United States naval officers, some of whom professed the single tax, took the Georges to dinner; and at sea Henry George was twice invited to explain his ideas to the people in the cabin. But this was all. The long run, south and west, from Honolulu to New Zealand was extremely quiet. The *Mariposa* slipped by Tutuila in the dark without a pause. Only at Auckland did Henry and Annie George get a first sign of the excitement to come.

Henry George's wish for that city was to see the seventy-eight-year-old Sir George Grey, who had spent four decades of his life as explorer, writer, and crown governor in Australia and New Zealand. During the last dozen years, and especially during 1877–9 as prime minister, he had emerged as a radical and philosophical-minded reformer. A present-day investigator, Mr. Peter Coleman, finds that, though Sir George lacked certain qualities which would have made him more effective in politics, he had a peculiar eloquence and power, not unlike Henry George's own, to make his countrymen aware of the economic dangers of land aggregation. Certainly he recommended *Progress and Poverty;* and before Henry George's arrival the book had been for a decade an influence in the land. Altogether the situation was favorable for the visitor; and we may anticipate that in years to come Henry George's ideas would again influence New Zealand tax policy.

Immediately on the *Mariposa's* putting in, Sir George took charge of Henry and Annie George. He charmed them. He took them to a gathering of the local Anti-Poverty Society and there publicly attested his belief in the visiting American's principles. George was presented with a handsome illuminated address. A few hours later, again at dockside, the two men could hardly part: the captain had to hold the *Mariposa* while they talked on the wharf. 'You have expanded a spark into a blaze of thought and unselfish conceptions which is spreading to every part and ennobling countless minds,' wrote Sir George Grey in a letter that followed.

On 6 March the outgoing voyage ended at Sydney. Every circumstance made this landing an exciting one: Sydney was Mrs. George's birthplace; and Australia meant rich associations for Henry George — memories of Hobson's Bay and Melbourne, 1855; his writing about the economic problems of the subcontinent in the San Francisco *Post;* the origin of the secret ballot; and recently a political venture into the public ownership of railroads and communications. Henry George called the return to Australia a honeymoon, and so it truly proved.

Mrs. George was accustomed to a quiet place in the background, but this time she was presented with a red-and-gold shoulder ribbon, with 'Welcome, Australia's Daughter' marked on it in large letters. In his first address Henry George, the missionary, asked for yet more return traffic in the ideas of democracy. He reported on the instances of American states adopting the Australian ballot. 'If you can teach us more, for God's sake teach us. Advance Australia!' The effect of this speech, according to the Sydney *Daily Telegraph,* was 'at once remarkable and indescribable.' John Farrell, who was about to become editor of the *Telegraph,* the city's largest paper, wrote to the New York *Standard* that George's brilliance as orator, and the charm which did not wear thin under all the tension and pressure, pleased those who heard and saw beyond all expectation.

The reception at Sydney more or less set a pattern according to which Henry George was treated for three solid months. He was welcomed by colonial and city officials; he was managed by local committees; he was scheduled to speak frequently, and then many times induced to speak still more often; his engagements were separated only when travel required. In Sydney he was taken in charge by Charles L. Garland, member of the parliament of New South Wales and president of the Single Tax League of that colony. The two had met in England in 1889; and indeed this visit had much in common with that one. As he had under Mr. Saunders' auspices in the mother country, George lectured most frequently before Protestant groups and in middle-class circumstances — of course the prevailing ones in Australia. During this first stop in Sydney, he appeared several times at such places as Protestant Hall, the Pitt Street Congregational Church, or at a meeting of a Presbyterian conference, while he had but one session with labor people.

After nearly a fortnight in Sydney — which must have been longer than any single stopover in any other city of his visits, unless London is the exception — George headed inland, at first west and then south. He made a dozen or so speeches, usually one a day, on the way to Melbourne, the capital of Victoria, and the city he remembered from the past. There he encountered at maximum force the principal hazard of his trip, the danger of falling out with people who would challenge his free-trade convictions and would perhaps reject him for those ideas though otherwise they might follow. As George analyzed the situation, in contrast with America, the masses were protectionist, partly he thought in protest against Great Britain. On the other hand, the landowners were the free-traders, and the people in closest touch and sympathy with home policy and ideas. But, as when dealing with the Irish in New York, George yielded nothing to the protectionists. Before a Melbourne Town Hall audience of working men, he spoke on 'Labour and the Tariff,' though he was advised not to do so. He surprised all concerned by winning an ovation; and he repeated the success a little later, in debate with a protectionist member of the colonial parliament.

There was more work to do, and more places to visit, than there was time to write his letters for the *Standard,* and accordingly our information runs a little short. Yet he was fascinated we know, and so was Mrs. George. Proud of her native land, she liked the cities better, as being neater and better kept, than American cities. In Melbourne, George ingratiated himself by reminiscing. There had been more ships in the harbor in 1855 than in 1890, he said, doubtless with a free-trade moral in mind; but he said also that a grim line of those vessels had been the transports for convicts out of England. He contrasted that grimness with the suburbs and villas now so pleasant along the waterfront, and with the changed face of the city.

After excursions out of Melbourne to places just west, George moved north to towns near Sydney, but much farther inland than he had gone on his way south. Then a week of travel took him to Adelaide, the capital of South Australia; and for the last ten days of April he was in and out of that city. The beauty of the place struck him; and so too did the power of a dour Scottish minister who was preaching the single tax there.

Before May was a week old, the traveler was back on the east coast again, where he had begun. From Sydney he went north, this time to Brisbane, capital of Queensland, where he was received by the mayor and by the Queensland Tax Reform Association. He made four or five speeches in the city. He seems to have discovered a special popularity in Marysborough, still farther up the coast. There, for one of several appearances, he was invited to talk to school children — an experience he had not had before, and one which terrified him. Along every leg of his Australian travels, various unfamiliar phenomena of nature caught his eye — the kangaroos, of course, and, here along the upper east coast, the great reef which stretches far to north and west.

On his final return to Sydney, Henry George closed the tour for which he had contracted, on the last day of May, just short of a quarter of a year after he had begun it. For that occasion he selected as his topic, 'Protection a Fallacy, Real Free Trade a Necessity'; and the president of the Free Trade League, though denying discipleship, saluted him as having made his name a household word in Australia. This can hardly have been an exaggeration. Two nights later he was honored by the mayor, who was also a member of parliament; and he was bid farewell at still another meeting in the city.

As in New Zealand, Henry George's ideas had entered public

consciousness deeply enough to make a difference. An early commentator credited two Americans with great influence on the rise
of collectivism in Australia — the larger influence to Edward Bellamy, and the lesser one to Henry George. But a recent scholar
discovers that Georgist ideas, in unusually doctrinaire form, were
written directly into a Queensland bill which, though not enacted,
had considerable importance; and that very soon South Australia,
New South Wales, and Queensland all enacted taxes on unimproved land, and so set a pattern which has become permanent in
Australian policy. George's follower, Max Hirsch, kept up the effort
for free trade, and his sizable book, *Democracy versus Socialism*,
first published in 1901, is more elaborate than anything George
ever wrote in setting forth the opposition of Georgist to socialist
principles.

—7—

In first planning the Australian trip, George had wanted the
homeward voyage, still west bound, to include a stop in Africa.
But now, at the actual point of departing, he would have liked still
better to turn south and west, as he was invited, first to Tasmania,
and then for a return visit to New Zealand. But he was very tired, and
perhaps felt too committed to attend the coming single-tax meeting
in New York to change direction. So the short stop the ship made
in Colombo was the last the Georges saw of the part of the world
they were so unlikely to return to. In Ceylon, as thirty-five years
earlier in and around Calcutta, Henry George observed Oriental
life. He visited a Buddhist temple and noticed the intelligence in
the dark faces.

The run up the Gulf of Suez gave a glimpse of Sinai, and of course
the African shore, but the Georges stopped neither for the Holy
Land nor for Egypt. Their plans called for three weeks, later July
and early August, crossing Europe, and for two weeks in England.
George had agreed to a couple of speeches there. They debarked
at Brindisi.

In Italy for the first time, the travelers saw the backbone of the
peninsula from a railroad-car window. The romantic in George
and the economist, both, were fascinated. The mountain scenery
and the hamlets, which he believed to be older than Rome, seized
his imagination. Then the engineering of the railroad took per-

spective from the type of labor which subserved its very operation — for instance, women carrying stones and mortar on their heads to masons building bridges. He compared Australian farming with the intensive olive raising of Italy. Stopping at Naples, the Georges visited Pompeii, Herculaneum, Capri, and Sorrento. George wrote home of this as a tourist, with few reflections, with little else than the delight of travel to express.

Like many Americans before and since, the Georges looked at paintings in the galleries more from duty than from satisfaction. 'You would get sick of old masters,' Henry George wrote Dr. Taylor, but said that they had 'had a good time in our own way, unknown and unknowing, and working our way by signs largely.' Mrs. George wrote Sister Teresa that St. John Lateran appealed to her more than any other church in Rome, and that she found St. Peter's not a place to pray. She visited the catacombs. But she made no effort to get an audience with the Pope — it was hard for Americans she said, not mentioning that Henry George's works had recently been put before the Inquisition.

From Rome the couple hurried north by way of Florence, Genoa, Venice, and Lugano. On the way out of Italy the 'silent and soft beauty' of Lake Como made an unforgettable impression. Their train took them through the St. Gothard to Luzerne; and by a failure of communication which may have been intentional they missed seeing Michael Flürscheim, who had been busy with single-tax writing and affairs, and who was anxious for a meeting as they passed so near to Germany. They had six days in Paris — Mr. George's third visit and Mrs. George's second, but the first for either with a real opportunity to look about.

There could have been no expectation that the fortnight in Britain, Henry George's sixth visit in less than a decade, would turn into a personal or ideological triumph, as the visits of 1884 and 1889 had done. There had been no planning for that kind of tour this time. This short visit took rather the form of a general's inspection of forces he himself had established on foreign soil but no longer commanded directly. George heard from Poultney Bigelow, who was now settled in England for writing; and not unlikely the two met and renewed old times. He certainly saw Father Huntington, who must have reported on the situation at New York headquarters, and the two went together to call on General and Mrs.

William Booth. George estimated the power of the Salvation Army more highly now than he had before, for he had seen it at work in Ceylon, and he hoped that the organization would in time become a rod and staff to him — a hope which was perhaps justified while Mrs. Booth lived, but which did not survive her early death. The Georges went to Birmingham and were entertained handsomely by Thomas Walker. The speeches this time were widely spaced: one in London, days after arrival; one in Glasgow, nearly a week later; one in Liverpool, on the eve of departure, before the Financial Reform Association once more.

This last visit in England, in 1890, confirms the picture of 1889, which showed him strongly entrenched among Radical and Protestant groups but out of the old familiarity with labor and socialist ones. Two interviews of the fortnight, however, raise new questions about old connections which were to have a bearing on his future. In London, George had a conference with Cardinal Manning, their second meeting. All that we are told about it is contained in Mrs. George's adjective put in a letter to her sister — it had been 'delightful.' One wonders. A year after the event, was Henry George uninformed that the Holy Office had found *Progress and Poverty* worthy of condemnation? Or, just possibly, could he have gone to the interview with that information and have come away with some nod which anticipated the decision, still many months in the future, that would lift Father McGlynn's excommunication? This seems improbable. One of the astonishing things about George's life was his capacity to make war on ideas and policies, and yet to keep in touch with people who believed in them.

Whatever the prince of the church may have said, George's visit with Thomas Walker produced definite results. In Birmingham the visitor was given a long memorandum, and it concerned the differences of opinion between visitor and host. George studied it while crossing the Atlantic, and he examined also a parcel of Fabian tracts which he had been given. The convictions of these Englishmen depressed him. He came home burdened with awareness of ideas he must somehow combat, on a larger scale than in the *Standard* office last year, and yet must do so without injuring the friends who held them.

Immediately on arrival in New York, on 1 September, he was taken to Cooper Union and presented to the first national single-tax conference. He had acquiesced in such a meeting before leaving; Croasdale had taken charge, and now the show of strength was timed precisely for his return. Five hundred delegates from thirty-odd states were present, and the Single Tax League of the United States was at the moment of birth. The presence of friends, the excitement of a meeting, and work to do were reassuring things to come home to.

George plunged in. On 2 September, his fifty-first birthday, he was greeted by an assembly of 3500, and Judge Maguire from San Francisco occupied the chair. Yet, from George's selection of subject for his own speech, one suspects a little detachment, a mood a shade different from simply wishing to acquiesce in the work at hand and from surrendering altogether to congratulation. He gave an address on free trade, not the single tax. The choice may have been directed entirely by its appropriateness for the voyager returned. But his son remembers George as having been somber at the conference. He noticed that when a voice at the birthday celebration cried out to wish him long life, George responded in intensity. 'But not too long. Life, long life, is not the best thing to wish for those you love. Not too long, but that in my day, whether it be long or short, I may do my duty, and do my best.'

Writing about the conference in the *Standard* of 10 September, George noted that the 'crank element' had departed, now, from his following, and that the general press, more friendly than earlier, was saying that the movement had abandoned its old extremism. He said he welcomed these changes. He believed that people's ideas were shifting, in a large way, in his own direction. He expected the movement to go forward, now, under its own power.

He himself planned to do some writing.

XVIII

———

Christian Democrat to the End

1890–1897

—1—

BETWEEN 1870 and 1897, Henry George wrote eight books. We are acquainted with five, already; three remain to be fitted into the story of his life. From first to last, George's books can be remembered conveniently by decades, and in that way be classified as to type and purpose.

During the '70s he found himself as a writer. In *Our Land and Land Policy* he rough-hewed his ideas; and in *Progress and Poverty* he polished them and gave them richness of context. During the first five years of the '80s he directed those theories toward practice. In *The Irish Land Problem* he made his *argumentum ad nationem;* and in *Social Problems* and *Protection or Free Trade* he developed, first, the practical collectivist side, and then the free-enterprise side, of his larger economic philosophy. Finally, during the '90s, he undertook the two tasks he had most wanted to do from the moment of completing *Progress and Poverty.* That is, he wrote answers to the philosophical materialism of his age, and he did a book which restated the principles of general economics in conformity with the ideas of his masterwork.

To be sure nothing turned out quite according to original plan. The 'primer' of economics, as he had first conceived it, ultimately became a two-volume treatise — though he never finished parts of it — *The Science of Political Economy,* which was published posthumously in 1898. The reply to materialism, though George had said that he held back much of his thought on that subject when he wrote *Progress and Poverty*, turned out to be not a general affirmation of idealism but a critique of Herbert Spencer: *A Perplexed Philosopher*, 1892. And before the busy author produced either of these works he took time, first, to do a short book, *The Condition of Labor*. This was his famous open letter to Pope Leo XIII, which set out to reconcile the social ideas of *Progress and Poverty* with those of Catholic Christianity.

George's entire writing effort of the final decade of his life reminds one of an engineering event of some years ago in Washington. When the huge Lincoln Memorial on the Mall, the marble temple which encloses the statue by John Chester French, threatened to go down because the ground around it was marshy, tons of fresh concrete were poured, to establish a sufficient foundation. Henry George had built *his* monument, and for a decade after 1879 it had held up beautifully, unthreatened. But experience was now persuading him that neighboring areas were unstable; and, much like the pourers of concrete into Potomac swamplands, he turned next to writing books intended to reinforce not so much *Progress and Poverty* itself as the terrain upon which it rested. Of the three new works of the '90s, two extended the reach of the moral sequence of thought set forth in *Progress and Poverty*. Only one book attempted to reinforce the inner logic of his economic proposals, and that book he left unfinished.

−2−

Readers who have sensed the degree of reorientation which occurred in George's activities when he abandoned labor politics will understand the better his wish to return to first principles, and to make those principles as clear and as practicable as he was able. Yet, to comprehend more completely his compulsion to fresh thought, a backward glance is required, a little to one side of the main road of reform affairs which the last few chapters have followed. We must now consider what did not concern him very much before 1890, namely, the meaning of the less partisan and more intellectual criticisms and estimations which had cumulated along the way. Thinkers who misapprehended or seemed to misapprehend him, and people who were lukewarm toward him or else coolly indifferent, any and all who might possibly be transformed into followers or sympathizers, or whose opposition might be neutral-ized — such persons naturally challenged Henry George to restate the fundamentals of his argument.

The time to look back to is the middle '8os. Though, as readers of Chapter XIV will remember, the country's awareness of the man derived in part from earlier causes than the political campaigns in New York city and state, the excitements of 1886 and 1887 must be understood as having heightened that awareness tremendously. The United Labor party created an American atmosphere in favor of recognizing him that compares with the effect of the Irish crisis on Britain's recognition, four or five years earlier.

As in England in 1883 and 1884, so in the United States a little later, criticisms and replies to Henry George increased to very large numbers. Individual items came out as pamphlet and book-size publications. The first such effort appeared in 1884, William Hanson's *The Fallacies of 'Progress and Poverty': in Henry Dunning Macleod's Economics, and in 'Social Problems.'* Though written by one who spoke rather against the compulsion of land-value taxation than against the merits of the case in economics, the little book seems to have disturbed George not at all. Perhaps it was too mild and glancing a blow to be concerned about, after Toynbee, Argyll, and the major British journals had struck their hardest.

By three years later, however, in the wake of the mayoralty campaign and during the year of the state campaign and of Father McGlynn's excommunication, two more books indicated an increase in both quantity and quality of counter-argument. In the instance of J. Bleecker Miller's 200 pages, *Trade Organizations in Politics, also, Progress and Robbery: an Answer to Henry George,* there is little, indeed, to be said about quality. The book simply incorporated two anti-George campaign addresses of 1886, and it carried forward the name-calling of that year. But Reuben C. Rutherford's *Henry George versus Henry George, a Review,* brought out by Appleton, George's own first New York publisher, was half again as long, and in its own way made telling points of objection. Beginning with a premise, opposite to George's own belief, that 'Equality is a dream that can never be realized . . . as undesirable as it is impossible,' and ending with a contention that George assumed too completely the perfectibility of the social order and considered too little the evil inherent in man, Rutherford's book illustrates the anti-egalitarian and anti-rationalistic assumptions which penetrated American criticism almost as frequently as they did British.

As might be anticipated, the year 1887 produced a good deal of Catholic commentary. Some of it cropped up far from the arch-diocese of New York. For instance, Father Edward A. Higgins was requested to lecture by students at Xavier University, in Cincinnati; and his ideas about the mentor of Father McGlynn were published in a pamphlet, *The Fallacies of Henry George*. At a more scholarly level, the *Catholic World* carried an article by Father Henry A. Brann, who noticed, as Archbishop Corrigan did not, George's distinction between private property in land and private property in things, but who condemned Henry George roundly, partly be-cause he found him 'essentially anti-American,' preaching 'a crusade against our republican rights of property.' A third Catholic writer considered George to belong, or almost belong, in the tradition of the best utopianism. But he reserved the thought that the mo-nastic orders of the Catholic Church were the only organizations capable of a 'true and practical' realization of utopia, and so in the end he dismissed George as a misleader. Still another writer, a parish priest of Pittsburgh, undertook in a pamphlet to make a kernel-sized reply to all of George's principal economic ideas.

Occasionally criticisms came from writers of such derivations in society as George liked to think would naturally be favorable to his ideas. Two of these were George Gunton and Robert Ellis Thompson. Gunton, though better remembered for the journal he edited under his own name, was at this time simply a labor spokes-man for the eight-hour program. In a *Forum* article of 1887, and in a book published a decade later, this writer criticized Henry George's theory of wages (and criticized F. A. Walker's also), and he offered a theory of his own. And the *Irish World,* which had turned against George when Father McGlynn defied church authority, deepened the rift by pushing the tariff question to the limit. During the election year, Patrick Ford employed Professor Thompson, whose book George had selected as target for *Protection or Free Trade,* to speak for the protective tariff. Along the way, the Phil-adelphia professor declared just as strongly against the single tax as he did against free trade; and the *Irish World*'s editorial page commented more savagely than did the special articles. From the point of view of the Henry George movement, the coincidence of opposition from priests, and from Irish and labor journalists, marked a real frustration. It set up a barrier beyond which George had a right to believe his ideas might carry. But the barrier held, apparently as unyielding in 1890 as three years earlier.

Among scholars, the most famous person to speak against him in this period was William Torrey Harris, the educator of St. Louis and a leader of the Concord School of Philosophy. In early September 1886, a date that indicates his decision to criticize was made before George became a candidate for mayor, Mr. Harris delivered a paper at a Saratoga meeting of the Social Science Association. His very adverse address, 'The Right of Property and the Ownership of Land,' was printed in the journal of the association.

Crediting Henry George with a true eloquence and with having achieved an influence on thought about equal to that of Ricardo or Malthus, Harris believed that land-value taxation, if ever put into actual operation, would lead to confiscations even greater than the amount of economic rent it intended to appropriate. The philosopher-critic said that George's style of thinking should be classified with that of Herbert Spencer. Though once again there is no evidence that George himself took any special notice of a critic, this kind of article was just the sort to seem answerable. As much as five years later, when Harris renewed his criticism, E. Benjamin Andrews of Brown did come forward with a kind of defense. 'Many of the objections raised against the George philosophy are in a way recommendations instead,' wrote the college president in the *International Journal of Ethics*. While stating doubts of his own about George's utopia, President Andrews called George 'clear-headed' and his economic analyses often 'very brilliant'; and he suggested that 'a stiff tax might be laid upon land without entirely destroying private income from rent, and involving no whit more confiscation than the forms of taxation now prevalent; in fact much less.'

Though estimations are bound to be impressionistic and generalizations must be tentative, it does seem that the middle and late '80s were the time when Henry George was least rejected by academic economists. Representative of the new institutional and historical branch of American economic thought, Richard Ely, whose later antipathy toward George impressed his students, made respectful comments in his *Recent American Socialism*, a Johns Hopkins study published in 1885; and, in a textbook and elsewhere, he said appreciative things about George as a stimulator of public thought and discussion. General Walker himself clearly referred to his old opponent in his presidential address before the American Economic Association. Even while condemning the vagaries of economic protest, he advised his brothers of the guild to pay attention. 'We ought to rejoice, with all our hearts, that the people, the whole people, are coming, for the first time, to take a deep, earnest, passionate interest in the subjects to which we have devoted our lives.'

Possibly the most revealing glimpse we can take in the academic direction is into the ideas of John Bates Clark, then of Smith College, bright rising star in neo-classical economics. The preface of his important book, *The Philosophy of Wealth*, was the place, 1886 the time, in which he stated the debt to George which we have already noted. In the fall of 1890, writing on 'The Ethics of Land Tenure,' however, Professor Clark rejected utterly the Georgist ideas that landholding is monopolistic and that the institution of private property in land operates to depress wages. That is to say, Professor Clark announced judgments different from those of George; the differences circumscribed but did not eradicate his old debt for insight into marginal theory.

Meanwhile Edward Bemis, Johns Hopkins-trained student of co-operation, made a fresh study of all of George's books and of his writings in the early *Standard*. He published his findings in the conservative pages of the *Andover Review*. Reversing John Bates Clark's criticism, Bemis admitted that he agreed 'fully with George, as did Mill, and as do all economists,' about the justice of land-value taxation, but he felt that the practical objections were overwhelming. He believed that such considerations, rather than those of theory, were what obliged conservative and radical schoolmen alike, the Sumners and Laughlins, and the Jameses and the Elys, to oppose with one voice the ideas of Henry George. The most that Bemis would concede in a practical way was that some form of land-value taxation might justly be applied in the big cities.

Replying to Clark's article in the *International Journal of Ethics*, and using the dissenting title 'Another View of the Ethics of Land Tenure,' Simon Newcomb Patten of the Wharton School came up with a judgment close to that of Bemis. Patten rejected George's program, yet spoke in a more friendly way than Clark did of his ethics; and he made the article mainly a plea for clearer thinking on everyone's part, along the lines that join and separate economics and ethics.

Only the most general words are inclusive enough to cover the various intellectual, more or less non-partisan, attitudes of academicians and others toward Henry George from 1886 to 1890: recognition, interest, criticism, opposition, usually distrust, but sometimes deep sympathy. Though George's own immediate reactions are hard to catch, it seems not too much to assume that he kept informed of current criticism; and the files of the *Standard* make it plain that his newspaper, at least, kept a sharp eye open for outside comment — especially for quotable items of approval. That paper reprinted in full, for example, the lawyer Samuel Clarke's review of criticisms, friendly to George, which appeared first in the *Harvard Law Review*. Likewise the *Standard* noticed when Arthur Twining Hadley, brilliant and philosophically minded economist at Yale, said something (apparently much like Bemis' position) that gave an opportunity for friendly comment. Even a conservative could go a considerable way with the idea of taxing urban land values and relieving capital improvements, said the *Standard*. The radical picture within a conservative frame was its judgment of Hadley's position.

With a world reputation, a newspaper, and the single-tax movement, Henry George in the United States about 1890 seems, on a magnified scale, very comparable to Henry George fifteen years earlier, after he had lost the *Post* in California. He had gone into retirement to write, at that time, even though there were many other possibilities open to him. This time his loss was the United Labor party, the vehicle of political expression most natural to him. Whatever other occupations might offer — whether in the single-tax movement at home, or in journalism abroad, for example — none was as important to him as a return to his desk once more.

This time he had the conviction of thought already tried, and he was more accustomed to advancing than to retreating in the international warfare of ideas.

—3—

In the preceding section, occasional uncertainty has been necessary about the effect on Henry George himself of the accumulating body of criticism. It is hard to be sure how much he knew or cared, while he was busy with politics or lecturing, about any except a few of the adverse articles and booklets. But there is no doubt about the fall months of 1890, immediately following the trip around the world. He then found himself under such pressure of controversy, outside politics, as never before or after; and the common-sense assumption is the only possible one, that that pressure contributed directly to the exhaustion and illness which came at the beginning of winter.

Indeed certain things George did and said in late 1889 and early 1890, before he left New York, indicate earlier efforts to answer the rising criticism. During September, for instance, he reprinted in the *Standard*, from the *Forum*, a reply to opponents written by Thomas Shearman. The title of the article was 'Henry George's Mistakes.' The 'mistakes' were the ideas chosen for dispute by half a dozen opponents: and the Shearman article amounted to a counterattack on the Duke of Argyll, William Mallock, Abram Hewitt, Edward Atkinson, and William T. Harris. Two months later Shearman again contributed to the same magazine an article on 'The Owners of the United States,' an examination of the new concentration of wealth, from a Georgist point of view. Endorsing this endorsement of his own ideas, Henry George reprinted it in the *Standard*, as he had the preceding article.

Drawing on a different type of reinforcement, the *Standard* republished from *Harper's Weekly* Hamlin Garland's now famous story with a Henry George moral, 'Under the Lion's Paw.' The paper announced at the same time that Garland was doing a single-tax play, 'Under the Wheel,' and that the distinguished playwright, James A. Herne, predicted a great reception for it.

The month of January 1890, before taking a train for San Francisco, was probably the time when Henry George wrote his reply to the most considerable piece of writing Edward Atkinson ever did against him. This was the Boston capitalist's 'A Single Tax on Land,' which would be published in the *Century* for July, and which George must have examined in manuscript or early galleys. In this instance the argument against George was placed principally on a statistical level; and the proposition, much like Harris's, was offered that land taxation alone could not support all the costs of government in the United States. Besides this, the critic challenged

the justice of George's remedy; and he hated the thought of the
administrative procedures which he believed the practice of land-
value taxation would require.

The *Century* gave George space for a full reply, and placed it
in the same issue, alongside Atkinson's article. Although Henry
George did make deft use of logic now familiar, building his argument on the automatism of economic rent, and reassuring readers
that his scheme would affect urban site-holders but disturb very
little the property rights of farmers, he hardly tried to answer Mr.
Atkinson in kind. He did little more with statistics than to incorporate some of Thomas Shearman's findings. Thus he practically
refused to enter into the kind of realistic controversy invited by
his businessman adversary. Not from this instance alone, the impression is given that, except for Shearman, spokesmen for land
reform were not very ready with facts and figures at the present
stage of controversy. In the October issue of the *Forum,* for instance,
Bishop Frederic Dan Huntington, of upstate New York, pronounced in broad but not very practical terms, in defense of George
and like-minded reformers.

But it would be untrue to imply that the rising criticism of
George and Georgism represented, in a general way, fact-minded
people *versus* the philosophically minded. On the contrary, about
the time George was leaving the country, two writers carried criticism right to the ground of ideas where he was always ready to
answer. In February Horace White, who now had worked with
Godkin for years, elected to quarrel with the single tax, largely
taking issue with its premises in natural-law and natural-rights
philosophy. White's ideas were of course in current style, and the
article, which was published in *Popular Science Monthly,* might
well have led to something considerable in George's life of controversy if he had remained in the country. In his absence Louis
Post answered in the *Standard.*

But then, almost simultaneously, Thomas Huxley raised the
same issues of philosophy, in a series of articles in the *Nineteenth
Century.* If George departed from home just too early to debate
with Horace White, his midsummer visit brought him to England
when the Huxley articles were several months old. Yet we know
they excited him greatly. 'Have you seen Thomas Huxley's articles?'
he demanded of Dr. Taylor about as soon as he returned to New

York. 'What do you think of him as philosopher? I am itching to get at him and will as soon as I can.'

The mere titles, which the great explicator of evolution had selected, go far to explain George's impulse: 'On the Natural In-equality of Man,' 'Natural Rights and Political Rights,' and 'Capital — the Mother of Labour.' The first article criticized Rousseau; but the second, which was published in February, made Henry George the modern intellectual villain. Taking up the early pages of *Progress and Poverty*, Book VIII, Huxley ridiculed the natural-rights underpinning of the argument. Then, in the final article he restated the wages-fund and Malthusian ideas, in opposition to George's eleven-year-old criticism. Compared with the early British reviews of *Progress and Poverty*, Huxley was temperate and re-spectful of George. But his economic presumptions were little different from, say, those of the critic in the *Edinburgh Review*, almost a decade earlier.

There is evidence which suggests that, within a month of men-tioning the matter to Dr. Taylor, Henry George found time to rough-hew an answer to the articles. That he never finished may be explained in the short run by the pressure of demands on him in the fall of 1890, and in the long run by the fact that, after his illness and recovery, Herbert Spencer would offer a more obvious occasion for a reply to modern materialism. Yet, in Henry George's own behalf, there is reason to regret that he did not complete im-mediately, and publish, his reply to Thomas Huxley. Such an essay would have placed in the record an important document in the modern collision of ideas between evolution-minded elitism and conservatism, and the natural-rights philosophy in the Jeffersonian tradition. Two or three answers to Huxley did actually get into prominent British print, one of them by a working man and one by Michael Flürscheim. But of course George's authority was lacking; and Huxley's anti-democratic philosophy seems not to have been much challenged or answered.[1]

[1] Though I have noticed no response, it is impossible to suppose that George was not troubled by an article by Goldwin Smith, famous historian of Toronto, a scholar of English origins and of Cornell connections, which appeared in the *Forum* for August 1890, a month before his arrival home. Calling them 'The Prophets of Unrest,' Mr. Smith bracketed George with Edward Bellamy and Henry Demarest Lloyd. This is a convenient point to note that George and Lloyd had come to their nearest relationship ever, not very close, in 1888. Ap-

Disturbed by the criticisms of the scientific-minded, George had hardly reached home when the attitudes of clergymen became, once more, a problem to him. In one of the sessions of the big single-tax conference, a minister-member of the new Single Tax Brother-hood of Religious Teachers rose to move that such organizations as his own be given special representation in the new committee. The motion had considerable support. But it drew fire which was dangerously sharp for the stability of a new organization. Were clergymen playing politics again, new McGlynns and Pentecosts in the making? The question produced especially convincing denials from John Filmer, one of the numerous Swedenborgians in the movement. No man or woman of that persuasion, he announced, wanted any 'recognition here on any other ground than manhood or womanhood.'

Not George, but Croasdale, spoke the opposition of the non-clergymen members, and the attitude that prevailed at the meeting. 'We represent in this movement in America what is understood by the word "state"; they represent what is understood by the word "church." The sound American doctrine is to let the church stand on its own bottom and let the state stand on its own bottom, each doing the work for which it is appointed, without any danger of complication or other responsibility of one for the other.' Though it must have been painful for George to receive, a little later, a sorrowful letter from a clergyman, who promised for the future that he and his kind would take a back seat, it is plain that George's own feeling went with the majority.

---

parently Lloyd offered a contribution to the *Standard* early that year which George did not print because he used a *nom de plume*. George wrote: 'I am much gratified, however, by your appreciation and sympathy, the more so as it came at a time when an almost universal chorus was going up that I had ruined myself [over the McGlynn issue]. I was attracted to you by your striking articles in the *North American Review*, and tried to see you when last in Chicago, but found you were in Europe. Should you ever come to New York, I hope you will call upon me.' When Lloyd brought out his article, 'The New Conscience,' in the *North American* for September that year, the *Standard* reprinted it. And at about that time Thomas Davidson, of Fabian Society fame, tried to bring George and Lloyd into association in some 'university scheme.' But for reasons, apparently trivial at first, George and Lloyd seem never to have met. And before long Lloyd was saying that, having let George's ideas 'lie "in soak" for a while,' he could discover neither cause nor cure in them, for the illnesses of society. By 1890, George must have been as unwilling to be bracketed with Lloyd as we know he was with Bellamy.

By this time the Protestant social-gospel movement had more than begun in the United States; and excellent histories assure us that Henry George had had much to do with impelling it. But events of the fall prove that he personally felt no happier about clergymen without, than about those within, the single-tax movement. When a new People's Municipal League of New York presently nominated a slate for a city election, and when socially conscious ministers assumed leading roles, George spoke out quite critically. He would vote with the League, he conceded. But, with reference to Heber Newton, he said that the reform platform had no vitality, and that he could find little heart in himself for such dilute reformism. Moderate reform had not changed San Francisco, he observed: 'Where Casey and Cora were hanged Boss Buckley now rules.'

A sense that clergymen were soft toward doctrines he hated entered Henry George's feeling about them. He voiced this anxiety to Father Dawson: 'It is very sad to see the general tendency on the part of all clergymen — and it is quite as marked, perhaps even more so, among the Protestant sects even to the Unitarian — to avoid the simple principle of justice . . . This is leading [the clergymen] to the advocacy of socialism and all sorts of dangerous things, even to the acceptance and even advocacy of principles which will lead ultimately to atheism.'

George's several-faceted concern about the role of Christian ministers in reform was matched, during this autumn of great pressures and anxieties, by yet a further concern about socialism. He sensed, correctly, that this movement was gaining in the United States. The situation had changed, not simply from the years of his collisions with Marxists of the SLP, but even from just a year earlier. In 1889, when he had blown back at what he called the cloud stuff of the Bellamy movement, he had also welcomed the cloud as a signal of America's social awareness. But now he felt uncomfortable, when the Bellamyites' journal, the *Nationalist,* discussed the possibilities of political co-operation with single-taxers. Thousands who do not go all the way with George, said one communication to that journal, do want 'the nationalization of land, railroads, telegraphs, etc., which is the rockbed of socialism,' and nationalists should recognize that George was the man who alerted the country to the need for those kinds of socialization.

To be enveloped in utopian socialism seemed to George a prospect hardly more attractive than to be identified with the Marxian variety of the movement. At home the difficulties he envisaged merged with his estimate of the clergy: a danger of false thinking, and a danger of reducing the zones of reformism. But the total problem seemed to him as international, not just American; and from England he learned of it in the most personal and affecting way.

Henry George and Thomas Walker had been discussing their disagreements about social theory for two years now; and by this time Walker's old argument, that interest on capital should be captured for the public as fully as the rent of land, had broadened, in his letters, into some vague general sympathy with socialism. The wealthy manufacturer contributed to a 'Labor Church,' supported the Fabian Society, and even showed some interest in Hyndman's Democratic Federation. He continued membership in the Land Nationalisation Society, though he confessed to George that the secretary of that organization knew no better than to be fuzzy-minded between nationalization and peasant proprietorships; and through all this he kept on with the Land Restoration League, and with affirmations of devotion, despite his disagreements, to Henry George. Writing to J. C. Durant, George explained what was worrying him about his friends in England. It was 'the wobbling, the compromising, the affiliating with socialists, and the admixture of our ideas with ideas that are directly opposed to them.'

In their correspondence of this autumn, Walker wrote long and troubled arguments of theory. In one letter he reached a conclusion very similar to that of William Torrey Harris, the Hegelian conservative. Urging George to 'trace the result of wise expenditures of Rent by the nation,' he said that the result would be *making all good things common,* which in my opinion will be seen to be the flavor of your teaching.' In an immediate reply George explained that the single tax embraced everything *Progress and Poverty* said in favor of capturing, for the community, the values created by the community. Do not be misled by socialism, he begged in a series of letters. 'As for Karl Marx he is the prince of muddleheads.' Other letters to England promised a full answer to socialism in future writings; and the next spring, after he had been ill, George told his son that he planned to use his coming

'Political Economy' to make that answer, as well as for other purposes.

Considering first certain differences of opinion within his own following, we have by-passed the most open sign of all that academic and general critical opinion in the United States bore heavily and personally on George, on the heels of the National Single-Tax Conference. On 5 September, as soon as he could get away from New York, he attended the annual meeting of the American Social Science Association in Saratoga. A 'Single Tax Debate' was the program; and speakers of opposite inclinations were scheduled, some of them old and some of them new to public discussion. Though scholars had by then organized, as at present, in national associations of economists, historians, and so on, the Social Science Association still brought together men of different kinds, non-professional students with professionals, and representatives of all the social studies with one another. The association combined in its learning a certain root flavor of idealism and reformism, as was appropriate to its origin and history.

The arrangements in this case indicate general fairness, if not fondness, for the single-tax movement. Besides George himself, two lawyers, Samuel B. Clarke and William Lloyd Garrison II, and a land-title expert of Boston, J. R. Carrett, were the invited speakers clearly on the single-tax side. Sure to take the negative side were Edward Atkinson, whom George had just debated in print, and William T. Harris, who was now United States commissioner of education.[2] Two college economists, John Bates Clark (whose paper we have already drawn on) and the young Edwin A. Seligman of Columbia, were perhaps as certain as any to speak on that side.

Others seem to have been less predictable, and plainly a few of them provided surprises. Thomas Davidson, whom we have met as a teasing friend of George, sent a paper which went entirely against the single tax. He spoke from somewhat state-solidarist, perhaps Hegelian, grounds. 'The true way to regard property,' he said, 'is as a gift of the state.' Professor Edmund J. James, of Pennsylvania, very recent founder of the American Academy of Social and Po-

[2] A side note concerning opinion, taken from a speech delivered in 1887 by Robertson James, brother of William and Henry, is in order here. While Mr. Harris was off from Concord refuting Henry George in Saratoga at that time, said Mr. James, the township famous in revolution and literature was reading *Progress and Poverty* as it had once read *Uncle Tom's Cabin*.

litical Science and soon to be a university president, pleased George and distressed Seligman by announcing a mild degree of approval. (His paper was not printed.) President Andrews took the friendly, middling position we know. He connected George's analysis with the recent *Analysis of Property under the Capitalist Regime* by Achille Loria, and said that 'an increasing number of able English and American writers share this view.' The record of the meeting gives the impression that the single tax gained more than it lost from those who might be called the uncommitted, or not clearly committed, speakers.

The fight of the meeting, the combat which left the scars, occurred between George and the Columbia professor. Seligman was just thirty years old, with his future great standing as tax expert and economist still to be attained. The antagonism, which sprang up when he spoke, seems to have derived as much from his manner as his argument. He spoke of 'the general science of finance' as though it were little understood, and as though understanding were reserved to readers of scholarly literature in foreign languages. He proposed to test the single tax by what he called the standards of universality, equality, and justice, and he found it lacking. He assured the audience that professors of political economy as a group rejected it.

George was stung. 'Let me say a direct word to you professors of political economy, you men of light and leading, who are fighting the single tax with evasions and quibbles and hair-splitting . . . You must choose the single tax, with its recognition of the rights of the individual, with its recognition of the province of government, with its recognition of the rights of property on the one hand, or socialism on the other.'

It was the anger of the reformer against the academician's assumption of the higher judgment. Yet Seligman's rejoinder won from George a half-apology for having called professors bartered minds. Seligman insisted that George overdid the distinction between property in land and property in things; and he said that Bellamy's socialism had grown at George's expense because it recognized that other values than land gained unearned increments. He demanded that social reformers 'not offer us schemes which are repugnant to our moral sense and repellent to our logic'; and he denounced *isms* and panaceas of all kinds. In later writings Seligman rounded off his case against the single tax — criticizing the singleness of it, and repudiating its natural-law foundation.

The battle of wits at Saratoga was George's third and last test by the measure of university men in America. Berkeley in 1877 was the first, and the magazine controversies with Sumner and Walker in 1883 the second. Ruefully he now wrote to Dr. Taylor that schoolmen rejected him. 'How persistent is the manner in which the professors and those who esteem themselves the learned class ignore and slur me; but I am not conscious of any other feeling about it than that of a certain curiosity.'

In the longer perspective we know that the total situation was not as unfriendly as he said. In the letter just quoted George added that he had 'been looking over some of the more recent politico-economic treatises. How clearly *Progress and Poverty* has influenced them, even though they ignore it.' This did not exaggerate. He may have been scanning some of Clark's writings, or Ely's. Even the writings of Edwin Seligman, Professor Dorfman now tells us, came to show some effect of Henry George. Though a reformer's bias must be discounted, it is worth anticipating that, a year later, when Bolton Hall as secretary of the New York Tax Reform Association was seeking support for that organization's mild Georgism he was able to say that he had received 143 answers to an inquiry addressed to 'leading political economists in our colleges. Of these 78 are highly favorable, including those of Bowdoin, Brown, Columbia, Harvard, New York University, Pennsylvania State University, University of Virginia, Union, Williams, and others.'

As of 1890, neither Henry George nor anyone else could count, before they became vocal, the sympathetic professors of the next generation, the young men whose minds were already being disturbed by *Progress and Poverty*. But the testimony of such future professional students of economics and society as Edward A. Ross, John R. Commons, and Thorstein Veblen tells us that they and their kind were affected. In the final chapter of this biography we shall encounter second-generation consciences stirred by Henry George, quite apart from any single-tax commitment; and in that afterphase professional economists were to have a considerable role.

–4–

The obligations of the controversies just discussed — the public appearances, the writing of letters, and apparently the planning and rough-sketching of articles — bore upon George in September and October principally. During November he went off to Texas on a two-week speaking trip. On the way out he stopped a couple of days in Memphis, where he made several addresses before women's organizations and Jewish groups which had invited him. Though he mentions one or two light audiences in Texas, there were single-tax clubs across the state — he went all the way to San Antonio — and he made $1200 or more on the tour. He was received by the mayor and council of Dallas; and he was obliged to cancel an engagement in Galveston in order to accept an invitation, and a $250 fee, to address the legislature in Austin. On the way home he stopped in Evansville, Indiana, for a speech arranged by the Central Labor Union — a kind of auspice not frequent on this journey. Altogether he had a hard trip, though doubtless also a good and reassuring one.

The chief incidental event of the fall of 1890 heightened the effect of pressures on the man, and of making high decisions. Since 1886 there had been snarled in the New Jersey courts the disposition of the so-called Hutchins legacy, $10,000 designated for Henry George. A widow's need, and opposition in the family complicated the situation. At an early stage of the litigation a judge had ruled that the money could not be delivered, because George's ideas were contrary to law. This amounted to a state inquisition and an Index in New Jersey. But during his own campaigning and travel, George's lawyers had won a reversal of that decision, and at this point he was offered the remnant of his legacy left after charges had been deducted — a net amount of $435. In this autumn of controversy, however, Henry George chose to fight his own lawyer rather than take the tiny amount, because the bases of settlement did not suit him. Meanwhile giving financial assistance to the widow of his admirer, he refused the money — and would wait four years longer to win a final token of $200.

The suggestion which the story of the Hutchins case conveys, that George was in an easy position as to money, at least, while life was otherwise so complicated, corresponds with other indications.

The house on Nineteenth Street, though his daughter remembers it as shabby, was costing $1000 a year, he told Thomas Briggs, and it required two servants. It is hard to believe that his recent earnings from lectures, abroad and at home, sufficed to account for his capacity to handle such costs; but it is easy to assume, either that he was already receiving direct subsidies from his wealthy followers, or that he had been assured he could have support, whenever he needed it.

Perhaps until December 1890, any subsidy he had took the form of salary from the *Standard*. The contributions which Tom Johnson, August Lewis, and Thomas Shearman were making to the paper now amounted, it seems, to $7000 or $8000 a year. But George apparently did not feel that he had to depend on the weekly; and he made arrangements, during the fall, for the final surrender of his position. His nearly eight months out of the country had convinced him that the *Standard* could carry on without him. To the guarantors he now stated that for some time his services had been only nominal, and that he could not go back to the old weight and haul. Did they want the paper continued, he inquired, or should the *Standard* and its deficits be at last put to rest? He left the decision to others.

A committee was set up. Agreement was quickly reached that George should be relieved, but that the paper should be continued for the benefit of single-taxers. Accordingly a new publishing firm was formed, to take over from Henry George and Company at the end of the calendar year. Fresh capital was supplied by the sale of shares of stock; Croasdale took the editorship; and he, until his death, and then Louis Post, would carry on the paper for twenty months longer.

On 5 December, two days after announcing in the *Standard* the change of proprietorship and control, and just as his activities were lightening, Henry George was struck down temporarily. The trouble began with a horrible headache; and for three days he could speak hardly at all. When the doctors came they called it aphasia: 'a slight hemorrhage in that part of the brain which presides over articulate speech.' As he himself came to recall the experience, though he lost all power to understand or express words, he felt perfectly clear of mind from first to last.

After the first few days he was a poor patient. Permitted to be up and around the house, he paid little attention to doctors' orders — four were consulted — to rest and not to try to write. Friends rallied round. John Russell Young called daily; Boston friends, Garrison and Louis Prang, wrote affectionate letters. From Birmingham, Thomas Walker, who had not yet replied to a long critique from George, wrote that his 'heart stood still' when he learned of the prostration. Very delicately he offered to take up any debt that might remain in George's name against the *Standard,* and offered any other assistance he could render. To Tom Johnson, whom he had never met, Walker wrote in anxiety, lest George return too soon to harness. 'Although I by no means accept slavishly all his conclusions, I recognize with deep gratitude that he has struck the keynote of the future universal harmony. For me, he has absolutely drawn aside the veil that hid the next stride in human progress, and has given to life a meaning and a brightness which previously it lacked.' Could Mr. Johnson persuade George, the Englishman inquired, to permit one or two of his followers to relieve him of financial worry? Walker implied a wish to make a sizable contribution.

Johnson and Lewis had already acted. Johnson wrote that George did not need help; and George, writing five weeks after the stroke, said that he felt entirely secure for the future. Recently he had had more invitations to lecture than he could accept, he said, at $125 per engagement. The letters to Walker did not say that Tom Johnson had provided for Mrs. George, in case of her husband's death; and it is not clear whether or not recent disagreements about ideas had anything to do with their refusing Walker.

As sensibly as generously, his rich American disciples wanted George to have a complete change of situation, and absolute separation from his desk. They selected Bermuda for a vacation. The arrangement proved just about perfect; and, amusingly, perhaps the only incongruity of the excursion was provided by Mr. Lewis' selection of a gift. He presented George with three volumes of Schopenhauer. The voyager actually managed a volume or more —'like a red flag to a bull,' he said.

Mr. and Mrs. George had as traveling companions the Simon Mendelsons, who were the parents of Mrs. Lewis and Dr. Walter Mendelson, who had attended him. Only it was about as hard to keep Henry George quiet in Bermuda as in Manhattan. One single-taxer, on from New York with a bicycle, taught him to ride; and he loved the popular sport. Other single-taxers — an army chaplain and the editor of a Bermuda paper — kept him talking — more than seems likely to have been good for George. He went sailing several times with Horace White's daughter, who became devoted to him. Except that, as an expatriated Californian, Mrs. George thought the Bermuda climate overrated, she especially loved the sojourn, and delighted in the rest her husband was getting.

For Henry George, himself, however, five or six weeks were enough, and all he wanted. By that time he felt that he must get home and be doing something, or at least preparing for work.

–5–

'I shall try to give a good account of the next few years if God spares me,' George had written Durant a week before the attack. Now he returned to duty in just that mood.

After taking time to visit Harry, in Washington, he plowed straight ahead. Within less than a month he had caught up with the preliminaries of major writing: getting settled at his desk, looking over old writings on subjects about to be undertaken, making plans. He sought Dr. Taylor's help in acquiring copies of his quarter-century-old pieces in the *Overland Monthly* — his memory was none too accurate about them. He considered a reprint edition of *Our Land and Land Policy*. Before April ended he had actually 'got to work' on the general treatise on political economy, which he had been contemplating for twenty years.

But on 15 May 1891, a world event in social thought and policy deflected his course. On that date appeared *Rerum Novarum*, Pope Leo XIII's encyclical 'On the Condition of Labour,' which has often been called the Magna Charta of the working man. It climaxed a series of ethical pronouncements. Leo's earlier letters had concerned *Political Power, Human Liberty,* and the *Christian Constitution of the State.* The series, and *Rerum Novarum* especially, is accounted by friendly scholarship to indicate a decision by the Catholic Church, 'in a democratic age to seek popular in place of princely support,' and a wish to establish 'a kind of truce of God in the industrial world, all towards a new organization of society based upon some conception of equality.' The central thought of the new encyclical recognized that the very poor of the age were

wretched and defenseless; it denied *laisser faire* economics of the
Malthus-Spencer variety; it condemned 'rapacious usury'; and it
regretted the passing away of guilds, as the ancient stabilizers of
the condition of labor. According to traditions of church thinking,
Leo repudiated the strong state, and so, socialism, as a solution for
labor; and equally he rejected social warfare, both the idea of
class struggle and the practice of strikes by labor unions. Of course
the encyclical has become established in the twentieth century as
the fundamental document of Catholic policy toward capital and
labor under the industrial system.

Though it offended him, so much of the encyclical conformed
with Henry George's ideas that it was possible, when he drew his
thoughts together, for him to acknowledge a certain basis of agreement. He appreciated, he said, 'the many wholesome truths' contained in *Rerum Novarum,* and felt, 'as all of us must feel, that
[the pope was] animated by a desire to help the suffering and oppressed.' This degree of confidence made his situation with Leo
different from his old situation with Archbishop Corrigan and
Catholics of that kind, in America and Ireland.

Unfortunately for George, the pope's letter had altogether too
little in common with Father McGlynn's old position — or Father
Dawson's or the Bishop of Meath's. It acknowledged class differences as unconquerable, a part of God's plan. 'Just as the symmetry of the human body is the result of the disposition of the
members of the body, so in a state is it ordained by nature that these
two classes should exist in harmony and agreement, and should,
as it were, fit into one another, so as to maintain the equilibrium
of the body politic.' Leo recommended workmen's associations, on
condition that the members pay 'special and principal attention to
piety and morality'; and he encouraged a necessary minimum of
state intervention in favor of fair wages, when economic need
might require. Sufficient wages and adequate accumulation for all
were the pope's main answers to the problem of poverty. Obliquely
but forcefully he resisted radical land reform. 'Man not only can
possess the fruits of the earth, but also the earth itself . . . And
to say that God has given the earth to the use and the enjoyment of
the universal human race is not to deny that there can be private
property.'

Perhaps there is suspicion of megalomania in Henry George's

hot individual reaction to a document drawn up for universal reading and guidance. The 'most strikingly pronounced condemnations of *Rerum Novarum* were directed against the ideas of *Progress and Poverty*' he declared. Three days after the encyclical was released he wrote to Father Dawson how distressed he was: 'You know the result in Ireland of ignoring principle.' But very soon he had confirmation from Henry George, Jr., who was in London on a journalistic assignment, that his first fears had been correct. The young man had gone to call on Cardinal Manning. Did the encyclical contain anything against his father's views, he had inquired. 'His name is not mentioned,' the cardinal replied. Did the encyclical censure the idea of the common ownership of land? 'Smooth as satin,' according to the caller, Manning had said that he believed it did. 'This knocked me endways,' wrote the son; and he had departed with no further questions. Thus the Henry George evidence does seem to indicate that not Karl Marx the materialist but a disturbing American idealist had been the great enemy in ideas, at whom Pope Leo was striking.

Making almost no speeches at all this year, George concentrated more intensely than at any time since 1878. In five months he completed his reply, *The Condition of Labor, an Open Letter to Pope Leo XIII*, a book a little over a hundred pages. It was published in October. Throughout the essay the author adopted such an editorial 'we' as few other Americans would have had either temerity or dignity to assume. He took advantage of the fact that he — unlike his more evolution-minded contemporaries — based his thinking, as much as anyone else, on religious assumptions.

In his own words: 'Our postulates are all stated or implied in your Encyclical. They are the primary perceptions of human reason, the fundamental teachings of the Christian faith.' Consider, he invited, what Bishop Nulty of Meath, 'who sees all this as clearly as we do,' has to say about property in land. 'In this beautiful provision [of economic rent] made by natural law for the social needs of civilization we see that God has intended civilization . . . Property that in itself has no moral sanction does not obtain moral sanction by passing from seller to buyer. If right reason does not make the slave the property of the slave hunter it does not make him the property of the slave buyer . . . For the justice of God laughs at the efforts of men to circumvent it, and the subtle law that binds

humanity together poisons the rich in the sufferings of the poor
. . . Failing to see the order and symmetry of natural law, [social-
ism] fails to recognize God . . . The whole tendency and spirit
of [*Rerum Novarum's*] remedial suggestions lean unmistakably to
socialism . . . Did not Christ in all his utterances and parables
show that the gross difference between rich and poor is opposed
to God's law? . . . Your encyclical gives the gospel to labourers
and the earth to the landlords . . . In your hands more than
those of any living man lies the power to say the word and make
the sign that shall end an unnatural divorce, and marry again to
religion all that is pure and high in social aspiration.'

As he wrote, Henry George took every precaution, making an
unusual form of argument, to reason as closely as possible. Father
Huntington advised him, thanking God as he did so that the
single tax was being presented as a law of nature; and Bishop
Huntington commended the book in his diocesan paper and wished
for 10,000 copies to be circulated as a tract. Proofs went out, with
requests for suggestions, to Sister Teresa, Thomas Walker, John
Russell Young, and William Lloyd Garrison. The son of the
liberator, the most recent friend in the group, responded at once.
'If the Pope don't read it Christians will,' wrote Garrison, and he
urged that clergymen be bombarded with copies. John Russell
Young, now in Philadelphia, never a single-taxer, had equal enthusiasm. 'It is a masterpiece,' he wrote, 'and explains problems
in your philosophy that never were clear in your book or your
conversation. I envy you the vigor and truth and splendor of your
style' — it surpassed all since Burke, this learned man added. None
was more delighted than Thomas Walker, so recently dissatisfied
with his friend. The book would be 'a crusher, a bombshell,' he
wrote. On the Catholic side, friends in San Francisco were pleased;
and Father Dawson, after some thought, praised George for the
'excellent use of a fine opportunity' and predicted that the book
would do much good, whether or not the pope would come to
understand it.

For Henry George himself, there was amusement and curiosity,
not much importance, in the point discussed in New York newspapers: Did the pope actually receive the letter? George learned
that he did, more than once. Besides proof sent by the author in
September, and a copy of the American edition, Leo received into

his own hands, from the prefect of the Vatican Library, a handsome copy of the Italian edition. There followed, within a couple of years, an edition in England, the first of three, and an edition in Germany. A Swedish, and apparently a Spanish one, followed much later.

Realizing that he could expect no reply from the pope himself or from a spokesman, George had hoped simply to put pressure on all socially minded Christians. 'What I have really aimed at,' he told Harry, 'is to make a clear brief explanation of our principles, to show their religious character, and to draw a line between us and the socialists. I have written really for such men as Cardinal Manning, General Booth, and religious-minded men of all creeds.' If as author he had been a bit disingenuous, and thought beforehand to stir up such cross-purposes within the Catholic Church as occurred in New York City in 1886, George did not announce any such intention, even to his closest correspondents.

Yet on a small scale that was the result. Some American Catholics of course sympathized with George's ethical argument, this time as earlier; and almost automatically these churchmen were obliged to raise questions of authority. Edward Osgood Brown, Catholic lawyer of Chicago, whom George had wanted to go over his manuscript before publication, said that no well-instructed Catholic supposed the encyclical to be such an utterance of the Holy See as is held infallible by Catholic doctrine. On the other side, as George reported to Father Dawson on 22 December, Archbishop Corrigan was openly proclaiming 'that all Catholics are bound by the Encyclical as well as by a well established doctrine of Holy Writ.' This led to as bitter a statement as George ever made, even in 1882 or in 1887, about the church. To the same friend and priest he continued: 'Catholic priests seem so thoroughly bulldozed that they are afraid to openly deny this teaching. I cannot but despise and hope for the downfall of a hierarchy that teaches so slavish a doctrine, and time will surely bring it . . . [I] wish that the spirituality of the Church could in some way be separated from its political and corrupt machine, which turns into merchandise the efforts and sacrifices of men and women who are really God's servants.'

Accidents of chronology now help us tie together the events of five years. Four years, to a day, before this bitter letter, Henry

George had written the same priest the hopeful news that Cardinal Manning and Archbishop Walsh were trying to get the McGlynn case reopened. Since that expectation had proved false, little that was friendly or favorable had occurred between the reformer and the church. But just a year after *The Condition of Labor*, 23 December 1892, George reported to Father Dawson a change. 'Something wonderful has happened on this side of the water. The Pope has quietly but effectively sat down on the ultramontane Toryism of prelates like Archbishop Corrigan. Their fighting the public school has stopped . . . I have for some time believed Leo XIII to be a very great man, but this transcends my anticipations. Whether he ever read my letter I cannot tell, but he has been acting as though he had not only read it, but had recognized its force.'

The most startling and newsworthy event of all was that Father McGlynn was now actually restored to his offices. As the priest himself presently told George the confidential story, the restoration was managed by a churchman close to Pope Leo. This was Archbishop Satolli, who had just come to the United States as papal nuncio. He invited the rebel of St. Stephen's to put into his own words the doctrines that had caused all the trouble. The resulting memorandum of beliefs, according to the man who wrote it, simply incorporated without quotation marks 'passages largely from [George's] own admirable letter to the Pope and partly from the Pope's encyclical.' The nuncio, who was himself a theologian, submitted McGlynn's essay to four theologians at Catholic University. When on 23 December they attested that there was nothing contrary to doctrine, Archbishop Satolli removed the censures. No retractions of economic opinion were asked, and very little, if anything, was made of McGlynn's refusals of 1886 and 1887 to obey orders.

On Christmas Day Father McGlynn said mass three times, and in the evening addressed the Anti-Poverty Society. To his old friend, Henry George wired congratulations — an overture toward their coming reconciliation. He and Father Dawson exchanged a pleasantry about a future Cardinal McGlynn. This was far enough from what would actually happen, as the two correspondents themselves must have known. Presently Father McGlynn was assigned an inconspicuous parish up the Hudson at Newburgh.

Nevertheless the Satolli decision marked a victory for freedom within the Catholic Church, and for freedom in America. One would like to penetrate behind the scenes and understand more closely the change of ruling. Recent Catholic scholarship assumes that George's book did have an effect within the church, and did help restore McGlynn. This seems the only plausible assumption. Yet if this is true, the outsider's little book helped to establish a very puzzling church situation. For the Satolli decision appears to contradict utterly the secret condemnation of George's works, by the Inquisition, three years earlier.[3]

Of the two policies, the Satolli decision is the one the church seems to have decided to live by. Since 1892 Catholic thinkers have contemplated as within reason George's distinction between property in land and other private property, and seem to have been positively affected. The writings of Father John A. Ryan of Catholic University, in this century American Catholicism's outstanding social thinker, are a case in point. This scholar rejected George's formulas, but agreed in part on taxation and on the social nature of rent. And for decades now, individual Catholics have acknowledged deep loyalty to George without being censured and have strongly advocated his proposals.

–6–

The Condition of Labor, though climactic, is only one instance of Henry George's success at marshaling Christian ideas in behalf of social reform. This strength had its corresponding weakness. As he himself came close to saying to Henry George, Jr., there were whole areas of society he could not expect to reach by the use of religious and natural-rights arguments.

An illustration of this came from California. 'There are many brilliant and many true things in Mr. George's book,' wrote President David Starr Jordan of Stanford, and 'I am not objecting to the idea of the public use of *land* rentals.' But this scientist and great citizen, who was readier than most scholars to speak for social improvement, could not stomach *The Condition of Labor's* underlying argument. 'A land tax is no more God-given than a beer tax!' he protested, and said that the reformer's metaphysics poisoned all the books he wrote.

[3] The *Tribune,* 24 February 1894, p. 1, indicates that Archbishop Corrigan made another effort to have George's works placed on the Index.

There is no precise name for the boundary of thought that separated George from the secular-minded, who were offended by the drafts he made on Christian and natural-rights ideas. Practical men abounded on the side opposite George. Huxley had represented them. Andrew Carnegie represented them in a different way, in 1891, in an article in the *Nineteenth Century*. The writing ironmaster asserted that all economists disagreed with Henry George and said also that the emergence of millionaires in America signified the well-being, not the hardship, of working men. Carnegie's real belief was in social progress of an almost automatic sort; and Henry George's own word which comprehended that philosophy, 'materialism,' though not precise was not inaccurate either. The phrase 'Social Darwinism,' which, as we have seen, scholars have adopted, comes close. George had had one collision with this *ism* in 1883, in the person of its high spokesman, William Graham Sumner. By now it was suffocatingly strong, in business and educational circles especially.

Perhaps Henry George regarded his old determination, to write a positive statement of idealism, as having been fulfilled by the letter to Pope Leo. The scope of that book makes it seem natural, at any rate, that he returned in 1892 to the polemic type of effort which he had planned and set aside two years earlier: a refutation of popular philosophy. The Huxley articles were old by now, but Herbert Spencer, whom George chose to call the 'Pope of the Agnostics,' offered a wide-open opportunity for controversy.

It will be recalled that George's first fondness for Spencer, from California days, had been chilled at a London party in 1882 and had been dissolved altogether when Spencer repudiated any identification with radical land doctrine. George's fresh occasion to give challenge came when Spencer at last changed certain writings to bring them into accord with his actual beliefs. During the early '90s he was especially troubled by the advance of Georgist ideas into the actual practice of local taxation in Britain. In 1891 he published his little book, *Justice;* and the next year he brought out a redoing of his first book as *Social Statics, Abridged and Revised.*

In *Justice* he specifically said that, though the 'equitable claim' of each citizen to the use of the earth resided in the discretion of legislatures, the operation of that claim was in fact 'traversed by established arrangement to so great an extent as to be practically suspended.' For the new *Social Statics* the author eliminated the objection he had made in 1850 to private property in land, and he filled space by inserting certain magazine articles of 1884, which were already well known under the general title, *Man* versus *the State*. This subtracting and adding of material gave the revised book consistency with the complete *laisser faire* of Spencer's later years. In George's opinion the changes so far overshot the philosopher's original individualism as to make 'a new departure' in his way of thought. Spencer was now assuming, George charged, that 'nothing at all is needed, in the nature either of palliative or remedy.'

George understood thoroughly how popular the doctrine was, and the figure, he was attacking. But, to him, Spencer's infidelity to his first judgment about property in land was part and parcel of the tardiness of the United States to accept *Progress and Poverty*. So once again the treatise on economics was left to wait, and a new book was given priority. Dr. Taylor urged caution. Henry George would be invincible against Herbert Spencer on the land question, the old friend counseled, but perhaps not so successful against the whole cosmogony of that philosopher. Yet George would not be persuaded. 'What I quarrel with is the essential materialism of Spencerian ideas, and this seems to me to inhere in them, in spite of all Spencer's denials.' He simply wanted to reassert the philosophy of *Progress and Poverty*, he explained, and not at all to deny 'the principle of evolution with which I do not quarrel.' He admired Darwin and Wallace, he said, because they wisely 'confined themselves so to speak to their muttons.' He most specifically did want to challenge the Spencerian extension of evolution into philosophy and into public policy.

In some degree George actually achieved his difficult goal. His chapter, 'The Synthetic Philosophy,' explains with uncommon force the materialism and fatalism so often implicit in evolutionary thinking. His footnote illustration from the case of E. L. Youmans, whom he described as wearing his Spencerian ideas 'like an ill-fitting coat he had accidentally picked up and put on,' is especially telling. He had once heard Mr. Youmans denounce corruption in New York politics. 'What do you propose to do about it?' George had asked. 'Nothing! You and I can do nothing. It's all a matter of evolution. We can only wait for evolution. Perhaps in four or five thousand years evolution may have carried men beyond this state of things. But we can do nothing.'

The writer achieved a kind of magnificence, too, in the field of his original quarrel with Spencer. In a chapter entitled 'Compensation,' he discussed again the question whether landlords should be paid by the state whenever land might be transformed from private into public property. He could hardly have changed his own mind on the subject. And yet, to state a firm no, at this time, was of course to imply great disagreement with his own followers of the 'single tax limited' persuasion. Their very existence challenged his doctrine. Notwithstanding the hazard, he wrote the most eloquent plea he had ever made, for confiscation. Followers at home and abroad were so struck by the chapter that they asked for separate publication.

For his own sake, it seems unfortunate that George did not act on that particular piece of advice. Though *A Perplexed Philosopher* contains two brilliant chapters, it is as a whole an unsatisfactory book, the only dull one the author ever wrote. The bulk of it traces interminably Spencer's various sayings about land, and attributes his recent conservatism to low motives. There can be little doubt that George proved Spencer to have contradicted himself, and to have displayed insincerity and even irresponsibility by keeping the old *Social Statics* in circulation for years after he had changed his opinions. Letters of approval from friends, notably Thomas Walker, Senator Carlisle, and Lloyd Garrison, can be understood to indicate an animus toward Spencer. But George's attack was too long and elaborate to be interesting, and so ill-spirited as to invite reply in the same tone.

Spencer himself made no response. But two years later, readers of the New York *Tribune* were treated to such a comment by a group which included Professor Youmans and John Fiske. *A Perplexed Philosopher* was translated only once, into Russian, and it was given very few reviews. From England, J. C. Durant wrote, even before publication, that the effort would prove 'somewhat of a waste of energy.' The real victory of the writer, he added, was the return of a radical county council for London, several members 'out and out Henry George men.' From an opposite corner of the earth, Professor Joseph Le Conte assured George that what he had said about evolution was sound enough, but that he had been too hard on Herbert Spencer.

A subtotaling of George's writings, since the trip to Australia, is in order. He had thus quickly gone as far as he was able in treating two subjects that had confronted him on his return to the country in September 1890. On the relation of Christianity to economic reconstruction, he had spoken against clericalism twice, once within his American reform movement, and once against the pope in Rome. Yet he had consistently maintained that faith is necessary for good works in society. On the dangers of evolutionary materialism to social thought, he had been equally definite. Though he challenged the mind of his age, he would remain to life's end an idealist.

Having been so definite with those who disagreed with him, Henry George logically returned once again to his treatise. He was now more than ever obliged to demonstrate, if he could, that the ideas he pronounced did actually belong to the science of political economy — and should be introduced into the policy of nations.

–7–

After the false starts of 1891 and 1892, and the interruptions caused by the excursions against Leo XIII and Herbert Spencer, George at last felt free in late 1892 to give much attention to the big commitment. Even so, he withdrew from affairs less completely than he had while he was doing *Progress and Poverty*. As we shall see, he gave time and attention to national politics in the exciting years 1892, 1894, and 1896. In late 1893 for the first time since the stroke, and again in early 1894 and during the following winter, he did a good deal of traveling and lecturing.

But he did settle at his desk for long intervals. Apropos of current hard times, he wrote an article on depression theory which was published in the *North American* for February 1894. It chanced to be printed next to a famous article by William Dean Howells, 'Are We a Plutocracy?' George's interpretation of unemployment was no different from the ideas he had discovered in California; but the article gave him the opportunity to say that New Zealand, which he called the most prosperous place in the world at the moment, owed its advantage to a partial policy of land-value taxation.

Writing articles and lectures may help with a book while an author's new ideas are germinating. But the restatement of old conceptions is useless; and one senses that, about the time of doing the depression article, George feared he would never complete the treatise. On the last day of 1894, writing to Thomas Walker who always sent him letters on Christmas and his birthday, he confessed recent discouragement. Though his courage returned, his expectations about finishing the work were several times put off. Nearly three years passed before he made up his mind he wanted 'The Science of Political Economy' as his title. He had waited to be sure, but he said at that time that he had made a science of the subject.

George's anxieties do him credit. He had changed, and the situation had changed, since he had last ventured to revise economics. In ways not again possible during the '90s, George as author of *Progress and Poverty* had conformed, not in ideas but by putting them on paper in the way economic ideas were usually written about. As he was a journalist then, so Malthus in his day had been a parson, Ricardo a businessman, and John Stuart Mill a civil servant; and, on the American side, Raymond had been a lawyer, and the Careys and Greeley had been editors and publishers. That is to say, big economic thinking and systematizing during the earlier nineteenth century had been non-academic, non-professional work, frequently, and had often had reformist or political purpose.

But by the time he got to work on *The Science of Political Economy*, the surrounding situation was different. Though we may have a good deal of sympathy for George's feeling, that the professors displayed considerable arrogance and animus against him, there could be no gainsaying that the new academic chairs and professional societies represented an enormous growth of economic literature which was strange to him. Importations and incorporations of ideas were taking place: from Jevons, from Marshall, from Schmoller and Wagner in Germany, and from Boehm-Bawerk and others of the Austrian school, for instance. Their influence, combining with native impulses, was making economic thought in the United States an infinitely more complex thing than the classical British economics, which was the only kind George ever mastered.

The problem came up in midsummer, 1897. George's friend, Lawson Purdy, had gotten for him, from Professor Hiram Loomis of Northwestern University, a memorandum on the Austrian economists for quick study. Though Professor Loomis wrote that he advocated the Austrians and said that he believed that, except for interest theory, their ideas actually reinforced George's, the toiling author could find no benefit in them. In this final text, George said that if the Austrian school was based on 'any principles, I have been unable to find them.' At the same point he dismissed his old antagonist, Alfred Marshall, as 'incomprehensible.' To George the new economics was a 'pseudo-science,' and was 'indeed, admirably calculated to serve the purpose of those powerful interests dominant in the colleges under our organization, that must fear a simple and understandable political economy, and who vaguely wish to have the poor boys who are subjected to it by their professors rendered incapable of thought on economic subjects.' [4]

Perhaps George's mood would have been better suited for writing an essay in irony than for composing a comprehensive treatise. But the treatise is what he persisted in trying to write. Before the final few months his correspondence supplies no more than occasional indications of his progress. Besides depression theory, he tackled money and banking. He looked over his old writings, as far back as the editorials on convertible bonds and greenbacks, in the San Francisco *Times* three decades earlier. But he did not attempt to write up such technical matter this time. When the treatise finally appeared, the tenor of its definitions of terms and the discussions of the functions of money were governed by the old anti-inflationist convictions of the author. The opposite of 'Coin' Harvey, and the large silver bloc now in Congress, George wanted no dependence on money reform as a means of economic stimulation. [5]

While *The Science of Political Economy* was still in the middle stages of composition, George had separate chapters, as he wrote them, put into galley proof for distribution. Louis Post, who was now working for the Cleveland *Recorder*, was able to make the arrangements. This gave the author the advantage of safety (he wanted no such loss again as occurred to the first manuscript of *Protection or Free Trade*), and gave him unusual freedom to invite friends to read and criticize. Louis Post was asked. His new wife, Alice Thacher, a religious person who was intensely interested in

[4] *The Science of Political Economy*, 208.
[5] Ibid. Bk. v.

the single tax, helped also. The author called on Dr. Edward Taylor once more, and on Lloyd Garrison — who had read and approved George's last two manuscripts.

Any preliminary criticisms, which might have been rendered at the stage when an author feels somewhat malleable, are not of record. But early in 1897, when George was estimating that he would probably need somewhat more than a year to finish, his intimates made comments which indicate them to have been baffled. Dr. Taylor praised 'great thought' and elevation of tone, once more, but said also that much of the manuscript seemed irrelevant. Tactfully the old associate enclosed a sonnet, the best he had ever written he was sure, and added that he wished no more than to leave one song that his fellow men would not forget.

But Post wrote in brutal candor. The sentences were too long — one contained 275 words — and the whole treatment lacked sharpness. George must not let himself think that the work was anywhere near done. Mrs. Post, with her Swedenborgian sensibilities at work, submitted her own separate criticism. She liked a certain opening passage on evolution, in which George discussed the special powers of reason and morality which elevate man above the animals. To the harsher criticisms, George's simple answer was that he would stick to his guns. 'I pit my own judgment against yours . . . and my own judgment is that this will be equal to Progress and Poverty.'

But it is doubtful that his confidence ran deep. In the latter part of the month in which these criticisms came in, the curtain dropped briefly, all too much like the attack of seven years earlier. Dizziness and nausea overcame Henry George, and utter weariness. To Dr. Taylor he wrote that he had had to stop work for a while, 'from fear of the prostration I had in 1890.' He resisted a doctor's suggestion that he take a sea rest again. This meant that he was at home, not quite recovered, when the saddest possible family event occurred. His daughter Jennie came on from her home in Baltimore, with her husband and new baby, for a visit. Typhoid struck like lightning and she died in her parents' house. The father bore the loss bravely, but the family sensed that he believed he had not much longer to live.

All this occurred in the spring of 1897, and events and conditions left sharp memories. His children noticed that Henry George reverted, again and again, to 'Rabbi Ben Ezra' and the Scriptures.

One day, while Richard George was doing a bust of him, the father said mildly, 'When I am dead you boys will have this bust to carry in my funeral procession as was the custom with the Romans.'

Yet George's letters of the summer show him back at work. He carried his draft through a series of chapters on economic value, notwithstanding his incapacity to read the extensive new scholarship in that field. Presently the call came, as it had in 1886, that he run for mayor of New York. He consulted his doctors and was told that a campaign would probably kill him. But he did not refuse the nomination and meanwhile continued with his writing. Three weeks before the vote he was sending out chapters for criticism and suggestion.

By doing the two things at once he indicates that he had made a remarkable decision. He would complete his book if he could. But he would take a huge risk of never finishing, in order to be candidate. That is, at final choice he preferred to dramatize his career in an appeal to voters in the general terms of politics rather than to reargue the technical background of reform.

From all that he said and did, the present writer believes the decision represents a tacit acknowledgment by George that he was unable to weld a new system of economics. When he lay down his pen, the six chapters on money still lacked recommendations for positive national policy. Chapters on wages and rent were wanting. In many other ways the book was not complete. Perhaps George reasoned that, whether or not he ran for mayor, his life would be too short to complete the writing. Or, just possibly, he admitted to himself alone that he had made a mistake of planning — that he was not the man, after all, to venture a compendious survey.

Unquestionably *The Science of Political Economy*, as Henry George, Jr., had it published in 1898, does not satisfy his father's first plan or the recent choice of title. Just as certainly, like the book against Herbert Spencer, it does contain passages of eloquence and of great logical power. The more interestingly because they had no great sympathy for Henry George otherwise, Charles and Mary Beard paid high tribute to this book's eloquence about the nature of civilization and humanity, and George's perception of the relation of economics to politics. 'The body economic, or Greater Leviathan,' he said, 'always precedes and underlies the body politic, or the Leviathan . . .' The author restated his religious and rationalist humanism: 'Is it not in [the] power "of thinking things out," of "seeing the way through" . . . that we find the essence of what we call reason? . . . Here is the true Promethean spark, the endowment to which the Hebrew Scriptures refer when they say that God created man in his own image; and the means by which we of all animals become the progressive animal. Here is the germ of civilization.'

If *A Perplexed Philosopher,* in 1892, was two books not one — short declarations of ideas and a long exposure of Herbert Spencer — the *Science of Political Economy* was several books. The parts that came intensely from the writer's experience were good; and the parts that came from his deferred studies were neither good nor successful. In some sections the book is autobiography. One chapter, an afterthought which George slipped in late, is really a short history of *Progress and Poverty* [6]; and other chapters in Book II, though listed as a survey of economic thought since the Physiocrats, are better understood as a review of certain books as sources of Henry George's ideas. The book is an arraignment in part. It completes Henry George's charge that economists in rejecting *Progress and Poverty* had rejected their consciences' best judgment. Though this passage is less self-righteous than the corresponding part of *A Perplexed Philosopher,* the signs of a reformer's frustrations are neither pleasant nor persuasive.

As a treatise for students and reviewers, *The Science of Political Economy* received about what its frailties deserved, not much consideration in the journals. Yet, a little paradoxically in view of how Henry George had been treated by Yale economists during his lifetime, a year after the author's death the book was reviewed, considerately and wisely if not favorably, by Arthur Twining Hadley. There are no contemporary words with which to take fairer leave of the latter-day Henry George, as writer, than Hadley's. They deserve quotation: 'Henry George was a great preacher . . . But in proportion as George passes from the field of oratory into the field of science, his work becomes less good . . . The book has little which is really new, unless it be a somewhat commonplace metaphysics within which the author tries to frame his economic system. Subtract this, and we have simply a new edition of *Progress and Poverty,* less well written, *plus* a number of rather disconnected ut-

[6] Ibid. Bk. II, ch. VII.

terances . . . For this reason it is quite impossible to review the book *in extenso*. This is not the first time a good preacher has proved himself a poor controversialist. Those of us who have admired George for his brilliant earlier work and for his unblemished personal character can only regret that this last book was ever written and desire that it may be forgotten as soon as possible.'

Neither Professor Hadley nor any other critic could have understood that he was reviewing an effort which had been sacrificed, rather than a text which the author thought he had mastered. *The Science of Political Economy* is read with comprehension of Henry George only when it is considered as a book that had several times yielded to other and more pressing interests. I think George would have been wise had he asked that it never be published; and his heirs would have served him better had they felt free either to make that decision themselves or to print the book as what it might have been if portions had been dropped and wise selections made — a distinguished series of memorial essays.

This final possible choice would have saved the book for its present best purpose. It would have preserved a conception of large strategy drawn by an aged fighter — by one who had died willingly, a volunteer on a different field of battle.

XIX

The Martyrdom of Henry George

1890–1897

—1—

AFTER Bermuda, during 1891 and 1892, Henry George gave a certain amount of time to the organized single-tax movement. He addressed the Manhattan Single Tax Club twice in 1891, once on the occasion of celebrating the club's fourth birthday; and in mid-1892 he spoke before the Chicago Single Tax Club. In 1893 he traveled more than he had and made a number of speeches, some of which have been mentioned above. For a writer, and for a man who had suffered aphasia, he did a great deal of speaking during the middle '90s, but of course less than earlier.

The most memorable meeting of the entire period occurred in Chicago, the second National Single Tax Conference. It was placed and timed in that city to take advantage of the Columbian Exposition. George had refused an invitation to speak before the Congress of Political and Social Science, held under the fair's own auspices; and he was reluctant about having a single-tax meeting at all. Since 1890 the accomplishments of the Single Tax League of the United States, the permanent national organization, had not been impressive. But George accepted anyhow and at the meeting created a moment of drama. There he met face-to-face, for the first time since their estrangement and reconciliation, Father Edward Mc-Glynn. At a mass meeting in the Art Institute, while the priest sat on the platform, George discussed the meaning of Archbishop Satolli's decision. Through the nuncio, George reasoned, the old practice of refusing Catholics freedom to preach the economic rights of man had been condemned by papal authority.

Otherwise the meeting hit the doldrums and even had special reverses for Henry George himself. A resolution favored the political reforms which were then rising in the country: the initiative and referendum, proportional representation, and votes for women. These were not points to disturb George, for he had favored them all for years, including even woman suffrage. But another resolution changed the economic program of the Single Tax League from formulas he himself had drawn in 1890. The national conference had then called for the public control and management of natural monopolies other than land — of telegraphs, railroads, city water, and gas, as proposed in *Social Problems* and in George's earlier writings. The resolution of 1893 reduced this demand. Louis Post records the change as a shift from the 'socialistic' toward the 'individualistic.'

George himself criticized the move more strongly. Whereas so many times he had had to contend with socialism, he wrote a California friend, 'at this meeting there was an outcropping of what was a strong tendency to anarchism.' It was a bitter pill. There is humor and pathos, both, in Henry George's voting No with the minority at a single-tax conference, the last one of his lifetime.

After Chicago in the exposition year, George withdrew about as completely as in 1891 from anything like organizational effort. Louis Post became the workhorse of the single-tax movement; and Thomas Shearman kept his role as theoretician. Post crossed and recrossed the continent, partly supporting himself by lecture fees, and partly backed by subsidies from Tom Johnson and others. Some of his speeches went into his book, *The Taxation of Land Values,* which was first published in 1894 under another title, and later republished many times. Meanwhile Shearman was continuing his thinking and writing; and in 1895 he produced *Natural Taxation,* a sort of single-tax textbook which would be issued and reissued for years. It completed the effort Shearman had begun, in 1887 or earlier, to concentrate land-value taxation on fiscal needs, and to make it acceptable to the minds of businessmen. The continuing difference, between Shearman's 'single tax limited' and Henry George's 'single tax unlimited,' is clearly indicated by the contrast between *Natural Taxation*'s moderateness, and *A Per-*

plexed Philosopher's demand for abolishing private property in land, without compensation to proprietors.

Besides his work as writer, his obligations as the father of the single tax, and his concern with politics, George acquired during the '90s yet another function to perform. It was a role of inspiration. Though the word *salon* is hardly right for the gatherings at Henry and Annie George's Nineteenth Street home, the place did become a center for kindred spirits to meet and talk — to ponder, in friendship, the plight and future of mankind. Cocoa was the beverage, and the household surroundings were homely in every detail. The distinction of the place was the grand old man, as he was now, at center. His wife, his beautiful daughter in her twenties, and his lively one in her teens each had capacities to make visitors comfortable and to draw them out.

Lawson Purdy, able young lawyer then and later a civic leader, speaks of having taken Henry Adams there as early as 1889. He himself was a recent convert to *Progress and Poverty,* and he remembers the talk he heard about the need to believe in immortality. One day there called William Sowden Sims, about ten years out of Annapolis and an impressive figure in uniform. The future lifeguard of the British Isles wanted to meet and talk with the man whose book had 'powerfully influenced' his mind. 'I can see no escape from the conclusions arrived at,' he confessed. Another evening a half-Maori dropped in, for similar reason; and yet another evening is remembered when Robertson James, brother of William and Henry, came as an admirer of Henry George.

For their summers during this period the Georges went to Merriewold, in Sullivan County, where a group of single-taxers had a vacation colony. Departure for there in the spring of 1895, however, involved a wrench, for at that time the family said good-by to the Nineteenth Street house. 'Afloat again,' was George's feeling. But in the fall they moved to Fort Hamilton, a high situation with a view, on the harbor side of New York. They loved the location. For about twenty months they occupied Tom Johnson's summer home as a regular residence. Meanwhile a legacy from England, about $14,000, and a gift of a piece of land by Mr. Johnson made possible a new and beautiful home in Fort Hamilton. Done in clapboard in the spacious suburban style then popular, it was the only house the family ever owned.

More handsomely than anything she could have expected, it fulfilled Annie George's old hope that they would some day have their own home. George himself must have felt deeply happy about the house. Here, as from the bayside houses in San Francisco, he watched the sky and water, and always the boats moving about the harbor. Then there was the reassurance of friends. August Lewis lived near by. It may be that Mr. Lewis's brother-in-law, Dr. Mendelson, participated in the arrangements that settled Henry George at Fort Hamilton, and that the rich men who made it possible were thinking that his health demanded a change from the city.

Pathetically, the move into a house of the Georges' own almost coincided with Jennie's death, and then with the special anxieties, which came up in early 1897, concerning Henry George's own condition. The handsome upstairs study, where many photographs of George were taken, never became a place of much writing; nor the downstairs living rooms the scene of many at-homes. Yet the new security must have helped account for Henry George's remarkable serenity and confidence in 1897 — as of course it would help his family later.

While George's more personal affairs were thus developing in patterns of old age, his connections were enlarging into literary circles where he had not penetrated earlier. Hamlin Garland in his thirties became the most remarkable personage of a whole group influenced by Henry George. Of course, if Garland's champion, William Dean Howells of the *Atlantic Monthly,* had gone strongly Georgist, he would have ranked first. The older writer did call, very pleasantly, at the Nineteenth Street house. The *Standard* may be judged to have stretched a point, however, when it discovered in a chapter of *A Hazard of New Fortunes* a plain reflection of a chapter of *Progress and Poverty*. Howells was a sympathetic acquaintance of Henry George and apparently not much more.

But there was nothing limited about Hamlin Garland's early interest in George and Georgism. He had been aroused by *Progress and Poverty* before leaving North Dakota and before Howells had become his mentor in any way. In Boston he experienced a real conversion, not unlike Bernard Shaw's. He heard George speak in Faneuil Hall, during 1886, George's great and critical year. In Garland's poignant memory: 'His first words profoundly moved me . . . Surprisingly calm, cold, natural, and direct . . . he spoke as gifted men write, with style and arrangement . . . This self-mastery, this grateful lucidity of utterance combined with a personal presence distinctive and dignified, reduced even his enemies to respectful silence . . . His questions were few and constrained, but his voice was resonant, penetrating, and flexible, and did not tire the ear . . . He had neither the legal swagger nor clerical cadence; he was vivid, individual, and above all *in deadly earnest.* He was an orator by the splendor of his aspirations, by his logical sequence and climax, by the purity and heat of his flaming zeal . . . I left that hall a disciple.'

The discipleship held. After backtrailing to the Middle West and getting out his first stories, Garland came on to New York, about the time the Georges returned from Australia. In 1890, he published 'Under the Lion's Paw'; and in 1891 this and other stories were gathered into *Main Travelled Roads,* a book which became a classic. As we have seen, the *Standard* reprinted certain of his writings. It discussed others, as they appeared in the magazines. And presently Garland was writing straight, non-fictional expositions of Georgism, and was making Georgist speeches before Farmers Alliances. His *Jason Edwards,* a none-too-successful novel of 1892, was in large degree a single-tax tract.

By this time, if not earlier, Hamlin Garland had entered the George discussion circle, and to those people he read his new stories as he composed them. Recollecting the exchange of affection and ideas, he says: 'The Georges, whom I had come to know very well, interested me greatly . . . Of course this home was doctrinaire, but then I liked that flavor, and so did the Hernes. Although Katherine's keen sense of humor sometimes made us all seem like thorough-going cranks — which we were.'

Garland's mention of the Hernes refers to a gifted couple, Katherine Corcoran, a beautiful and distinguished actress, and her husband, James A. Herne, actor and playwright. The husband's writings, though little-remembered, occupy about the same position in the history of the realistic drama as Garland's do in the history of the short story and essay. The couple were close to Garland personally, for his brother Franklin played in their company; and James Herne's loyalty to George's ideas was enriched by his having worked his professional way in San Francisco, at the time George was writing *Progress and Poverty.* The earliest letters we have between George and Herne were written during the '90s while Herne was playing on the West coast. He assured George that good seed had been planted out there, and he ventured some cultivating of the soil himself. He discussed the single tax with actors, and read 'Under the Lion's Paw' to labor audiences.

For reasons, natural in his profession, Herne was at first more interested in other varieties of realism than economic for portrayal on the stage. In 1890 he had just written the play, *Margaret Fleming*, which now occupies a niche in history as one of the early important American dramas to discuss marriage with modern candor. Its failure makes the more notable, for this history, the success Herne scored just afterward with *Shore Acres*, the first Henry George drama on record. It was a down-East, local-color, family-problem play in which events hinge on the disposition of a piece of land. When he saw it, Henry George was too deeply moved even to speak to his friends after the curtain went down. Its realism surpassed *Margaret Fleming*, he wrote the author, yet the moral truth came through. In Mr. Herne's own mind *Shore Acres* captured the language and the spirituality of old Maine; and the intensity of the situation on the stage dissolved theater traditions and made theater history.

In two or three ways the theater people were the ones, among George's literary and artistic champions, who came to mean the most to his family and following. Through these connections they became friends with members of the now famous de Mille family, among them William, who later married Anna Angela. And Francis Neilson, who, as editor of the interesting New York *Freeman* of three decades ago, was the head of the best literary journal ever produced in the tradition of Georgism, gives stage people credit for inspiration in the '90s. American actors, with whom he worked in his youth, says Mr. Neilson in his autobiography, turned him to *Progress and Poverty*.

Though there is no need to examine the more dilute solutions of Georgism that were to be found in American novels during the '90s, the geographic spread of George's influence on literary people and his knowledge of that spread have a real biographical importance. Probably the farthest contact to the east that George had with a literary American was his correspondence with a friend of a dozen years, Poultney Bigelow. The young man in his thirties was now pursuing a free-lance career, more or less expatriated, in England. He found it possible, he wrote in 1893, to insert Henry George ideas, somewhat surreptitiously, into the pieces he contributed to British and Continental journals. In the West, Henry George's literary frontier seems to have been located in San Luis Obispo, a place just as far away as London. With Mrs. Frances Milne, poet of that city, George had a long but intermittent correspondence. An oversentimental and pious disciple, Mrs. Milne was one of several who sent George hero-worshipping verse.

Since George often visited Chicago, he may well have known about intellectuals there who loved to talk his ideas. We learn of two circles. One was a group of architects, members of a profession which was lively in that city, among whom Louis Sullivan, the early modernist, was an interested member. For the other, Brand Whitlock, at the time a young journalist, is spokesman. There was a circle of men, he says somewhat vaguely, who had read Henry George, or who, without reading him, 'had looked on life intelligently and gained a concept of it . . . But these men were not in politics . . . and the only man in politics who understood them at all was Altgeld.'

In the case of literary people like Whitlock and Neilson, or among students like John R. Commons, reading Henry George meant discovering a loyalty that would last. Those young men signified in America an inspirational spread of his ideas, parallel and overlapping, but not confined to, the organized single-tax movement.

–2–

At home, where examination can be more exact, we see that certain more or less literary minds were shifted by Henry George during the '90s toward making an effort for social improvement. Among his followers overseas, on whom our perspective is more distant, the accents of the picture are different. In England and the British antipodes, where George had spoken and where political doctrine had been influenced, the results seem to have been pretty purely political. But elsewhere the story is the opposite. In Russia Georgism achieved surprisingly great ideological results, students of the literature of that country tell us, though political efforts were frustrated.

Henry George received personally the good news from the South

Pacific. Letters from Sir George Grey in New Zealand, and from Max Hirsch and others in Australia, told him of land reforms achieved and of fights against the tariff. And similarly from the mother country, such reports reached him as made it possible for George to continue hoping that Britain would be the first country to make land-value taxation national policy. In 1891 he was informed, at the request of a member of Parliament, on the occasion when the Commons came within twenty-six votes of resolving that the ground values of London 'ought to contribute directly a substantial share of Local Taxation.' Another report, mentioning the biggest political personalities to speak on his side so far, came to George the next year from James Durant, who himself was then a member of Parliament. Haldane spoke recently for 'our ideas,' wrote the old friend and publisher, and he was brilliantly seconded by Asquith. Besides these men in the Commons, Durant named others who, previously critical, he believed to be now going Georgist — Charles Harrison, the brother of Frederic, and H. W. Massingham, the journalist, among them. Also: 'The better class of socialists — Sidney Webb and that crowd — are now all working with us, but they as well as ourselves are still opposed to the lower shades of socialism.' The Fabians, Durant reported, 'come from being opponents back to being supporters of our views.'

British news of this kind all came in earlier than 1895, when the Salisbury government took over. For the remainder of George's life such optimistic reports would be politically impossible. But he did receive invitations to come again to lecture; and such news as that of work being done by a Henry George Institute in Glasgow kept him informed that his ideas were still growing in Scotland and England. *The Science of Political Economy* was written with Britain very much in mind.

It is hard to speak in a general way about Georgism in western Europe during this decade. The Henry George papers indicate no continuation at all from the practical undertakings of the 1889 conference in Paris. Perhaps George managed to forget that he had been elected president of an international organization of radicals. Letters to him do indicate, however, certain quickenings of interest in his writings. Translations were made into Romance languages — for the southerly lands of low industrialism and high Catholicism, where George's ideas had so far had little reception.

Though, as we have seen, the Italian edition of *The Condition of Labor* came out, as was almost necessary, as early as the American edition, *Progress and Poverty* had been published in Italy only in 1888. A translation of the major book was brought out in Spain in 1893, not long after George had had a request for permission to translate in Havana; and in 1892 a self-styled 'sectary' wrote from Rio de Janeiro, requesting permission to make a Portuguese translation.

Though tardy, the Italian and Spanish translations were gains. But from France and Holland, George learned of discouragement. An admirer and translator at the University of Bordeaux (whose name was Plato) wrote sorrowfully that after ten years only 1670 copies 'of your famous work' had been sold. Jan Stoffels reported in 1892 that neither *The Condition of Labor,* which he had just translated, nor *Progress and Poverty* was selling at all well. Only the Anglo-Saxons are ripe for your principles, wrote the Dutchman, and England and America will have to lead the way.

Yet Stoffels should have mentioned the Scandinavian countries, for they were continuing their early show of interest. Henry George himself was kept somewhat informed, though he never visited there. In 1890 the Copenhagen publisher of *Social Problems* wrote that, though Norway had responded first, there was real 'evidence of the spread of the Gospel and the progress of the Single Tax' in his own 'remote corner of the planet.' This corresponds with an undated memorandum in the George collection, written by Georg Brandes, the distinguished literary critic and historian of Denmark. 'What has made the deepest impression on my mind,' said this student of the French *philosophes* and of romanticism, 'is the profound truth that I should not be compelled to pay a tax on . . . my work, but . . . from that wealth or value which I have received from no merit or exertion on my own part.'

Unfortunately George never discovered a follower in Germany sufficiently like Walker and others in England to help him bridge the gap between reformism in the republic and reformism in the empire. Probably in 1891 and perhaps earlier, he broke with Flürscheim permanently. When Bernhard Eulenstein, a devotee who introduced himself by mail as a 'strict Landliger,' took the initiative, a new connection was established, for a moment. George may have been pleased at first by this man's criticisms of Flürscheim, as at once too socialistic and too conservative, and by his criticism of the publishers for keeping *Fortschritt und Armuth* too costly for mass sale and circulation. But George can only have disliked intensely the bizarre political procedures which Eulenstein recommended. He wanted Henry George, first of all, to visit Germany and have an audience with William II. The young Kaiser had many ideas on the social question, Eulenstein said, and anyway the interview would be a grand advertisement for *Landligers*. Second, he proposed — to the American lecturer on Moses, now a protégé of August Lewis — that in Germany the single tax be identified with the anti-Semitic party. 'The British relies too much on his political liberty for which I do not give a fig today,' went on Eulenstein.

For the second time George came to a cul-de-sac in his personal relations with Germans. He seems never to have made contact with Theodor Hertzka, Austrian land reformer and writer of utopian economics; and, unfortunately, he had none with Adolph Damaschke. This younger man entered the land-reform movement the year before George died and became a devoted follower; in the twentieth century he would be an influential worker for improved urban housing, and a leader to infuse in *Bodenreform* a new humanity and power.

In Russia *Social Problems* and *The Condition of Labor* were published almost as soon as in the United States, and an astonishing number of Henry George's minor writings were translated also. But *Progress and Poverty* was not published there until after the turn of the century; and, though George heard, some years before he died, that Count Leo Tolstoy was saying wonderful things about him, it is doubtful that he had any understanding at all of the following he had already achieved in that dark land.

Curiously enough, it was the German Eulenstein who told him in 1894 that Tolstoy was reading *Progress and Poverty* to his peasants. And it was the same promoter who wrote two years later that, if George would come to Berlin for a land-reform convention, timed for the exposition, Tolstoy would be present. But this was an election year at home, and in any case George would probably have refused another experience that promised to be like the Paris conference. He turned down the invitation before he heard that Tolstoy had told Jane Addams that, if George would come, he himself would 'break his habit of never traveling,' and come in a 'box,' as he called a railroad car.

But George did write to Tolstoy. The reply he received is as suggestive as the early acceptances of Henry George in England, say those by Bernard Shaw and Philip Wicksteed. It deserves a full quotation. 'The reception of your letter gave me a great joy for it is a long time that I know you and love you. Though the paths we go are far different, I do not think we differ in the foundations of our thoughts.

'I was very glad to see you mention twice in your letter the life to come.

'There is nothing that widens as much the horizon, that gives such firm support nor such a clear view of things as the consciousness that although it is but in this life that we have the possibility and the Duty to act, nevertheless this is not the whole of life but that bit of it only which is open to our understanding.

'I shall wait with great expectation for the appearance of your new book which will contain the so much needed criticism of the orthodox political economy. The reading of every one of your books makes clear to me more and more the truth and practicability of your system. Still more do I rejoice at the thought that I may possibly see you. My summers I invariably spend in the country near Tala. With sincere affection.'

One would like to picture Henry George's going to Tala, or at least maintaining a long correspondence with Count Tolstoy. He did neither, and one guesses that he missed understanding either the Russian's sincerity or his greatness. As, a dozen years earlier, *Progress and Poverty* had given faith to certain Englishmen that the power of the state could be used for social reconstruction, so, in this instance, George and his book worked a similar persuasion. Tolstoy became deeply convinced that his philosophical anarchism should yield, and that land-value taxation should be made the one exception to his distrust of all state action. He wished in 1894 that he could persuade the new tsar to assign the rent of the crown estates to the workers; and he actually prevailed on his daughter to do just that on certain family holdings. He wrote the same doctrine to a Siberian peasant, and he made the same appeal to the prime minister and Duma in 1906 and 1907. He stated his conviction in an eloquent essay of that period, 'The Great Iniquity,' and predicted that the Henry George idea would succeed.

Tolstoy was far from being alone with such aspirations in Russia. Long before Karl Marx became a great influence in the land, and before the wars and suppressions of this century destroyed the possibilities of humane methods of social reconstruction, Georgism entered the thought of social students and reformers. As a recent study of Russian populism of the early twentieth century indicates, George communicated both political hope and economic ideas. More than Bellamy, the American socialist, who was also known in Russia, and more than any other American, George was read and absorbed by thinkers in the Romanov empire.

George's actual influence in Russia recalls the prophecy he made about the destiny of that land, in one of his earliest editorials. One wonders how the future rivalry he contemplated between the United States and Russia, the first political fact of our own day, might have developed or not developed, if Georgism had succeeded better, and Marxism less well, during the second and third decades of the twentieth century.

–3–

While waves of appreciation of Henry George were extending at home and abroad, in the world of thought and letters, a political tornado occurred in America. Though there were Georgists in both the West and the South, few words are necessary to explain that he individually had very little to do with the immediate building up of political discontent and protest. He visited the South only once or twice, and in the West his personal role had never been other than that of occasional lecturer. Deeply as he believed that land-value taxation would be as correct in the country as in the city, since California days his practice of politics, except for 1887, had all been urban. In campaigning for Cleveland in 1888 he had not gone so far out of his own state, even, as to speak for Tom Johnson in Cleveland. The fall of 1890, when Johnson tried again for Congress, and succeeded, was of course the time of George's own greatest preoccupations and pressures. While the new People's party ran candidates, he saw an opportunity for doctrine. 'Politically things in the United States look splendidly,' he wrote Thomas Walker that October, 'radical free trade is rapidly gaining ground, and our single tax men everywhere are doing good work.'

When the returns came in the Populists had made startling gains: three governors in the South, two senators from the West, about fifty congressmen, and strong delegations in fifteen or sixteen state legislatures. But to George, and the *Standard*, all this seemed, not without reason, ephemeral. To George the great events were that Tom Johnson, as complete a free-trader as anyone, was elected to Congress, and William McKinley, whose name was attached to the high-tariff act of the spring, had been retired. In New York, though William Croasdale, George's successor on the *Standard*, was defeated, John de Witt Warner, a limited-single-taxer, was elected. Perspective does confirm George's judgment that the election of 1890 brought to Washington a great enlargement of anti-tariff conviction. But of course this sentiment, like Populist sentiment, would be for the next few years only: different from George's long-run expectation, by the later '90s big business would consolidate, as not before, behind protectionism.

Under the old system of 'lame-duck' sessions, Tom Johnson did not take his seat in the House of Representatives until December 1891. George had recovered from his illness and had written *The Condition of Labor* by that time, and the millionaire pleasantly insisted that he come to Washington, for a bicycle ride and talk, and that he be present at the swearing-in. On this trip George began to have a little influence on federal patronage: his first and successful effort was to get Annie's relative, Will McCloskey, a place in the Government Printing Office.

Meanwhile during the summer, though single-taxers recognized that Populist doctrines and organizations were not for them, efforts were made to have George men lined up for nominations in the Middle West, in the hope that they would be chosen in the coming big election. Thomas Shearman paid Louis Post's expenses to go to Kansas to sound the possibilities of Professor James H. Canfield's running for the Senate. Though the emissary decided that the move could not succeed — and the professor (Dorothy Canfield Fisher's father) became instead the chancellor of the University of Nebraska — the trip was not in vain.

In Kansas, Post established a friendship with 'Sockless' Jerry

Simpson. And when that famous personage came east, in 1891, to take his seat in the House of Representatives, he visited Henry George 'to declare his discipleship.' He spoke at a free-trade meeting in Cooper Union and was much publicized for attending a champagne supper with millionaires present — several were single-taxers, one of them Tom Johnson. At about the same time this middle-western connection was established, George began to have letters from young Franklin Lane, future Democratic secretary of the interior. Lane reported that Georgist ideas were making headway among Scandinavian working men in the state of Washington.

The special stimulation of having Henry George men in Congress, taking an active part in national affairs, appeared first in the spring of 1892. Those members cared intensely — more in a doctrinaire way than any other group in the country — whether Grover Cleveland, if nominated a third time, would, or would not, reassume his role of 1888, as leader against protectionism. Now seemed the time of times to hit hard against that policy.

Tom Johnson, all vigor and nerve, conceived a stroke of propaganda. He arranged with five other representatives — one each from Kentucky, Tennessee, Illinois, Iowa, and Kansas (Jerry Simpson) — to have read into the *Congressional Record,* as an extension of their remarks, a section of George's book of 1886, *Protection or Free Trade.* By proper arrangement the whole text would be reproduced in the *Record.* This did not mean free printing, but very cheap printing; and it did mean free distribution, by means of the members' franking privilege. The trick was quickly turned. The most the Republicans could do, after failing to have the book expunged from the *Record,* was to have a book by George Gunton, Henry George's old critic, distributed (not very widely) in the same way.

Henry George loved the coup. In New York he took charge of the printing. Six weeks after the vote, he was able to report that the book was coming off the press at a rate of 9000 a day. Many contributions pleased him: money from Walker for sending 10,000 copies to Britain; and funds in the United States, from Johnson principally. The thousands of copies sent to Ohio and Pennsylvania, ancient strongholds of protectionism, delighted him especially. Altogether more than a million copies went out before the election;

and according to Henry George, Jr., they were sent to all the news-papers in the country.

Hardly second to the quantity of this operation, George loved the idea that Democratic party action had been the force to put it over. A partisan vote had saved the reading into the *Record,* and by that token *Protection or Free Trade* took the color of Democratic doctrine. The press gallery of the House was stunned, wrote Henry George, Jr. Congressmen were awakening to the fact that the single tax was in politics, according to the same reporter, and he believed that the Democratic party, allowing exceptions, was 'galloping towards free trade. Our work is to spur that gallop.'

Of course the national convention in Chicago was not so subject to stampede. As in 1888, the tariff plank caused a prolonged battle in committee; and once more the committee reported a weak and two-minded proposition. Again Tom Johnson, as mighty new-comer in politics, seized the lead. Joining with Henry Watterson, who represented the southern tradition for free trade and who had had his Louisville paper serialize *Protection or Free Trade* when it was first published, Johnson managed to have the tariff plank debated on the floor of the convention. He won something of what he wanted. The Democrats officially declared the McKinley Act to be a 'culminating atrocity of class legislation.' But the party made no such clear-cut affirmation as Johnson desired, or as would have been consistent with *Protection or Free Trade*.

A compromise would seem to have been all that the free-traders had a right to hope for, in the convention. But they did permit themselves to expect that 'Mr. President,' now nominated, would be persuaded to resume the line of his most historic message to Congress. Watterson wrote Cleveland that in Chicago he had opposed 'what was represented as your judgment and desire in the adoption of the tariff plank,' and he added that he did 'not think that you appreciate the overwhelming force of the revenue reform issue, which has made you its idol.' He tried pressure. 'You cannot escape your great message of 1887 if you would . . . Emphasize it, am-plify it, do not subtract a thought, do not erase a word.'

But Grover Cleveland was not a man to be managed. He and Watterson never spoke after this letter. Tom Johnson and Henry George approached the candidate. Probably they were not as in-considerate as the Kentuckian, but they felt rebuffed. It can be estimated that the Georgists overstrained, alike in Congress and convention and with Cleveland, asking for more than they could demand. The impression of political opportunities lost at home is heightened by the Liberal victories in England. In that country, during the same summer, was created the Parliamentary situation already reported, which was favorable to Georgist ideas.

Shortly after the convention, Henry George on his own responsibility ordered 200,000 new copies of *Protection or Free Trade* to be printed. The propaganda went on. But after Cleveland's rebuff there ceased to be heart in the effort. George retired quietly to Merriewold. For the summer he even stopped trying to keep informed about the campaign. His one remaining hope, he told Shearman during the second week of September, was that a stunning vote for Tom Johnson would strengthen the radical line.

But once again, as in 1888, his faith in Cleveland was renewed. He met the ex-president, and a remark Cleveland dropped convinced him that the candidate was not 'crawfishing' after all. Understanding now that Cleveland truly believed in the revenue-only idea of the tariff, George advised Johnson that 'for the present he has gone far enough,' and that 'the Radical wing is on top,' after all. To his Republican intimate, John Russell Young, George said that there was no need to go to the Populists 'while the Democratic Party can be made to work.'

Late in October, according to this reconciliation, Henry George took a political speaking trip into the Middle West. Though he went as far as Minneapolis, as a Democrat for Cleveland, his main concern was for Ohio. He had become anxious about Johnson, whose district had been gerrymandered. As in George's own case in 1887, possible long-run results seemed more important than immediate ones. Radical hopes reached farther than just re-election; another term in Congress, George thought, might open the way to the governorship; and the governorship in turn might lead to making Ohio the first single-tax state. Then, in 1896 or whenever might be, Tom Loftin Johnson for President.

In this frame of mind, Henry George made no concessions, either to Populist doctrine or to Populist strength. The *Standard* printed the Georgist criticism: that, though the party represented 'widespread and well founded discontent,' its platform was no better than a 'patchwork.' Later, when the vote was in, George attributed no deep importance to the large increase of Populist showing. Though some of his judgments seem sectarian and ungenerous, and though he was far too optimistic about certain victories he cherished, he did, in November, have much cause to celebrate. Cleveland was returned to the White House. Tom Johnson, Jerry Simpson, and John de Witt Warner were re-elected; and his old friend Judge Maguire was chosen a member of Congress from San Francisco. The Republican party is now destroyed, Henry George wrote his lady-poet admirer in San Luis Obispo, and before long the Democratic party, too, will crumble. A true party will appear. Yet the truth we work for does not reside in parties, 'it is the progress of our idea . . . The future believe me is ours.'

A campaign year in which he allowed himself a host of exaggerated hopes was poor preparation for the political realities of 1893 and after. With the worsening depression, national politics shifted from anti-tariff to money problems and to income tax. Henry George as anxious observer and doctrinaire had no quarrel of principle with the President's demand for the repeal of the Sherman Silver Purchase Act. It was doubtless the old editor in him, once sold out by Senator Jones of Nevada, who now resented the silver lobby. And it was the old spokesman for the gold standard, and for limited greenbacks and interconvertible bonds, who opposed new varieties of inflationism. He talked and corresponded with Tom Johnson, in 1893, about bonds and paper money and, in general terms, about working out an 'elastic currency' as national policy. Depression exigencies by no means forced George out of the swim, but the special session of Congress of the summer of 1893 made him heartsick that opportunity for tariff reform was rapidly slipping away.

The situation came to a head in the winter, after the Fifty-third Congress reassembled. The President's message called for a reduction in schedules of duties, and the Wilson Bill was introduced. Hope persisted for reform, and at one dramatic point Henry George had a moment of glory. He was seated in the gallery of the house, and Tom Johnson was speaking — himself a manufacturer — against the tariff on steel rails. But a member pointed to the gallery, and spoke in contempt of the 'master' above, directing his 'pupil on the floor of the house.' In reply a number of Democrats marched up the steps and shook hands with the free-trade thinker.

Later that winter, when the famous and short-lived income tax of 1894 was passed as an amendment to the tariff bill, Henry George's ideas were acknowledged a second time. The measure was enacted, of course, by reason of the agreement of nearly every variety of liberalism: the President favored it; so did the People's party, and farmer and labor groups generally; and Tom Johnson reluctantly agreed. But for Georgists there was very particular reason for regret, and Representative James Maguire moved an amendment. Place the tax on land values exclusively, he proposed. Make the tax fall on the states in proportion to population, precisely as the constitution requires of any direct taxation by Congress, he argued. Different from George's opinion when once asked by a Senate committee, Judge Maguire believed a constitutional amendment to be entirely unnecessary.[1]

This was the first time that Henry George's reform had been considered in a legislature as possible policy for an entire nation. George appreciated the event in those terms. The six members who voted for the Maguire amendment were twice the number he expected: Maguire, Johnson, Simpson, Warner, and Charles Tracey of New York and Michael Harter of Ohio. Though he was pleased, he did not think he saw the future coming in Washington. 'The direct line of our advance,' he wrote Richard McGhee of Glasgow, 'is however in State legislation, and the single tax may in that way be brought into political issue at any time.' When the Supreme Court threw out the new income tax, George thought the majority judges to be more right than wrong.[2]

The events that honored Henry George in Congress were the deeds of tiny minorities. To his distress, the fears of the summer of 1893 were more than realized during the winter. Not only did the Mills tariff wither into a 'final defeat of long-deferred hopes,' but the administration took the side of capital in a shocking labor

[1] As we have seen, while he called income taxes second-best, George always judged them to be inquisitorial and unwise. He thought it unfair to levy either on a citizen's earnings by labor, or on his income from capital, at least as long as there remained sources of taxation in rent. In *A Perplexed Philosopher* he spoke indirectly but strongly against income taxes.

[2] Probably George noticed that the court reasoned much as Maguire did. It decided that the income tax was unconstitutional because it would tax income from rent (among all sources) without apportionment among the states according to population. See George, Jr., 579; compare Swisher, *American Constitutional Development*, 449–51.

affair. At campaign time 1892, Cleveland had said, for the ears of labor sympathizers, the right things about the recent Homestead strike. But when, in the more famous crisis of two years later, the President not only broke a strike but used such a mighty exercise of federal power to do so as no earlier administration ever had, and none has since, liberals and pro-labor people were alarmed in the extreme.

The Pullman strike and Cleveland's ordering troops to Chicago, requires no retelling. To Henry George the issues were the gravest the country had to confront, and they were utterly plain. The President's famous dictum, that if it took 'the entire army of the United States to deliver a postal card in Chicago, that postal card will be delivered,' seemed to him irrelevant and needless. His admiration went to Governor Altgeld, who protested that Cleveland was being too precipitate, and that federal troops were not necessary.

In New York George assumed the role of a kind of tribune of the people. He returned to Cooper Union, where during labor campaigns he had spoken so frequently. Perhaps 10,000 tried to hear him. Under the title, 'Peace by Standing Army,' he spoke for the freedom of working men. 'There is something more important, even, than law and order, and that is liberty. I yield to nobody in my respect for the rights of property; yet I would rather see every locomotive in this land ditched, every car and every depot burned and every rail torn up, than to have them preserved by means of a Federal standing army. That is the order that reigned in Warsaw [long applause]. That is the order in the keeping of which every democratic republic before ours has fallen. I love the American Republic better than I love such order.' Of a handful of letters preserved from those that came to George after the address, the best were from writers who were old abolitionists and wrote in that vein.

The reformer never changed his mind again, to be favorable to Grover Cleveland. He quarreled with him once more, in 1896. In an event famous in diplomatic relations, the President said some very sharp things against Britain, in the matter of the Guiana-Venezuela boundary dispute. As the question before the public was how to apply the Monroe Doctrine, we may wonder whether George remembered his own plan to intervene in Latin America, from the Pacific side, thirty years earlier. But he was a sober man now, a leader with followers in England whom he had indoctrinated in natural rights. He made an eloquent anti-imperialist speech, once again in Cooper Union. It won praise from directions not usual. 'You have rendered your country a noble service,' wrote Horace White, 'your speech last night was very effective.'

Meanwhile, over a period of two years, George's dissents and his associations with other radicals had ripened in him the most bitter feeling about the administration and the conservative branch of the Democratic party. The sympathy with Governor Altgeld in 1894 had led to a correspondence, though they had never met. George assured the governor that the issues he had fought over would surely rise again. In the summer of 1894, as the congressional elections approached, the only hope he had was the old one, that conservative blunders would lead to radical gains. 'Does political history show any parallel to the Democratic stultification?' he demanded of Lloyd Garrison.

Once again he rejected the third-party possibility. He would not change his mind about the People's party, or encourage a new party of his own. When single-taxers in New York and Brooklyn made a motion toward organizing, he said publicly that he would accept no nomination if offered. 'The Single Tax is not a party or an organization,' he told a *Tribune* reporter. 'It is a perception of a great truth.'

In Chicago his attitude made difficulties. Eugene Debs, the recent leader of the Pullman strike, Henry Demarest Lloyd, whose *Wealth versus Commonwealth* had just appeared, Clarence Darrow, and others had fabricated a united front of Populist and labor forces. Even single-taxers and socialists were pulling weight together in that city. But when Henry George visited, a month before the elections, he talked single-tax ideas unadulterated. According to Professor Destler's close study, his opposition so weakened the labor and Populist alliance as to assist the coming Republican victory in Illinois.

Neither united-front, nor third-party, nor George's own type of intra-Democratic insurgency succeeded at the polls that year. In New York, John de Witt Warner was not even nominated for Congress. Jerry Simpson and Tom Johnson, who had judged it best that George not make campaign speeches in the West, were both defeated. Of the Georgist group in Congress, only Judge Maguire survived. Champ Clark — with whom George was acquainted — called 1894 the greatest slaughter of the innocents since Herod.

The way ahead darkened suddenly, after brightness. George had no function, any longer, as adviser to congressmen. The next election seemed crucial. Professor Nevins has given us President Cleveland's haunting fear: should the Democratic party go wrong on the money issue now, as it had once gone wrong on slavery, it might wander in the wilderness another thirty years. From his own point of view, almost as opposed as Cleveland's to monetary inflation but governed by a different sense of history, George shared the sense of fatality.

Yet when 1896 came he could do what the retiring President could not. He could stay with the party when it named an inflationist candidate. William Jennings Bryan 'certainly did not represent my views,' he told Dr. Taylor. 'But I had to take the best offered, and he came nearest it.' He had little to say at first.

George's situation is represented perfectly by the fact that for the campaign he resumed the role of correspondent. He was outside history, rather than in it, this time. The New York *Journal* hired him. He had had some slight acquaintance with William Randolph Hearst earlier, but there seems to have been no personal connection this time. His real associations were much less with the proprietor of the new paper than with Arthur McEwen, old friend and ace reporter, and with the editor-in-chief, Willis J. Abbot. Abbot was a believer in George's doctrines and had been active in Chicago labor politics until recently.

The job took George to both the Republican and the Democratic conventions, and it allowed him freedom to write as he pleased. While in Chicago he saw much of Tom Johnson, and he heard Bryan give the 'Cross of Gold' address. Perhaps a letter to his employer was the first estimate he made of the 1896 leftward movement of the Democratic party — the first such movement for decades. He congratulated Hearst on committing the *Journal* to Bryan. The platform stops short, he said, and in certain respects he disagreed with it: he was not a silver man, and he did not like the income tax. Yet Bryan had the better cause, and he was glad to serve.

In September he spoke much more warmly. He endorsed Bryan

in a letter to the *Arena,* and many times he said publicly how he would vote. In his belief, monopoly not gold was the cross that must be removed — and would be, if Bryan won.

Besides his writing, George did a little platform work for the candidate. He prevailed on Governor Altgeld to come east and make a speech against government by injunction, and against federal domination in any sphere of power. This proved to be a major campaign event, and thousands stood outside the hall. So far as George as a public man was concerned, moreover, it indicated a real change of style. By arranging the meeting, by sitting on the platform with Mary Ellen Lease and others, he demonstrated that he had rejoined the general forces of insurgency and change.

This was a little hard for some of the businessmen and lawyers of the single-tax movement. Not Tom Johnson, who was for Bryan, but Thomas Shearman and August Lewis of New York, George's generous patrons, and Louis Prang and Lloyd Garrison, both of Boston, disagreed. To Garrison George explained that he believed it 'quite as well, if not somewhat better, that some of us single-taxers should be on different sides, though I wish you and I at least were together . . . You and I can talk, after this madness is over.' As if to act on this advice, a group of single-taxers, who differed from George, published a kind of manifesto of their views.

Despite his tolerance, the conservatism of his followers led to George's climactic piece of campaign journalism. Under the title, 'Shall the Republic Live,' it was printed in the *Journal* on the day before the vote. It shows that he had caught the passion, and shared the exaltation, of one of America's four or five most crucial presidential campaigns. He demanded to know of those few single-taxers, who, 'deluded, as I think, by the confusion, propose to separate from the majority of us on the vote,' how they expected to recognize 'the great struggle to which we have all looked forward as inevitable,' if not by present indications? 'For all the great struggles of history have begun on subsidiary and sometimes on what seemed at the moment irrelevant issues . . . Would [the single-taxers] not expect to hear predictions of the most dire calamity overwhelming the country, if the power to rob the masses was lessened ever so little? . . . The larger business interests have frightened each other, as children do when one says "Ghost!" Let them frighten no thinking man.'

George's more leftward and literary followers were thrilled. Post stood right beside him, as always. John Swinton, with whom there had been a recent reconciliation, was delighted. Hamlin Garland sent his compliments; and James Herne said that no one but the author of *The Condition of Labor* could have written that final article.

For George and those like him, perhaps even more than for those Bryan men who had no anxieties about silver, the campaign of 1896 achieved a special glory. Twentieth-century progressivism would draw from its dedications and gathering of forces. So, too, did Henry George, personally, just one year later. The Bryan campaign in some degree canceled for him the retirement of 1887. It returned him to politics. It prepared him to make a second campaign, a most tragic fight to be mayor of New York.

–4–

After the battle was over the *Journal* offered Henry George more writing at very good pay. Because there had been no central single-tax journal since the *Standard* died in 1892, the proposition must have been tempting. George could have $50 for a weekly column — or could contribute an occasional column at convenience — in which he would have the opportunity to address single-taxers and sympathizers with 'absolute freedom of expression' guaranteed.

But George refused the offer, in favor of working on *The Science of Political Economy*. His decision conforms also with the quiet role he retained, with respect to the single-tax movement. In recent years his organized followers had been developing the techniques of propaganda: they were starting chain letters, using single-tax stickers, establishing new organizations, and so on. But George himself made only one notable exception to his general habit of keeping apart. In 1895 and 1896, he joined Post and Shearman and Lawson Purdy and others, who were trying by concentration of forces to capture Delaware — one small state to be made a pilot for the single tax. The campaign effort meant simply traveling to Philadelphia, crossing the state line, and making speeches. But George seems to have had no heart for the work. When an issue of free speech arose, he refused to dare arrest and become a member of the 'Dover Jail Single Tax Club.' The veteran of Loughrea and

Athenry decided that his friends had drummed up a none-too-valid case.

George held back too, in January 1897, when he began to hear rumors that he would be nominated a second time for mayor of New York. 'Are your congratulations as to the mayoralty sarcastic?' he demanded after a letter from Post; 'I am a little uneasy about being pulled off my course.' Five months later — after illness and his daughter's death had intervened — he wrote Thomas Walker that he was giving no countenance to the proposed candidacy; and he told another correspondent that he wished his friends would abandon the idea.

The inner question, as we saw in the last chapter, was whether George should give all to the book he intended to be final, or dramatize his cause once more in a city election that would be reported round the world. The considerations in favor of politics were enlarged now because of the reorganization which had just been enacted for New York. On 1 January 1898, the old city would become the borough of Manhattan; and by combination with Brooklyn and other boroughs, Greater New York would be organized under one government, the second city in population, the most cosmopolitan city on earth. In other respects different from 1886, the mayor would hold office for four years; his patronage would be second only to the President's; and both practically and symbolically his authority would be unique. The new blueprint of city government corresponded well with Henry George's early ideas about city reform, as he had put them in editorials in the San Francisco *Post*. James Bryce saluted the coming election as of international significance; and, just after the campaign closed, an American expert called it 'a stupendous experiment in city government, such as the world had never seen before.'

So far as Henry George's medical advisers were concerned, to run or not to run was a black-and-white decision: either keep on writing and live, or run for mayor and die. Dr. Kelly and Dr. Leverson said the same thing. With the latter, a friend of twenty-five years standing, George discussed the decision as they walked the Shore Road at Fort Hamilton. The physician remembered the reformer's words: 'But I have got to die. How can I die better than serving humanity? Besides so dying will do more for the cause than anything I am likely to be able to do for the rest of my life.' George omitted asking the advice of the physician who had attended him in 1890. When Dr. Mendelson, agitated by what he saw in the newspapers, implored his friend not to run — there have been thousands of mayors but only one *Progress and Poverty*, he begged — George answered that he would take that advice, 'unless as I see it duty calls.' But he wrote those words on 30 September, and by that time the answer must have been crystal clear in his own mind.

As in 1886, he discussed — this time hardly shared — the decision with his friends. Tom Johnson took charge, at a meeting of about thirty, in his office in New York. George allowed no one to discuss his health; and, when the book was mentioned, he said that the essentials were now complete — an exaggeration which indicates his state of mind. After the meeting he asked his wife whether she remembered his saying at the time of the Phoenix Park murders that Michael Davitt should go straight to Dublin, even though it cost his life? I ask you now, the husband went on, 'will you fail to tell me to go into this campaign? The people want me; they say they have no one else on whom they can unite. It is more than a question of good government. If I enter the field it will be a question of natural rights, even though as mayor I might not directly be able to do a great deal for natural rights. New York will become the theatre of the world, and my success will plunge our cause into world politics.'

Annie George hesitated less than her husband had done, and the decision brought no remorse. The family noticed that the candidate's old optimism came back, that his eye lit again and spring returned to his step. His pictures show an emaciated man, but those who knew him best recall a rekindled one.

The first obvious result of the reorganization of New York was that, contrary to what was usual, the campaigning began early in the city. Those who were first to move were reformist independents in politics, the members of the recently established Citizens Union. The union wished to be bi-partisan, but the impulse had come from liberal Republicans, and the nominee was of just that kind. President Seth Low of Columbia University was blessed with about all the advantages, and burdened with the disadvantages, that a man of wealth and education has in American mass politics. He was the heir of a clipper-ship fortune and had served in the family business; he had been reform mayor of Brooklyn and a leader in the public-charities movement. Though he gave every sign of really wanting to run, President Low took a leaf from Henry George's book. He did not commit himself entirely until 125,000 signatures indicated that there was popular interest in his cause. Had a momentum developed from this careful preparation, there can be no question but what Greater New York would have had as first mayor — President Low was actually elected in 1901 — an executive with capacities and merits in proportion to the office.

But, to the crucial question, whether Republican party regulars would vote for Low, and so perhaps smash Tammany, Boss Thomas Platt gave the answer which denied 100,000 votes. Under his orders, at the end of September, the party nominated General Benjamin F. Tracy, who had been President Harrison's secretary of navy, and since then law partner of Mr. Platt's son. Simultaneously, when Richard Croker returned after three years at his home in England, he dictated the Tammany ticket. Judge Robert A. van Wyck, a party hack, became the regular Democratic nominee. This left the Bryan Democrats of 1896, the groups known as the Democratic Alliance and the United Democracy, as discontented as were the Republican liberals. They were the ones who had sounded Henry George.

The situation differed from 1886, and yet was capable of being built into likeness. Devotion to Bryan and the Chicago free-silver platform had hardly the compulsion and self-consciousness that labor had had, in Henry George's first campaign. Yet last year's emotion did have political effect. At the meeting at which George accepted the nomination of the Democratic Alliance, Mary Ellen Lease of Kansas sat on the platform, and the candidate addressed himself to 'Fellow Democrats, who last year voted for William Jennings Bryan.' Though he had nearly fainted before the meeting, George put eloquence into saying that 'into the common people would come a power that would revivify not merely this imperial city . . . but the world.' The meeting sent greetings to Bryan. We learn as a campaign secret, which leaked to the Republicans, that Bryan approved the nomination as though George, and not Tammany's van Wyck, were the regular Democratic candidate. A majority of the national committee are said to have felt the same way.

As in 1886 Henry George wrote his own platform, and he made

it virtually the same. He stressed municipal ownership and municipal home rule, and called for tax reform and the end of government by injunction. Striving more than ever to universalize his message, he named his party 'The Democracy of Thomas Jefferson.' It was not a labor party, this time, though it sought the votes of labor; and it was not a single-tax party, though many but by no means all the single-taxers of New York went with their leader. George believed that this effort had the same goals as the one of 1886 — purification in politics and democratization in economics, to begin in New York, and to be spread gradually elsewhere, as politics might make possible.

The immediate enemy, now as before, was Croker's Tammany Hall. For George this was the determining point of strategy in a campaign where little else was clear. As candidate he was concerned, though as radical Democrat not governed in his tactics, by the vast enigma, how Low and Tracy would divide the Republican vote. Memory of his last campaign must have helped him believe that neither of these two would win. His Republican opponent of 1886, who had had the support of both wings of that party, regular and liberal, was greatly concerned this time. Viewing the city election from the perspective of Washington, Roosevelt conceded 'what the populists say,' that his party in New York did represent 'corrupt wealth.' He favored Low. But he criticized the academic man sharply for not having consolidated with Platt and accused him of being 'hand in glove with Henry George.' The total situation, from George's point of view, was that Tracy was a candidate to neglect, Low was one to respect but not to concede to, and Judge van Wyck was the one to defeat — for the good of city and party alike.

As was entirely natural, George's own thoughts reached back eleven years. 'I won the race,' he said publicly and definitely, as he had not spoken in 1886. 'I know, as you know, that the votes cast for me were counted out by the system that prevailed then.' Making this early effort to establish continuity between the present campaign and his last one, George was taking long chances. What he said brought reply not from Croker but from Hewitt and Ivins. The ex-mayor was quoted from abroad as saying again that Henry George was leading forces of anarchy and destruction. The name-calling seemed to be striking once more.

This prompted George to review publicly for the first time the whole history of his relations with Hewitt, from employee to rival, and to tell the story of the Democrats' effort to divert him from the first mayoralty campaign with an offer to elect him to Congress. George's accusations of bribery evoked the reply of Ivins, which was discussed in Chapter xv. Whatever the exact fact about 1886 may have been, it seems unlikely that recriminations in 1897 made very effective campaigning. Certainly Mr. Hewitt's fear words did not have their earlier power. When George demanded retractions, Hewitt returned a soft answer. He had been misquoted from overseas, he said, and had not meant what had been printed. Hewitt, whom Tammany had elected in 1886 and dropped in 1888, announced for Low this time.

Though his energies were limited, George fought an aggressive campaign and loved the fight. As in all recent years, financial support came from Tom Johnson and August Lewis. Father McGlynn wrote in a friendly way but counseled George against taking the stump too vigorously. If there was no labor support to compare with that of 1886, the shortage was somewhat filled by Jerome O'Neill, the Central Labor Union man who ran for president of the council, on the Democracy of Thomas Jefferson ticket. Apparently the strongest lieutenant George had from the Democratic party was Charles N. Dayton. A former postmaster of New York, he was expected to make a real subtraction from Tammany strength.

From single-tax ranks, besides the senior allies already mentioned, Lawson Purdy and Charles Frederic Adams were the most prominent men. Hamlin Garland, who got into the thick of the fight, tried to mobilize literary manpower. He asked Henry Demarest Lloyd for an endorsement 'to be used in a very literary meeting we are organizing,' at which Herne and he were going to make speeches. He hoped that Howells would return from Europe in time to take part in the campaign.

Though there appeared no special campaign paper, like the *Leader,* in 1897, there was less need for one. Willis J. Abbot of the New York *Journal* took hold as chairman of the campaign committee. Hearst gave him leave with pay. And, though the *Journal* supported the Tammany candidate, star writers such as Arthur Brisbane and Arthur McEwen, who contributed a splendid character study of George to the then current November *Review of Reviews,* spoke favorably of George in Hearst's own paper. In general the metropolitan press behaved in a much friendlier way than in 1886. The best papers of both parties went for Low: the *Times,* the *Tribune,* the *World,* and the Brooklyn *Eagle.* Naturally the *Tribune* was especially eager to have George take as many Tammany votes as he could.

In his own role as speaker and leader, George tried desperately to perform as he had once performed. He was persuaded to conserve his strength by going daily, from campaign headquarters at the Union Square Hotel, to August Lewis's downtown house for lunch and an afternoon rest. People noticed his reduced vigor, and his wife says that he became spiritually withdrawn. Despite everything, he outdid as fighter every one of his adversaries; and for a dozen days, from 16 to 28 October, his record was truly heroic. He made thirty speeches. And on five of those days, one of them the day he died, he spoke four times.

As of 8 October, professional betting odds were ten to seven in favor of van Wyck, three to one against Tracy, four to one against Low, and eight to one against George. How realistic this was at the time and whether or not George's fortnight of hard campaigning developed any sizable current his way are of course questions not subject to present-day estimate.

For civic reformers like Heber Newton, George's candidacy, as it was launched later than Low's, presented a terrible contradiction. This was of course the thought, which has been shared by students since, that the two reform elements, one derived from each party, would cancel each other out. But the fear seems to have been unrealistic. There is evidence to support as fact what Theodore Roosevelt charged — a considerable mutuality between the two. The Democracy of Thomas Jefferson supported the county candidates of the Citizens Union, and the two nominees behaved with extraordinary respect toward one another. Low retracted a comment made in error about George; and George said many things which after his death the Citizens Union was able to use to indicate that if Henry George could speak again he would advise his people to vote the ticket led by President Low.

Though there is much to justify the Citizens Union claim, Henry George's last statement about Low was perhaps the most explicit.

He was far from a merger at that time. He spoke the following words at Flushing, five days before the election, and about twelve hours before he died. 'Let me say a word about Mr. Low. On election day as between Mr. Low and myself, if you are yet undecided you must vote for whom you please. I shall not attempt to dictate to you. I do entertain the hope, however, that you will rebuke the one-man power by not voting for the candidate of the bosses. I am not with Low. He is a Republican and he is fighting the machine, which is all very good as far as it goes. But he is an aristocratic reformer; I am a democratic reformer. He would help the people; I would help the people to help themselves.'

This valedictory echoes much of the life intention of Henry George. It is barely possible that Greater New York would have had a more creditable administrative history for the coming four years, if, on the last Friday of the campaign, the Democracy of Thomas Jefferson had shifted to President Low. But Henry George, Jr., was nominated on that day of anguish, and any other choice would seem to have been humanly impossible. Political momentums were too great, personal loyalties too emotional for any other choice to have been right.

On election day, the next Tuesday, President Low received 151,000 votes. Henry George, Jr., received 22,000. Justice Tracy had 101,000; and Judge van Wyck won, with a 234,000 plurality vote. The regular parties had almost twice as many votes as the reform parties combined.

Poignant letters by grieving George men tell us that some strength did shift from the Democracy of Thomas Jefferson to the Citizens Union vote. An informed contemporary believed that about 60,000 made the change. If as few as half that number did so, Low received a smaller number of votes of his own than the number who had signed the pre-campaign petitions which requested him to run.

In their own retrospect, the Citizens Union leaders believed that the death of Henry George had destroyed the Columbia president's last hope of victory in that campaign. If George had lived, for Low to have won, the Democracy of Thomas Jefferson would have had to take about 85,000 votes that went to the Tammany candidate. And this calculation subtracts nothing from Low's actual vote, as strength that would have belonged to George.

Altogether it seems improbable that George's continued candidacy could have meant victory for Low and the Citizens Union in 1897.

As for the most optimistic tabulation of Henry George's own chances, if we allow him 85,000 Tammany votes (as Low's advisers imply they did), we may allow him 50,000 Citizen's Union votes as well (less than our contemporary's estimate). Such a poll, combined with what Henry George, Jr., did receive, would have made him the mayor of New York.

The only cautious estimate is that reform, by schism in the parties, could in no circumstances have won in 1897. Henry George's belief that the fight would be a battle of symbols, one last venture in education in democratic theory and practice, seems entirely right.

–5–

On Thursday, the day before he died, George spoke three times on Long Island. Considerable traveling was required. He appeared first at Whitestone, then at College Point, and then at Flushing, where Dan Beard, of Boy Scout fame, was in the chair. At that place he made the statement about Low, which is quoted above. At College Point he had seemed dazed and exhausted; and his final remarks, made at the Manhattan Opera House, where he arrived after most of the crowd had departed, were so rambling as to distress the audience that remained.

He died in his hotel, early the next morning, after brief suffering. Mrs. George found him in their sitting room, a hard stroke of apoplexy upon him. Dr. Kelly came and could do nothing; his Irish grief was the most uncontrolled of all. The women stood firm. The oldest son, who was to have been married within a few days, had to give first attention to the campaign. The family behaved, and the martyrdom had occurred, just as Henry George had invited, in the dignity of duty and great love.

There followed on Sunday the amazing salute, obsequies which the New York *Herald* called 'unique,' and the *Times* compared with Abraham Lincoln's. 'Call it what you will, hero worship,' that paper said, 'but its object was truly a hero.' In the early morning the body was taken to lie in state at Grand Central Palace. Richard George accompanied it; and Anna Angela, now nearly twenty, insisted that she go too. Beginning at seven the mourners started the procession that lengthened with the day. Estimates of those who passed the bier vary from 30,000 to 100,000.

From three to five-thirty the public services were held. Heber Newton read the Episcopal service, his and his friend's legacy from old St. Paul's. Lyman Abbot spoke, and the choir from Plymouth Church sang the hymns. The later speakers were Rabbi Gottheil, John S. Crosby, and Father McGlynn. Mayor Strong and Seth Low had seats on the platform. The break of tension came when Father McGlynn declared his belief in Henry George's ideas. The cheers of thousands rang, shocking and yet appropriate too, across the body of Henry George.

In the late-fall evening the funeral procession moved south. The open hearse was drawn by sixteen horses draped in black. The bronze bust by Richard George was carried Roman style, just as Henry George had wanted. A white rose, dropped from a Madison Avenue window, clung to the casket in the waning light. A military band had volunteered; it led the way with 'Chopin's Funeral March' and 'The Marseillaise.' The procession passed City Hall, then crossed Brooklyn Bridge; and at the Borough Hall in Brooklyn the body was returned to the family.

The next day, privately, the interment service was read at Greenwood Cemetery. Two Episcopalian clergymen, John Kramer and George Latimer, the cousin who helped him get passage to India when he was fifteen, took charge. Father McGlynn spoke, about immortality.

Almost required, one thinks, were the words the family chose to have set in bronze on the stone that marks the grave. They come from the conclusion of *Progress and Poverty*. 'The truth that I have tried to make clear will not find easy acceptance . . . It will find friends . . . This is the power of truth.'

XX

The Triple Legacy of Georgism

—1—

In California, during the later '70s, while he was studying and writing, Henry George believed that *Progress and Poverty* would be a book for the twentieth century. His career on the West coast, it will be recalled, had given him little reason to hope that his ideas would spread at all rapidly.

George's change of mind, to expect immediate effects, which occurred on the heels of his first visit in Ireland and England, was no one-sided result, either of his natural optimism or of his inner shift of emphasis from a prophetic role to an almost messianic one. Events encouraged his hopes. A social revolution in his own day suddenly seemed altogether likely to occur. The questions in George's mind during the middle '80s were whether the United Kingdom or the United States would be the first to achieve a new economic order, and whether that change would be induced by Christian and rational measures or by doctrines of materialism and methods of violence.

But after the political setbacks of 1887, 1890, and 1894, at home, Henry George's expectations receded almost to the original estimation. His willingness to die in 1897 recalls his thought of two decades earlier. He believed once more that his ideas would have a stronger effect on men and nations in the future than on his exact contemporaries. Calculating the risks of the campaign for the Democracy of Thomas Jefferson, he turned to Johnson. 'Tom, wouldn't that be a glorious way to die?' he demanded.

The memorial services, meetings, editorials, and articles of appreciation, which appeared everywhere after his death, were of course the first stage of the carrying-on of the effort of Henry George. Perhaps the tribute, the personal estimate and assignment to a place in history that George would have liked best of all, however, was a private one. George W. Julian inscribed it in his diary. He spoke with as complete an authority, in the line of thought he chose, as anyone alive could have mustered. With a trembling hand the octogenarian abolitionist wrote: 'The death of Henry George in the midst of his grand fight against political thieving has touched the hearts of the whole world as no other death has done since that of Lincoln. George was a real saint and Martyr. He was the most religious man I have ever known, with his whole heart he loved the toiling poor, and he freely gave his life as a sacrifice. He was absolutely pure and unselfish, and his exalted place among the heroes of humanity is already perfectly assured . . . I think he overvalued his scheme of Land reform, but his books, and especially those dealing with the tariff, will probably influence public opinion in the years to come.'

–2–

When the leader died he left behind three types of belief in his ideas: the fiscal-reform Georgism of the single tax, of which Thomas Shearman was still the central figure; the political Georgism which entered into many varieties of reform activity, and which Tom Loftin Johnson represented most completely; and the moral and intellectual Georgism, of which Tolstoy and Hamlin Garland were eloquent early figures. The three categories overlap, of course, but we have noticed cases of the first without the second, and of the third without the first or second. Among Henry George's early prominent followers, perhaps Tom Johnson and Father McGlynn were the only ones who had the capacity to enter energetically into all three forms of Georgism.

In fairness to the accomplishment of the men who were Henry George's immediate successors, it should be said that the climate of American opinion after 1897 did not favor the growth of the Georgist political effort. Had the master himself lived in vigor a dozen years longer than he did, it is impossible to suppose that he could have played, during the administrations of McKinley, Theodore Roosevelt, and Taft, any political part equal to the one

he assumed during the Cleveland period of American history. Even
the most progressive Republicans of the first decade of the present
century, and there were never too many of them, were nationalistic
pro-tariff men and overseas imperialists. On the home front, the
advanced Republicans who fought for conservation of the federal
domain and natural resources, spoke they ever so strongly in the
public interest, were more concerned to have the government
manage the land than they were to have the people use it. Although Henry George's ideas may seem at first thought to have
been logically perfect to give philosophical support to the con-
servationism of Roosevelt and Pinchot, all three forms of Georgism
were in political fact quite remote from the reforms which early
Progressivism introduced in Washington.

Under the circumstances of Republican domination in the
country, there can have been few choices for the legatees of
Henry George to make when they asked themselves the question,
in the months and years after 1897, what they should do to carry
on. The natural answer was to continue with what they had been
doing previously, in different localities and in individual ways, as
followers of their leader while he lived. Sometimes the result was
ingenuous, as in the case of Charles Fillebrown of Boston, who was
a businessman devotee and one who, like William Lloyd Garrison
II, regretted Henry George's politics of 1896 and 1897. Mr.
Fillebrown tried to become a sort of schoolmaster for twentieth-
century Georgists. He wrote a primer, the *ABC of Taxation with
Boston Object Lessons;* and he made a habit of entertaining at
banquets professors and public men, and of presenting them with
speakers for the single tax. This effort drew sharp criticism from
within the single-tax movement itself.

In New York City, on the other hand, later Georgism, though
conservative and fiscal-minded in emphasis, was aggressive, and it
had power. The line of continuity from before 1897 descended
through the Manhattan Single Tax Club; and in 1901 the *Single
Tax Review* came to the city from the Middle West. After the
death of Thomas Shearman in 1900, Lawson Purdy became a
practical and thoughtful developer, in the direction of the single
tax, limited. More gifted as a leader than Shearman, Purdy in
time contributed to the defeat of the general property tax. During
the second decade of the present century, he became the principal

spokesman for the policy the city adopted, of assessing the value of land separately from improvements on the land. More than any other Georgist, moreover, Mr. Purdy has studied the administrative implications which inhere in the program of taxing land values. He has examined the bearing of taxation on land classification and land-use planning in the modern city; and he has asserted the need of cities sometimes to develop areas under a policy of public ownership.

During the early part of this century Georgists in other cities helped achieve tax reforms similar to those in New York. Under political circumstances which will be explained shortly, Cleveland adopted the system of separate assessments; and in Pennsylvania Georgists led in the fights, one of them recently, for the legislation which has brought about the higher taxation of land values and the lower taxation of buildings in Pittsburgh and certain other cities. Separate assessment has become a widespread practice in America, during the last half-century.

The sizable exception to the rule, that broader political Georgism faced impossible adversities during the decade after George's death, occurred, as seems entirely natural, in Tom Johnson's state of Ohio. While Henry George was living, Johnson had become a kind of field commander, west of New York at least, deploying Georgist forces at strategic centers, as his money made it possible. He had moved Warren W. Bailey, a journalist, from Chicago to Pennsylvania and made him editor of the Johnstown *Democrat*. The plan was to have a paper to compare with the *Springfield Republican,* to develop the radical side of the Democratic party. During the early '90s, he had brought Louis Post from New York to Cleveland, it will be recalled, to carry on with newspaper work when the *Standard* of New York was discontinued.

After George's death Johnson sent Post on to Chicago, to undertake a major effort. This was *The Public,* a liberal weekly which lasted fifteen years. Among many whom Mr. Post names, Jane Addams, Ben B. Lindsay, Lincoln Steffens, Professor Edward Bemis, and Jerry Simpson warmly supported the journal, and some of them contributed articles. *The Public* criticized the Roosevelt administration severely. Though Post objected to William Jennings Bryan's ideas on the trust problem, *The Public* and Bryan's own paper, *The Commoner*, were friendly; and Bryan once contributed to *The Public* an appreciation of Henry George. Though the honor of having been the most brilliant general and literary magazine of Georgist inclination should probably be withheld from *The Public*, in favor of Francis Neilson's short-lived *Freeman* of the 1920s, *The Public* deserves credit for having been a substantial journal of opinion. It belonged to the political and moral traditions of Georgism, more than to the fiscal one. The single tax has been served, during the twentieth century, by a dozen or so ephemeral papers.

In his home city, Johnson personally resumed the burden of practical politics, four years after Henry George laid it down. In 1901 the Democratic ex-congressman became mayor of Cleveland; and, three times re-elected, he held that office for eight years while Washington was dominated by Republicans. Johnson used the methods of a democratic reformer, one who on George's pattern would help the people to help themselves. He conducted public meetings in a huge circus tent; he encouraged all manner and kind of persons to speak and won a reputation for being a scrupulous presiding officer. As victor at the polls he had to go beyond George's old role of political educator, however, and become a people's administrator. For this he had great talent. Newton Baker's judgment, reinforced by that of Lincoln Steffens, that Tom Johnson should be ranked as 'the outstanding municipal executive so far produced in United States history,' and that he made Cleveland 'the best governed city in America,' is probably still a true judgment today, over two decades after it was written.

On the side of policy, much of Johnson's effort as mayor was concentrated on establishing in Cleveland a municipally owned transportation system which would render free services to the working community. Fighting Mark Hanna on this issue, Mayor Johnson did not win the battle, nor did he lose altogether. He believed in an idea George had advanced in his own mayoralty campaign of 1886, that a city's growth, like a building made higher, is justified only when size increases efficiency and service. As a tall building includes elevators in its free services, George had argued, so a large city should supply, through a charge to be made against land values, free transportation to laborers. At the end of his campaign, Johnson did win a reduction to a three-cent fare. Though the public utility remained privately owned, the city had heard a remarkable discussion of the reasons for the public ownership of monopolies created by technology, and it had gained cheap transportation.

As for land-value taxation, Johnson made little progress earlier than his last term in office. At that time he succeeded in having a young and dedicated colleague, Frederic C. Howe, elected to the city's tax commission. That body, first conferring with Lawson Purdy, installed the system of separate assessment; and, a little later, a new change in procedure, which placed high assessments on lands and low assessments on buildings, brought about a practical advance toward Georgist tax policy. 'It confirmed my belief,' confesses Howe, the reformer, 'in the results that would follow the taxation of land values and the exemption of improvements from taxation.'

When Tom Johnson retired from office in 1909, not long before his death, his combined record as congressman and mayor made him the American who had gone farther than anyone else to advance into practical politics all three of George's main economic proposals. His advocacy of free trade, in Congress and in Democratic conventions, and before the people; his campaign for municipally owned, free utilities; and the achievement of land-value taxation, however limited, in Cleveland, brought Georgism nearer to being established in the statute books than Henry George himself had managed in New York or California.

-3-

By 1909 signs were increasing that Georgist efforts of the twentieth century would not be as isolated, and not as unsympathetic with main currents of politics, as they had been a few years earlier. As in George's own day, encouragement came from across the ocean. Notably in 1906 and after, the single tax and land nationalization were taken up once more in serious English journals; and the newly victorious Liberal party, whose leaders, Campbell-Bannerman, Asquith, and Lloyd George derived many of their ideas from the Radicalism of Gladstone's day, was more than favorable to Georgism. The famous Lloyd George budget, the taxation and social-reform features of which led to Britain's constitutional crisis of 1909–10, contained substantial influence from the ideas of the American George. Tom Johnson and Louis Post went to England, quite in Henry George style, to do what they could to help in the fight and to share in the celebrations of victory.

One of the achievements of Johnson's years as mayor had been the building of a team of younger associates. Councilman Frederic C. Howe and Newton D. Baker, who would become mayor of Cleveland in 1912, both of them lawyers, were the two most important members. But Brand Whitlock, whom we encountered during the '90s in Chicago, served, after 1905, first as right-hand man, then as successor, of Mayor 'Golden Rule' Jones of Toledo; and he too belonged to the group. Recollections weave around political discussions which were held in Tom Johnson's mansion, and which Clarence Darrow and Lincoln Steffens and other liberals sometimes attended. Howe tells us of the mayor's capacity to transmit to his younger associates the ideas that impelled his own reformism. Johnson, he says, 'had talked every phase of his philosophy through' with Henry George himself, and he had its 'deeper social significances at his fingertips . . . He was not a sectarian . . . His mind was a garden rather than a safe-deposit box.'

The Ohio group included several writing members. Brand Whitlock had produced a novel of political realism before he entered city politics. But Frederic Howe's books of 1905 and 1910, *The City the Hope of Democracy* and *Privilege and Democracy in America*, which are the best of all books that have developed the Georgist critique since George, were almost certainly indebted to the reform group in which he shared. A brief quotation from *Privilege and Democracy in America* will be the best indication of the continuity. 'Private land ownership is now complete,' wrote Howe. 'Those who come after us must come as trespassers . . . The railway question is at bottom a land question . . . Two hundred thousand men from the workers of the metropolis must work for ten long years, ten hours a day, and three hundred days every year to pay the annual incomes of the few thousand men who own the land underlying the city . . . It is the unskilled laborer who suffers most . . . He does not organize . . . The agricultural worker falls in the same class . . . The same is true of the salaried and professional classes.'

The year 1909 would have been a natural time for the disintegration, or at least the withering, of the Ohio group. But just when Tom Johnson quit as mayor, a gift of money from Joseph Fels, of Cincinnati, created new work for him and his associates. In a way a latter-day Francis Shaw, Mr. Fels set up a commission and assigned to the members all responsibility for distributing the money. Johnson himself became the Fels Fund's first treasurer; Daniel C. Kiefer of Cincinnati was president; and Frederic Howe and Lincoln Steffens were members of the board. The assignment was exciting, according to Steffens, who noted that the immediate problem was to spend $50,000 a year 'so that radical economic reforms of the system would result.' Though this same commissioner felt obliged to explain to his colleagues, who seemed not to understand the motives of the creative artist very well, that offering a large prize would not be a good way to secure the writing of a social-protest novel, he lacked no sympathy for the spirit of the undertaking. 'When they are thoughtful as they are today,' Steffens wrote to Warren W. Bailey, 'the real artists are likely to be propagandists or muckrakers.'

Thus, at the point of the Fels Fund, more distinctly than earlier the Georgist impulse entered the stream of Progressivism. By now, that movement had become a broad intellectual and moral current, which included members of both parties, and which extended itself beyond the limits of any political party. To be sure the fund supported the *Single Tax Review,* which represented the narrower Georgism. But it also underwrote translations of *Progress and Poverty* into Swedish and Bulgarian, Yiddish and Chinese, and assisted the distribution of Henry George works at home; and it helped *The Public* of Chicago.

The fund contributed to political protest in addition. Money was sent to Rhode Island, where George's old admirer, Dr. Garvin, was governor. The largest contributions were sent to Oregon, because a vote of 1908 had indicated a sizable single-tax minority. W. S. U'Ren, the reform leader in that state, believed in working for political reforms, direct legislation especially, as a necessary first step to deeper, Georgist, legislation. On that basis three subsidized campaigns were fought, in 1910, 1912, and 1914; and the results were pretty crushing. Yet, although Mr. U'Ren suffered remorse that he and his associates had been too cautious and wished they had worked for 'the full Single Tax philosophy,' he did derive satisfaction from thinking that the campaigns had saved Oregon from a complete political reaction.

Before the presidential election of 1912, at least a few Republican conservationists awoke to Georgist theories. The star case, here, is Congressman William Kent of California, who gave Muir Woods to the United States as a national park. Never a single-taxer but a reader of George and a sympathizer, he wrote the following to Louis Post, as early as 1909, when he sent his check for *The Public*. 'Inasmuch as my fear and hatred of Wall Street and its affiliated highways in other cities has driven me to seek investment in land and products of the soil, I have been brought to do a lot of thinking about this land-owning privilege which seems to me as absurd and as unjust as a privilege can be. For the sins in which I am compelled to indulge I am endeavoring to make reparation in terms of land, and hope that others will see the point and do likewise until such time as the privilege is abolished.' A year later, when he was about to be candidate for the house, as independent Republican, Mr. Kent crossed party lines to tell Louis Post that Gifford Pinchot — Roosevelt's appointee as chief forester, who had just been ousted by President Taft — had sought advice about building a program 'that would stand for human welfare.' Bowing himself out, the Westerner offered the opinion that 'the time is not ripe for a radical assault on the land-owning privilege, which I have come to believe takes up more of the result of human invention and human cooperation than any other privilege.' But in case Mr. Post might judge action to be possible, Kent proposed that he frame a platform and send it to Pinchot, as the person 'in a position to do more good in this country than any other man.'

During the next few years, Congressman Kent's own 'lot of thinking' led him to prefer an inheritance tax to land-value taxation, and ultimately to prefer a partial nationalization of land. Especially during the session of 1915, he worked for a system of leasing the grazing lands of the domain; and he drew his ideas together in an article for the *American Economic Review*. 'In my philosophy,' he told a friend, 'I hold that the land of the nation ought not to be in the hands of those who will not use it productively — ought not to be held by those who selfishly preclude others from the enjoyment of a privilege which ought to be national . . . It may have been unfortunate for the cause that I, a radical in the matter of land tenure, should have been attacked at once as a beef baron, as a tool of the beef trust, and as a public land thief.'

The colorful and reform-minded Californian who wrote these words, and who, very much a free-trader, was later appointed by President Wilson to the United States Tariff Commission, of course represented neither the center of Georgism nor the center of his old political party. But Kent did represent with eloquence the cross-connecting of ideas, the conscience and will to act, which were the best of the Progressive movement and a true part of the Georgist one.

—4—

Among the three great Progressive leaders, La Follette, Roosevelt, and Wilson, who gave the election of 1912 its character as a turning point in national history, there seems to have been lacking any consciousness of obligation to the ideas of Henry George. In *La Follette's Autobiography* the one acknowledgment of *Progress and Poverty* is the terse sentence: 'I read the book.' More than this we learn only that he had friends who remember his saying that he really avoided *Progress and Poverty* for fear of falling under a spell.

Though, of the three leaders, the Bull Mooser would have been the last to borrow doctrines from his rival of 1886, we do have a story of his own platform building, which resembles the correspondence between William Kent and Louis Post. At midsummer, 1912, the Reverend Heber Newton, whom Henry George had judged to be a soft reformer, approached Theodore Roosevelt from a Georgist angle of thought. 'I am sure you recognize, with all reformers who have the gift of vision,' wrote the clergyman to the ex-President, 'the fundamental nature of the land question in a reconstructed commonwealth . . . The thin edge of the wedge in this case seems to be a measure providing that all mineral resources to be discovered on and after a given date in the future should be held by the State for the people at large . . . the profits to create an educational fund for the State . . . It would inevitably lead to further applications of the general principle.' The fact that such a policy would be for the states to execute, rather than the nation, would not prevent using it for the Progressive platform, Mr. Newton urged.

Roosevelt agreed completely. 'I am absolutely in sympathy with you on your proposition about the mineral lands,' he replied at once, 'and I shall forward your letter to Dean Kirchwey and ask if he cannot put in the plank substantially as you recommend it.' Heber Newton's proposal seems possibly to represent the origin of the Progressive party plank of 1912, which called for retaining in public ownership all domain lands that had water, forest, oil, coal, or other mineral resources.

The bearing of Georgist ideas on the Democratic campaign and victory of 1912, and on the administration that followed, is a somewhat complex problem, and one to be posed rather than solved in this book. The plainest fact is a negative one. No more than La Follette and Roosevelt did Woodrow Wilson owe conscious debts for ideas to *Progress and Poverty*, or to any of Henry George's writings. Historian and political scientist, the academician president did have a set of economic ideas which combined *laisser faire* and control; but he had derived them from English sources principally, and apparently not at all from the American ideologue who had tried so hard to influence the Democratic party.

Yet Wilson's political history, if not his reading and thinking one, contains essential elements of Georgism. Up to 1910, when he resigned as president of Princeton, he had been a social and religious conservative, politically inactive. But his crucial two years in New Jersey politics, the one-term governorship which comprised his amazing short cut from academic life to the White House, took Wilson through Georgist terrain. The important man who more than any other guided this transition was George L. Record, a lawyer, politician, and reformer, a Republican at this stage of his life, and the leading Georgist in the state. Though at first disliking Woodrow Wilson, Mr. Record was challenged by his campaign to be governor. Before the campaign was far advanced, the two became friends, and Mr. Record rendered services of advice and counsel which compared with the famous services to be rendered Wilson by Louis Brandeis during the 1912 campaign. Among many acts which helped make a political progressive of Wilson, Mr. Record drafted the utilities control bill which became one of Wilson's triumphs in Trenton. Meanwhile, from across the continent, William U'Ren tutored the candidate, as Mr. Record did also, in the new ideas and practices of direct democracy. A primary law was the principal political reform of the Wilson administration in New Jersey; and in this direction the governor was particularly guided by Georgists.

The reader may already have collected in his mind several loyal believers in Henry George's ideas, whom Woodrow Wilson called to high place in Washington. From recent connections, the new President appointed his idealistic and personable secretary, Joseph Tumulty, who was a younger member of the New Jersey Georgist group. The President's alter ego, Colonel Edward House of Texas, exhibited in his novel, *Philip Dru, Administrator,* a diluted Georgist social philosophy. At cabinet level, the new secretary of the interior, Franklin K. Lane of California, was the only Georgist before 1916; but in that year Newton Baker came on from Ohio to take office as secretary of war, as the nation's ordeal drew near. From the Middle West, Herbert Quick, Georgist mayor of Sioux City, was appointed to the Farm Loan Bureau. In a backward-looking mood, at the end of his conservationist-minded administration of the Department of Interior, Lane told a friend that he believed that Emerson, Henry George, and William James were a 'singular trio' in history, who in the future would be 're-garded not as literary men but as American social, spiritual, and economic philosophers'; and he thought also that William James, Theodore Roosevelt, and Henry George were 'the three greatest forces of the last thirty years.'

As for the old associates of Tom Johnson, besides Baker, Brand Whitlock was sent at once to Brussels, and Frederic Howe was made commissioner of immigration. He would be sent in due time to Paris on a semi-official assignment concerning the peace negotiations with the central powers. Louis Post became the assistant secretary of labor. Yet before Post accepted, Warren W. Bailey solicited Lane and Whitlock and others to urge him for the full secretaryship of that department. The effort failed, but Mr. Bailey was comforted to learn that the President expressly wanted Post because he was a Henry George man. 'Mr. Wilson thoroughly understands what Mr. Post represents,' Bailey informed Daniel Kiefer, still the Fels Fund head, 'and both he and Mr. Bryan

frankly recognize the importance of bringing the single-tax people
into closer touch with the administration.'

In 1913, as twenty years earlier, two or three Georgists entered
the House of Representatives. Warren W. Bailey of Pennsylvania
was one; and Henry George, Jr., still of New York, was another.
Since 1897 he had edited his father's writings and written the
biography so often drawn on for this book; and, more or less as his
father's successor, he had traveled for the movement and had even
visited Tolstoy. He had pursued his career as journalist and had
written a book of social criticism, *The Menace of Privilege,* and a
third-rate novel which may have been inspired by his father's life.
These new members, and Congressman William Kent also, voted
with the majority, of course, on the Underwood low tariff of 1913,
the first great reduction of rates since before the Civil War.

Apparently the one time President Wilson was presented with
Georgist reform proposals in a large way was in 1919, long after
his own program of domestic reform had been enacted and put into
practice. The President sent a message to the Democrats of New
Jersey, which George L. Record read as an opportunity to render
a reformer's suggestions. He proposed that the President recommend to Congress a policy of government ownership of all
monopolies of federal size and interest. He specified railroads,
pipelines, and resources owned by trusts. He urged federal legislation against land speculation and monopoly, a statutory limitation
on the inheritance of great fortunes, and even income taxes.

Record spoke with a bluntness, and with an assumption of
mutual understanding such as Henry George could never have
used in addressing President Cleveland. 'In my judgment nothing
that you are proposing in the League of Nations idea, will give you
a place in history as a great man, because at the end of your term
you will have rendered no great and lasting service that will lift
you above the average of our Presidents, and you have ignored
the great issue which is slowly coming to the front, the question of
economic democracy, abolition of privilege, and securing to men
the full fruits of their labor or service.'

Like George, but not much like Woodrow Wilson, Record saw in
economics the source of political conditions, domestic and international alike, and he drew his morals in those terms. 'Wars are
caused by privilege . . . I do not criticize your going abroad . . .

But my point is that you ought not neglect the bigger domestic questions . . . You should become the real leader of the radical forces in America, and present to the country a constructive program of radical reform which shall be an alternative to the program presented by the socialists and the Bolsheviki, and then fight for it . . . You could so educate the public that you could force this radical program into the platform of the Democratic party.'

Before this letter was written, President Wilson had told Tumulty that the advanced opinions he held about land and government ownership might be right after all; and it is not unlikely that the secretary had hinted to Record that the time was ripe to urge economic reform. At any rate Tumulty himself wrote an endorsement, and speaking 'as a Democrat,' he pleaded, in phrases reminiscent of Henry George's speeches half a century earlier, for a 'realignment of parties' and 'a fight between the Federalist and anti-Federalist, between the Whig and Tory' once more.

Wilson was in the midst of peacemaking when the recommendations reached him, and already the pressures were gathering which would break him within half a year. He acknowledged Record's letter in a friendly way, but he said nothing to indicate what even his flash judgment was on the merits of the plea his Georgist colleagues had made. He seems never to have had another occasion to speak. As 1919 advanced, his preoccupation with the Treaty of Versailles, and then his illness, turned him from domestic reform for the last year of his administration and for the short remainder of his life.

The men and influences considered in this section make clear that, in larger part than has often been noticed, the idealism of the administration of Woodrow Wilson was Henry George idealism renewed.

−5−

Returning to the terms with which the present discussion opened, the Georgism that came to Washington in 1913 was moral and intellectual, rather than political; and of course it was not fiscal Georgism.

Political Georgism, in the sense of leaders, organizations, and campaigns dedicated to Georgist ends, we may count as having passed from the scene when Tom Johnson's career as mayor closed.

Perhaps Newton Baker's administration of Cleveland should be thought of as a residue; and certainly the election to Congress of Henry George, Jr., and Warren W. Bailey should be considered that way. We do not need to disregard the little enclaves of Georgist communities, such as Fairhope, Alabama, which have been established in this century; nor to forget such events of the early '20s as the introduction of several Georgist bills in Congress and the serious effort, aided by John R. Commons, to introduce a 'farmers' single tax' in Wisconsin. Such programs, however, were not inclusive enough, or such successes and failures of the vote significant enough, to fit the pattern of Henry George's campaigns in New York City, or Tom Johnson's campaigns in Cleveland. The presidential election of 1912 had assimilated political Georgism in the larger progressive movement. The epitaph was composed on ambassadorial stationery and addressed to Newton Baker when Brand Whitlock learned, in June 1920, that he was wanted to run for President on a single-tax ticket, with Carrie Chapman Catt as running mate. 'I may be a single-taxer, but I am not a damn fool.'

After the war, when America's political climate shifted violently, nearly every change was adverse to Georgist growth of any kind. Georgists in the government at the end of the Wilson administration were embittered by the anti-liberal reaction, as Louis Post and Frederic Howe most eloquently testified. Their group was close to the retirement age. They had no role in the Republican victories of the '20s. And if any later Georgists had the opportunity to introduce ideas into the New Deal or Fair Deal, in a way that at all compared with the work of the introducers of the ideas of Veblen, Keynes, and even Henry C. Carey, they are indeed the forgotten men and ideas of those epochs of our history. Perhaps the one specific instance of Georgism, cropping out in the new policy of great nations in recent days, is the dilute variety that the British Labour government wrote into its Town and Country Planning Act of 1947.

The quiet influence of Henry George, then, during the agony and revolution of the last four decades, is to be discovered on two levels. On the visible surface of affairs is the persevering work of the fiscal Georgists, who win occasional reforms in city tax policy. Very close to that effort, yet different, is the continuing task of the propagation of ideas, in the line which Henry George and Francis

Shaw began in 1882. The work done in America centers in New York, where the Schalkenbach Foundation supplies subsidies, and where George's books and speeches are distributed and journals issued year after year. To the old habit of giving and selling Henry George's writings, the Henry George schools, in several cities, have added free instruction in *Progress and Poverty* and a number of other writings. The overseas work carries on in London, in the organization and journal of the International League for Land Value Taxation and Free Trade. If the present-day life of intellectual Georgism seems anemic by the standards of the last century, it is nonetheless wonderfully persistent; and we may suppose that no book except the Bible has been so widely and devotedly distributed as *Progress and Poverty* has been.

The deeper level of Henry George's influence on the modern world is the one described in the earlier part of this book but so often forgotten to be his. The participation of free governments in the processes of social justice is now accepted everywhere as policy to be maintained. A desire for world-wide free trade recurs in our day; and many believe that a greater equality among the peoples of the earth, of access to its resources, would increase mankind's hope for mankind. For the United States and the United Kingdom, for Australia and New Zealand, for many in Norway and Denmark, for early liberals in Russia, and for others around the world, Henry George has been the incomparable prophet of these three goals.

NOTES ON THE SOURCES

A DUAL DEFENSE OF THE TEXT

The footnotes above are few in number, a tiny fraction of those first put in the text as it was written. In most cases they have been inserted at points that invite immediate and specific reinforcement. In some cases, especially in Chapter x, citations have been placed where they will help a reader who may want to find the way from this book to important passages in George's writings.

The footnotes represent the first tactic in defending the argument. For the deeper strategy of documentation, I rely on the bibliographical notes which follow. First there is a description of those source materials which I have used from beginning to end. Thereafter, in subdivisions which correspond to the twenty chapters of text, I present the other documents which have bearing. I mention the more important rare materials, either at the point where they are first drawn on, or where they are first drawn on extensively.

This defense in depth gives up as needless the conventional Maginot Line of protective scholarship. Doubtless the best reason for abandoning footnotes for every quotation and for a great many facts is the reason of practicality which Darwin offered in the introduction to his most famous work of scientific controversy: 'I cannot here give references and authorities for my several statements; and I must trust to the reader reposing some confidence in my accuracy.' Any who are not satisfied with this are informed that I retain in my own possession a heavily footnoted typescript.

SOURCES USED THROUGHOUT

The principal sources of this biography are Henry George's own writings. The unpublished materials are: his letters, his diaries and memoranda, and drafts or notes for some of his lectures. The printed writings are: his newspaper editorials and reports; his magazine articles and letters to editors; his major lectures and addresses; and his eight books.

HENRY GEORGE COLLECTION, NEW YORK PUBLIC LIBRARY

Most of the Henry George manuscripts known to exist, a large number of his newspaper and magazine writings, all his books in a large collection of editions and translations, and his own and his family's collection of what was contemporaneously written about him are deposited in the New York Public Library. The great amount of these materials was given, as the Henry George Collection, by Mrs. Anna George de Mille, about 1925; and other correspondence, much of it between Henry George and his wife, was added after Mrs. de Mille's death in 1947 by her daughter Agnes de Mille.

In 1926 the library published *Henry George and the Single Tax, A Catalogue of the Collection in the New York Public Library*, by Rollin A. Sawyer, chief of the Economics Division. This very full bibliography gives not only a catalogue of the original de Mille gift, but it lists book and magazine writings by and about Henry George, and about the single tax, which are to be found in the general collections of the library. The Sawyer *Catalogue* is useful in any library with rich collections in the field. There is no other Henry George bibliography worthy of the name.

The manuscript part of the Henry George Collection, which is deposited in the Manuscript Division of the library, divides into two approximately equal parts. One of these consists of Henry George's correspondence, I think about 2500 pieces. About one-third of the lot concerns 1854–80, the correspondence of the period of the present Part One; and two-thirds concern Part Two. But the earlier letters, as the product of the years when George was in private life, are more revealing of the man and his ideas than those written later. The letters after 1880 are more often from George's correspondents than to them, and are frequently humdrum stuff.

Of the second major part of the manuscript collection, about one-third consists of letters of other members of the George family. A considerable series is the correspondence of Henry George, Jr., about editing his father's works and gathering the data for his biography. There are also sizable batches of Henry George's lecture notes and drafts, book manuscripts, and miscellaneous memoranda and memorabilia, which include photographs. The one greatly disappointing part of the collection is the series of about thirty diaries. After the sea journals of his youth, George commonly neglected diary keeping, or else reduced his diaries to engagement books.

The printed materials in the Henry George Collection are deposited in special cases in the Economics Division of the library. They include newspaper files of high biographical importance: George's San Francisco *Daily Evening Post* for 4 December 1871 through 21 October 1873; and the other San Francisco papers he owned, the *Morning Ledger* for 20 August through 8 November 1875, and the weekly *State* for 5 April through 14 June 1879; and George's weekly New York *Standard* for 8 January 1887 through 31 August 1892. Except for the file of the *Post*, which covers only the first half of the period of George's proprietor-editorship, these are complete files. But I have used the complete file of the *Post* in the Bancroft Library of the University of California in Berkeley, and the complete file of the *Standard* in the Johns Hopkins Library; and I have actually handled only fractions of the newspaper part of the Henry George Collection.

A large proportion of the other printed materials of the Henry George Collection is made up of 29 volumes of Henry George Scrapbooks. The most valuable parts of the thousands of clippings they contain are such sequences as the following: George's letters of 1882 to the *Irish World*, which are not fully available elsewhere; certain series of his California editorials of the 1860s, before he became a newspaper proprietor; and collections of reviews of his books, especially *Progress and Poverty,* including notices from distant and minor papers which could hardly be recovered in any other way. But many hundreds of clippings, from the years of George's lecture travels, seem to represent nothing better than the industry of clipping services in turning up brief reports in provincial papers; and, partly because many items are undated or unlocated or both, they are of little value to history. Apparently George himself gathered the earlier and more valuable scrapbooks. I have used them; but I have preferred to study George's editorials in the newspaper files themselves, and even to read the reviews in the original locations, whenever practicable.

The remainder of the Henry George Collection is a miscellany of books by him, of books he owned, and of photographs and other memorabilia.

THE WORKS OF HENRY GEORGE

Immediately following George's death, Henry George, Jr., set about collecting his father's works and writing a substantial biography. The results were published in ten volumes, between 1906 and 1911, as *The Complete Works of Henry George,* Fels Fund, library edition (Garden City, N.Y.). The first eight volumes are Henry George's own. His longer books require entire volumes in this edition; the shorter ones are bound with a selection of his principal addresses. In the present biography, all Henry George's writings cited are from this edition unless other editions are indicated. Problems of text are very minor ones in Henry George studies, but there is a special interest in the original California editions of his two first books, which he wrote in that state.

BIOGRAPHIES AND GENERAL TREATMENTS

The Life of Henry George by Henry George, Jr., which was first published by itself, in New York, 1900, comes nearer to actually belonging as two volumes in *The Complete Works of Henry George,* as it was later issued, than would logically seem likely. Many letters of Henry George are quoted at length, and so are passages from early diaries and later speeches and writings. This *Life* is a source book in a second sense, also. As Henry George, Jr., was the first child of his parents' youthful marriage, and as he was intimately associated with his father's work from his middle teens, his biography is in great degree a memoir; and it is always a close if somewhat dull mirror of his father's values and ideas.

There is more life but less event in the second biography of Henry George, which was also written by one of his children. This is Anna George de Mille's *Henry George, Citizen of the World,* edited by Don C. Shoemaker, brightened by an introduction by Agnes de Mille, and published at Chapel Hill in 1950. Mrs. de Mille had a keen mind to match her dedication to her father's cause, and there is no derogation in saying that hers is a feminine account. As she was hardly out of her teens when her father died, her book is less a memoir than her brother's is. It gives more attention to their mother, and more to Henry George as a family man, than anything else in print.

I have drawn on both these family biographies; and the more extensively, of course, from the earlier book.

Of the hundreds of writings about Henry George, from outside the family, it is strange that there are only two which endeavor to interpret the man in any large way. Albert Jay Nock's *Henry George, an Essay* (New York, 1931) is a brilliant appreciation of character and mind; and George R. Geiger's *Philoso-*

phy of Henry George (New York, 1933) is an able study by a philosopher of generally pragmatic persuasion. Long ago I read both books with admiration, and owe them gratitude, especially for confirming my early judgment that George deserves more serious attention from scholarship than he has often received. But as I wanted to hew my own road, I have referred to those books infrequently in recent years.

SYMBOLS FOR THE MAJOR SOURCES

In the notes which follow I use symbols for the main sources just described, and symbols for the library locations of other major collections. They are:

HGC: manuscript in the Henry George Collection, New York Public Library.

NYPL: item in the printed part of the Henry George Collection, in that library.

Complete Works: item printed in *The Complete Works of Henry George,* in the volume indicated.

George, Jr.: Henry George, Jr., *Life of Henry George.*

de Mille: Anna George de Mille, *Henry George, Citizen of the World.*

LC: manuscript in Library of Congress.

UCBL: manuscript or rare printed item in Bancroft Library, University of California, Berkeley.

HL: manuscript or rare printed item in Huntington Library, San Marino, California.

JHU: item in the Hutzler Collection, Johns Hopkins University Library.

I. A BOY FROM A CHRISTIAN HOME, 1839–1855

PHILADELPHIA FAMILY AND HOME. Here and throughout the book I draw many of the particulars of family background from George, Jr., and de Mille. Letters to HG, after his early departures of the 1850s from home, also contain information, for instance about the legacy, in a letter from Caroline George, 3 March 1858, HGC.

FINANCIAL CONDITION OF THE GEORGES. Mr. George reviewed his affairs in a letter to HG, 19 July 1858, HGC. The impression of an $1100 salary is confirmed in a letter to HG from his mother, 2 February 1858; and a letter from Jane George (1858?) mentions $3000 as the value of the house next to theirs. The comparison of R. S. H. George's income with teachers' salaries is made from information generously supplied by Mr. William M. Duncan, from the minutes of the Controllers of Public Schools, First District of Pennsylvania, 9 March 1852, 30 June 1853; and from other information, supplied by Mr. Greville Haslam, from the records of the Episcopal Academy. The comparison with clergymen's incomes is from letters of this period, HGC, and from Franklin S. Edmonds, *History of St. Matthew's Church, Francisville, Philadelphia* (Philadelphia, 1925), 12, 81, 100. On price levels during HG's childhood, see Jesse M. Cutts, 'One Hundred and Thirty-Four Years of Wholesale Prices,' *Monthly Labor Review,* 41:250.

ST. PAUL'S CHURCH AND THE GEORGES. Edmonds' *History of St. Matthew's Church* contains 'Reminiscences of old St. Paul's' by the Rev. George A. Latimer, Mrs. George's nephew, with a mention of R. S. H. George and his Sunday School work, p. 60. Morris Stanley Barratt, *Outline of the History of old St. Paul's Church, Philadelphia, Pennsylvania* (Philadelphia, 1917), has historical background, and mentions the Latimers. See also Henrietta M. Larson, *Jay Cooke, Private Banker* (Cambridge, 1936), 57, 85. On Dr. Newton, see William H. Newton, *Yesterday with the Fathers* (New York, 1910), 36–7. Dr. Newton's institutional radicalism is mentioned in a discussion of a book he wrote, in E. Clowes Chorley, *Men and Movements in the American Episcopal Church* (New York, 1946), 69–70, 89, 92–3. Though the diocesan records in Philadelphia do not list the confirmations at St. Paul's in HG's day, I feel that the family's fears for his salvation adequately support my point that he was not confirmed there. Evidence of their anxiety appears in letters to HG from his parents, 18 March, 3 April, 3 May 1858, and from Caroline George, 18 January 1858; and HG's attitudes toward Dr. Newton are recorded in a memorandum, n.d., and a letter to Caroline George, 4 January 1859; all HGC. HG's editorial appreciation of Episcopalianism is in SF *Post*, 12 May 1873.

EDUCATION OF HENRY GEORGE. Background materials in James P. Wickersham, *A History of Education in Pennsylvania* (Lancaster, 1886), 98–9, 289, and *passim*. For the data on the curriculum of the Episcopal Academy, and on fees charged, I am indebted to Mr. Haslam, who took them from the academy's records. HG's score on entering the public high school was taken from the school's records, by Mr. Duncan. The school's qualities, in this period, are described in Franklin S. Edmonds, *History of Central High School, Philadelphia* (Philadelphia, 1902), 61, 63–5, 99–100, 102, 158–9.

II. INDEPENDENCE BY SEA, 1855–1857

DECISION TO GO TO SEA. Concerning the decision to go and the departure, there is, over and above contemporary materials quoted in George, Jr., a number of family letters, HGC. Those with the following dates are drawn on: 27 February, 3 April, 5 April, 9 May, 31 May, 7 June 1855, 11 December 1861. Florence Curry's poem is dated 1 April 1855. There is also Captain Miller's Ms. account of the Voyage of the Hindoo. The writer indicates that he had a close friendship with relatives and friends of the Georges; and this corresponds with Caroline George's idea that he was in love with one of the Latimer girls (letter to HG, 18 July 1859).

INDIA VOYAGE. HG's Sea Journal is quoted in different drafts, and the drafts are described, in George, Jr., 24–39, and in de Mille, 'Henry George: Childhood and Early Youth,' *American Journal of Economics and Sociology*, 1:292–302 (April 1942). I have used the originals, as well as these quotations. His children's associating the Hobson's Bay episode with George's later reformism is to be found in George, Jr., 32, and de Mille, 12–13. The letters here drawn on, which HG received or sent in Calcutta, are dated as follows: 4 April, 4 May, 10 May, 31 May, 1 June, 4 June, 7 June 1855; and 12 December 1855, 28 January, 4 February, 5 February 1856; HGC. Captain Miller's letter of parting advice is dated 25 July 1856, HGC.

BETWEEN VOYAGES IN PHILADELPHIA. This passage is largely based on unprinted correspondence, 1857, between HG and the Currys, as they encouraged the move to the West. The following letters are important: HG to Mrs. Rebecca D. Curry, 3 April, 1 June; Mrs. Curry to HG, 19 April; HG to Emma Curry, 16

March, 29 June; Emma Curry to HG, 19 April, 19 May; Florence Curry to HG, 17 August. Tension over religion at home is suggested in the Sea Journal, 27 July 1856; and HG's financial anxieties appear, besides in the letters to the Currys, in diary entries of 12, 14, 15, 20 June, 9 July 1857, and in a draft of a letter not sent to B. F. Ely, 30 September 1857, all HGC. The boyish activities of the Lawrence Society are represented by the essays, 'Mormonism,' 23 June 1857, and 'Composition: The Poetry of Life,' 1857. They are somewhat described in letters, HG to B. F. Ely, 30 September 1857; Jo Jeffreys to HG, 4 January 1858; Charles Walton to HG, 29 July 1863, HGC.

WESTWARD Ho! HG's efforts to win the *Shubrick* appointment are represented or described in letters he wrote, during the fall of 1857, HGC: to Rep. T. B. Florence, 5 October; to his uncle, Thomas Latimer, 10 October; to Captain Thornton A. Jenkins, Secretary of the Light House Bureau, 23 November 1857. The phrenological examination is printed in George, Jr., 53–5; in quoting it I have used the ellipsis to indicate breaks in the thought, which are indicated by paragraphing in the full text, as well as breaks in the quoting.

III. NEW CALIFORNIAN: IMMIGRANT AND WAGE EARNER, 1858–1861

THE VOYAGE OF THE SHUBRICK. About the *Shubrick* and HG's appointment as a steward, present Lighthouse Service records are not as full as those which Henry George, Jr., investigated in 1899 and incorporated in his account, pp. 56–7. But Lyle J. Holverstott, Chief of the Treasury Section, National Archives, who generously searched the remaining records, discovered that two appointments as steward were contemplated, one for a 'middle-aged man' at $40 per month, and one as a cabin steward at $25. Possibly HG expected the higher position, but was given the lower. His own comment is in a letter of 6 January 1858, HGC, printed in part in George, Jr., 58. The hurricane is reported in the Philadelphia *Evening Journal*, 30 January 1858; and the tempest in the George home in letters to HG from Jo Jeffreys and Charles Walton, 1 and 16 February 1858, HGC. HG reported the stops in St. Thomas and at Rio, the yellow fever, and the death of Martin in letters to Walton (18 February, not sent), and to his parents, 6 January and n.d., HGC; see George, Jr., 58. 'Dust to Dust' was written for the *Philadelphia Saturday Night*, his friend Ned Wallazz's little paper; it was republished in the San Francisco *Californian*, 14 July 1866; and all except five paragraphs are reproduced in George, Jr., 63–7. The earlier story referred to in the text, which also derived from *Shubrick* experiences, is 'The Boatswain's Story,' *Californian*, 5 August 1865; about it, see Franklin Walker, *San Francisco's Literary Frontier* (New York, 1939), 200. HG's impressions of the Strait of Magellan are recorded in the biographical 'Meeker Notes,' clipping from the Harrisburg *Patriot* (?), 18 November 1897, HG Scrapbook 29, NYPL.

SAN FRANCISCO: ARRIVAL AND TEMPORARY DEPARTURE. HG's arrival in California, the factors in his decision making, and his departure, 1858, are described in his correspondence. For letters printed in part, see George, Jr., 70–71, 75–7. The following unprinted letters, HGC, are drawn on: to HG from his parents, 1 January, 3 April, 2, 4 August; from members of the Curry family, 22 May; from Jeffreys, 31 July. On California's depression and the call of the Frazer River: Rodman W. Paul, *California Gold: The Beginning of Mining in the*

Far West (Cambridge, 1947), 177–8; John S. Hittell, *A History of San Francisco and Incidentally of the State of California* (San Francisco, 1878), 277. The contemporary comments cited are: Henry Haight to F. M. Haight, 6 April 1857, Haight Collection, HL; and the *Hesperian*, 1:57 (15 June 1858).

HARD TIMES IN BRITISH COLUMBIA AND CALIFORNIA. HG's adventure into the Pacific Northwest appears mainly in his correspondence of late 1858. See George, Jr., 76–8, 80. Other letters with important data are the one from Jeffreys, 1 November, and one to Caroline George, 10 October, HGC. HG recollected the miner's economics, 4 February 1890, when he made an address in San Francisco. See George, Jr., 80; and Complete Works, VIII, 297–321. He told the story more fully in a Chicago address, 25 August 1893, HGC. The temporary break with James George, the tapering-off with the Currys, and the death of Jeffreys are matters which appear in letters between HG and members of his family and friends, 21 September 1858–1 August 1859, HGC. On 23 February 1864, Caroline George wrote HG (HGC) what seems to have been his final word about the Currys: Mrs. Curry and Emma had died, and Florence was happily married. Jeffrey's advice to HG is contained in letters of 19 May 1858 and 3 February 1859, HGC, the latter quoted in George, Jr., 87–8. HG's stopgap jobs and his unemployment, in San Francisco 1858–9, are accounted for in George, Jr., 83–4, 93; and comparable experiences appear in James J. Ayers, *Gold and Sunshine, Reminiscences of Early California* (Boston, 1922?), 167, and in Thaddeus S. Kenderdine, *A California Tramp and Later Footprints . . .* (Newtown, Pa., 1888), ch. XVI.

FINDING HIMSELF. HG's satisfaction in an opportunity to read again and his delight in living in San Francisco appear in letters to members of his family, 20 November 1859, 4 January, 18 April 1860, and in a reminiscence, 'The Noble View from Telegraph Hill,' Ms. *c.* 1870, HGC. What Cheer House is discussed in Joseph Weed, *California as It Is* (San Francisco, 1874), 144; and in articles in *Hutching's California Magazine* (San Francisco), 5:206–8, 294–5 (November 1860, January 1861). The literary papers, of the kind which hired HG, are discussed in Walker, *San Francisco's Literary Frontier*, especially chs. v–VII; and California's regionalism, especially in chs. I and XIII. The issue of the *California Home Journal* is that of 16 October 1859, HL. The family letters, HGC, which tell the story of HG's decision to remain awhile in California, and which report his conversion, were for the most part written in 1860.

IV. SUFFERING AND EXALTATION, 1861–1865

CALIFORNIA LOYALTIES AT THE OPENING OF THE CIVIL WAR. For the state's recent politics and votes, see Hubert Howe Bancroft, *History of California*, VI (Works, XXIII [1887]), 701–3; Ayers, *Gold and Sunshine*, 153–7, 180, 192–3; Edward S. Stanwood, *History of the Presidency* (Boston and New York, 1928), I, 276, 297. On loyalties and disloyalties which worried HG, see John J. Earle, 'The Sentiment of the People of California with Respect to the Civil War,' American Historical Association *Annual Report*, I, 127–9, 134, and *passim* (1908). Several family letters about the crisis are quoted in George, Jr., 97, 112.

ANXIETY AND LOVE. Concerning the San Francisco *Daily Evening Journal*, HG's hope and disappointment in 1861, I draw on copy, 11 June 1861, UCBL, and on letters between HG and his sisters, 10 April, 19 August, and November (?)

1861, HGC. Letters to HG from parents, aunt, two sisters, and one brother, 10 June–30 November 1861, HGC, describe the financial adversities of the family in Philadelphia. HG's 'Millennial Letter' to Jane George, 15 September 1861, HGC, is quoted at about three-quarter length in George, Jr., 116–18. Their children tell the story of HG's and Annie Fox's courtship and marriage (without mention of HG's boyhood fondness for Florence Curry), in George, Jr., 105–7, 122–7, and de Mille, chs. v–vi. Annie's retrospect is in a letter to HG, 3 December 1868; and other McCloskey family information in Sister Teresa to HG, 15 September 1865, HGC.

FIRST RESIDENCE IN SACRAMENTO. Annie George wrote as many of the letters as HG did, mostly to the Philadelphia family, which tell the story of their family affairs, 1862. They are in HGC; but passages are taken from quotations in George, Jr., as are certain letters from Philadelphia, pp. 128, 129, 131, 134. HG's projects and speculations appear in correspondence with his California friends, 1863 and 1864, HGC and George, Jr., 138. On politics in Sacramento, see George T. Clark, *Leland Stanford* (Stanford, 1931), ch. VI; and on journalism, contemporary statements by Paul Morrill of the *Union*, and E. A. Waite, Bowman Mss., Newspaper Matter, pp. 40–41, 81, 85–7, UCBL. Morrill is the proprietor quoted in criticism of the railroads. HG's comment on Watson is in his pamphlet, *The Press. Should It be Personal or Impersonal?* (Sacramento, 1876 or 1877).

ORDEAL IN SAN FRANCISCO. For the depression background of HG's ordeal of 1864–5, see Hittell, *San Francisco*, 340, 346–7; and Ayers, *Gold and Sunshine*, 214. The Hinckley letter, 22 December 1864, is in the Hinckley Collection, HL. On the *American Flag*, see John J. Young, *Journalism in California* (San Francisco, 1915), 60; there is one issue of HG's period of working on the paper, 23 April 1864, UCBL. The Christmas diary is quoted in George, Jr., 146; and that biography, 148–9, and de Mille, 31n, 41, tell slightly varying stories of desperation at the time of Richard George's birth. HG's memoranda of new plans for life are printed in George, Jr., 150, 154; and in 'On the Profitable Employment of Time,' 156–8.

BEGINNING AS A WRITER. I have discovered no file of the *Journal of Trades and Workmen*, but HG's first article is clipped in HG Scrapbook 25, NYPL, excerpted in George, Jr., 159; and the paper is discussed in Ira B. Cross, *A History of the Labor Movement in California*, University of California Publications in Economics, XIV (Berkeley, 1935), 37. California's interest in the occult, the vein to which HG shifted, is discussed in Walker, *San Francisco's Literary Frontier*, ch. VII. HG's 'Plea for the Supernatural' is in the *Californian*, 2:9 (8 April 1865). On San Francisco's reaction to Lincoln's death, see *Alta California*, 16 April 1865; Bancroft, *California*, VII, 311–14; Hittell, *San Francisco*, 351; George, Jr., 161. HG's 'Sic Semper Tyrannis' is clipped, n.d., in HG Scrapbooks 25–6, NYPL; though printed, I do not find it in the *Alta* files. But the *Alta's* reports of Lincoln mourning on 16, 17, 18, 19, and 20 April were probably all HG's writing; and there is no doubt about the editorial of 23 April. The filibustering projects are related in George, Jr., 166–7; and Professor Walker's comment is in *San Francisco's Literary Frontier*, 114–15.

V. SAN FRANCISCO EDITOR VERSUS CALIFORNIA IDEAS, 1865-1868

1. GEORGE'S WRITING AND THINKING IN SACRAMENTO. George, Jr., 168–72, tells the story and prints the documents quite fully, for late 1865 and early 1866. HG's retrospect of his early protectionism appears in his *Protection or Free Trade* (1885), Complete Works IV, 29–30. 'The Prayer of Kakonah' is in the *Californian*, 5:9 (28 July 1866); HG's 'Proletarian' articles, in the Sacramento *Union*, 13, 22 August, 29 September 1866; and the reports on the state fair I think I identify correctly as the articles signed 'Adios' in the San Francisco *Call*, 12–18 September 1866. See George, Jr., 171. Henry Watson of the *Union* wrote the recommendation for HG, 28 August 1866, HGC.

ON THE SAN FRANCISCO TIMES. HG's decision for San Francisco appears in a letter from A. A. Stickney, 15 August 1866 (HGC), and one to his father, 8 August 1866, George, Jr., 172. On McClatchy's claim to having assigned HG to editorial writing, ibid. 173, and Sacramento *Bee* editorial, 18 March 1899; on the role of Brooke, see his own article, 'Henry George in California,' *Century*, n.s., 57:549–50 (February 1899), and George, Jr., 174–5. On the SF *Times*, see Anna L. Marston, ed., *Records of a California Family, Journals and Letters of Lewis C. Gunn and Elizabeth Le Breton Gunn* (San Diego, 1928), 265–6; for what Wells stood for, see Fred B. Joyner, *David Ames Wells, Champion of Free Trade* (Cedar Rapids, 1939), 44–53. The comment on the *Times* from the side of the SF *Bulletin* is Loring Pickering's, in letters to his partner, G. K. Fitch, 7 February, 20, 28 March 1868, Fitch Collection, Box 16, UCBL. That of the Oakland *Transcript* is in the issue of 2 November 1869 and may have been written by HG.

2. ECONOMIC THOUGHT IN CALIFORNIA. The only work that seriously examines a part of this subject is the doctoral dissertation of Professor Claude W. Petty, of San Mateo Junior College, 'Gold Rush Intellectual: John S. Hittell' (accepted by the University of California, Berkeley, 1952). Mr. Petty let me see a draft, but the present chapter was written before then, and I took no borrowings earlier than those indicated below, in the note on ch. IX. In a general way Mr. Petty's findings and mine run parallel. In the present chapter I use again ideas that I put into an article, 'Henry George and the California Background of *Progress and Poverty*,' *California Historical Society Quarterly*, 24:97–115 (1945). Professor Paul S. Taylor's analysis of leading issues of social thought is to be found in his 'Foundations of California Rural Society,' ibid. 194–202. There are many illustrations of social thought in Walker, *San Francisco's Literary Frontier;* and Doris Bepler, 'Descriptive Catalogue of Western Historical Materials in California Periodicals, 1854–1890,' M.A. thesis, UCBL, is useful in the field.

PLANS AND VIEWS OF THE STATE. The moralizing estimates of the two ministers are: William Taylor, *California Life Illustrated* (New York, 1858), 277; and Horace Bushnell, *Characteristics and Prospects of California* (San Francisco, 1858), 13–21. Gadsden's southern notion is printed, from the Leidesdorff Papers, HL, in *Huntington Library Bulletin* no. 8 (October 1935), 173–5; and Taylor, loc. cit., gives a beautiful instance of southern development.

LAND PROBLEMS AND STATE DEVELOPMENT. The best historical introduction to California's land problems is Robert G. Cleland, *The Cattle on a Thousand Hills* (San Marino, 1941), especially chs. I–III, VI. See also Bancroft, *California*, VI, ch. XX; and for the comment of a contemporary lawyer, see *Memoirs of Elisha Oscar Crosby*, ed. by Charles A. Barker (San Marino, 1945), 65–73. There is some mention of California matters in Benjamin Horace Hibbard's standard *History of the Public Land Policies* (New York, 1924), but not much of present concerns in W. W. Robinson, *Land in California* (Berkeley, 1950).

SAN FRANCISCO PUEBLO QUESTION. The general statements on this issue, made in the text, are based on a survey of primary materials as far back as the reports made by General Halleck for the army and W. C. Jones for the General Land Office: Henry W. Halleck, *Report on the Laws and Regulations Relative to Grants or Sales of Public Lands in California* (Washington, 1850); William Carey Jones, *Report on the Subject of Land Titles in California, Made in Pursuance of Instructions from the Secretary of State and the Secretary of the Interior* (Washington, 1850). The following lawyers' briefs are drawn on, as being practically histories of San Francisco titleholding: Nathaniel Bennett, *Land Titles in San Francisco* (San Francisco, 1862); John W. Dwinelle, *Colonial History of San Francisco* (San Francisco, 1863); William J. Shaw, *Argument in the Case of Hart vs. Burnett* (San Francisco, 1860). Historical comment in: Bancroft, *California*, III, 229–33; VII, 230; Robinson, *Land in California*, ch. XVII; and Cleland, *California, American Period* (New York, 1922), 290. On Judge Field's role: Carl B. Swisher, *Stephen J. Field, Craftsman of the Law* (Washington, 1930), 98–101.

3. GEORGE'S FIRST EDITORIAL PROGRAM: THE TIMES. The *Times'* position on economic questions, just before HG took charge, is derived from editorials mainly of the first five months of 1867. The event behind HG's discussing analogies between American and European developments is described in B. F. Gilbert, 'Welcome to the Czar's Fleet, an Incident of Civil War Days in San Francisco,' *California Historical Society Quarterly*, 26 (1947):13–19. HG's editorials on Russia, identified as his by internal evidence, are in SF *Times*, 16, 23, 27 November 1866; see George, Jr., 173. HG's support of the Democratic mayor, on land policy, appeared in the *Times* 23 July 1868; and Mayor McCoppin's letters to him are dated 18 April, 23 July 1868, HGC. For the California background of the railroad matters about which HG editorialized, see Stuart Daggett, *Chapters in the History of the Southern Pacific* (New York, 1922); and for Pennsylvania's earlier public-works-and-private system, see A. L. Bishop, 'The State Works of Pennsylvania,' *Transactions of the Connecticut Academy of Arts and Sciences*, XIII (1907), 149–297. The claim that HG's monetary ideas were indebted to Ferris was made by Charles H. Shinn, in 'Early Books, Magazines, and Book-Making' (in California), *Overland Monthly*, 2d series, 12:349 (October 1888); Ferris's own *Financial Economy of the United States Illustrated, and Some of the Causes Which Retard the Progress of California Demonstrated* (San Francisco, 1867) sets forth the strict gold-base idea of currency, and argues for free trade. Ferris was more in a hurry for specie resumption than HG was. On this economist, see Joseph Dorfman, *The Economic Mind in American Civilization*, III (New York, 1949), 5, vii. On the 'Ohio Idea' of monetary reform, see Chester McA. Destler, *American Radicalism, 1865–1901*,

Essays and Documents, Connecticut College Monographs, no. 3. (New London, 1946), chs. II–III, especially 34–42, 47; and on Edward Kellogg, ch. IV.

VI. FIGHTING MONOPOLY AND PLEDGING UTOPIA,
1869–1871

1. ON THE SAN FRANCISCO CHRONICLE, 1868. The account of family affairs is based in part on George, Jr., and de Mille; but Annie George's children were more reticent than need be about her illness, and their accounts confuse this water trip with her next trip, by rail, from California east. I draw on family letters, mostly Annie George to HG, 2 September–8 December 1868, HGC. The comment on the *Chronicle* is made from the paper itself; but Young, *Journalism in California,* is useful.

2. NEWS MONOPOLIZATION IN CALIFORNIA. HG's trip east, his chance to see communications monopolies firsthand, he discussed in a letter to the NY *Tribune,* 5 March 1869; see George, Jr., 181. Concerning his antimonopoly employer, Nugent, I draw on two comments by contemporaries: memorandum by Frank Soulé, 1878, Bowman Mss., Newspaper Matter, UCBL; Ayers, *Gold and Sunshine,* 155, 158–61. For historical treatments of Nugent's battles for freedom, and of surrounding California history, see: H. H. Bancroft, *Popular Tribunals* (Works, XXXVI–XXXVII), and his *Retrospection Political and Personal* (New York, 1912), 184–93; and Caughey, *California,* 348–53, and Cleland, *Wilderness to Empire,* 264–8. Nugent's own plans for the second *Herald* appear in editorials, SF *Daily Herald,* 19 January, 17 October 1869. The present account of California newspaper economics rests in part on sources just cited, and in part on HG's retrospects in the NY *Herald,* 25 April 1869, and the SF *Post,* 27 June 1874.

GEORGE VERSUS AP AND WESTERN UNION. For a historical account of HG's Goliath, see Oliver Gramling, *AP: The Story of the News* (New York and Toronto, 1940), 64–78. HG's hot public review of his fight appeared in the NY *Herald,* 25 April 1869; and his later recollections, in *Report of the Committee of the Senate upon the Relations between Labor and Capital,* 1 (1883), 481–5, and in NY *Standard,* 28 September 1889. HG's earlier criticisms of the SF *Bulletin* occurred in the SF *Times,* 11 April, 23 July 1868; and his comment on Grant's cabinet in SF *Herald,* 12 April 1869. My narrative of HG's fight is supplied from about 25 of his own letters, principally to Nugent and Charles A. Sumner in San Francisco, dated between 14 January and 29 April 1869, HGC.

3. VISION AND DEDICATION. John Hasson's record of the phrenological examination, with comment, 1869, is preserved, HGC. J. R. Young's reminiscence of HG at this time is in his *Men and Memories* (New York and London, 1901), II, 417–26; and HG's reminiscences of New York, in his Chicago Art Institute Speech, 29 August 1893, HGC. HG's recollections of his vision appear in George, Jr., 192–3. The Chinese problem of the time is stated in Elmer C. Sandmeyer, *The Anti-Chinese Movement in California,* Illinois Studies in the Social Sciences, XXIV, no. 3 (Urbana, 1939), especially chs. II–III; and Mary R. Coolidge, *Chinese Immigration* (New York, 1909). George's Chinese letter appeared in the NY *Tribune,* 1 May 1869; and it was reprinted with comment, SF *Herald,* 23, 24 May 1869. My guess is that he derived his wage ideas from J. S. Mill, *Principles of Political Economy* (New York, 1864), I, 511; he acknowledged the

political ambitions he placed in the Chinese letter, in letters to Sumner, 26 April, 2 May 1869, HGC.

4. ON THE SAN FRANCISCO SIDELINES. Copies of HG's contract with the NY *Tribune*, 1 May 1869, appear in both HGC and John Russell Young Papers, LC. The account of his trip to San Francisco and of the deterioration of his affairs is drawn from his memoranda and his letters to Sumner, Hasson, Sinclair, and Caroline George, May–August 1869, HGC; and from a letter to Young, 16 May 1869, John Russell Young Papers, LC. The Philadelphia side of the family story is from Annie George's letters to him, July–September 1869, HGC. HG's estimate of the situation of the Irish in San Francisco appeared in the *Monitor*, 14, 21 August 1869; his figures are sustained by Hugh Quigley, *The Irish Race in California* (San Francisco, 1878), 149–51.

5. PROGRAM OF THE CALIFORNIA IMMIGRANT UNION. The immigrant union is sketched from President Hopkins' own data: 'The California Reflections of Caspar T. Hopkins,' serialized in *California Historical Society Quarterly*, vols. 25–7, especially 27:169–70 (1948); and his principal pamphlet, *Common Sense Applied to the Immigration Question: Showing Why the 'California Immigrant Union' was Founded and What It Expects to Do* (San Francisco, 1869). Other important publications of the union were: Alexander D. Bell, *Arguments in Favor of Immigration, with an Explanation of the Measures Recommended by the Immigrant Union* (1870); and *All About California and the Inducements to Settle There* (San Francisco, 1870), which included an essay by J. S. Hittell.

6. RETURN TO POLITICAL JOURNALISM. On HG's becoming acquainted with Governor Haight, and the symbolism of the event, see: George, Jr., 207–8; de Mille, 57; Destler, *American Radicalism*, 5–6. On Haight, see Bancroft, *California*, VII, 325–36, 363, 370; there is comment on him by his law partner, in a Ms. biographical statement, UCBL. The Mill letter is reprinted in full, and HG's comment is largely reprinted, George, Jr., 198–201. HG's letter of 1893 to Garrison is quoted at length also, ibid. 202–3; there are other letters between the two on the same subject: HG to Garrison, 19 May 1888, Garrison Collection, Smith College; and Garrison to HG, 4 December 1893, HGC.

ILLUMINATION IN OAKLAND. HG's fullest account of the event, written in the Meeker Notes, 1897, is printed in George, Jr., 210; his other reminiscences are quoted from his Chicago Art Institute Speech, 29 August 1893, HGC, and from *Science of Political Economy*, 162–3. HG's letter to Mill, 16 July 1870, appears in the John Stuart Mill Correspondence, JHU.

7. POSITION AS LEADING DEMOCRATIC EDITOR. For the personal and family aspects of the move to Sacramento, George, Jr., 211; and Annie George to HG, 2 April 1870, HGC. For HG's success with the American Press Association, his correspondence with Hasson and Young, May–July 1870, HGC; and Thompson and West, *History of Sacramento County, California* (Oakland, 1880), 92. About having been bought out of the *Reporter*, HG seems to have been reticent for years; but in the SF *Post*, 14 January 1873, he placed the responsibility on Stanford; and he told his story elaborately in the SF *State*, no. 1, 5 April 1879.

THE ANTI-MONOPLY PROGRAM OF THE REPORTER. (1) Concerning railroad regulation, Governor Haight summed up his position, as quoted, in a letter to L. I. Carr, 25 January 1871, Haight Paper, HL. HG's position, in the *Reporter*, 9, 12 May 1870. (2) Concerning taxation: ibid. 28 February, 5 April, 14 April 1870; compare J. A. Ferris, *Political Economy of the United States*, ch. xx. (3) Concerning labor's real earnings and frontier opportunities: Sacramento *Reporter*, 12 April, 9 August 1870; compare Wesley C. Mitchell, *Gold, Prices, and Wages under the Greenback Standard*, University of California Publications in Economics, 1 (Berkeley, 1908), 122-3, 237-48, 275-6, 283; and compare also Fred A. Shannon, *The Farmer's Last Frontier* (New York and Toronto, 1945), 356-9, and his 'A Post-Mortem on the Labor-Safety-Valve Theory,' *Agricultural History*, 19:31-7 (January 1945). (4) On the Chinese problem: HG renewed his attack in the *Reporter*, 4, 7 March, 15, 18 April, 11 June 1870; he wrote Mill, 16 July 1870, John Stuart Mill Correspondence, JHU; and the encouragement he received from Mill and Horace White is to be found in their respective letters of 13 August and 20 July 1870, HGC. (5) On HG's theme of the continuing Civil War: *Reporter*, in the order of the quotations in the text, 4 May, 20 April, 4 July, 1 August 1870; R. S. H. George to HG, 2 June 1870, HGC.

8. OUR LAND AND LAND POLICY. HG's *Subsidy Question* pamphlet is now rare; no place or date of publication is indicated but the UCBL copy is marked 1871, and the NYPL copies are identified, San Francisco, 1871. For the timeliness of it, see David M. Ellis, 'The Forfeiture of Railroad Land Grants, 1867-1894,' *Mississippi Valley Historical Review*, 33:27, 34-6, 38 (June 1946). *Our Land and Land Policy* was published in two editions in San Francisco, 1871, and they also are rare; it appears in Complete Works, VIII, 1-131. HG's colored map, with diagrammatic representation of railroad grants, may be compared with a modern map, also controversial, in Robert S. Henry, 'The Railroad Land Grant Legend in American History Texts,' *Mississippi Valley Historical Review*, 32 (1945): 171-94. Horace Greeley's quoted statement about swamp lands, from *Recollections of a Busy Life* (New York, 1869), 231, corresponds with *Our Land and Land Policy*, 59-62. For the historians' acceptance of HG's criticisms, see: Bancroft, *California*, VI, 580; Shannon, *Farmer's Last Frontier*, 389; Gates, 'The Homestead Law in an Incongruous Land System,' *American Historical Review*, 41 (1936): 657, 668-9. Concerning HG's connection with E. T. Peters, who is mentioned in Dorfman, *Economic Mind*, III, 35, xi, and whose idea, expressed in 1871, that 'every dollar' obtained from city land values is 'taken out of other men's pockets' certainly indicates convictions like those animating HG, I think that the timing indicates minimum ideological influence of one land radical on the other. Mr. Peters' articles appeared in the NY *National Standard* between spring and fall, 1871, the idea just quoted on 2 September, too late to affect *Our Land and Land Policy*. In a letter of 12 March 1880 (HGC), however, HG told Dr. E. R. Taylor that he had known Peters from some lectures (did he mean articles?) but had never met him. *Our Land and Land Policy*, 5, gives credit to Peters' statistical work for the Treasury.

VII. TRYING OUT RADICAL IDEAS: THE SAN FRANCISCO
DAILY EVENING POST, 1871-1874

1. PERSONAL SITUATION, 1871. HG's role in the Democratic convention is indicated in Winfield J. Davis, *History of Political Conventions in California* (Sacramento, 1893), 298-300, and in a notation on a copy of the platform, HG

Scrapbook 3, NYPL. His pieces in the *Overland* were: 'How Jack Breeze Missed Being a Pasha,' and 'Bribery in Elections,' 6:164–77 (February), and 7:497–504 (December, 1871). Annie George's illness is reported from her own letters, from the autumn of 1871 until the next summer, HGC. Eastern responses to *Our Land and Land Policy* are indicated in the following letters: Julian to HG, 16 August 1871, HGC; Wells to HG, quoted in George, Jr., 234, and HG to Wells, 19 September, 26 October 1871, Wells Collection, LC; White to HG, 11 September 1871, HGC. California comment occurs in: SF *Bulletin*, 31 July; SF *Call*, 1 August; Sacramento *Bee*, 31 July; Sacramento *Union*, 1 August 1871. Governor Haight's report, 5 December 1871, and Governor Booth's address, 8 December 1871, appear in *California Assembly Journal*, 1871–2 (Sacramento, 1872), 62, 123. For the legislative committee's declaration, see *Report of the Joint Committee to Inquire Into and Report Upon the Condition of the Public and State Lands Lying Within the Limits of the State* (Sacramento, 1872), 5–7.

2. LAUNCHING THE POST. The memorandum of HG's partner, William Hinton, in George, Jr., 237, describes the earliest financial arrangements. My facts and figures on the newspaper business are from: SF *Call*, 9 September 1866, 4 August 1871; SF *Post*, 25 May 1874; Fitch to Simonton, 12 May 1871, Fitch Mss., UCBL. On the history of penny journalism, see Mott, *American Journalism*, 220–24. HG's statements of political orientation are found in: letter to Wells, 19 September 1871, Wells Collection, LC; SF *Post*, 4 December 1871. For the background of HG's labor politics, see Commons, *History of Labour*, I, 153–5; Cross, *Labor Movement in California*, 96. On his role as delegate to the Baltimore convention: Davis, *Political Conventions in California*, 316; SF *Post*, 10, 11, 12 June 1872; George, Jr., 240. HG's opinions on the campaign, in the order mentioned in the text: SF *Post*, 24 June, 26 July 1872; letters to Whitelaw Reid, 24 September, 11 October 1872, Reid Mss., Herald Tribune Building, New York City, copies supplied by Professor Jeter A. Iseley of Princeton; SF *Post*, 6, 30 November, 7 December 1872.

2–3. WITHDRAWAL, RETURN, AND PROSPERITY. HG's immediate success with the *Post* is attested by the appearance of the paper, and by announcements, printed 30 December 1871 and 9–10 January 1872. Terms of sale, in George, Jr., 238–9. Of later success, the principal announcements occur in the *Post*, 11 December 1872, 29 November 1873; HG's overture to Reid in letter of 24 September 1872, Reid Mss., Herald Tribune Building, copy supplied by Professor Iseley. The report on HG's office life is supplied from de Mille, 66–7, and Mrs. C. F. McLean, 'Henry George, a Study from Life,' *Arena* (Boston), 20:299–300 (1918); that on his club life, from HG to John Swinton, 27 March 1873, HGC, and Robert H. Fletcher, *Annals of the Bohemian Club* (San Francisco, 1898), 159, 167 (for access to which, and to the club's membership record, I thank Mr. Henry L. Perry, the club's historian); and that on his home life, from his own and his wife's letters, 16 October, 7 November 1874, HGC.

3. CONTINUITIES OF REFORM THOUGHT. HG's attitude toward California's liberal Republicans appears in the *Post* of: 8 December 1871; 1 September, 6, 12, 18 December 1873; 1 April 1874; 2 April, 21 May, 21 June 1875. For HG's current ideas on railroad policy, ibid. 20, 26 February, 28 June, 6, 17 July, 9, 24 September, 19 October 1872; 24 January, 6 March, 13 November 1873. For an opinion he liked, see W. A. Grosvenor, 'The Railroads and the Farms,' *Atlantic*

Monthly, 32:591–610 (November 1873); concerning the Atlantic and Pacific possibility, information from Bancroft Ms., Caspar T. Hopkins, UCBL, and Hopkins 'Memoirs,' *California Historical Society Quarterly*, 27:339–41. Concerning the APA: the hard competition it gave the *Bulletin* and the *Call* is acknowledged in G. K. Fitch to J. W. Simonton, 12 May 1871, Fitch Ms., UCBL; HG's embarrassment about APA is stated in SF *Post*, 24 October 1874; and his fury toward AP, ibid. 20 January 1873. His reply to Wells, proposing the public ownership of the telegraph and other utilities, ibid. 18 January 1873. HG's acuteness in speaking of natural monopolies appears by reference to George T. Brown's chapter on 'The Theory of Natural Monopoly,' in *The Gas Light Company of Baltimore*, Johns Hopkins University Studies in Historical and Political Science, Series 54 (Baltimore, 1936).

4. CONVICTION AGAINST PRIVATE PROPERTY IN LAND. The report of the criticism in *Green's Land Paper* is written from the six-month file, UCBL, and the quotations are drawn from the issues of 6 January, 3 February, and 5 June 1872. HG's socialist-meeting defense of private landholding, in SF *Post*, 27 February 1872. Assemblyman Days's reformist position is indicated in his bill, 7 March 1872 (after similar resolutions introduced by another assemblyman), *California Assembly Journal*, 1871–2, 607; and HG's approval, in SF *Post*, 8, 15 February, 29 March, 15 October 1872. Days's memorandum, on having changed HG's mind, in George, Jr., 230, 232–3. For instances of HG's publicizing cases of land engrossment, see the *Post*, 6, 16 December 1871, 3 June 1875; and for his policy recommendations, 29 December 1871; 29 January, 23 March 1872; 16 January, 24 February 1874.

5. CALIFORNIA TAXES AND AMERICAN THEORY. The description of the tax environment in which HG's key reform idea was born borrows from William C. Fankhauser, *A Financial History of California, Public Revenues, Debts, and Expenditures*, University of California Publications, III (Berkeley, 1913). New York reform ideas are taken directly from D. A. Wells, E. Dodge, G. W. Cuyler, *Second Report* . . . (Albany, 1872), 7, 14, 35–6, 47, and *passim;* see also Herbert R. Ferleger, *David A. Wells and the American Revenue System* (New York, 1942). For a brief statement of Wells's ideas, see his 'Rational Principles of Taxation,' *Journal of Social Science*, 6 (1874): 120–33. The *Post* is considered as background of single-tax ideas in Arthur N. Young, *The Single Tax Movement in the United States* (Princeton, 1916), 54–60.

IMMEDIATE DEVELOPMENT OF GEORGE'S TAX PROPOSAL. The early responses of the San Francisco papers, except those taken from the *Chronicle* and the *Call*, respectively of 16 February, and 5, 12 November 1873, are traced from information in the *Post*, 1873–4. Essential *Post* editorials, discussing the application of the proposal in rural areas, appear in the issues of 22 July, 5 August, 10 October 1874, 13 March 1875; those discussing its application in urban areas, in the issues of 14 July, 10, 19 November 1873, 23 January, 13 August, 30 October 1874, 13 February, 17 November 1875.

STATE CAPITAL REACTIONS. Governor Booth's 1873 ideas about landholding were voiced in his message, 1 December 1873, *California Assembly Journal*, 1873–4, 122. The reactions of the Sacramento press are taken occasionally from reports in the *Post*, but principally from the journals themselves, as follows:

Bee, 27 January, 4, 29 November 1873; *Union,* 25 October, 4 November 1873. The *Record* figures, as reported in the text, correspond with those in the *State Board of Equalization Report* (Sacramento, 1873), 23, 27; but they differ a little from the figures Governor Booth used in his biennial address. The report of the Murphy committee of the assembly was printed, apparently in full, in the *Post,* 4 May 1874; and HG's optimistic reaction appeared the next day. HG's current fondness for Mill is represented in the *Post* of 17 April 1873 and 1 May 1874; and his strong statements, which are quoted, against private property in land were made in the same newspaper, 29 October 1874, 30 April, 16 July 1875.

VIII. ROUNDING OUT AN EDITOR'S THOUGHT: THE *POST*'S UTOPIA, 1872–1875

2. FIELDS FOR IMMEDIATE REFORM. The editorials on tariff policy, drawn on for illustrations, are to be found, in the order of the text, in the SF *Post* for: 16 January 1874, 24 October 1873, 3 March, 3 November 1874, 27 September 1875. HG's identification of tariff reform with free trade and the review of the Butts book appear, respectively, ibid. 22 December 1873, 5 June 1875. On the question of municipalizing San Francisco's water system, HG's diagnosis appears ibid. 20 November 1873, 12, 17, 22 March, 27 June, 13, 20 November 1874. Other opinions in: SF *Call,* 22 March, 27 June 1874; SF *Bulletin,* 9, 10 April 1875; SF *Chronicle,* 2 April 1873. HG's economic prescriptions appear in SF *Post:* 6 January 1872, 2 December 1873, 28 March 1874.

BELIEF IN LABOR AND CAPITALISM. HG's ideas about unions, strikes, and the eight-hour program appear in SF *Post,* 14 June 1872, 16 July 1874. The Sunrise story is to be found ibid. October–November 1873 *passim;* see also George, Jr., 241, Young, *Journalism in California,* 79. HG's notions about the prevention and cure of depressions appear in the *Post,* 15 January, 28 November 1874, 4 February 1875; his financial ideas, ibid. 23, 25 February, 5 October, 29 December 1874, 11 January, 16 July 1875; and his ideas about banking, building-and-loan, and other credit services, ibid. 5, 7 December 1871, 1 August, 24 September, 7 October 1872, 25 October 1873, 29 April, 27 November 1874, 7 July 1875. The appreciation of Ralston and other imaginative capitalists, ibid. 2 December 1872, 4 June 1874, 28 August, 13 September 1875; SF *Ledger,* 28 August 1875.

3. ENLARGEMENT OF PERSONAL FAITH. On HG's religious inclinations at home, George, Jr., 252. His critical reflections against moral relativism and agnosticism appear in SF *Post,* 1 May, 12 September 1874, 6 February 1875. His favorable response to idealistic history appears ibid. 11, 21 November 1874; and his vein of moral pessimism is represented, ibid. 8 November 1872, 15 February, 14, 16, 17, 21 June, 7 August 1873, 6 March 1875. Aspects of his international awareness, in the order of the text, appear in SF *Post,* 16 October 1874, 12 December 1871, 20 November 1875, 6, 10 June 1874, 14 June 1873.

4. THE JUST STATE. George's criticisms of militarism and bureaucracy appear ibid. 13, 20 April, 23 June 1874. His dream of extended federalism, ibid. 9 July 1874; his anxieties about overgovernment, ibid. 4 April 1872, 4 June 1873, 15 November 1875; and his preferences for localized power, fixed executive responsibility, and economy, ibid. 26 March, 10 April 1872, 22 October, 26 December 1873, 17 February 1874, 27 February, 5 June 1875. For HG's first effort for

the Australian ballot, see 'Bribery in Elections,' *Overland Monthly*, 7:497–504 (December 1871), and de Mille, 65. His other ideas and reservations about electoral reform, SF *Post*, 4, 19 December 1871, 4 April 1872, 3, 23 January, 31 March, 13 April 1874. His wish for a new California constitution appears ibid. 13 January, 17 February, 16 March, 6 April 1874, 9 August 1875.

5. EFFORTS TO DO GOOD. HG's preliminary battle with police corruption appears in SF *Alta California*, 10, 13 May 1873, and SF *Post*, 10 April 1875; see also George, Jr., 244. The story of the Cockrill affair is told in almost every issue of the *Post* during the three weeks beginning 10 April 1875; I draw also on the SF *Call* and *Bulletin* for the second half of the month. On the Industrial School exposure, besides the *Post*, 3 December 1872–10 January 1873, see George, Jr., 241–2. The frame of the story of the *Post*'s attack on the administration of the University of California is drawn in William S. Ferrier, *Origin and Development of the University of California* (Berkeley, 1930); there is information in Fabian Franklin, *Life of Daniel Coit Gilman* (New York, 1910), 145–7, 150, 151, 155 (unfortunately the Gilman Mss. at Johns Hopkins and Yale add nothing here); and there is much testimony, if not much conclusion, in the 'Investigation of the Alleged Frauds in the Construction of the College of Letters. Testimony Taken by the Assembly Committee on Public Buildings and Grounds,' *California Assembly Journal*, 1873–4, Appendix IV (Sacramento, 1874). On the character of Professor Carr, see Merle E. Curti and Vernon Carstenson, *The University of Wisconsin, A History*, I (Madison, 1949), 180–81. See George, Jr., 208–9. Besides these background sources, I draw on the *Post*, especially 8, 22 January, 9, 16 March, 9 June 1874.

6. SUCCESSES AND DOWNFALL OF THE POST. HG's battle with the liquor interests appears in the *Post*, July 1874, *passim;* see also Arthur Mc Ewen, 'Henry George, a Character Sketch,' *Review of Reviews*, 16 (1897): 551. The plans, conditions, and achievement involved in the *Post*'s new plant are told from the paper's own announcements, especially during June 1874, and October 1874–January 1875. George, Jr., pp. 247–8, note 2, says that Senator Jones's $30,000 purchased 30 of 100 shares of the newspaper's stock, but probably this should be translated to mean 300 of 1000. The *Bulletin*'s unfriendly opinion of Jones is taken from the issue of 30 December 1874; and this conforms with the notion of the *Call*, 26 June 1874, that the *Post* really belonged to creditors. On the other side of the antagonism, the *Post* frequently denounced those papers, and sometimes predicted (4 June 1873, 19 June 1874, 7 October 1875) the fall of the *Bulletin*. But the Fitch Mss., Exhibits K and L, 1875, UCBL, contain a statement about that paper's earning power. HG's hopes for the *Weekly Post* and the *Morning Ledger* he stated to John Swinton, 6 October 1875, HGC; the account of the *Ledger* is based mainly on the paper itself, but see also George, Jr., 248, de Mille, 71–2. HG's immediate reactions to the loss of his paper are quoted from letters to Swinton, 28 November, 27 December 1875, HGC; the later reminiscence, from a letter to Charles Nordhoff, 31 January 1880, HGC.

IX. FROM ISOLATION: SPEAKING AND WRITING IN TIME OF CRISIS, 1876–1879

1. HOLDING A SINECURE. The letters in which HG stated his satisfactions at being free of newspaper obligations are family ones, 31 March (?), 26 May 1876, HGC.

His being appointed to a state job is the subject of a memorandum by E. W. Maslin, George, Jr., 262–3; the formal record of confirmation appears in California Legislature, *Senate Journal*, 1875–6, 99, and the description of that event is from McLean, 'Henry George, A Study from Life,' *Arena*, 20:304. For HG's acknowledgment that the inspectorship was a sinecure, see *Science of Political Economy*, 201; his discussions of the practical politics, duties, and pleasures of the job occur in letters to James Coffey, and to his wife and his mother, January–May 1876, printed in part, George, Jr., 257–9. His pamphlet, *The Press. Should It Be Personal or Impersonal?* was almost certainly published in San Francisco, 1876.

2. BEGINNING A SPEAKING CAREER. HG's first major speech was printed as *The Question before the People, What Is the Real Issue in the Presidential Campaign?* (San Francisco, 1876); the quoted passages are from pp. 3, 15, 6. The San Luis Obispo event is taken from the *Gazette* of that city, 9 October 1876, HG Scrapbook 6, NYPL; and HG's improved style appears in his Ms. address, 'Why I Am a Democrat,' HGC. Other details of his campaign of 1876 efforts, including the self-estimate quoted, from George, Jr., 268–71. HG's 4 July address, 'The American Republic: Its Dangers and Possibilities,' is in Complete Works, VIII, 157–84, the quoted passages on pp. 157–8, 159, 160, 161, 162, 168, 170, 171, 173. The events of the 4 July celebrations are taken from the *Alta California*, 5 July 1876, 5 July 1877. The circumstances surrounding HG's university lecture are related in George, Jr., 274–5; and C. T. Hopkins' preceding address is printed, *Business versus Speculation* (San Francisco, 1876). HG's own text, 'The Study of Political Economy,' is in Complete Works, VIII, 135–53; the passages quoted, on pp. 135, 136, 140–41, 153. The lecture was first printed in *Popular Science Monthly*, 16:601–12 (March 1880). For the analysis by George, Jr., see p. 282.

3. ARGUING WITH UNREASON. On the immediate economic-political background, see HG, 'The Kearney Agitation in California,' *Popular Science Monthly*, 17 (1880): 433–53; and the chapter on the same subject in James Bryce, *American Commonwealth* (New York and London, 1895), II, which, pp. 429n, 444–5, draws on HG's 'brilliant' article. For scholarly treatments, see: Bancroft, *California*, VII, ch. XIV; Cross, *Labor Movement in California*, chs. VI–VII; Sandmeyer, *Anti-Chinese Movement in California*, ch. IV; and Ralph Kauer, 'The Workingmen's Party of California,' *Pacific Historical Review*, 13 (1944): 278–91. Kearneyite overtures to HG are contained in a letter from T. W. Dennis and Edward Connolly, 25 August 1877, HGC; his other choices are indicated in diary and letters, HGC, partly reproduced in George, Jr., 288, 298. See also Sandmeyer, 79–80. On the gathering of the California Land Reform League, George, Jr., 293–4, and Louis F. Post, *Prophet of San Francisco* (New York, 1930), 46. HG's keynote address, *Why Work Is Scarce, Wages Low, and Labor Restless*, was printed (San Francisco, 1885); quotations in the text from pp. 1–9, 11, 13. The *Argonaut*'s version appeared 17, 24 August 1878. To see the ideas in the perspective of HG's growth, compare *Progress and Poverty*, Bk. V, ch. I, and his article, 'Causes of the Business Depression,' 1894, in Complete Works, VIII, 325–31. HG's own explanation of the address to Swinton, 2 June 1878, HGC, is quoted in de Mille, 80; Mr. Waite's objection, referring to his article in *Overland Monthly*, 15: 446–55 (November 1875), is in memorandum, Bowman Mss., Newspaper Matter, p. 64, UCBL. The 'Moses' address is printed,

Complete Works, VII; pp. 6, 9, 13, 16, 24 are quoted. There is an account of the event in SF *Alta California*, 21 February 1878; and Mrs. de Mille's comment is in 'Henry George, The *Progress and Poverty* Period,' *American Journal of Economics and Sociology*, 2:551 (July 1943).

4. WRITING WHILE CALIFORNIA WAS REORGANIZED. For the origins of the constitutional convention, I draw on Kauer, loc. cit. 282–3, and on Carl B. Swisher, *Motivation and Political Technique in the California Constitutional Convention 1878–1879* (Claremont, 1930), 10–14, 17–18. HG's original interest is voiced in letters to Coffey, 5, 28 March 1878, HGC; and his broadside appeal 3 May 1878 is preserved, HGC and UCBL. For the terms set by the Kearneyites, and HG's refusal, see Davis, *Political Conventions in California*, 388, and George, Jr., 299; for the terms on which he undertook candidacy, letter to Democratic convention, 6 June 1878, HGC. On the election of delegates, slightly different figures in Kauer, loc. cit., 283, from those in Davis, *Political Conventions in California*, 390–92. Information on the physical circumstances in which *Progress and Poverty* was written is from: George, Jr., 300–305; de Mille, 81; and undated clipping, HG Scrapbook 8, p. 25, NYPL. On the help of friends, data from: letter from the governor's son, Samuel C. Haight, to B. W. Burgess, 12 August 1927, HGC; Linnie Wolfe Marsh, *Son of the Wilderness, The Life of John Muir* (New York, 1946), 182–3; John Swett, *Public Education in California* (New York, 1911), 233–4; Judge James Maguire, address, NY *Standard*, 8 October 1887; Sacramento *Bee*, 23 August 1915; reminiscences by James H. Barry, *The Bee, Annual for 1903*, 4.

THE OBJECTIONABLE REORGANIZATION. For the background of HG's 1879, I have borrowed ideas, and a few editorial quotations from the *Alta California*, from ch. XIII, 'The Alta and the Big Red Scare of 1877–1879,' of Dr. Petty's 'Gold-Rush Intellectual: John S. Hittell,' all with the permission of the author. I draw again on the studies mentioned above as discussing Kearneyism; and on J. C. Stedman and R. A. Leonard, *The Workingmen's Party of California* (San Francisco, 1878), especially chs. II, V–VIII. The economic opinion of Mr. Beale appears in his letter to R. S. Baker, 17 April 1879, R. S. Baker Collection, HL. *Hall's Land Journal* (Los Angeles, 1876, San Francisco, 1876–8) is drawn on, HL file. The new constitution is most readily found in Francis N. Thorpe, *Federal and State Constitutions, Colonial Charters and Other Organic Laws* (Washington, 1909), I, 412–51; but the present chapter was written with reference to the full *Debates and Proceedings of the Constitutional Convention of California* (3 vols., Sacramento, 1880), and I am convinced that HG's ideas were thoroughly disregarded there. Ex-governor Haight, who died before the convention began, was the only elected delegate whom I can connect with HG.

AUTHOR REJECTED AT HOME. HG's opinions, in the *State*, are reported from the paper itself. For his children's belief, that the paper paid its way, see George, Jr., 317; de Mille, 83. His own summing up of the California situation, for Swinton, is in a letter of 6 May 1879, HGC. His denunciation of the new railroad commission refers to the Constitution, Article XII, Sections 22–3; the SF *State* condemned railroad influence, 5 April 1879. His later condemnations are quoted from 'The Kearney Question in California,' loc. cit., 446, 451–2; *Social Problems*, 182. For the advice his friends gave HG, see Swett, *Public Education in California*, 233–4; Young, *Men and Memories*, II, 417–26.

X. BEFORE THE WORLD: *PROGRESS AND POVERTY*, 1879

1. SALIENT FEATURES OF THE BOOK. This chapter might have gained in historical feeling if I had made my references to the San Francisco 'author's edition' of 1879, but convenience would have been sacrificed. All page references are to Complete Works, I; and they are valid also for the many editions which reproduce that one. A printed sheet (HGC) announced the sober title that HG first gave the book. George, Jr., p. 321n, may be correct in supposing that the author used it to conceal the real title, until copyright was established; but it may as easily be supposed that HG first thought to make the book sound scientific, and then preferred to make it more appealing. Dr. Taylor's early appreciation of *P and P*'s regional character appeared in the *Californian* (San Francisco, 1880–81), 1:183. For a recent exposition of the author's broader range of thought, see leaflet of the Henry George School of Social Science, 'Henry George the Scholar,' by Francis Neilson. HG's knowledge of Buckle is indicated, *P and P*, 92–3; and passages of Buckle which may possibly be echoed in George occur in the *History of Civilization in England* (London, 1873), III, 309, 312, 314. HG's ignorance of the Physiocrats is indicated by the little he said about them, *P and P*, 421–2, 431; see also his *Science of Political Economy*, Bk. II, ch. IV; and Emile Rivaud, *Henry George et la Physiocratie* (Paris, 1907), and Charles Gide, 'The Single Tax and the Impôt Unique,' *Quarterly Journal of Economics*, 5:494–5 (July 1891).

2. THE CONTEXT OF GEORGE'S CRITIQUE OF CLASSICAL ECONOMICS. HG's comment on Walker's attack on the wages fund seems adequate and just and more timely than he knew. In a review of 1869 John Stuart Mill recanted the wages-fund idea, but he failed to change the later edition of his text to express his change of mind. See Mill, *Principles of Political Economy* (Ashley ed.), 343–4, 991–2. HG's objection to the Malthusianism in *The Wages Fund* seems timely, too, by comparison with Bowen's anti-Malthusian article, 'Malthusianism, Pessimism, and Darwinism,' *North American Review*, November 1879, reprinted in his *Gleanings from a Literary Life, 1838–1880* (New York, 1880), see pp. 356, 361–74. On the prevalence of Malthusianism, see Dorfman, *Economic Mind in American Civilization*, II–III, *passim*. A letter of 1893, HG to Byron W. Holt, an admirer who disagreed about Malthusianism, indicates that HG refused to change his mind about the validity of *P and P*, Bk. II (letter kindly supplied by Professor W. Stull Holt of the University of Washington).

THE INFLUENCE OF RICARDIAN THEORY. For the staying power, in economic thought, of Ricardo's law of rent, see Carl M. Bye, *Developments and Issues in the Theory of Rent* (New York, 1940), especially 104–6. For an approving comment on a Ricardian idea which HG adopted, that rent does not enter the price-making process but is determined by price, see Alfred Marshall, *Principles of Economics* (6th ed., London, 1898), 484–5n. On radical developments from Ricardian bases, see Esther Lowenthal, *The Ricardian Socialists* (New York, 1911).

A SAN FRANCISCO THEORY OF INTEREST. Mr. del Mar's charge of plagiarism is contained in his *Science of Money* (London, 1885), 98–9n; and that book mentions his earlier writings. His lecture, which coincided with *P and P*'s publication, was published: *Usury and the Jews* (San Francisco, 1879), 16 pp. On del

Mar see C. T. Hopkins, 'Memoirs,' *California Historical Society Quarterly*, 27:345–7 (December 1948); and Dorfman, *Economic Mind*, III, 98–101, xxii, which wisely calls attention to this forgotten man. The possibility that del Mar and HG developed their similar ideas independently is suggested by a case that occurred later in HG's life. In a letter of 22 August 1916 (HGC), René Brossière, a French writer, told August Lewis that his own theory of interest, 'which I thought was a new one, was exactly the same as Henry George's (in *Progress and Poverty*) — only I go much farther than the great author.' HG's interest theory in *P and P* drew criticisms for many years. For friendly but severe criticism, see D. M. Lowrey, 'The Basis of Interest,' *Annals of the American Academy of Social and Political Science*, 2 (1892): 629–52. For friendly doubt: Bolton Hall to R. T. Ely, 19 August 1900, R. T. Ely Collection, Wisconsin Historical Society. For single-tax comment: Joseph Faidy, 'Henry George's Theory of Interest,' *Single Tax Review*, 3 (1903): 20–23; P. H. Elback, 'Interest and the Reform of Henry George,' ibid. 13 (1913): 1–12; Charles A. Green, *The Profits of the Earth* (Boston, 1934).

3. GEORGE'S DEPRESSION THEORY IN RETROSPECT. Compare Eugen von Bergmann, *Die Wirtschaft Krisen: Geschichte der Nationalökonimischen Krisen Theorien* (Stuttgart, 1895), 353–9, and Jean Lescure, *Des crises generales et periodiques de production* (Paris, 1910), 474–6, with Paul Barnett, 'Business Cycle Theory in the United States, 1860–1900,' in University of Chicago, School of Business, *Studies in Business Administration*, XI, no. 3 (1938).

4. GEORGE'S REALISM ABOUT THE SOUTH. Compare *P and P*, 347, with Roger Shugg, *Origins of Class Struggle in Louisiana* (University, La., 1939), and with C. Vann Woodward, *The Rise of the New South* (University, 1952), ch. VII.

6. GEORGE AND MARGINALISM. For the uses of the term 'margin' in books from which HG may have borrowed, see: Henry Fawcett, *Manual* (1864 ed.), 140; (1876 ed.), 121; Millicent Garrison Fawcett, *Political Economy for Beginners* (1876 ed.), 97; Mill, *Principles of Political Economy* (Ashley ed.), 690, 716. For a learned summary of European beginnings and early American developments of the marginal ideas, see Dorfman, *Economic Mind*, III, 84–7, 145, 188–205, and *passim*. Clark's acknowledgment of debt to HG appears in his *Distribution of Wealth, A Theory of Wages, Interest and Profits* (New York, 1902), viii. For highly critical comment, see Edgar N. Johnson, 'The Economics of Henry George's *Progress and Poverty*,' *Journal of Political Economy*, 18 (1910):729; see also George C. Stigler, *Production and Distribution Theories, The Formative Period* (New York, 1941), 302.

GEORGE AS FRONTIER THEORIST. Dr. F. Lee Benson suggested some of my inquiry on this point. Professor Mood's findings derive from Turner's copy of *Progress and Poverty* deposited in HL, and from the Minutes of the Johns Hopkins Seminar in History, 17 May 1889, JHU. Professor Merle E. Curti permits me to quote the following, from a letter written him by Turner, 5 January 1931: 'I . . . think I never read his *Progress and Poverty* before writing the "Frontier." Since reading your chapter I have read the *Progress and Poverty* discussion of the public domain and its influence upon the question of labor and capital. It is clear that, so far as the land question and legislation on its taxation goes, he had the idea before my "Frontier"; but the single-tax conception never met with my assent.' It seems that Turner, writing at the age of seventy, had forgotten reading done nearly half a century earlier. Elsewhere in the letter he justly claims greater breadth than George, in using the frontier idea.

XI. IN THE TIDE OF IDEA AND OPPORTUNITY, 1880–1881

2. PUBLISHING PROGRESS AND POVERTY. The story is told quite fully in George, Jr., 315–22; my version draws on additional letters of negotiation and arrangement with the publishers, 1879, HGC. See also McLean, 'Henry George: a Study from Life,' *Arena*, 20:305 (July 1898).

EARLY RECEPTION OF THE BOOK. The letters from George W. Julian, Sir George Grey, and the British Liberals, sent in response to gift copies of the SF edition, are quoted in George, Jr., 323–4, and in de Mille, 85. Professor Leslie's letters, dated 26 November [1879], and 26 September and 24 November [1880], are in HGC; his printed observations on HG, in *Fortnightly Review*, 1 October 1880, New Series, 28:127, 147–9. The earlier HG letter to Nordhoff appears in George, Jr., 328–9; the later one, 31 January [1880], and Horace White's letter, 17 December 1879, are in HGC. The earliest New York reviews were: *Tribune*, 5 December 1879; *Herald*, 15 December 1879 (these and others a little later, in HG Scrapbook 24, NYPL).

CALIFORNIA REVIEWS. There is a description of 'the reception of *Progress and Poverty* in California' in Young, *Single Tax Movement*, 67–9. The SF *Examiner* and *Bee* reviews (apparently of 8 and 12 November 1879, respectively) are preserved in HG Scrapbook 24, NYPL; Dr. Taylor's review is in *Californian*, 1:182–7 (February 1880), and there is a sketch of HG by him in Ella Sterling Cummins [Mighels], *The Story of the Files, a Review of California Writers and Literature* (San Francisco, 1893), 174–5. Dr. Leverson's salute and 'Ex-Rebel's' letter appeared in the *Argonaut* of 14(?) February and 6 March 1880, HG Scrapbook 24, NYPL; comment on them in Sacramento *Bee*, 2 (?) February 1880. Besides the reviews mentioned, there may have appeared by April 1880 an adverse comment made in the *Berkeley Quarterly* (date not clear); in July 1881 that journal (2:210–23) carried a severely critical article, John J. Dwyer, 'Henry George on Taxation.' HG's own impressions of first responses to *P and P* appear in *Science of Political Economy*, 170–71, and letter to Dr. Taylor, 17 February 1880, HGC.

3. EASTERN RECEPTION OF NEW YORK EDITION. The special interest in *P and P* in the Appleton office during early 1880 is evident in letters to HG from the firm, 20 February, 5, 27 March, 1, 9 April; from Youmans, 12 March, and from Steers, 27 March, HGC. The lead article on *P and P* was by C. M. Lungren, *Popular Science Monthly*, 16:721–37; and one suspects similar strategy of publicity in the Editor's Table of *Appleton's Journal*, May and June 1881, when criticism was offered and HG replied (New Series, 10:472–4, 552–9, 569–70). The locations of the important reviews are: NY *Times*, 6 June 1880; NY *Nation*, 31: 65–6, 117–18 (22 July, 12 August 1880); *Christian Register*, 9 and 19 February 1880; Springfield *Republican*, 27 June 1880; *Atlantic Monthly*, 46 (1880): 847, 851, 854. Some of these are in HG Scrapbook 24, NYPL; and I draw most of the comment from minor journals from that collection. HG's own attitudes appear in George, Jr., which prints some of his letters to Dr. Taylor,

334, 340, 344; I draw also on letters to John Swinton, 29 April, HGC, and to D. A. Wells, 3 April, 1, 9 December 1880, Wells Collection, LC.

4. AUTHOR's HARD TIMES IN NEW YORK. HG's life in New York during 1880–81 is told mostly from letters to Dr. Taylor, 31 August, 27 September, 28 November, 4, 18 December 1880, 4 January, 6 March, 12 May 1881, HGC. Family letters are few, but HG's to Richard George, aged fifteen, 2 September, 17 December 1880, HGC, are eloquent. So are Bigelow's account of HG in *Seventy Summers*, II, 16–17, and Young's reminiscence, from NY *Herald*, 30 October 1897. HG's campaign efforts are recounted in George, Jr., 336–8; and there is a draft of the article Youmans rejected, one may think too reformist for *Popular Science Monthly*, preserved in HGC. HG reviewed his relations with Hewitt in a draft letter, 1897, HGC. In his *Abram S. Hewitt, With Some Account of Peter Cooper* (New York and London, 1935), 418–19, Allan Nevins offers evidence which supports HG's own idea that Hewitt had liked *P and P*. I have scanned the HGC draft of HG's report done for Hewitt, and, as nearly as I can tell (the report is partly in HG's shorthand), it contains little or nothing to justify Hewitt's later charge that it was full of single-tax ideas. The other best contemporary documents on the Hewitt affair are HG's letters to Dr. Taylor 28 November 1880, 6 March 1881, HGC.

SECURING A FOOTHOLD. On Young's efforts for *P and P* in England, see his *Men and Memories*, II, 423. HG's new friendships, including Shearman's, are attested in George, Jr., 350–51; and in letters, HG to Bigelow, 15 April 1881, and to Taylor, 25 May, 23 June 1881. As for the unpleasant side of the visit to San Francisco, a note to Dr. Taylor, 11 August 1881, HGC, indicates HG's anxiety lest someone would 'garnishee proceeds' of his lecture in Metropolitan Temple. The nomination for the Senate is recorded in the California Legislature *Senate Journal*, 1881, 46–7, 52; see George, Jr., 352n.

5. PROGRESS AND POVERTY OVERSEAS. The Laveleye review, 'La Propriété terrienne et le paupérisme,' *La Revue scientifique*, 25:708–10 (24 January 1880), was praised in the *Bee*, 18 February 1880; and HG immediately wrote Dr. Taylor; see George, Jr., 331. Another Belgian, Agathon de Potter, wrote HG a complimentary letter. The *Economist*, 38:472, reviewed the NY edition, 24 April 1880; it reviewed the British edition, 39:540–41, 30 April 1881, and at that time praised HG's free-trade ideas while resisting his ideas about land. *Statist* review, 10 April 1880, in HG Scrapbook 24, NYPL. Concerning German distribution: letters, Gütschow to HG, 6 January 1881, and Elwin Staude to Gütschow, 5 May 1881, HGC. The German reviews referred to are: Wagner's in *Zeitschrift für die Gesamte Staatswissenschaft* (Tübingen), Bd. 37 (1881): 619–24; one by E. Heitz (complaining of HG's lack of proper method), *Jahrbucher für Nationalökonomie und Statistik* (Jena), 38–9:123–6; and one by Schmoller, in Schmoller's *Jahrbuch für Gezetzgebung, Verwaltung, und Vokswirtschaft* (Leipsic), 6 (1882):i, 354–9.

GEORGE's CONNECTION WITH IRELAND. I draw on Norman D. Palmer, *The Irish Land League Crisis* (New Haven, 1940), for Irish and *Irish World* backgrounds. At first entitled *The Irish Land Question* (New York, 1881, and many early editions), HG's little book later became simply *The Land Question*, as in Complete Works, III. HG's success with this book, and with NY Irishmen, he described in letters, especially those to McClatchy, 27 January, 22 February, 9 October 1881, HGC. George, Jr., tells the story fully, 341–57.

THE SUPPORT OF NEW FRIENDS. F. G. Shaw turned to HG in a letter of 18 July 1881, HGC; HG's letters to him, 13 September, 4, 9 October 1881, HGC, are printed in part, in George, Jr., 353–4, 403. The interest of Louis Post, at this stage, appears in his *Prophet of San Francisco*, chs. II–V; for comment on his paper *Truth*, see Mott, *American Journalism*, 502. HG's knowledge of A. R. Wallace's endorsement appears in letters to Dr. Taylor and Shaw, respectively 7 September, 9 October 1881, HGC; see George, Jr., 354–5.

XII. PROPHET IN THE OLD COUNTRY: IRELAND AND ENGLAND, 1881–1882

1. THE CONDITION OF IRELAND. For the opening paragraphs, and for background throughout, I draw especially on: Palmer, *Irish Land League Crisis;* John E. Pomfret, *The Struggle for Land in Ireland, 1800–1923* (Princeton, 1930); and R. C. K. Ensor's volume in the Oxford History of England, *England 1870–1914* (Oxford, 1936). I have used also: Herbert Paul, *History of Modern England*, III, IV; John Morley, *Life of William Ewart Gladstone,* III (New York and London, 1903). The opinions on the Irish Land Act of 1881 are drawn from: Hammond, *Gladstone and the Irish Nation* (London, 1938), 167; and J. L. Garvin, *Life of Joseph Chamberlain,* 1 (London, 1932), 336.

2. THREE MONTHS AMONG THE IRISH, 1881–2. HG rendered a public report of his visit in the *Irish World,* beginning with a letter written 3 November and printed 3 December. He sent home also what amounts to a supplementary report, a parallel series of private letters to Patrick Ford, HGC. The one file of the newspaper, deposited in the New York Public Library, is badly damaged and broken; and I have drawn on the clippings of HG's *Irish World* letters, in HG Scrapbooks, 12–13, NYPL, a collection I believe to be complete. Some letters, both public and private, are quoted in George, Jr., and de Mille; but I have gone directly to the collected sources. Annie George's observations, written for the boys, also HGC, are quoted in George, Jr., 366, and de Mille, 101. Concerning the Rotunda lecture, HG wrote to Dr. Taylor, 20 November 1881, as well as to Ford; that letter and copy of the address, 'Land and Labour,' 14 November 1881, are in HGC; see George, Jr., 362. Pomfret, op. cit. 104–8, discusses the radical ideological background which HG discovered in Ireland. HG's account of the Bishop of Clonfert's salute is in NY *Standard,* 8 January 1887; and he reprinted the Bishop of Meath's diocesan letter, ibid. 18 June 1887. HG's difficult relations with Meath appear in letters between them, 12, 13 November 1881, 27, 28 February 1882, and in HG letters to Ford, 9, 15, 22 November, 12, 28 December 1881, HGC; and in HG letter, 2 January, in *Irish World,* 28 January 1882. See Palmer, op. cit. 118–20.

3. RADICALIZING IN ENGLAND, 1882. HG's estimations of a revolution rising in England were made in letters to Dr. Taylor, 11 January, 6 June, to Steers, 11 February, to Shaw, 28 April, 30 May 1882, HGC. His information about the sales of his books he reported to Shaw, more than to anyone else; and the account of Shaw's subsidies is drawn from correspondence between the two men, 28 April–18 July 1882, HGC, partly printed in George, Jr., 389–91. HG's second speech in Dublin was reported in the London *Times,* 12 June 1882, p. 3; his meeting

with J. Morrison Davidson is reported in that writer's *Concerning Four Precursors of Henry George* (London and Glasgow, 1899?), 1–2.

FIRST CONNECTIONS WITH SOCIALISTS ABROAD. HG's English influence, especially on the socialists, is the object of a study in process by Dr. Elwood Lawrence of Michigan State College. On the early stages, see his 'Uneasy Alliance, the Reception of Henry George by British Socialists in the Eighties,' *American Journal of Economics and Sociology*, 11:63. For immediate background see: H. M. Hyndman, *Record of an Adventurous Life* (London, 1911), ch. xv and *passim;* Max Beer, *A History of British Socialism* (London, 1919–20), II, 246–53; Edward R. Pease, *History of the Fabian Society* (London, 1925), 23–4. For Marx's opinion of HG, as quoted, see letter no. 175, *Karl Marx and Friedrich Engels Correspondence, A Selection with Commentary and Notes,* translated and edited by Dora Torr (New York, 1934?), 394–6. Hyndman's attitude toward HG as possible convert is stated in his *Record of an Adventurous Life,* 282, 290–92; and HG's, toward Hyndman, in letter to Ford, 9 March 1882, HGC. For the drawing-room event, which under Hyndman's auspices opposed HG to Spencer, I use HG to A. J. Steers, 25 August 1882, HGC; see George, Jr., 369–70.

CONNECTIONS WITH RADICALS AND LAND NATIONALIZERS. Miss Taylor's acceptance of *P and P* is related in letters, HG to Henry George, Jr., 22 March 1882, and Henry George, Jr., to F. G. Shaw, 17 April 1882, HGC; see George, Jr., 367–8, and de Mille, 102. A. R. Wallace approached HG in letters of 3, 7 June 1882; his political preferences appear in his reply to a double review of *Land Nationalisation* and *Progress and Poverty* by Professor Fawcett, reprinted in Wallace, *Studies Scientific and Social* (London and New York, 1900), ch. XVII. The Wallace-Darwin exchange of ideas about HG was made in letters of 9, 12 July 1881, in James Marchant, *Alfred Russel Wallace, Letters and Reminiscences* (2 vols., London, New York, Toronto, and Melbourne, 1916), I, 316, 317. See also Wallace, *My Life, a Record of Events and Opinions* (New York, 1905), II, ch. xxxv. On the correspondence of ideas among the three writers, compare: Wallace, *Land Nationalisation* (1892 ed.), 172; Cairnes, *Some Leading Principles of Political Economy Newly Expounded* (London, 1872), 333; *P and P,* 20–22; and for Wallace's identifying his thought with HG's, as quoted, *Land Nationalisation,* 173–4. HG reported to Ford his associations with Joseph Chamberlain and John Morley, in letters of 6, 22, 27 April 1882; the article he did for the latter was 'England and Ireland, an American View,' *Fortnightly Review,* 37:780–94 (1 June 1882). For a kind of intellectual history, see Morley, *Recollections* (2 vols., New York, 1917), I. For immediate political backgrounds, see Garvin, *Joseph Chamberlain,* I, chs. xv–xvii; the passage quoted is on pp. 385–6.

4. IRISH CRISIS OF 1882. My account of Liberal policy in Ireland during the spring of 1882 draws mainly on Hammond, *Gladstone and the Irish Nation,* ch. xv, and Garvin, *Joseph Chamberlain,* I, chs. xvi–xvii. The London *Times,* 4 September 1882, p. 5, supplies the information that, up to 31 July 1882, the Land Act of 1881 had operated to bring 79,455 applications before the statutory commission on fair rents; that 11,964 fair-rent agreements had been recorded, as made out of court; and that the commission had fixed 14,945 rentals. HG's letter in the *Irish World,* 26 August 1882, mentions such improvements. His

new attitude toward Parnell appears in letters to Ford, 6, 30 June 1882, HGC; his reports of the bitter day after Phoenix Park were printed in the *Irish World*, 3, 10 June 1882. My account draws also from Michael Davitt, *The Fall of Feudalism in Ireland, or the Story of the Land League Revolution* (London and New York, 1902), 357, 361, and *passim*. The attitudes represented there encourage the interpretation of HG's role which de Mille indicates, p. 256, note 9, as being Father Dawson's idea.

IDENTIFICATION WITH DAVITT AND MCGLYNN. HG's reactions to Davitt's speeches in England appear in his letters of May and June to Ford, Annie George, and Shaw, HGC. See George, Jr., 382, 383. For Davitt's own statement of his land program, see *Leaves from a Prison Diary* (London, 1885), II, lectures XXV–XXVII. HG's warning to Ford, lest Davitt be made to seem too much a *P and P* man, appears in letters of 27 May, 27 June, 4 August 1882, HGC. McGlynn's speech which forced the issue, and identified the speaker as a HG man, is quoted in George, Jr., 385.

ARRESTED TWICE IN IRELAND. The account of the venture to Athenry and Loughrea is based on HG's letter printed in the *Irish World*, 23 September 1882, and on Joynes's letter, London *Times*, 4 September 1882, p. 4. Letters from Joynes to HG, 14 November, 7 December 1882, 25 March 1883, HGC, which tell of his losing a job as a result of the episode, make HG's irony about him seem unkind. HG's acknowledgment that Secretary Trevelyan eased his case appears in the London *Times*, 6 September 1882, p. 6; and his letter to President Arthur is printed, ibid. 2 October 1882, p. 8. See George, Jr., 394–5. The essential out-letters in the State Department Archive, National Archives, from which I draw the diplomatic phase of this story, are the following: Secretary of State (or acting secretary), letters or telegrams to Lowell (or to W. J. Hoppin of the legation), 18, 21, 23, 26 August, 3 October 1882, in State Department, Great Britain, Ms. Instructions, vol. 36. The essential in-letters are the following: Lowell (or Hoppin) to the Secretary of State, 14 July, 22, 30 August, 9, 29 September, 17 October 1882, in State Department, Great Britain, Ms. vol. 145. This volume contains Lowell to Foreign Minister, Earl Granville, 29 August 1882; and Granville to Hopkins, 27 September 1882.

5. THE TIMES's AND OTHER APPRECIATIONS. J. R. Young's response to the review of *P and P* in *The Times* was dated 26 November 1882, HGC. HG's Land Nationalisation Society speech was reported in *The Times*, 6 September 1882, p. 5. Shaw wrote about it, 24 January 1905, letter quoted in Archibald Henderson, *George Bernard Shaw, His Life and Works* (London, 1911), 152–3. For the festive occasion of this reminiscence, a *P and P* dinner, see *Single Tax Review*, 4 (1905):26–8. For other comment on the 1882 meeting, see: de Mille, 115, 257; William S. Irvine, *The Universe of GBS* (New York, 1949), 40–43; A. R. Wallace, *My Life*, II, 274. HG's reflections on having found his place in England appear in letters to F. G. Shaw, 17, 21 September, and to Father Thomas Dawson, 23 October 1882, HGC.

XIII. PROPHET IN THE OLD COUNTRY: ENGLAND AND SCOTLAND, 1884–1885

1. ENGLISH FONDNESS FOR THE ABSENT GEORGE, 1883. HG learned about the Land Reform Union from letters from Thomas Walker, 5, 7 June 1883, HGC;

see George, Jr., 398, 422. The Olivier letter, 15 November 1882, is printed in Margaret Olivier, ed., *Sydney Olivier, Letters and Selected Writings* (New York, 1948), 54. Wicksteed's letters to HG, 29 October 1882, 4 February 1883, are in HGC. For data on the Economic Circle, see Charles H. Herford, *Philip Henry Wicksteed, His Life and Work* (London and Toronto, 1881), 193, 196, 199, 205–7; for Wicksteed's influence in English socialism, G. B. Shaw, 'On the History of Fabian Economics,' in Edward R. Pease, *History of the Fabian Society* (London, 1925), 275–6. The lasting Georgist element in Wicksteed is discussed in Herford, op. cit. 213–14; and in Wicksteed, *Common Sense of Political Economy*, ed. by Lionel Robbins (London, 1933), I, vi–vii; II, 686–90. Hyndman's challenge to HG was written 6 April 1883, HGC; see comment in Destler, *American Radicalism*, 80–81. For the Positivist attitude toward HG, quite ambiguous, see Frederic Harrison's address, 'The Views on the Labour Problem of our Positivist School,' printed as ch. IV of his *National and Social Problems* (New York, 1908), Pt. II.

2. MAJOR BRITISH REVIEWS OF PROGRESS AND POVERTY. The figures on the sales of *P and P* were gathered from Kegan Paul company records by Dr. Lawrence and appear in his 'Henry George's British Mission,' *American Quarterly*, 3 (1951):233. The first two reviews discussed are: Laveleye, ' "Progress and Poverty," a Criticism,' *Contemporary Review*, 42:786–806; and Sarson, *Modern Review*, 4:52–80, reprinted as *Land Reform Union Tract*, no. 4 (London, 1884). Mallock's review appeared in the *Quarterly Review*, 155:35–74 (the long quotation is from pp. 36–7); this and three other anti-George pieces by him are assembled in his book, *Property and Progress or a Brief Enquiry into Contemporary Social Agitation in England* (London, 1884). Mallock's own account of his anti-radical activity, from which I quote, appears in his *Memoirs of Life and Literature* (New York and London, 1920), 181–2, and *passim;* for a sympathetic discussion of Mallock, see Russell Kirk, *The Conservative Mind from Burke to Santayana* (Chicago, 1953), 345–57. For the *Edinburgh Review* criticism, see vol. 157:134–48; my quotations are from pp. 146, 148. Herbert Spencer's letter, printed at once in the *St. James Gazette,* is reprinted in HG's *A Perplexed Philosopher*, Complete Works, V, 58–60; that book, p. 57, contains HG's reminiscence of the Edinburgh review.

PUBLIC DISCUSSION AND CRITICISM. For the British trade unionists' discussion of HG, see Sidney and Beatrice Webb, *History of Trade Unionism* (New York and London, 1920 ed.), 375–6. A famous labor leader's acknowledgment of debt appears in *Tom Mann's Memoirs* (London, 1923), 27–8, 33. HG had some information concerning this kind of following, from A. C. Swinton, 22 October 1883, HGC. Alfred Marshall's lectures were printed in the Bristol *Times and Mirror*, 20, 27 February, 6 March 1883, certified transcript, NYPL. Concerning Toynbee, see F. C. Montague, *Arnold Toynbee*, Johns Hopkins University Studies in Historical and Political Science, VII (1889), 51–2 and *passim;* and memoir by Benjamin Jowett, in Toynbee, *Lectures on the Industrial Revolution* (1896 ed.), v–xix. The St. Andrews Hall lectures are printed as an appendix to this book, the quoted passage appearing on p. 318; Wicksteed's letter to HG, 4 February 1883, and Kegan Paul's circular, HGC.

GATHERING RESISTANCE. Fawcett's article in *Macmillan's*, 48:182–94 (and Fawcett, *Manual of Political Economy*, 1883 ed., Bk. II, ch. XI), was answered by

A. R. Wallace in 'The "Why" and "How" of Land Nationalization,' *Macmillan's*, 48:357–67. Mallock's second *Quarterly Review* HG article appears in vol. 156:353–93, reprinted in *Property and Progress*, 83–166. The quoted passages from the *Fortnightly Review*, 1 September 1883, are from vol. 34:444, 445.

3. AMERICAN ORATOR IN ENGLAND. Academic overtures to HG, before this arrival, were contained in letters from Müller, 28 February, 15 July, and in one from J. E. Symes, 22 November 1883, HGC. *The Times* reported the stunt arrival in London and commented on the St. James Hall speech, 6 January, p. 10, and 10 January 1884, p. 4. On these London days, see also: George, Jr., 422–7, and Lawrence, 'Henry George's British Mission,' *American Quarterly*, 3 (1951), 236; Algar Labouchere Thorold, *The Life of Henry Labouchere* (London, 1913), 214; NY *Free Soiler*, May 1884. As to HG's speaking procedures, as he swung into the English tour, I am indebted to suggestions of Dr. A. J. Croft, who has made technical studies of HG's oratory; and about HG's position in the battle of ideas, I am indebted to Dr. Lawrence's articles, *American Quarterly*, 3:236, and *American Journal of Economics and Sociology*, 11:64–6. Professor Müller's criticism is in a letter to HG, 23 January 1884, HGC. *Punch's* HG cartoon appeared on 26 January 1884, p. 43; and the *Saturday Review*, 57:97 (26 January 1884) said that Englishmen were foolish to be so respectful to a quoter of the American Declaration. Joseph Chamberlain's article appeared in *Fortnightly Review*, 34:775 (1 December 1883). For all stages of this trip I draw on HG's current letters to his wife, HGC.

4. FIRST SUCCESS IN SCOTLAND. On the condition of labor there, see Webb, *History of Trade Unionism* (1902 ed.), 334. There is a full account of the first Glasgow appearance in de Mille, 128–9; on the influence of the visit, see George, Jr., 434, 437, 578–9; and William Stewart, *J. Keir Hardie, A Biography* (London, New York, Toronto, Melbourne, 1921), 65.

5. HARD TREATMENT IN THE UNIVERSITIES. The first university visit is reported by Dr. Lawrence in 'Henry George's Oxford Speech,' *California Historical Society Quarterly*, 30 (1951):118–21, which draws on *Jackson's Oxford Journal*, 15 March 1884. Max Müller's letters arranging the visit, and HG's letter during it, March 1884, are in HGC; this last one is quoted in de Mille, 130. The written apology came from William Unwin, 8 March 1884, HGC. For the Oxford episode, I draw also from George, Jr., 435–6; and NY *Free Soiler*, May 1884. The assurances HG had about Cambridge, beforehand, came from F. S. Oliver, 5 March 1884, HGC; I have caught no evidence that HG knew about a learned and temperate book against him, George B. Dixwell's, *Progress and Poverty, a Review of the Doctrines of Henry George*, which Cambridge University Press had published, 1882. The comment of the premier's daughter is from Lucy Masterman, ed., *Mary Gladstone (Mrs. Drew) Her Diaries and Letters* (New York, 1930), 293, 306–8. Miss Clarke's comment, March 1884, is preserved, HGC.

RESPECT FOR A DEPARTING GUEST, 1884. Davitt's good wishes appear in a letter to HG, 19 March 1884, HGC; Cardinal Manning's appreciation, in George, Jr., 438, and in Shane Leslie, *Henry Edward Manning, His Life and Labours* (London, 1921), 353; and that of the young Gladstone group, in Masterman, *Mary Gladstone*, 310. HG's letters to his wife, 25 March, 4 April 1884, HGC, supply part of the story of farewell.

6. GEORGE ATTACKED AND DEFENDED, 1884. The *Saturday Review* attack appeared 12 April and 11 October 1884, vol. 57:465–6, 58:460–61; more of the same, 1885, in vol. 59:75–6, and 60:583–4. The defensive biography was Henry Rose's, *Henry George, A Biographical, Anecdotal, and Critical Sketch* (London, 1884), a book about which HG once showed some annoyance but otherwise seems to have had little to say. Concerning the author of the principal attack on HG, see *George Douglas, Eighth Earl of Argyll, K.G., K.T. (1823–1900) Autobiography and Memoirs* (2 vols., London, 1906), though it omits any mention of his HG affair. 'The Prophet of San Francisco' appeared in *The Nineteenth Century*, 15:537–58; and HG's reply, ibid. 16:134–55. Both are reprinted in Complete Works, III, 'Property in Land, A Passage at Arms between the Duke of Argyll and Henry George,' 7–40, 41–74.

RETURN TO SCOTLAND, 1884–5. The narrative of this trip is based largely on HG's letters to his wife, November–January, HGC. His idea that the press boycotted him is supported by Poultney Bigelow, who at the time was a NY *Herald* correspondent, in his *Seventy Summers*, II, 15. The significance of the Royal Exchange meeting, London, is discussed by Dr. Lawrence, in *American Journal of Economics and Sociology*, 11:67; and the London *Times* reported the Belfast meeting, 23 January 1885, p. 9.

7. A LASTING INFLUENCE IN BRITAIN. HG's dialogue with Hyndman appeared as 'Socialism and Rent Appropriation, A Dialogue,' *The Nineteenth Century*, 17 (1885), 369–77; see Hyndman, *Record of an Adventurous Life*, 267. Webb's comments on HG's influence of about this time appear in *Socialism in England* (London, 1890), 21, and *History of Trade Unionism* (1894 ed.), 362; and Pease's estimate is in his *History of the Fabian Society* (London, 1925), 20, 21. Lib Lab interest in HG is represented in Great Britain, Royal Commission on Housing of the Working Classes, *First Report* (London, 1885), 42, 61, 76–81; see George, Jr., 453n. Spencer's distress at HG influence appears in *Various Fragments* (New York, 1898), 134–6. Hobson's famous appreciation is in the *Fortnightly Review*, 62: my quotations, which I have adjusted a little in syntax and paragraphing but not in meaning, are from pp. 836–7, 839, 841–2, 844.

XIV. NOT WITHOUT HONOR IN HIS OWN LAND, 1882–1886

1. AS HERO IN NEW YORK, 1882. The story of HG's reception at home, as a figure of the Irish resistance, is told by participators in George, Jr., 400–401, and in Post, *Prophet of San Francisco*, ch. VI. I have also used Young, *Single Tax Movement*, 79, and de Mille, 117; and draw on HG's letters of 23 October 1882 to Dr. Taylor and Father Dawson, HGC.

AS WRITER WHOSE IDEAS WERE READ, 1882–3. HG's correspondence of June and August, 1882, while he was still abroad, especially his exchanges with F. G. Shaw, is the source of the story of the reprinting of *P and P*. Miss Peabody's tribute, 4 March 1883, occurs in HGC; so do all the letters mentioned in the text, except the Joseph Labadie letter, 12 January 1883, Labadie Collection, University of Michigan. On Lovell's interests, see Edward and Eleanor Marx Aveling, *The Working-Class Movement in America* (London, 1891), 193. Letters to HG from A. J. Steers, 26 September 1882, and from Lovell, 28 November, and HG to James McClatchy, 28 March 1883, HGC, bear on HG's shift from Appleton to Lovell, publisher of cheap editions. See George, Jr., 404–5. C. D. F.

Gütschow, in a letter of 16 February 1883, and L. P. Nelson, in letters of June 1883, HGC, were the proposers of new translations of *P and P*.

2. Invited Contributor to Major Journals, 1883. HG's *North American* articles of 1883 are located: 'Money in Elections,' vol. 136:201–11; 'Overproduction,' vol. 137:584–93. Concerning Sumner, as HG's rival in economic journalism, I draw on Harris E. Starr, *William Graham Sumner* (New York, 1925), 436, and Hofstadter, *Social Darwinism*, ch. III. Sumner's own *What Social Classes Owe to Each Other* (New York, 1883), pp. 48, 50–52, 68, 116, 134, illustrates his interest in combatting HG. HG's contract with *Leslie's* was negotiated through H. L. Bridgman, and his difficulties with *Leslie's* appear in dealings with the same representative and with J. Y. Foster: letters of 7 March, 28 June, 31 July 1883; memorandum of conversation with Bridgman, 14 August 1883 — all in HGC. See also Post, *Prophet of San Francisco*, ch. VI. The passages used from the *Leslie's* articles appear in *Social Problems*, Complete Works, II, 7, 13, 15, 17, 38, 63, 188–91; see also pp. 55–6, 140, 142, 158.

Critic of Francis A. Walker. Tenth Census, *Compendium*, farm-acreage figures on p. 657, was the starting point of HG's attack; Walker's *Princeton Review* article is reprinted in Tenth Census, *Statistics of Agriculture*, xxviii–xxxi. HG's criticism appears in *Social Problems*, 40–41; and the entire controversy in *Leslie's* is reprinted as an appendix of that book, pp. 248–75. Walker's concessions appear in *Statistics of Agriculture*, ix. HG's concession, in 'More about American Landlordism,' *North American Review*, 142:387, 391 (February 1886). The passages specially used, from Walker's *Land and Its Rent*, are chs. III–v, and particularly pp. 127–9, 141, 147 ff. Dr. Garvin's effort to have the two minds meet appears in his letter to HG, 28 July 1883, HGC; and the conflict between editor and HG, in *Leslie's*, 56:214, 230, 334, 366; and 57:2 (26 May, 2 June, 14, 28 July, 25 August 1883).

3. In Search of a New Career, 1883. HG's refusals of good jobs appear in letters to Dr. Taylor, 7, 25 March, 28 April 1883, and one to his wife, 28 April, HGC. See George, Jr., 405–10. For relevant material concerning the man HG cultivated, see *The Path I Trod, The Autobiography of Terence V. Powderly*, edited by Harry J. Carman, Henry David, and Paul N. Guthrie (New York, 1940), 182–3. HG's overtures to Powderly, as quoted, are contained in letters of 19 April, 25 July 1883, in the Powderly Collection, Catholic University, for access to which I thank Father Henry J. Browne, in charge. The Baltimore *Sun*, 2 August 1883, describes the occasion of their meeting.

Leader in a New York Group. The Senate committee hearing in New York was reported in the NY *Tribune*, 23, 25 August 1883; I follow also the printed testimony, *Report of the Committee of the Senate upon the Relations between Labor and Capital*, I (Washington, 1885), especially pp. 467, 480–85, 512–13. The New York beginnings of the American Free Soil Society are recorded in the *Free Soiler*, May, June 1884; California developments, in J. G. Maguire to HG, 2 September 1883, HGC; and HG's hopes in letter to Labadie, 24 August 1883, Labadie Collection, University of Michigan. For reminiscent accounts of the society, see George, Jr., 406–7, and Post, *Prophet of San Francisco*, 47–9. HG's connections with pro-labor writers appear in: HG to Dr. Taylor, 25 March, HGC; Gronlund to Ely, 28 September 1883, Newton to Ely, 24 September 1883, Ely Papers, Wisconsin Historical Society.

4. LECTURER EMBARRASSED, 1884. HG's lecture contract with Brooks and Ditson, 25 April 1884, is in HGC; on his performance, under that contract and otherwise, see George, Jr., 442–4, and Post, op. cit. 62–3. The Detroit church-congress speech was reported in the *Churchman*, 25 October 1884. The events of HG's summer, 1884, I take from his letters to Dr. Taylor and Thomas Walker, May–September, HGC.

5. PRO-LABOR WRITER, 1885–6. The case story of HG's lecturing, in Burlington, is based on letters: David Love to R. T. Ely, 27 June 1884, 12 April 1885, Ely Papers, Wisconsin Historical Society; HG to his wife, 3, 4 April 1885, HGC. The address there is printed in Complete Works, VIII, 189–219, and in pamphlet form. Later HG letters in April voice his decision to turn to writing. HG's earlier articles in the *North American Review*, written at this time, are located: the dialogue with Field, vol. 141:1–14; 'England and Ireland,' vol. 142:185–93 (February 1886); 'More about American Landlordism,' vol. 142:384–401. Compare HG's criticism of the agricultural-ladder theory, ibid. 393, with the criticism in Lawanda F. Cox, 'The American Agricultural Wage Earner, 1865–1900,' *Agricultural History*, 22:95–114 (April 1948), and with the more favorable view in Henry C. and Anna D. Taylor, *The Story of Agricultural Economists in the United States, 1840–1932* (Ames, Iowa, 1952), 820–29. HG's Ohio and Pennsylvania travels, in the spring of 1886, are reported from his letters to his wife, April–June, HGC; on the visit with Tom Johnson and its significance, see: George, Jr., 457–8; Tom Loftin Johnson, *My Story* (New York, 1911), 49–51; Frederic C. Howe, *Confessions of a Reformer* (New York, 1925), 95–7. The 'Labor in Pennsylvania' articles appeared in the *North American Review*, 143:165–82 (August), 268–77 (September), 360–70 (October 1886); 144:86–95 (January 1887); I draw especially on 143:167, 172, 273, 368–9; 144:88, 95.

6. AUTHOR OF PROTECTION OR FREE TRADE. HG voiced his hopes for the manuscript in letters to Nordhoff, 5 September, and to Dr. Taylor, 19 September 1885, HGC. Many letters, September–October, HGC, concern serialization; about the new publishing company, see George, Jr., 456. The book, *Protection or Free Trade, an Examination of the Tariff Question with Especial Regard to the Interests of Labor* (New York, Henry George and Company, 1886), is reprinted in Complete Works, III. For the background of tariff opinion in which HG wrote, see Ida Tarbell, *All in a Day's Work* (New York, 1911), 278, and *The Tariff in Our Times* (New York, 1911), 141; for his own awareness of problems involved, see *Protection or Free Trade*, 250–52, ch. XXVIII. The reviews mentioned are located: Newcomb's in *Political Science Quarterly*, 1:341–3 (June 1886); Shaw's, in the *Dial*, 7:389 (June 1886); *Critic*, new series, 5:230 (8 May 1886). A review much like Newcomb's appeared in *Jahrbücher für Nationalökonomie und Statistik*, 50:304 (1888). Many newspaper and other reviews are clipped in HG Scrapbooks, 8, 23, 27, NYPL. On the editions, see Sawyer, *Henry George and the Single Tax*, 18; on sales, George, Jr., 573–4.

XV. CONQUEST IN NEW YORK CITY: LABOR LEADER AND ALMOST MAYOR, 1886

1. READY FOR POLITICS AT HOME. HG's information about English politics, 1885–6, appears in his correspondence with friends overseas. The urgent letters to come to England were from Durant, 24 February, 30 March 1886. HG's revela-

tions of his home strategy were to Walker, 4 March, 4 September 1885, 18 January 1886; and to McGhee, 4 June 1886 — all HGC.

2. THE CONDITION OF AMERICAN LABOR. Post's story of a labor interest in HG appears in a political article, really a memoir, 'The United Labor Party,' *The Public* (Chicago), 14:1127 (3 November 1911). For labor background, in this chapter, I draw on: Selig Perlman, Pt. v, chs. VII–XII, in Commons, *History of Labour in the United States*; Henry David, *History of the Haymarket Affair* (New York, 1936), especially chs. I–II, VII; Norman J. Ware, *Labor Movement in the United States, 1860–1895* (New York, 1929); and the autobiographies of the principal leaders, Powderly, *The Path I Trod*, especially chs. X–XII, and Samuel Gompers, *Seventy Years of Life and Labor* (New York, 1925), I, especially chs. VII–XIV. For scholarly studies of the awakening conscience of this period, see, for the churches: May, *Protestant Churches and Industrial America* (New York, 1949), especially pp. 101–3, and earlier histories in the same field by C. Howard Hopkins and Aaron Abell. Concerning the new crop of social novels, Walter F. Taylor, *Economic Novel in America* (Chapel Hill, 1942), 40–41; and, concerning the economists, Dorfman, *Economic Mind*, III, ch. VIII. The fullest treatment of the NY Central Labor Union is ch. II of Peter A. Speek, *Singletax and the Labor Movement*, University of Wisconsin *Bulletin*, Economic and Political Science Series, VIII, no. 3 (Madison, 1917). The same author contributes the passage in Commons, *History of Labor*, II, from which, p. 442, I quote the CLU's class-conscious declaration.

3. EMERGENCE AS LEADER FOR LABOR. For the Theiss case, see Speek, *Singletax and the Labor Movement*, 58–61. My account of the whole campaign draws on this book, though I disagree with many of the author's judgments. I depend most of all on L. F. Post and F. C. Leubuscher, *An Account of the George-Hewitt Municipal Election of 1886* (New York, 1887), which is practically a documentary history and reproduces many platforms, speeches, and other documents. Hereafter in these notes I cite the two books as Speek, and Post and Leubuscher. The key HG documents, discussed in the text, are the following, in the pages indicated in Post and Leubuscher: letter conditionally accepting nomination, 26 August, 7–11; HG's platform for the labor party, 23 September, 13–15; speech of acceptance, 5 October, 19–29. Gompers' self-justifying account of his participation is in *Seventy Years*, I, 312–18.

DECISIONS MADE IN PRIVATE. HG's story of the Ivins interview appears in an open letter to A. S. Hewitt, draft in HGC, printed in NY *Tribune*, 18 October 1897, p. 2, and in other papers, and quoted, George, Jr., 463. Mr. Ivins' counter-statement in NY *Tribune*, 19 October 1897, p. 3. Frederick J. Zwierlein, *Life and Letters of Bishop McQuaid*, III (Rochester, 1927), ch. XXIX, gives a very full and sympathetic account of Archbishop Corrigan at this time; but Patrick J. Walsh, *William J. Walsh, Archbishop of Dublin* (London, New York, Toronto, 1928), 227–8, 230, justifies my comment on the churchman's mental operations. HG's account of his interview with the archbishop is in the NY *Standard*'s first issue, 8 January 1887. HG's letter challenging Corrigan, 30 September 1886, is in the archive of St. Joseph's Seminary, Yonkers; Father Jeremiah J. Brennan generously sent me a copy. See George, Jr., 465–6.

4. DEMOCRATIC AND REPUBLICAN OPPONENTS. For accounts of HG's rivals, 1886, see: Nevins, *Hewitt*, ch. XXIII; Henry F. Pringle. *Theodore Roosevelt, a Biog-*

raphy (New York, 1931), 110–15; Howard L. Hurwitz, *Theodore Roosevelt and Labor in New York State* (New York, 1943), chs. III–IV. Hewitt's allowing his decisions about candidacy to be made by Croker appears in two letters preserved in the library of Cooper Union: Hewitt to Richard Croker, 7 October 1886, Hewitt Papers; Hewitt to R. E. Henry, 9 October 1886, Hewitt Transcripts, Biography 2. His address of acceptance is in Post and Leubuscher, 32–43. Roosevelt's private opinions appear in letters to Lodge, 17, 20 October, 1 November 1886, Elting Morrison, ed., *Letters of Theodore Roosevelt*, 1 (Cambridge, 1951), 111–13, 115. The cases cited of Republicans for HG appear in: Peter Eichele to HG, 27 October 1886, HGC; groups and individuals named in NY *Leader*, 26–9 October 1886; Eva Ingersoll Wakefield, ed., *Letters of Robert Ingersoll* (New York, 1951), 662–3; HG, in NY *Tribune*, 30 October 1886. The story of sympathy for HG among the Peabody trustees is from C. W. Garrison, ed., 'Conversations with Hayes, a Biographer's Notes,' *Mississippi Valley Historical Review*, 25:377–8; see also Charles R. Williams, *Life of Rutherford B. Hayes* (Columbus, 1914), II, 282–3.

LABOR'S RESOURCES. HG's address to Irving Hall is in Post and Leubuscher, 125–7. On the support tendered by visiting Englishmen, see: concerning A. R. Wallace, *My Life*, II, 107, and NY *Leader*, 26 October 1886; concerning the Avelings, see their book, *The Working-Classes in America* (London, 1891), 184, 186–7, 193, and NY *Nation*, 43:280 (7 October 1886); and Sidney Webb to HG, 8 March 1889, HGC. The strain between the former associates appears in Davitt to HG, 4 November 1886, HGC. My estimate of the *Leader* is based on the file, Columbia University Library; and on comment in Speek, 73–5.

TIDE OF BATTLE. Hewitt's campaign attack, and HG's reply, which challenged a spoken debate and led to a printed one, 19–24 October, are all in Post and Leubuscher, 32–71. For comment on the campaign procedures Croker favored, see Morris R. Werner, *Tammany Hall* (Garden City and New York, 1928), 311–12. The contemporary comment cited is from: NY *Tribune*, 22 October 1886, p. 4; *Leslie's Weekly*, 63:130, 162–3 (16, 30 October); *Public Opinion* (Washington), 2:21–4 (23 October). HG's Chickering Hall speech is in Post and Leubuscher, 62–84. Dr. Croft's Ms. list of speeches by HG, which I have seen with certain other parts of his Ms. dissertation on George as public speaker (Northwestern University, 1952), helps me through the maze of HG's speaking activities. Concerning Catholic elements on HG's side: about Powderly and McGlynn, I follow principally Father Henry J. Browne's excellent *Catholic Church and the Knights of Labor* (Washington, 1949), 182–5, 190–93, 218, 222–3; and about public opinion, Florence E. Gibson, *The Attitudes of the New York Irish towards State and National Affairs, 1848–1892* (New York, 1951), 398. For Father Preston's effort against HG, see Post and Leubuscher, 133; Speek, 85–6. On the close of the labor campaign, Gompers, *Seventy Years*, 318–19; Powderly, *The Path I Trod*, 150; Post and Leubuscher, 153; NY *Leader*, 30 October, 1 November 1886.

5. THE RESULTS. For a tabulation of votes, and an account of labor's immediate follow-up, see Post and Leubuscher, 168–70. For other meetings and pledges to carry on: NY *Leader*, 3, 8, 27 November 1886; *John Swinton's Paper*, 1 November 1886; Gompers, *Seventy Years*, I, 320, 434–5.

THE QUESTION OF STOLEN VICTORY. Seventeen alleged cases of illegal conduct at the polls appear in NY *Leader*, 4, 6 November 1886. Bigelow's assessment of corruption is in *Seventy Summers*, II, 12. For the liberal Catholic comment cited, see Davitt to Archbishop Walsh, 4 November 1887, in Walsh, *William J. Walsh, Archbishop of Dublin*, 229; and Thomas Sugrue, *A Catholic Speaks His Mind on America's Religious Conflict* (New York, 1951), 44–5. Varying judgments or evidences of abuse at the polls occur in: George, Jr., 481; de Mille, 152; Post, *Prophet of San Francisco*, 79; Stephen Bell, *Rebel, Priest, and Prophet* (New York, 1937), 40; Charles Edward Russell, *Bare Hands and Stone Walls* (New York, 1933), 46–8, 50–51 (Miss Dorothy Fay Duffy, of the University of Maryland, has checked the Russell Papers, LC, and finds no mention of this point); Gustavus Myers, *History of Tammany Hall* (New York, 1917), 270; Lothrop Stoddard, *Master of Manhattan* (New York and Toronto, 1931), 86; Nevins, *Hewitt*, 469; Perlman, in Commons, *History of Labour*, II, 453.

XVI. NO NATIONAL LABOR PARTY TO LEAD, 1887

1. GEORGE'S HIGHEST POLITICAL HOPE. Many of HG's personal satisfactions and dissatisfactions of the winter and spring, 1886–7, are recorded in his letters, especially those to his wife, December and March-April, HGC. For a sampling of the newspapers' speculation about HG's becoming a candidate for president, see *Public Opinion*, 2:86, 188 (13 November, 18 December 1886). HG's wish that labor organize for self-education is in Post and Leubuscher, 172–3; Powderly's decision not to carry on with political labor is in NY *Leader*, 21 December 1886. The Clarendon Hall convention was reported in the NY *Tribune*, 7 January 1887, p. 1. The ULP, as there organized, is described in Speek, 90–96. HG correspondence with Thomas Briggs, December 1886, HGC, shows that the story of financing the new *Standard* given in George, Jr., 484–5, needs a little revision. There are other accounts of beginning the paper in Speek, 98–100, and by Post in *The Public*, 14:1174–5 (17 November 1911).

2. ROMAN CATHOLIC CONDEMNATION OF PROGRESS AND POVERTY. Corrigan's condemnation of HG's ideas is contained in pastoral letter, 19 November 1886, Zwierlein, *Bishop McQuaid*, III, 7–11. His approach to Cardinal Manning is in a letter of 23 December 1886, in Leslie, *Henry Edward Manning*, 356–7; and Manning's reconsidered judgment of HG is printed in Zwierlein, III, 12–13. Archbishop Walsh's criticism of Corrigan occurs in letters to Manning, 28 December 1886, 9 January 1887, Walsh, *William J. Walsh, Archbishop of Dublin*, 227–8, 230. The surrounding labor problems, which concerned the bishops while they considered HG, I describe from the scholarship of churchmen: Browne, *Catholic Church and the Knights of Labor*, especially pp. 218–19, 223–5, 229, 237–53, 256; Allen S. Will, *Life of James Cardinal Gibbons* (New York, 1922), I, chs. XIX–XXI, especially pp. 336, 370–71; John Tracy Ellis, *Life of James Cardinal Gibbons* (Milwaukee, 1952), I, chs. XII–XIII. For the Holy Office's ultimate condemnation of HG's writings, 9 April 1889, see Father Ellis, *Cardinal Gibbons*, I, 336, 584, note 86.

GEORGE'S COUNTERATTACK. The following issues of the NY *Standard*, 1887, contain high points of HG's case against Archbishop Corrigan and his supporters: 8 January, the original attack; 22 January, the observation about

Catholic voters defying the hierarchy (which is confirmed from a source friendly to Corrigan, Hurlburt, *Ireland under Coercion*, I, xliv, lvi); 29 January, the doctrinal argument; 18 June, the Bishop of Meath's letter reprinted. The reaction in other journals is from *Public Opinion*, 2:288–9, 313–14 (15, 22 January 1887); the *Standard*'s fluctuating popularity is estimated from data in its own columns, 12 February, 31 December 1887; and from HG letters to Richard McGhee and Gütschow, February–October 1887, HGC.

3. THE ANTI-POVERTY SOCIETY. For a detailed account of Father McGlynn in 1887, see Bell, *Rebel, Priest, and Prophet*, chs. II, III. Most of the data on the society are from the *Standard*, especially 7 May, 17 September, 10 December 1887. See also George, Jr., 491–2. For an estimate of Anti-Poverty's potential for schism, see Sugrue, *A Catholic Speaks His Mind*, 44.

4. GEORGE'S BREAK WITH THE NEW YORK SOCIALISTS. For HG's attitude toward the Union Labor Party, see NY *Standard*, 12, 26 February, 9 July 1887; for the attitudes of socialist elements, *John Swinton's Paper*, 31 July, and NY *Leader*, 5 August 1887. For an account of the midsummer change of attitudes between HG and the socialists in the ULP, see Quint, *Forging of American Socialism*, 44–8. HG's private comments on the separation are in letters to Gütschow, 29 August, 25 November 1887, HGC, the latter quoted in George, Jr., 501n. The detail of party meetings, schisms, and declarations I largely borrow from Speek, 106–17. Gompers' role appears in *Seventy Years*, I, 322; his letter, which I quote, was addressed to John O'Brian, 7 February 1889, Gompers Letterbook 3, AF of L Building, Washington.

5. THE NEW YORK STATE CAMPAIGN. For a contemporary account of the Syracuse convention, see NY *World*, 16–20 August 1887; for a reminiscent one, Post in *The Public*, 14:1151 (10 November 1911). For older accounts, see George, Jr., 499, and Speek 127, 136–7; for a recent one, which includes an account of the Progressive Labor Party, Quint, op. cit. 48, 50–53. For my account of the canvass, I borrowed again from Dr. Croft's checklist of HG speeches; and used the NY *Standard*, 3 September–5 November 1887. HG's challenge to debate and Governor Hill's reply are in letters of 24, 27 September 1887, HGC. The vote is given in Speek, 140; Irish Catholic reactions are stated in Browne, *Catholic Church and the Knights of Labor*, 285–6, 305, 307, and in Gibson, *Attitudes of the New York Irish*, 399–400.

6. GEORGE AND THE HAYMARKET TRIALS. David's *History of the Haymarket Affair* is the fullest scholarly treatment; ch. x of Richard Morris, *Fair Trial* (New York, 1952), is a judicious brief review. The criticisms of HG in the text, for having accepted the decision of the Illinois Supreme Court, are from: Chicago *Labor Enquirer*, 29 October 1887 (Labadie Collection, University of Michigan); NY *Leader*, 11 November 1887; David, op. cit. 402. The early date of HG's consulting Judge Maguire is indicated in H. D. Miller to Harry Weinburger, 5 October 1931, copy in Labadie Collection; Maguire's first opinion about the trial, in Gütschow to HG, 13–15 November 1887, HGC. My account values more highly than Professor David's does, the influence of the Maguire opinion on HG; see *History of the Haymarket Affair*, 402. This takes the date of the judge's letter, which was printed in the *Standard*, 19 November, as the date of the influence; but the fact of the earlier consultations of the two men

requires a revision of the story. The Maguire letter was not written *to* George but was presented *by* him, to clarify matters. HG's letter to Governor Oglesby was written 5 November 1887; and his later thoughts, to Gütschow, 22 October 1888; these letters are all in the HGC.

XVII. THE FATHER OF THE SINGLE TAX, 1888–1890

2. GEORGE EXCLUDED FROM THE ULP. HG's confused hopes and anxieties for his party after the 1887 defeat appear in the NY *Standard*, 3, 31 December 1887, 4 February 1888; and in a letter to Gütschow, 25 November 1887, HGC. On McGlynn's arrogance and assumption of party power, data in Browne, *Catholic Church and the Knights of Labor*, 308; *Standard*, 14 January 1887. George's exclusion is discussed in an editorial by W. T. Croasdale, L. F. Post, J. W. Sullivan, ibid. 18 February 1888. The political history of the ULP, and of McGlynn, during later 1888, are taken from: Speek, 149–50, 154; Young, *Single Tax Movement*, 131–2; *Standard*, 12, 26 May, 7 July 1888; HG to Father Dawson, 6 June 1888, HGC.

THE COLLAPSE OF ANTI-POVERTY. Data from: NY *Tribune*, 14 March 1888, p. 3; NY *Standard*, 21 January, 4, 25 February, 17 March, 7 July 1888; HG to Gütschow, 22 October 1888, HGC.

GEORGE AS CLEVELAND DEMOCRAT. On the tariff policy, which reconciled HG to his old party, see Allan Nevins, *Grover Cleveland, A Study in Courage* (New York, 1932), 379. HG's analysis of the Mills Bill was printed in the *Standard*, 10 March 1888. His increasingly favorable comments occur, ibid. *passim*, especially 25 February, 10 March, 7 April, 9 June 1888. Those comments are strikingly close to Professor Nevins' judgments of the bill in retrospect of half a century, in *Cleveland*, 385, 387–9, 391–3. For HG's weaving tariff reform into free-immigration and land-value-taxation connections, see *Standard*, 12 May, 18 August 1888; and for his optimism following the nomination, ibid. 30 June, 7 July 1888. HG's late-campaign ideas and efforts appear ibid. 15 September, 13, 27 October, 3 November 1888; and in letters to Thomas Briggs, 31 August, 15 October 1888, HGC. His post-election ideas appear in the NY *Standard*, 10 November, 8 December 1888; for support for the idea that *P and P* affected a presidential message, see Nevins, *Cleveland*, 444.

3. THE BIRTH OF THE SINGLE TAX. HG's letter to Garrison, assessing his shift from labor politics to single tax, 14 January 1888, is in the Garrison Papers, Smith College. My account of the new reform in the pre-organizational stage is drawn from the *Standard*, 1888, especially 3 March, 16, 23 June, 11, 25 August, 1, 8, 15 September. At the organizational stage, after the national election, I draw on Young, *Single Tax Movement*, 132–4, 138–9, 215–16, and *passim*, and on Post, *Prophet of San Francisco*, 52–3, 140–41, 146. The Warren Worth Bailey Collection of manuscripts in the Princeton University Library, from which I take a little information here, would bear considerable study by an investigator of grass-roots reform during the Progressive period. On HG's speechmaking in the Mississippi Valley: NY *Standard*, 19, 26 January 1889; HG to his wife, 14 January, and to Thomas Briggs, 24 January 1889, HGC.

4. INVITED TO BRITAIN. The account of the brief visit of late fall 1888 is based on: NY *Standard*, 17 November 1888–12 January 1889; and on Thomas Walker

to HG, 4, 11 December 1888. Symes's *A Short Textbook of Political Economy* (London, 1889) follows HG's distribution theory; but there is no direct reference to him, at least in the edition I have seen, and there are prominent references to Mill and Marshall. The letters of invitation and political evaluation, which HG received, for the big trip of 1889, are: from Thomas Walker, 13 February; from Helen Taylor, 12 April; from Sidney Webb, 8 March — all HGC.

WELCOMED BY MIDDLE-CLASS GROUPS. HG's debate with Hyndman, the trip's late symbol of his new separation from old Marxist connections, is described from HG's side in NY *Standard*, 13 July 1889, and in an undated letter to his wife, HGC; and, from Hyndman's side, in *Record of an Adventurous Life*, see chs. XVIII–XXI; and see also G. B. Shaw, in *Essays in Fabian Socialism* (London 1932), 155. HG reported his meetings and events in England and Scotland, NY *Standard*, 30 March–8 June 1888; and in his Coney Island address, ibid. 28 July 1888. His comments on Thorold Rogers occur in letter to Thomas Walker, 13 June 1884, HGC, and in death notice, *Standard*, 22 October 1890.

ACCEPTED IN NORTHERN EUROPE. On the *Land Liga* and German *Bodenreform* generally, see Young, *Single Tax Movement*, 11–12; and Heinrich Freese, *Die Bodenreform, Ihre Vergangenheit und Ihre Zukunft* (Berlin, 1918). Flürscheim's statement about joining HG is quoted from a translation given HG, HGC. For translators, dates, and other bibliographical data on European editions of HG's works, see Sawyer, *Henry George and the Single Tax*, 16, 19, 21. But the list omits the French translation of *Social Problems* by Louis Voisson: see NY *Standard*, 21 January 1888, and George, Jr., 519n. HG's information about Norway and Denmark came in letters from Tugjald Kjennerud, 10 May 1886, John Svenson, 24 June 1886, and Jacob Lange, 22 August 1888, HGC; for Koht's comment, made with the Scandinavian countries in mind, see his *American Spirit in Europe* (Philadelphia, 1949), 202–3.

LIONIZED IN PARIS. HG's invitation, from Flürscheim, was dated 18 May 1889, HGC. The meeting of land reformers was reported, London *Times*, 12 June 1889, p. 5; NY *Standard*, 29 June 1889. HG discussed his Holland visit, and his ideological difficulties, ibid. 13, 27 July 1889. Leroy-Beaulieu was reported, from *Journal des Debats*, 24 June 1889, in NY *Standard*, 13 July 1889.

5. IDEOLOGICAL PURGE OF THE STANDARD. The financial background of the paper is drawn from: HG letters to Gütschow, 29 January 1887, 22 October 1888; to T. A. Briggs, 19 January 1888; to Richard McGhee, May 1888; circular (?) June 1888, all HGC; and from NY *Standard*, 31 December 1887. The NY *Tribune*'s appreciations appeared 7 January 1887; 1, 3 November 1889. HG's knowledge of the M'Cready-Sullivan *versus* Post-Croasdale conflict came from a long series of long letters, spring 1889, HGC, some from his son and some from the disputants. On the Bellamy Nationalist background, see Quint, *Forging of American Socialism*, ch. III. Sullivan's 'Ideo Kleptomania, the Case of Henry George, with Henry George's Denial of Plagiarism from Patrick Edward Dove' was reprinted separately from *Twentieth Century*, 10 October 1889, copy in Labadie Collection, University of Michigan. Outside concern in the issues of the editorial-room fight is represented in the HGC by letters to HG from: J. O. H. Huntington, 31 July 1889; Thomas Walker, 27 June 1889; Thomas Davidson, 16 September 1889. The summary statements by the contenders were

printed in the *Standard*, 13, 20 July; and HG's opinions, ibid. 10, 17 August 1889. HG on Bellamy, ibid. 31 August, 28 September 1889.

6. READY FOR A WORLD TOUR. HG's estimates of his own growing strength at home, and his intimations of Populism, are in NY *Standard*, November–December 1889; Dr. Quint supplied the datum that the *Journal of the Knights of Labor* was critical of him. HG's expectations from Australia were set by a letter from E. W. Foxall (Sydney), 27 November 1889; and HG's pre-departure activities appear in personal letters, HGC, and in the NY *Standard*, 4 December 1889, 15, 22, 29 January 1890. See Lyman Abbot, *Reminiscences* (Boston and New York, 1915), 420–21. Accounts of the transcontinental trip and the Pacific voyage in: *Standard*, 5, 12 February, 26 March, 23 April 1890; HG to Anna Angela George, 31 January 1890, HGC; George, Jr., 523–9; de Mille, 173–6.

TRIUMPHANT IN THE ANTIPODES. My comment on HG in New Zealand borrows information from a student of New Zealand history, Mr. Peter Coleman. I have also used: James E. Rossignol and William D. Stewart, *State Socialism in New Zealand* (New York, 1910), especially ch. VIII; Hugh H. Lusk, 'The Single Tax in Operation in New Zealand,' *Arena*, 18 (1897): 79–87; Arthur Withy, 'New Zealand . . . the Single Tax Movement,' *Single Tax Review*, 12 (1912):1–69; and P. J. O'Regan, article on New Zealand, in Joseph Dana Miller, ed., *Single Tax Yearbook* (New York, 1917), 122–7. For a survey which brings the matter to recent date: *Christian Science Monitor*, 17 November 1950, p. 11. Concerning the day-to-day events of the visit in Australia, there is a wealth of information in HG's letters, and in Farrell's, in the *Standard*, April–July 1890. HG Scrapbook 1 contains many Australian clippings. These sources are quoted in George, Jr., 529–38, and de Mille, 177–9. For estimates of HG influence in Australia, see: A. St. Ledger, *Australian Socialism* (London, 1909), 6–7, 65; Brian Fitzpatrick, *The British Empire in Australia, an Economic History, 1834–1939* (Melbourne, etc., 1941), 283–4, 364–5, 368–9; articles on South Australia and Queensland by E. J. Craigee, and on New South Wales by A. G. Huie, in *Single Tax Yearbook* (1917), 128–41; and a report on the pattern of site taxation, compared with other countries, in *Henry George News* (New York), August 1946.

7. GOING HOME. The story of the trip to and across Europe is told from: HG memorandum, n.d., and letters to William Saunders, 15, 28 July, and to E. R. Taylor, 16 September 1890; Annie George to Sister Teresa Fox, 21 July, 21 August (all HGC); and NY *Standard*, 6 August 1890. On the visit in England generally, ibid. 24 September 1890. On HG's hopes from the Salvation Army, see George, Jr., 540; a letter from Ballington Booth, 17 March 1893, HGC, assured him of the 'strong sympathy Mrs. Booth felt for your views and work.' HG's early responses to Thomas Walker's criticisms, in letters to Walker, 23, 28 August, 25 September 1890; in a letter to J. C. Durant, 27 November 1890 — both HGC. On the single-tax meeting in New York: George, Jr., 541; Louis Post, 'First American Single Tax Conference,' *The Public*, 14:903–13 (1 September 1911), and *Prophet of San Francisco*, 145–7; and Young, *Single Tax Movement*, 139–40.

XVIII. CHRISTIAN DEMOCRAT TO THE END, 1890–1897

2. IN THE STREAM OF CRITICAL OBJECTION. In the order of the text, the following give the titles and locations of the principal criticisms discussed: Miller,

Trade Organizations in Politics, also, Progress and Robbery: an Answer to Henry George (New York, 1887); Rutherford, *Henry George versus Henry George* (New York, 1887); Higgins, *The Fallacies of Henry George* (Cincinnati, 1887); Henry A. Brann, 'Henry George and His Land Theories,' *Catholic World* (New York), 44:810-28 (March 1887); James M. Cain, 'Individualism and Exclusive Ownership,' *American Catholic Quarterly Review* (Philadelphia), 13:82-95 (January 1888); F. L. Tobin, *Notes on Progress and Poverty, A Reply to Henry George* (Pittsburgh, 1887); Gunton, 'Henry George's Heresies,' *Forum,* 3:15-28 (March 1887), and *Wealth and Progress, a Critical Examination of the Labor Problem* (New York, 1897); Thompson in *Irish World,* 24 December 1887, 21 January, 14 July 1888 (for these references I thank Dr. Alexander Butler of Michigan State College); Harris, in *Journal of the American Social Science Association,* 22 (1887):120 ff., and ' Henry George's Mistakes about Land,' *Forum,* 3:435-42 (July 1887); Andrews, 'Economic Reform Short of Socialism,' *International Journal of Ethics,* 2:281-2 (April 1892); Ely, *Recent American Socialism* (Baltimore, 1885), 16-27, and *Labor Movement in America* (New York, 1905), 125, 283-4, and in *Christian Advocate,* 25 December 1890, quoted in Young, *Single Tax Movement,* 316n; Walker quoted, ibid. 316, full address, 'The Tide of Economic Thought,' American Economic Association *Publications,* VI (1891), 15-38; Clark, in *International Journal of Ethics,* 1:62-79 (October 1890); Bemis, 'Henry George's Tax on Land Values,' *Andover Review,* 8:592-600 (December 1887); Patten, *International Journal of Ethics,* 1:354-70 (April 1891); Clarke, 'Criticisms upon Henry George, reviewed from the standpoint of justice,' *Harvard Law Review,* 1:265-93 (January 1888), reprinted *Standard,* 28 January 1888.

3. GEORGISTS VERSUS THE CRITICS. Shearman's reply to certain HG critics and his next article were printed in the *Forum,* 8:40-52, 262-73, and reprinted in the *Standard,* 31 August, 9 November 1889. Atkinson's critique, and HG's reply, in *Century Illustrated Monthly Magazine,* 40:385-403; Max Hirsch answered more fully for HG, in *Democracy versus Socialism,* Pt. v, ch. VI, 'Mr. Edward Atkinson's Objections.' White's criticism 'Agriculture and the Single Tax,' *Popular Science Monthly,* 36:481-500, was answered by Post in the *Standard,* 5 February 1890. Thomas Huxley's series appeared in *The Nineteenth Century,* 27:1-23, 172-95, 513-32 (January, February, April 1890); and the following replies were published in England: J. D. Christie, 'A Workingman's Reply to Professor Huxley,' *The Nineteenth Century,* 27:476-83; Michael Flürscheim, 'Professor Huxley's Attacks,' ibid. 27, 639-50; Andreas Scheu, 'Professor Huxley and His Natural Rights,' *Commonweal* (London), 6:84-5 (1890). Goldwin Smith's article is located in the *Forum,* 9:599-614; the other sources drawn on for the footnote are: HG to Lloyd, 11 October, Davidson to Lloyd, 14 November, Lloyd to Davidson, 23 November 1888, all Lloyd Collection, Wisconsin Historical Society; and Caroline Lloyd, *Henry Demarest Lloyd* (New York and London, 1912), I, 115, 301-2.

GEORGE VERSUS UTOPIANS AND CLERGYMEN. The conference debate over clerical influence in the single-tax movement is recorded by Post, in *The Public,* 14:910. HG's current feeling about clergymen as reformers, in the *Standard,* 15 October 1890, and in a letter to Father Dawson, 18 May 1891, HGC. The wish of American Bellamyites to make common cause with HG is represented in the *Nationalist,* 3:6-7, 188 (August, October 1899, references supplied by Dr. Quint). The like-minded effort of English friends appears in Walker to HG, 23 August 1890, 2 May 1892; and HG's resistance, in letters to Walker, 25 September, and to Durant, 27 November 1890 — all HGC.

GEORGE VERSUS ACADEMIC ECONOMISTS. The Saratoga meeting is recorded by Frank Sanborn in the *Journal of Social Science* (Boston and New York), 27 (1890); for background of the American Social Science Association, see Luther Lee Barnard and Jessie Barnard, *Origins of American Sociology* (New York, 1943), 527–607. The passages of the Saratoga discussion treated in the text appear in the *Journal* as follows: from James, p. 8; from Andrews, 29–30; from the HG-Seligman exchange, 34–44, 85, 89, 98. Seligman's ultimate criticisms of the single tax appear in his *Essays on Taxation* (New York, 1921), 66–97, and *Studies in Public Finance* (New York, 1925), 226–52. Post replied in *Prophet of San Francisco,* ch. XXIII. HG's quoted comment on academicians is in a letter of 28 April 1891, HGC; Bolton Hall's findings, 7 December 1891, copy in Gilman Collection, JHU; and later academic acknowledgments in: Ross, *Seventy Years of It* (New York and London, 1936), 15; Joseph Dorfman, *Thorstein Veblen and His America* (New York, 1934), 32; Commons, *Myself* (New York, 1934), 39–40.

4. THE NEED TO SETTLE DOWN. HG's Texas tour is described in the NY *Standard,* 26 November 1890, and in letters to his wife, 12, 16 November, HGC. Summary of the Hutchins case, George, Jr., 509–11; detail in Judge James E. Minturn, 'Tale of a Suit,' *Single Tax Review,* 15:342–6 (November–December 1915); many documents of the case, HGC; comment, NY *Tribune,* 14 February 1894. HG's general financial condition and the reorganization of the *Standard* appear, HGC, in letters to Briggs, 28 September 1890, 18 November 1891, and Briggs to HG, 30 November, 28 December 1891 (when Briggs forgave his $1000 loan). For HG's attack, I draw on Dr. Peterson's notes, quoted in George, Jr., 541–2; and on Jennie George to Thomas Briggs, 15 December 1890, HG to Thomas Walker, January 1891, HGC. Financial arrangements appear in letters among friends: Walker to George, 26 December, to Johnson, 27 December 1890; HG to Walker, 8 January, Johnson to Walker, 21 January 1891; HG to his wife, n.d. — all HGC. The Bermuda trip is reported in NY *Standard,* 17 January 1891; further data in: Annie George to Henry George, Jr., 5 February 1891, notes by Simon Mendelson, n.d. — both HGC.

5. CONTROVERSIALIST OF LEO XIII. Letters to Dr. Taylor of 3, 14, 28 April 1891, HGC, describe HG's return to the desk. Of many editions and commentaries on *Rerum Novarum,* I use Oswald von Nell-Breuning, S. J., *Reorganization of Social Economy, the Social Encyclical Developed and Explained* (New York, 1937); Bernhard Eulenstein wrote HG, 18 April 1893, HGC, that Professor Pedrazzini of the University of Fribourg was the actual author of the encyclical. I draw on Aaron I. Abell, 'The Reception of Leo XIII's Labor Encyclical in America, 1891–1919,' *Review of Politics,* 7 (1945):467, 477–8, and *passim.* Henry George, Jr.'s report of Cardinal Manning's comment was made in a letter to his father, 30 May 1891, HGC; see George, Jr., 565. HG's *The Condition of Labor* was published in the United States, 1891, by two firms, Doubleday and McClure and the United States Book Company; it is in Complete Works, III, from which the following pages are quoted: 68, 3, 15, 19–20, 25, 48, 61, 70–71, 98, 104.

THE MORAL SUPPORT OF FRIENDS. Protestant support came to HG in the following letters, 1891, HGC: from J. O. H. Huntington, 30 July, 3 November; from Garrison, 5 September; from Young, 3 September; from Thomas Walker, 11 November. Catholic support, HGC, from: Joseph Legett, 31 October; from Father Dawson, 20 July, 16 November, 12 December 1891.

VICTORY FOR CATHOLIC FREEDOM. McGlynn told HG the story of his reinstatement in a letter of 3 January 1893, HGC. The text of his statement to Satolli is printed in Sylvester L. Malone, *Dr. Edward McGlynn* (New York, 1918). I draw also on Bell, *Rebel, Priest, and Prophet*, ch. v; Browne, *Catholic Church and Knights of Labor*, 350; and John A. Ryan, *Distributive Justice*, especially chs. II, VI; and 'Henry George and Private Property,' *Catholic World*, 93:289–300 (June 1911).

6. GEORGE VERSUS HERBERT SPENCER. My illustrations of opposition to HG's piety are drawn from: Jordan, *True Basis of Economics* (New York, 1899); Carnegie, 'The Advantages of Poverty,' March 1891, reprinted in *Gospel of Wealth* (New York, 1900), 47–82. Spencer's anxiety, before he redid *Social Statics*, appears in a letter to Earl of Wemyss, 10 June 1890, David Duncan, *Life and Letters of Herbert Spencer* (New York, 1908), 299–300. HG's *Perplexed Philosopher*, published in New York and London, 1893, is in Complete Works, V; my quotations are from pp. 66, 135–6. The reluctance of some of HG's friends about the effort appears in letters of spring 1893, HGC: HG to Dr. E. R. Taylor, February and April; Durant to HG, 16 May; HG to J. E. Mills, 12 April. The satisfaction of others, in the 'Compensation' chapter, in: Bernhard Eulenstein to HG, 20 February 1893, HGC, and HG to Byron Holt, 27 March 1893, kindly lent by W. S. Holt; see also Harry Gunnison Brown, 'The Perplexed Economists,' in *Henry George News*, October 1946. For Spencer's quiet reaction to HG's attack: Duncan, *Life and Letters of Herbert Spencer*, 338–43; and 'Unpublished Letters' to James A. Skilton, *Independent*, 56 (1904):1169–74, 1471–8. For his friends' open ones: NY *Tribune*, 23, 30 September, 12, 18 November 1894.

7. BIG TREATISE NOT FINISHED. The personal and general problems that enter the story of writing *The Science of Political Economy* are drawn from personal letters, HGC, in the order of the text as follows: HG to Walker, 31 December 1894; to (William ?) Burbage, 9 September 1897; to Dr. Taylor, 10 February and 8 April, and from him, 10 March 1897; from Louis Post, 3 March, from Alice Post, 5 February, to Louis Post, 6 March 1897. Technical problems are discussed in the Loomis memorandum, in Purdy to HG, 21 July 1897, HGC. For the appreciation by the Beards, see *American Spirit*, 367–73; compare *Science of Political Economy*, 15, 21, 27, 33–4. For Hadley's criticism, *Yale Review*, 7:231 (August 1893).

XIX. THE MARTYRDOM OF HENRY GEORGE, 1890–1897

1. GEORGE AS DISSENTER WITHIN THE SINGLE-TAX MOVEMENT. Concerning HG's speaking activities, 1891–3, and finally for 1897, I am guided again by Dr. Croft's Ms. checklist; and I draw from letters and memoranda, March–June 1893, HGC. About the Chicago Single Tax Conference: typescript of HG speech, 29 August 1893, HGC; Post, in *The Public*, 14:911–12 (1 September 1911), and *Prophet of San Francisco*, 150; HG to J. E. Mills, 27 September 1893, HGC. Data on

Post's activities, from Ms. autobiography, LC; on Shearman's, from memorial issue of *Single Tax Review*, 1901.

As PHILOSOPHER AND FRIEND TO LIBERALS. Concerning the 'salon,' I draw on reminiscences in the following locations: Purdy's, in *Henry George News*, October 1946; Elting E. Morrison, *Admiral Sims* (New York, 1942), 28; Mrs. J. S. Lowell to HG, 14 December 1891, HGC. On the connection of Howells with HG, see Mildred Howells, *Life in Letters of William Dean Howells* (New York, 1928), II, 21–2; the NY *Standard*, 12 March 1890, compared *A Hazard of New Fortunes* (1890), Pt. II, ch. XII, with *P and P*, Bk. IX, ch. III. Garland's reminiscence of HG in Faneuil Hall is in South Carolina *Libertarian*, November 1925, pp. 281–2; his reminiscence of the HG home, in *Son of the Middle Border*, 431. His Georgism in non-fiction appears in 'A New Declaration of Rights,' 'The Single Tax in Actual Operation,' and 'The Land Question and its Relation to Art and Literature,' *Arena*, 3 (1891), 157–84; 10 (1894), 52. Concerning Garland, I have benefitted from letters generously written by Professor Eldon C. Hill of Miami University. See Walter Taylor, *Economic Novel in America*, ch. IV; and Grant C. Knight, *The Critical Period in American Literature* (Chapel Hill, N.C., 1951), 53, 56, 58, and *passim*. Concerning Herne: his own appreciation of his Georgist play is in 'Art for Truth's Sake in the Drama,' *North American Review*, 17:367–8 (February 1897); I draw also on letters he wrote to HG, 29 September, 15 October 1890, 17 November 1891, HGC. On other theater Georgists, see de Mille, 187–8, and Francis Neilson, *My Life in Two Worlds* (Appleton, Wis., 1952), I, 67, 241; and on the Georgism of the *Freeman*, see *The Freeman Book* (New York, 1924), 34–5, 42–3, 45–9, 159–62, and *passim*. On dilute Georgism in literature see Taylor, *Economic Novel in America*, 105, and Claude R. Flory, *Economic Criticism in American Fiction, 1792–1900* (Philadelphia, 1936), 171, 181, 190–95, and *passim*. For indications of the Chicago groups: Louis Sullivan, *Autobiography of an Idea* (New York, 1924), 251–2; Whitlock, *Forty Years of It* (New York and London, 1925), 94–6.

2. As GROWING INFLUENCE OVERSEAS. The near-success of a Georgist tax policy for London was a resolution introduced in the Commons by James Stuart, 13 March 1891 (defeated 149–26, after six and a half hours of debate), *Hansard's Parliamentary Debates*, 3d Series, 351:933–1013; Durant's letter, 16 May 1892, HGC, probably refers to remarks made by Haldane and Asquith concerning a Small Agricultural Holdings Bill, 5 April 1892, *Hansard*, 4th Series, 3:735, 737. What is said about Eulenstein in Germany is drawn from his own letters to HG, HGC:2, 26 December 1891; 9 January, 23 December 1892; 18 April, 15 May, 31 July 1893; 24 March 1894. On Damaschke, see article in *Der Grosse Brockhaus* (Leipzig, 1929), IV, 344; among his writings, which say much in appreciation of HG, see *Die Bodenreform* (1918) and *Geschichte der Nationalökonomie* (1920).

ESPECIALLY IN RUSSIA. For surrounding data, and much about Georgism in Russia, see Max M. Laserson, *The American Impact on Russia, Diplomatic and Ideological, 1784–1917* (New York, 1950), 269–90. HG's knowledge of Tolstoy's interest in him came from letters, HGC, from Eulenstein, especially 24 March 1894, 29 February 1896; from W. L. Garrison, II, 14 February 1897; and the one of 8 April 1896, which is quoted, from Tolstoy himself. Concerning Tolstoy's Georgism see: Ethel Wedgwood, *Tolstoy on Land and Slavery* (London, 1909);

Ernest Simmons, *Leo Tolstoy* (Boston, 1946), 394, 501, 503–4, 651, 675; L. N. Tolstoy, ed., 'Count Tolstoy on the Doctrines of Henry George,' *American Monthly Review of Reviews*, 17:73–4 (January 1898); *Tolstoy Centenary Edition*, Aylmer Maude, trans. (London), 21 (*Recollections and Essay*, 1921): 189–94 ('Letters on Henry George'), 272–306 ('A Great Iniquity').

3. FREE-TRADE IDEOLOGUE OF CONGRESSMEN. HG's political estimations of campaign time are taken from a letter to Walker, 17 October 1890, HGC; NY *Standard*, 6 November 1890. On Georgist efforts to influence middle-western radicalism, Post's Ms. Autobiography, p. 422, LC, and *Prophet of San Francisco*, 124. On the publication of *Protection or Free Trade* in the *Congressional Record*, see ibid. 14 April 1892, 3299–3306; Young, *Single Tax Movement*, 142–3; Johnson, *My Story*, 68–9; George, Jr., 571–4; and Henry George, Jr., letters to HG, n.d., HGC, and to W. W. Bailey, 13 May 1892, Bailey Collection, Princeton University Library. For the Democratic policy of 1892, see *Official Proceedings of the National Democratic Convention* (Chicago, 1892), 82–92, and Nevins, *Cleveland*, 491; for something of the backstage pressures on the tariff question, see Henry Watterson to Cleveland, 7 July 1892, in Nevins, ed., *Letters of Grover Cleveland, 1850–1908* (Boston and New York, 1933), 631, and C. E. Russell, *Bare Hands and Stone Walls*, 40–43; Johnson, *My Story*, 71–3. HG's alternations of hope and despair for Democratic radicalism appear in letters to Johnson, Shearman, J. R. Young, Thomas Walker, and Mrs. Frances Milne, June–July, September–December 1892, HGC. For HG's small victories in the House, see George, Jr., 570, which refers I think to the time of the debate of 10 January 1894, *Congressional Record*, 53d Congress, 26 (1): 632–88; and ibid. 31 January 1894, vol. 26 (2):1739, which is treated in Young, *Single Tax Movement*, 143.

ANTI-POPULIST FOR BRYAN. HG's speech during the Pullman strike is reported in NY *Tribune*, 13 July 1894, p. 5; see also George, Jr., 577; and for background, Nevins, *Cleveland*, ch. XXXIII, especially 624–8. Letters to HG from Tom Johnson, 10, 23 October, 7 November 1894, HGC, gave HG a close view of their political defeat. For the ambivalent roles of the single tax and HG in Illinois labor-Populist politics, see Destler, *American Radicalism*, 170, 172, 193, 197–211; see also Henry Barnard, *Eagle Forgotten* (Indianapolis, 1938), 382. HG's decision for Bryan appears in letter to W. R. Hearst, 1896, HGC; and in public, in *Arena*, 16:705 (September 1896). For the nearer background of his journalism, see Willis J. Abbot, *Watching the World Go By* (Boston, 1934), 194, and *passim*. See also Mott, *American Journalism*, 520–24. For HG's association with Altgeld: his letter of 14 October 1895, Schilling Collection, Illinois State Historical Society (copy kindly supplied by the librarian), and account of the New York anti-injunction meeting, Barnard, op. cit. 380–82. For HG's political differences of 1896 with one wing of his following: letter to Garrison, 31 October 1896, Garrison Collection, Smith College; Shearman to HG, 4 November 1896, HGC. For the political sympathy of others: letters from Swinton, 4 November, Garland, 10 November, Herne, 10 November 1896, HGC. See Post, *Prophet of San Francisco*, 127–9.

4. THE LAST CAMPAIGN. The NY *Journal's* offer to HG is in a letter, W. J. Abbot to HG, 1 May 1897, HGC. Concerning the single-tax invasion of Dela-

ware, see Young, *Single Tax Movement*, 147–52. On the special nature of the New York City campaign, see: Bryce, 'The Mayoralty Election in New York,' *Contemporary Review*, 72 (1897):751–60; Delos F. Wilcox, 'The First Municipal Campaign of Greater New York,' *Municipal Affairs* (New York), 2 (1898): 207. HG's first feeling about candidacy in letters to: Post, 25 January, Walker, 27 May, T. E. Willson, 3 June 1897, HGC. The decision to act against doctors' orders is recorded in Dr. Leverson's notes, and in an exchange with Dr. Mendelson, George, Jr., 594–5; de Mille, 224–5. On the preliminaries of the campaign, *Review of Reviews*, 16:394–7 (October 1897); for a party and machine history, see Alexander, *Political History of the State of New York*, III. I draw passages of HG's opening address from George, Jr., 600. The message to Bryan is mentioned in the NY *Tribune*, 6 October 1897, pp. 1–2; Bryan's endorsement of HG was asserted in the Cuyler Ten Eyck letter to Seth Low, 24 October 1897, Seth Low Collection, Columbia University Library. Roosevelt's opinion, as stated to Lodge, 16, 29 October 1897, is in Morison, ed., *Letters of Theodore Roosevelt*, I, 697–8, 703–4. HG's charges and Hewitt's and Ivins' denials, concerning 1886, appeared in the NY *Tribune*, 6 October, p. 2, 20 October 1897, p. 3. Garland's overture to Lloyd, 19 October 1897, in Lloyd Collection, Wisconsin Historical Society. On newspaper opinion during the campaign: Abbot, *Watching the World Go By*, 195–6; *Review of Reviews*, 16:520; *Leslie's Weekly*, 85:276; *Public Opinion*, 23:453–5, 486, 518–19, 551, 581–2 (all journals, October–November 1897). HG's final word about Low is quoted from George, Jr., 605–6; the Citizen's Union claim to Georgist support was elaborated for Low by Richard H. Clarke, the secretary of the Citizen's Union, 30 October 1897, Low Collection, Columbia University. My guesses of what the election might have been, if HG had lived, are made from: estimates in Edward M. Shepard, 'Political Inauguration of Greater New York,' *Atlantic Monthly*, 81 (1898):116; and R. W. Alsop's opinion, sent Low, 2 November 1897, that HG's death must have sent 'almost the entire Democratic vote' to van Wyck, and Low's idea, 3 November, that, 'If Mr. George had lived, I think there might have been a chance of success. With his death, I, personally, felt that the chances for victory had become very small' (letters in Low Collection, Columbia University).

XX. THE TRIPLE LEGACY OF GEORGISM

1. EARLY APPRECIATION OF GEORGE. Julian's estimate is taken from G. W. Julian Journal, 1 December 1897, Ms. pp. 251–2, Indiana State Library, Indianapolis, copy supplied by Miss Lila Brady.

2. WHILE TOM JOHNSON LED: FISCAL AND POLITICAL GEORGISM. On Fillebrown in Boston, see Young, *Single Tax Movement*, 105–6, 160–62, 244–6, 265–76, and *passim;* his writings are listed in Sawyer, *Henry George and the Single Tax*, 30–31, 58–9. On Purdy's New York career and thought, see *American Journal of Economics and Sociology*, October 1947 issue dedicated to him. Concerning *The Public* in Chicago, I drew from letters in the Post Collection, LC: Post to W. J. Bryan, 13 June 1900, 26 December 1906, 13 July 1908; to Charles Bryan, 18 July 1911. Bryan on HG, in 'Equal Opportunity and Moral Truth,' *The Public*, 7:702–4. Concerning Johnson, beyond *My Story*, the need for a biography is supplied only in miniature by Newton D. Baker's article in *Dictionary of American Biography*, x (1933), 124–5; see also *Autobiography of*

Lincoln Steffens (New York, 1931), chs. XVI–XVII. For Cleveland's approach to Georgist policy, see F. C. Howe, *Confessions of a Reformer* (New York, 1925), chs. X, XXII, 230.

3. AS PROGRESSIVISM INCREASED: MORAL AND POLITICAL GEORGISM. The Georgist renewal in Britain is indicated, 1907–9, by many articles in the *Westminster,* the *Fortnightly,* and other reviews. The influence of HG's ideas in English politics, 1909–10, is testified to in Charles S. Orwin and W. R. Peel, *The Tenure of Agricultural Land* (Cambridge, England, 1942), 41. See also accounts of Americans in England, in Post, Ms. Autobiography, 334, LC; Tom Johnson, *My Story,* 298. At about the same time, Henry George's ideas were being assimilated by Sun Yat Sen into the revolutionary program in China. See Paul M. A. Linebarger, *Political Doctrines of Sun Yat Sen,* Johns Hopkins University Studies in Historical and Political Science, Extra Volumes, new series, no. 24 (Baltimore, 1937), 137. For the circle of reformers who followed Johnson, in Cleveland and Toledo, see Brand Whitlock, *Forty Years of It, passim,* and Howe, *Confessions of a Reformer,* 129, and *passim;* see also the series of articles on 'The Civic Revival in Ohio,' by Robert H. Bremmer, *American Journal of Economics and Sociology* beginning April 1949, as follows: 8:299–309, 413–22; 9:239–54, 369–76, 477–82; 10:87–91, 185–206. Information concerning the Fels Foundation in: Mary Fels, *Joseph Fels and His Life-Work* (New York, 1916), ch. XIII, and *passim;* Young, *Single Tax Movement,* ch. IX; Steffens letter to Laura Steffens, 9 April 1910, *Letters of Lincoln Steffens,* ed. by Ella Winter and Granville Hicks (New York, 1938), I, 242, and Steffens to W. W. Bailey, 29 September 1910, Bailey Collection, Princeton University Library. Concerning political activities subsidized by Fels money, I draw on Young, *Single Tax Movement,* 168–83, and W. S. U'Ren in *Single Tax Yearbook,* 42–6. The William Kent materials used are the following: Kent letters to Louis Post, 13 April 1909 and 13 April 1910, and to T. W. Tomlinson, 18 March 1915 (?); and his 'Land Tenure and Public Policy,' *American Economic Review Supplement,* 9:225 (March 1919). I draw on the manuscript material with the permission of Mrs. William Kent and her son, Professor Sherman Kent, and that of the officials of the Sterling Memorial Library of Yale University, where the William Kent Collection is deposited.

4. IN WOODROW WILSON'S DAY: MORAL GEORGISM. As for the political leaders of 1912: La Follette confessed his fear of *P and P* to Mr. Edward Nordmann of Madison. The letters between Newton and Roosevelt, of 30 July–2 August 1912, are in Newton Miscellany, New-York Historical Society Library. I draw general ideas about Wilson's thought from William Diamond, *Economic Thought of Woodrow Wilson* (Baltimore, 1944). For the New Jersey transformation of Wilson's politics, including the Georgist influences, see Arthur S. Link, *Wilson, the Road to the White House* (Princeton, 1947), chs. IV–IX; Ransom E. Noble, *New Jersey Progressivism before Wilson* (Princeton, 1946); Noble, 'Henry George and the Progressive Movement,' and 'G. L. Record's Struggle for Economic Democracy,' *American Journal of Economics and Sociology,* 8:259-63 (April 1949), 10:71–83 (October 1950); James Kerney, *The Political Education of Woodrow Wilson* (New York and London, 1926); Joseph Tumulty, *Woodrow Wilson as I Knew Him* (London, 1922), chs. V–IX. Secretary Lane's appreciations of George as a continuing force appear in letters he wrote

G. W. Wickersham, 18 November 1920, and to J. W. Hallowell, 9 December
1920; *Letters of Franklin K. Lane, Personal and Political,* Anna Winternute
Lane and Louise Herrick Wall, eds. (New York, 1922), 368, 375. Record's exhortation, 31 March 1919, and Tumulty's effort to radicalize Wilson appear
in Kerney, op. cit. 437–46, 448; see Record's comment of 1930 on Wilson and
the whole generation of Progressives in Noble, 'Henry George and the Progressive Movement,' loc. cit. 268–9.

5. SINCE MEMORY OF GEORGE HAS FADED: FISCAL AND MORAL GEORGISM. Concern-
ing the enclaves, see Charles White Huntington, *Enclaves of Single Tax or
Economic Rent* (Cambridge, Mass., 1922). The Georgist Ralston-Nolan and
Keller Bills, before Congress, 1921, were analyzed by B. H. Hibbard, Legislative
Reference Library, Madison; see also S. H. Patterson, 'The Ralston-Nolan Bill,
A Proposed Tax on Unimproved Land Values,' American Academy of Social
and Political Science, *Annals,* 95:188–93 (May 1921). On the Grimstad Bills in
Wisconsin, 1923, see Commons, *Myself,* 39–40, 53, 100; and his 'A Progressive
Tax on Bare Land Values,' *Political Science Quarterly,* 38:41–68 (March 1922).
Brand Whitlock's dismissal of Georgist politics is in a letter of 23 June 1920,
Letters of Brand Whitlock, Allan Nevins, ed. (New York, 1936), 304; see also
Journal of Brand Whitlock, 612. On the bitterness of Georgists, about 1920,
see Howe, *Confessions of a Reformer,* chs. XVII–XVIII, 319; Post, Ms. Auto-
biography, LC; Post, *Deportations Delirium of 1920, a personal narrative of an
official experience,* introduction by Moorfield Storey (Chicago, 1923). On the
Georgism of Parliament's act of 1947, see Charles M. Haar, *Land Planning Law
in a Free Society* (Cambridge, 1951), 163, and *passim.*

Editor's Note: Among the many books about Henry George published
after Professor Barker's book first appeared, readers may want to
consult:

Andelson, Robert V., ed., *Critics of Henry George.* Cranbury, NJ:
Fairleigh Dickinson U. Press., 1979

Cord, Steven B., *Henry George: Dreamer or Realist?* New York:
Robert Schalkenbach Foundation (originally published by U. of
Pennsylvania Press), 1985

Hellman, Rhoda, *Henry George Reconsidered.* New York: Carlton
Press, 1987

Lissner, Will and Dorothy, eds., *George and the Scholars.* Robert
Schalkenbach Foundation, 1991

Lissner, Will and Dorothy, eds., *George and Democracy in the British
Isles.* New York: (forthcoming) Robert Schalkenbach Foundation, 1992

Noyes, Richard, ed., *Now the Synthesis.* New York: Holmes & Meier
Publishers, Inc., 1991

Silagi, Michael, *Henry George and Europe: His Influence on Land
Reform Movements.* (New York: Robert Schalkenbach Foundation, forthcoming.)

Thomas, John L., *Alternative America.* Cambridge: Harvard U. Press,
1983

INDEX

Hill, Governor David B., 459, 500–501

Hindoo, 67; see also George, Henry: Voyages

Hinton, William M., 161, 165–6, 217–18, 227, 303, 313, 319, 437

Hirsch, Max, 548, 595

Hittell, John S., 92, 129; Calif. criticism, 1864, 84–9; spokesman of red scare, 1878–9, 257

Hobson, J. A., on HG's influence in England, 415–16, 664

Hopkins, Caspar T., 172–3, 257–8; president Immigrant Union, 128; ideas, 129–30; lecturer Univ. of Calif., 240–41

'How Jack Breeze Missed Being a Pasha,' 157, 649

Howe, Frederic C., 625, 626–7, 635

Howells, William Dean, 311, 478, 591

Huntington, Bishop Frederic Dan, 538, 560, 574

Huntington, Father James O. H., 538, 549, 574

Hutchins legacy, 568

Huxley, Thomas, 560–61, 578

Hyndman, Henry M., 353, 381, 393, 406, 412, 660; cultivates HG, 355–7; approves *Social Problems*, 426–7; debate with HG, 527; see also Marxism

I

Immigrant Union, Calif., origin, 128; policy, 129–30; HG's attack, 132–3

Income tax, 288, 604, 605

International League for Land Value Taxation and Free Trade, 402, 635

Ireland, 1881–2, ch. XII; leadership of protest, 341–2; economic condition, 342; Parliamentary policy toward, 343–5, 361, 363, 373; ancient critique of property in land, 350–52; see also George, Henry: Correspondent in Ireland; Irish Land League; Irish land problem; 'The Irish Land Question'; *names of leaders*

Irish Land League, 335, 336–7, 342, 344; No Rent movement, 345–6, 351, 363; role of women in, 347–8; underground, 348; finances, 358–9; disintegration, 363; see also George, Henry: Correspondent in Ireland; Irish land problem

Irish land problem, analogy with California, 126, 210, 320, 341; condition of, 1881, 344, 1882, 363–4, 660; see also Irish Land League; *The Land Question*

'Irish Land Question, The,' 320, 322, enlarged into book, 335, 658; see also *The Land Question*

Irish World, 336, 357, 441; reviews *P & P*, 322; employs HG as correspondent in Ireland, 339, 352, 361, 368; supports Land League, 358; celebrates HG, 418; see also Irish Land League

Irwin, Governor William, 195, 232

'Is Our Civilisation Just to Workingmen,' 440, 666

Ivins, William, 541, 614–15; urges HG against 1886 campaign, 463–4

J

Jackson, age of, source of HG's standards, 3–4, 77, 98, 101, 102, 145–6, 162, 167, 213, 251, 307, 456

Jackson, Joseph, 455, 458

James, Professor Edmund, 457–8, 565–6

James, Robertson, 565n., 590

Jeffreys, Joseph, 26–7, 38–9; estimate of HG, 42–3

John Swinton's Paper, 460, 467, 472, 479, 495; see also Swinton, John

Johnson, Tom Loftin, 449, 541, 609, 612, 621, 626; beginning with HG, 446; supports HG 1886, 455, 471; guarantor *Standard*, 535, 536, 569; gives HG security, 570, and home, 590–91; single-tax leader and subsidizer, 589, 605; Ohio representative, 599–605, 606–7, leader free-trade Democrats, 600, 601, 602; presidential hope, 603; subsidizer 1897 campaign, 615; leader 'political Georgism,' 623–5, and of Ohio reformers, 626–7

Jones, Senator John Percival, 223, 227, 229

Jordan, President David Starr, 577

Journal, NY, 608–10

Journal of Trades and Workmen, 66, 68, 259, 643

Joynes, J. L., 368–9, 380, 401; arrested with HG, 370

Julian, George W., 77, 137n., 164–5, 215, 312, 314, 621

K

Kearneyism, early overtures refused by HG, 243–4, 251; development and reaction, 256–7; success 1879, 258–9; HG critique, 258, 261–3, 653; see also Land Reform League

Kelly, George Fox, 87

Rice, Allen Thorndike, offers journal to HG, 432; HG's appreciation, 469–70
Rogers, Thorold, 285, 528–9
Roosevelt, Theodore, 331, 614, 629–30; Republican nominee 1886, 468; estimate of campaign, 469
Rose, Henry, 664
Ruskin, John, 397
Russell, Charles Edward, 480–81, 669
Russia, HG's early ideas about, 92, 95, 210; influence in, 597–9
Ryan, Father John A., 577, 676

S

Sacramento, 58, 60, 61; see also *Bee;* California; George, Henry: Employment and Unemployment, California Editor, Economic Thought; McClatchy, James; *Record; Reporter; Union;* Stanford, Leland
St. Paul's Episcopal Church, Philadelphia, 10, 11–12, 619
San Francisco, 543–4; HG's appreciation, 46, 103, 164, 253; *pueblo* question, 89–91, 93–5, 103–4, 148, 152; see also California; George, Henry: Voyages, Employment and Unemployment, California Editor, Conflicts and Protests, While Writing *P & P; newspapers and magazines by name*
Satolli, Professor Francesco, 576, 588
Saunders, William, 379, 380, 410, 411, 419, 523–4, 525
Schevitsch, Serge, 486, 495, 498, 501
Schmoller, Gustav, 334
Science of Political Economy, The, 552, 595, 610; yields to other things, 581, 584, 585; intellectual environment of, 582–3; problems of authorship of, 583–4, 585; contents and omissions, 585–6; criticism, 586–7
Scotland, see George, Henry: In England and Scotland, 1883–4, In Scotland and England, 1884–5; Land Restoration League; *names of HG associates there*
Seligman, E. R. A., 479, 565–6, 567, 675
Senate Committee on Labor, 1884, 119, 435–6, 665
Seyd, Ernst, 83, 85
'Shall the Republic Live?' 609–10
Shannon, Professor Fred A., 149, 648
Shaw, Francis G., 340, 368, 371, 421; subsidies of *P & P,* 337, 354–5, 358–9, 420
Shaw, George Bernard, 311, 382, 413; converted by HG, 376–7
Shearman, Thomas G., 331, 418–19, 450,

521, 559, 600, 609, 621; 'The Single Tax' speech, 518; textbook, 589; guarantor of *Standard,* 535, 536, 569; differences from HG, 539–41; see also Single tax
Sherman, John A., 100
Shubrick, 31, 34; see also George, Henry: Voyages
'Sic Semper Tyrannis!' 68–9, 643
Simonton, James W., 115–17, 218
Simpson, 'Sockless' Jerry, 600–601, 604, 605, 607, 622
Sims, William Sowden, 590
Single tax, significant occurrence of phrase, 291, 444, 454, 510, 607; 'single tax, limited,' 331, 539–41, 589–90; role in HG's thought, 508–11, 517–18; clubs, 521; rival political strategies, 521–2; national conferences, 542, 588–9; in twentieth century, 621–2, 625; see also George, Henry: Single-Tax Leader; Shearman, Thomas; *names of other leaders*
Smith, Adam, *Wealth of Nations,* 45, 194, 195, 267, 450; used in *P & P,* 274
Social Darwinism, 425, 578; see also Spencer, Herbert; Sumner, William Graham
Social gospel, 307, 563; see also Newton, Rev. Heber
Social Problems, 378–9, 407, 552; developed from articles in *Leslie's,* 425–6; U.S. publication, 426, 431; ideas, 426–7; translations, 531, 532; see also George, Henry: Economic Ideas in Later Writings
Social Science Association, 565–7
Socialism, see Bellamy Nationalism; Fabianism; Gronlund, Laurence; Hyndman, Henry M.; Marx, Karl; Marxism; Progressive Labor party; Socialist Labor party; Webb, Sidney; *names of other leaders*
'Socialism and Rent Appropriation,' 412–13, 664
Socialist Labor party, 458, 460, 499; expelled from ULP, 496–8; see also Marxism; Progressive Labor party
Spence, Thomas, 357
Spencer, Herbert, 374, 387, 581, 676; HG's borrowings, 204, 267, 291–2, 298; HG meeting, 357–8; repudiates land nationalization, 388–9; see also *A Perplexed Philosopher*
Spread the Light, a Journal of Social Progress and Tax Reform, 454–5
Spring Valley Water Co., 199–200

Webb, Sidney, 311, 382, 471, 527, 595;
estimate of HG influence, 413; warning
as to Fabianism, Radicalism, Georgism,
525–6; see also Fabianism
Wells, David Ames, 152, 174–5, 325, 450;
influences SF Times, 78; on Our Land
and Land Policy, 158, 163; author NY
tax reports, 183
Werth, J. J., 82
Western Union, deals with SF Herald,
113, 115–16; connection with AP, 115,
118, 173–4; refuses SF Herald, 117;
HG's attack, 118–19; see also George,
Henry: Economic Thought, Conflicts
and Protests
What Cheer House, 43, 45, 62
'What the Railroad Will Bring Us,' 102–4,
128, 145, 151, 244

White, Horace, 144, 469, 607; on Our
Land and Land Policy, 159; on P & P,
316, review, 323; on HG philosophy,
560
Whitlock, Brand, 594, 626, 634
'Why Work Is Scarce, Wages Low, and
Labor Restless,' 245–8, 653
Wicksteed, Philip, 380, 391, 392, 397, 406,
662; debt to P & P, 381
Wilson, Woodrow, 630–33
Wren, Walter, 360, 406

Y

Youmans, E. L., 321, 325–6, 327, 579, 580
Young, Professor Arthur N., 317, 650, 652
Young, John Russell, 117, 120, 124–5, 139,
264, 320, 322–3, 327, 330, 375, 422, 485,
570, 574